TRICKED

A graphic novel by
Alex Robinson

Top Shelf Productions
Atlanta / Portland

Cover design by Brett Warnock and Alex Robinson, with background paintings by Bwana Spoons.

ISBN 1-891830-73-2
1. Fiction
2. Music / Bands
3. Graphic Novels

First Printing, July 2005. Printed in Canada.

For Bochi,
even though she would not have liked the
naughty bits.

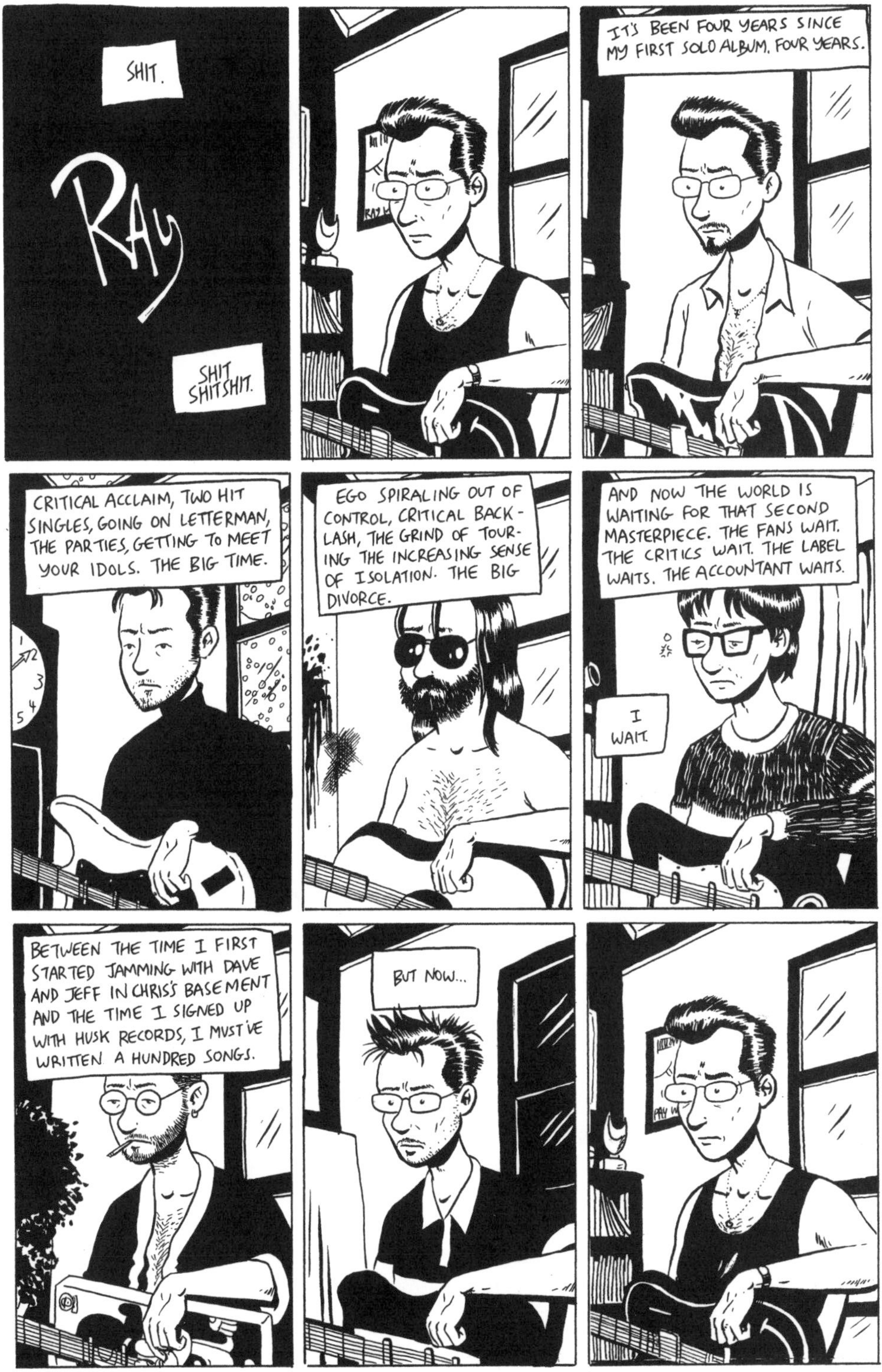
SHIT.
RAY
SHIT SHITSHIT.
IT'S BEEN FOUR YEARS SINCE MY FIRST SOLO ALBUM. FOUR YEARS.
CRITICAL ACCLAIM, TWO HIT SINGLES, GOING ON LETTERMAN, THE PARTIES, GETTING TO MEET YOUR IDOLS. THE BIG TIME.
EGO SPIRALING OUT OF CONTROL, CRITICAL BACK-LASH, THE GRIND OF TOUR-ING THE INCREASING SENSE OF ISOLATION. THE BIG DIVORCE.
AND NOW THE WORLD IS WAITING FOR THAT SECOND MASTERPIECE. THE FANS WAIT. THE CRITICS WAIT. THE LABEL WAITS. THE ACCOUNTANT WAITS.
I WAIT.
BETWEEN THE TIME I FIRST STARTED JAMMING WITH DAVE AND JEFF IN CHRIS'S BASEMENT AND THE TIME I SIGNED UP WITH HUSK RECORDS, I MUST'VE WRITTEN A HUNDRED SONGS.
BUT NOW...

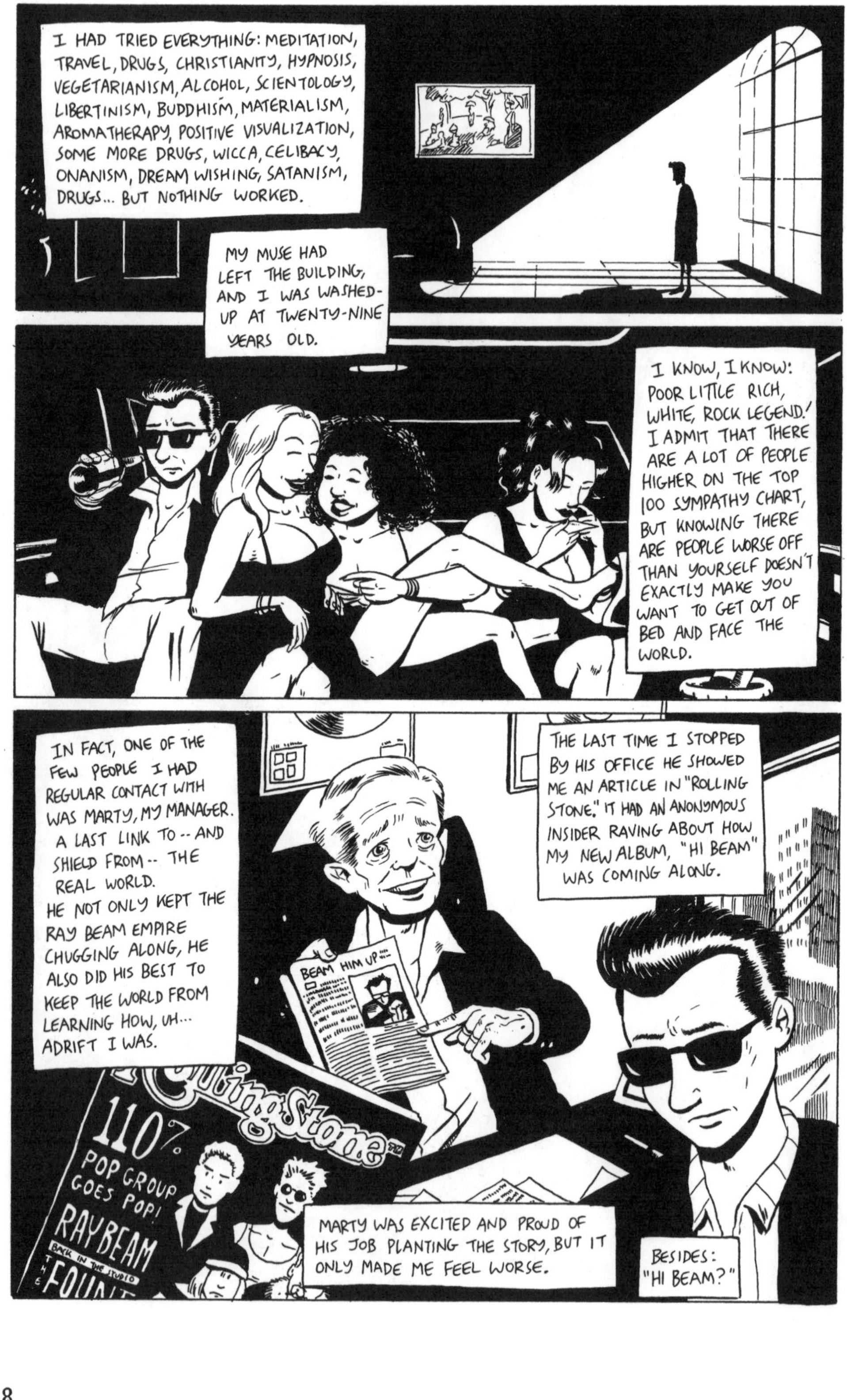
I HAD TRIED EVERYTHING: MEDITATION, TRAVEL, DRUGS, CHRISTIANITY, HYPNOSIS, VEGETARIANISM, ALCOHOL, SCIENTOLOGY, LIBERTINISM, BUDDHISM, MATERIALISM, AROMATHERAPY, POSITIVE VISUALIZATION, SOME MORE DRUGS, WICCA, CELIBACY, ONANISM, DREAM WISHING, SATANISM, DRUGS... BUT NOTHING WORKED.
MY MUSE HAD LEFT THE BUILDING, AND I WAS WASHED-UP AT TWENTY-NINE YEARS OLD.
I KNOW, I KNOW: POOR LITTLE RICH, WHITE, ROCK LEGEND! I ADMIT THAT THERE ARE A LOT OF PEOPLE HIGHER ON THE TOP 100 SYMPATHY CHART, BUT KNOWING THERE ARE PEOPLE WORSE OFF THAN YOURSELF DOESN'T EXACTLY MAKE YOU WANT TO GET OUT OF BED AND FACE THE WORLD.
IN FACT, ONE OF THE FEW PEOPLE I HAD REGULAR CONTACT WITH WAS MARTY, MY MANAGER. A LAST LINK TO -- AND SHIELD FROM -- THE REAL WORLD.
HE NOT ONLY KEPT THE RAY BEAM EMPIRE CHUGGING ALONG, HE ALSO DID HIS BEST TO KEEP THE WORLD FROM LEARNING HOW, UH... ADRIFT I WAS.
THE LAST TIME I STOPPED BY HIS OFFICE HE SHOWED ME AN ARTICLE IN "ROLLING STONE." IT HAD AN ANONYMOUS INSIDER RAVING ABOUT HOW MY NEW ALBUM, "HI BEAM" WAS COMING ALONG.
BEAM HIM UP
RollingStone
110%
POP GROUP GOES POP!
RAY BEAM
BACK IN THE STUDIO
MARTY WAS EXCITED AND PROUD OF HIS JOB PLANTING THE STORY, BUT IT ONLY MADE ME FEEL WORSE.
BESIDES: "HI BEAM?"

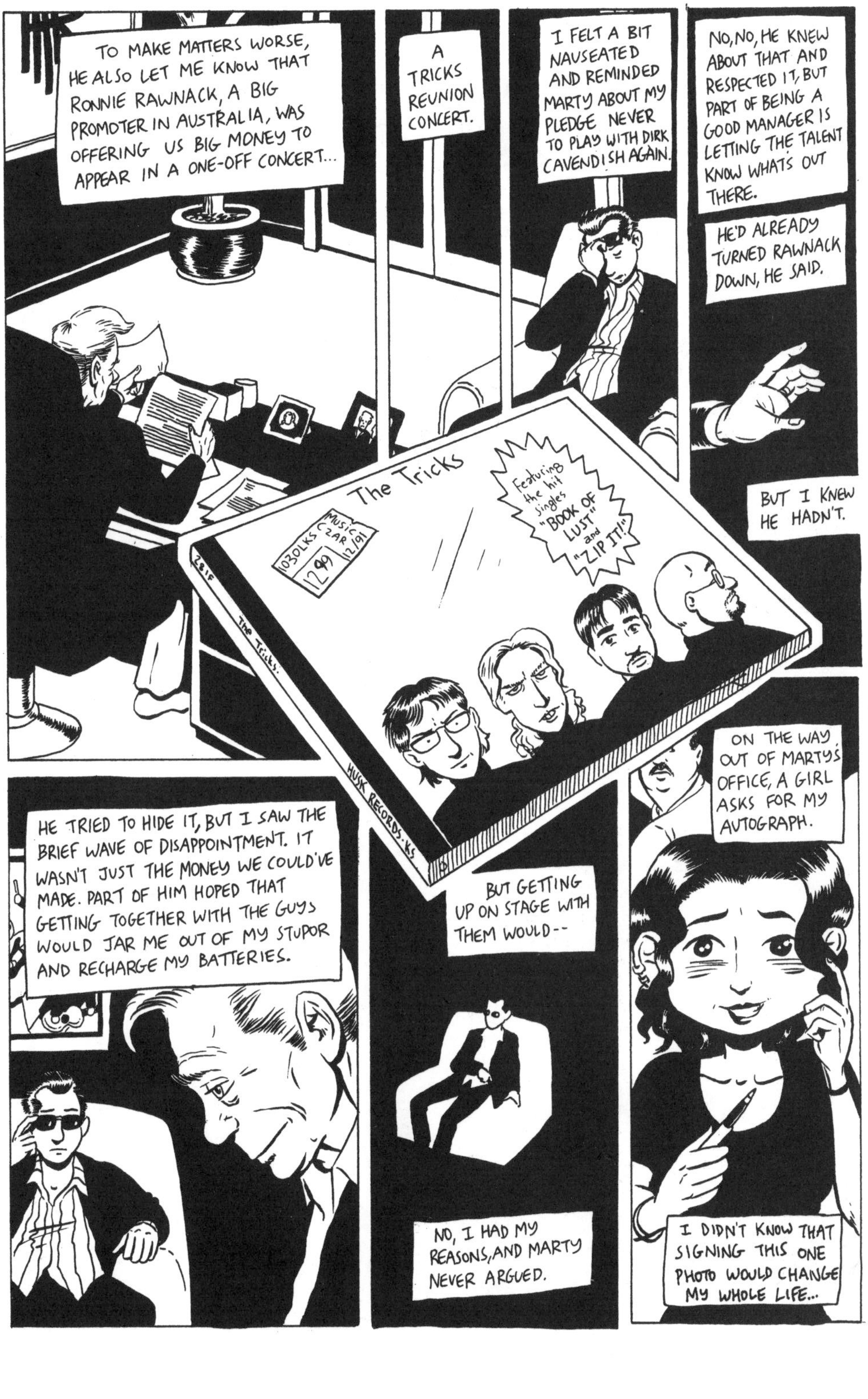
TO MAKE MATTERS WORSE, HE ALSO LET ME KNOW THAT RONNIE RAWNACK, A BIG PROMOTER IN AUSTRALIA, WAS OFFERING US BIG MONEY TO APPEAR IN A ONE-OFF CONCERT...
A TRICKS REUNION CONCERT.
I FELT A BIT NAUSEATED AND REMINDED MARTY ABOUT MY PLEDGE NEVER TO PLAY WITH DIRK CAVENDISH AGAIN.
NO, NO, HE KNEW ABOUT THAT AND RESPECTED IT, BUT PART OF BEING A GOOD MANAGER IS LETTING THE TALENT KNOW WHAT'S OUT THERE.
HE'D ALREADY TURNED RAWNACK DOWN, HE SAID.
BUT I KNEW HE HADN'T.
The Tricks
Featuring the hit singles "BOOK OF LUST" and "ZIP IT!"
MUSIC CZAR
1030LKS
12/91
12.99
The Tricks
HUSK RECORDS
HE TRIED TO HIDE IT, BUT I SAW THE BRIEF WAVE OF DISAPPOINTMENT. IT WASN'T JUST THE MONEY WE COULD'VE MADE. PART OF HIM HOPED THAT GETTING TOGETHER WITH THE GUYS WOULD JAR ME OUT OF MY STUPOR AND RECHARGE MY BATTERIES.
BUT GETTING UP ON STAGE WITH THEM WOULD--
NO, I HAD MY REASONS, AND MARTY NEVER ARGUED.
ON THE WAY OUT OF MARTY'S OFFICE, A GIRL ASKS FOR MY AUTOGRAPH.
I DIDN'T KNOW THAT SIGNING THIS ONE PHOTO WOULD CHANGE MY WHOLE LIFE...

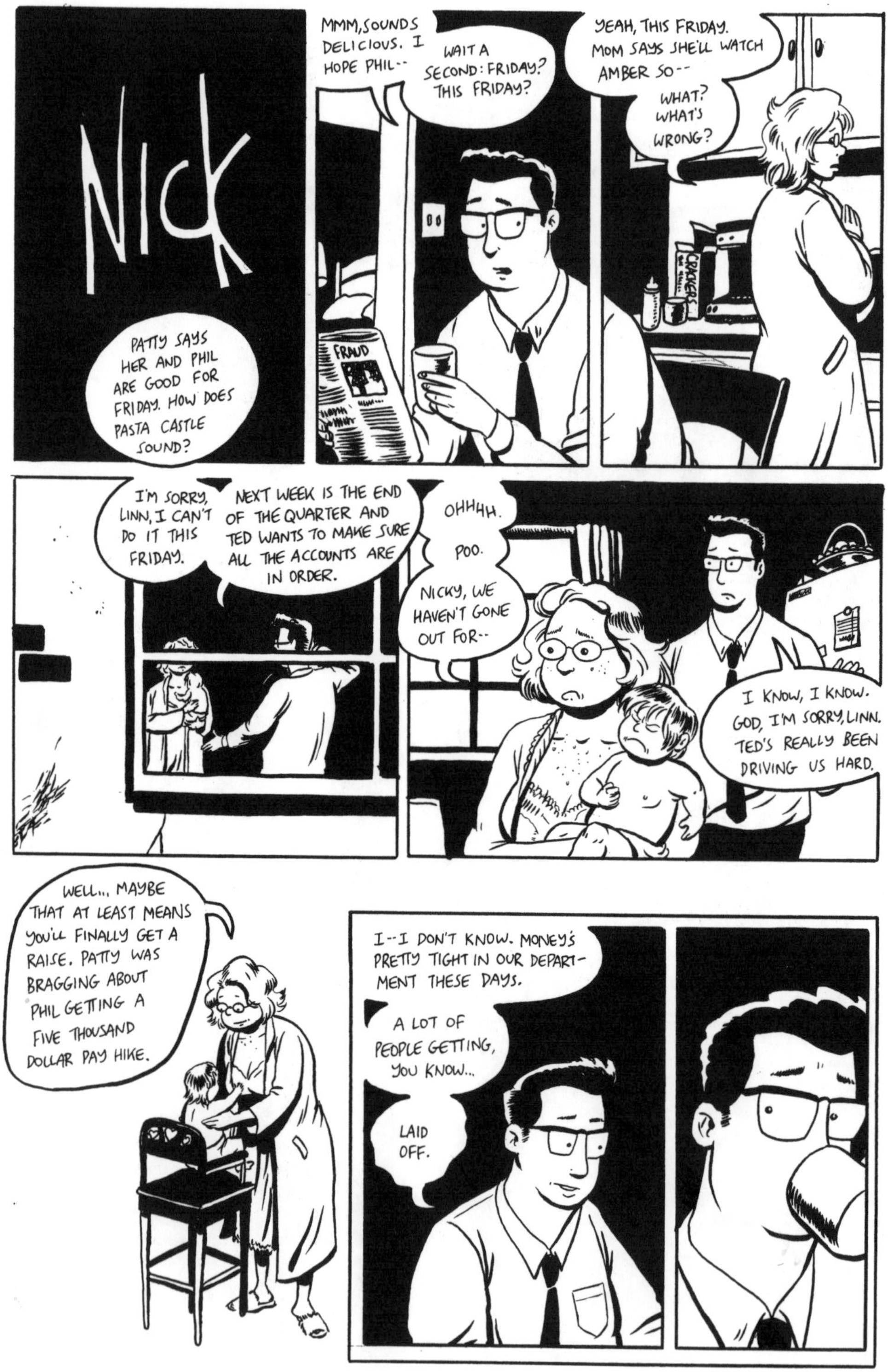
NICK
PATTY SAYS HER AND PHIL ARE GOOD FOR FRIDAY. HOW DOES PASTA CASTLE SOUND?
FRAUD
MMM, SOUNDS DELICIOUS. I HOPE PHIL--
WAIT A SECOND: FRIDAY? THIS FRIDAY?
YEAH, THIS FRIDAY. MOM SAYS SHE'LL WATCH AMBER SO--
WHAT? WHAT'S WRONG?
CRACKERS
I'M SORRY, LINN, I CAN'T DO IT THIS FRIDAY.
NEXT WEEK IS THE END OF THE QUARTER AND TED WANTS TO MAKE SURE ALL THE ACCOUNTS ARE IN ORDER.
OHHHH.
POO.
NICKY, WE HAVEN'T GONE OUT FOR--
I KNOW, I KNOW. GOD, I'M SORRY, LINN. TED'S REALLY BEEN DRIVING US HARD.
WELL... MAYBE THAT AT LEAST MEANS YOU'LL FINALLY GET A RAISE. PATTY WAS BRAGGING ABOUT PHIL GETTING A FIVE THOUSAND DOLLAR PAY HIKE.
I--I DON'T KNOW. MONEY'S PRETTY TIGHT IN OUR DEPARTMENT THESE DAYS.
A LOT OF PEOPLE GETTING, YOU KNOW...
LAID OFF.

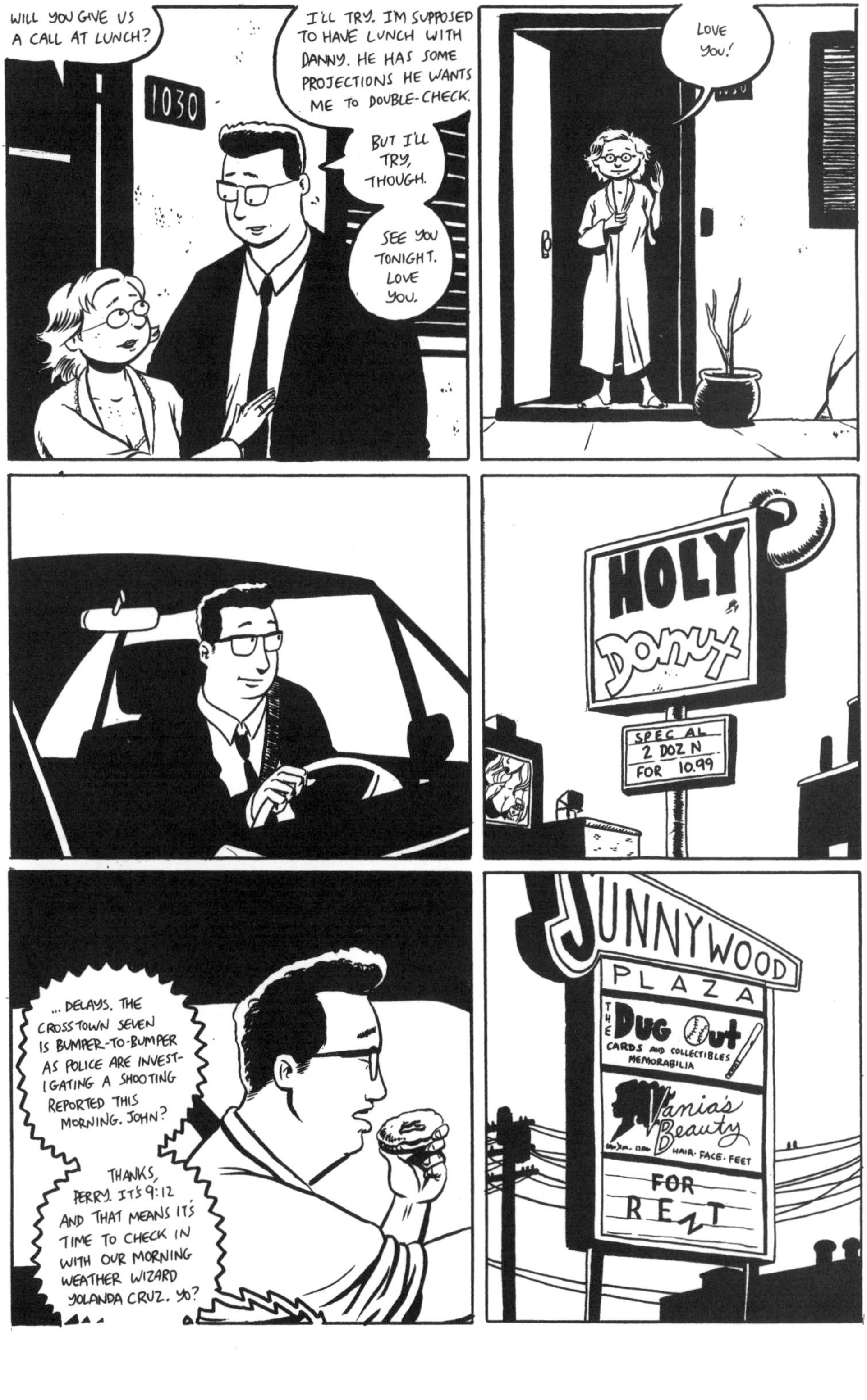
WILL YOU GIVE US A CALL AT LUNCH?
1030
I'LL TRY. I'M SUPPOSED TO HAVE LUNCH WITH DANNY. HE HAS SOME PROJECTIONS HE WANTS ME TO DOUBLE-CHECK.
BUT I'LL TRY, THOUGH.
SEE YOU TONIGHT. LOVE YOU.
LOVE YOU!
HOLY DONUT
SPEC AL 2 DOZ N FOR 10.99
... DELAYS. THE CROSSTOWN SEVEN IS BUMPER-TO-BUMPER AS POLICE ARE INVESTIGATING A SHOOTING REPORTED THIS MORNING. JOHN?
THANKS, PERRY. IT'S 9:12 AND THAT MEANS IT'S TIME TO CHECK IN WITH OUR MORNING WEATHER WIZARD YOLANDA CRUZ. YO?
UNNYWOOD PLAZA
THE DUG OUT CARDS AND COLLECTIBLES MEMORABILIA
Vania's Beauty HAIR · FACE · FEET
FOR RE T

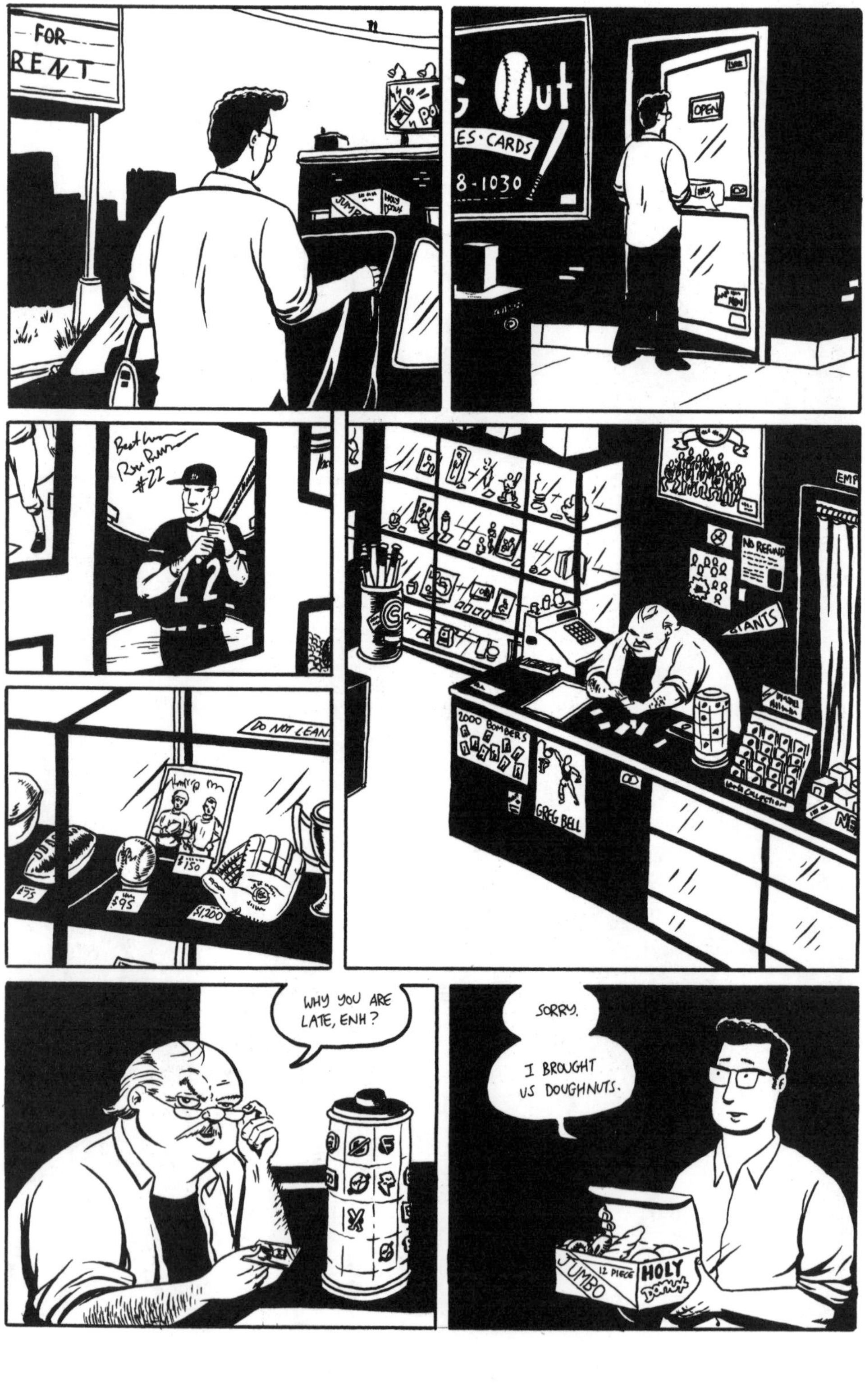
FOR
RENT
ES·CARDS
8-1030
OPEN
#22
DO NOT LEAN
$75
$95
$150
$1,200
NO REFUNDS
GIANTS
2000 BOMBERS
GREG BELL
WHY YOU ARE LATE, ENH?
SORRY.
I BROUGHT US DOUGHNUTS.
JUMBO
12 PIECE
HOLY
Donut

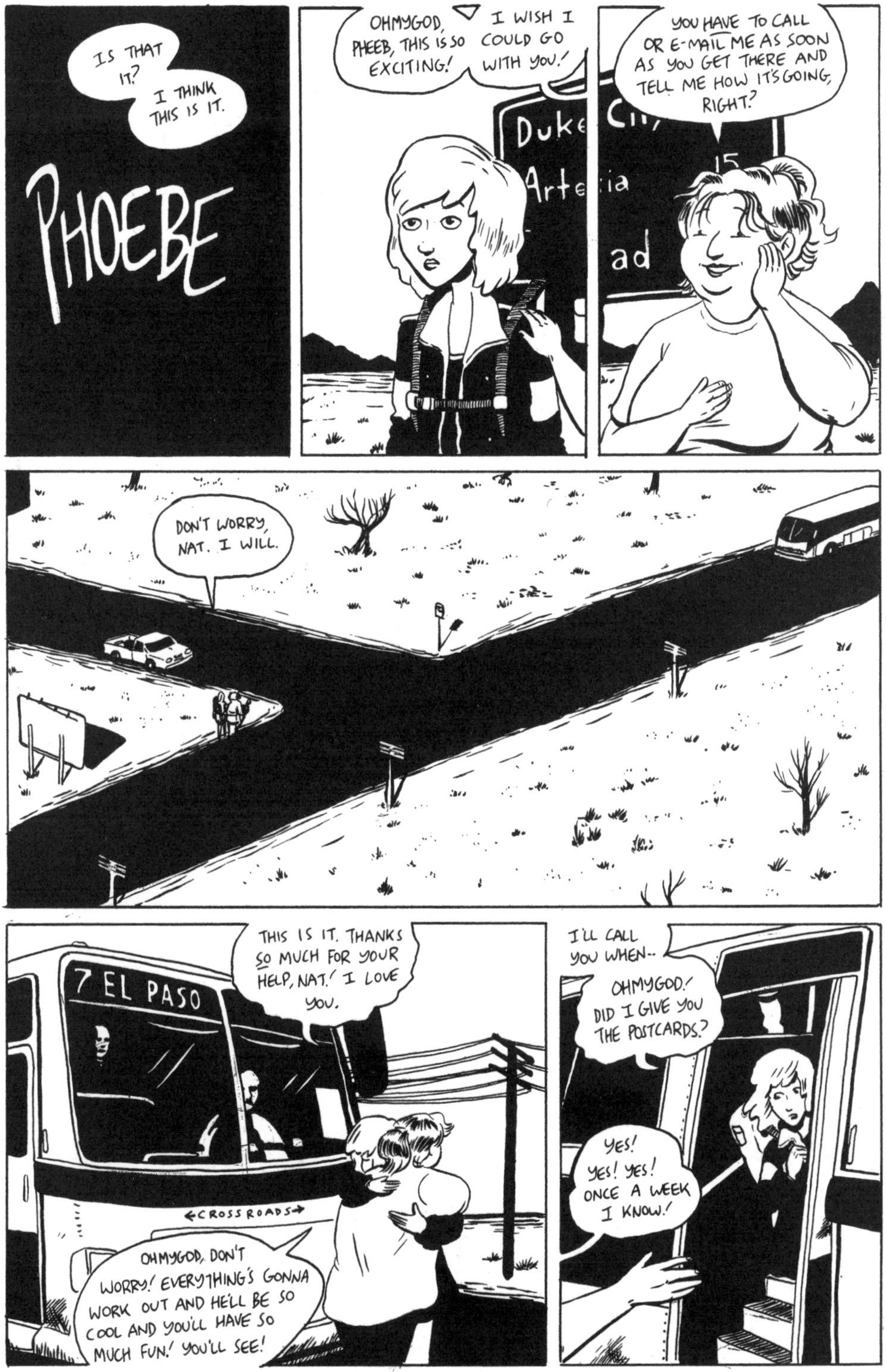
IS THAT IT?
I THINK THIS IS IT.
PHOEBE
OHMYGOD, PHEEB, THIS IS SO EXCITING!
I WISH I COULD GO WITH YOU.
YOU HAVE TO CALL OR E-MAIL ME AS SOON AS YOU GET THERE AND TELL ME HOW IT'S GOING, RIGHT?
DON'T WORRY, NAT. I WILL.
7 EL PASO
THIS IS IT. THANKS SO MUCH FOR YOUR HELP, NAT. I LOVE YOU.
←CROSSROADS→
OHMYGOD, DON'T WORRY! EVERYTHING'S GONNA WORK OUT AND HE'LL BE SO COOL AND YOU'LL HAVE SO MUCH FUN! YOU'LL SEE!
I'LL CALL YOU WHEN--
OHMYGOD! DID I GIVE YOU THE POSTCARDS?
YES! YES! YES! ONCE A WEEK I KNOW!

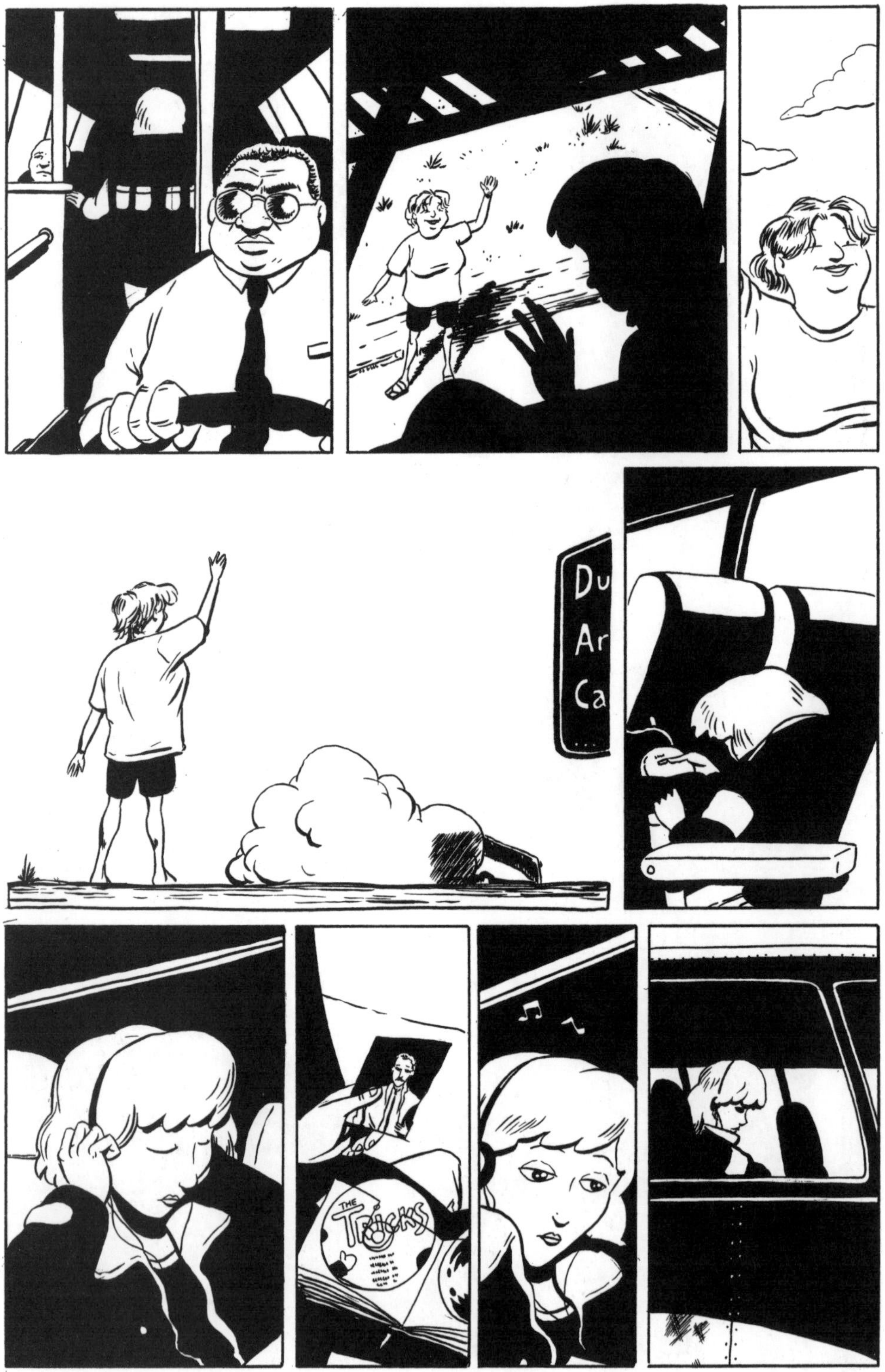
Du
Ar
Ca
THE TRICKS

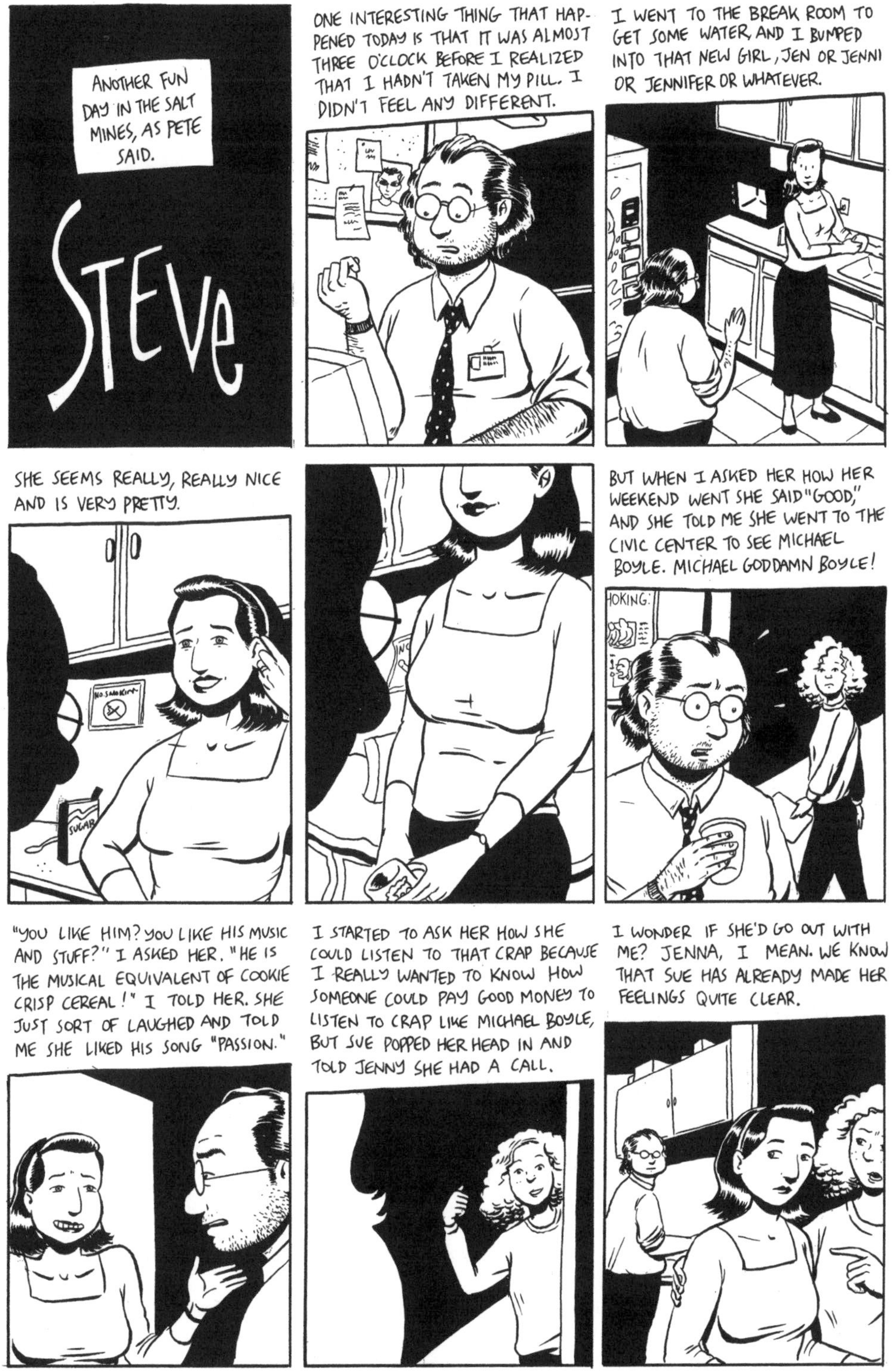
ANOTHER FUN DAY IN THE SALT MINES, AS PETE SAID.
STEVE
ONE INTERESTING THING THAT HAPPENED TODAY IS THAT IT WAS ALMOST THREE O'CLOCK BEFORE I REALIZED THAT I HADN'T TAKEN MY PILL. I DIDN'T FEEL ANY DIFFERENT.
I WENT TO THE BREAK ROOM TO GET SOME WATER, AND I BUMPED INTO THAT NEW GIRL, JEN OR JENNI OR JENNIFER OR WHATEVER.
SHE SEEMS REALLY, REALLY NICE AND IS VERY PRETTY.
SUGAR
BUT WHEN I ASKED HER HOW HER WEEKEND WENT SHE SAID "GOOD," AND SHE TOLD ME SHE WENT TO THE CIVIC CENTER TO SEE MICHAEL BOYLE. MICHAEL GODDAMN BOYLE!
"YOU LIKE HIM? YOU LIKE HIS MUSIC AND STUFF?" I ASKED HER. "HE IS THE MUSICAL EQUIVALENT OF COOKIE CRISP CEREAL!" I TOLD HER. SHE JUST SORT OF LAUGHED AND TOLD ME SHE LIKED HIS SONG "PASSION."
I STARTED TO ASK HER HOW SHE COULD LISTEN TO THAT CRAP BECAUSE I REALLY WANTED TO KNOW HOW SOMEONE COULD PAY GOOD MONEY TO LISTEN TO CRAP LIKE MICHAEL BOYLE, BUT SUE POPPED HER HEAD IN AND TOLD JENNY SHE HAD A CALL.
I WONDER IF SHE'D GO OUT WITH ME? JENNA, I MEAN. WE KNOW THAT SUE HAS ALREADY MADE HER FEELINGS QUITE CLEAR.

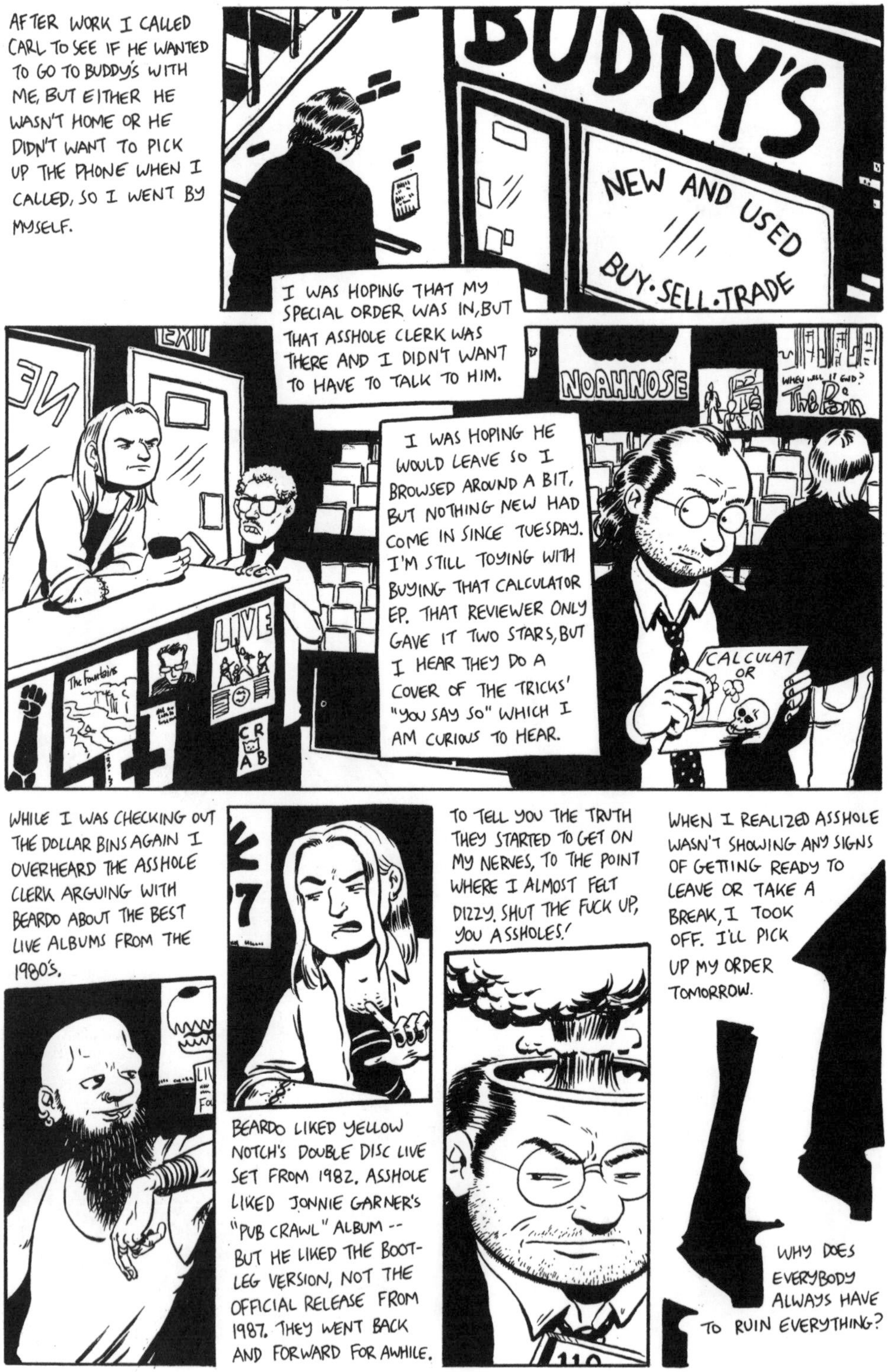
AFTER WORK I CALLED CARL TO SEE IF HE WANTED TO GO TO BUDDY'S WITH ME, BUT EITHER HE WASN'T HOME OR HE DIDN'T WANT TO PICK UP THE PHONE WHEN I CALLED, SO I WENT BY MYSELF.
BUDDY'S
NEW AND USED
BUY·SELL·TRADE
I WAS HOPING THAT MY SPECIAL ORDER WAS IN, BUT THAT ASSHOLE CLERK WAS THERE AND I DIDN'T WANT TO HAVE TO TALK TO HIM.
EXIT
NOAHNOSE
The Pain
I WAS HOPING HE WOULD LEAVE SO I BROWSED AROUND A BIT, BUT NOTHING NEW HAD COME IN SINCE TUESDAY. I'M STILL TOYING WITH BUYING THAT CALCULATOR EP. THAT REVIEWER ONLY GAVE IT TWO STARS, BUT I HEAR THEY DO A COVER OF THE TRICKS' "YOU SAY SO" WHICH I AM CURIOUS TO HEAR.
LIVE
The Fountains
CRAB
CALCULATOR
WHILE I WAS CHECKING OUT THE DOLLAR BINS AGAIN I OVERHEARD THE ASSHOLE CLERK ARGUING WITH BEARDO ABOUT THE BEST LIVE ALBUMS FROM THE 1980'S.
BEARDO LIKED YELLOW NOTCH'S DOUBLE DISC LIVE SET FROM 1982. ASSHOLE LIKED JONNIE GARNER'S "PUB CRAWL" ALBUM -- BUT HE LIKED THE BOOT-LEG VERSION, NOT THE OFFICIAL RELEASE FROM 1987. THEY WENT BACK AND FORWARD FOR AWHILE.
TO TELL YOU THE TRUTH THEY STARTED TO GET ON MY NERVES, TO THE POINT WHERE I ALMOST FELT DIZZY. SHUT THE FUCK UP, YOU ASSHOLES!
WHEN I REALIZED ASSHOLE WASN'T SHOWING ANY SIGNS OF GETTING READY TO LEAVE OR TAKE A BREAK, I TOOK OFF. I'LL PICK UP MY ORDER TOMORROW.
WHY DOES EVERYBODY ALWAYS HAVE TO RUIN EVERYTHING?

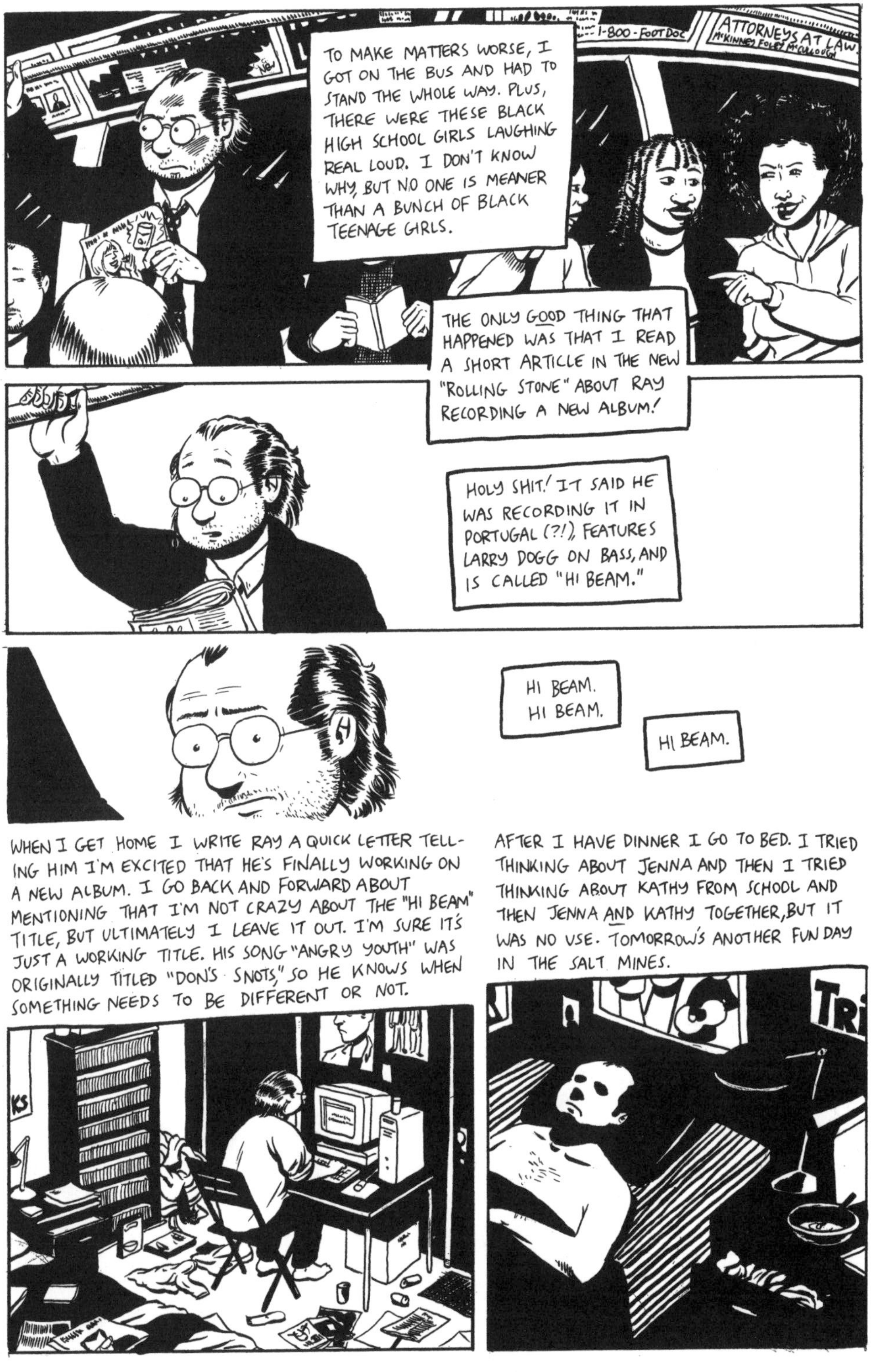
1-800-FOOT DOC
ATTORNEYS AT LAW
TO MAKE MATTERS WORSE, I GOT ON THE BUS AND HAD TO STAND THE WHOLE WAY. PLUS, THERE WERE THESE BLACK HIGH SCHOOL GIRLS LAUGHING REAL LOUD. I DON'T KNOW WHY, BUT NO ONE IS MEANER THAN A BUNCH OF BLACK TEENAGE GIRLS.
THE ONLY GOOD THING THAT HAPPENED WAS THAT I READ A SHORT ARTICLE IN THE NEW "ROLLING STONE" ABOUT RAY RECORDING A NEW ALBUM!
HOLY SHIT! IT SAID HE WAS RECORDING IT IN PORTUGAL (?!), FEATURES LARRY DOGG ON BASS, AND IS CALLED "HI BEAM."
HI BEAM. HI BEAM.
HI BEAM.
WHEN I GET HOME I WRITE RAY A QUICK LETTER TELLING HIM I'M EXCITED THAT HE'S FINALLY WORKING ON A NEW ALBUM. I GO BACK AND FORWARD ABOUT MENTIONING THAT I'M NOT CRAZY ABOUT THE "HI BEAM" TITLE, BUT ULTIMATELY I LEAVE IT OUT. I'M SURE IT'S JUST A WORKING TITLE. HIS SONG "ANGRY YOUTH" WAS ORIGINALLY TITLED "DON'S SNOTS," SO HE KNOWS WHEN SOMETHING NEEDS TO BE DIFFERENT OR NOT.
AFTER I HAVE DINNER I GO TO BED. I TRIED THINKING ABOUT JENNA AND THEN I TRIED THINKING ABOUT KATHY FROM SCHOOL AND THEN JENNA AND KATHY TOGETHER, BUT IT WAS NO USE. TOMORROW'S ANOTHER FUN DAY IN THE SALT MINES.

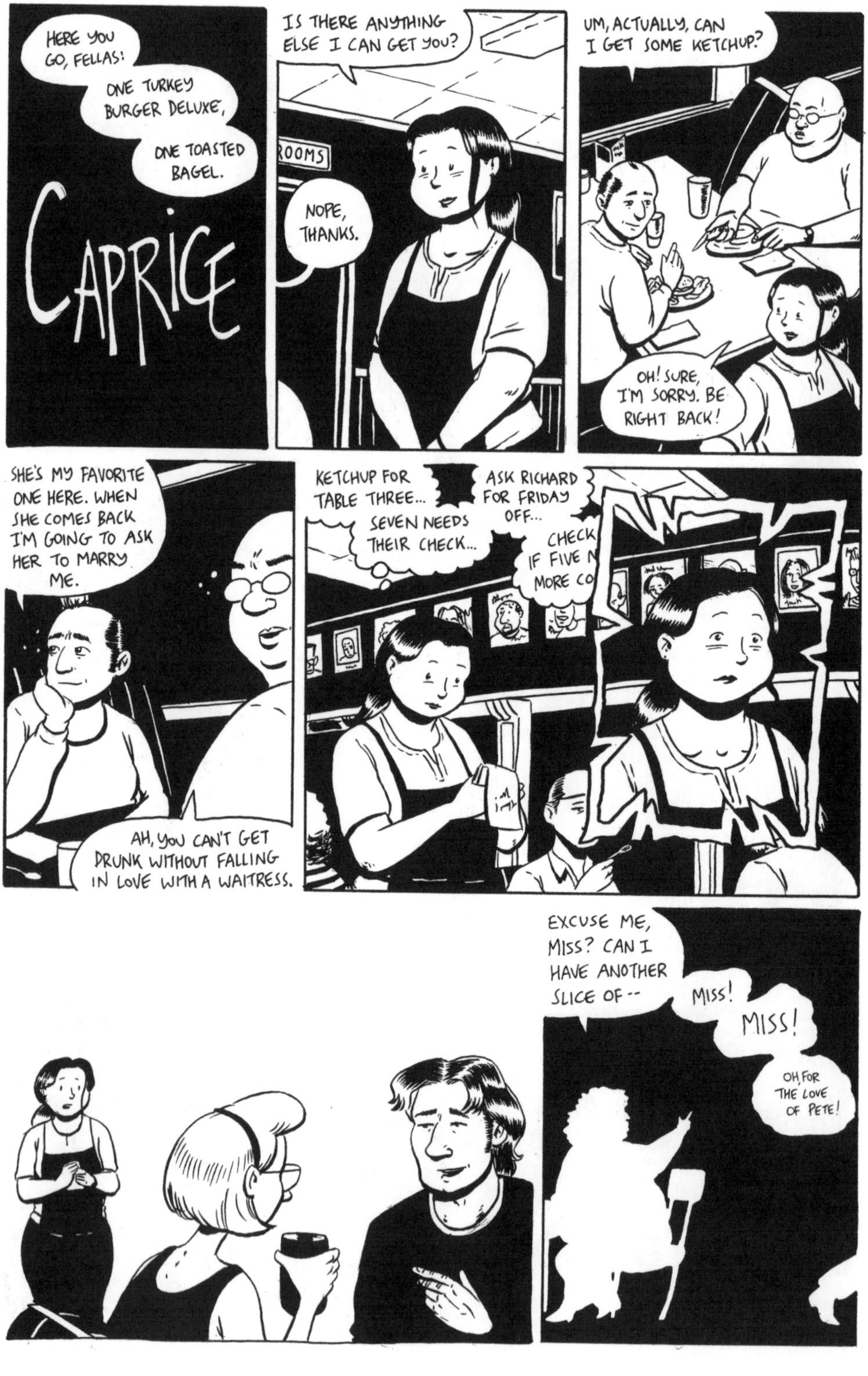
HERE YOU GO, FELLAS!
ONE TURKEY BURGER DELUXE,
ONE TOASTED BAGEL.
CAPRICE
IS THERE ANYTHING ELSE I CAN GET YOU?
ROOMS
NOPE, THANKS.
UM, ACTUALLY, CAN I GET SOME KETCHUP?
OH! SURE, I'M SORRY. BE RIGHT BACK!
SHE'S MY FAVORITE ONE HERE. WHEN SHE COMES BACK I'M GOING TO ASK HER TO MARRY ME.
AH, YOU CAN'T GET DRUNK WITHOUT FALLING IN LOVE WITH A WAITRESS.
KETCHUP FOR TABLE THREE...
SEVEN NEEDS THEIR CHECK...
ASK RICHARD FOR FRIDAY OFF...
CHECK IF FIVE N MORE CO
EXCUSE ME, MISS? CAN I HAVE ANOTHER SLICE OF --
MISS!
MISS!
OH, FOR THE LOVE OF PETE!

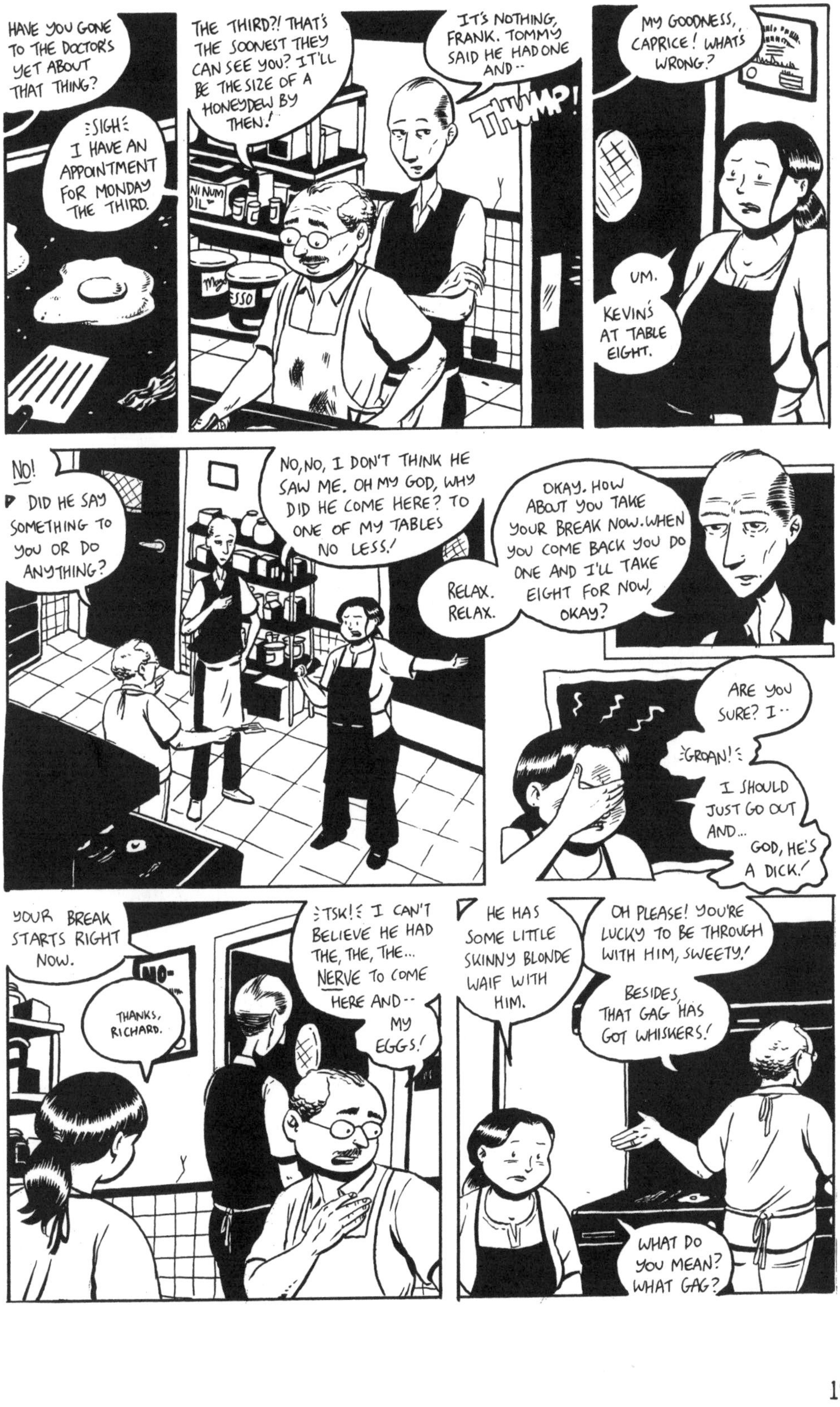
HAVE YOU GONE TO THE DOCTOR'S YET ABOUT THAT THING?
SIGH I HAVE AN APPOINTMENT FOR MONDAY THE THIRD.
THE THIRD?! THAT'S THE SOONEST THEY CAN SEE YOU? IT'LL BE THE SIZE OF A HONEYDEW BY THEN!
IT'S NOTHING, FRANK. TOMMY SAID HE HAD ONE AND--
THUMP!
MY GOODNESS, CAPRICE! WHAT'S WRONG?
UM.
KEVIN'S AT TABLE EIGHT.
NO!
DID HE SAY SOMETHING TO YOU OR DO ANYTHING?
NO, NO, I DON'T THINK HE SAW ME. OH MY GOD, WHY DID HE COME HERE? TO ONE OF MY TABLES NO LESS!
RELAX. RELAX.
OKAY. HOW ABOUT YOU TAKE YOUR BREAK NOW. WHEN YOU COME BACK YOU DO ONE AND I'LL TAKE EIGHT FOR NOW, OKAY?
ARE YOU SURE? I--
GROAN!
I SHOULD JUST GO OUT AND...
GOD, HE'S A DICK!
YOUR BREAK STARTS RIGHT NOW.
THANKS, RICHARD.
TSK! I CAN'T BELIEVE HE HAD THE, THE, THE... NERVE TO COME HERE AND--
MY EGGS!
HE HAS SOME LITTLE SKINNY BLONDE WAIF WITH HIM.
OH PLEASE! YOU'RE LUCKY TO BE THROUGH WITH HIM, SWEETY!
BESIDES, THAT GAG HAS GOT WHISKERS!
WHAT DO YOU MEAN? WHAT GAG?

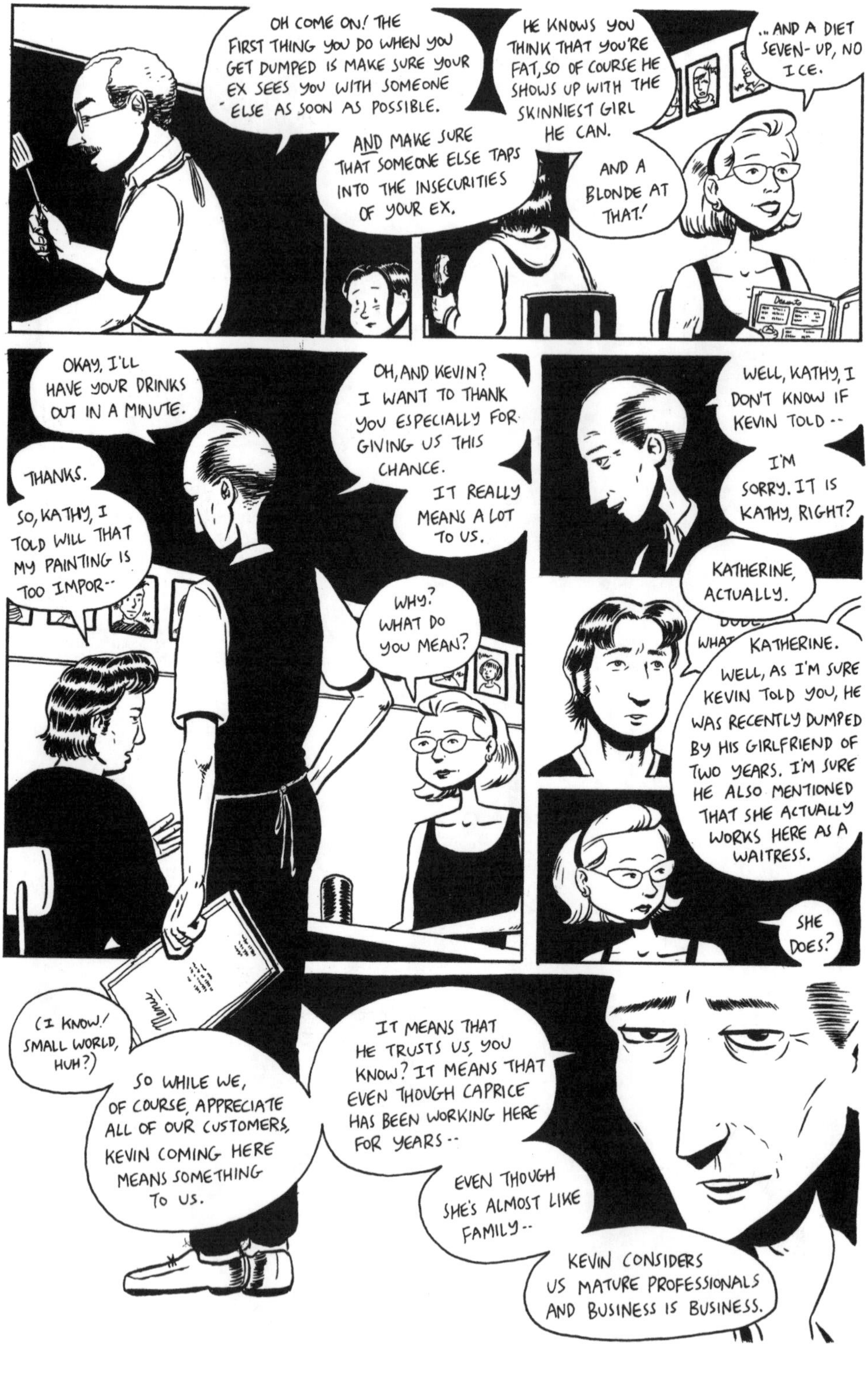
OH COME ON! THE FIRST THING YOU DO WHEN YOU GET DUMPED IS MAKE SURE YOUR EX SEES YOU WITH SOMEONE ELSE AS SOON AS POSSIBLE.
AND MAKE SURE THAT SOMEONE ELSE TAPS INTO THE INSECURITIES OF YOUR EX.
HE KNOWS YOU THINK THAT YOU'RE FAT, SO OF COURSE HE SHOWS UP WITH THE SKINNIEST GIRL HE CAN.
AND A BLONDE AT THAT!
...AND A DIET SEVEN-UP, NO ICE.
OKAY, I'LL HAVE YOUR DRINKS OUT IN A MINUTE.
THANKS.
SO, KATHY, I TOLD WILL THAT MY PAINTING IS TOO IMPOR--
OH, AND KEVIN? I WANT TO THANK YOU ESPECIALLY FOR GIVING US THIS CHANCE.
IT REALLY MEANS A LOT TO US.
WHY? WHAT DO YOU MEAN?
WELL, KATHY, I DON'T KNOW IF KEVIN TOLD --
I'M SORRY. IT IS KATHY, RIGHT?
KATHERINE, ACTUALLY.
KATHERINE.
WELL, AS I'M SURE KEVIN TOLD YOU, HE WAS RECENTLY DUMPED BY HIS GIRLFRIEND OF TWO YEARS. I'M SURE HE ALSO MENTIONED THAT SHE ACTUALLY WORKS HERE AS A WAITRESS.
SHE DOES?
(I KNOW! SMALL WORLD, HUH?)
SO WHILE WE, OF COURSE, APPRECIATE ALL OF OUR CUSTOMERS, KEVIN COMING HERE MEANS SOMETHING TO US.
IT MEANS THAT HE TRUSTS US, YOU KNOW? IT MEANS THAT EVEN THOUGH CAPRICE HAS BEEN WORKING HERE FOR YEARS --
EVEN THOUGH SHE'S ALMOST LIKE FAMILY --
KEVIN CONSIDERS US MATURE PROFESSIONALS AND BUSINESS IS BUSINESS.

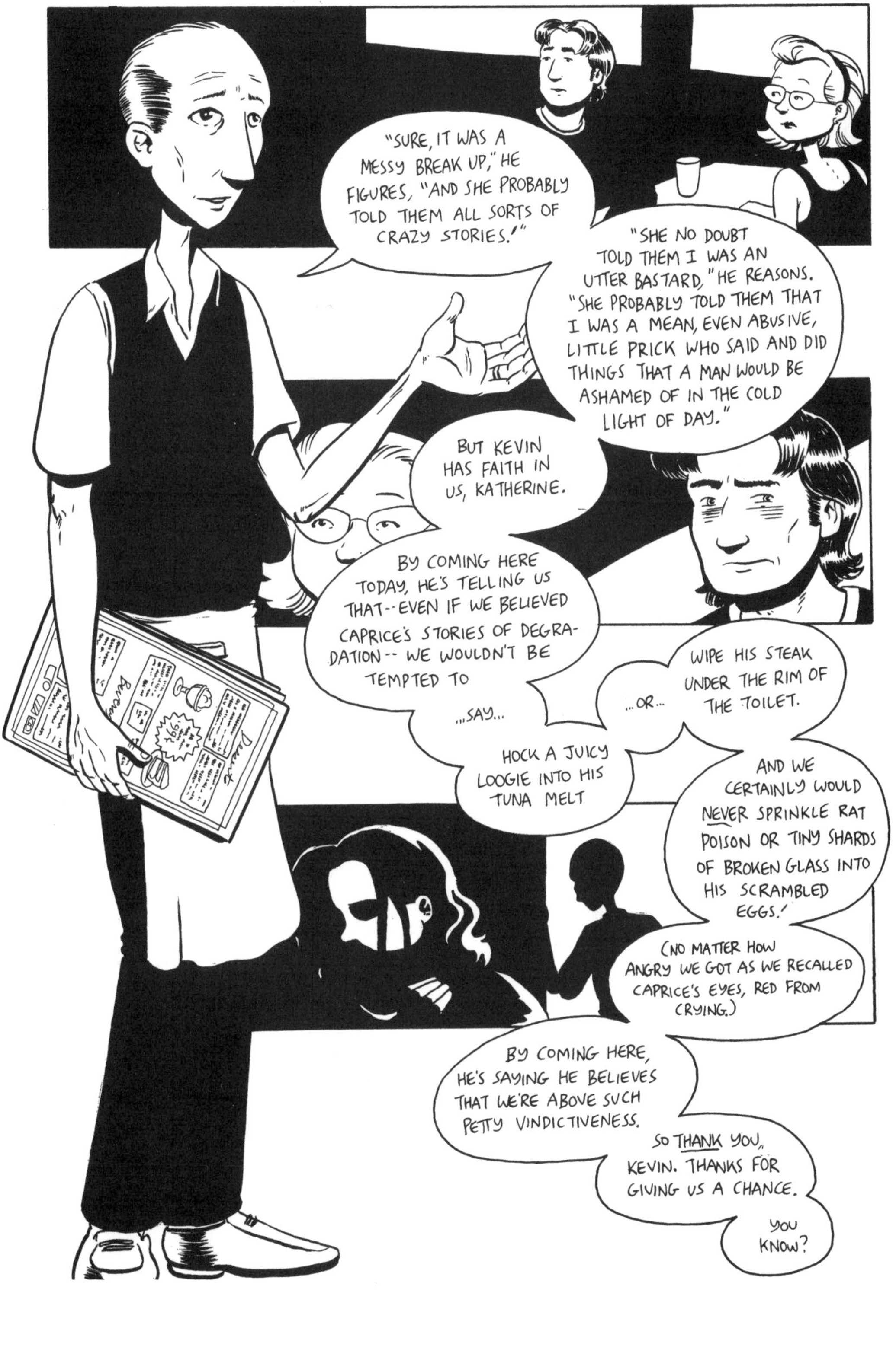
"SURE, IT WAS A MESSY BREAK UP," HE FIGURES, "AND SHE PROBABLY TOLD THEM ALL SORTS OF CRAZY STORIES!"
"SHE NO DOUBT TOLD THEM I WAS AN UTTER BASTARD," HE REASONS. "SHE PROBABLY TOLD THEM THAT I WAS A MEAN, EVEN ABUSIVE, LITTLE PRICK WHO SAID AND DID THINGS THAT A MAN WOULD BE ASHAMED OF IN THE COLD LIGHT OF DAY."
BUT KEVIN HAS FAITH IN US, KATHERINE.
BY COMING HERE TODAY, HE'S TELLING US THAT--EVEN IF WE BELIEVED CAPRICE'S STORIES OF DEGRADATION-- WE WOULDN'T BE TEMPTED TO
...SAY...
HOCK A JUICY LOOGIE INTO HIS TUNA MELT
...OR...
WIPE HIS STEAK UNDER THE RIM OF THE TOILET.
AND WE CERTAINLY WOULD NEVER SPRINKLE RAT POISON OR TINY SHARDS OF BROKEN GLASS INTO HIS SCRAMBLED EGGS!
(NO MATTER HOW ANGRY WE GOT AS WE RECALLED CAPRICE'S EYES, RED FROM CRYING.)
BY COMING HERE, HE'S SAYING HE BELIEVES THAT WE'RE ABOVE SUCH PETTY VINDICTIVENESS.
SO THANK YOU, KEVIN. THANKS FOR GIVING US A CHANCE.
YOU KNOW?

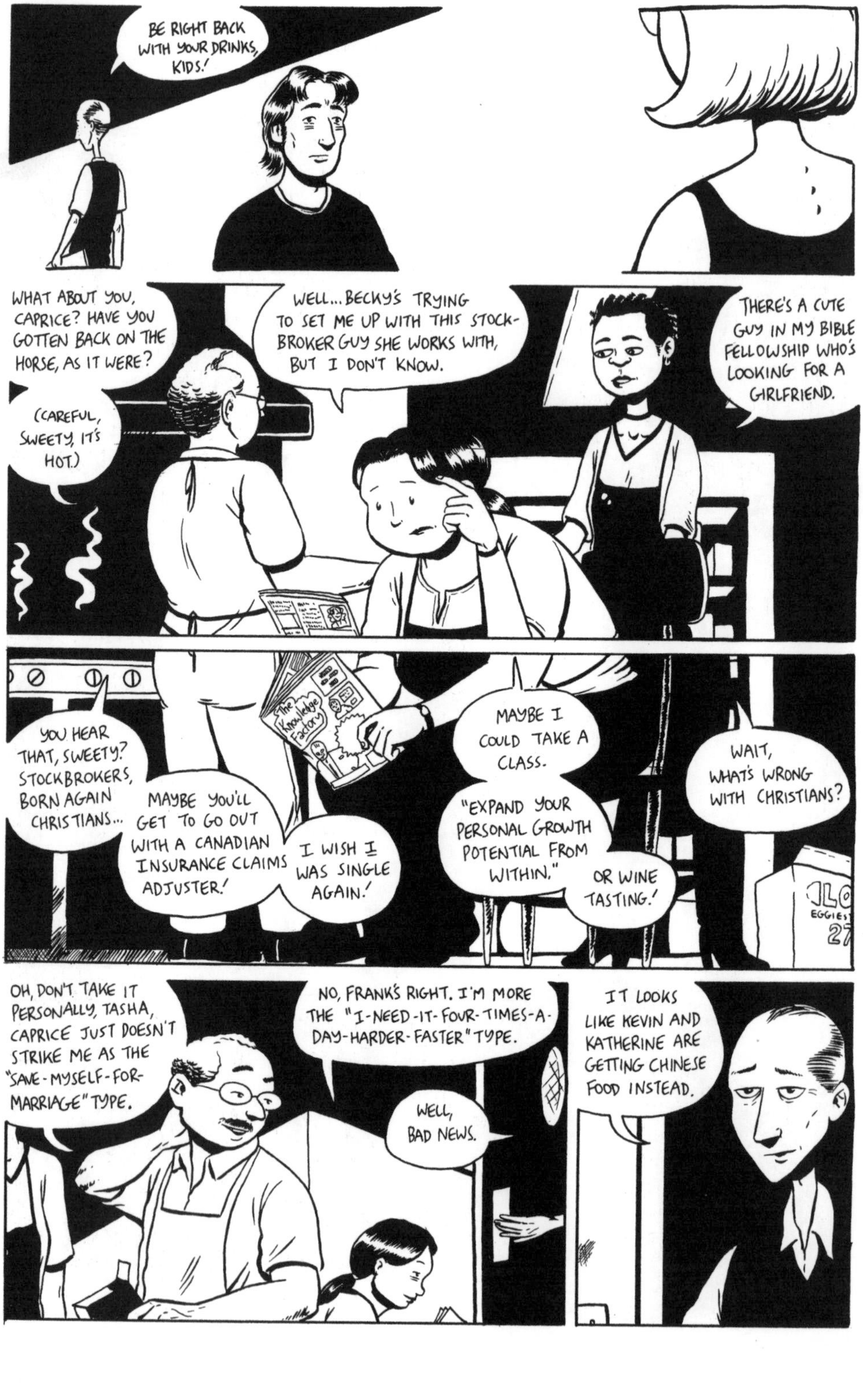
BE RIGHT BACK WITH YOUR DRINKS, KIDS!
WHAT ABOUT YOU, CAPRICE? HAVE YOU GOTTEN BACK ON THE HORSE, AS IT WERE?
(CAREFUL, SWEETY, IT'S HOT.)
WELL... BECKY'S TRYING TO SET ME UP WITH THIS STOCK-BROKER GUY SHE WORKS WITH, BUT I DON'T KNOW.
THERE'S A CUTE GUY IN MY BIBLE FELLOWSHIP WHO'S LOOKING FOR A GIRLFRIEND.
The Knowledge Factory
YOU HEAR THAT, SWEETY? STOCKBROKERS, BORN AGAIN CHRISTIANS...
MAYBE YOU'LL GET TO GO OUT WITH A CANADIAN INSURANCE CLAIMS ADJUSTER!
I WISH I WAS SINGLE AGAIN!
MAYBE I COULD TAKE A CLASS.
"EXPAND YOUR PERSONAL GROWTH POTENTIAL FROM WITHIN."
OR WINE TASTING!
WAIT, WHAT'S WRONG WITH CHRISTIANS?
OH, DON'T TAKE IT PERSONALLY, TASHA, CAPRICE JUST DOESN'T STRIKE ME AS THE "SAVE-MYSELF-FOR-MARRIAGE" TYPE.
NO, FRANK'S RIGHT. I'M MORE THE "I-NEED-IT-FOUR-TIMES-A-DAY-HARDER-FASTER" TYPE.
WELL, BAD NEWS.
IT LOOKS LIKE KEVIN AND KATHERINE ARE GETTING CHINESE FOOD INSTEAD.

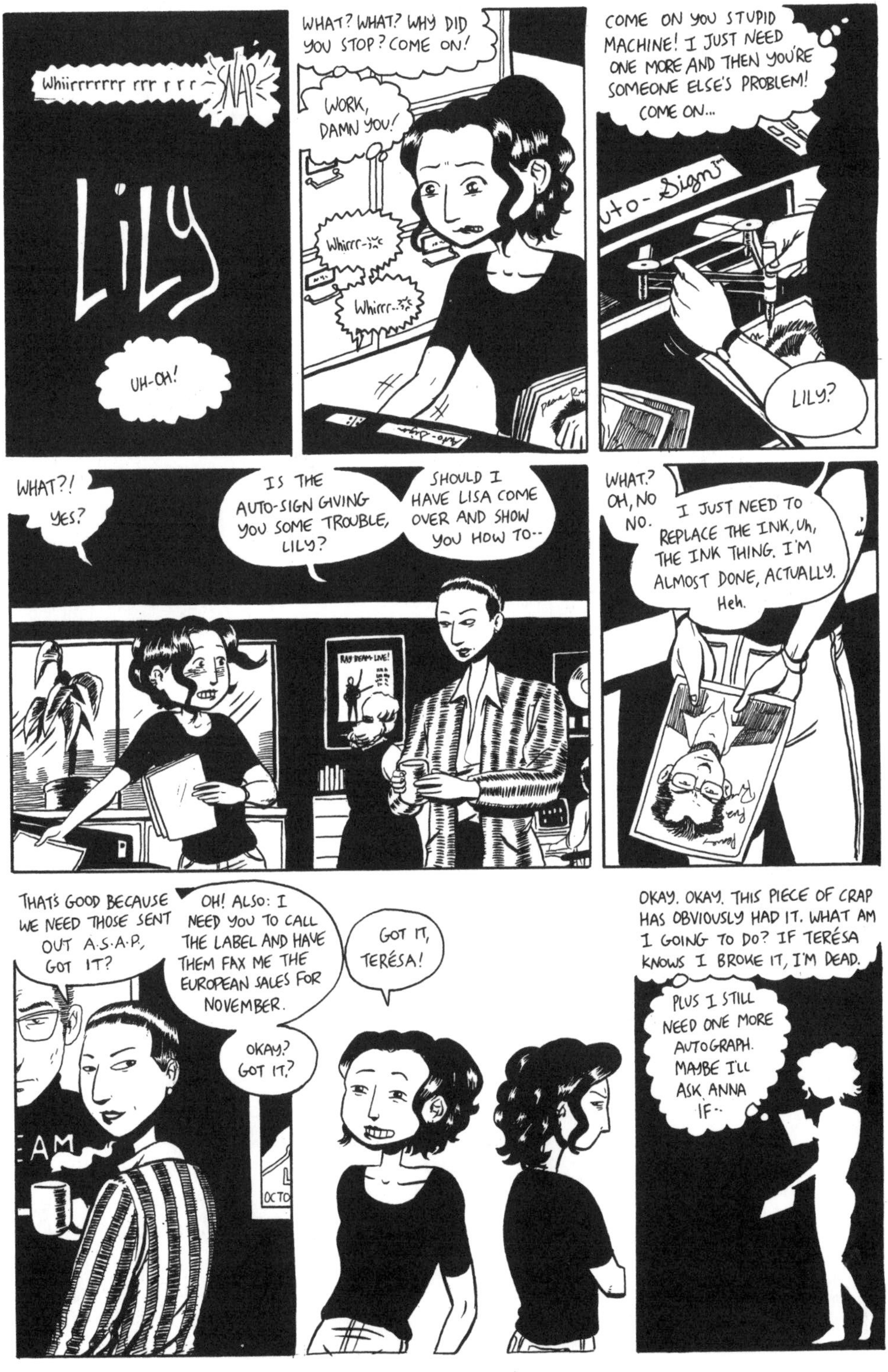
Whiirrrrrrr rrr r r r SNAP
LiLy
UH-OH!
WHAT? WHAT? WHY DID YOU STOP? COME ON!
WORK, DAMN YOU!
Whirrr--
Whirrr--
COME ON YOU STUPID MACHINE! I JUST NEED ONE MORE AND THEN YOU'RE SOMEONE ELSE'S PROBLEM! COME ON...
Auto-Sign
LILY?
WHAT?! YES?
IS THE AUTO-SIGN GIVING YOU SOME TROUBLE, LILY?
SHOULD I HAVE LISA COME OVER AND SHOW YOU HOW TO--
RAY BEAM LIVE!
WHAT? OH, NO NO.
I JUST NEED TO REPLACE THE INK, Uh, THE INK THING. I'M ALMOST DONE, ACTUALLY. Heh.
THAT'S GOOD BECAUSE WE NEED THOSE SENT OUT A.S.A.P., GOT IT?
OH! ALSO: I NEED YOU TO CALL THE LABEL AND HAVE THEM FAX ME THE EUROPEAN SALES FOR NOVEMBER.
OKAY? GOT IT?
GOT IT, TERÉSA!
OKAY. OKAY. THIS PIECE OF CRAP HAS OBVIOUSLY HAD IT. WHAT AM I GOING TO DO? IF TERÉSA KNOWS I BROKE IT, I'M DEAD.
PLUS I STILL NEED ONE MORE AUTOGRAPH. MAYBE I'LL ASK ANNA IF--

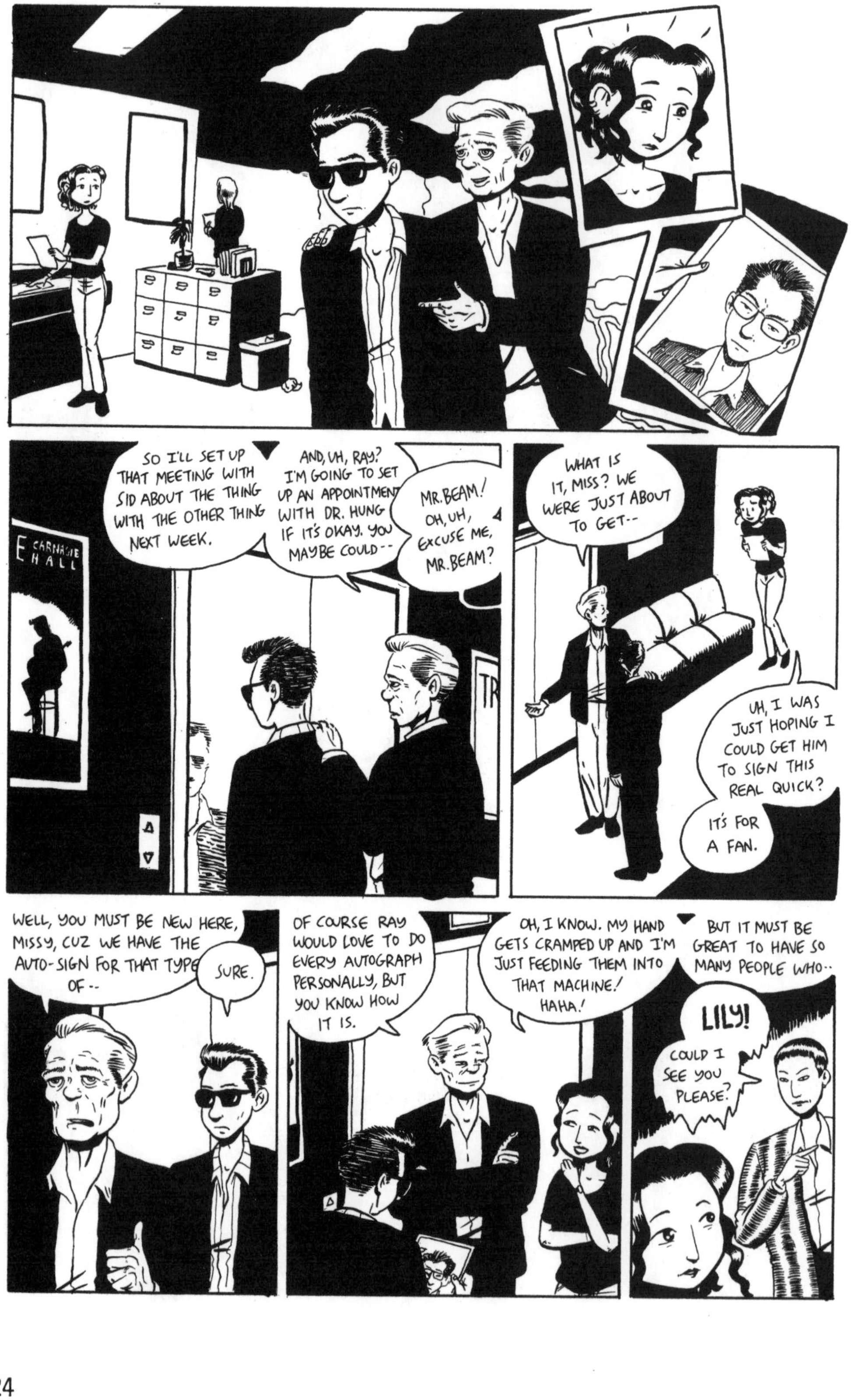
CARNAGIE HALL
SO I'LL SET UP THAT MEETING WITH SID ABOUT THE THING WITH THE OTHER THING NEXT WEEK.
AND, UH, RAY? I'M GOING TO SET UP AN APPOINTMENT WITH DR. HUNG IF IT'S OKAY. YOU MAYBE COULD--
MR. BEAM! OH, UH, EXCUSE ME, MR. BEAM?
WHAT IS IT, MISS? WE WERE JUST ABOUT TO GET--
UH, I WAS JUST HOPING I COULD GET HIM TO SIGN THIS REAL QUICK?
IT'S FOR A FAN.
WELL, YOU MUST BE NEW HERE, MISSY, CUZ WE HAVE THE AUTO-SIGN FOR THAT TYPE OF--
SURE.
OF COURSE RAY WOULD LOVE TO DO EVERY AUTOGRAPH PERSONALLY, BUT YOU KNOW HOW IT IS.
OH, I KNOW. MY HAND GETS CRAMPED UP AND I'M JUST FEEDING THEM INTO THAT MACHINE! HAHA!
BUT IT MUST BE GREAT TO HAVE SO MANY PEOPLE WHO..
LILY!
COULD I SEE YOU PLEASE?

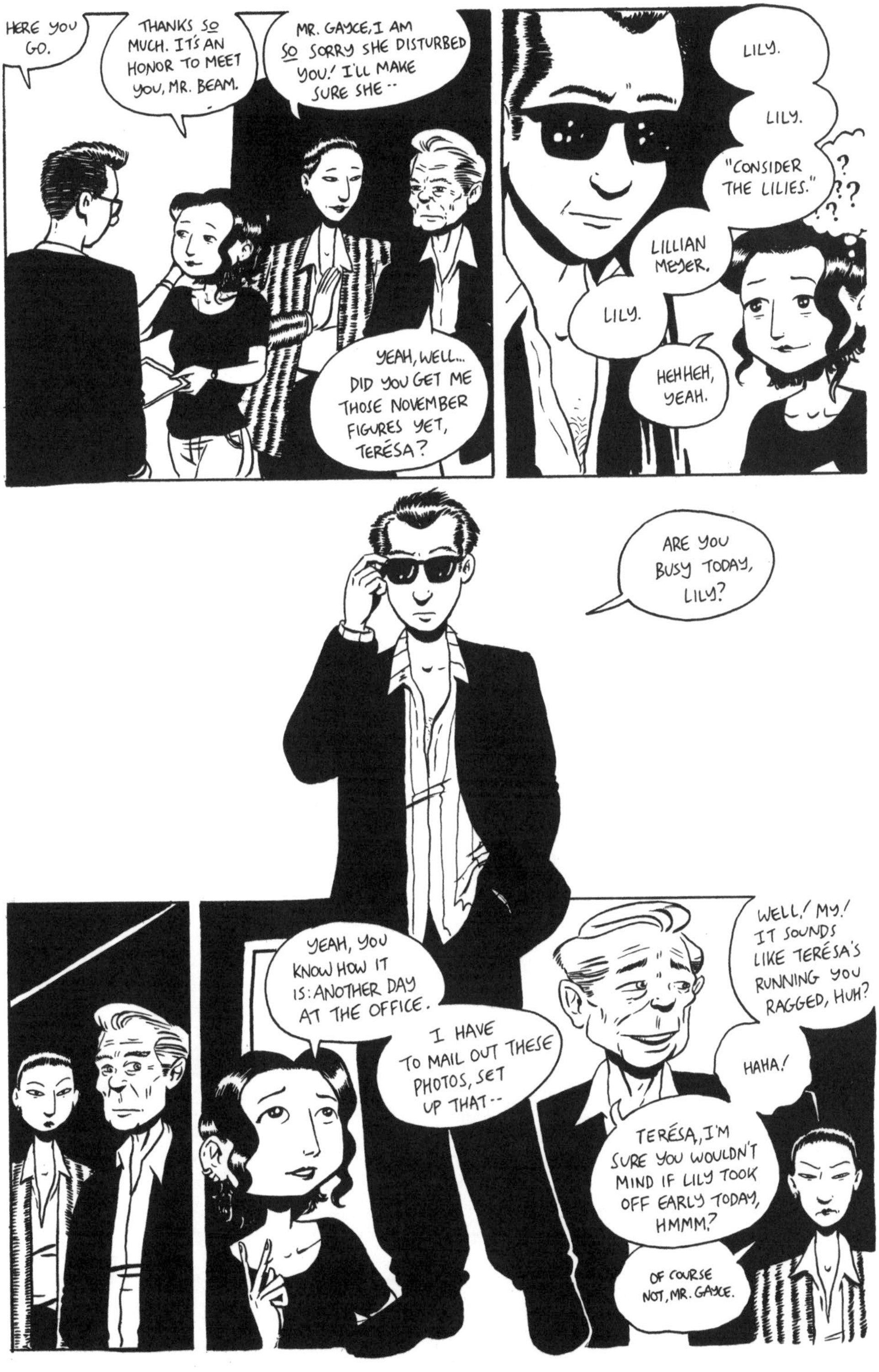
HERE YOU GO.
THANKS SO MUCH. IT'S AN HONOR TO MEET YOU, MR. BEAM.
MR. GAYCE, I AM SO SORRY SHE DISTURBED YOU! I'LL MAKE SURE SHE--
YEAH, WELL... DID YOU GET ME THOSE NOVEMBER FIGURES YET, TERÉSA?
LILY.
LILY.
"CONSIDER THE LILIES."
???
LILLIAN MEYER.
LILY.
HEHHEH, YEAH.
ARE YOU BUSY TODAY, LILY?
YEAH, YOU KNOW HOW IT IS: ANOTHER DAY AT THE OFFICE.
I HAVE TO MAIL OUT THESE PHOTOS, SET UP THAT--
WELL! MY! IT SOUNDS LIKE TERÉSA'S RUNNING YOU RAGGED, HUH?
HAHA!
TERÉSA, I'M SURE YOU WOULDN'T MIND IF LILY TOOK OFF EARLY TODAY, HMMM?
OF COURSE NOT, MR. GAYCE.

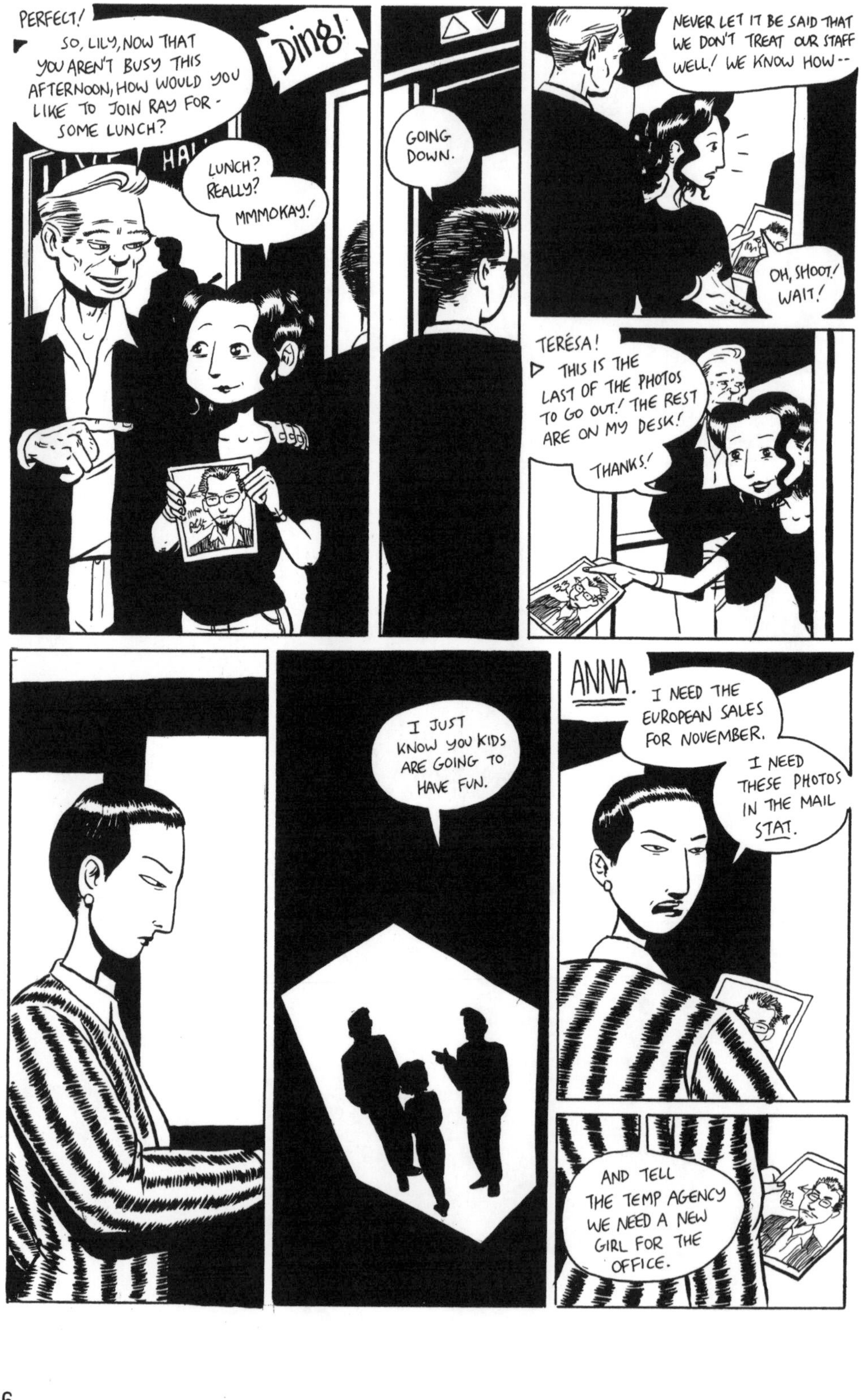
PERFECT!
SO, LILY, NOW THAT YOU AREN'T BUSY THIS AFTERNOON, HOW WOULD YOU LIKE TO JOIN RAY FOR - SOME LUNCH?
Ding!
LUNCH? REALLY? MMMOKAY!
GOING DOWN.
NEVER LET IT BE SAID THAT WE DON'T TREAT OUR STAFF WELL! WE KNOW HOW--
OH, SHOOT! WAIT!
TERÉSA!
THIS IS THE LAST OF THE PHOTOS TO GO OUT! THE REST ARE ON MY DESK!
THANKS!
I JUST KNOW YOU KIDS ARE GOING TO HAVE FUN.
ANNA.
I NEED THE EUROPEAN SALES FOR NOVEMBER.
I NEED THESE PHOTOS IN THE MAIL STAT.
AND TELL THE TEMP AGENCY WE NEED A NEW GIRL FOR THE OFFICE.

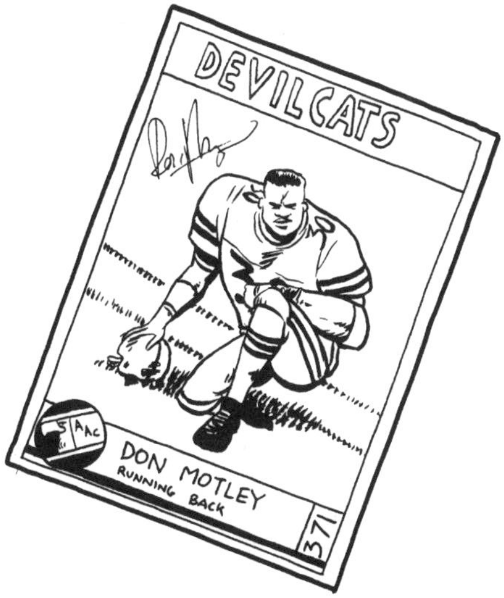
DEVIL CATS
DON MOTLEY
RUNNING BACK
371

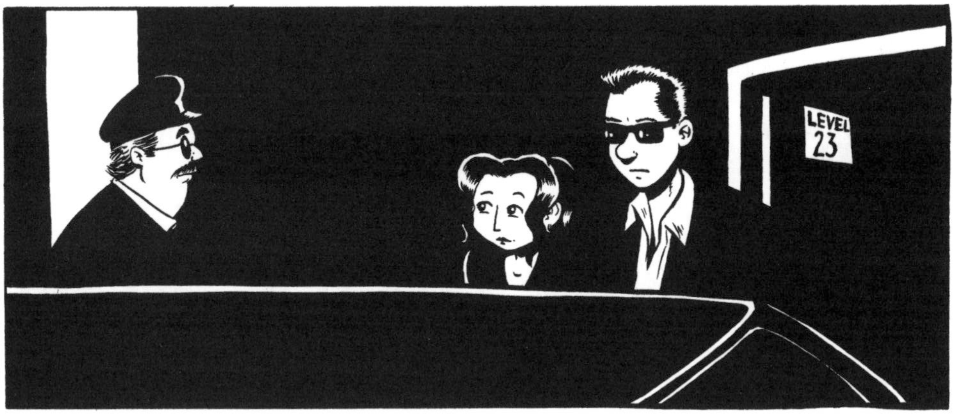
LEVEL
23

49

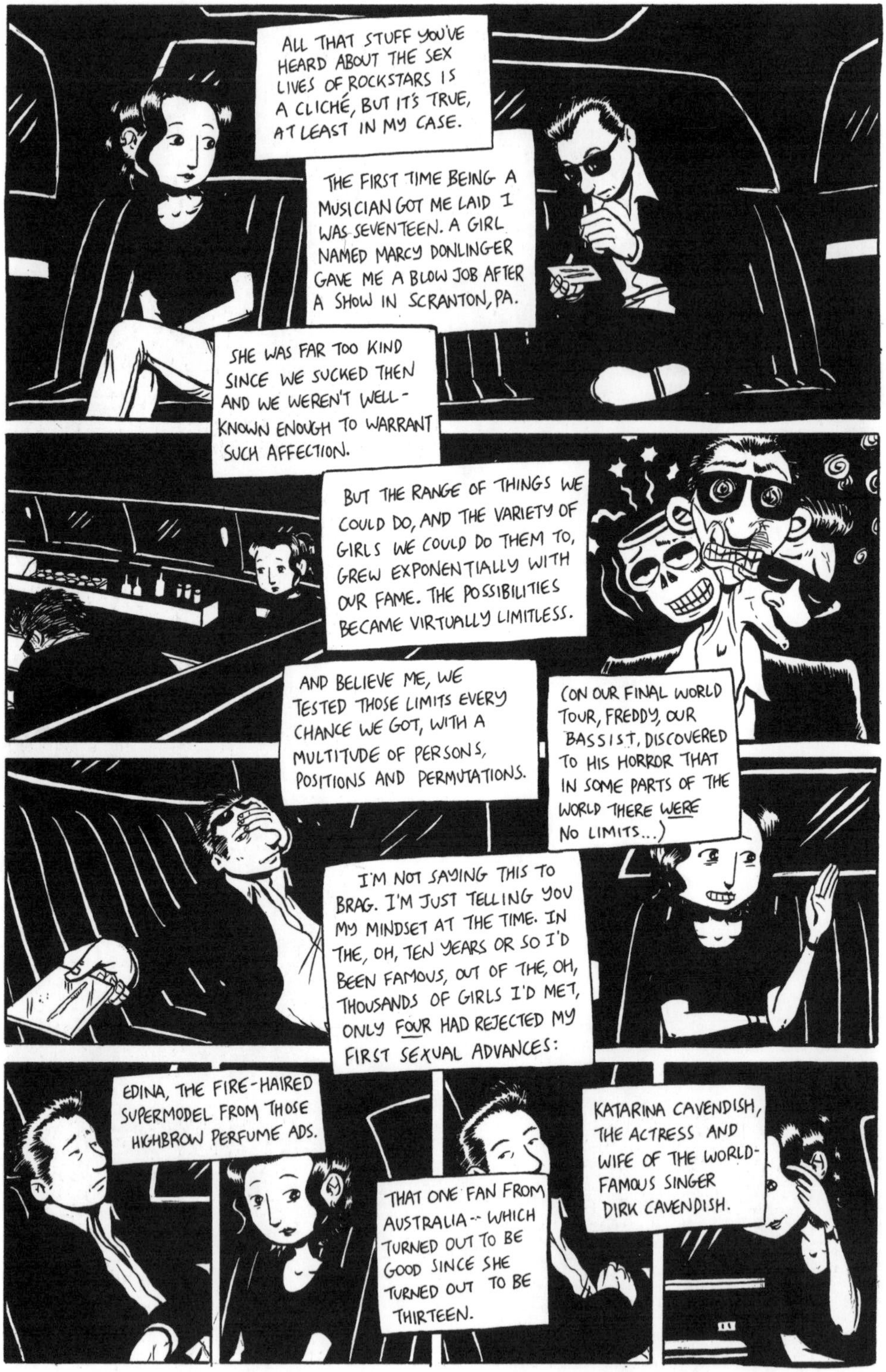
ALL THAT STUFF YOU'VE HEARD ABOUT THE SEX LIVES OF ROCKSTARS IS A CLICHÉ, BUT IT'S TRUE, AT LEAST IN MY CASE.
THE FIRST TIME BEING A MUSICIAN GOT ME LAID I WAS SEVENTEEN. A GIRL NAMED MARCY DONLINGER GAVE ME A BLOW JOB AFTER A SHOW IN SCRANTON, PA.
SHE WAS FAR TOO KIND SINCE WE SUCKED THEN AND WE WEREN'T WELL-KNOWN ENOUGH TO WARRANT SUCH AFFECTION.
BUT THE RANGE OF THINGS WE COULD DO, AND THE VARIETY OF GIRLS WE COULD DO THEM TO, GREW EXPONENTIALLY WITH OUR FAME. THE POSSIBILITIES BECAME VIRTUALLY LIMITLESS.
AND BELIEVE ME, WE TESTED THOSE LIMITS EVERY CHANCE WE GOT, WITH A MULTITUDE OF PERSONS, POSITIONS AND PERMUTATIONS.
(ON OUR FINAL WORLD TOUR, FREDDY, OUR BASSIST, DISCOVERED TO HIS HORROR THAT IN SOME PARTS OF THE WORLD THERE WERE NO LIMITS...)
I'M NOT SAYING THIS TO BRAG. I'M JUST TELLING YOU MY MINDSET AT THE TIME. IN THE, OH, TEN YEARS OR SO I'D BEEN FAMOUS, OUT OF THE, OH, THOUSANDS OF GIRLS I'D MET, ONLY FOUR HAD REJECTED MY FIRST SEXUAL ADVANCES:
EDINA, THE FIRE-HAIRED SUPERMODEL FROM THOSE HIGHBROW PERFUME ADS.
THAT ONE FAN FROM AUSTRALIA -- WHICH TURNED OUT TO BE GOOD SINCE SHE TURNED OUT TO BE THIRTEEN.
KATARINA CAVENDISH, THE ACTRESS AND WIFE OF THE WORLD-FAMOUS SINGER DIRK CAVENDISH.

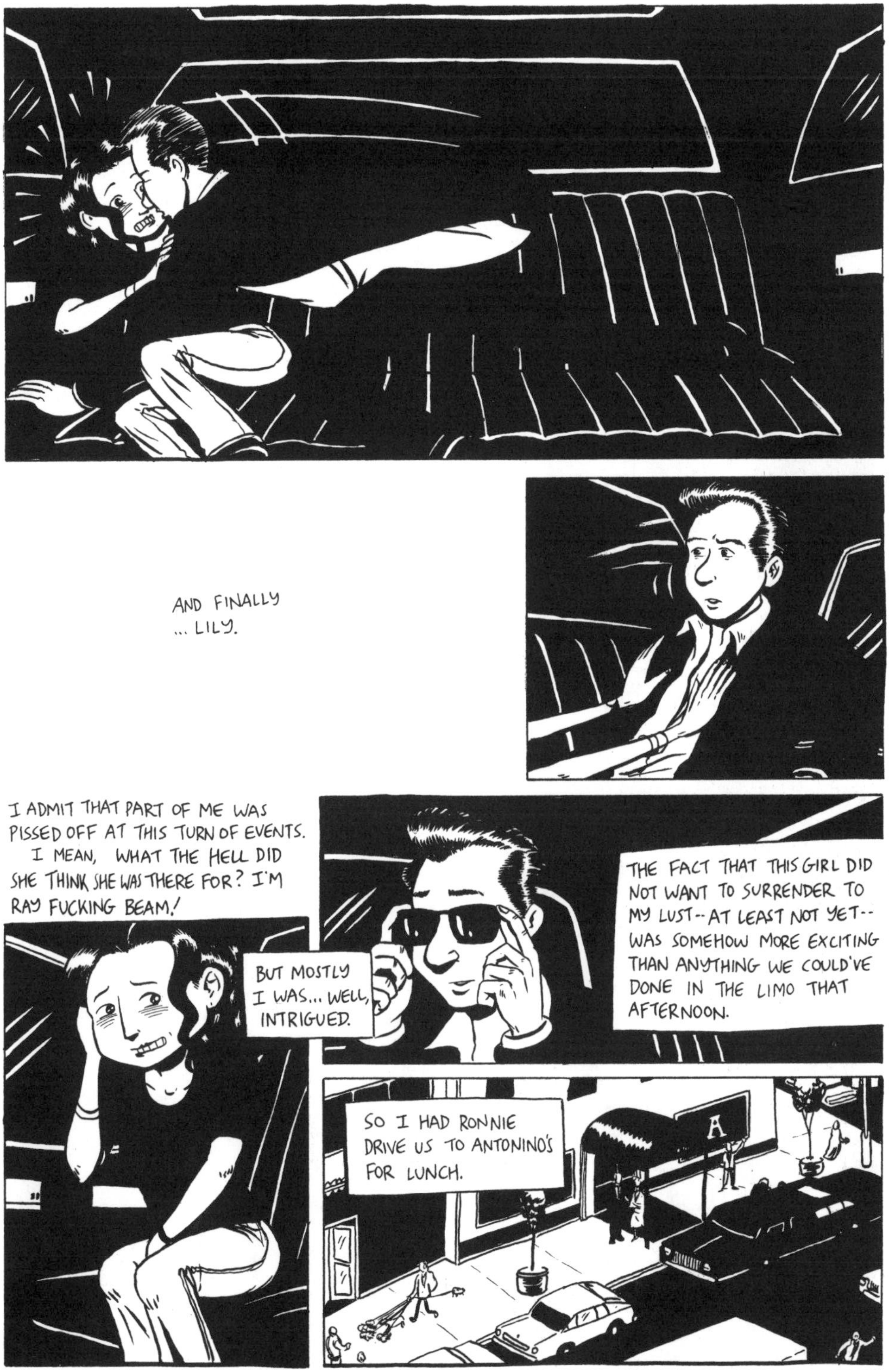
AND FINALLY ... LILY.
I ADMIT THAT PART OF ME WAS PISSED OFF AT THIS TURN OF EVENTS. I MEAN, WHAT THE HELL DID SHE THINK SHE WAS THERE FOR? I'M RAY FUCKING BEAM!
BUT MOSTLY I WAS... WELL, INTRIGUED.
THE FACT THAT THIS GIRL DID NOT WANT TO SURRENDER TO MY LUST--AT LEAST NOT YET--WAS SOMEHOW MORE EXCITING THAN ANYTHING WE COULD'VE DONE IN THE LIMO THAT AFTERNOON.
SO I HAD RONNIE DRIVE US TO ANTONINO'S FOR LUNCH.
A

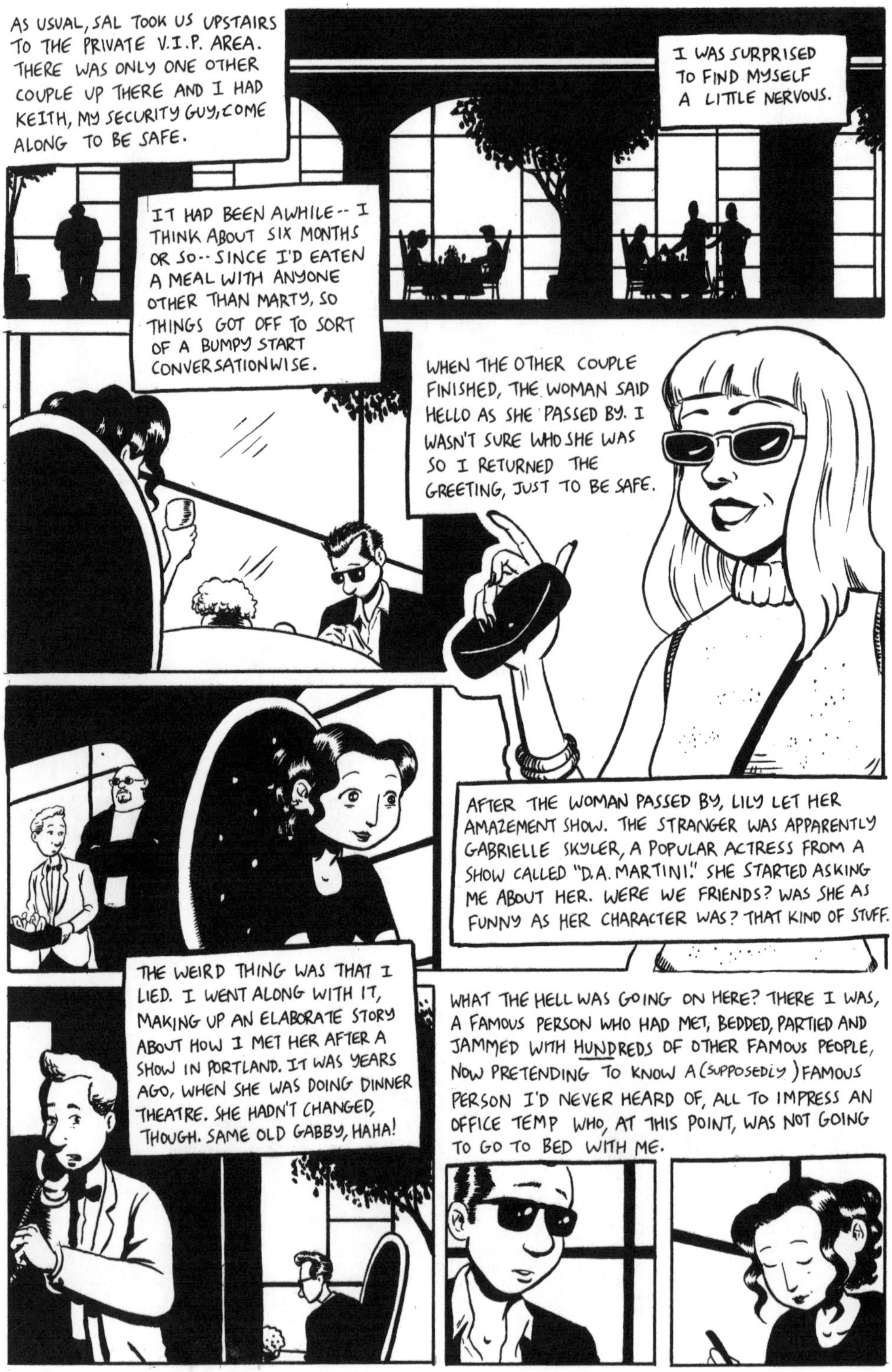
AS USUAL, SAL TOOK US UPSTAIRS TO THE PRIVATE V.I.P. AREA. THERE WAS ONLY ONE OTHER COUPLE UP THERE AND I HAD KEITH, MY SECURITY GUY, COME ALONG TO BE SAFE.
I WAS SURPRISED TO FIND MYSELF A LITTLE NERVOUS.
IT HAD BEEN AWHILE -- I THINK ABOUT SIX MONTHS OR SO -- SINCE I'D EATEN A MEAL WITH ANYONE OTHER THAN MARTY, SO THINGS GOT OFF TO SORT OF A BUMPY START CONVERSATIONWISE.
WHEN THE OTHER COUPLE FINISHED, THE WOMAN SAID HELLO AS SHE PASSED BY. I WASN'T SURE WHO SHE WAS SO I RETURNED THE GREETING, JUST TO BE SAFE.
AFTER THE WOMAN PASSED BY, LILY LET HER AMAZEMENT SHOW. THE STRANGER WAS APPARENTLY GABRIELLE SKYLER, A POPULAR ACTRESS FROM A SHOW CALLED "D.A. MARTINI." SHE STARTED ASKING ME ABOUT HER. WERE WE FRIENDS? WAS SHE AS FUNNY AS HER CHARACTER WAS? THAT KIND OF STUFF.
THE WEIRD THING WAS THAT I LIED. I WENT ALONG WITH IT, MAKING UP AN ELABORATE STORY ABOUT HOW I MET HER AFTER A SHOW IN PORTLAND. IT WAS YEARS AGO, WHEN SHE WAS DOING DINNER THEATRE. SHE HADN'T CHANGED, THOUGH. SAME OLD GABBY, HAHA!
WHAT THE HELL WAS GOING ON HERE? THERE I WAS, A FAMOUS PERSON WHO HAD MET, BEDDED, PARTIED AND JAMMED WITH HUNDREDS OF OTHER FAMOUS PEOPLE, NOW PRETENDING TO KNOW A (SUPPOSEDLY) FAMOUS PERSON I'D NEVER HEARD OF, ALL TO IMPRESS AN OFFICE TEMP WHO, AT THIS POINT, WAS NOT GOING TO GO TO BED WITH ME.

I TRIED TO GET THINGS BACK ON TRACK BY TALKING ABOUT FAMOUS PEOPLE I REALLY DID KNOW. THAT'S WHEN THE SECOND WEIRD THING HAPPENED:

I STARTED TELLING HER ABOUT DAVEY GOLIATH AND THE POOL.

NOW, I'M NOTORIOUSLY TOUCHY ABOUT TALKING ABOUT MY LIFE WITH THE TRICKS. BACK WHEN I USED TO DO INTERVIEWS, THE SUREST WAY TO GET ME TO CLAM UP WAS TO ASK ME ABOUT LIFE WITH FREDDY, DIRK AND DAVE.

GAME OVER.
THANKS FOR PLAYING.
G'NIGHT.

BUT THERE I WAS, TELLING HER ABOUT THE TIME OUR DRUMMER EMPTIED THE CONTENTS OF HIS HOTEL ROOM INTO THE SWIMMING POOL SEVEN FLOORS BELOW. AND THIS WAS A SUITE, MIND YOU, SO YOU CAN IMAGINE THE AMOUNT OF LABOR--AND NARCOTICS-- THIS WOULD ENTAIL.

IT'S A GREAT GODDAMN STORY.

LILY SEEMED TO THINK SO TOO, AND THAT'S WHEN THE THIRD AND FINAL WEIRD THING HAPPENED, THE THING THAT CHANGED EVERYTHING.

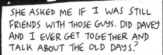
SHE ASKED ME IF I WAS STILL FRIENDS WITH THOSE GUYS. DID DAVEY AND I EVER GET TOGETHER AND TALK ABOUT THE OLD DAYS?

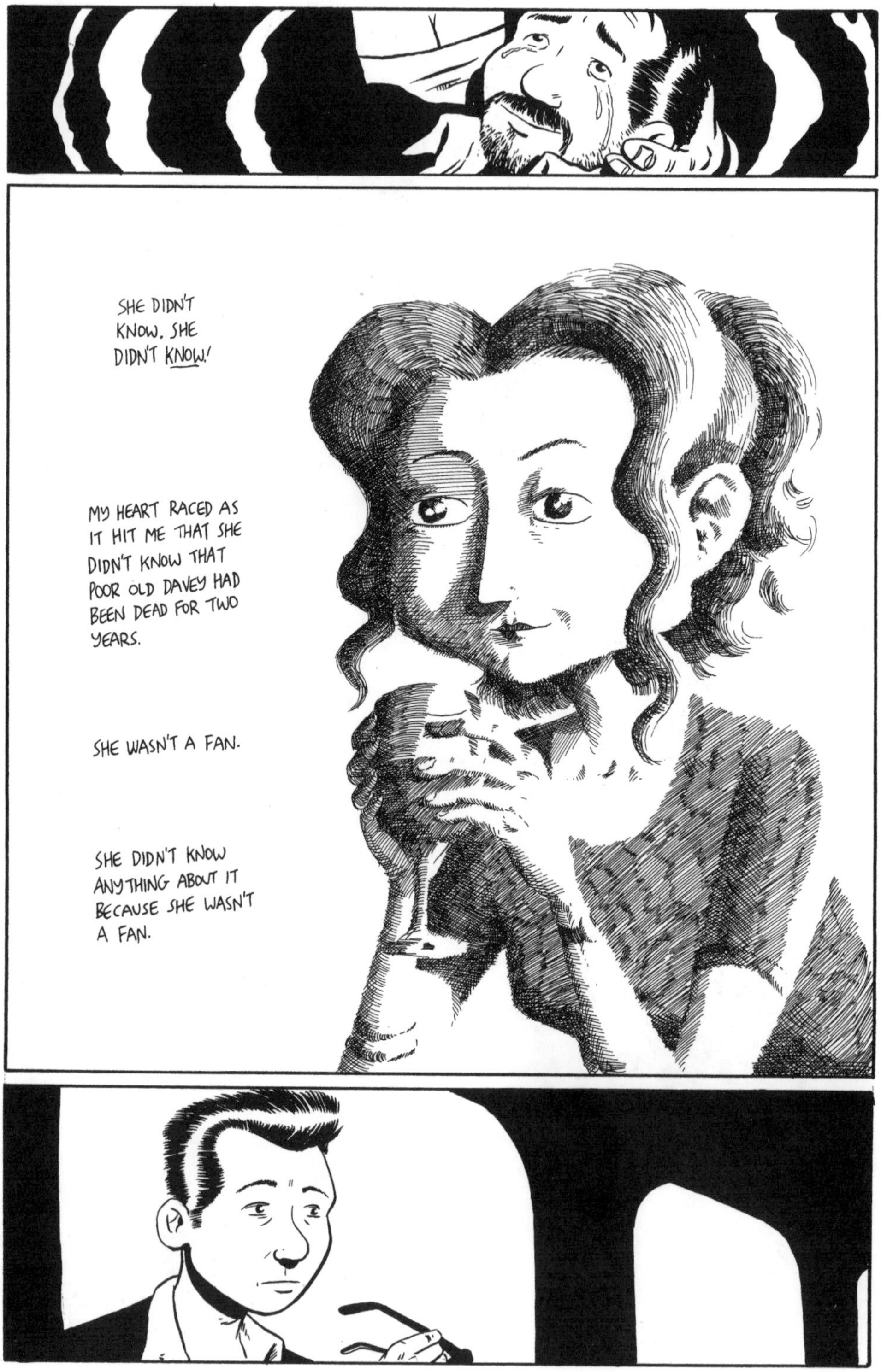
SHE DIDN'T KNOW. SHE DIDN'T KNOW!
MY HEART RACED AS IT HIT ME THAT SHE DIDN'T KNOW THAT POOR OLD DAVEY HAD BEEN DEAD FOR TWO YEARS.
SHE WASN'T A FAN.
SHE DIDN'T KNOW ANYTHING ABOUT IT BECAUSE SHE WASN'T A FAN.

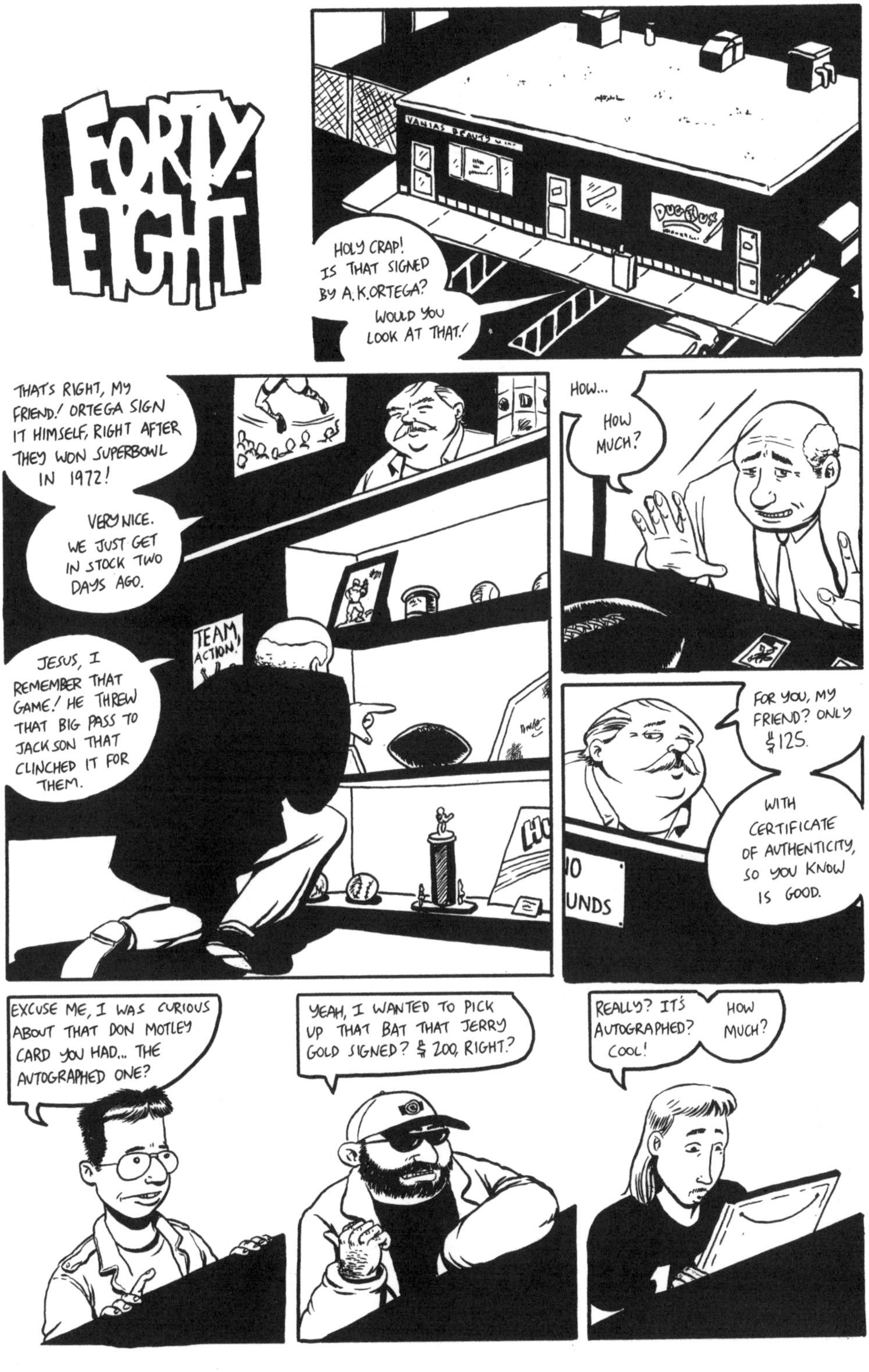
FORTY-EIGHT
VANIA'S BEAUTY
DUGOUTS
HOLY CRAP! IS THAT SIGNED BY A.K. ORTEGA?
WOULD YOU LOOK AT THAT!
THAT'S RIGHT, MY FRIEND! ORTEGA SIGN IT HIMSELF, RIGHT AFTER THEY WON SUPERBOWL IN 1972!
VERY NICE. WE JUST GET IN STOCK TWO DAYS AGO.
TEAM ACTION!
JESUS, I REMEMBER THAT GAME! HE THREW THAT BIG PASS TO JACKSON THAT CLINCHED IT FOR THEM.
HOW...
HOW MUCH?
FOR YOU, MY FRIEND? ONLY $125.
WITH CERTIFICATE OF AUTHENTICITY, SO YOU KNOW IS GOOD.
EXCUSE ME, I WAS CURIOUS ABOUT THAT DON MOTLEY CARD YOU HAD... THE AUTOGRAPHED ONE?
YEAH, I WANTED TO PICK UP THAT BAT THAT JERRY GOLD SIGNED? $200, RIGHT?
REALLY? IT'S AUTOGRAPHED? COOL!
HOW MUCH?

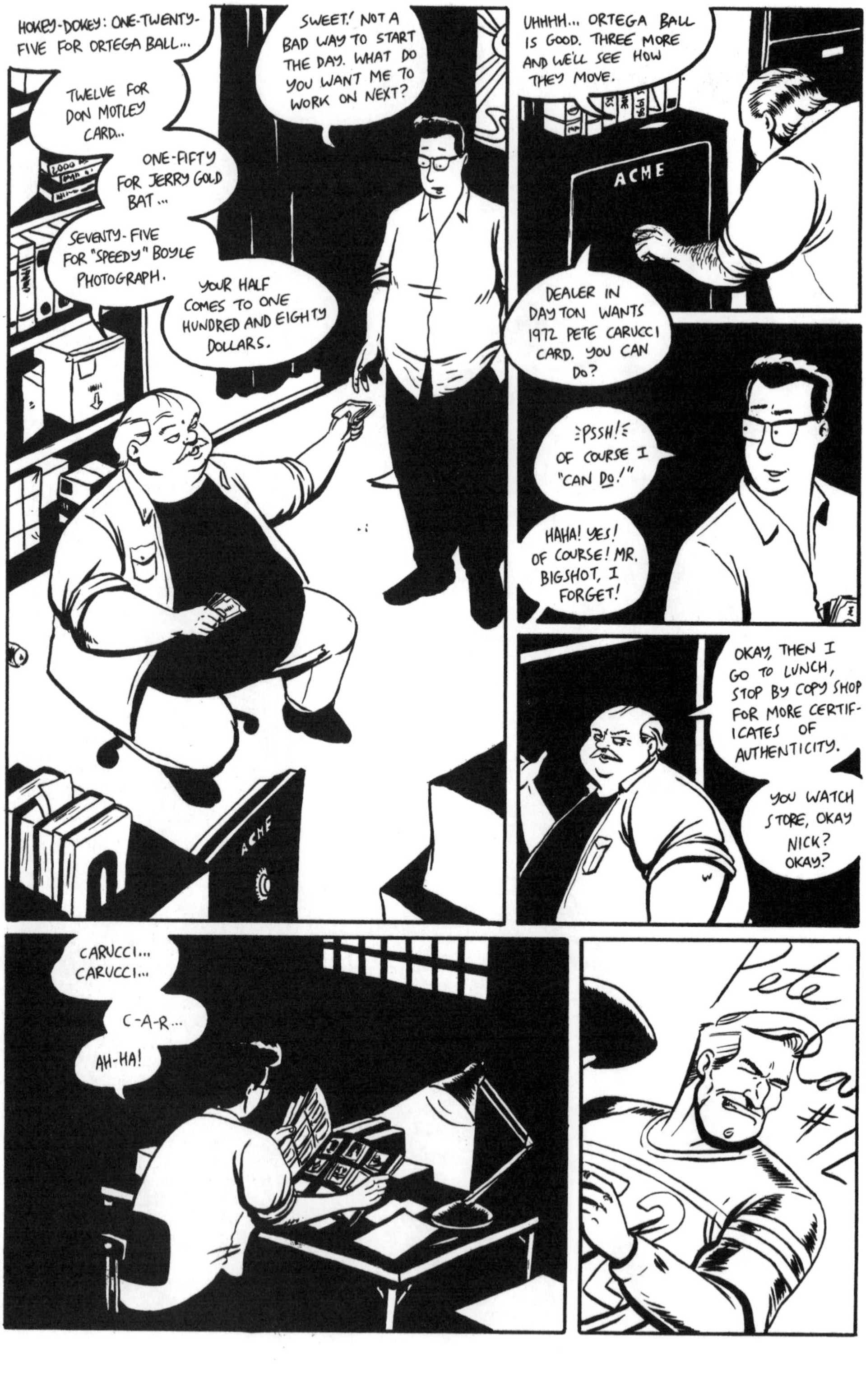
HOKEY-DOKEY: ONE-TWENTY-FIVE FOR ORTEGA BALL...
TWELVE FOR DON MOTLEY CARD...
ONE-FIFTY FOR JERRY GOLD BAT...
SEVENTY-FIVE FOR "SPEEDY" BOYLE PHOTOGRAPH.
YOUR HALF COMES TO ONE HUNDRED AND EIGHTY DOLLARS.
SWEET! NOT A BAD WAY TO START THE DAY. WHAT DO YOU WANT ME TO WORK ON NEXT?
UHHHH... ORTEGA BALL IS GOOD. THREE MORE AND WE'LL SEE HOW THEY MOVE.
ACME
DEALER IN DAYTON WANTS 1972 PETE CARUCCI CARD. YOU CAN DO?
PSSH!
OF COURSE I "CAN DO!"
HAHA! YES! OF COURSE! MR. BIGSHOT, I FORGET!
OKAY, THEN I GO TO LUNCH, STOP BY COPY SHOP FOR MORE CERTIFICATES OF AUTHENTICITY.
YOU WATCH STORE, OKAY NICK? OKAY?
ACME
CARUCCI... CARUCCI...
C-A-R...
AH-HA!
Pete

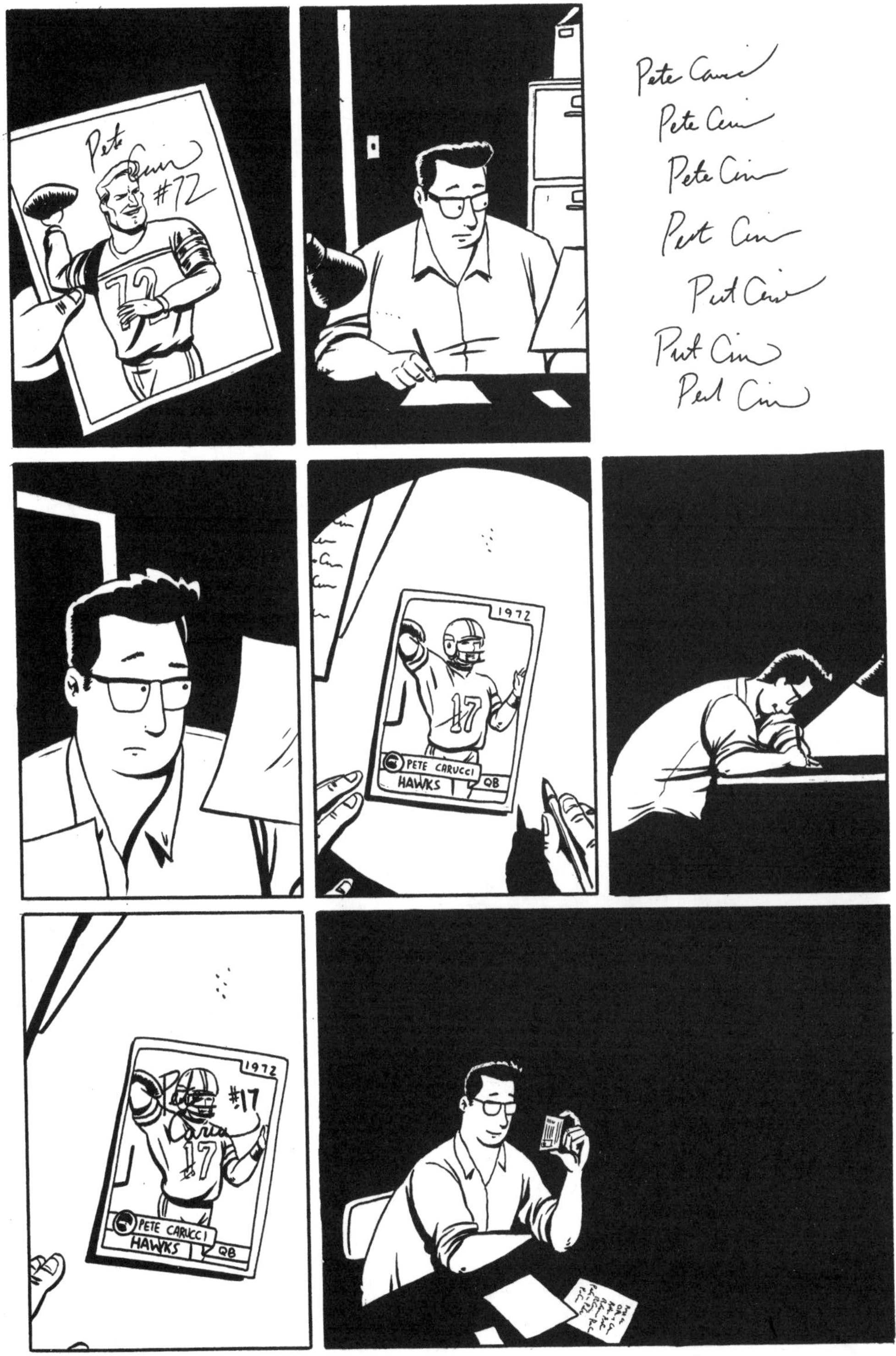
Pete
#72
72
1972
17
PETE CARUCCI
HAWKS
QB
1972
#17
17
PETE CARUCCI
HAWKS
QB

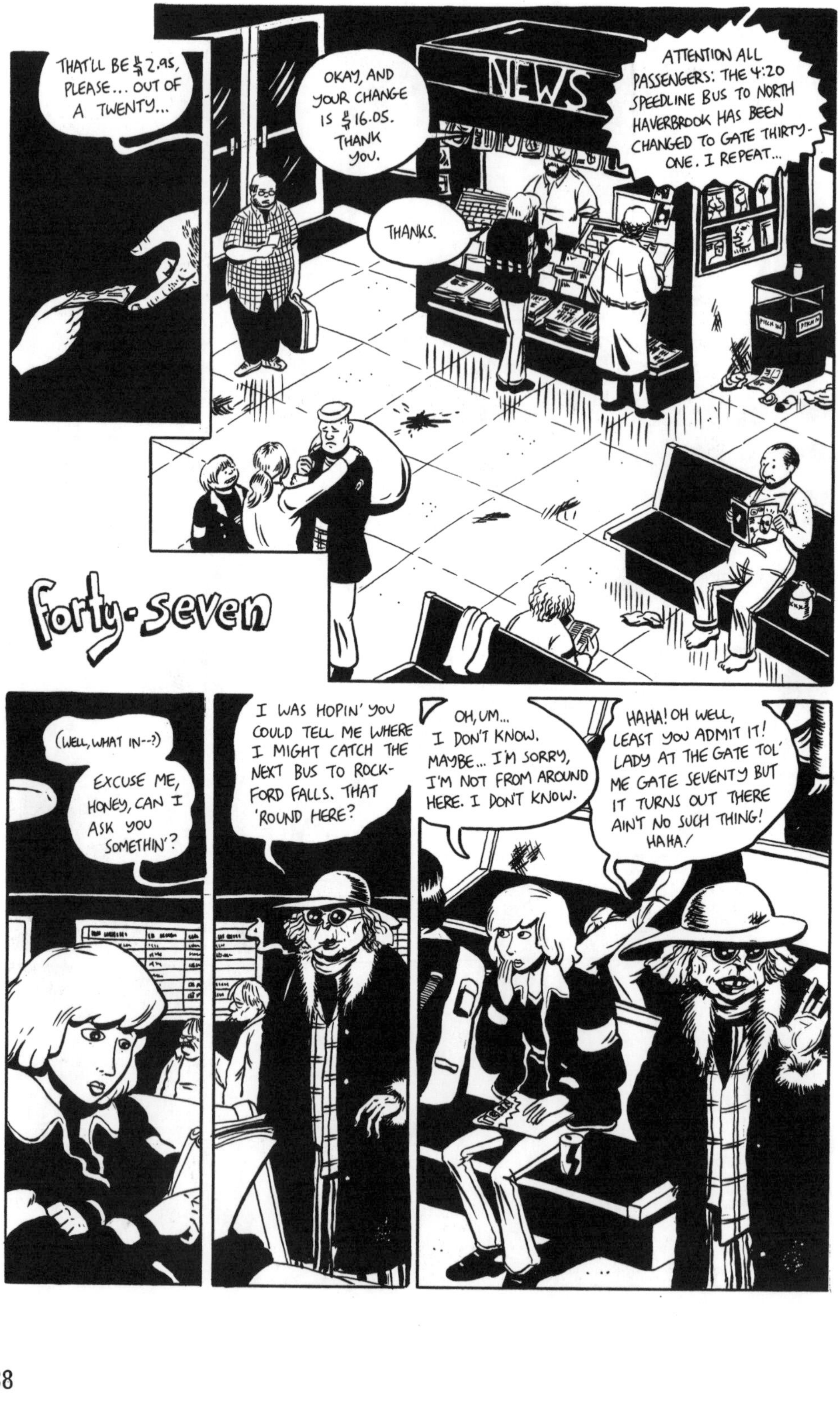
THAT'LL BE $2.95, PLEASE... OUT OF A TWENTY...
OKAY, AND YOUR CHANGE IS $16.05. THANK YOU.
ATTENTION ALL PASSENGERS: THE 4:20 SPEEDLINE BUS TO NORTH HAVERBROOK HAS BEEN CHANGED TO GATE THIRTY-ONE. I REPEAT...
NEWS
THANKS.
forty-seven
(WELL, WHAT IN--?)
EXCUSE ME, HONEY, CAN I ASK YOU SOMETHIN'?
I WAS HOPIN' YOU COULD TELL ME WHERE I MIGHT CATCH THE NEXT BUS TO ROCK-FORD FALLS. THAT 'ROUND HERE?
OH, UM... I DON'T KNOW. MAYBE... I'M SORRY, I'M NOT FROM AROUND HERE. I DON'T KNOW.
HAHA! OH WELL, LEAST YOU ADMIT IT! LADY AT THE GATE TOL' ME GATE SEVENTY BUT IT TURNS OUT THERE AIN'T NO SUCH THING! HAHA!
...

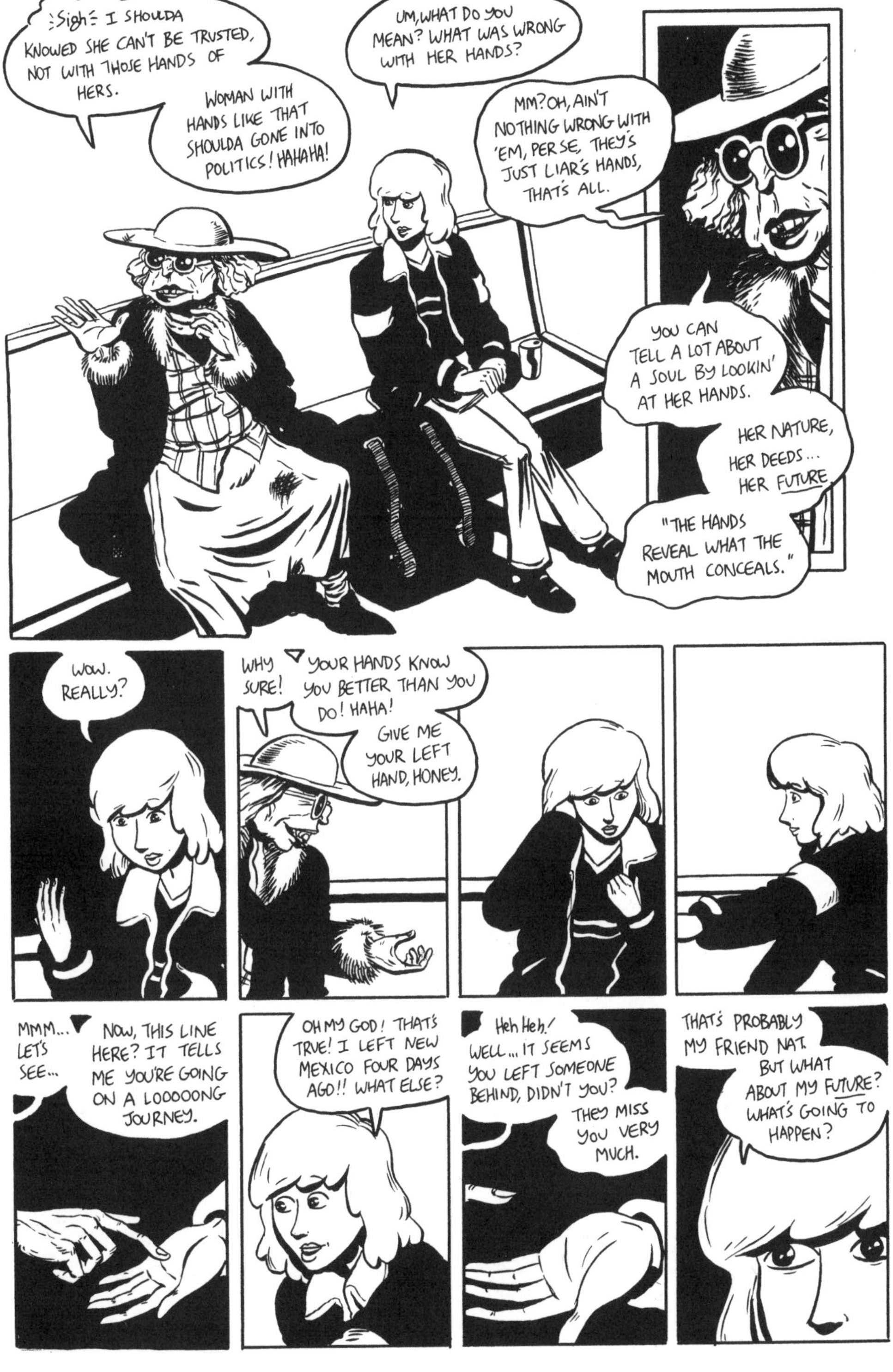

:Sigh: I SHOULDA KNOWED SHE CAN'T BE TRUSTED, NOT WITH THOSE HANDS OF HERS.
WOMAN WITH HANDS LIKE THAT SHOULDA GONE INTO POLITICS! HAHAHA!
UM, WHAT DO YOU MEAN? WHAT WAS WRONG WITH HER HANDS?
MM? OH, AIN'T NOTHING WRONG WITH 'EM, PER SE, THEY'S JUST LIAR'S HANDS, THAT'S ALL.
YOU CAN TELL A LOT ABOUT A SOUL BY LOOKIN' AT HER HANDS.
HER NATURE, HER DEEDS... HER FUTURE.
"THE HANDS REVEAL WHAT THE MOUTH CONCEALS."
WOW. REALLY?
WHY SURE!
YOUR HANDS KNOW YOU BETTER THAN YOU DO! HAHA!
GIVE ME YOUR LEFT HAND, HONEY.
MMM... LET'S SEE...
NOW, THIS LINE HERE? IT TELLS ME YOU'RE GOING ON A LOOOOONG JOURNEY.
OH MY GOD! THAT'S TRUE! I LEFT NEW MEXICO FOUR DAYS AGO!! WHAT ELSE?
Heh Heh! WELL... IT SEEMS YOU LEFT SOMEONE BEHIND, DIDN'T YOU?
THEY MISS YOU VERY MUCH.
THAT'S PROBABLY MY FRIEND NAT.
BUT WHAT ABOUT MY FUTURE? WHAT'S GOING TO HAPPEN?

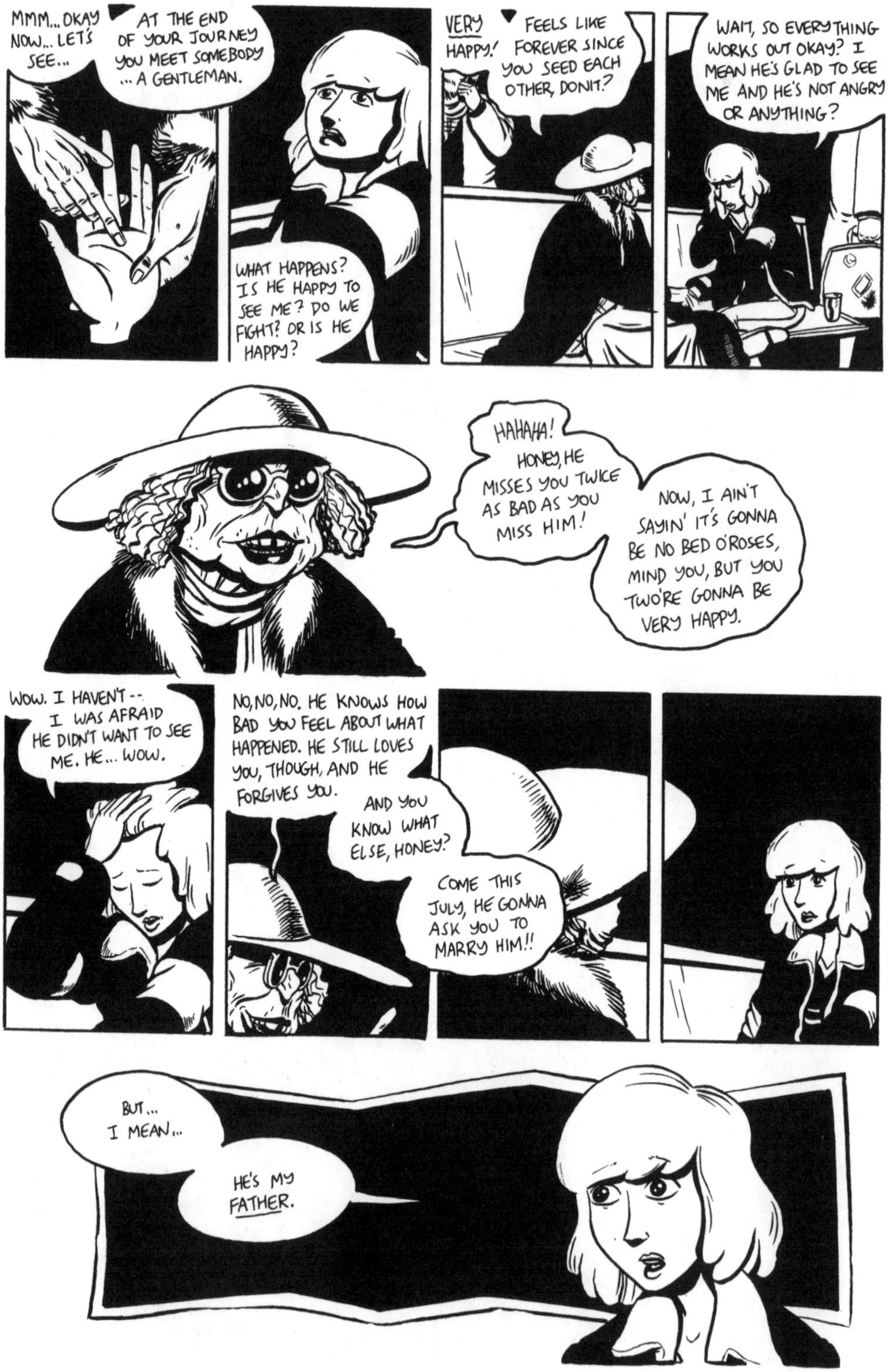
MMM... OKAY NOW... LET'S SEE...
AT THE END OF YOUR JOURNEY YOU MEET SOMEBODY ... A GENTLEMAN.
WHAT HAPPENS? IS HE HAPPY TO SEE ME? DO WE FIGHT? OR IS HE HAPPY?
VERY HAPPY!
FEELS LIKE FOREVER SINCE YOU SEED EACH OTHER, DON'T?
WAIT, SO EVERYTHING WORKS OUT OKAY? I MEAN HE'S GLAD TO SEE ME AND HE'S NOT ANGRY OR ANYTHING?
HAHAHA!
HONEY, HE MISSES YOU TWICE AS BAD AS YOU MISS HIM!
NOW, I AIN'T SAYIN' IT'S GONNA BE NO BED O'ROSES, MIND YOU, BUT YOU TWO'RE GONNA BE VERY HAPPY.
WOW. I HAVEN'T -- I WAS AFRAID HE DIDN'T WANT TO SEE ME. HE... WOW.
NO, NO, NO. HE KNOWS HOW BAD YOU FEEL ABOUT WHAT HAPPENED. HE STILL LOVES YOU, THOUGH, AND HE FORGIVES YOU.
AND YOU KNOW WHAT ELSE, HONEY?
COME THIS JULY, HE GONNA ASK YOU TO MARRY HIM!!
BUT... I MEAN...
HE'S MY FATHER.

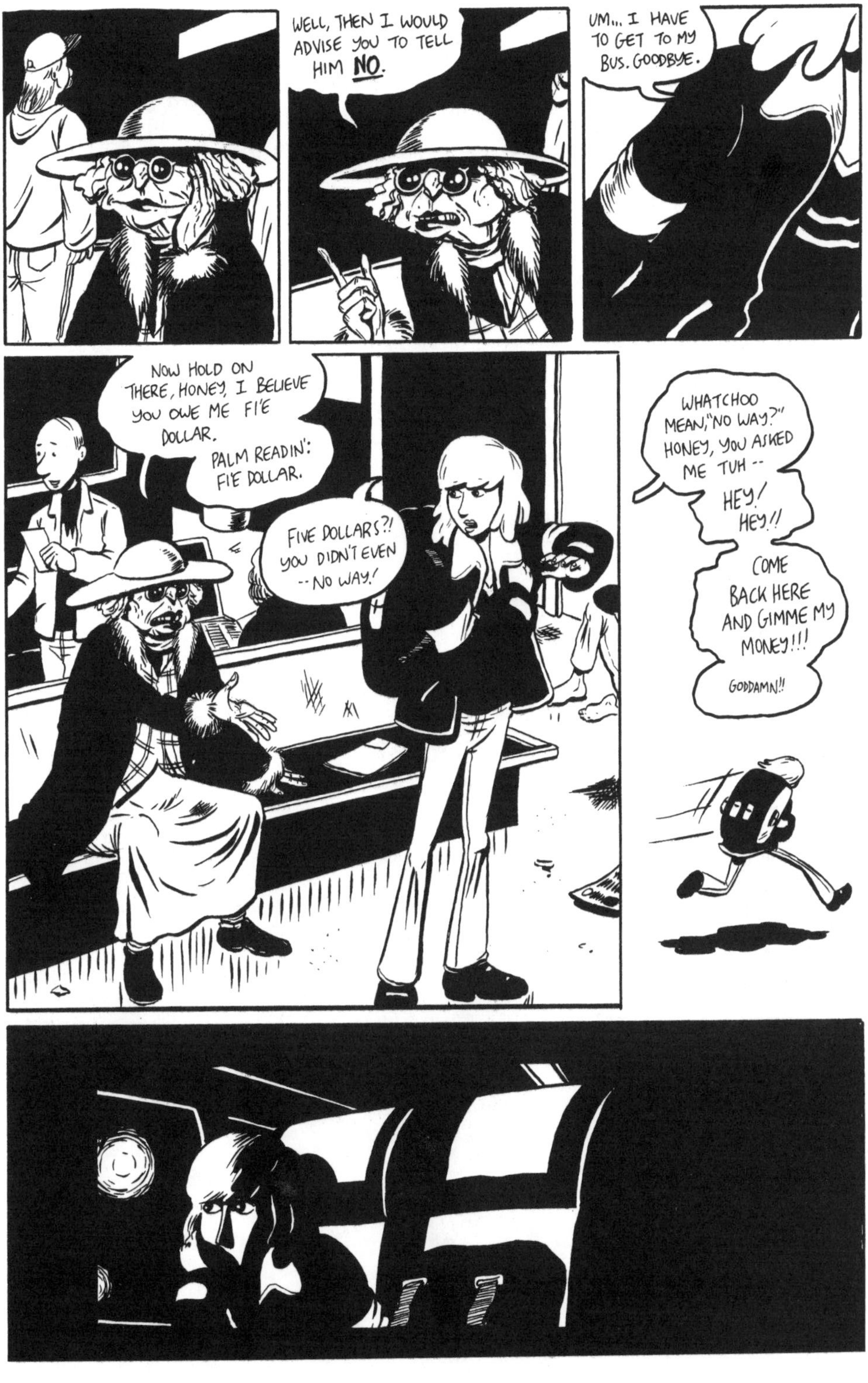
WELL, THEN I WOULD ADVISE YOU TO TELL HIM NO.
UM... I HAVE TO GET TO MY BUS. GOODBYE.
NOW HOLD ON THERE, HONEY, I BELIEVE YOU OWE ME FI'E DOLLAR.
PALM READIN': FI'E DOLLAR.
FIVE DOLLARS?! YOU DIDN'T EVEN -- NO WAY!
WHATCHOO MEAN, "NO WAY?" HONEY, YOU ASKED ME TUH --
HEY! HEY!!
COME BACK HERE AND GIMME MY MONEY!!!
GODDAMN!!

-FORTY-SIX-

GARY'S COMPUTER GOT FROZEN YET AGAIN AT WORK TODAY, SO NATURALLY I WAS CALLED IN TO CLEAN UP HIS MESS. IF PEOPLE REALIZED THE STUPIDITY OF THE PEOPLE HANDLING THEIR RETIREMENT FUND INVESTMENTS THEY'D BE TERRIFIED. SPIDER MONKEYS WITH DART BOARDS COULD DO JUST AS GOOD A JOB.

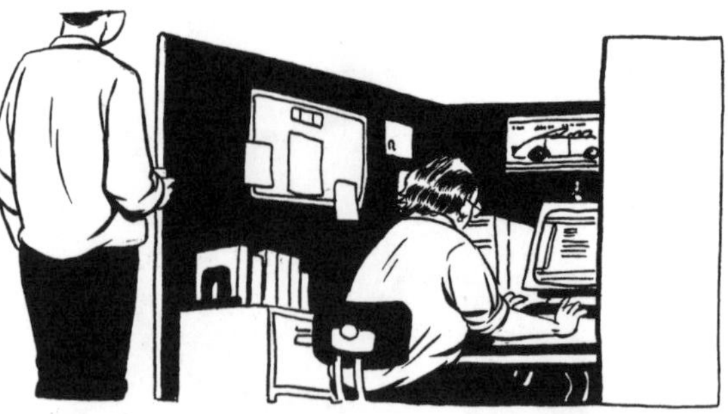

SO I'M WORKING ON FIXING THE PROBLEM AND NEXT THING YOU KNOW ALLISON GOBE POPS HER STUPID FACE UP OVER THE CUBICLE WALL. SHE STARTS ASKING ALL THESE QUESTIONS AND GIVING ME ADVICE AND EVERYTHING.

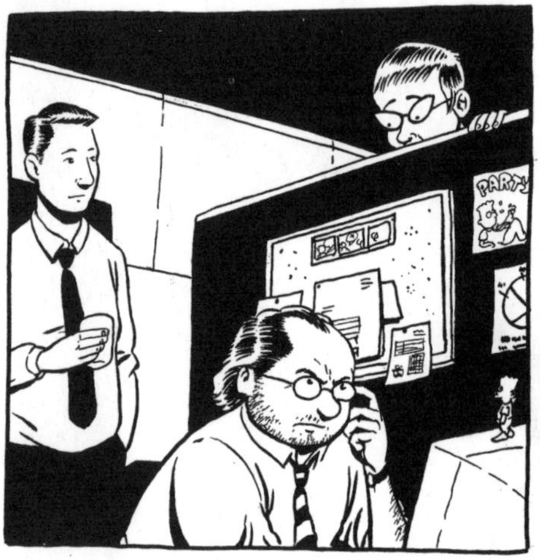

DID I TRY PRESSING THIS? DID I CLICK ON THAT? I SHOULD CLOSE SUCH-AND-SUCH A FILE AND THEN I SHOULD OPEN THIS OTHER FILE. DID I TRY THAT?

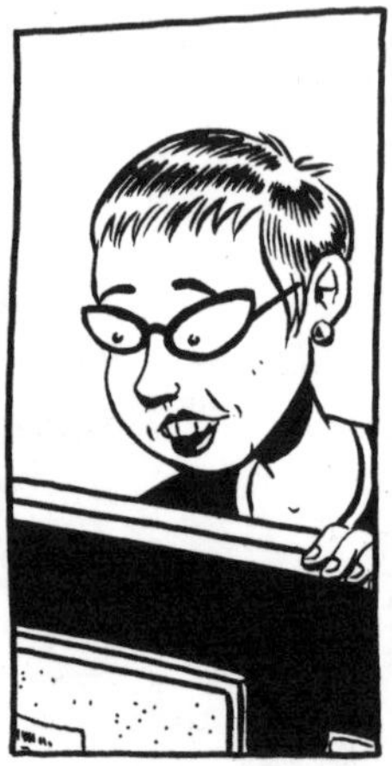

I DIDN'T EVEN PAY ATTENTION, OF COURSE, BUT CAN YOU BELIEVE THE BALLS ON HER? WHO THE FUCK DID SHE THINK SHE WAS? WHY DOESN'T SHE LEAVE THE TECHNICAL STUFF TO THE TECH GUYS AND WE'LL LEAVE THE SUCKING DICK, OR WHATEVER SHE'S PAID FOR, TO HER? HOW ABOUT WE TRY THAT?

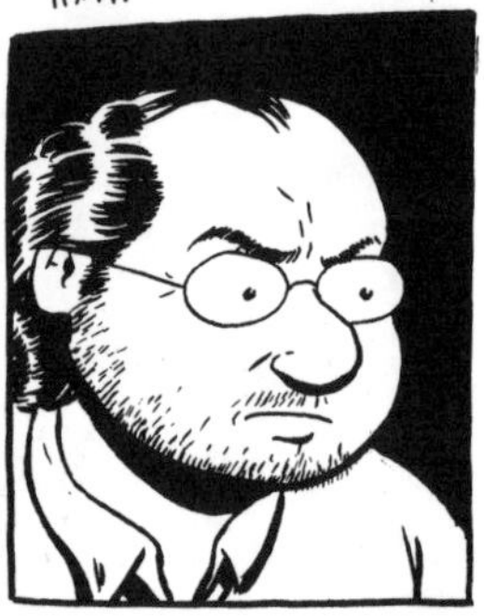

BUT TO MAKE MATTERS EVEN WORSE, GARY, THE GUY WHOSE COMPUTER I'M FIXING, SIDES WITH HER! HE SAID MAYBE I SHOULD CLOSE THE SUCH-AND-SUCH FILE LIKE SHE SUGGESTED. AT ONE POINT HE EVEN CALLED ME "DUDE." I SWEAR TO GOD. THEN THEY STARTED JOKING AROUND WITH EACH OTHER, SAYING THEY DIDN'T KNOW HOW TO FIX COMPUTERS. NO SHIT, EINSTEIN!!!

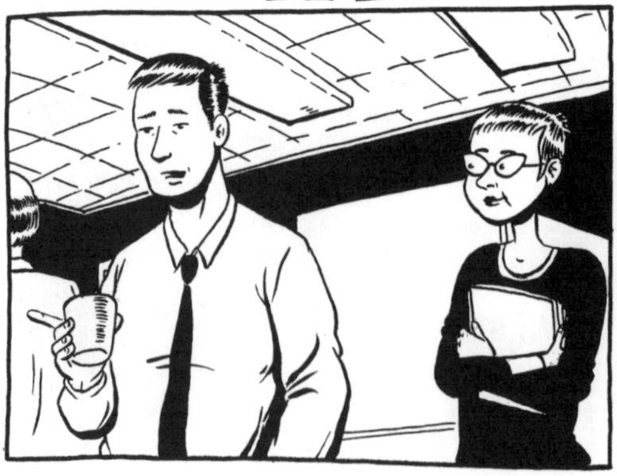

THE IMPLICATION, OF COURSE, WAS THAT THEY WERE TOO COOL AND HIP, TOO BUSY LIVING IT UP AT THE FUCKING GAP AND STARBUCKS TO BOTHER WITH EVEN BASIC COMPUTER SKILLS... UNLIKE SOME GEEKS. ANYONE WHO KNOWS A MOUSE FROM A MODEM IS CLEARLY TOO BIG A NERD TO EVEN TALK TO. MR. AND MRS. KING AND QUEEN OF THE FUCKING PROM.

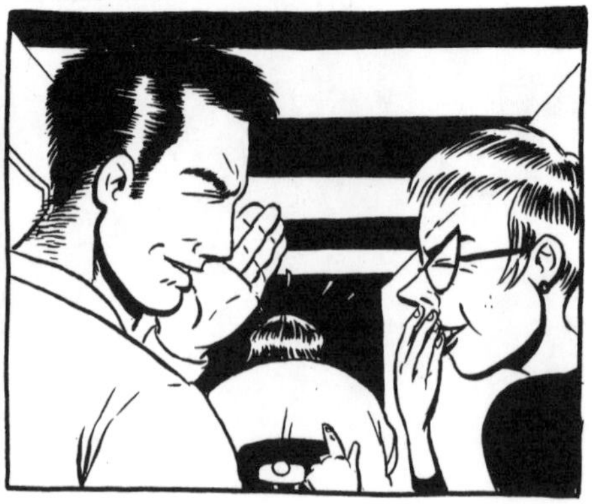

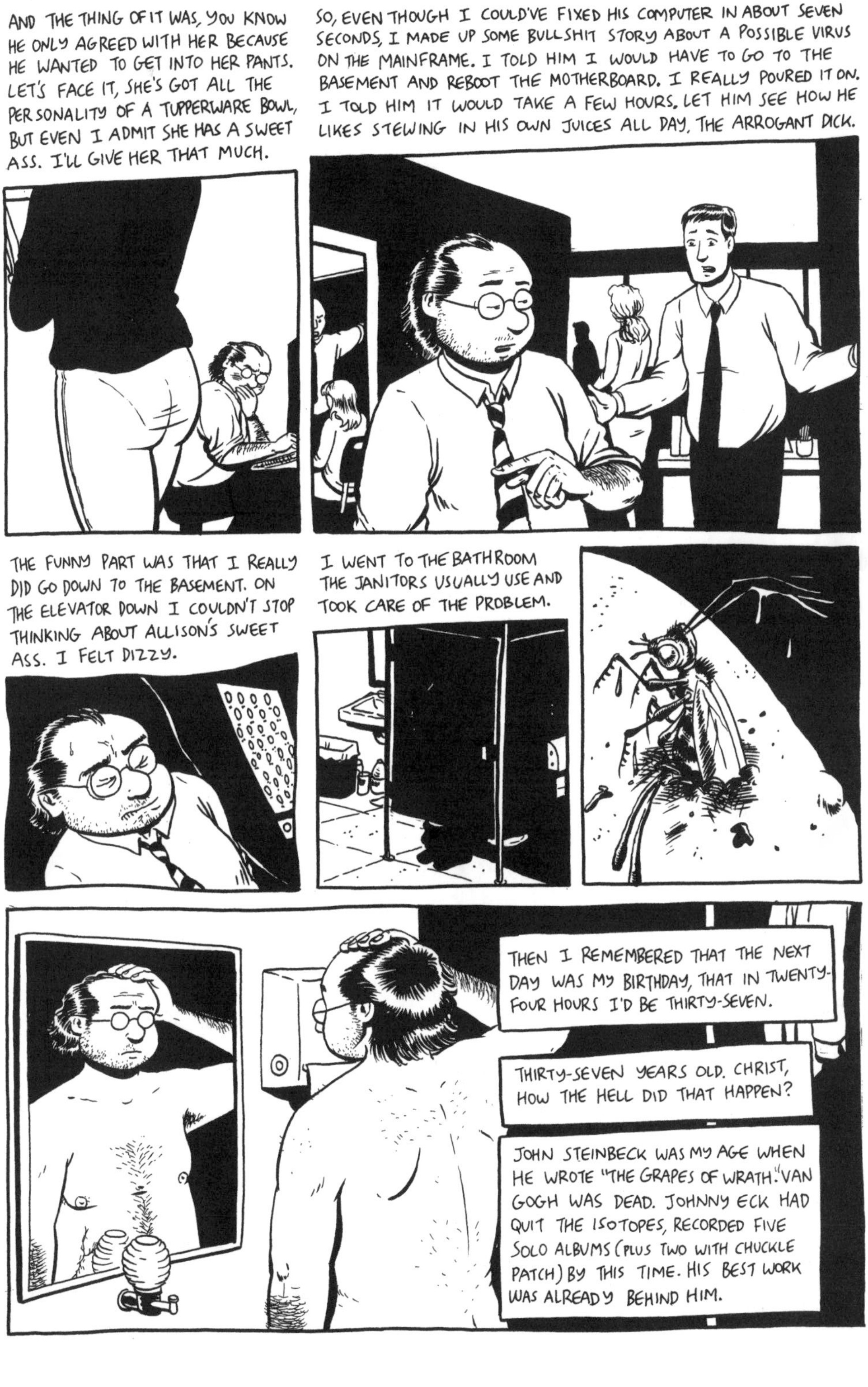
AND THE THING OF IT WAS, YOU KNOW HE ONLY AGREED WITH HER BECAUSE HE WANTED TO GET INTO HER PANTS. LET'S FACE IT, SHE'S GOT ALL THE PERSONALITY OF A TUPPERWARE BOWL, BUT EVEN I ADMIT SHE HAS A SWEET ASS. I'LL GIVE HER THAT MUCH.
SO, EVEN THOUGH I COULD'VE FIXED HIS COMPUTER IN ABOUT SEVEN SECONDS, I MADE UP SOME BULLSHIT STORY ABOUT A POSSIBLE VIRUS ON THE MAINFRAME. I TOLD HIM I WOULD HAVE TO GO TO THE BASEMENT AND REBOOT THE MOTHERBOARD. I REALLY POURED IT ON. I TOLD HIM IT WOULD TAKE A FEW HOURS. LET HIM SEE HOW HE LIKES STEWING IN HIS OWN JUICES ALL DAY, THE ARROGANT DICK.
THE FUNNY PART WAS THAT I REALLY DID GO DOWN TO THE BASEMENT. ON THE ELEVATOR DOWN I COULDN'T STOP THINKING ABOUT ALLISON'S SWEET ASS. I FELT DIZZY.
I WENT TO THE BATHROOM THE JANITORS USUALLY USE AND TOOK CARE OF THE PROBLEM.
THEN I REMEMBERED THAT THE NEXT DAY WAS MY BIRTHDAY, THAT IN TWENTY-FOUR HOURS I'D BE THIRTY-SEVEN.
THIRTY-SEVEN YEARS OLD. CHRIST, HOW THE HELL DID THAT HAPPEN?
JOHN STEINBECK WAS MY AGE WHEN HE WROTE "THE GRAPES OF WRATH." VAN GOGH WAS DEAD. JOHNNY ECK HAD QUIT THE ISOTOPES, RECORDED FIVE SOLO ALBUMS (PLUS TWO WITH CHUCKLE PATCH) BY THIS TIME. HIS BEST WORK WAS ALREADY BEHIND HIM.

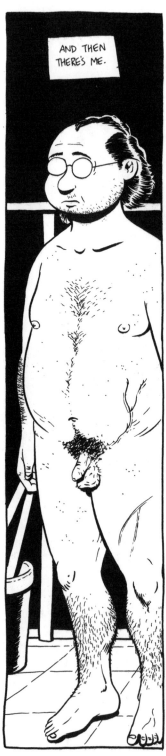

AND THEN THERE'S ME.

HAVE YOU EVER HAD THAT WEIRD SENSATION WHERE YOU AREN'T SURE IF SOMETHING REALLY HAPPENED OR NOT? HAPPENED TO YOU?

I WAS SITTING AT HOME LISTENING TO BLUE CADBURY'S "YOUTH IN REVOLT" ALBUM AND I STARTED THINKING ALL ABOUT A MOVIE. A GUY DROVE HIS WIFE AWAY BY ACTING LIKE A BIG ASSHOLE. THE THING WAS, I COULD NOT REMEMBER WHAT MOVIE IT WAS AND IT WAS DRIVING ME CRAZY.

I COULDN'T EVEN REMEMBER THE LEAD ACTORS. THE GUY, AS I SAID, WAS A TOTAL PRICK. THE AUDIENCE HATED HIM. HE WAS UNBEARABLE AND OBNOXIOUS AND YOU CAN TOTALLY SYMPATHIZE WITH THE WIFE, WHO LEAVES HIM. BUT WHAT MOVIE WAS IT? THAT'S WHEN IT CLICKED: IT WAS ME. IT WAS MY LIFE, AND SHERYL WAS THE WOMAN WHO LEFT.

THE OTHER DAY I WAS EATING AT THAT NEW CHINESE PLACE THAT THEY OPENED ON LAZERNE STREET. THE FOOD WAS OKAY, BUT THERE WAS THIS MORON YAPPING ON HIS CELL PHONE NEARBY. ACTUALLY, HE WAS NOT TALKING TOO LOUD, BUT IT WAS STILL ANNOYING. I WONDER WHY?

I THINK ON A SUBCONSCIOUS LEVEL PEOPLE ARE DISTURBED WHEN THEY CAN ONLY HEAR ONE END OF A CONVERSATION LIKE THAT. I MEAN, FOR MOST OF HUMAN HISTORY IF YOU HAD A CHAT WITH SOMEONE NO ONE ELSE COULD SEE OR HEAR, YOU WERE EITHER A SHAMAN OR INSANE.

YEAH, OR BOTH.

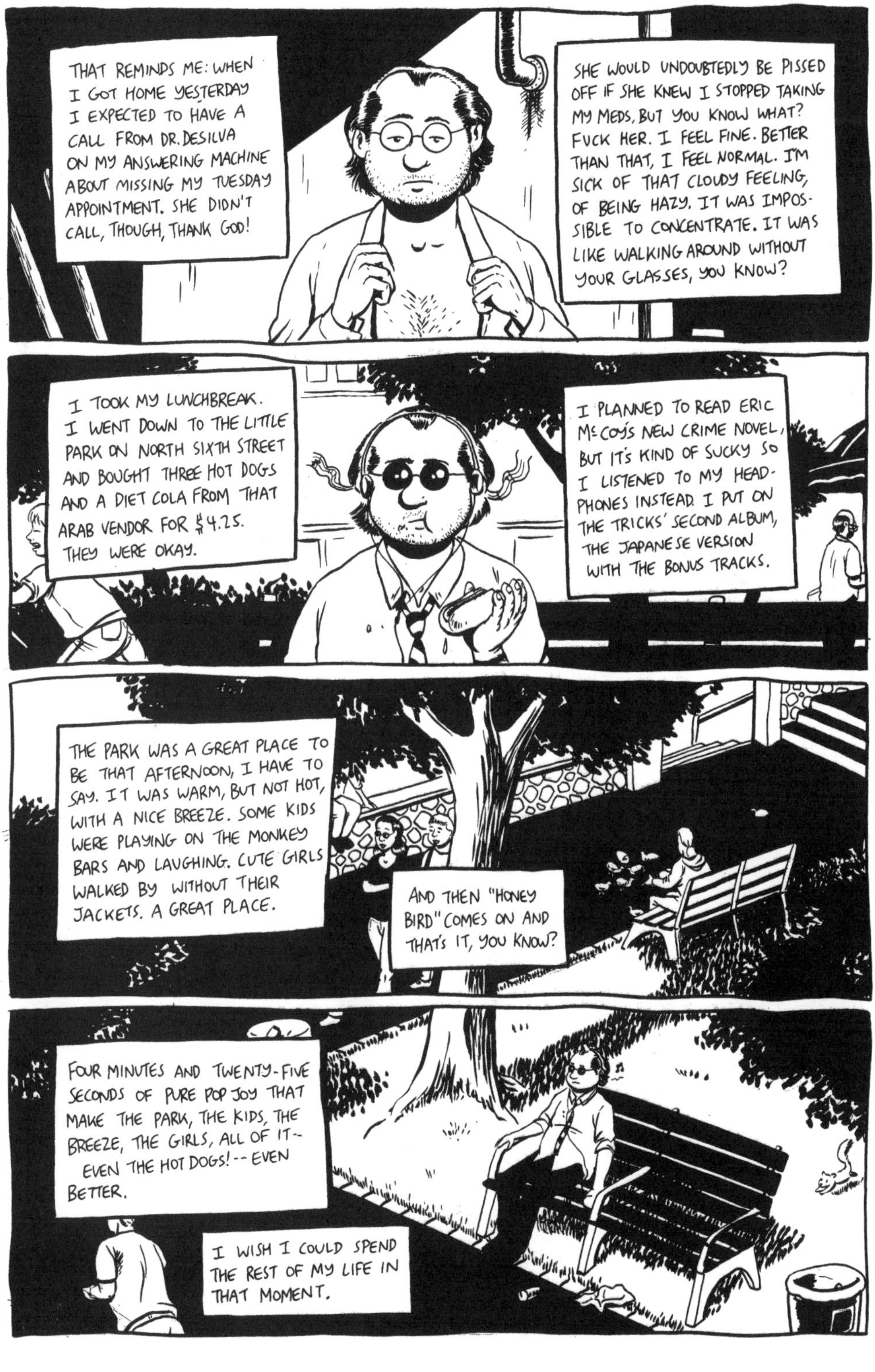
THAT REMINDS ME: WHEN I GOT HOME YESTERDAY I EXPECTED TO HAVE A CALL FROM DR. DESILVA ON MY ANSWERING MACHINE ABOUT MISSING MY TUESDAY APPOINTMENT. SHE DIDN'T CALL, THOUGH, THANK GOD!
SHE WOULD UNDOUBTEDLY BE PISSED OFF IF SHE KNEW I STOPPED TAKING MY MEDS, BUT YOU KNOW WHAT? FUCK HER. I FEEL FINE. BETTER THAN THAT, I FEEL NORMAL. I'M SICK OF THAT CLOUDY FEELING, OF BEING HAZY. IT WAS IMPOSSIBLE TO CONCENTRATE. IT WAS LIKE WALKING AROUND WITHOUT YOUR GLASSES, YOU KNOW?
I TOOK MY LUNCHBREAK. I WENT DOWN TO THE LITTLE PARK ON NORTH SIXTH STREET AND BOUGHT THREE HOT DOGS AND A DIET COLA FROM THAT ARAB VENDOR FOR $4.25. THEY WERE OKAY.
I PLANNED TO READ ERIC McCOY'S NEW CRIME NOVEL, BUT IT'S KIND OF SUCKY SO I LISTENED TO MY HEADPHONES INSTEAD. I PUT ON THE TRICKS' SECOND ALBUM, THE JAPANESE VERSION WITH THE BONUS TRACKS.
THE PARK WAS A GREAT PLACE TO BE THAT AFTERNOON, I HAVE TO SAY. IT WAS WARM, BUT NOT HOT, WITH A NICE BREEZE. SOME KIDS WERE PLAYING ON THE MONKEY BARS AND LAUGHING. CUTE GIRLS WALKED BY WITHOUT THEIR JACKETS. A GREAT PLACE.
AND THEN "HONEY BIRD" COMES ON AND THAT'S IT, YOU KNOW?
FOUR MINUTES AND TWENTY-FIVE SECONDS OF PURE POP JOY THAT MAKE THE PARK, THE KIDS, THE BREEZE, THE GIRLS, ALL OF IT-- EVEN THE HOT DOGS! -- EVEN BETTER.
I WISH I COULD SPEND THE REST OF MY LIFE IN THAT MOMENT.

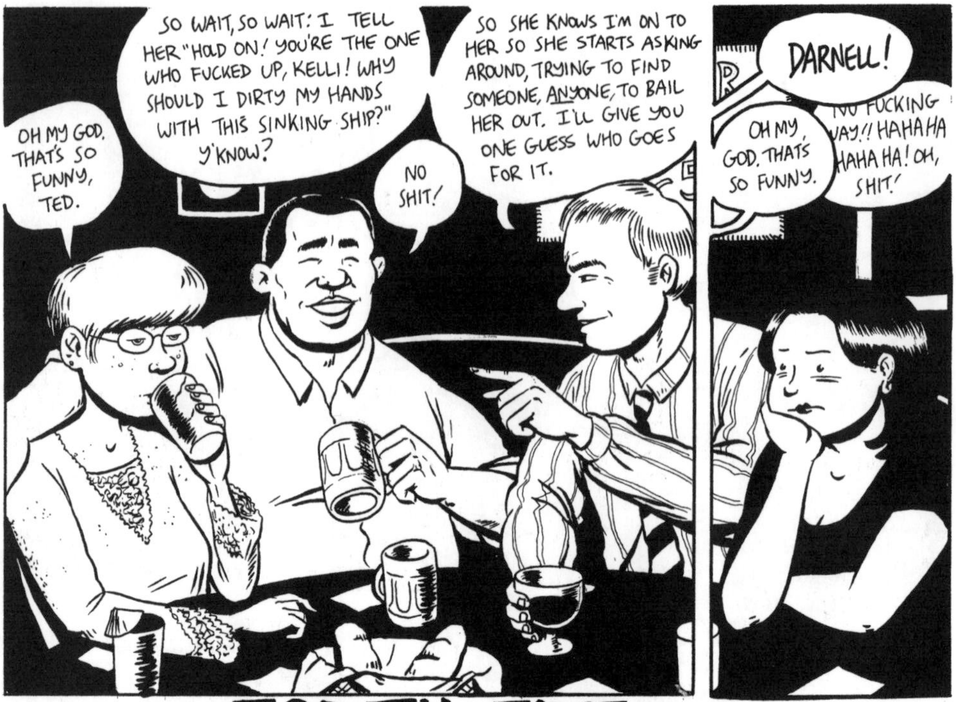
SO WAIT, SO WAIT: I TELL HER "HOLD ON! YOU'RE THE ONE WHO FUCKED UP, KELLI! WHY SHOULD I DIRTY MY HANDS WITH THIS SINKING SHIP?" Y'KNOW?
OH MY GOD. THAT'S SO FUNNY, TED.
NO SHIT!
SO SHE KNOWS I'M ON TO HER SO SHE STARTS ASKING AROUND, TRYING TO FIND SOMEONE, ANYONE, TO BAIL HER OUT. I'LL GIVE YOU ONE GUESS WHO GOES FOR IT.
DARNELL!
NO FUCKING WAY!! HAHAHA HAHA HA! OH, SHIT!
OH MY, GOD. THAT'S SO FUNNY.

FORTY-FIVE

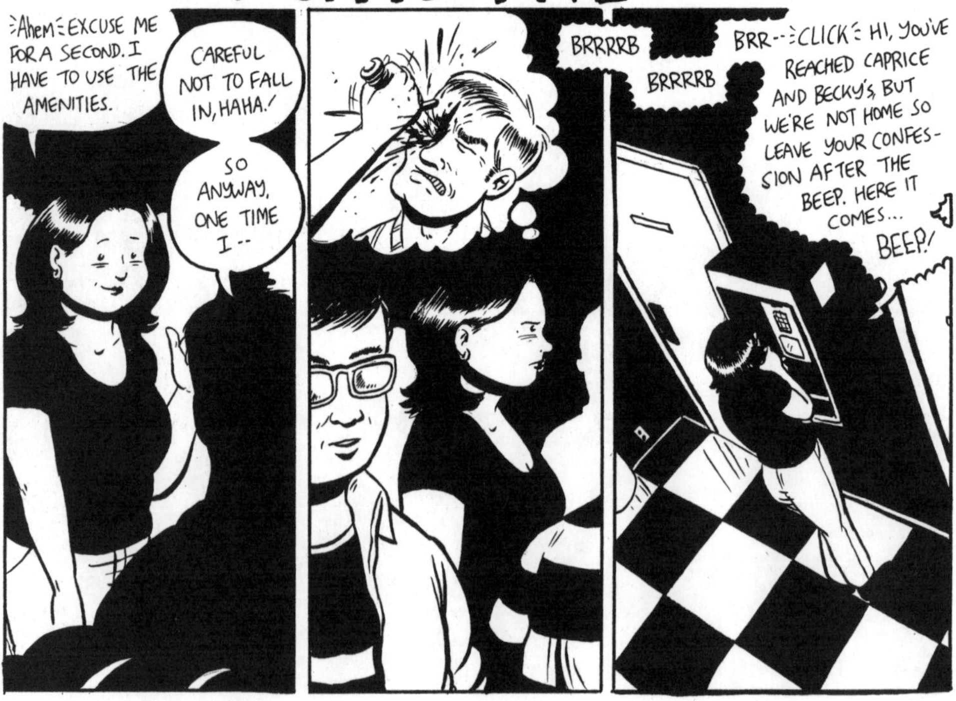
AHEM EXCUSE ME FOR A SECOND. I HAVE TO USE THE AMENITIES.
CAREFUL NOT TO FALL IN, HAHA!
SO ANYWAY, ONE TIME I--
BRRRRB
BRRRRB
BRR--CLICK HI, YOU'VE REACHED CAPRICE AND BECKY'S, BUT WE'RE NOT HOME SO LEAVE YOUR CONFESSION AFTER THE BEEP. HERE IT COMES...
BEEP!

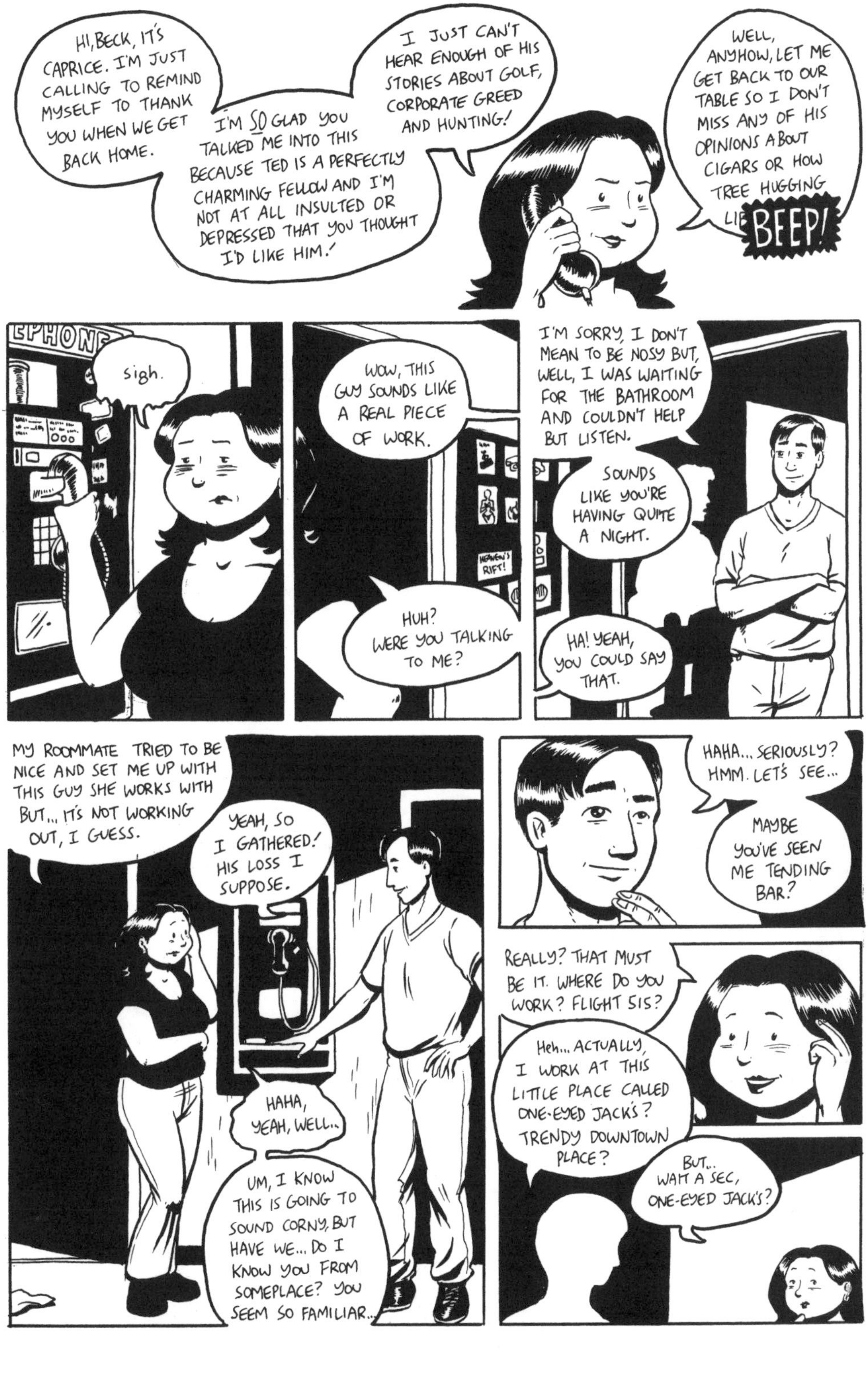
HI, BECK, IT'S CAPRICE. I'M JUST CALLING TO REMIND MYSELF TO THANK YOU WHEN WE GET BACK HOME.
I'M SO GLAD YOU TALKED ME INTO THIS BECAUSE TED IS A PERFECTLY CHARMING FELLOW AND I'M NOT AT ALL INSULTED OR DEPRESSED THAT YOU THOUGHT I'D LIKE HIM!
I JUST CAN'T HEAR ENOUGH OF HIS STORIES ABOUT GOLF, CORPORATE GREED AND HUNTING!
WELL, ANYHOW, LET ME GET BACK TO OUR TABLE SO I DON'T MISS ANY OF HIS OPINIONS ABOUT CIGARS OR HOW TREE HUGGING LI
BEEP!
sigh.
WOW, THIS GUY SOUNDS LIKE A REAL PIECE OF WORK.
HUH? WERE YOU TALKING TO ME?
I'M SORRY, I DON'T MEAN TO BE NOSY BUT, WELL, I WAS WAITING FOR THE BATHROOM AND COULDN'T HELP BUT LISTEN.
SOUNDS LIKE YOU'RE HAVING QUITE A NIGHT.
HA! YEAH, YOU COULD SAY THAT.
MY ROOMMATE TRIED TO BE NICE AND SET ME UP WITH THIS GUY SHE WORKS WITH BUT... IT'S NOT WORKING OUT, I GUESS.
YEAH, SO I GATHERED! HIS LOSS I SUPPOSE.
HAHA, YEAH, WELL...
UM, I KNOW THIS IS GOING TO SOUND CORNY, BUT HAVE WE... DO I KNOW YOU FROM SOMEPLACE? YOU SEEM SO FAMILIAR...
HAHA... SERIOUSLY? HMM. LET'S SEE...
MAYBE YOU'VE SEEN ME TENDING BAR?
REALLY? THAT MUST BE IT. WHERE DO YOU WORK? FLIGHT 515?
Heh... ACTUALLY, I WORK AT THIS LITTLE PLACE CALLED ONE-EYED JACK'S? TRENDY DOWNTOWN PLACE?
BUT... WAIT A SEC, ONE-EYED JACK'S?

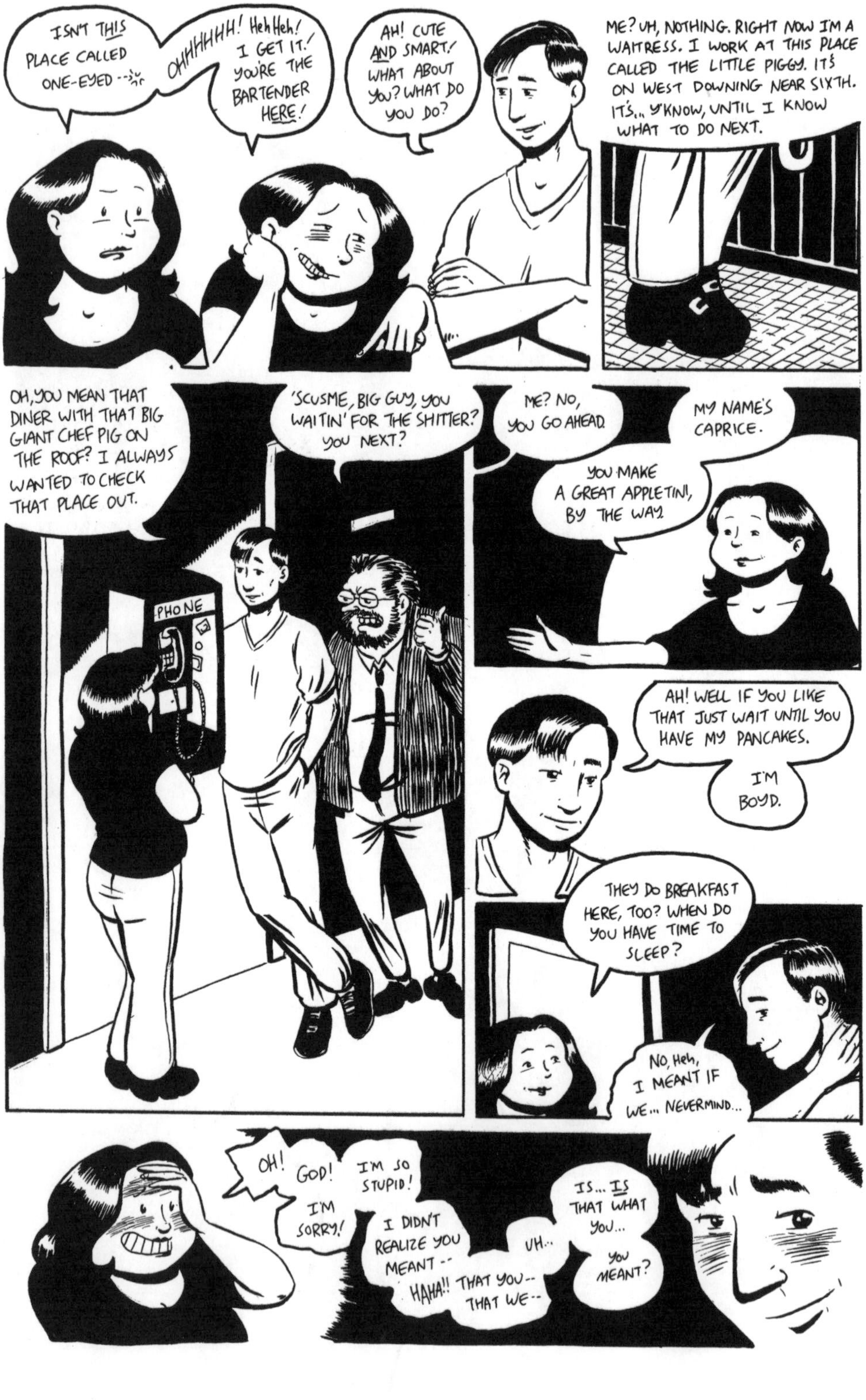

ISN'T THIS PLACE CALLED ONE-EYED --
OHHHHHH! HehHeh! I GET IT! YOU'RE THE BARTENDER HERE!
AH! CUTE AND SMART! WHAT ABOUT YOU? WHAT DO YOU DO?
ME? UH, NOTHING. RIGHT NOW I'M A WAITRESS. I WORK AT THIS PLACE CALLED THE LITTLE PIGGY. IT'S ON WEST DOWNING NEAR SIXTH. IT'S... Y'KNOW, UNTIL I KNOW WHAT TO DO NEXT.
OH, YOU MEAN THAT DINER WITH THAT BIG GIANT CHEF PIG ON THE ROOF? I ALWAYS WANTED TO CHECK THAT PLACE OUT.
'SCUSME, BIG GUY, YOU WAITIN' FOR THE SHITTER? YOU NEXT?
PHONE
ME? NO, YOU GO AHEAD.
MY NAME'S CAPRICE.
YOU MAKE A GREAT APPLETINI, BY THE WAY.
AH! WELL IF YOU LIKE THAT JUST WAIT UNTIL YOU HAVE MY PANCAKES.
I'M BOYD.
THEY DO BREAKFAST HERE, TOO? WHEN DO YOU HAVE TIME TO SLEEP?
NO, Heh, I MEANT IF WE... NEVERMIND...
OH!
GOD!
I'M SO STUPID!
I'M SORRY!
I DIDN'T REALIZE YOU MEANT --
HAHA!! THAT YOU-- THAT WE--
UH...
IS... IS THAT WHAT YOU...
YOU MEANT?

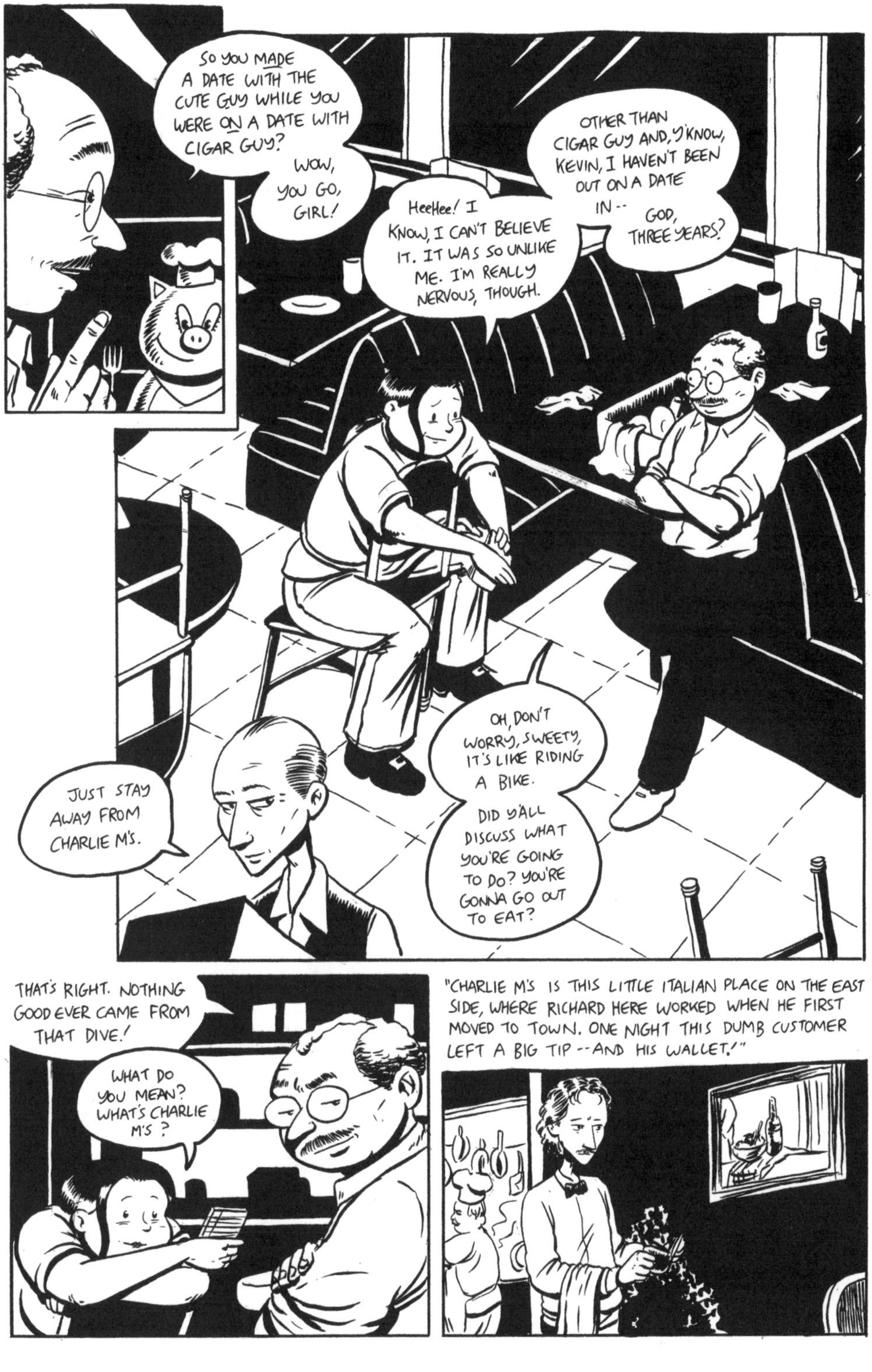
SO YOU MADE A DATE WITH THE CUTE GUY WHILE YOU WERE ON A DATE WITH CIGAR GUY?
WOW, YOU GO, GIRL!
HeeHee! I KNOW, I CAN'T BELIEVE IT. IT WAS SO UNLIKE ME. I'M REALLY NERVOUS, THOUGH.
OTHER THAN CIGAR GUY AND, Y'KNOW, KEVIN, I HAVEN'T BEEN OUT ON A DATE IN --
GOD, THREE YEARS?
OH, DON'T WORRY, SWEETY, IT'S LIKE RIDING A BIKE.
DID Y'ALL DISCUSS WHAT YOU'RE GOING TO DO? YOU'RE GONNA GO OUT TO EAT?
JUST STAY AWAY FROM CHARLIE M'S.
THAT'S RIGHT. NOTHING GOOD EVER CAME FROM THAT DIVE!
WHAT DO YOU MEAN? WHAT'S CHARLIE M'S?
"CHARLIE M'S IS THIS LITTLE ITALIAN PLACE ON THE EAST SIDE, WHERE RICHARD HERE WORKED WHEN HE FIRST MOVED TO TOWN. ONE NIGHT THIS DUMB CUSTOMER LEFT A BIG TIP -- AND HIS WALLET!"

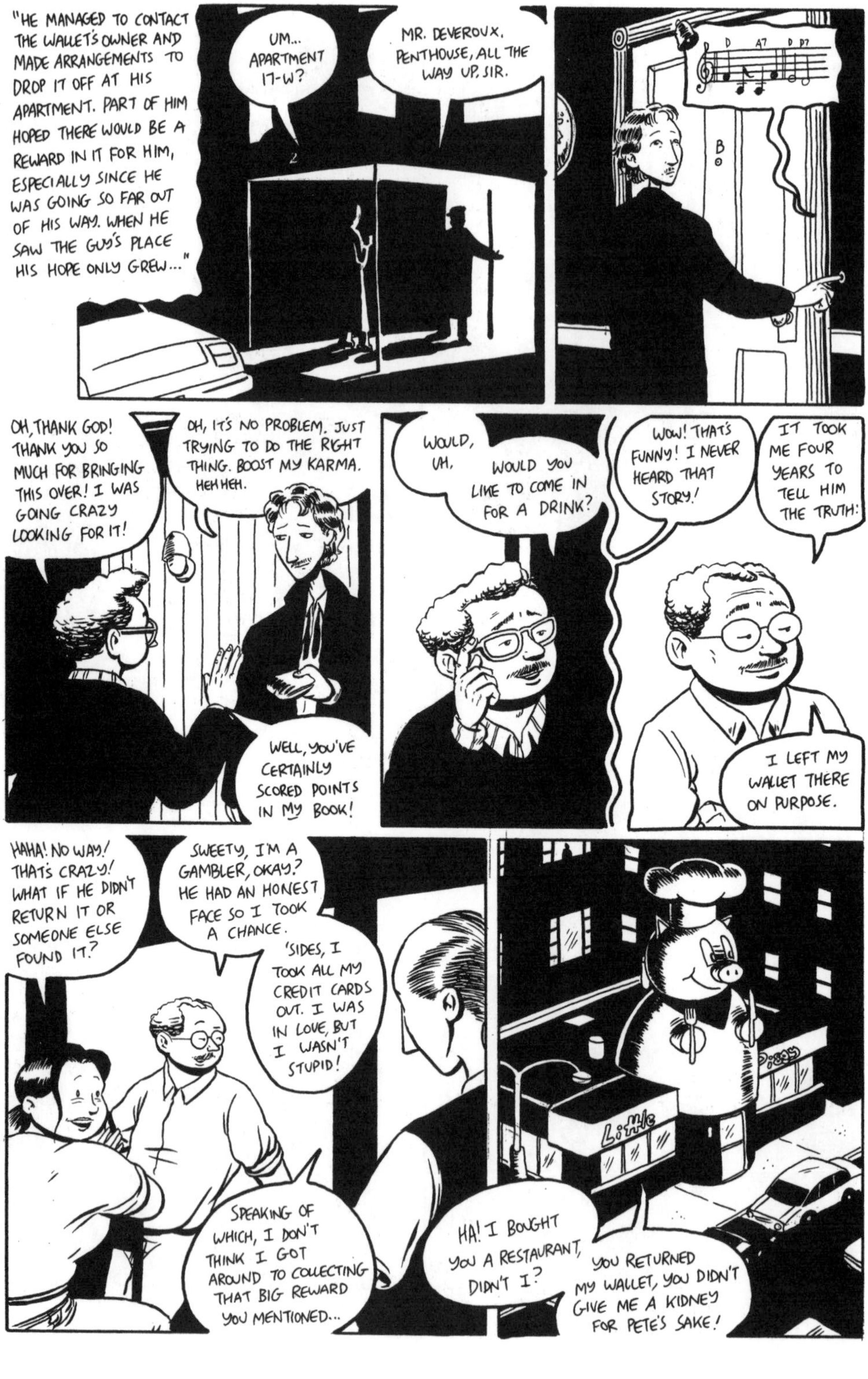
"HE MANAGED TO CONTACT THE WALLET'S OWNER AND MADE ARRANGEMENTS TO DROP IT OFF AT HIS APARTMENT. PART OF HIM HOPED THERE WOULD BE A REWARD IN IT FOR HIM, ESPECIALLY SINCE HE WAS GOING SO FAR OUT OF HIS WAY. WHEN HE SAW THE GUY'S PLACE HIS HOPE ONLY GREW..."
UM... APARTMENT 17-W?
MR. DEVEROUX. PENTHOUSE, ALL THE WAY UP, SIR.
OH, THANK GOD! THANK YOU SO MUCH FOR BRINGING THIS OVER! I WAS GOING CRAZY LOOKING FOR IT!
OH, IT'S NO PROBLEM. JUST TRYING TO DO THE RIGHT THING. BOOST MY KARMA. HEH HEH.
WELL, YOU'VE CERTAINLY SCORED POINTS IN MY BOOK!
WOULD, UH,
WOULD YOU LIKE TO COME IN FOR A DRINK?
WOW! THAT'S FUNNY! I NEVER HEARD THAT STORY!
IT TOOK ME FOUR YEARS TO TELL HIM THE TRUTH:
I LEFT MY WALLET THERE ON PURPOSE.
HAHA! NO WAY! THAT'S CRAZY! WHAT IF HE DIDN'T RETURN IT OR SOMEONE ELSE FOUND IT?
SWEETY, I'M A GAMBLER, OKAY? HE HAD AN HONEST FACE SO I TOOK A CHANCE.
'SIDES, I TOOK ALL MY CREDIT CARDS OUT. I WAS IN LOVE, BUT I WASN'T STUPID!
SPEAKING OF WHICH, I DON'T THINK I GOT AROUND TO COLLECTING THAT BIG REWARD YOU MENTIONED...
HA! I BOUGHT YOU A RESTAURANT, DIDN'T I?
YOU RETURNED MY WALLET, YOU DIDN'T GIVE ME A KIDNEY FOR PETE'S SAKE!
Little
Piggy

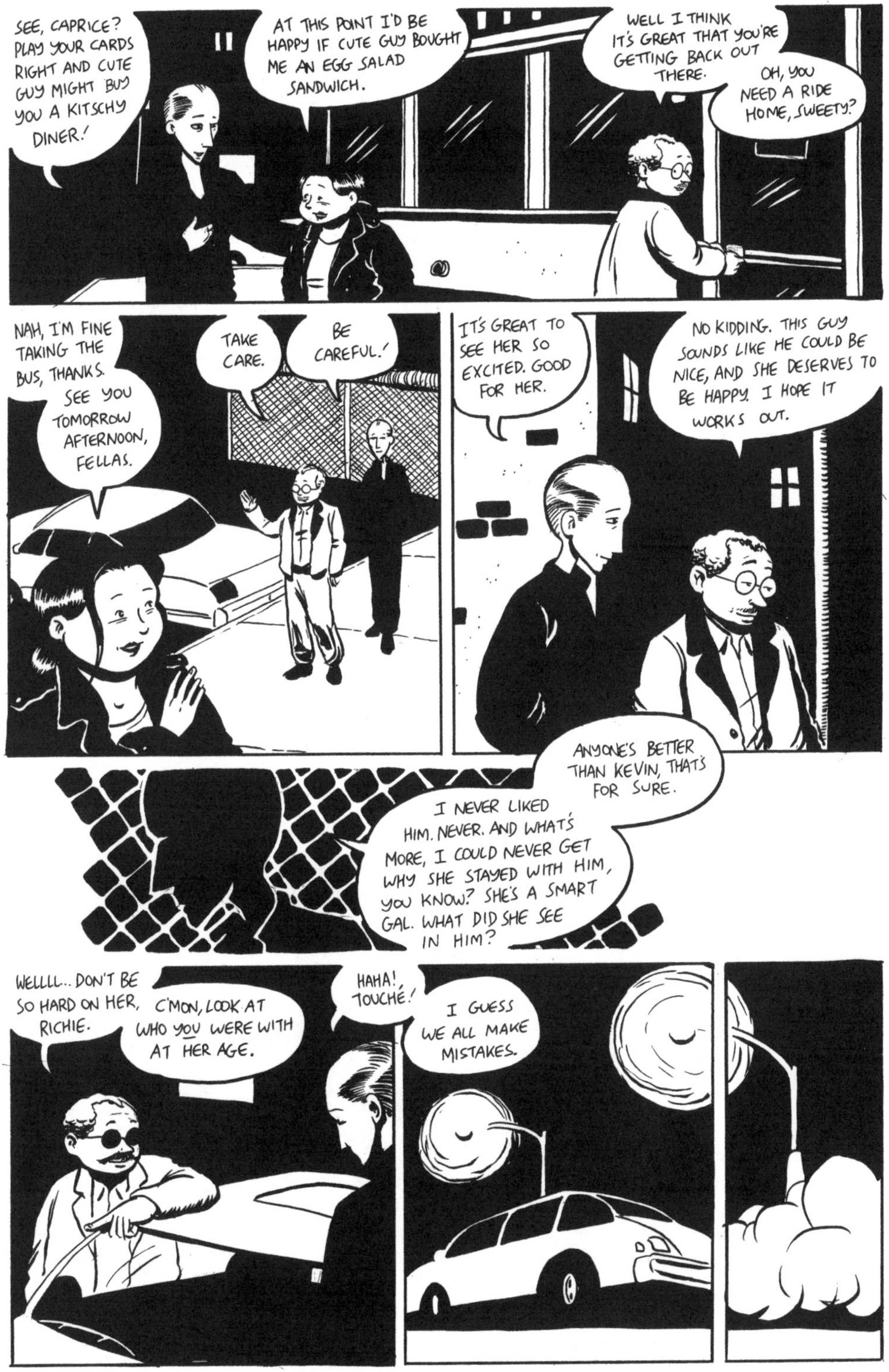
SEE, CAPRICE? PLAY YOUR CARDS RIGHT AND CUTE GUY MIGHT BUY YOU A KITSCHY DINER!
AT THIS POINT I'D BE HAPPY IF CUTE GUY BOUGHT ME AN EGG SALAD SANDWICH.
WELL I THINK IT'S GREAT THAT YOU'RE GETTING BACK OUT THERE.
OH, YOU NEED A RIDE HOME, SWEETY?
NAH, I'M FINE TAKING THE BUS, THANKS.
SEE YOU TOMORROW AFTERNOON, FELLAS.
TAKE CARE.
BE CAREFUL!
IT'S GREAT TO SEE HER SO EXCITED. GOOD FOR HER.
NO KIDDING. THIS GUY SOUNDS LIKE HE COULD BE NICE, AND SHE DESERVES TO BE HAPPY. I HOPE IT WORKS OUT.
ANYONE'S BETTER THAN KEVIN, THAT'S FOR SURE.
I NEVER LIKED HIM. NEVER. AND WHAT'S MORE, I COULD NEVER GET WHY SHE STAYED WITH HIM, YOU KNOW? SHE'S A SMART GAL. WHAT DID SHE SEE IN HIM?
WELLLL... DON'T BE SO HARD ON HER, RICHIE.
C'MON, LOOK AT WHO YOU WERE WITH AT HER AGE.
HAHA! TOUCHÉ!
I GUESS WE ALL MAKE MISTAKES.

FORTY-FOUR

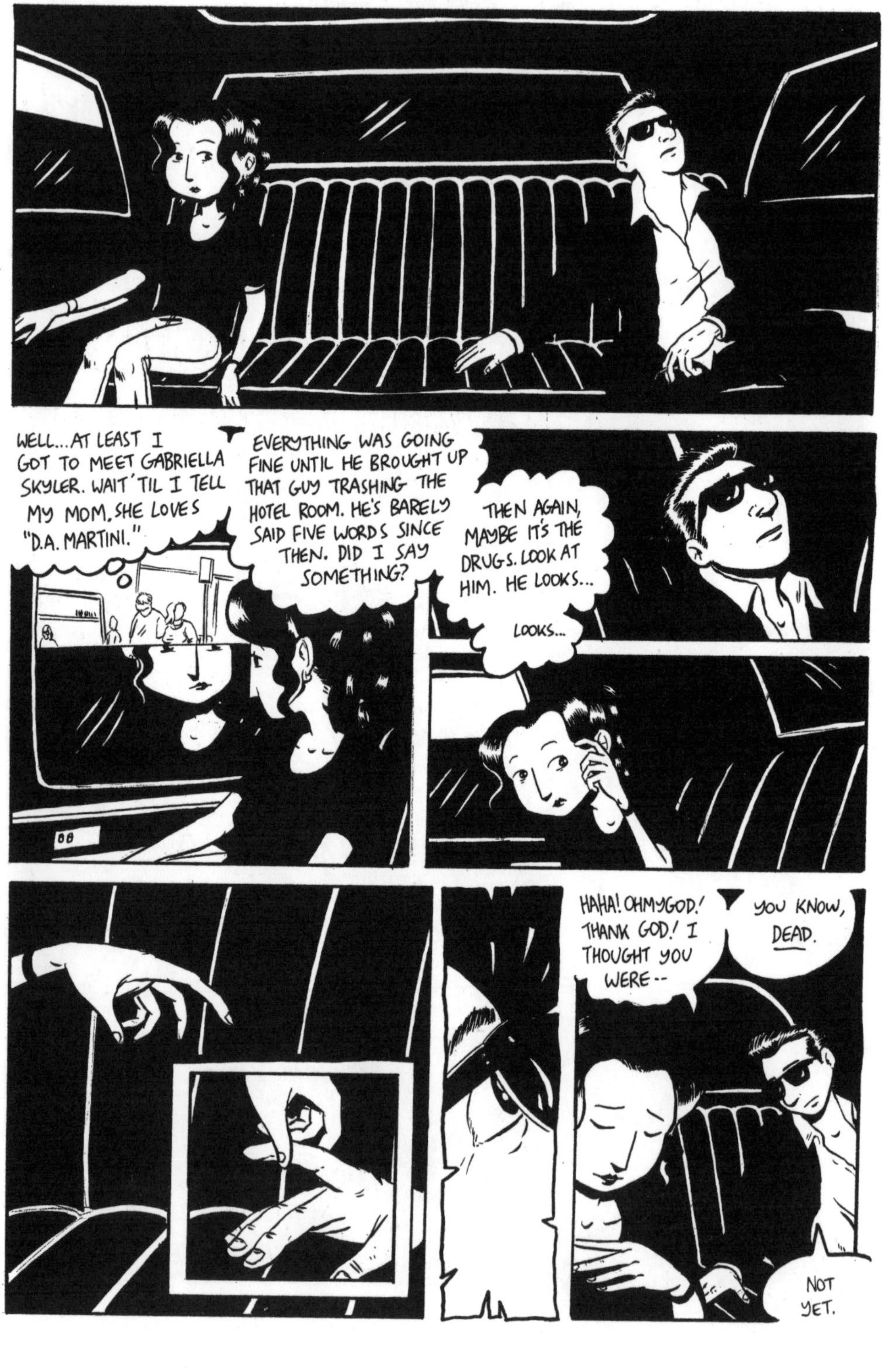
WELL... AT LEAST I GOT TO MEET GABRIELLA SKYLER. WAIT 'TIL I TELL MY MOM. SHE LOVES "D.A. MARTINI."
EVERYTHING WAS GOING FINE UNTIL HE BROUGHT UP THAT GUY TRASHING THE HOTEL ROOM. HE'S BARELY SAID FIVE WORDS SINCE THEN. DID I SAY SOMETHING?
THEN AGAIN, MAYBE IT'S THE DRUGS. LOOK AT HIM. HE LOOKS...
LOOKS...
HAHA! OHMYGOD! THANK GOD! I THOUGHT YOU WERE --
YOU KNOW, DEAD.
NOT YET.

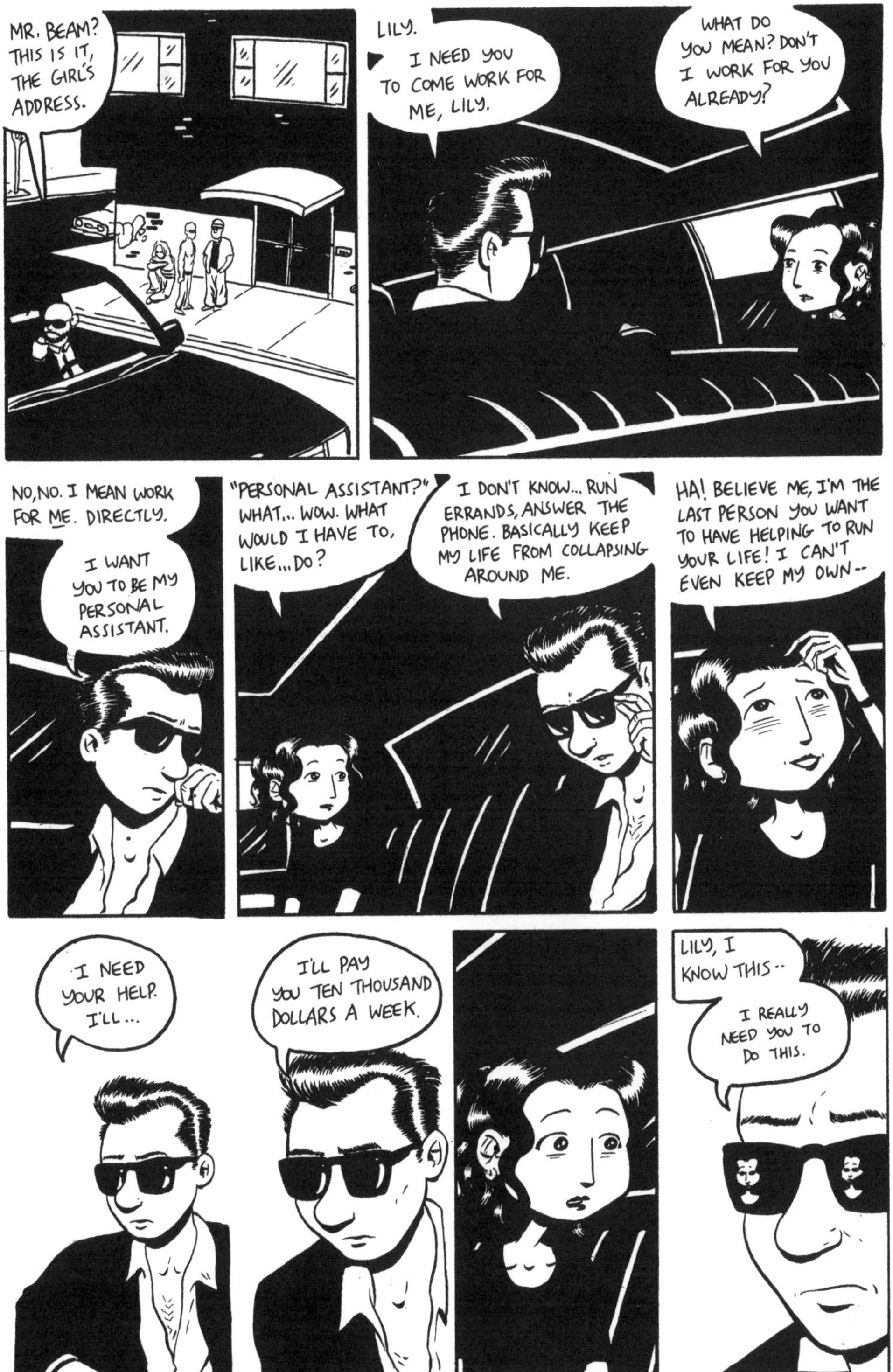
MR. BEAM? THIS IS IT, THE GIRL'S ADDRESS.
LILY.
I NEED YOU TO COME WORK FOR ME, LILY.
WHAT DO YOU MEAN? DON'T I WORK FOR YOU ALREADY?
NO, NO. I MEAN WORK FOR ME. DIRECTLY.
I WANT YOU TO BE MY PERSONAL ASSISTANT.
"PERSONAL ASSISTANT?" WHAT... WOW. WHAT WOULD I HAVE TO, LIKE... DO?
I DON'T KNOW... RUN ERRANDS, ANSWER THE PHONE. BASICALLY KEEP MY LIFE FROM COLLAPSING AROUND ME.
HA! BELIEVE ME, I'M THE LAST PERSON YOU WANT TO HAVE HELPING TO RUN YOUR LIFE! I CAN'T EVEN KEEP MY OWN--
I NEED YOUR HELP. I'LL...
I'LL PAY YOU TEN THOUSAND DOLLARS A WEEK.
LILY, I KNOW THIS--
I REALLY NEED YOU TO DO THIS.

WOW. UH...
WELL...

HAHAHA!
OKAY!

GREAT.

SO...UH...
WHAT HAPPENS
NOW?

OH.
UH...

I GUESS
MARTY WILL CALL
YOU TONIGHT TO
WORK OUT THE,
UH, DETAILS.

AND I GUESS
TOMORROW YOU START,
Y'KNOW, ASSISTING ME.
PERSONALLY.

OKAY. I'LL SEE YOU
TOMORROW, THEN,
MR. BEAM!

ERT!!

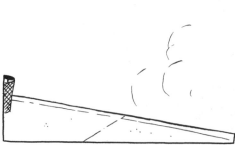

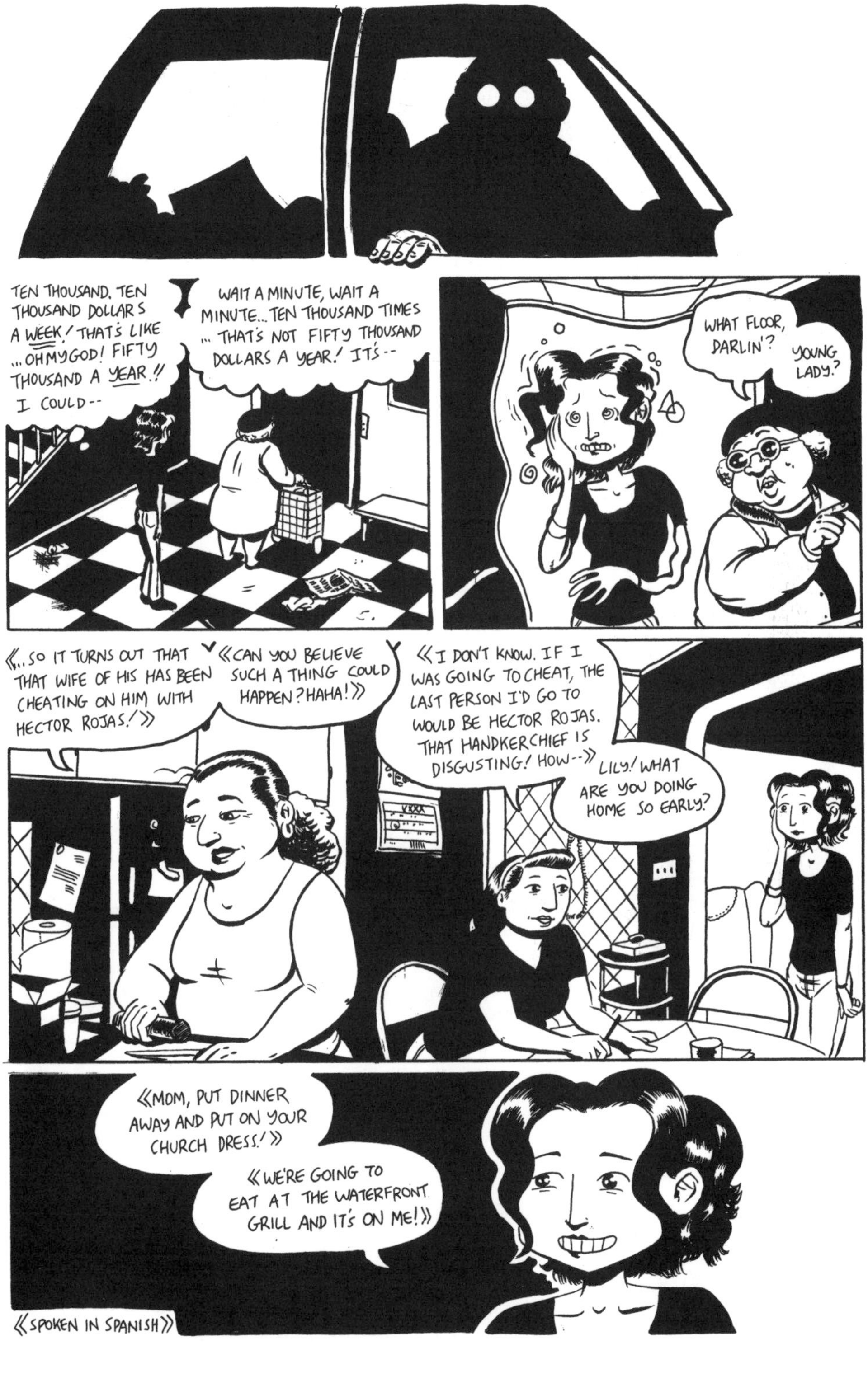
TEN THOUSAND. TEN THOUSAND DOLLARS A WEEK! THAT'S LIKE ...OHMYGOD! FIFTY THOUSAND A YEAR!! I COULD--
WAIT A MINUTE, WAIT A MINUTE... TEN THOUSAND TIMES ... THAT'S NOT FIFTY THOUSAND DOLLARS A YEAR! IT'S--
WHAT FLOOR, DARLIN'?
YOUNG LADY?
«...SO IT TURNS OUT THAT THAT WIFE OF HIS HAS BEEN CHEATING ON HIM WITH HECTOR ROJAS!»
«CAN YOU BELIEVE SUCH A THING COULD HAPPEN? HAHA!»
«I DON'T KNOW. IF I WAS GOING TO CHEAT, THE LAST PERSON I'D GO TO WOULD BE HECTOR ROJAS. THAT HANDKERCHIEF IS DISGUSTING! HOW--»
LILY! WHAT ARE YOU DOING HOME SO EARLY?
«MOM, PUT DINNER AWAY AND PUT ON YOUR CHURCH DRESS!»
«WE'RE GOING TO EAT AT THE WATERFRONT GRILL AND IT'S ON ME!»
«SPOKEN IN SPANISH»

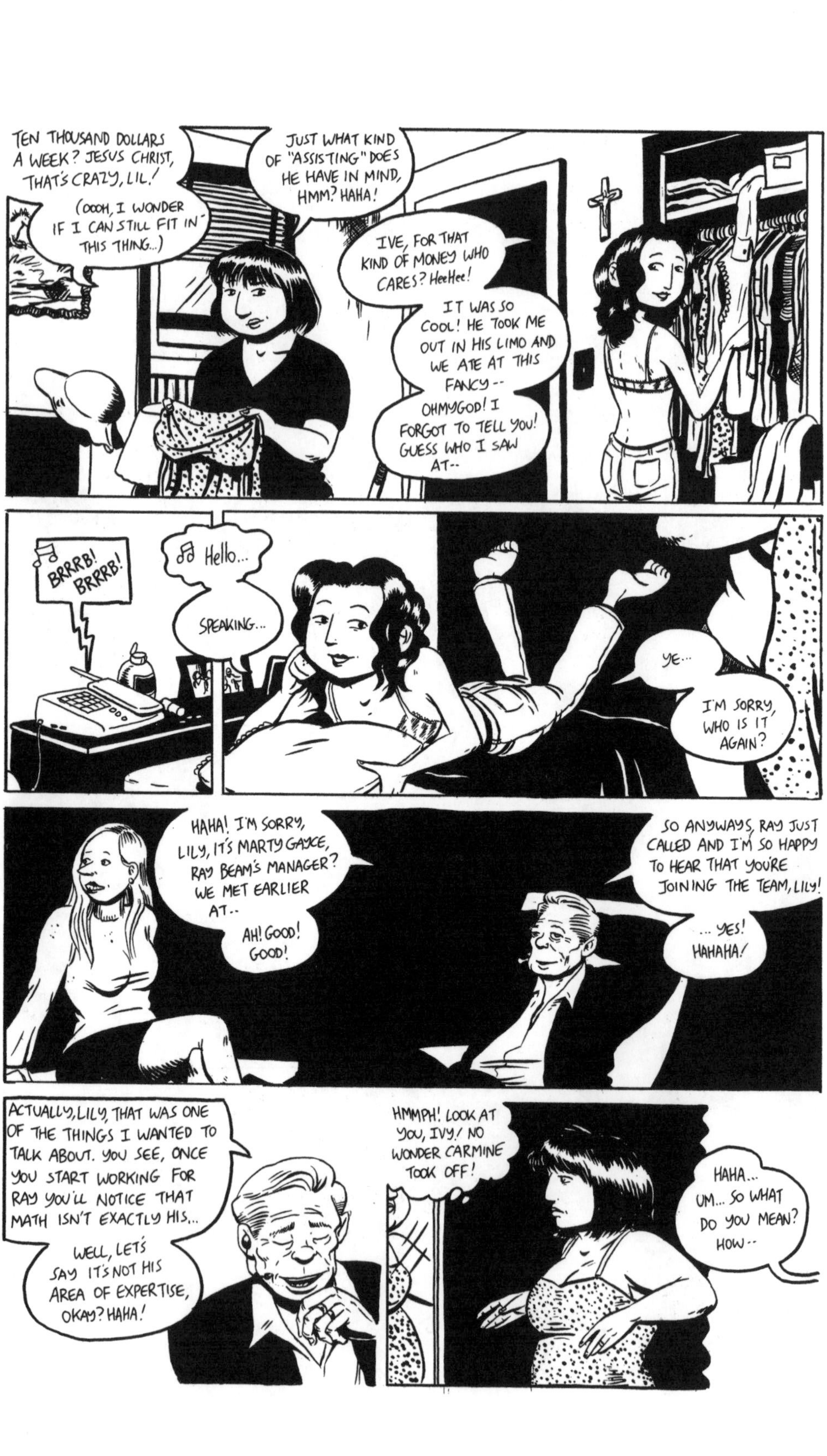
TEN THOUSAND DOLLARS A WEEK? JESUS CHRIST, THAT'S CRAZY, LIL!
(OOOH, I WONDER IF I CAN STILL FIT IN THIS THING...)
JUST WHAT KIND OF "ASSISTING" DOES HE HAVE IN MIND, HMM? HAHA!
IVE, FOR THAT KIND OF MONEY WHO CARES? HeeHee!
IT WAS SO COOL! HE TOOK ME OUT IN HIS LIMO AND WE ATE AT THIS FANCY --
OHMYGOD! I FORGOT TO TELL YOU! GUESS WHO I SAW AT--
BRRRB! BRRRB!
Hello...
SPEAKING...
YE...
I'M SORRY, WHO IS IT AGAIN?
HAHA! I'M SORRY, LILY, IT'S MARTY GAYCE, RAY BEAM'S MANAGER? WE MET EARLIER AT..
AH! GOOD! GOOD!
SO ANYWAYS, RAY JUST CALLED AND I'M SO HAPPY TO HEAR THAT YOU'RE JOINING THE TEAM, LILY!
... YES! HAHAHA!
ACTUALLY, LILY, THAT WAS ONE OF THE THINGS I WANTED TO TALK ABOUT. YOU SEE, ONCE YOU START WORKING FOR RAY YOU'LL NOTICE THAT MATH ISN'T EXACTLY HIS...
WELL, LET'S SAY IT'S NOT HIS AREA OF EXPERTISE, OKAY? HAHA!
HMMPH! LOOK AT YOU, IVY! NO WONDER CARMINE TOOK OFF!
HAHA... UM... SO WHAT DO YOU MEAN? HOW--

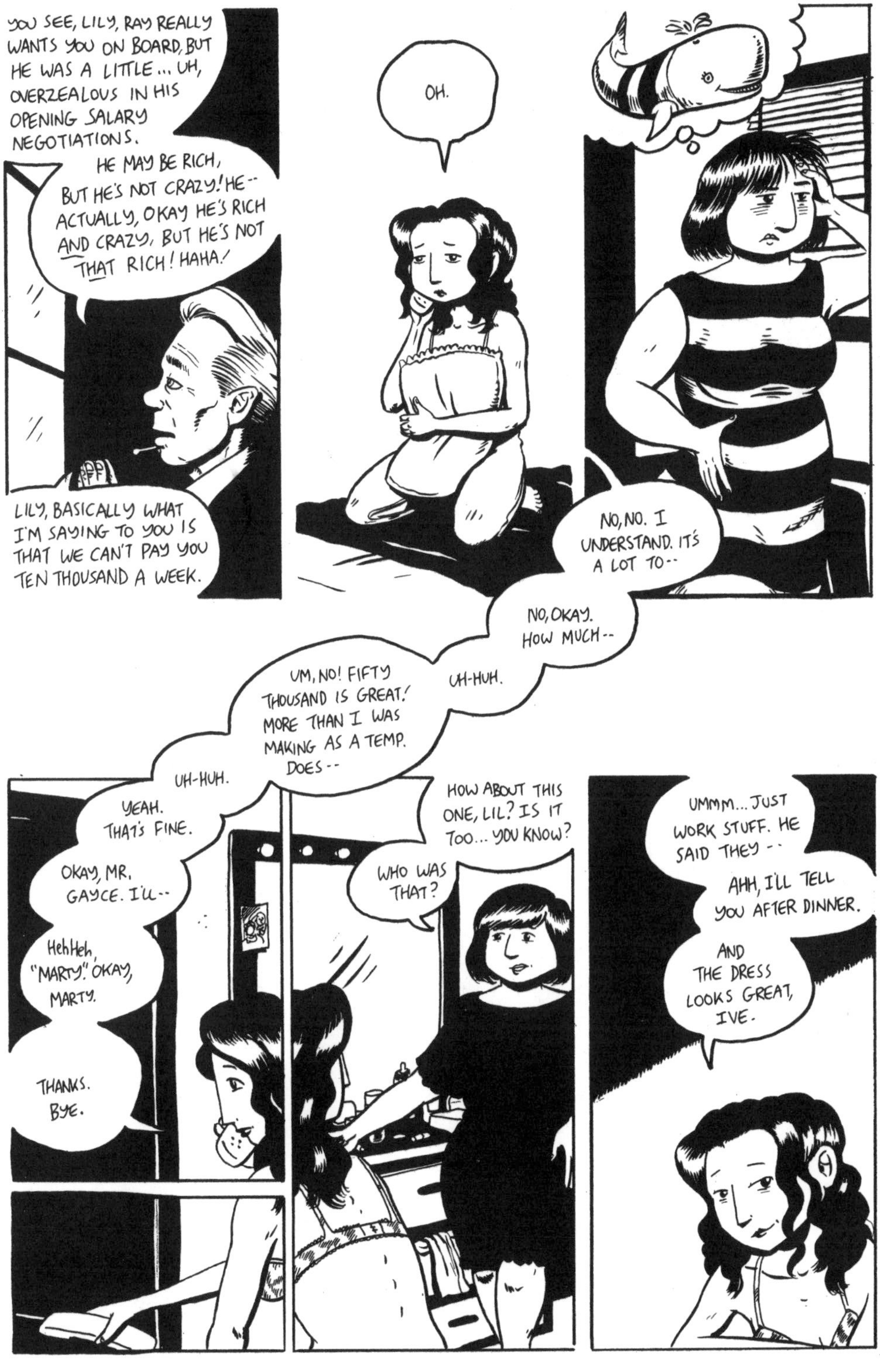
YOU SEE, LILY, RAY REALLY WANTS YOU ON BOARD, BUT HE WAS A LITTLE... UH, OVERZEALOUS IN HIS OPENING SALARY NEGOTIATIONS.
HE MAY BE RICH, BUT HE'S NOT CRAZY! HE-- ACTUALLY, OKAY HE'S RICH AND CRAZY, BUT HE'S NOT THAT RICH! HAHA!
LILY, BASICALLY WHAT I'M SAYING TO YOU IS THAT WE CAN'T PAY YOU TEN THOUSAND A WEEK.
OH.
NO, NO. I UNDERSTAND. IT'S A LOT TO--
NO, OKAY. HOW MUCH--
UH-HUH.
UM, NO! FIFTY THOUSAND IS GREAT! MORE THAN I WAS MAKING AS A TEMP. DOES--
UH-HUH.
YEAH. THAT'S FINE.
OKAY, MR. GAYCE. I'LL--
HehHeh, "MARTY." OKAY, MARTY.
THANKS. BYE.
HOW ABOUT THIS ONE, LIL? IS IT TOO... YOU KNOW?
WHO WAS THAT?
UMMM... JUST WORK STUFF. HE SAID THEY--
AHH, I'LL TELL YOU AFTER DINNER.
AND THE DRESS LOOKS GREAT, IVE.

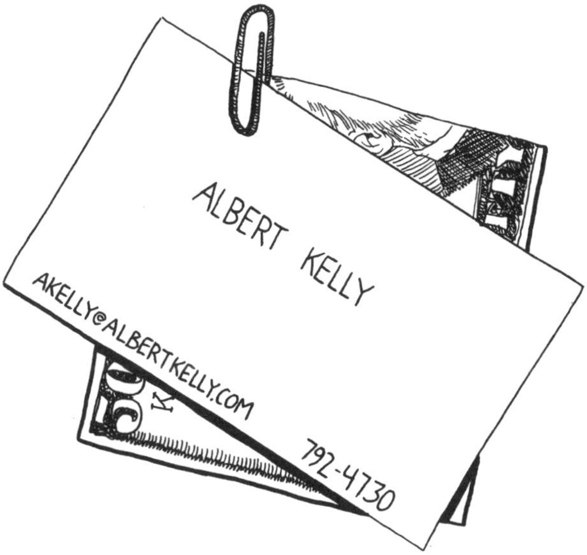
ALBERT KELLY
AKELLY@ALBERTKELLY.COM
792-4730

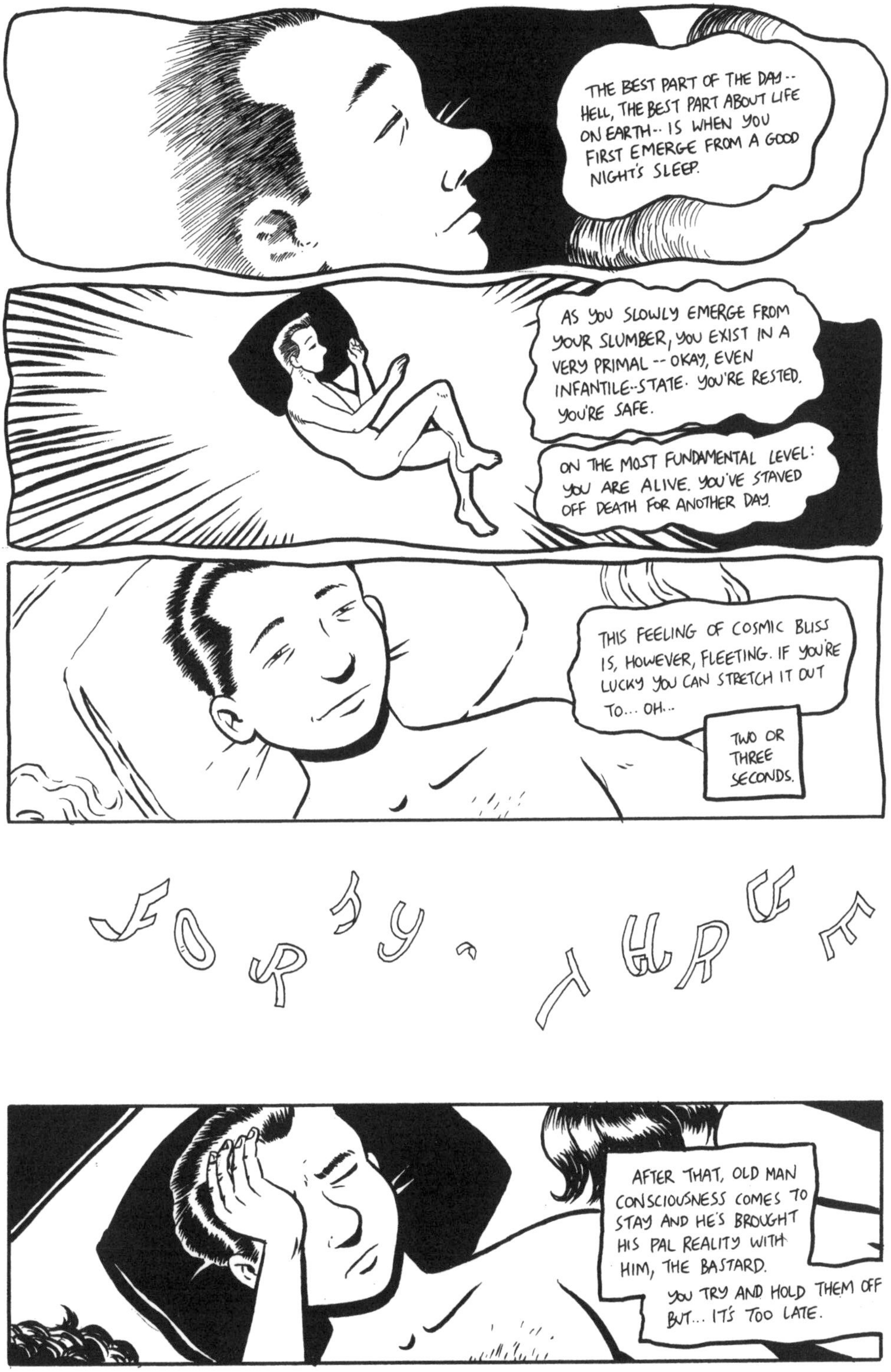
THE BEST PART OF THE DAY -- HELL, THE BEST PART ABOUT LIFE ON EARTH -- IS WHEN YOU FIRST EMERGE FROM A GOOD NIGHT'S SLEEP.
AS YOU SLOWLY EMERGE FROM YOUR SLUMBER, YOU EXIST IN A VERY PRIMAL -- OKAY, EVEN INFANTILE -- STATE. YOU'RE RESTED. YOU'RE SAFE.
ON THE MOST FUNDAMENTAL LEVEL: YOU ARE ALIVE. YOU'VE STAVED OFF DEATH FOR ANOTHER DAY.
THIS FEELING OF COSMIC BLISS IS, HOWEVER, FLEETING. IF YOU'RE LUCKY YOU CAN STRETCH IT OUT TO... OH...
TWO OR THREE SECONDS.
FORTY-THREE
AFTER THAT, OLD MAN CONSCIOUSNESS COMES TO STAY AND HE'S BROUGHT HIS PAL REALITY WITH HIM, THE BASTARD.
YOU TRY AND HOLD THEM OFF BUT... IT'S TOO LATE.

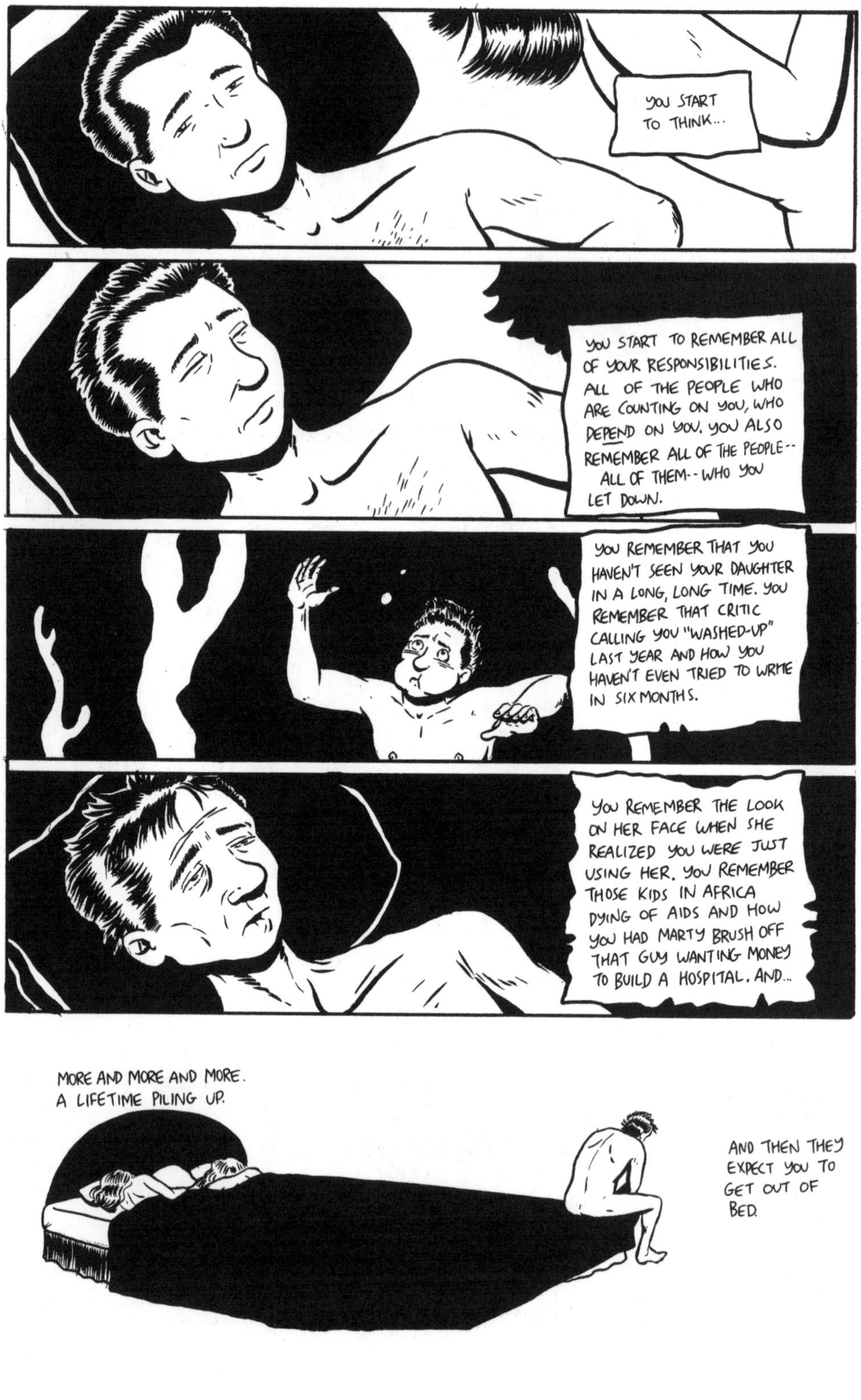
YOU START TO THINK...
YOU START TO REMEMBER ALL OF YOUR RESPONSIBILITIES. ALL OF THE PEOPLE WHO ARE COUNTING ON YOU, WHO DEPEND ON YOU. YOU ALSO REMEMBER ALL OF THE PEOPLE-- ALL OF THEM--WHO YOU LET DOWN.
YOU REMEMBER THAT YOU HAVEN'T SEEN YOUR DAUGHTER IN A LONG, LONG TIME. YOU REMEMBER THAT CRITIC CALLING YOU "WASHED-UP" LAST YEAR AND HOW YOU HAVEN'T EVEN TRIED TO WRITE IN SIX MONTHS.
YOU REMEMBER THE LOOK ON HER FACE WHEN SHE REALIZED YOU WERE JUST USING HER. YOU REMEMBER THOSE KIDS IN AFRICA DYING OF AIDS AND HOW YOU HAD MARTY BRUSH OFF THAT GUY WANTING MONEY TO BUILD A HOSPITAL. AND...
MORE AND MORE AND MORE. A LIFETIME PILING UP.
AND THEN THEY EXPECT YOU TO GET OUT OF BED.

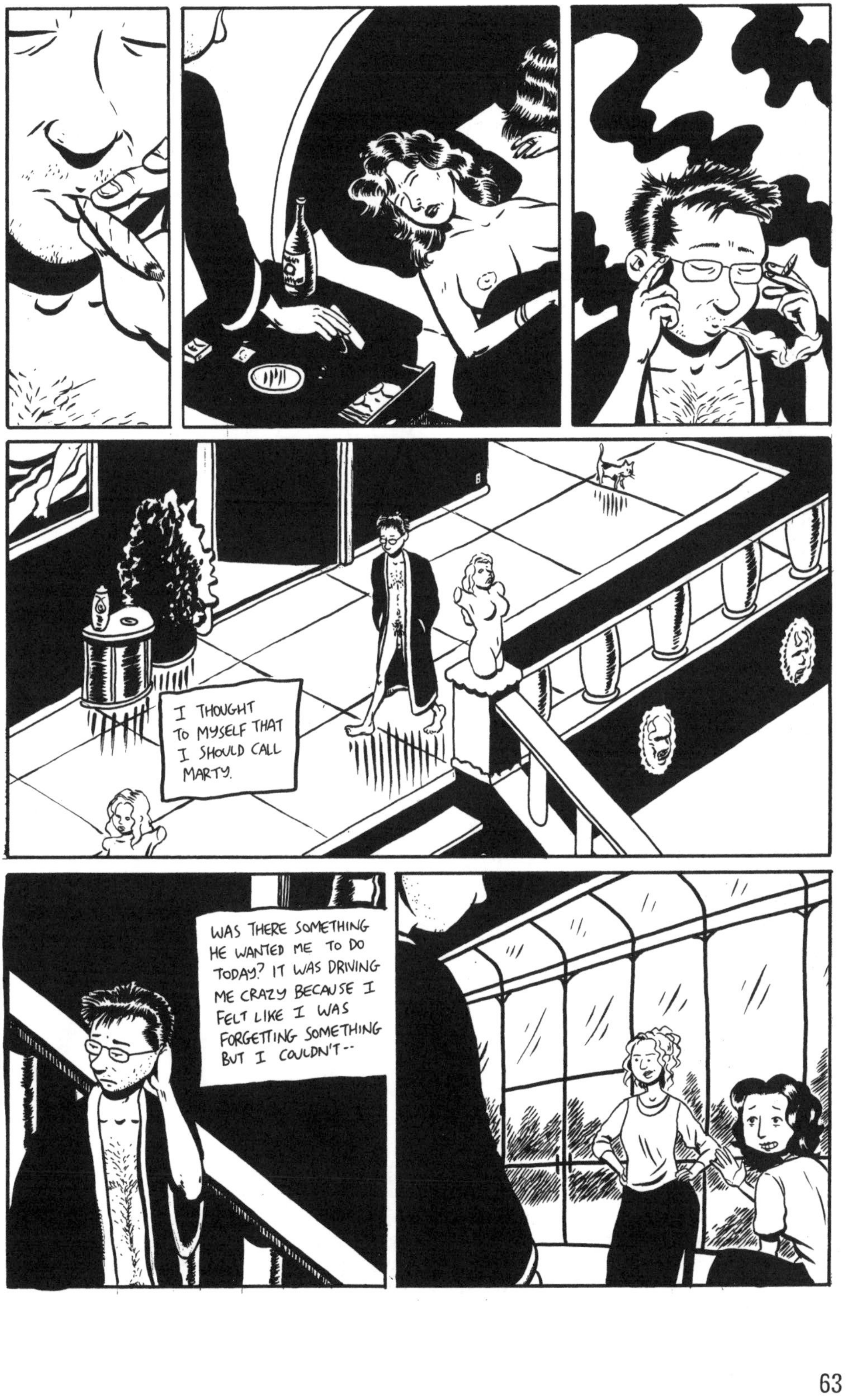
I THOUGHT TO MYSELF THAT I SHOULD CALL MARTY.
WAS THERE SOMETHING HE WANTED ME TO DO TODAY? IT WAS DRIVING ME CRAZY BECAUSE I FELT LIKE I WAS FORGETTING SOMETHING BUT I COULDN'T--

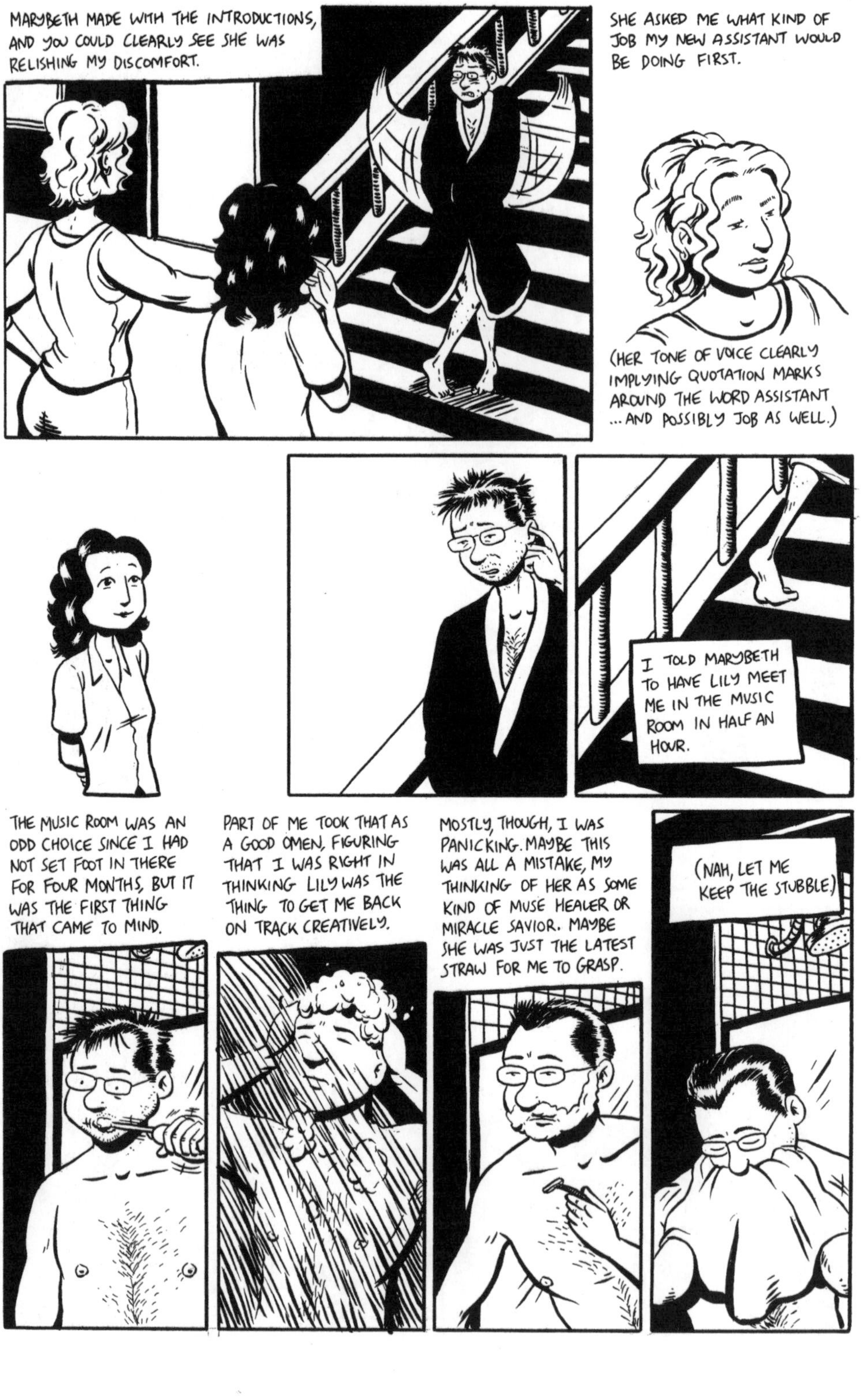
MARYBETH MADE WITH THE INTRODUCTIONS, AND YOU COULD CLEARLY SEE SHE WAS RELISHING MY DISCOMFORT.
SHE ASKED ME WHAT KIND OF JOB MY NEW ASSISTANT WOULD BE DOING FIRST.
(HER TONE OF VOICE CLEARLY IMPLYING QUOTATION MARKS AROUND THE WORD ASSISTANT ...AND POSSIBLY JOB AS WELL.)
I TOLD MARYBETH TO HAVE LILY MEET ME IN THE MUSIC ROOM IN HALF AN HOUR.
THE MUSIC ROOM WAS AN ODD CHOICE SINCE I HAD NOT SET FOOT IN THERE FOR FOUR MONTHS, BUT IT WAS THE FIRST THING THAT CAME TO MIND.
PART OF ME TOOK THAT AS A GOOD OMEN, FIGURING THAT I WAS RIGHT IN THINKING LILY WAS THE THING TO GET ME BACK ON TRACK CREATIVELY.
MOSTLY, THOUGH, I WAS PANICKING. MAYBE THIS WAS ALL A MISTAKE, MY THINKING OF HER AS SOME KIND OF MUSE HEALER OR MIRACLE SAVIOR. MAYBE SHE WAS JUST THE LATEST STRAW FOR ME TO GRASP.
(NAH, LET ME KEEP THE STUBBLE.)

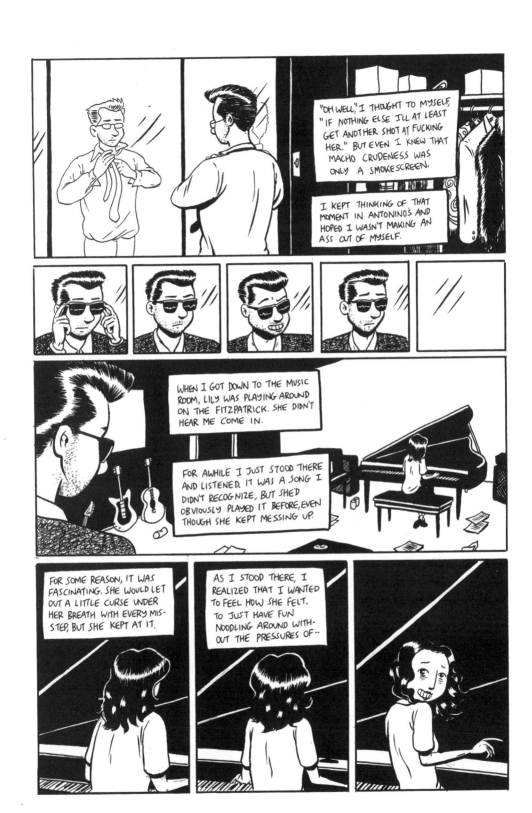

"OH WELL," I THOUGHT TO MYSELF, "IF NOTHING ELSE I'LL AT LEAST GET ANOTHER SHOT AT FUCKING HER." BUT EVEN I KNEW THAT MACHO CRUDENESS WAS ONLY A SMOKESCREEN.

I KEPT THINKING OF THAT MOMENT IN ANTONINO'S AND HOPED I WASN'T MAKING AN ASS OUT OF MYSELF.

WHEN I GOT DOWN TO THE MUSIC ROOM, LILY WAS PLAYING AROUND ON THE FITZPATRICK. SHE DIDN'T HEAR ME COME IN.

FOR AWHILE I JUST STOOD THERE AND LISTENED. IT WAS A SONG I DIDN'T RECOGNIZE, BUT SHE'D OBVIOUSLY PLAYED IT BEFORE, EVEN THOUGH SHE KEPT MESSING UP.

FOR SOME REASON, IT WAS FASCINATING. SHE WOULD LET OUT A LITTLE CURSE UNDER HER BREATH WITH EVERY MIS-STEP, BUT SHE KEPT AT IT.

AS I STOOD THERE, I REALIZED THAT I WANTED TO FEEL HOW SHE FELT. TO JUST HAVE FUN NOODLING AROUND WITH-OUT THE PRESSURES OF--

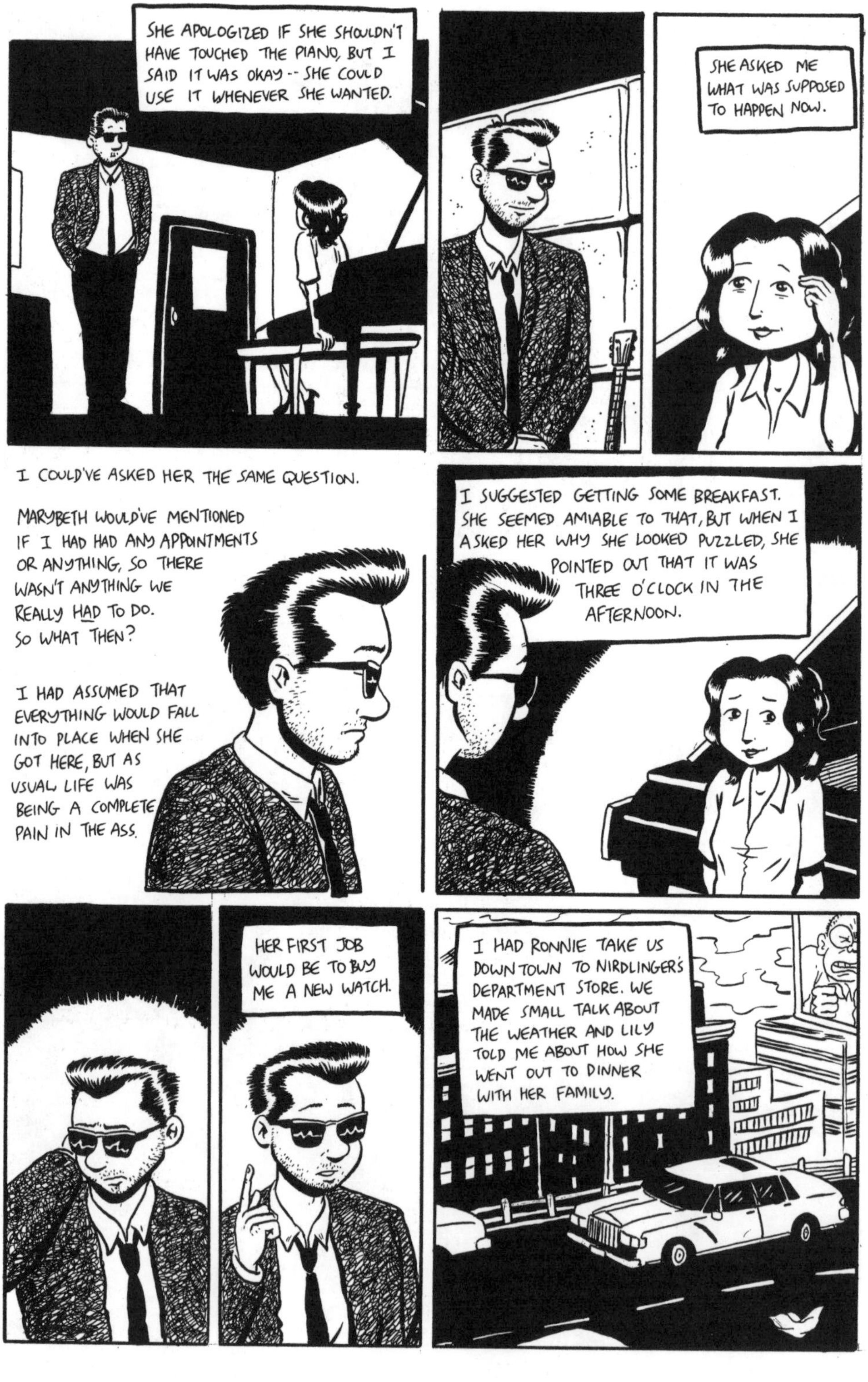
SHE APOLOGIZED IF SHE SHOULDN'T HAVE TOUCHED THE PIANO, BUT I SAID IT WAS OKAY -- SHE COULD USE IT WHENEVER SHE WANTED.
SHE ASKED ME WHAT WAS SUPPOSED TO HAPPEN NOW.
I COULD'VE ASKED HER THE SAME QUESTION.
MARYBETH WOULD'VE MENTIONED IF I HAD HAD ANY APPOINTMENTS OR ANYTHING, SO THERE WASN'T ANYTHING WE REALLY HAD TO DO. SO WHAT THEN?
I HAD ASSUMED THAT EVERYTHING WOULD FALL INTO PLACE WHEN SHE GOT HERE, BUT AS USUAL LIFE WAS BEING A COMPLETE PAIN IN THE ASS.
I SUGGESTED GETTING SOME BREAKFAST. SHE SEEMED AMIABLE TO THAT, BUT WHEN I ASKED HER WHY SHE LOOKED PUZZLED, SHE POINTED OUT THAT IT WAS THREE O'CLOCK IN THE AFTERNOON.
HER FIRST JOB WOULD BE TO BUY ME A NEW WATCH.
I HAD RONNIE TAKE US DOWNTOWN TO NIRDLINGER'S DEPARTMENT STORE. WE MADE SMALL TALK ABOUT THE WEATHER AND LILY TOLD ME ABOUT HOW SHE WENT OUT TO DINNER WITH HER FAMILY.

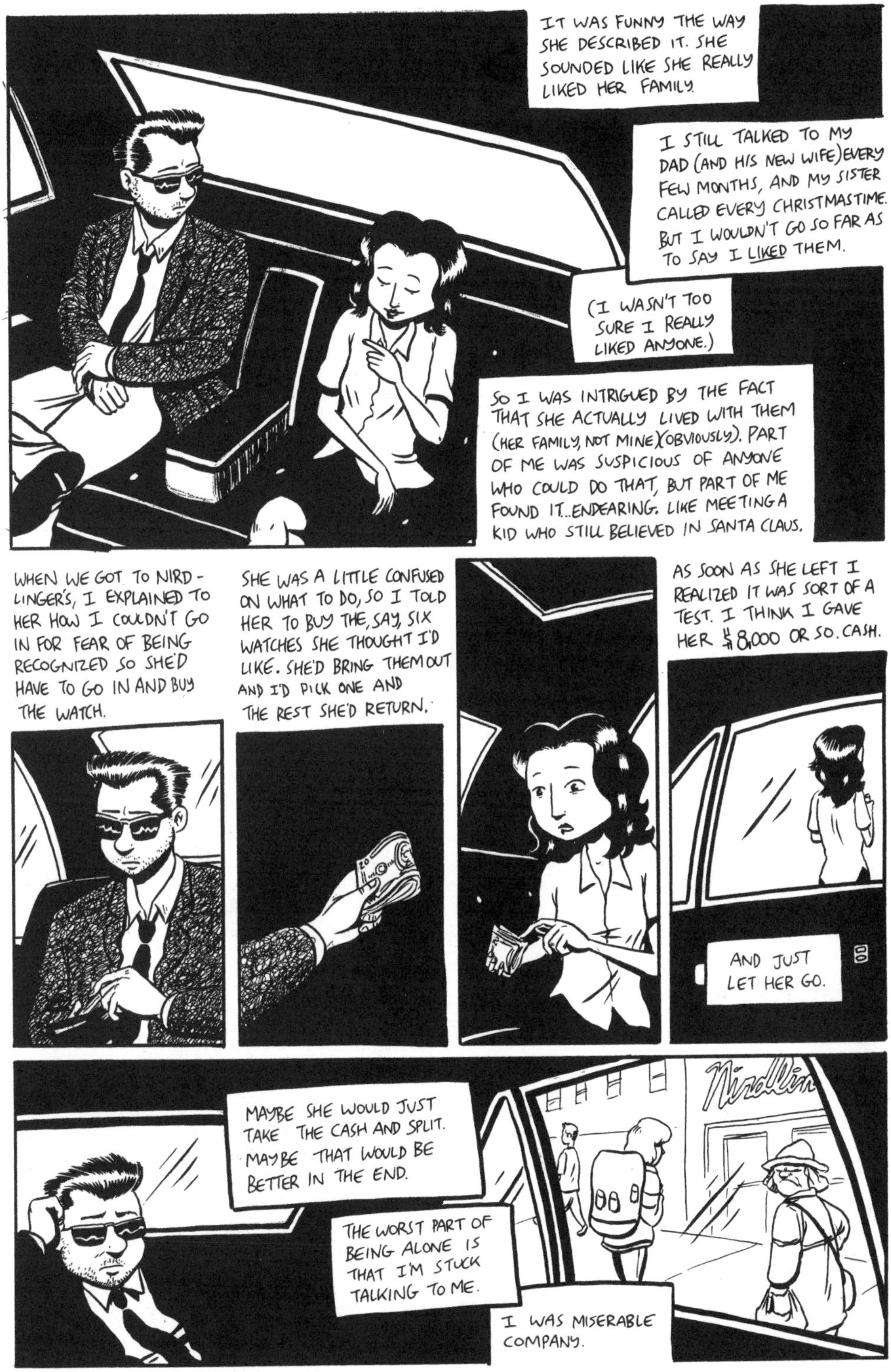
IT WAS FUNNY THE WAY SHE DESCRIBED IT. SHE SOUNDED LIKE SHE REALLY LIKED HER FAMILY.
I STILL TALKED TO MY DAD (AND HIS NEW WIFE) EVERY FEW MONTHS, AND MY SISTER CALLED EVERY CHRISTMASTIME. BUT I WOULDN'T GO SO FAR AS TO SAY I LIKED THEM.
(I WASN'T TOO SURE I REALLY LIKED ANYONE.)
SO I WAS INTRIGUED BY THE FACT THAT SHE ACTUALLY LIVED WITH THEM (HER FAMILY, NOT MINE) (OBVIOUSLY). PART OF ME WAS SUSPICIOUS OF ANYONE WHO COULD DO THAT, BUT PART OF ME FOUND IT...ENDEARING. LIKE MEETING A KID WHO STILL BELIEVED IN SANTA CLAUS.
WHEN WE GOT TO NIRD-LINGER'S, I EXPLAINED TO HER HOW I COULDN'T GO IN FOR FEAR OF BEING RECOGNIZED SO SHE'D HAVE TO GO IN AND BUY THE WATCH.
SHE WAS A LITTLE CONFUSED ON WHAT TO DO, SO I TOLD HER TO BUY THE, SAY, SIX WATCHES SHE THOUGHT I'D LIKE. SHE'D BRING THEM OUT AND I'D PICK ONE AND THE REST SHE'D RETURN.
AS SOON AS SHE LEFT I REALIZED IT WAS SORT OF A TEST. I THINK I GAVE HER ¥8,000 OR SO. CASH.
AND JUST LET HER GO.
MAYBE SHE WOULD JUST TAKE THE CASH AND SPLIT. MAYBE THAT WOULD BE BETTER IN THE END.
THE WORST PART OF BEING ALONE IS THAT I'M STUCK TALKING TO ME.
I WAS MISERABLE COMPANY.

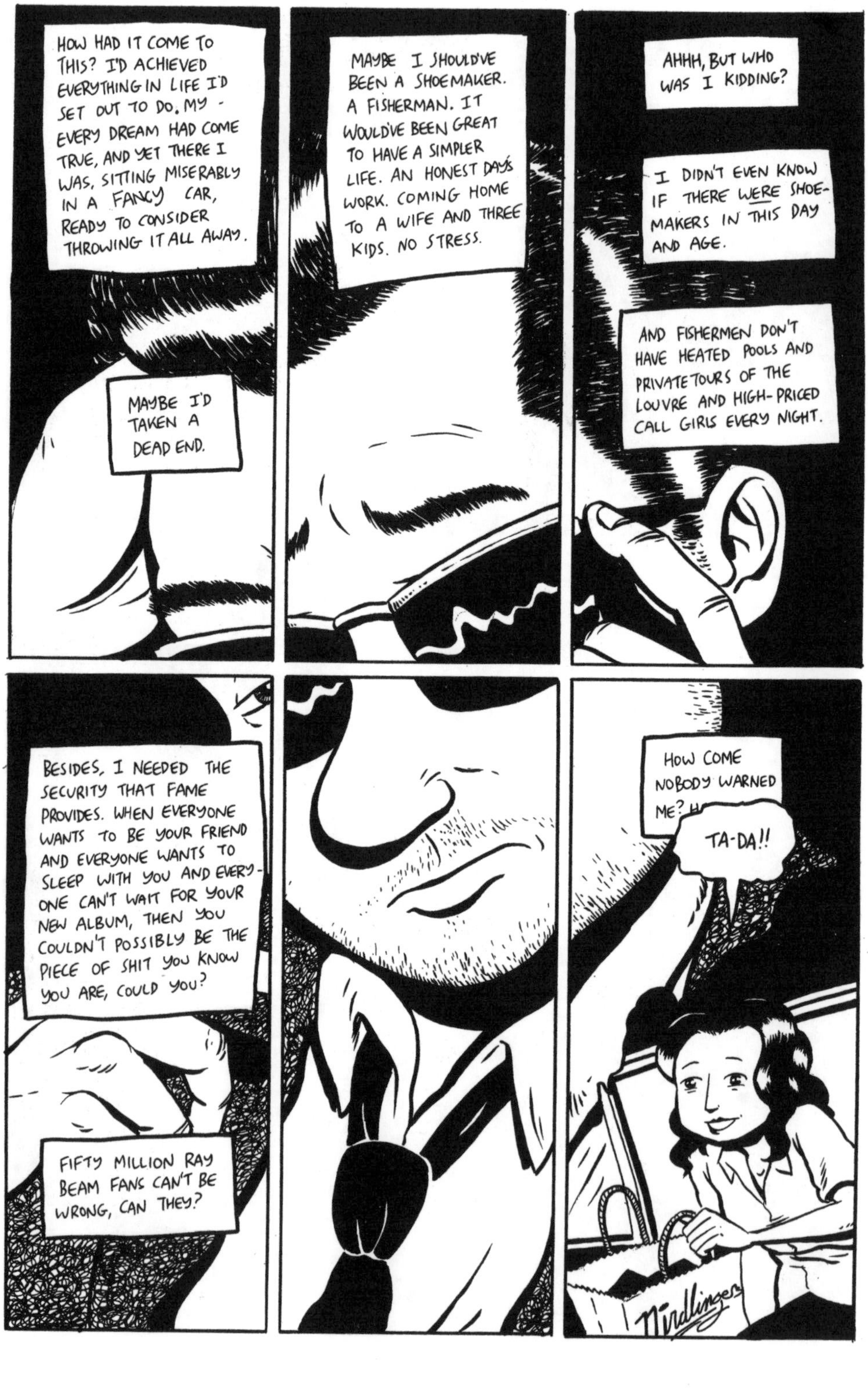
HOW HAD IT COME TO THIS? I'D ACHIEVED EVERYTHING IN LIFE I'D SET OUT TO DO. MY - EVERY DREAM HAD COME TRUE, AND YET THERE I WAS, SITTING MISERABLY IN A FANCY CAR, READY TO CONSIDER THROWING IT ALL AWAY.
MAYBE I'D TAKEN A DEAD END.
MAYBE I SHOULD'VE BEEN A SHOEMAKER. A FISHERMAN. IT WOULD'VE BEEN GREAT TO HAVE A SIMPLER LIFE. AN HONEST DAY'S WORK. COMING HOME TO A WIFE AND THREE KIDS. NO STRESS.
AHHH, BUT WHO WAS I KIDDING?
I DIDN'T EVEN KNOW IF THERE WERE SHOEMAKERS IN THIS DAY AND AGE.
AND FISHERMEN DON'T HAVE HEATED POOLS AND PRIVATE TOURS OF THE LOUVRE AND HIGH-PRICED CALL GIRLS EVERY NIGHT.
BESIDES, I NEEDED THE SECURITY THAT FAME PROVIDES. WHEN EVERYONE WANTS TO BE YOUR FRIEND AND EVERYONE WANTS TO SLEEP WITH YOU AND EVERYONE CAN'T WAIT FOR YOUR NEW ALBUM, THEN YOU COULDN'T POSSIBLY BE THE PIECE OF SHIT YOU KNOW YOU ARE, COULD YOU?
FIFTY MILLION RAY BEAM FANS CAN'T BE WRONG, CAN THEY?
HOW COME NOBODY WARNED ME?
TA-DA!!
Nirdlingers

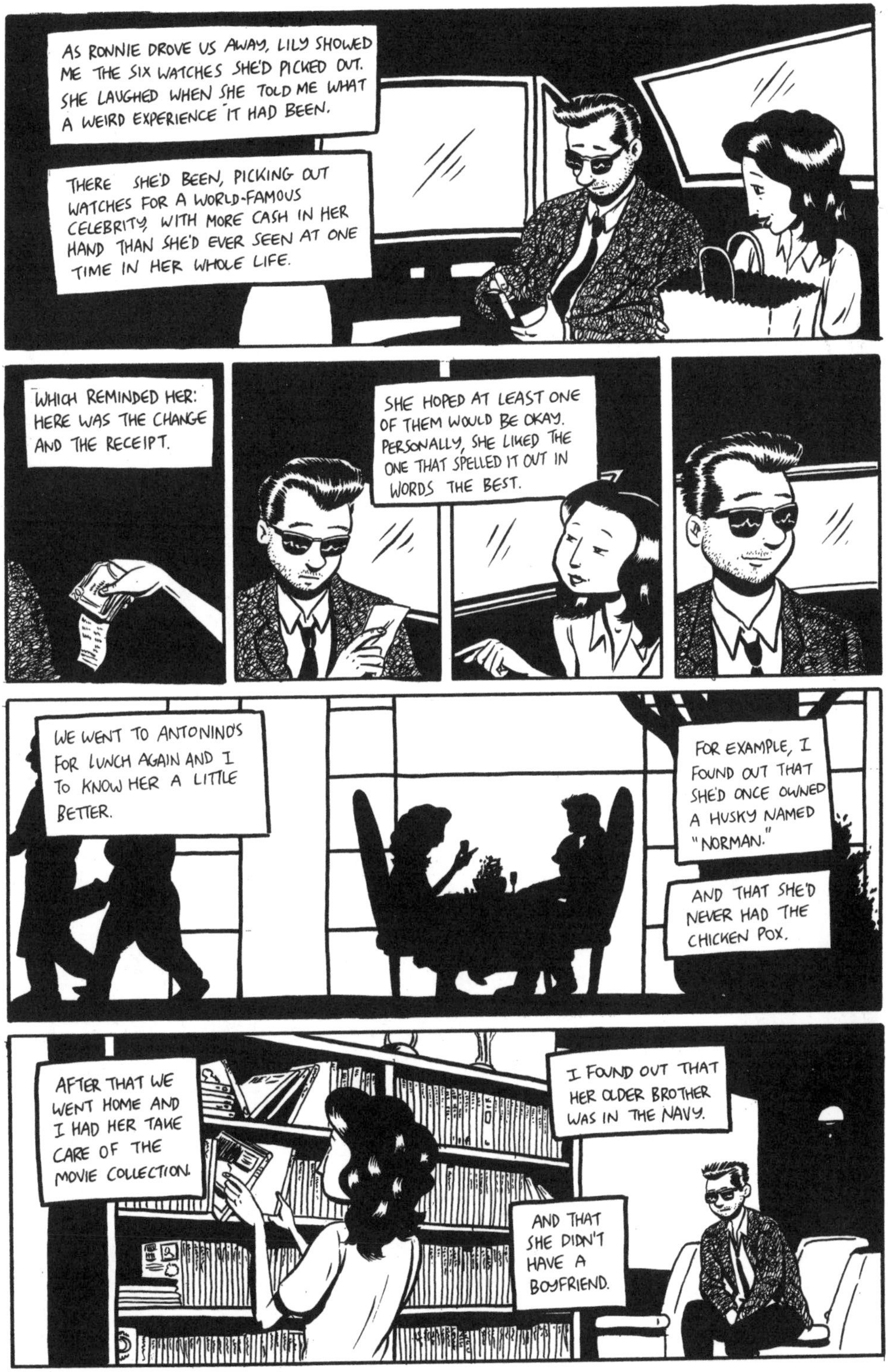
AS RONNIE DROVE US AWAY, LILY SHOWED ME THE SIX WATCHES SHE'D PICKED OUT. SHE LAUGHED WHEN SHE TOLD ME WHAT A WEIRD EXPERIENCE IT HAD BEEN.
THERE SHE'D BEEN, PICKING OUT WATCHES FOR A WORLD-FAMOUS CELEBRITY, WITH MORE CASH IN HER HAND THAN SHE'D EVER SEEN AT ONE TIME IN HER WHOLE LIFE.
WHICH REMINDED HER: HERE WAS THE CHANGE AND THE RECEIPT.
SHE HOPED AT LEAST ONE OF THEM WOULD BE OKAY. PERSONALLY, SHE LIKED THE ONE THAT SPELLED IT OUT IN WORDS THE BEST.
WE WENT TO ANTONINO'S FOR LUNCH AGAIN AND I TO KNOW HER A LITTLE BETTER.
FOR EXAMPLE, I FOUND OUT THAT SHE'D ONCE OWNED A HUSKY NAMED "NORMAN."
AND THAT SHE'D NEVER HAD THE CHICKEN POX.
AFTER THAT WE WENT HOME AND I HAD HER TAKE CARE OF THE MOVIE COLLECTION.
I FOUND OUT THAT HER OLDER BROTHER WAS IN THE NAVY.
AND THAT SHE DIDN'T HAVE A BOYFRIEND.

I ASKED HER IF SHE WANTED TO SEE THE NEW ROCK LANDERS MOVIE (IT HADN'T BEEN RELEASED YET, BUT I HAD A COPY ON DVD) WHEN SHE--SOMEWHAT AWKWARDLY-- ASKED ME WHEN SHE WAS "ON" UNTIL.

I HADN'T THOUGHT ABOUT IT.

SO I ASKED WHAT TIME SHE USUALLY GOT TO GO HOME, BACK WHEN SHE WORKED IN MARTY'S OFFICE.

SHE USUALLY WENT HOME AROUND FIVE O'CLOCK, SHE TOLD ME.

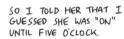

SO I TOLD HER THAT I GUESSED SHE WAS "ON" UNTIL FIVE O'CLOCK.

THEN SHE TOLD ME IT WAS ALREADY SIX FORTY-FIVE. AND MADE A JOKE ABOUT MY NEW WATCHES.

SO MARY BETH DROVE HER HOME.

I'VE GOT TO ADMIT THAT I WAS A LITTLE CONFUSED. AS I WATCHED THEM DRIVE AWAY, PART OF ME REFLECTED THAT IT HAD BEEN A PLEASANT WAY TO SPEND AN AFTERNOON.

BUT PART OF ME WAS PISSED OFF: IF SHE WAS GOING TO CHANGE MY LIFE, WHAT IN HELL WAS SHE WAITING FOR?

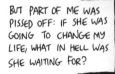

Forty-Two

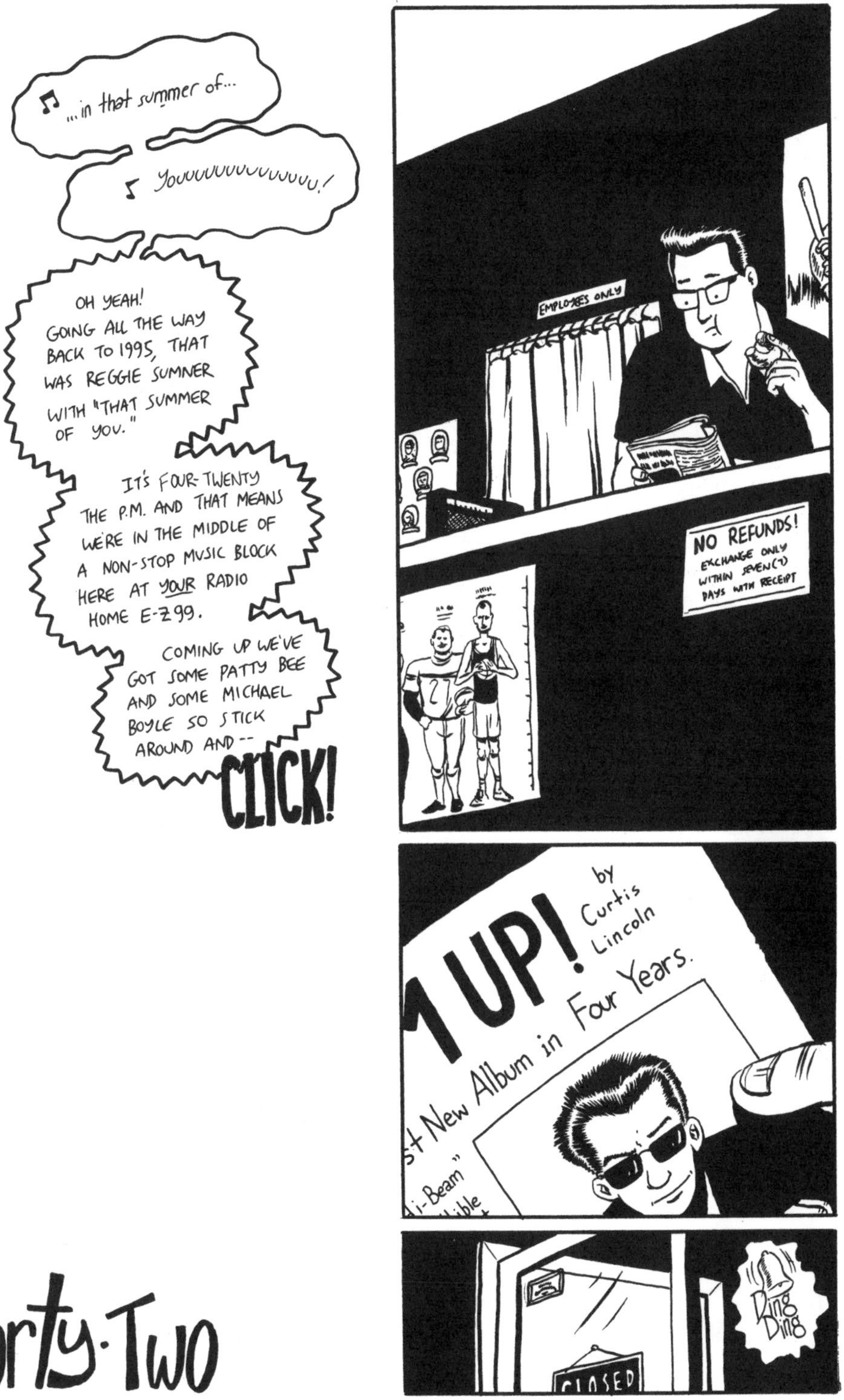
♫ ...in that summer of...
♪ Youuuuuuuuuuuuu!
OH YEAH! GOING ALL THE WAY BACK TO 1995, THAT WAS REGGIE SUMNER WITH "THAT SUMMER OF YOU."
IT'S FOUR-TWENTY THE P.M. AND THAT MEANS WE'RE IN THE MIDDLE OF A NON-STOP MUSIC BLOCK HERE AT YOUR RADIO HOME E-Z99.
COMING UP WE'VE GOT SOME PATTY BEE AND SOME MICHAEL BOYLE SO STICK AROUND AND--
CLICK!
EMPLOYEES ONLY
NO REFUNDS! EXCHANGE ONLY WITHIN SEVEN(7) DAYS WITH RECEIPT
1UP! by Curtis Lincoln
New Album in Four Years
CLOSED
Ding Ding

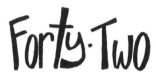

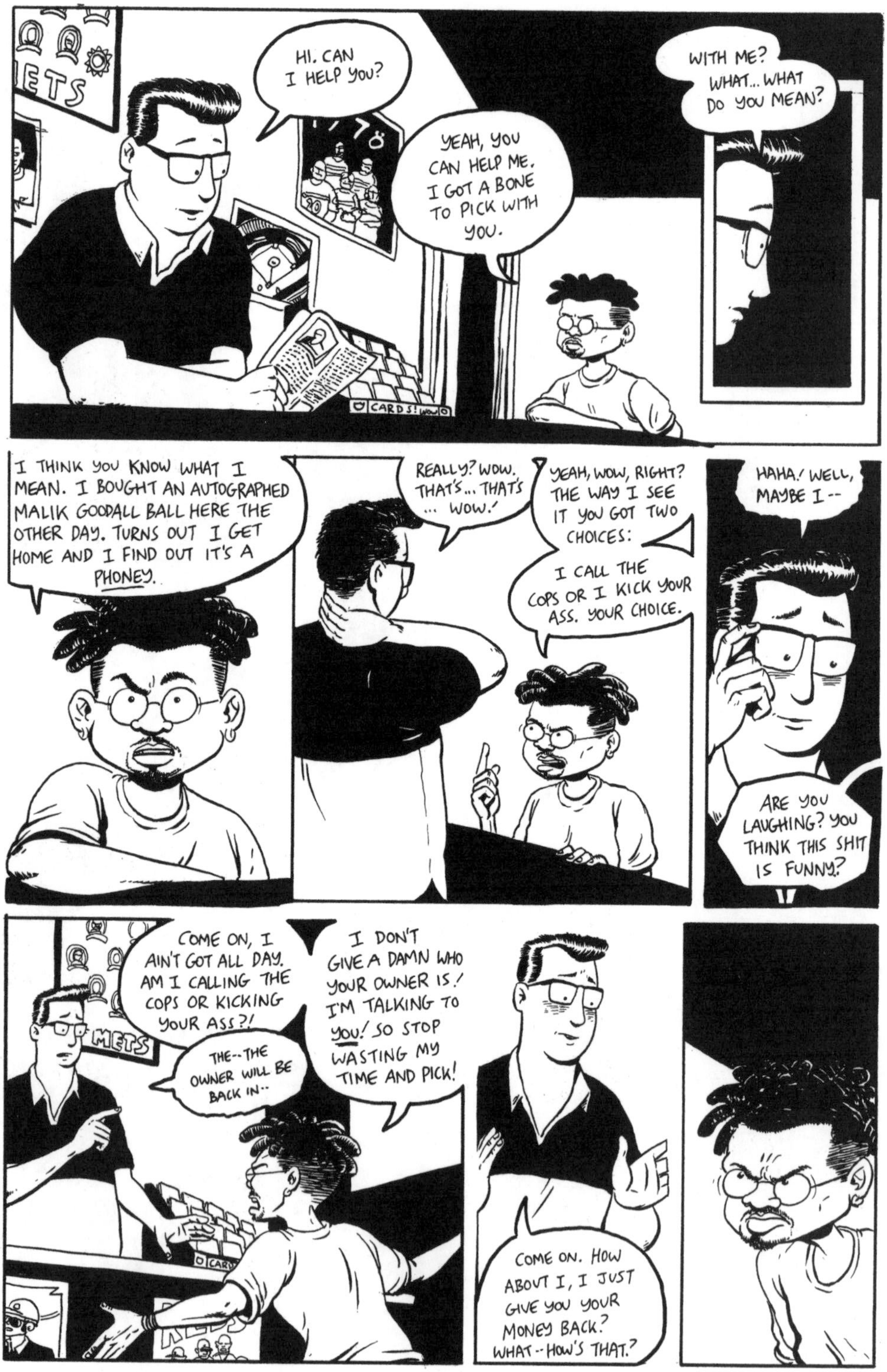
HI. CAN I HELP YOU?
YEAH, YOU CAN HELP ME. I GOT A BONE TO PICK WITH YOU.
CARDS! WOW
WITH ME? WHAT... WHAT DO YOU MEAN?
I THINK YOU KNOW WHAT I MEAN. I BOUGHT AN AUTOGRAPHED MALIK GOODALL BALL HERE THE OTHER DAY. TURNS OUT I GET HOME AND I FIND OUT IT'S A PHONEY.
REALLY? WOW. THAT'S... THAT'S ... WOW.!
YEAH, WOW, RIGHT? THE WAY I SEE IT YOU GOT TWO CHOICES:
I CALL THE COPS OR I KICK YOUR ASS. YOUR CHOICE.
HAHA.! WELL, MAYBE I --
ARE YOU LAUGHING? YOU THINK THIS SHIT IS FUNNY?
COME ON, I AIN'T GOT ALL DAY. AM I CALLING THE COPS OR KICKING YOUR ASS?!
METS
THE--THE OWNER WILL BE BACK IN--
I DON'T GIVE A DAMN WHO YOUR OWNER IS! I'M TALKING TO YOU! SO STOP WASTING MY TIME AND PICK!
COME ON. HOW ABOUT I, I JUST GIVE YOU YOUR MONEY BACK? WHAT--HOW'S THAT?

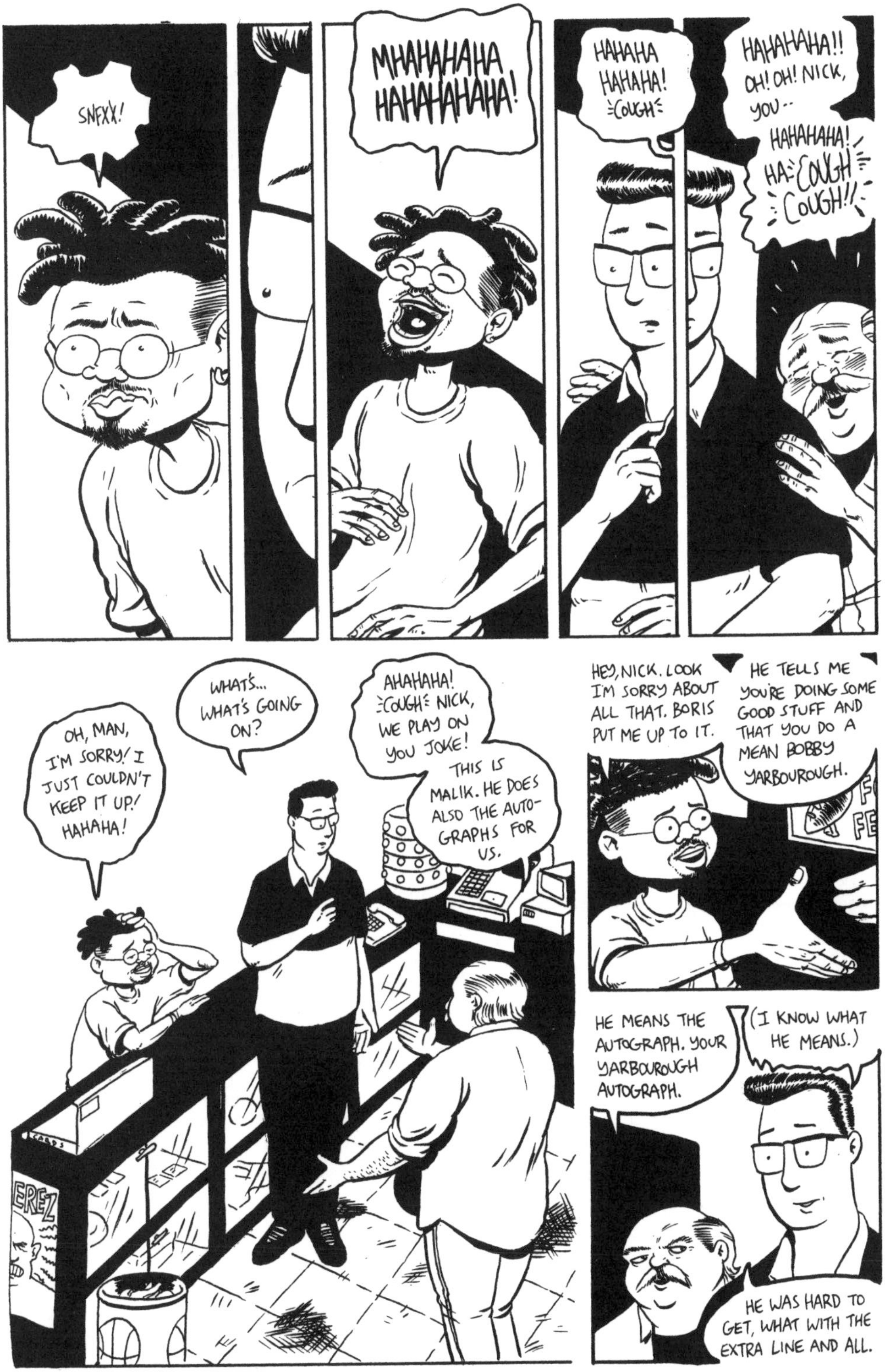
SNFXX!
MHAHAHAHA HAHAHAHAHA!
HAHAHA HAHAHA! COUGH
HAHAHAHA!! OH! OH! NICK, YOU--
HAHAHAHA! HA- COUGH COUGH!!
OH, MAN, I'M SORRY! I JUST COULDN'T KEEP IT UP! HAHAHA!
WHAT'S... WHAT'S GOING ON?
AHAHAHA! COUGH NICK, WE PLAY ON YOU JOKE!
THIS IS MALIK. HE DOES ALSO THE AUTO-GRAPHS FOR US.
HEY, NICK. LOOK I'M SORRY ABOUT ALL THAT. BORIS PUT ME UP TO IT.
HE TELLS ME YOU'RE DOING SOME GOOD STUFF AND THAT YOU DO A MEAN BOBBY YARBOUROUGH.
HE MEANS THE AUTOGRAPH. YOUR YARBOUROUGH AUTOGRAPH.
(I KNOW WHAT HE MEANS.)
HE WAS HARD TO GET, WHAT WITH THE EXTRA LINE AND ALL.

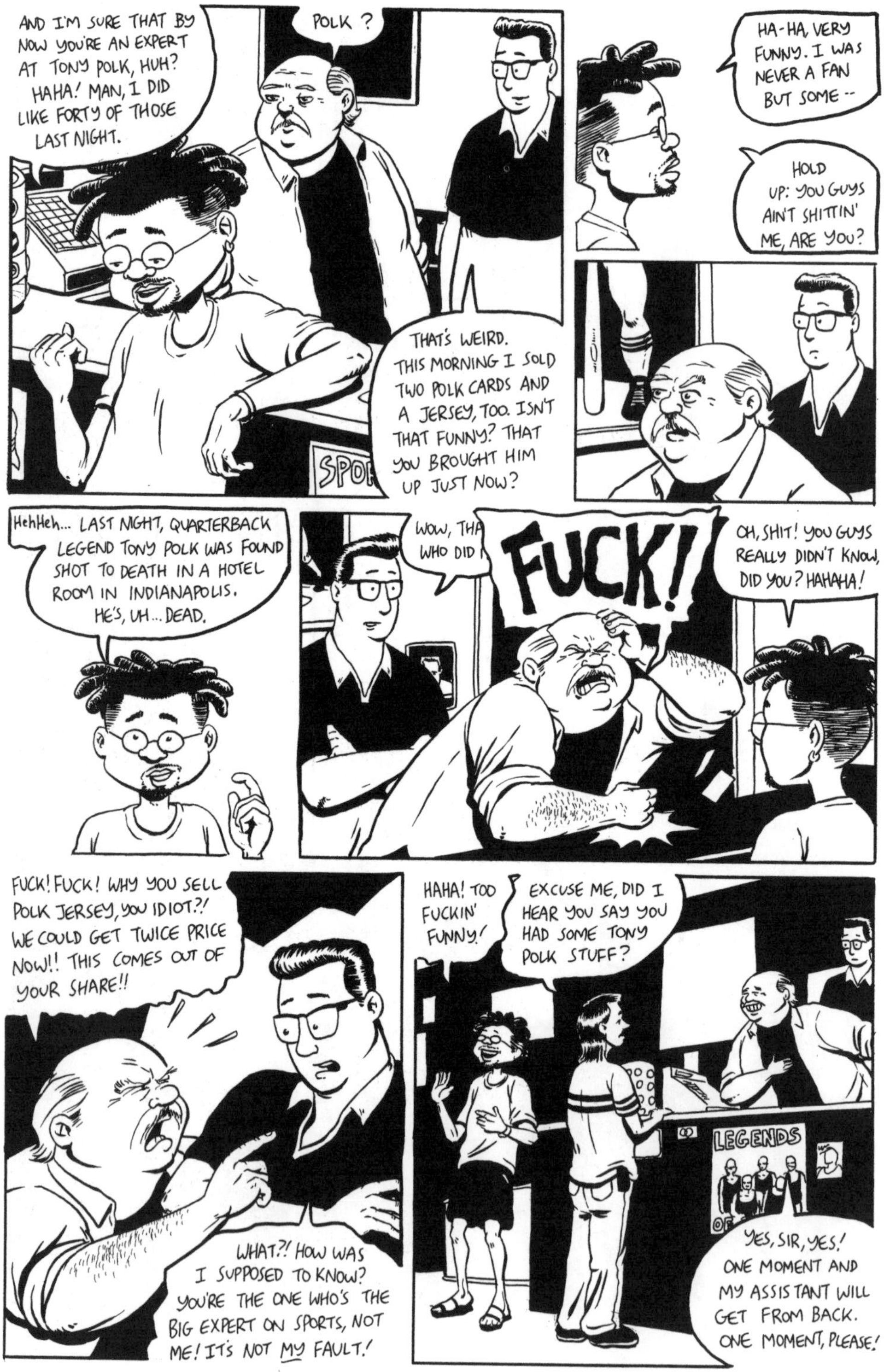
AND I'M SURE THAT BY NOW YOU'RE AN EXPERT AT TONY POLK, HUH? HAHA! MAN, I DID LIKE FORTY OF THOSE LAST NIGHT.
POLK ?
THAT'S WEIRD. THIS MORNING I SOLD TWO POLK CARDS AND A JERSEY, TOO. ISN'T THAT FUNNY? THAT YOU BROUGHT HIM UP JUST NOW?
SPOR
HA-HA, VERY FUNNY. I WAS NEVER A FAN BUT SOME --
HOLD UP: YOU GUYS AIN'T SHITTIN' ME, ARE YOU?
HehHeh... LAST NIGHT, QUARTERBACK LEGEND TONY POLK WAS FOUND SHOT TO DEATH IN A HOTEL ROOM IN INDIANAPOLIS. HE'S, UH... DEAD.
WOW, THA WHO DID
FUCK!
OH, SHIT! YOU GUYS REALLY DIDN'T KNOW, DID YOU? HAHAHA!
FUCK! FUCK! WHY YOU SELL POLK JERSEY, YOU IDIOT?! WE COULD GET TWICE PRICE NOW!! THIS COMES OUT OF YOUR SHARE!!
WHAT?! HOW WAS I SUPPOSED TO KNOW? YOU'RE THE ONE WHO'S THE BIG EXPERT ON SPORTS, NOT ME! IT'S NOT MY FAULT!
HAHA! TOO FUCKIN' FUNNY!
EXCUSE ME, DID I HEAR YOU SAY YOU HAD SOME TONY POLK STUFF?
LEGENDS
OF
YES, SIR, YES! ONE MOMENT AND MY ASSISTANT WILL GET FROM BACK. ONE MOMENT, PLEASE!

ASSISTANT! GO IN BACK ROOM AND GET AUTOGRAPHED POLK FOOTBALL, OKAY? FOR GENTLEMAN? HAHA!

OKAY! OKAY! QUIT SHOVING!

IS GREAT LOSS TO SPORT, ANH? POLK WAS GREAT MAN... GREAT MAN...

RAZZA FRAZZINMY FAULT I DON'T FOLLOWSTUPID SPORTSCRAP... GRUMBLE...

Best Wishes
John Polk
"#31"

?

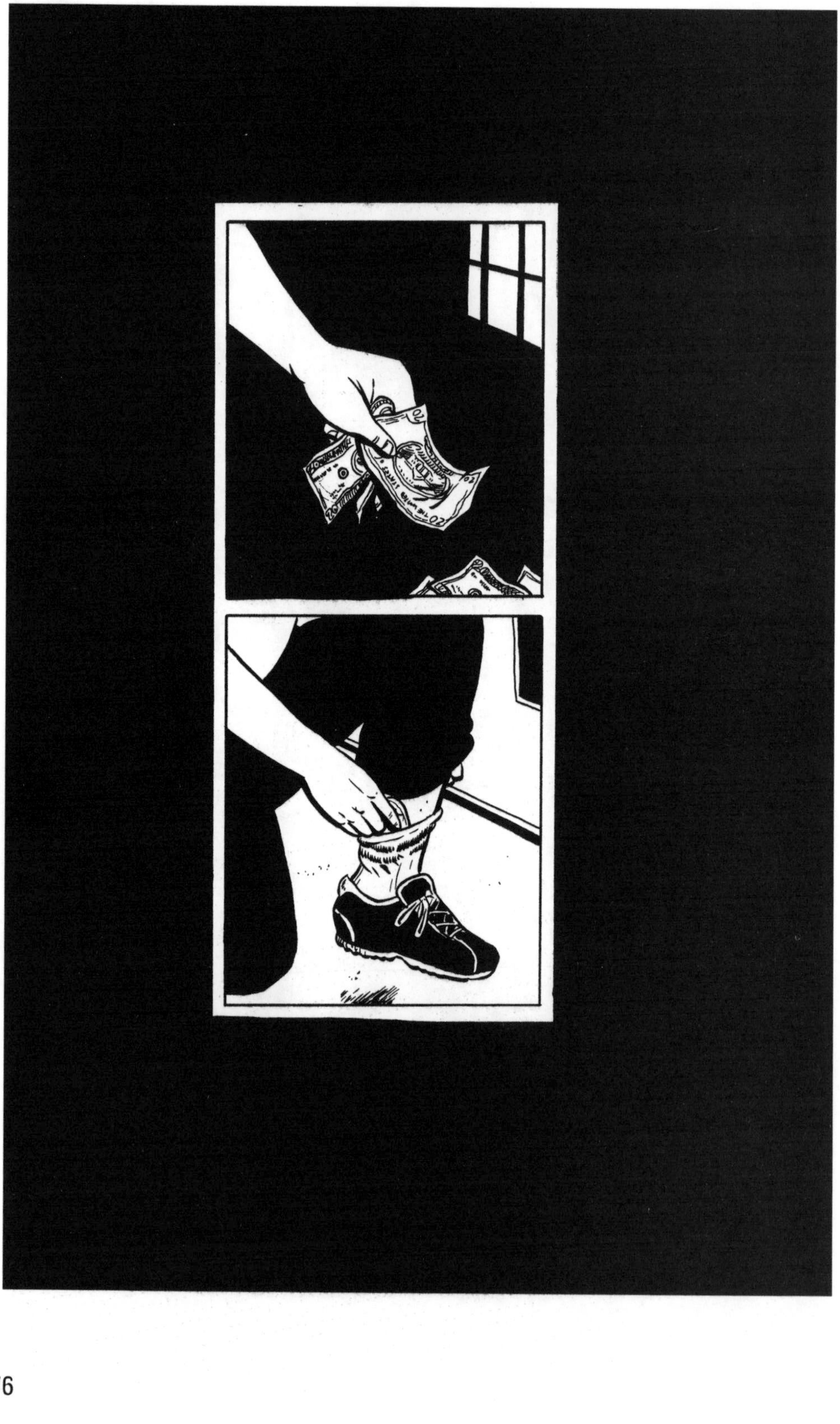

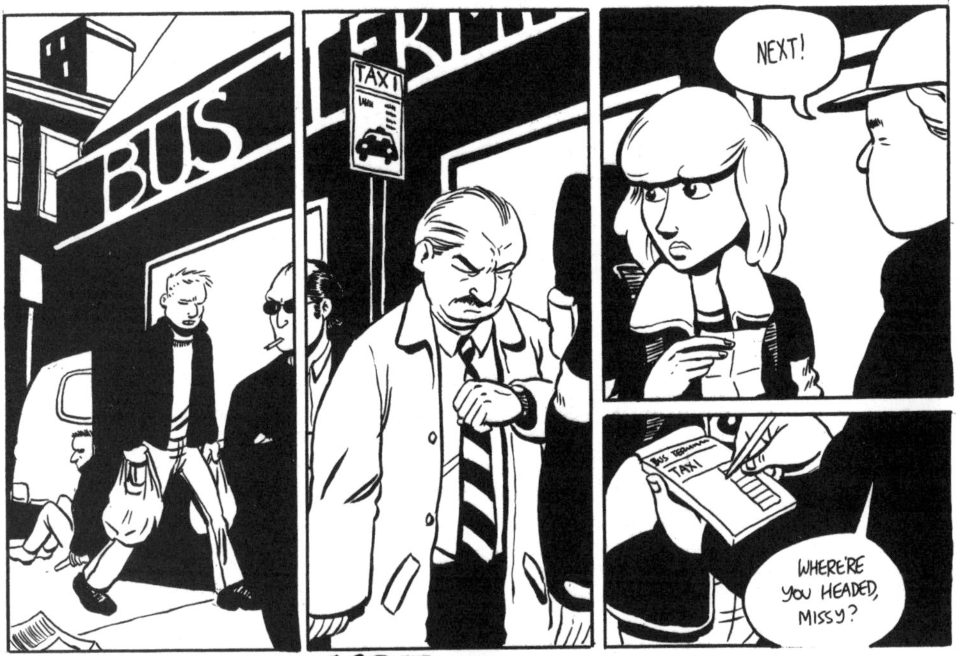
BUS
TAXI
NEXT!
TAXI
WHERE'RE YOU HEADED, MISSY?

FORTY·ONE

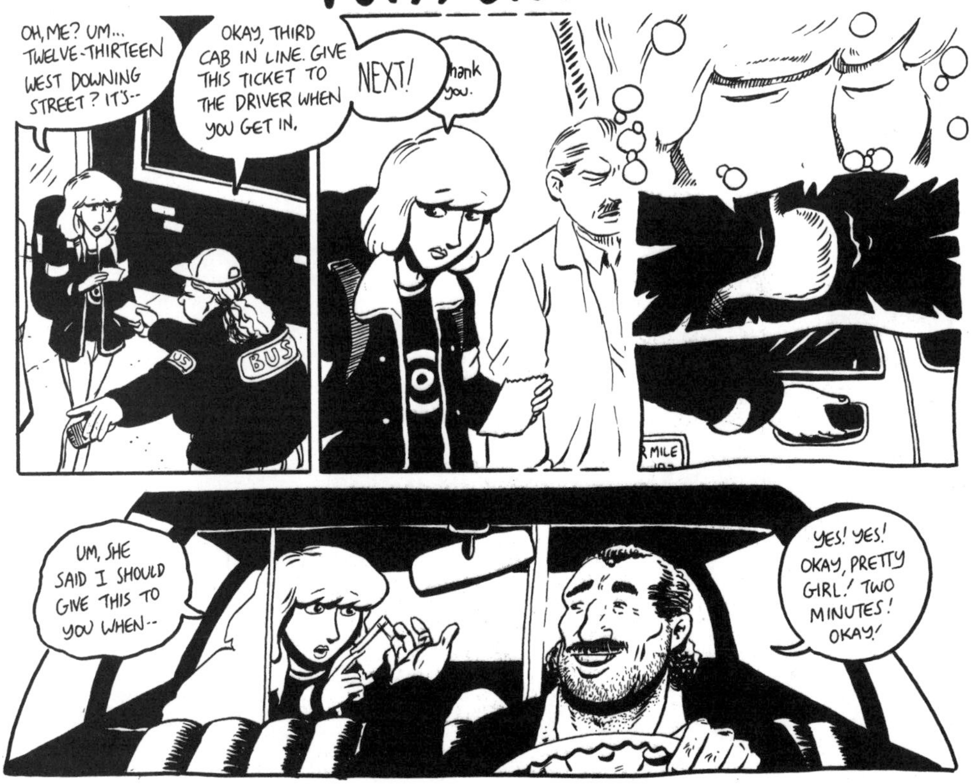
OH, ME? UM... TWELVE-THIRTEEN WEST DOWNING STREET? IT'S--
OKAY, THIRD CAB IN LINE. GIVE THIS TICKET TO THE DRIVER WHEN YOU GET IN.
BUS
NEXT!
hank you.
UM, SHE SAID I SHOULD GIVE THIS TO YOU WHEN--
YES! YES! OKAY, PRETTY GIRL! TWO MINUTES! OKAY!

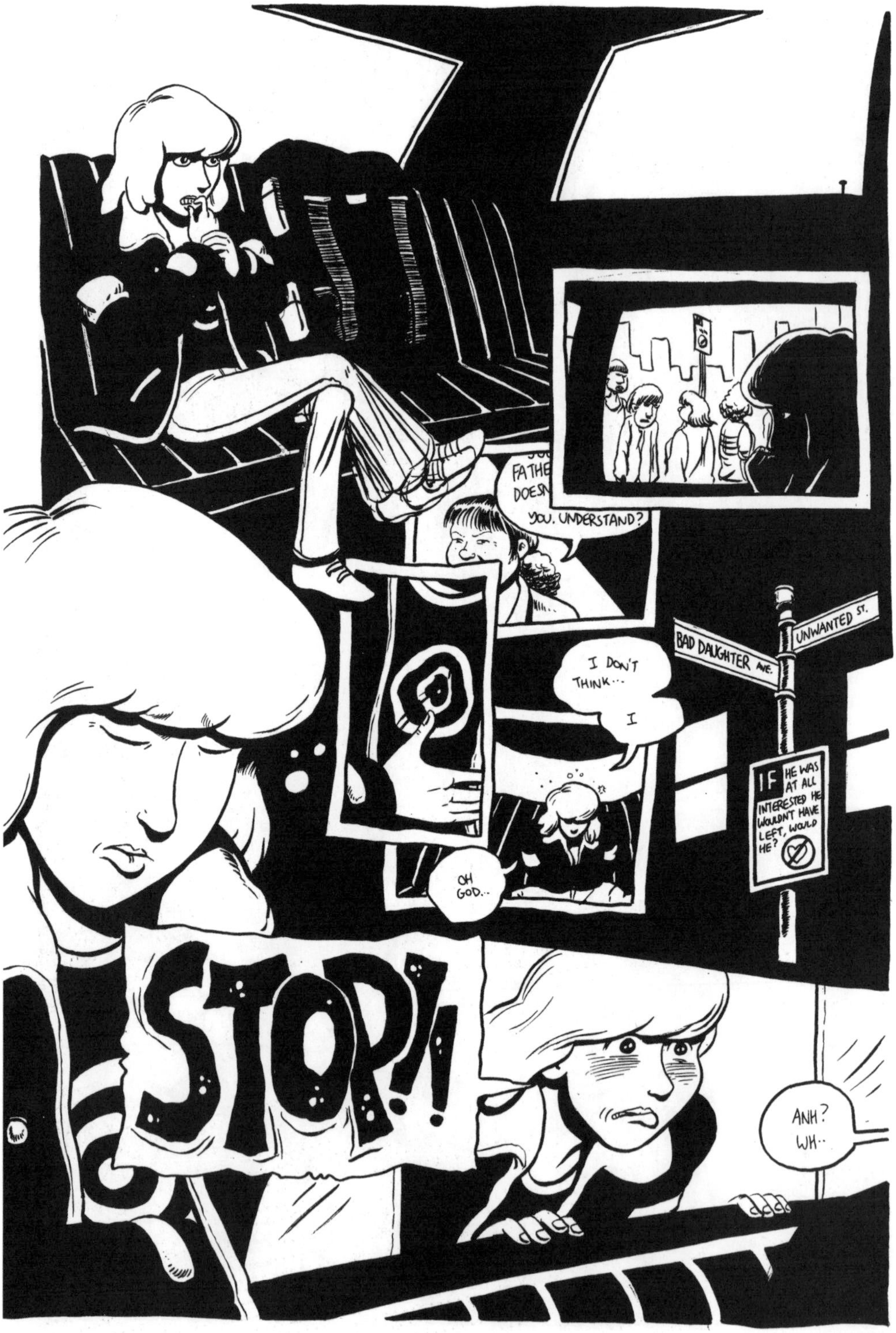
FATHE DOESN
YOU. UNDERSTAND?
BAD DAUGHTER AVE.
UNWANTED ST.
I DON'T THINK...
I
IF HE WAS AT ALL INTERESTED HE WOULDN'T HAVE LEFT, WOULD HE?
OH GOD...
STOP!!
ANH? WH..

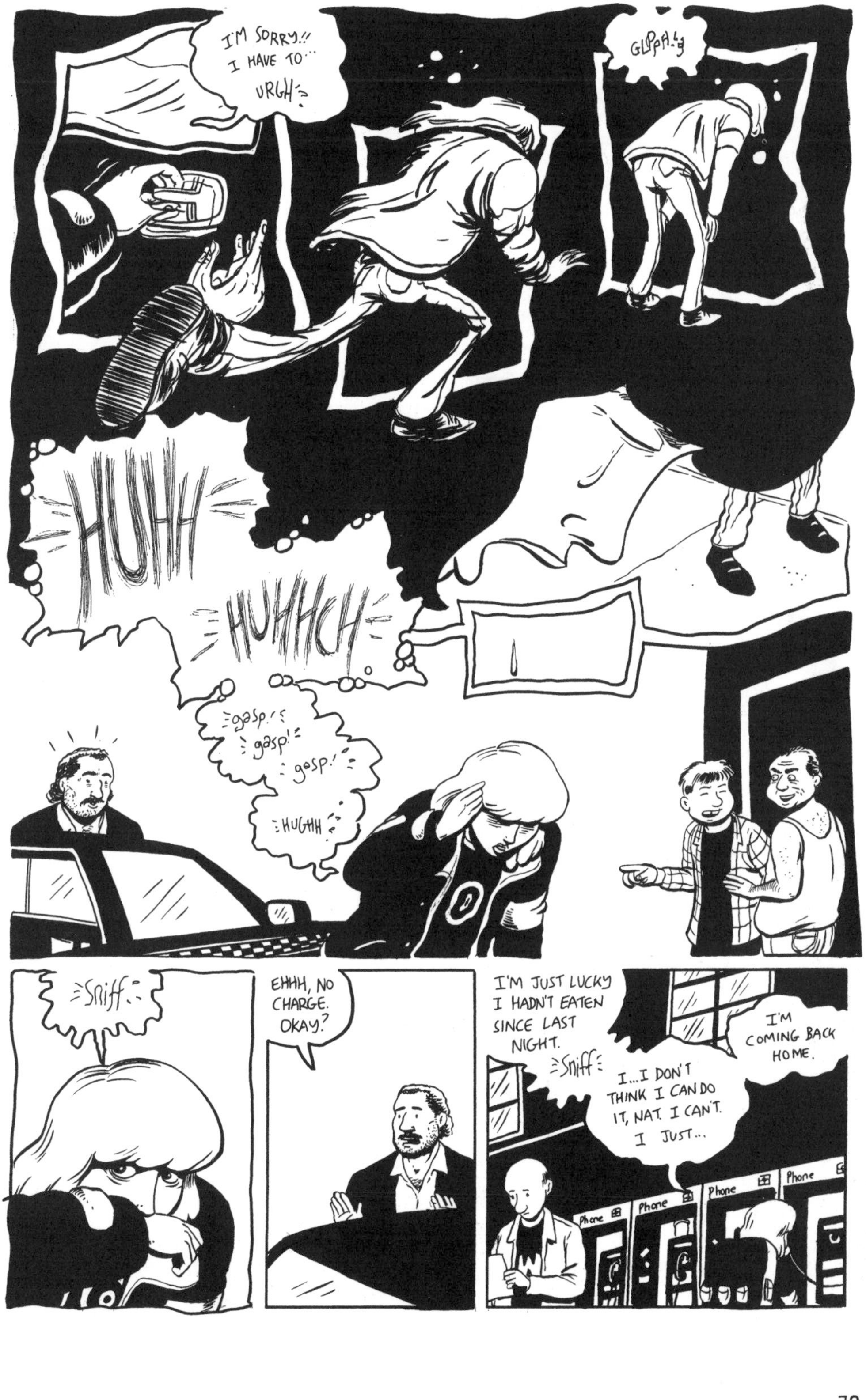
I'M SORRY!! I HAVE TO... URGH
GLPPAH
HUHH
HUHHCH
gasp! gasp! gasp!
HUGHH
Sniff
EHHH, NO CHARGE. OKAY?
I'M JUST LUCKY I HADN'T EATEN SINCE LAST NIGHT.
Sniff
I'M COMING BACK HOME.
I...I DON'T THINK I CAN DO IT, NAT. I CAN'T. I JUST...
Phone
Phone
Phone
Phone

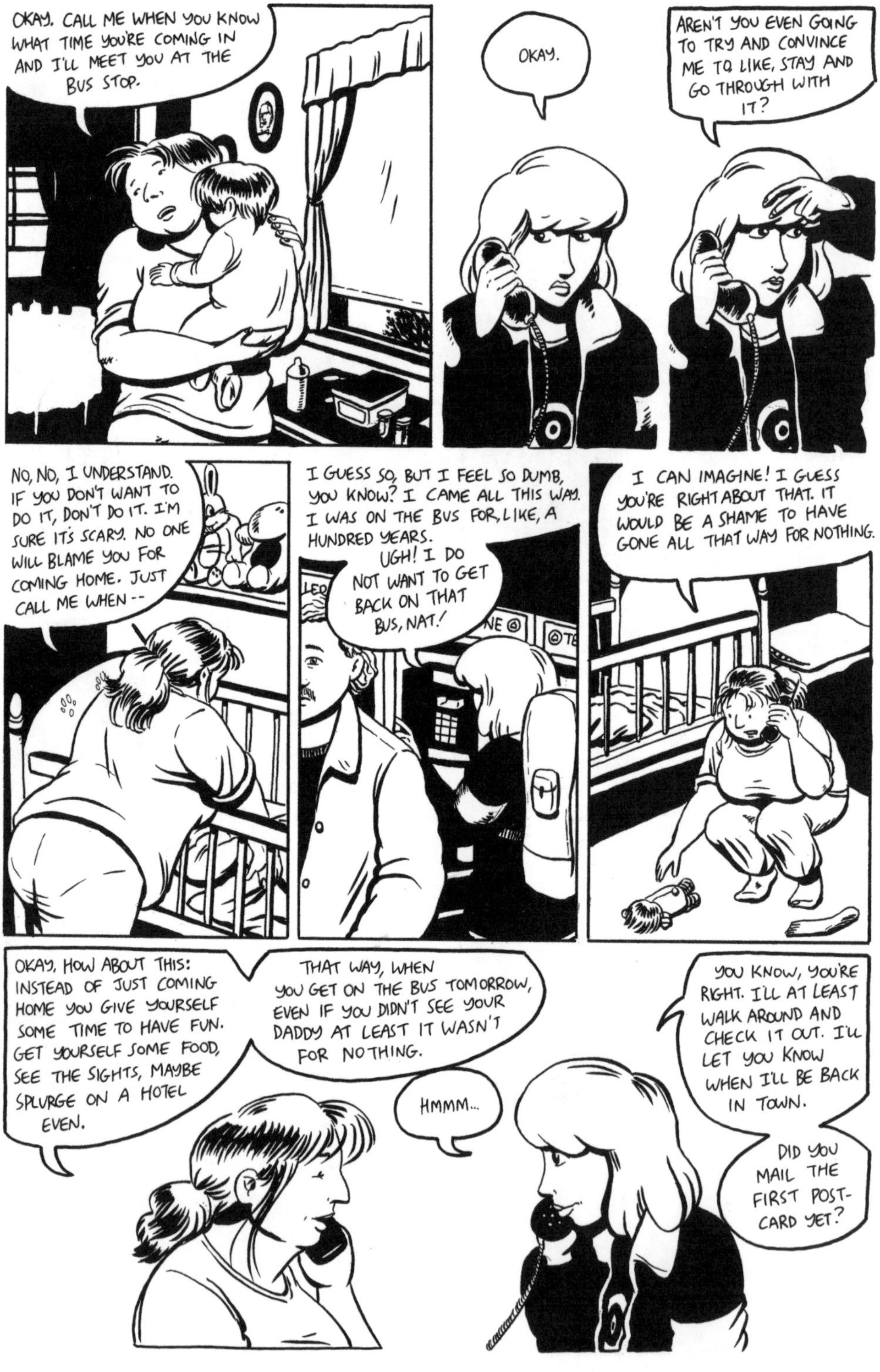
OKAY. CALL ME WHEN YOU KNOW WHAT TIME YOU'RE COMING IN AND I'LL MEET YOU AT THE BUS STOP.
OKAY.
AREN'T YOU EVEN GOING TO TRY AND CONVINCE ME TO LIKE, STAY AND GO THROUGH WITH IT?
NO, NO, I UNDERSTAND. IF YOU DON'T WANT TO DO IT, DON'T DO IT. I'M SURE IT'S SCARY. NO ONE WILL BLAME YOU FOR COMING HOME. JUST CALL ME WHEN --
I GUESS SO, BUT I FEEL SO DUMB, YOU KNOW? I CAME ALL THIS WAY. I WAS ON THE BUS FOR, LIKE, A HUNDRED YEARS.
UGH! I DO NOT WANT TO GET BACK ON THAT BUS, NAT!
I CAN IMAGINE! I GUESS YOU'RE RIGHT ABOUT THAT. IT WOULD BE A SHAME TO HAVE GONE ALL THAT WAY FOR NOTHING.
OKAY, HOW ABOUT THIS: INSTEAD OF JUST COMING HOME YOU GIVE YOURSELF SOME TIME TO HAVE FUN. GET YOURSELF SOME FOOD, SEE THE SIGHTS, MAYBE SPLURGE ON A HOTEL EVEN.
THAT WAY, WHEN YOU GET ON THE BUS TOMORROW, EVEN IF YOU DIDN'T SEE YOUR DADDY AT LEAST IT WASN'T FOR NOTHING.
HMMM...
YOU KNOW, YOU'RE RIGHT. I'LL AT LEAST WALK AROUND AND CHECK IT OUT. I'LL LET YOU KNOW WHEN I'LL BE BACK IN TOWN.
DID YOU MAIL THE FIRST POST-CARD YET?

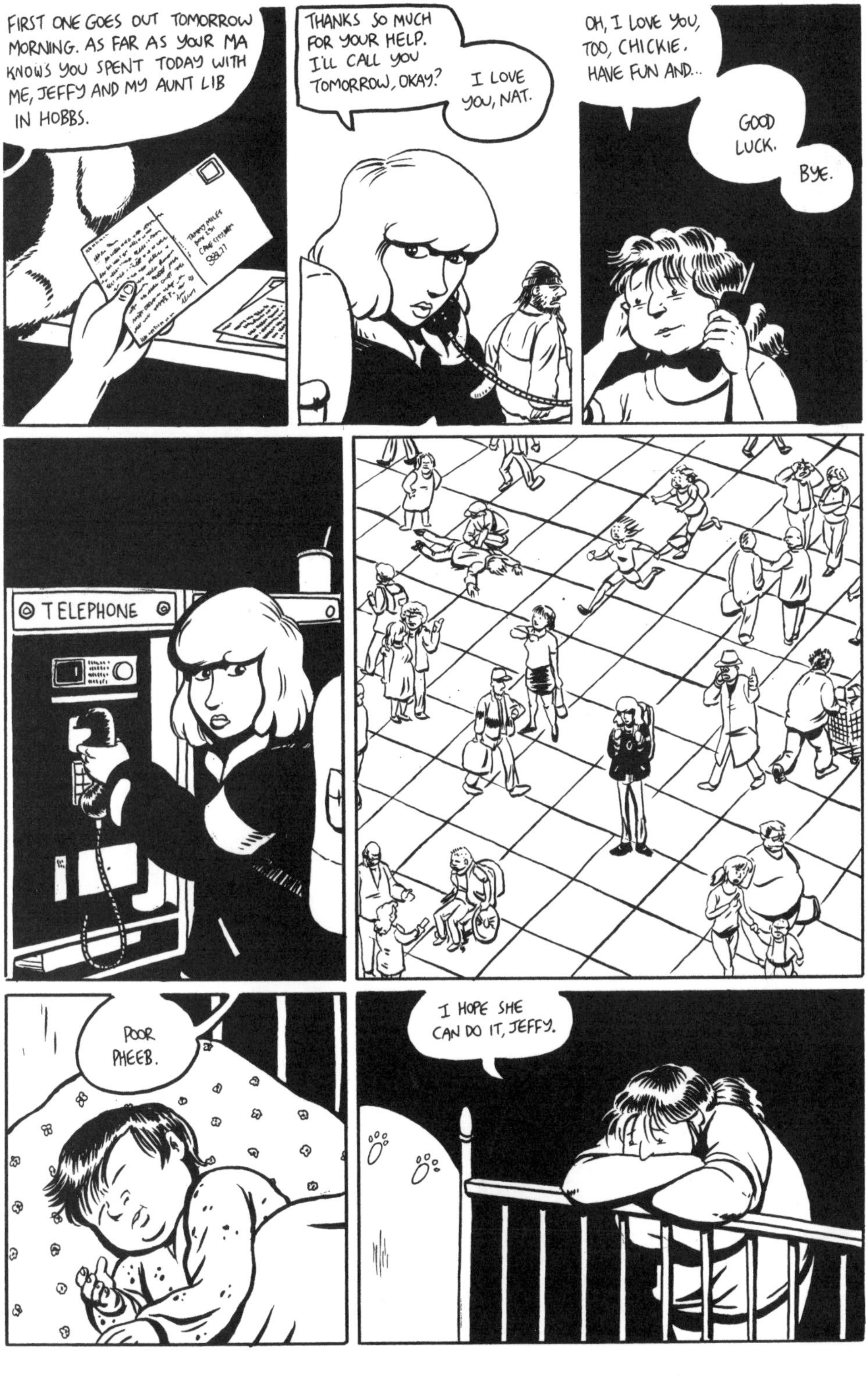
FIRST ONE GOES OUT TOMORROW MORNING. AS FAR AS YOUR MA KNOWS YOU SPENT TODAY WITH ME, JEFFY AND MY AUNT LIB IN HOBBS.
THANKS SO MUCH FOR YOUR HELP. I'LL CALL YOU TOMORROW, OKAY?
I LOVE YOU, NAT.
OH, I LOVE YOU, TOO, CHICKIE. HAVE FUN AND...
GOOD LUCK.
BYE.
TELEPHONE
POOR PHEEB.
I HOPE SHE CAN DO IT, JEFFY.

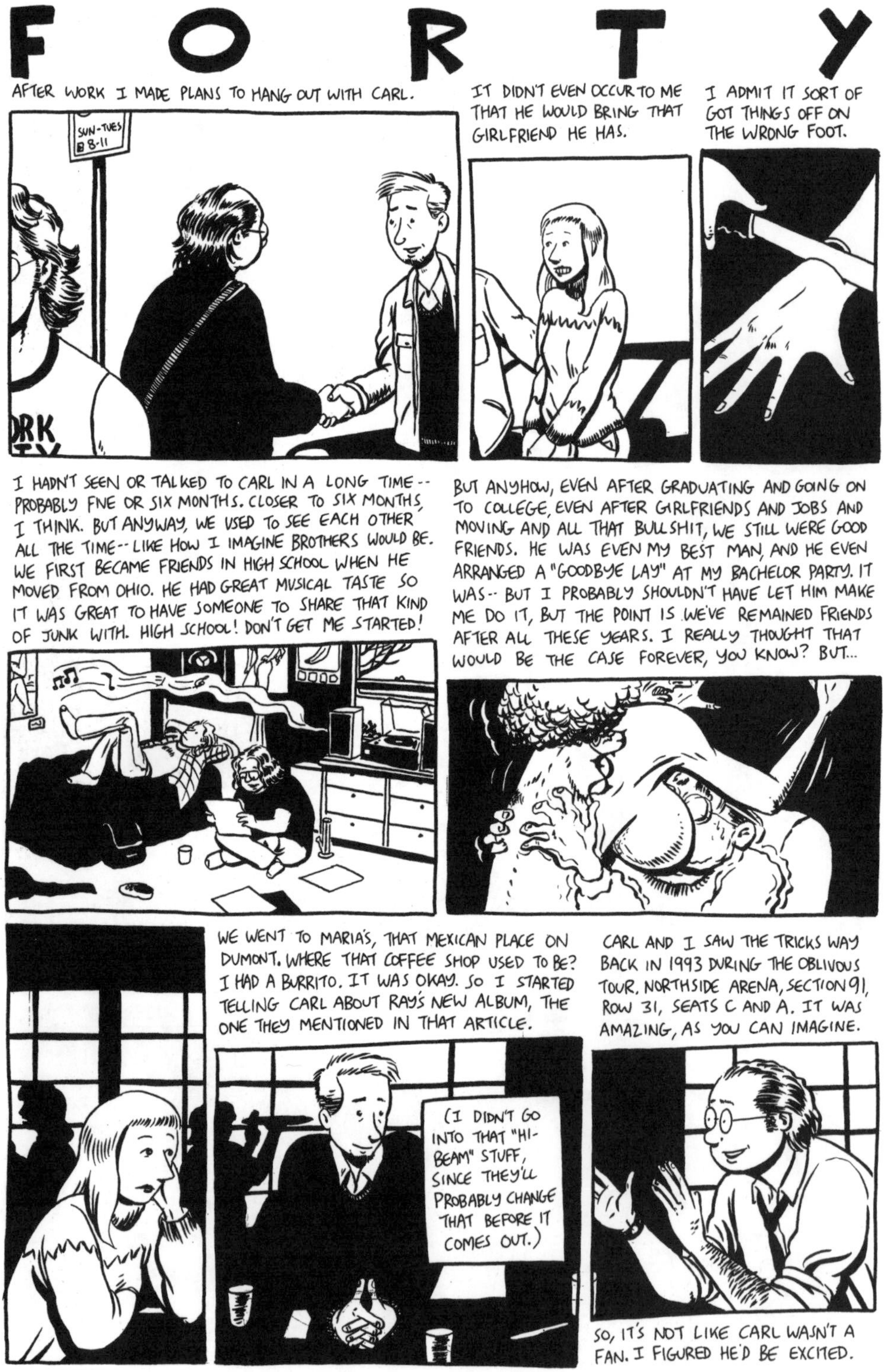
FORTY
AFTER WORK I MADE PLANS TO HANG OUT WITH CARL.
SUN-TUES 8-11
IT DIDN'T EVEN OCCUR TO ME THAT HE WOULD BRING THAT GIRLFRIEND HE HAS.
I ADMIT IT SORT OF GOT THINGS OFF ON THE WRONG FOOT.
I HADN'T SEEN OR TALKED TO CARL IN A LONG TIME-- PROBABLY FIVE OR SIX MONTHS. CLOSER TO SIX MONTHS, I THINK. BUT ANYWAY, WE USED TO SEE EACH OTHER ALL THE TIME-- LIKE HOW I IMAGINE BROTHERS WOULD BE. WE FIRST BECAME FRIENDS IN HIGH SCHOOL WHEN HE MOVED FROM OHIO. HE HAD GREAT MUSICAL TASTE SO IT WAS GREAT TO HAVE SOMEONE TO SHARE THAT KIND OF JUNK WITH. HIGH SCHOOL! DON'T GET ME STARTED!
BUT ANYHOW, EVEN AFTER GRADUATING AND GOING ON TO COLLEGE, EVEN AFTER GIRLFRIENDS AND JOBS AND MOVING AND ALL THAT BULLSHIT, WE STILL WERE GOOD FRIENDS. HE WAS EVEN MY BEST MAN, AND HE EVEN ARRANGED A "GOODBYE LAY" AT MY BACHELOR PARTY. IT WAS-- BUT I PROBABLY SHOULDN'T HAVE LET HIM MAKE ME DO IT, BUT THE POINT IS WE'VE REMAINED FRIENDS AFTER ALL THESE YEARS. I REALLY THOUGHT THAT WOULD BE THE CASE FOREVER, YOU KNOW? BUT...
WE WENT TO MARIA'S, THAT MEXICAN PLACE ON DUMONT. WHERE THAT COFFEE SHOP USED TO BE? I HAD A BURRITO. IT WAS OKAY. SO I STARTED TELLING CARL ABOUT RAY'S NEW ALBUM, THE ONE THEY MENTIONED IN THAT ARTICLE.
(I DIDN'T GO INTO THAT "HI-BEAM" STUFF, SINCE THEY'LL PROBABLY CHANGE THAT BEFORE IT COMES OUT.)
CARL AND I SAW THE TRICKS WAY BACK IN 1993 DURING THE OBLIVIOUS TOUR, NORTHSIDE ARENA, SECTION 91, ROW 31, SEATS C AND A. IT WAS AMAZING, AS YOU CAN IMAGINE.
SO, IT'S NOT LIKE CARL WASN'T A FAN. I FIGURED HE'D BE EXCITED.

I STARTED TO SPECULATE ON WHAT RAY'S NEW STUFF WOULD SOUND LIKE. AFTER THE INTROSPECTIVE MATERIAL OF HIS FIRST SOLO ALBUM (1996), WITH HIS PERSONAL, ALMOST AUTOBIOGRAPHICAL SONGS, I WAS THINKING HE MIGHT RETURN TO AN EARLIER, POP-ORIENTED MODE. MAYBE EVEN SOUNDING LIKE THE FIRST TRICKS STUFF.' AFTER ALL, HE'D TAKEN HIS SELF-EXPLORATION STUFF AS FAR AS IT COULD GO, RIGHT? I MEAN, IT WAS BRILLIANT, OF COURSE, BUT IT MADE SENSE TO GO FULL CIRCLE, BACK TO THE STUFF THAT MADE HIM A HOUSEHOLD NAME.

BUT THEN AGAIN, GIVEN THE HARD KNOCKS RAY GAVE TO DIRK'S SOLO STUFF (1997'S "HOUSE OF HOMES" PARTICULARLY!) MAYBE A RETURN TO CATCHY HOOKS AND CHORUSES WAS A STRETCH. BUT ANYTHING IS POSSIBLE, RIGHT? MAYBE HE'D TAKE US IN A WHOLE NEW DIRECTION. "MY MIND HAS TAKEN ME PLACES/THAT MY HEART DIDN'T WANT TO GO."

I TOLD CARL ABOUT THAT WEBSITE THAT SAID RAY WAS WORKING ON A FRIGGING JAZZ ALBUM! FUCK, I HOPED NOT. THAT'S NOT TRUE. I MEAN, OKAY, JAZZ CAN BE OKAY, USUALLY AS, LIKE, BACKGROUND MUSIC IN A MOVIE OR SOMETHING, BUT WHO HAS THE PATIENCE TO ACTUALLY SIT AND LISTEN TO THAT MASTURBATORY NOODLING? I JOKED THAT IF I'M LISTENING TO SOMEONE JERK OFF IT BETTER BE ME!

I KNOW CARL HAS SOMETIMES DABBLED IN JAZZ, BUT HE KNOWS THERE'S NO WAY IT COULD MOVE HIM, SPEAK TO HIM, THE WAY ROCK MUSIC COULD. I JUST WANTED HIM TO ADMIT THIS WAS TRUE, YOU KNOW? JUST TO HEAR HIM SAY IT. I EVEN GAVE HIM A CHALLENGE: HE NAMES THE TOP...FIVE BEST JAZZ SONGS, AND FOR EVERY ONE HE PICKED I WOULD NAME... SEVEN, NO! EIGHT! ROCK SONGS WHICH WERE BETTER! COME ON, I SAID. I WOULD NAME FORTY ROCK/POP SONGS BETTER THAN EVEN THE BEST JAZZ SONG EVER!!

WE USED TO HAVE THESE DISCUSSIONS ALL THE TIME SO I WAS SURPRISED THAT HE DIDN'T EVEN TRY. HE SAID HE'D NEED TO THINK ABOUT IT AND THEN, TO THROW ME OFF THE TRACK, HE STARTING TALKING ABOUT THE FOOD, WONDERING WHERE THE WAITRESS WAS!

THEN, OF COURSE, SHE CHIMES IN ABOUT SOME STUPID MOVIE SHE SAW AND ASKS ME IF I'VE SEEN ANYTHING GOOD.

I TOLD HER THAT A) I DON'T GO TO THE MOVIES BECAUSE THEY GIVE ME MIGRAINES, AND MORE IMPORTANTLY, B) WOULD SHE MIND IF I FINISHED WHAT I WAS SAYING BEFORE WE LET HER RAMBLE ON ABOUT SOME CHICKFLICK SHE SAW AT THE MALL?

I WASN'T ABOUT TO LET CARL OFF THE HOOK THAT EASILY!

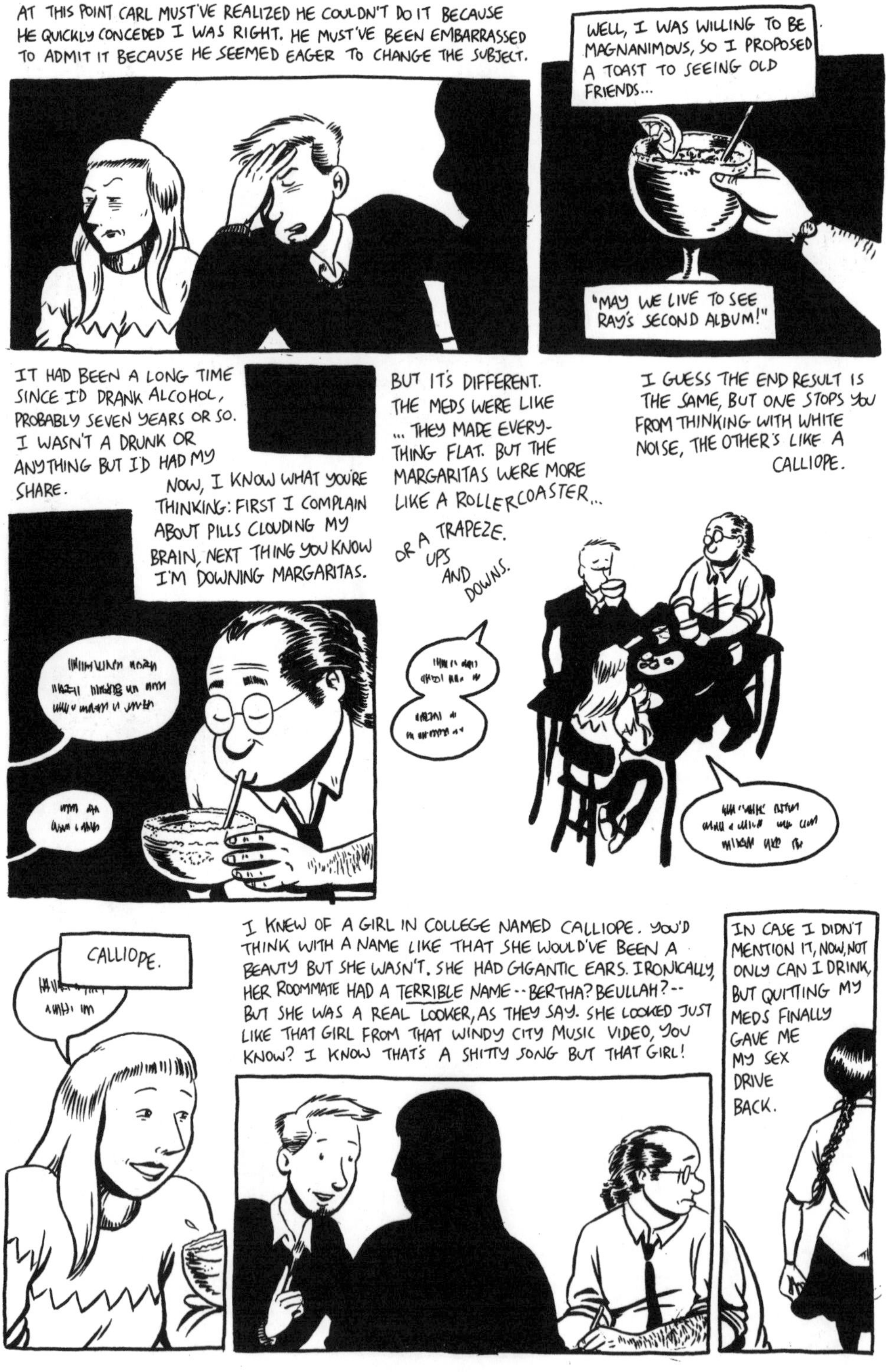

AT THIS POINT CARL MUST'VE REALIZED HE COULDN'T DO IT BECAUSE HE QUICKLY CONCEDED I WAS RIGHT. HE MUST'VE BEEN EMBARRASSED TO ADMIT IT BECAUSE HE SEEMED EAGER TO CHANGE THE SUBJECT.
WELL, I WAS WILLING TO BE MAGNANIMOUS, SO I PROPOSED A TOAST TO SEEING OLD FRIENDS...
"MAY WE LIVE TO SEE RAY'S SECOND ALBUM!"
IT HAD BEEN A LONG TIME SINCE I'D DRANK ALCOHOL, PROBABLY SEVEN YEARS OR SO. I WASN'T A DRUNK OR ANYTHING BUT I'D HAD MY SHARE.
NOW, I KNOW WHAT YOU'RE THINKING: FIRST I COMPLAIN ABOUT PILLS CLOUDING MY BRAIN, NEXT THING YOU KNOW I'M DOWNING MARGARITAS.
BUT IT'S DIFFERENT. THE MEDS WERE LIKE ... THEY MADE EVERYTHING FLAT. BUT THE MARGARITAS WERE MORE LIKE A ROLLERCOASTER...
OR A TRAPEZE. UPS AND DOWNS.
I GUESS THE END RESULT IS THE SAME, BUT ONE STOPS YOU FROM THINKING WITH WHITE NOISE, THE OTHER'S LIKE A CALLIOPE.
CALLIOPE.
I KNEW OF A GIRL IN COLLEGE NAMED CALLIOPE. YOU'D THINK WITH A NAME LIKE THAT SHE WOULD'VE BEEN A BEAUTY BUT SHE WASN'T. SHE HAD GIGANTIC EARS. IRONICALLY, HER ROOMMATE HAD A TERRIBLE NAME--BERTHA? BEULLAH?--BUT SHE WAS A REAL LOOKER, AS THEY SAY. SHE LOOKED JUST LIKE THAT GIRL FROM THAT WINDY CITY MUSIC VIDEO, YOU KNOW? I KNOW THAT'S A SHITTY SONG BUT THAT GIRL!
IN CASE I DIDN'T MENTION IT, NOW, NOT ONLY CAN I DRINK, BUT QUITTING MY MEDS FINALLY GAVE ME MY SEX DRIVE BACK.

SUDDENLY, IT WAS LIKE I WAS SIXTEEN YEARS OLD AGAIN. I WAS JERKING OFF LIKE SEVEN TIMES A DAY -- EVEN MORE ON THE WEEKENDS -- AND IMAGINING WHAT IT WOULD BE LIKE TO FUCK EVERY WOMAN I MET.

EVEN UGLY ONES AND EVEN SOME OLD LADIES AND GIRLS WITH HORRIBLE SOULS. JUST ABOUT EVERY GIRL HAS HER GOOD QUALITIES IF YOU LOOK HARD ENOUGH OR IMAGINE THEIR SWEATY FACES CONTORTED WITH ECSTACY.

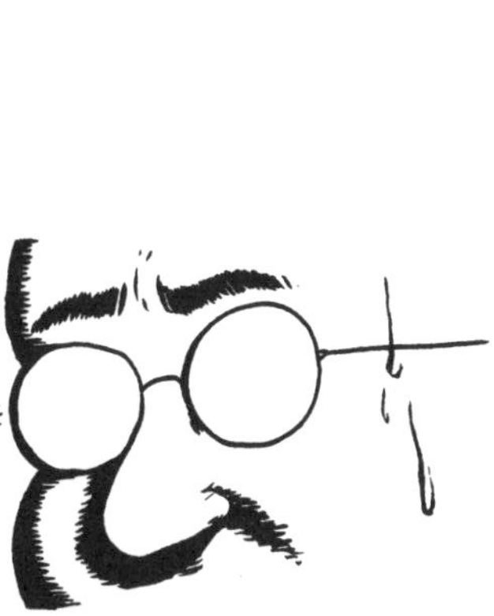

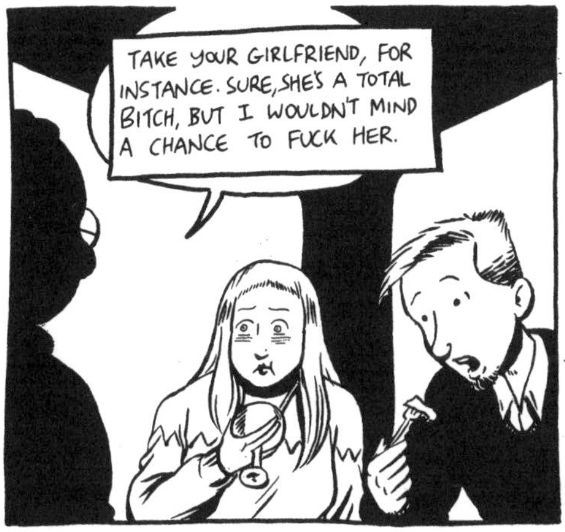
TAKE YOUR GIRLFRIEND, FOR INSTANCE. SURE, SHE'S A TOTAL BITCH, BUT I WOULDN'T MIND A CHANCE TO FUCK HER.

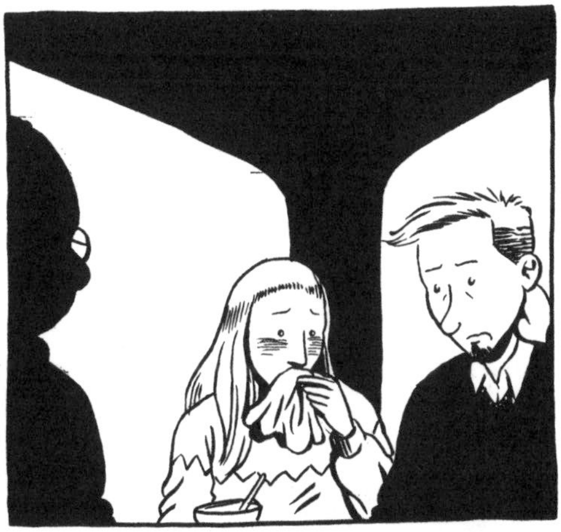

DINNER ENDED A BIT EARLY WHEN CARL'S EVIL GIRLFRIEND REMEMBERED SOME "THING" SHE HAD TO BE AT EARLY THE NEXT MORNING. TOTAL BULLSHIT. I THINK SHE WAS JUST PISSED OFF THAT CARL AND I HAVE MORE IN COMMON THAN THEY DO. BASIC JEALOUSY.

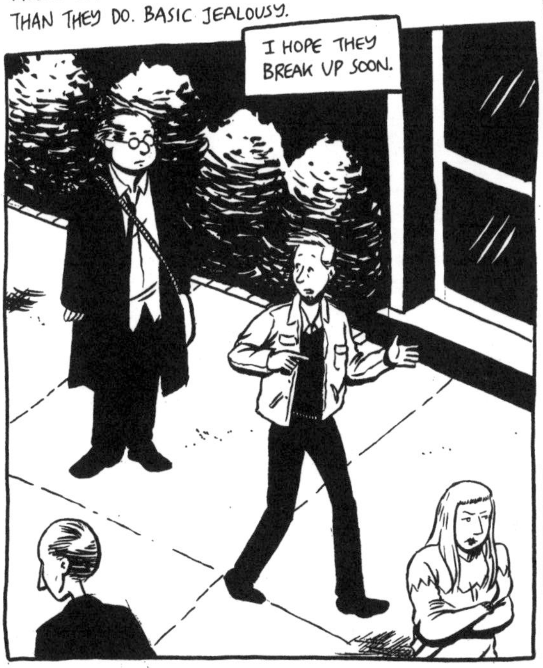
I HOPE THEY BREAK UP SOON.

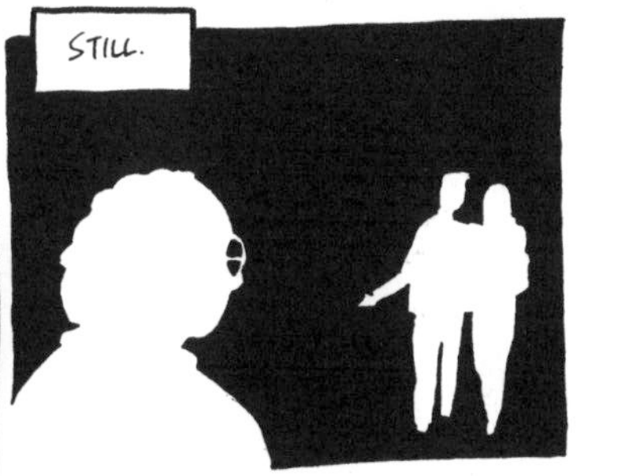
STILL.

I WASN'T GOING TO LET HER RUIN MY NIGHT. THOSE MARGARITAS HAD ME FEELING PRETTY GOOD AND RELAXED. RATHER THAN CATCH THE BUS STRAIGHT HOME I THOUGHT I'D WALK HOME. MAYBE I'D STOP AT BUDDY'S AND SEE IF THAT CD I ORDERED CAME IN YET. I WAS IN A GOOD MOOD.

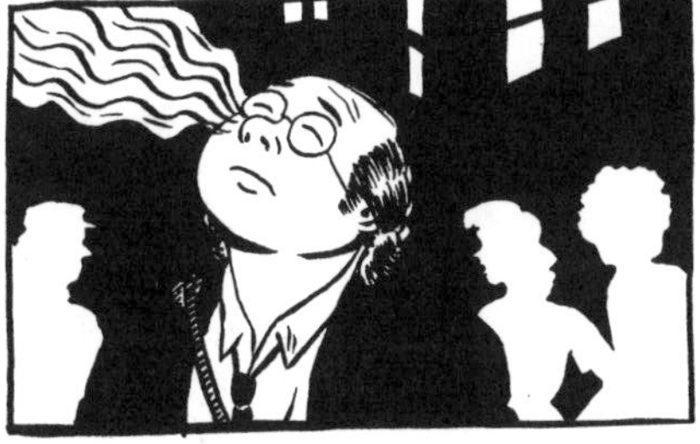

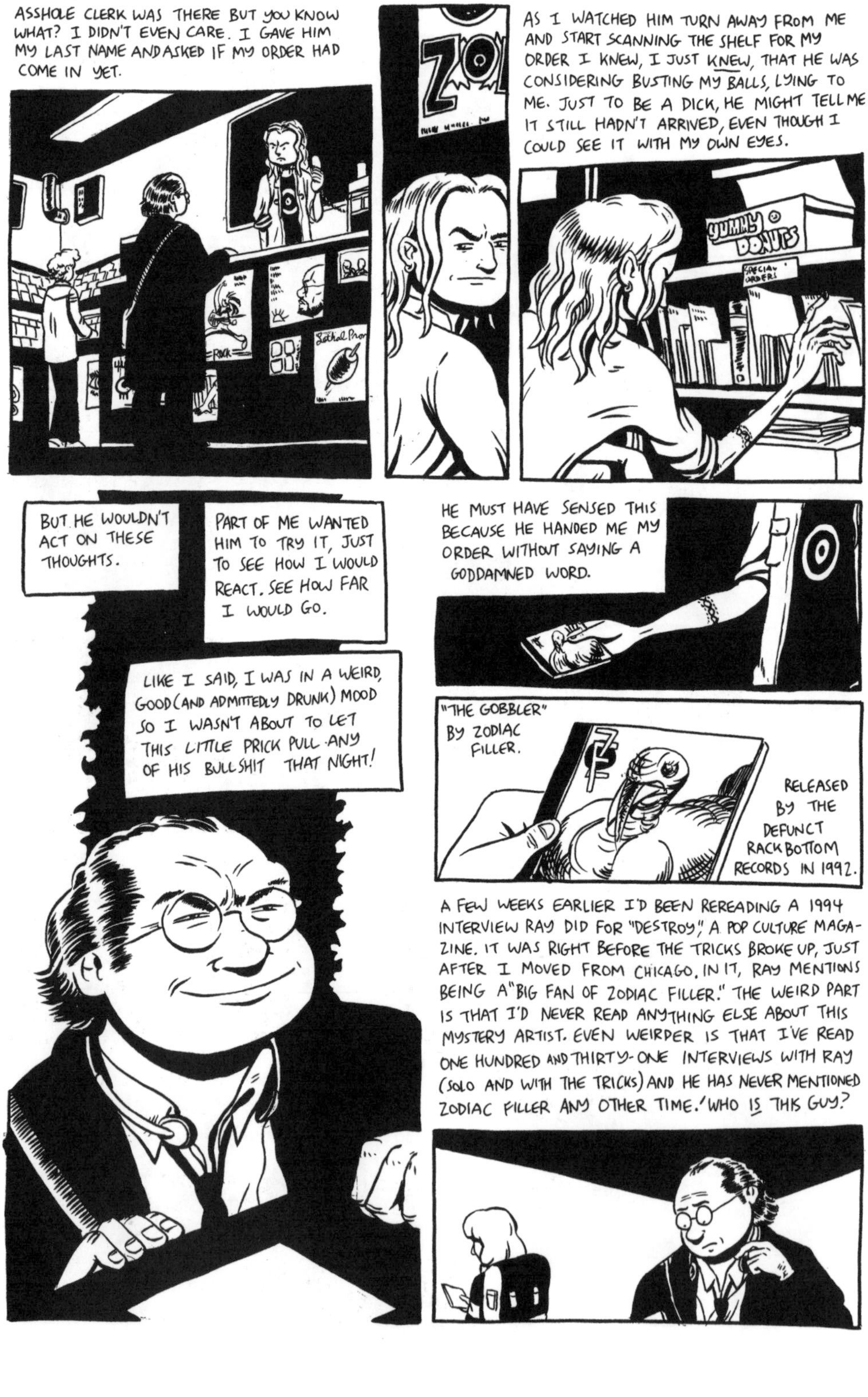
ASSHOLE CLERK WAS THERE BUT YOU KNOW WHAT? I DIDN'T EVEN CARE. I GAVE HIM MY LAST NAME AND ASKED IF MY ORDER HAD COME IN YET.
AS I WATCHED HIM TURN AWAY FROM ME AND START SCANNING THE SHELF FOR MY ORDER I KNEW, I JUST KNEW, THAT HE WAS CONSIDERING BUSTING MY BALLS, LYING TO ME. JUST TO BE A DICK, HE MIGHT TELL ME IT STILL HADN'T ARRIVED, EVEN THOUGH I COULD SEE IT WITH MY OWN EYES.
YUMMY DONUTS
SPECIAL ORDERS
BUT HE WOULDN'T ACT ON THESE THOUGHTS.
PART OF ME WANTED HIM TO TRY IT, JUST TO SEE HOW I WOULD REACT. SEE HOW FAR I WOULD GO.
LIKE I SAID, I WAS IN A WEIRD, GOOD (AND ADMITTEDLY DRUNK) MOOD SO I WASN'T ABOUT TO LET THIS LITTLE PRICK PULL ANY OF HIS BULLSHIT THAT NIGHT!
HE MUST HAVE SENSED THIS BECAUSE HE HANDED ME MY ORDER WITHOUT SAYING A GODDAMNED WORD.
"THE GOBBLER" BY ZODIAC FILLER.
RELEASED BY THE DEFUNCT RACK BOTTOM RECORDS IN 1992.
A FEW WEEKS EARLIER I'D BEEN REREADING A 1994 INTERVIEW RAY DID FOR "DESTROY," A POP CULTURE MAGAZINE. IT WAS RIGHT BEFORE THE TRICKS BROKE UP, JUST AFTER I MOVED FROM CHICAGO. IN IT, RAY MENTIONS BEING A "BIG FAN OF ZODIAC FILLER." THE WEIRD PART IS THAT I'D NEVER READ ANYTHING ELSE ABOUT THIS MYSTERY ARTIST. EVEN WEIRDER IS THAT I'VE READ ONE HUNDRED AND THIRTY-ONE INTERVIEWS WITH RAY (SOLO AND WITH THE TRICKS) AND HE HAS NEVER MENTIONED ZODIAC FILLER ANY OTHER TIME. WHO IS THIS GUY?

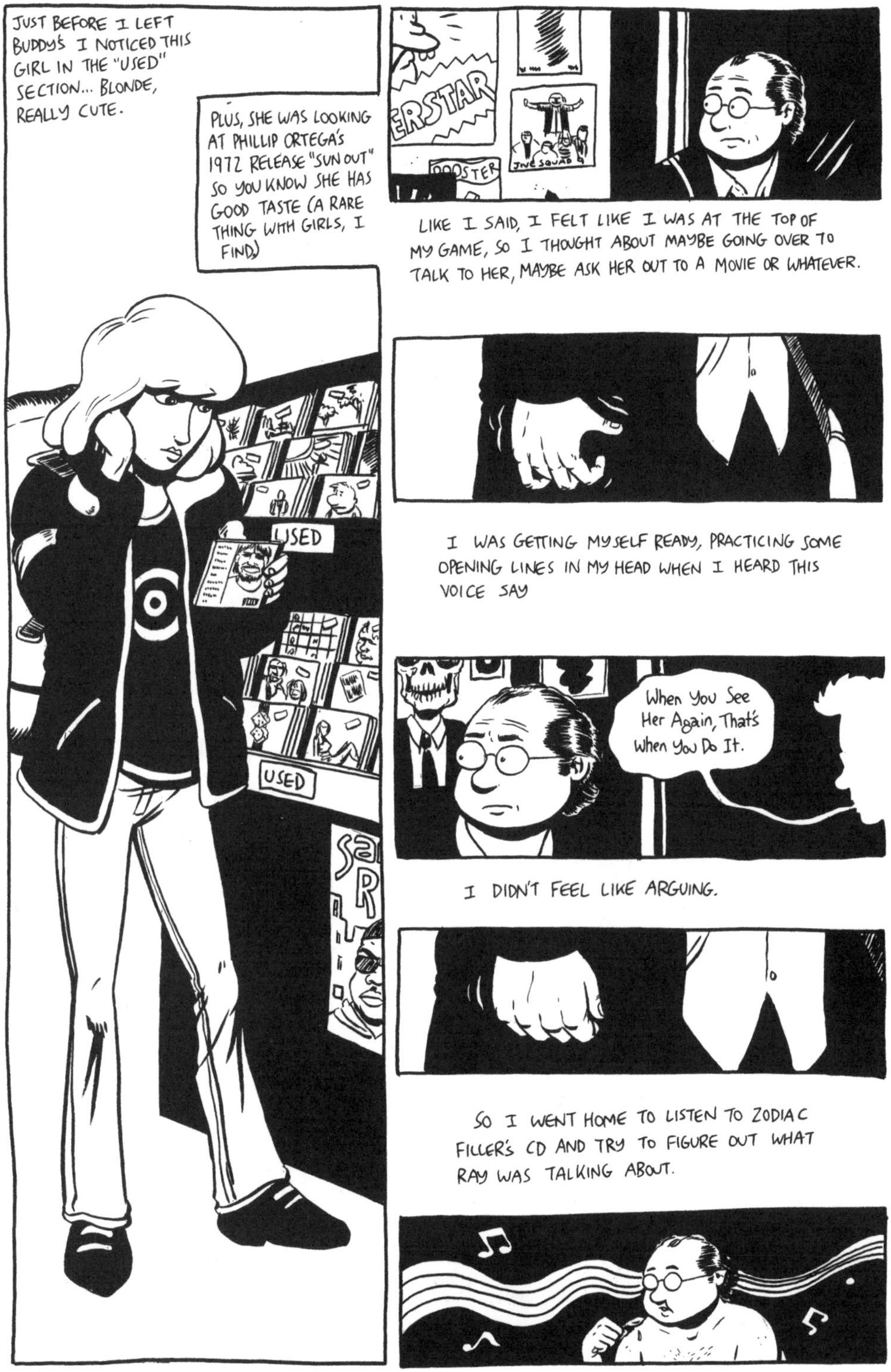
JUST BEFORE I LEFT BUDDY'S I NOTICED THIS GIRL IN THE "USED" SECTION... BLONDE, REALLY CUTE.
PLUS, SHE WAS LOOKING AT PHILLIP ORTEGA'S 1972 RELEASE "SUN OUT" SO YOU KNOW SHE HAS GOOD TASTE (A RARE THING WITH GIRLS, I FIND.)
USED
USED
JIVE SQUAD
ROOSTER
LIKE I SAID, I FELT LIKE I WAS AT THE TOP OF MY GAME, SO I THOUGHT ABOUT MAYBE GOING OVER TO TALK TO HER, MAYBE ASK HER OUT TO A MOVIE OR WHATEVER.
I WAS GETTING MYSELF READY, PRACTICING SOME OPENING LINES IN MY HEAD WHEN I HEARD THIS VOICE SAY
When You See Her Again, That's When You Do It.
I DIDN'T FEEL LIKE ARGUING.
SO I WENT HOME TO LISTEN TO ZODIAC FILLER'S CD AND TRY TO FIGURE OUT WHAT RAY WAS TALKING ABOUT.

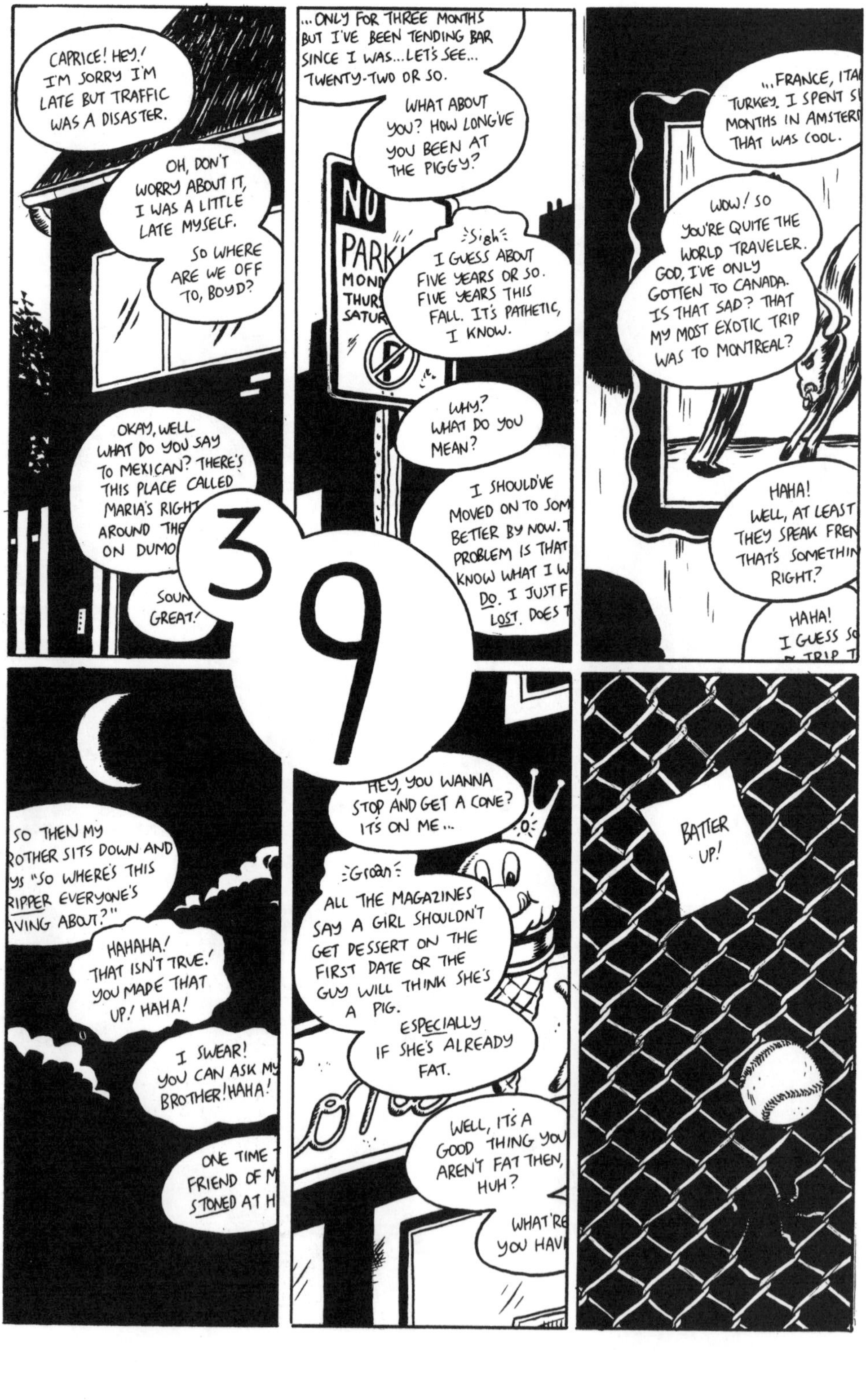
CAPRICE! HEY! I'M SORRY I'M LATE BUT TRAFFIC WAS A DISASTER.
OH, DON'T WORRY ABOUT IT, I WAS A LITTLE LATE MYSELF.
SO WHERE ARE WE OFF TO, BOYD?
OKAY, WELL WHAT DO YOU SAY TO MEXICAN? THERE'S THIS PLACE CALLED MARIA'S RIGHT AROUND THE ON DUMO
SOUN GREAT!
...ONLY FOR THREE MONTHS BUT I'VE BEEN TENDING BAR SINCE I WAS...LET'S SEE... TWENTY-TWO OR SO.
WHAT ABOUT YOU? HOW LONG'VE YOU BEEN AT THE PIGGY?
NO PARK MOND THURS SATUR
SIGH
I GUESS ABOUT FIVE YEARS OR SO. FIVE YEARS THIS FALL. IT'S PATHETIC, I KNOW.
WHY? WHAT DO YOU MEAN?
I SHOULD'VE MOVED ON TO SOM BETTER BY NOW. T PROBLEM IS THAT KNOW WHAT I W DO. I JUST F LOST. DOES T
39
...FRANCE, ITA TURKEY. I SPENT S MONTHS IN AMSTER THAT WAS COOL.
WOW! SO YOU'RE QUITE THE WORLD TRAVELER. GOD, I'VE ONLY GOTTEN TO CANADA. IS THAT SAD? THAT MY MOST EXOTIC TRIP WAS TO MONTREAL?
HAHA! WELL, AT LEAST THEY SPEAK FREN THAT'S SOMETHIN RIGHT?
HAHA! I GUESS SO
SO THEN MY ROTHER SITS DOWN AND YS "SO WHERE'S THIS RIPPER EVERYONE'S AVING ABOUT?"
HAHAHA! THAT ISN'T TRUE! YOU MADE THAT UP! HAHA!
I SWEAR! YOU CAN ASK MY BROTHER! HAHA!
ONE TIME FRIEND OF M STONED AT H
HEY, YOU WANNA STOP AND GET A CONE? IT'S ON ME...
GROAN
ALL THE MAGAZINES SAY A GIRL SHOULDN'T GET DESSERT ON THE FIRST DATE OR THE GUY WILL THINK SHE'S A PIG. ESPECIALLY IF SHE'S ALREADY FAT.
WELL, IT'S A GOOD THING YOU AREN'T FAT THEN, HUH?
WHAT'RE YOU HAVI
BATTER UP!

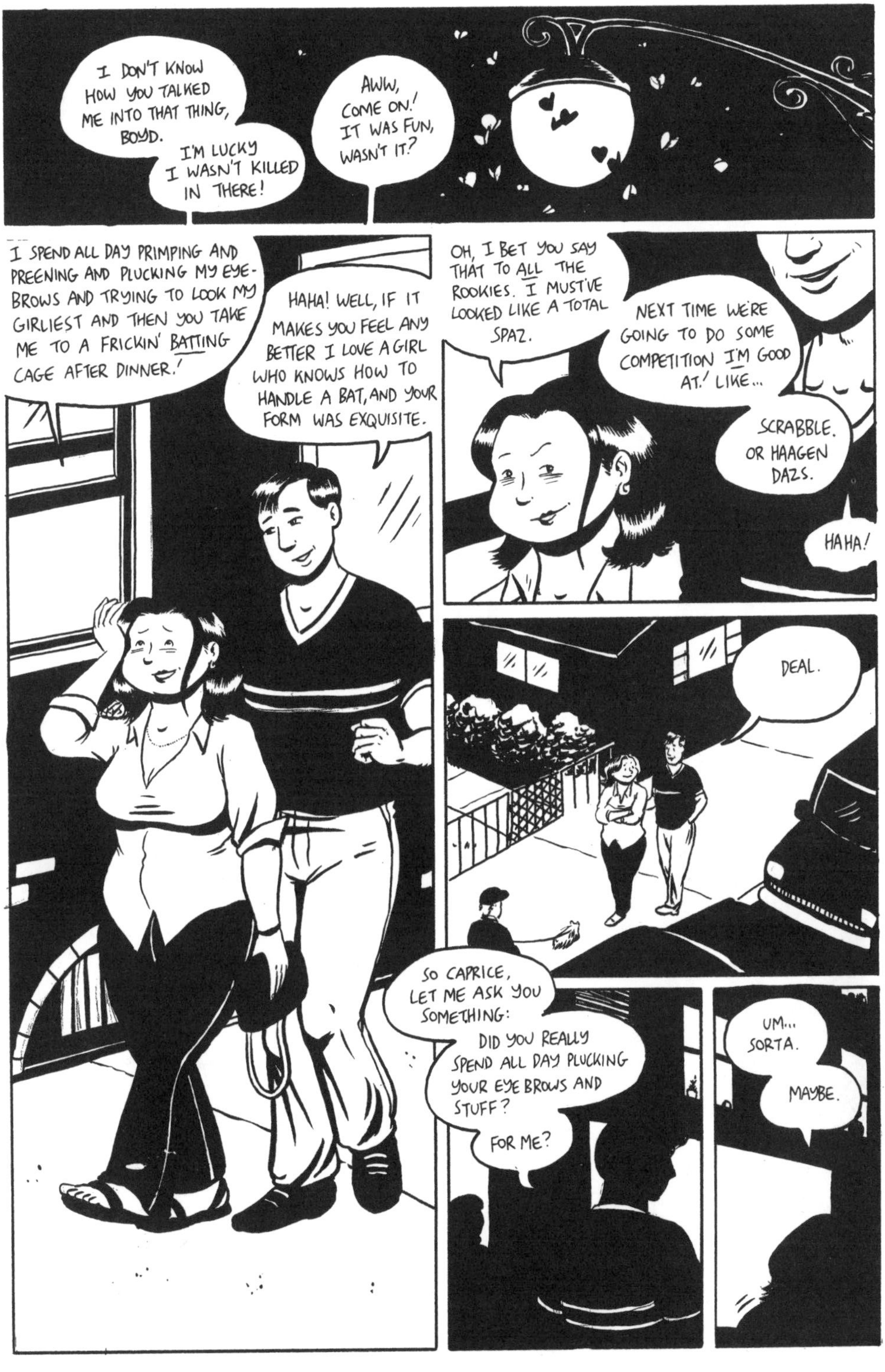
I DON'T KNOW HOW YOU TALKED ME INTO THAT THING, BOYD.
I'M LUCKY I WASN'T KILLED IN THERE!
AWW, COME ON! IT WAS FUN, WASN'T IT?
I SPEND ALL DAY PRIMPING AND PREENING AND PLUCKING MY EYE-BROWS AND TRYING TO LOOK MY GIRLIEST AND THEN YOU TAKE ME TO A FRICKIN' BATTING CAGE AFTER DINNER!
HAHA! WELL, IF IT MAKES YOU FEEL ANY BETTER I LOVE A GIRL WHO KNOWS HOW TO HANDLE A BAT, AND YOUR FORM WAS EXQUISITE.
OH, I BET YOU SAY THAT TO ALL THE ROOKIES. I MUST'VE LOOKED LIKE A TOTAL SPAZ.
NEXT TIME WE'RE GOING TO DO SOME COMPETITION I'M GOOD AT! LIKE...
SCRABBLE. OR HAAGEN DAZS.
HAHA!
DEAL.
SO CAPRICE, LET ME ASK YOU SOMETHING:
DID YOU REALLY SPEND ALL DAY PLUCKING YOUR EYE BROWS AND STUFF?
FOR ME?
UM... SORTA.
MAYBE.

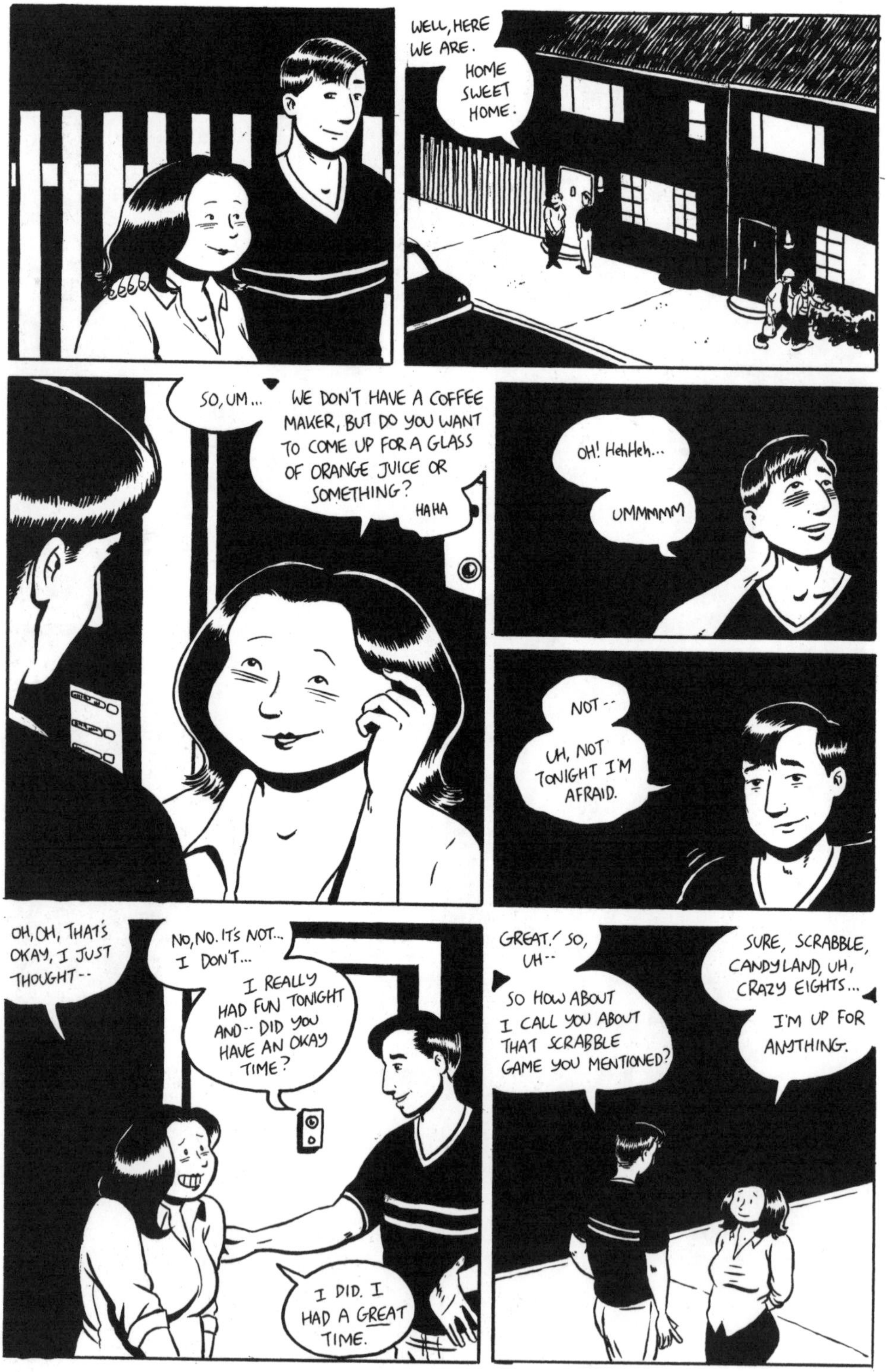
WELL, HERE WE ARE.
HOME SWEET HOME.
SO, UM...
WE DON'T HAVE A COFFEE MAKER, BUT DO YOU WANT TO COME UP FOR A GLASS OF ORANGE JUICE OR SOMETHING?
HAHA
OH! HehHeh...
UMMMMM
NOT--
UH, NOT TONIGHT I'M AFRAID.
OH, OH, THAT'S OKAY, I JUST THOUGHT--
NO, NO. IT'S NOT... I DON'T...
I REALLY HAD FUN TONIGHT AND-- DID YOU HAVE AN OKAY TIME?
I DID. I HAD A GREAT TIME.
GREAT! SO, UH--
SO HOW ABOUT I CALL YOU ABOUT THAT SCRABBLE GAME YOU MENTIONED?
SURE, SCRABBLE, CANDYLAND, UH, CRAZY EIGHTS...
I'M UP FOR ANYTHING.

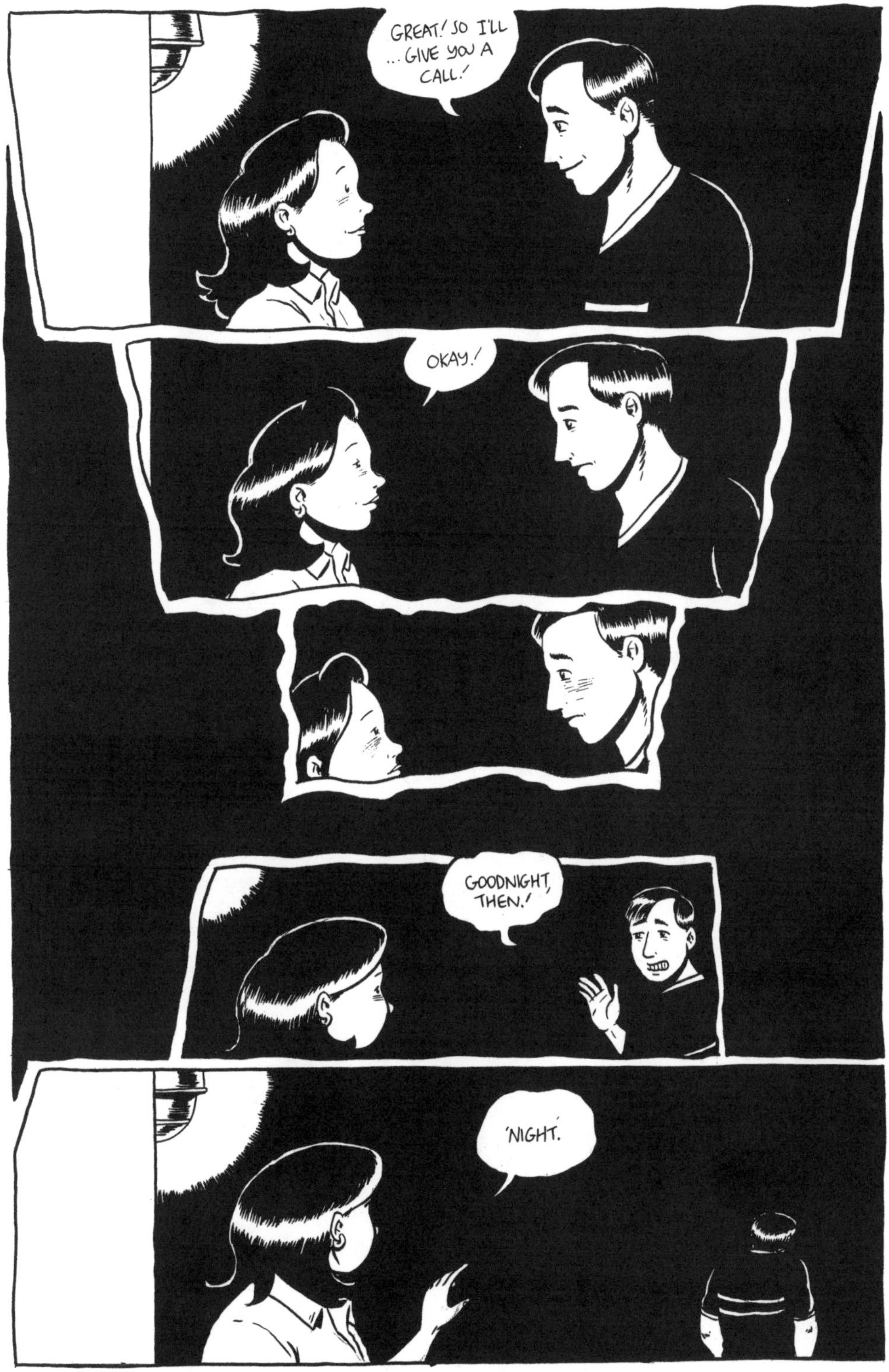
GREAT! SO I'LL ...GIVE YOU A CALL!
OKAY!
GOODNIGHT, THEN!
'NIGHT.

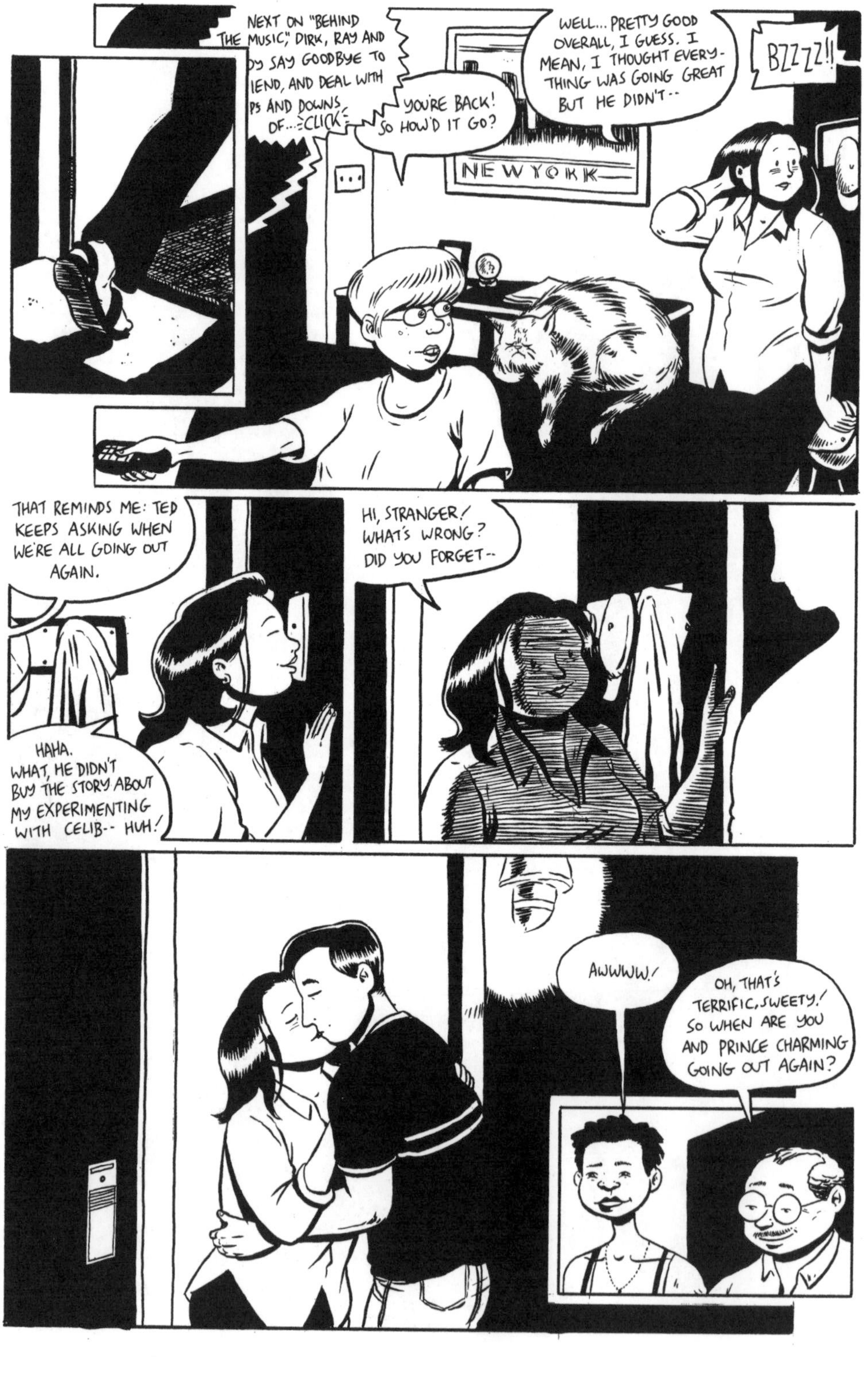
NEXT ON "BEHIND THE MUSIC," DIRK, RAY AND
SAY GOODBYE TO
AND DEAL WITH
AND DOWNS
OF... CLICK
YOU'RE BACK! SO HOW'D IT GO?
WELL... PRETTY GOOD OVERALL, I GUESS. I MEAN, I THOUGHT EVERY-THING WAS GOING GREAT BUT HE DIDN'T--
BZZZZ!!
THAT REMINDS ME: TED KEEPS ASKING WHEN WE'RE ALL GOING OUT AGAIN.
HAHA. WHAT, HE DIDN'T BUY THE STORY ABOUT MY EXPERIMENTING WITH CELIB-- HUH!
HI, STRANGER! WHAT'S WRONG? DID YOU FORGET--
AWWWW!
OH, THAT'S TERRIFIC, SWEETY! SO WHEN ARE YOU AND PRINCE CHARMING GOING OUT AGAIN?

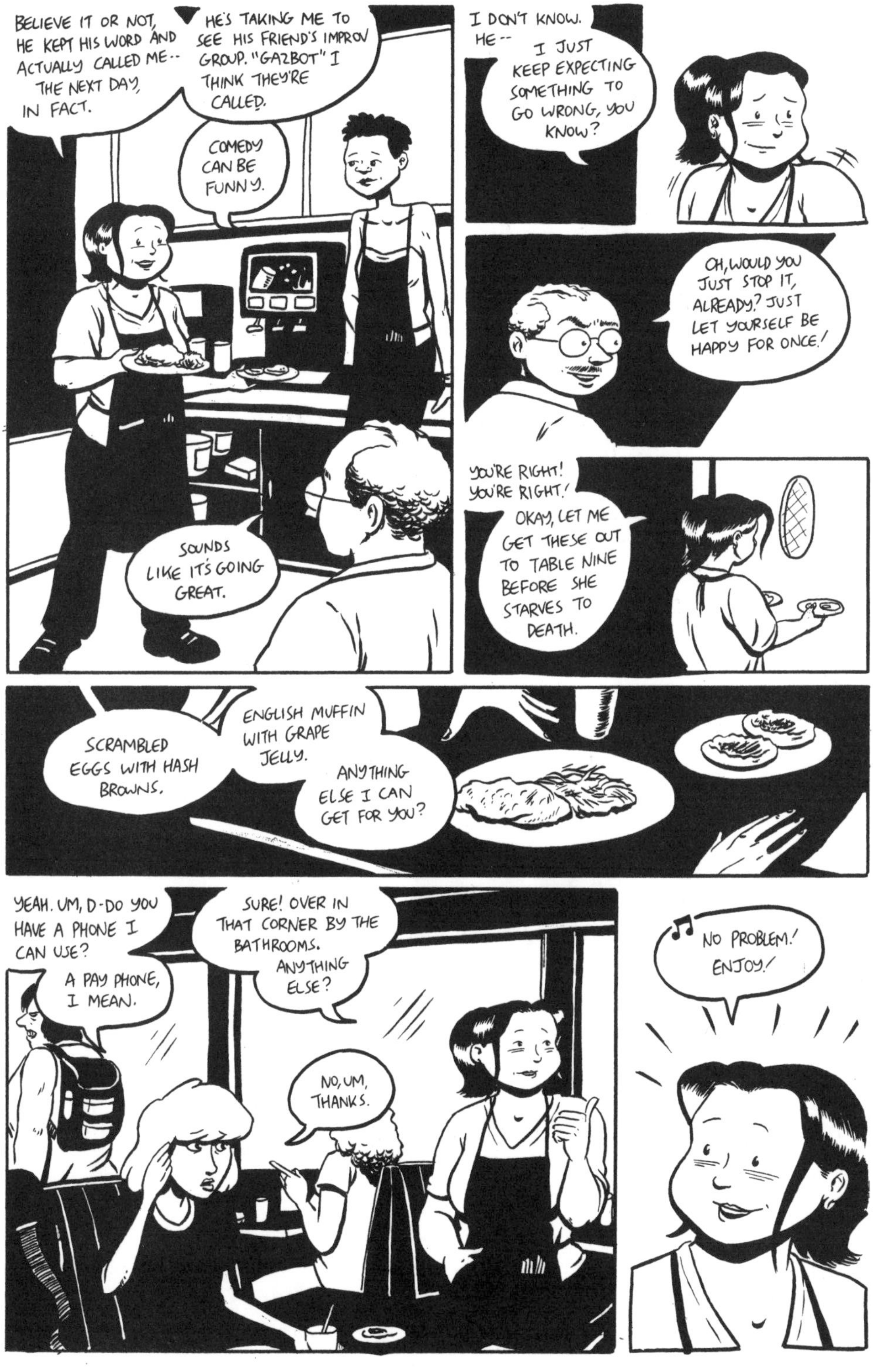
BELIEVE IT OR NOT, HE KEPT HIS WORD AND ACTUALLY CALLED ME -- THE NEXT DAY, IN FACT.
HE'S TAKING ME TO SEE HIS FRIEND'S IMPROV GROUP. "GAZBOT" I THINK THEY'RE CALLED.
COMEDY CAN BE FUNNY.
SOUNDS LIKE IT'S GOING GREAT.
I DON'T KNOW. HE --
I JUST KEEP EXPECTING SOMETHING TO GO WRONG, YOU KNOW?
OH, WOULD YOU JUST STOP IT, ALREADY? JUST LET YOURSELF BE HAPPY FOR ONCE!
YOU'RE RIGHT! YOU'RE RIGHT!
OKAY, LET ME GET THESE OUT TO TABLE NINE BEFORE SHE STARVES TO DEATH.
SCRAMBLED EGGS WITH HASH BROWNS.
ENGLISH MUFFIN WITH GRAPE JELLY.
ANYTHING ELSE I CAN GET FOR YOU?
YEAH. UM, D-DO YOU HAVE A PHONE I CAN USE?
A PAY PHONE, I MEAN.
SURE! OVER IN THAT CORNER BY THE BATHROOMS.
ANYTHING ELSE?
NO, UM, THANKS.
NO PROBLEM! ENJOY!

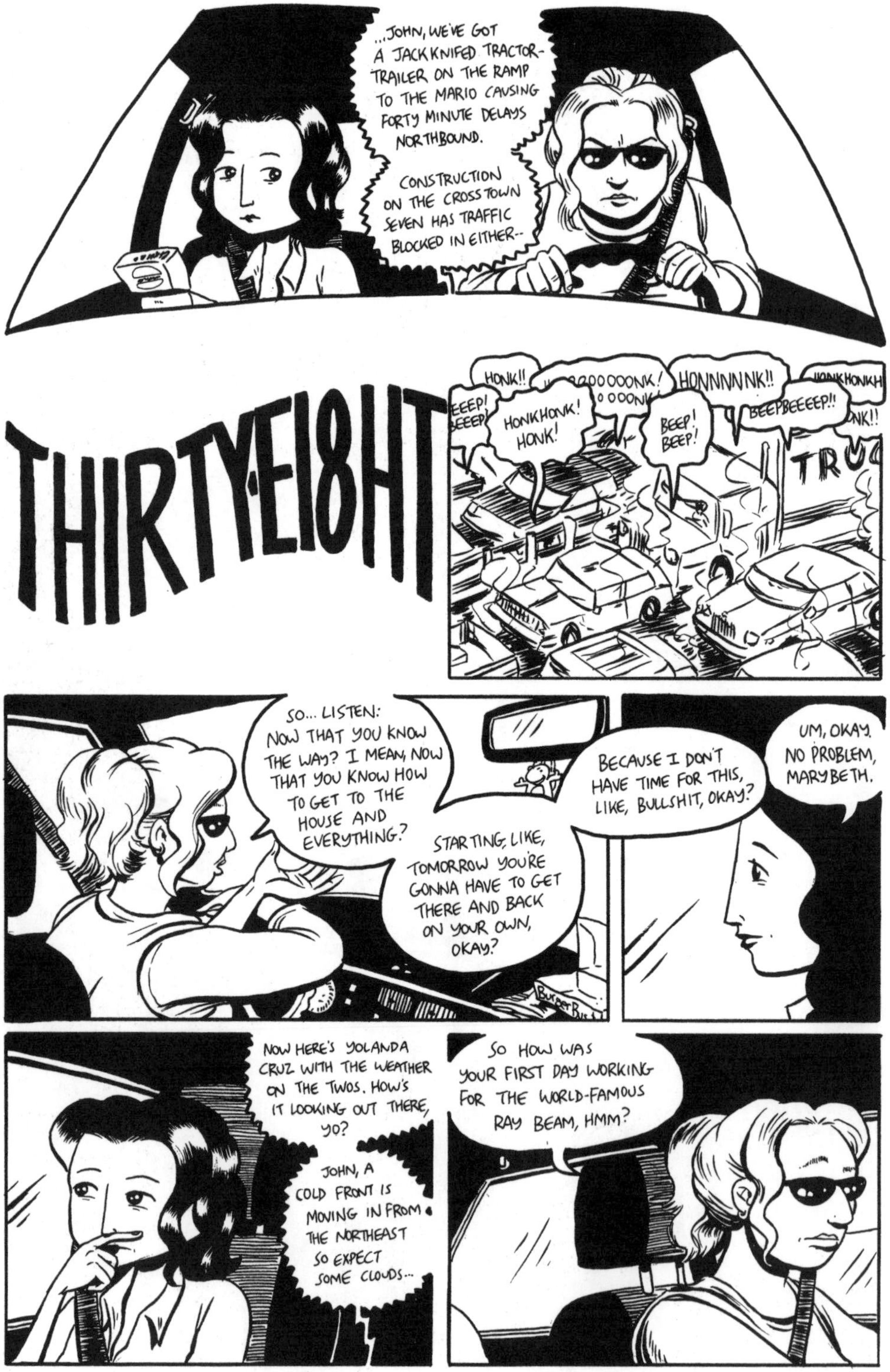
...JOHN, WE'VE GOT A JACKKNIFED TRACTOR-TRAILER ON THE RAMP TO THE MARIO CAUSING FORTY MINUTE DELAYS NORTHBOUND.
CONSTRUCTION ON THE CROSSTOWN SEVEN HAS TRAFFIC BLOCKED IN EITHER--
THIRTY-EI8HT
HONK!!
HONKHONK! HONK!
HONNNNNK!!
BEEP! BEEP!
BEEPBEEEEP!!
SO... LISTEN: NOW THAT YOU KNOW THE WAY? I MEAN, NOW THAT YOU KNOW HOW TO GET TO THE HOUSE AND EVERYTHING?
STARTING, LIKE, TOMORROW YOU'RE GONNA HAVE TO GET THERE AND BACK ON YOUR OWN, OKAY?
BECAUSE I DON'T HAVE TIME FOR THIS, LIKE, BULLSHIT, OKAY?
UM, OKAY. NO PROBLEM, MARYBETH.
NOW HERE'S YOLANDA CRUZ WITH THE WEATHER ON THE TWOS. HOW'S IT LOOKING OUT THERE, YO?
JOHN, A COLD FRONT IS MOVING IN FROM THE NORTHEAST SO EXPECT SOME CLOUDS...
SO HOW WAS YOUR FIRST DAY WORKING FOR THE WORLD-FAMOUS RAY BEAM, HMM?

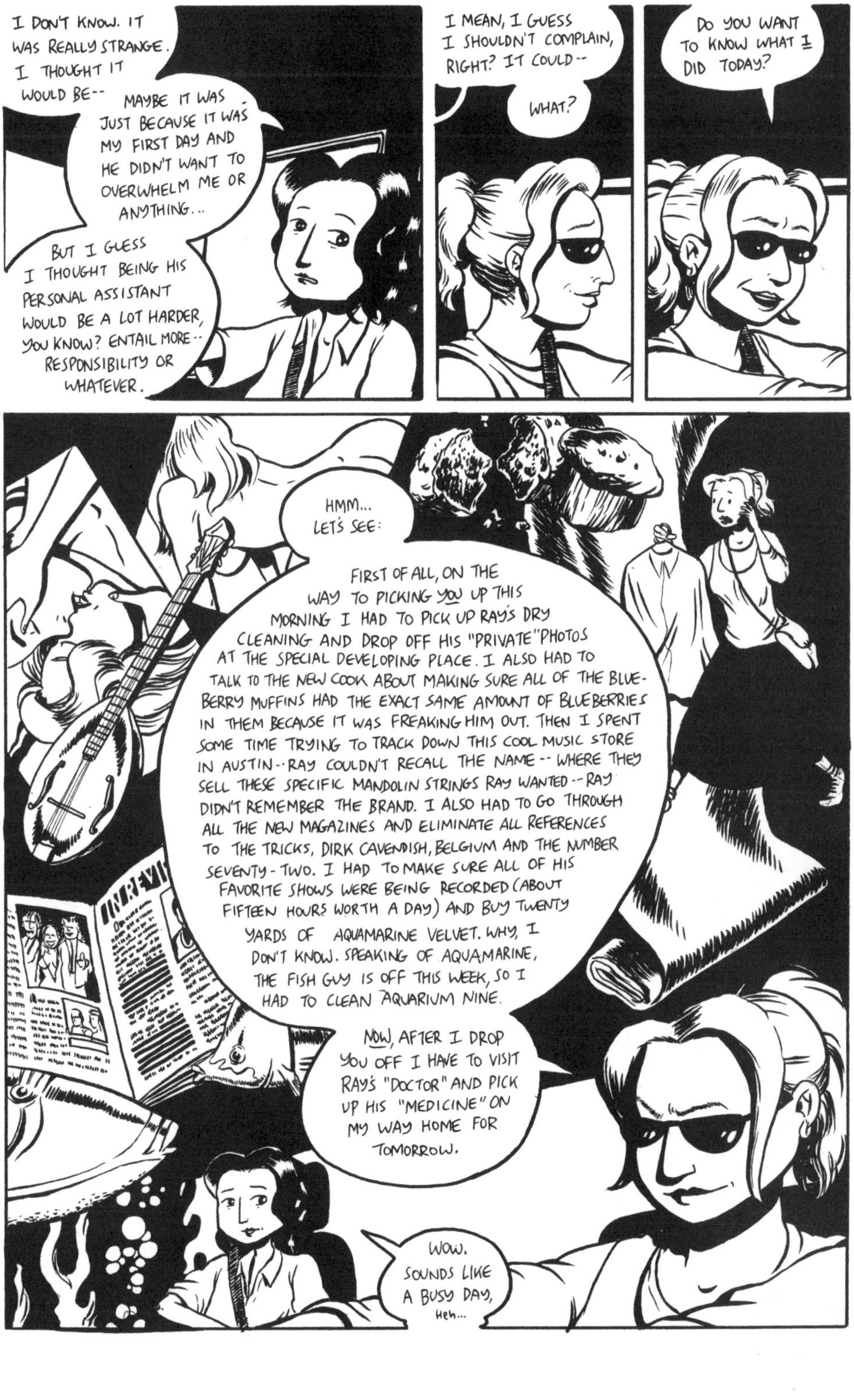
I DON'T KNOW. IT WAS REALLY STRANGE. I THOUGHT IT WOULD BE--
MAYBE IT WAS JUST BECAUSE IT WAS MY FIRST DAY AND HE DIDN'T WANT TO OVERWHELM ME OR ANYTHING...
BUT I GUESS I THOUGHT BEING HIS PERSONAL ASSISTANT WOULD BE A LOT HARDER, YOU KNOW? ENTAIL MORE-- RESPONSIBILITY OR WHATEVER.
I MEAN, I GUESS I SHOULDN'T COMPLAIN, RIGHT? IT COULD--
WHAT?
DO YOU WANT TO KNOW WHAT I DID TODAY?
HMM... LET'S SEE:
FIRST OF ALL, ON THE WAY TO PICKING YOU UP THIS MORNING I HAD TO PICK UP RAY'S DRY CLEANING AND DROP OFF HIS "PRIVATE" PHOTOS AT THE SPECIAL DEVELOPING PLACE. I ALSO HAD TO TALK TO THE NEW COOK ABOUT MAKING SURE ALL OF THE BLUE-BERRY MUFFINS HAD THE EXACT SAME AMOUNT OF BLUEBERRIES IN THEM BECAUSE IT WAS FREAKING HIM OUT. THEN I SPENT SOME TIME TRYING TO TRACK DOWN THIS COOL MUSIC STORE IN AUSTIN--RAY COULDN'T RECALL THE NAME--WHERE THEY SELL THESE SPECIFIC MANDOLIN STRINGS RAY WANTED--RAY DIDN'T REMEMBER THE BRAND. I ALSO HAD TO GO THROUGH ALL THE NEW MAGAZINES AND ELIMINATE ALL REFERENCES TO THE TRICKS, DIRK CAVENDISH, BELGIUM AND THE NUMBER SEVENTY-TWO. I HAD TO MAKE SURE ALL OF HIS FAVORITE SHOWS WERE BEING RECORDED (ABOUT FIFTEEN HOURS WORTH A DAY) AND BUY TWENTY YARDS OF AQUAMARINE VELVET. WHY, I DON'T KNOW. SPEAKING OF AQUAMARINE, THE FISH GUY IS OFF THIS WEEK, SO I HAD TO CLEAN AQUARIUM NINE.
NOW, AFTER I DROP YOU OFF I HAVE TO VISIT RAY'S "DOCTOR" AND PICK UP HIS "MEDICINE" ON MY WAY HOME FOR TOMORROW.
WOW. SOUNDS LIKE A BUSY DAY, HEH...

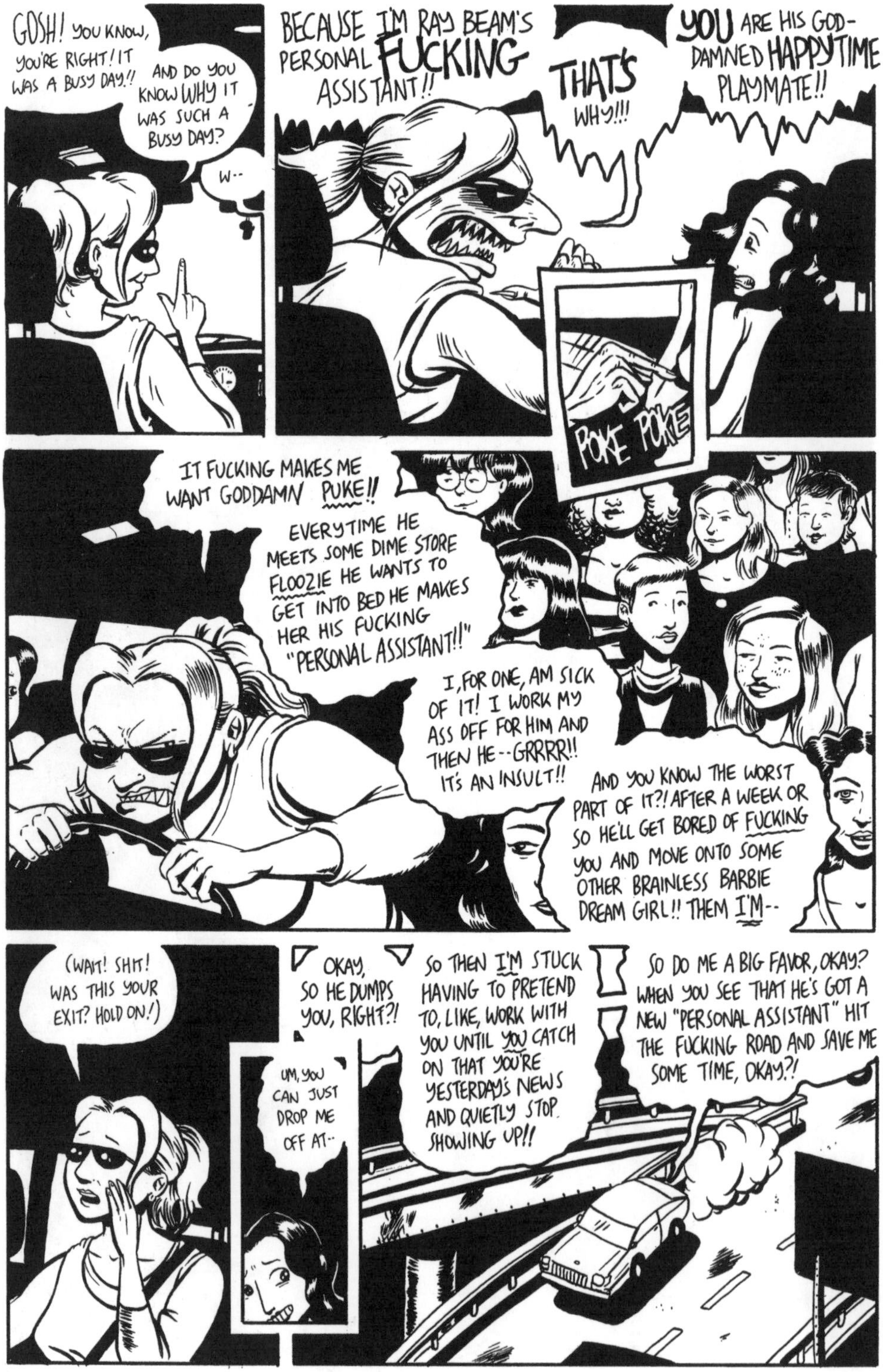
GOSH! YOU KNOW, YOU'RE RIGHT! IT WAS A BUSY DAY!!
AND DO YOU KNOW WHY IT WAS SUCH A BUSY DAY?
W--
BECAUSE I'M RAY BEAM'S PERSONAL FUCKING ASSISTANT!!
THAT'S WHY!!!
YOU ARE HIS GOD-DAMNED HAPPYTIME PLAYMATE!!
POKE POKE
IT FUCKING MAKES ME WANT GODDAMN PUKE!!
EVERYTIME HE MEETS SOME DIME STORE FLOOZIE HE WANTS TO GET INTO BED HE MAKES HER HIS FUCKING "PERSONAL ASSISTANT!!"
I, FOR ONE, AM SICK OF IT! I WORK MY ASS OFF FOR HIM AND THEN HE--GRRRR!! IT'S AN INSULT!!
AND YOU KNOW THE WORST PART OF IT?! AFTER A WEEK OR SO HE'LL GET BORED OF FUCKING YOU AND MOVE ONTO SOME OTHER BRAINLESS BARBIE DREAM GIRL!! THEM I'M--
(WAIT! SHIT! WAS THIS YOUR EXIT? HOLD ON!)
OKAY, SO HE DUMPS YOU, RIGHT?!
UM, YOU CAN JUST DROP ME OFF AT--
SO THEN I'M STUCK HAVING TO PRETEND TO, LIKE, WORK WITH YOU UNTIL YOU CATCH ON THAT YOU'RE YESTERDAY'S NEWS AND QUIETLY STOP SHOWING UP!!
SO DO ME A BIG FAVOR, OKAY? WHEN YOU SEE THAT HE'S GOT A NEW "PERSONAL ASSISTANT" HIT THE FUCKING ROAD AND SAVE ME SOME TIME, OKAY?!

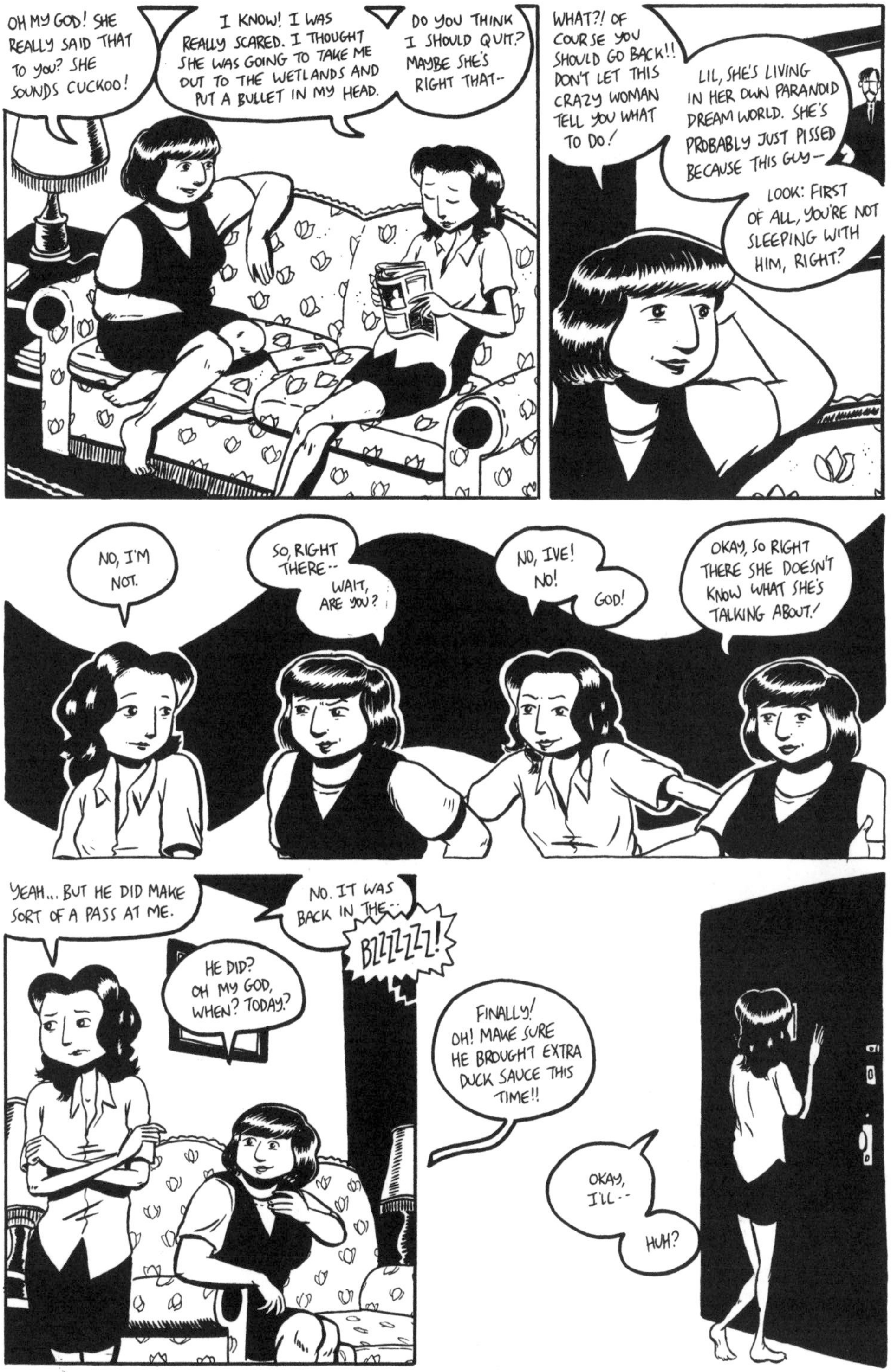
OH MY GOD! SHE REALLY SAID THAT TO YOU? SHE SOUNDS CUCKOO!
I KNOW! I WAS REALLY SCARED. I THOUGHT SHE WAS GOING TO TAKE ME OUT TO THE WETLANDS AND PUT A BULLET IN MY HEAD.
DO YOU THINK I SHOULD QUIT? MAYBE SHE'S RIGHT THAT--
WHAT?! OF COURSE YOU SHOULD GO BACK!! DON'T LET THIS CRAZY WOMAN TELL YOU WHAT TO DO!
LIL, SHE'S LIVING IN HER OWN PARANOID DREAM WORLD. SHE'S PROBABLY JUST PISSED BECAUSE THIS GUY--
LOOK: FIRST OF ALL, YOU'RE NOT SLEEPING WITH HIM, RIGHT?
NO, I'M NOT.
SO, RIGHT THERE--
WAIT, ARE YOU?
NO, I'VE! NO!
GOD!
OKAY, SO RIGHT THERE SHE DOESN'T KNOW WHAT SHE'S TALKING ABOUT!
YEAH... BUT HE DID MAKE SORT OF A PASS AT ME.
NO. IT WAS BACK IN THE--
HE DID? OH MY GOD, WHEN? TODAY?
BZZZZZZ!
FINALLY! OH! MAKE SURE HE BROUGHT EXTRA DUCK SAUCE THIS TIME!!
OKAY, I'LL--
HUH?

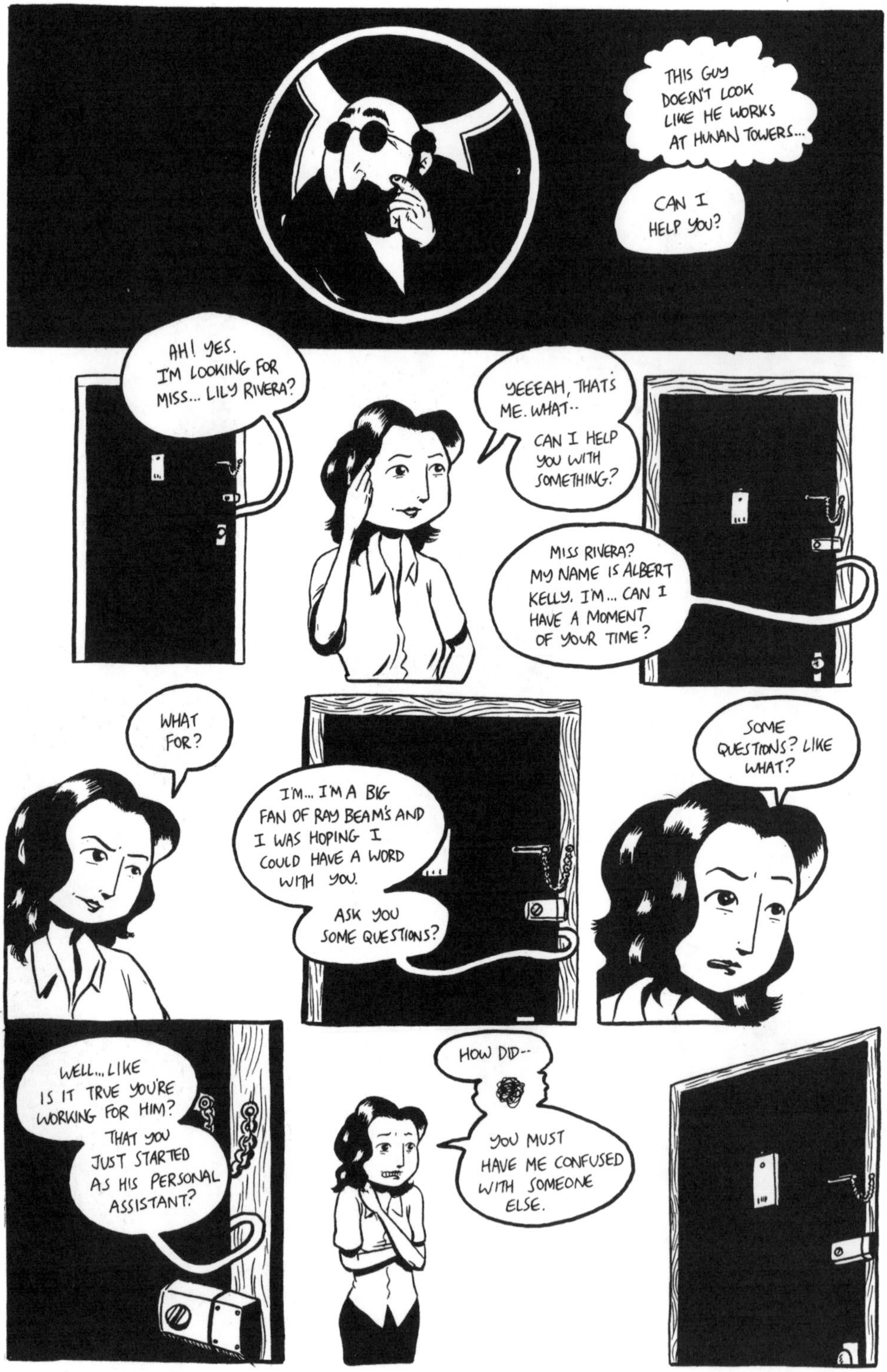
THIS GUY DOESN'T LOOK LIKE HE WORKS AT HUNAN TOWERS...
CAN I HELP YOU?
AH! YES. I'M LOOKING FOR MISS... LILY RIVERA?
YEEEAH, THAT'S ME. WHAT.. CAN I HELP YOU WITH SOMETHING?
MISS RIVERA? MY NAME IS ALBERT KELLY. I'M... CAN I HAVE A MOMENT OF YOUR TIME?
WHAT FOR?
I'M... I'M A BIG FAN OF RAY BEAM'S AND I WAS HOPING I COULD HAVE A WORD WITH YOU.
ASK YOU SOME QUESTIONS?
SOME QUESTIONS? LIKE WHAT?
WELL... LIKE IS IT TRUE YOU'RE WORKING FOR HIM? THAT YOU JUST STARTED AS HIS PERSONAL ASSISTANT?
HOW DID--
YOU MUST HAVE ME CONFUSED WITH SOMEONE ELSE.

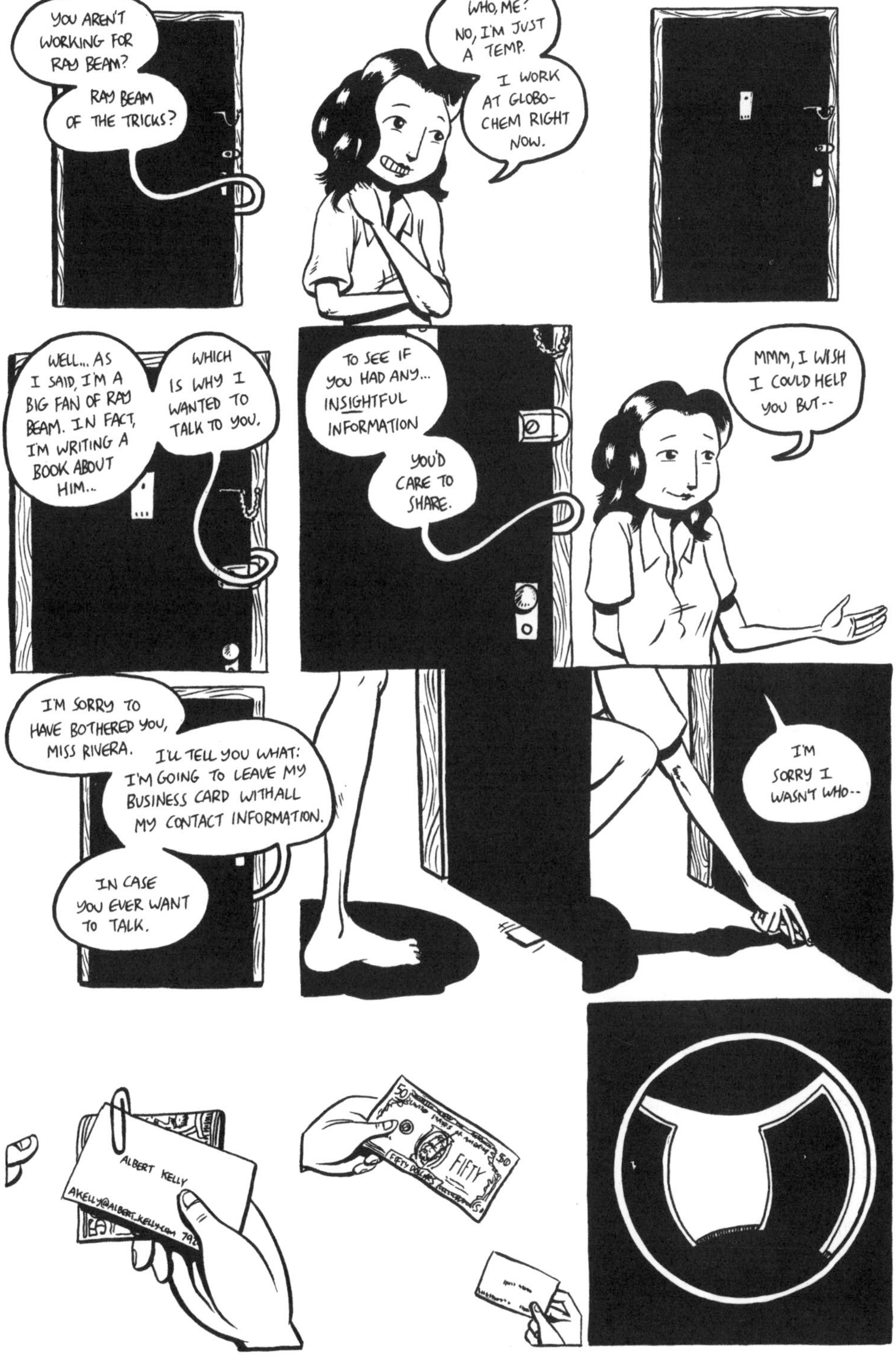
YOU AREN'T WORKING FOR RAY BEAM?
RAY BEAM OF THE TRICKS?
WHO, ME? NO, I'M JUST A TEMP.
I WORK AT GLOBO-CHEM RIGHT NOW.
WELL... AS I SAID, I'M A BIG FAN OF RAY BEAM. IN FACT, I'M WRITING A BOOK ABOUT HIM..
WHICH IS WHY I WANTED TO TALK TO YOU.
TO SEE IF YOU HAD ANY... INSIGHTFUL INFORMATION
YOU'D CARE TO SHARE.
MMM, I WISH I COULD HELP YOU BUT--
I'M SORRY TO HAVE BOTHERED YOU, MISS RIVERA.
I'LL TELL YOU WHAT: I'M GOING TO LEAVE MY BUSINESS CARD WITH ALL MY CONTACT INFORMATION.
IN CASE YOU EVER WANT TO TALK.
I'M SORRY I WASN'T WHO--
ALBERT KELLY
AKELLY@ALBERT_KELLY.COM
FIFTY
50
FIFTY DOLLARS

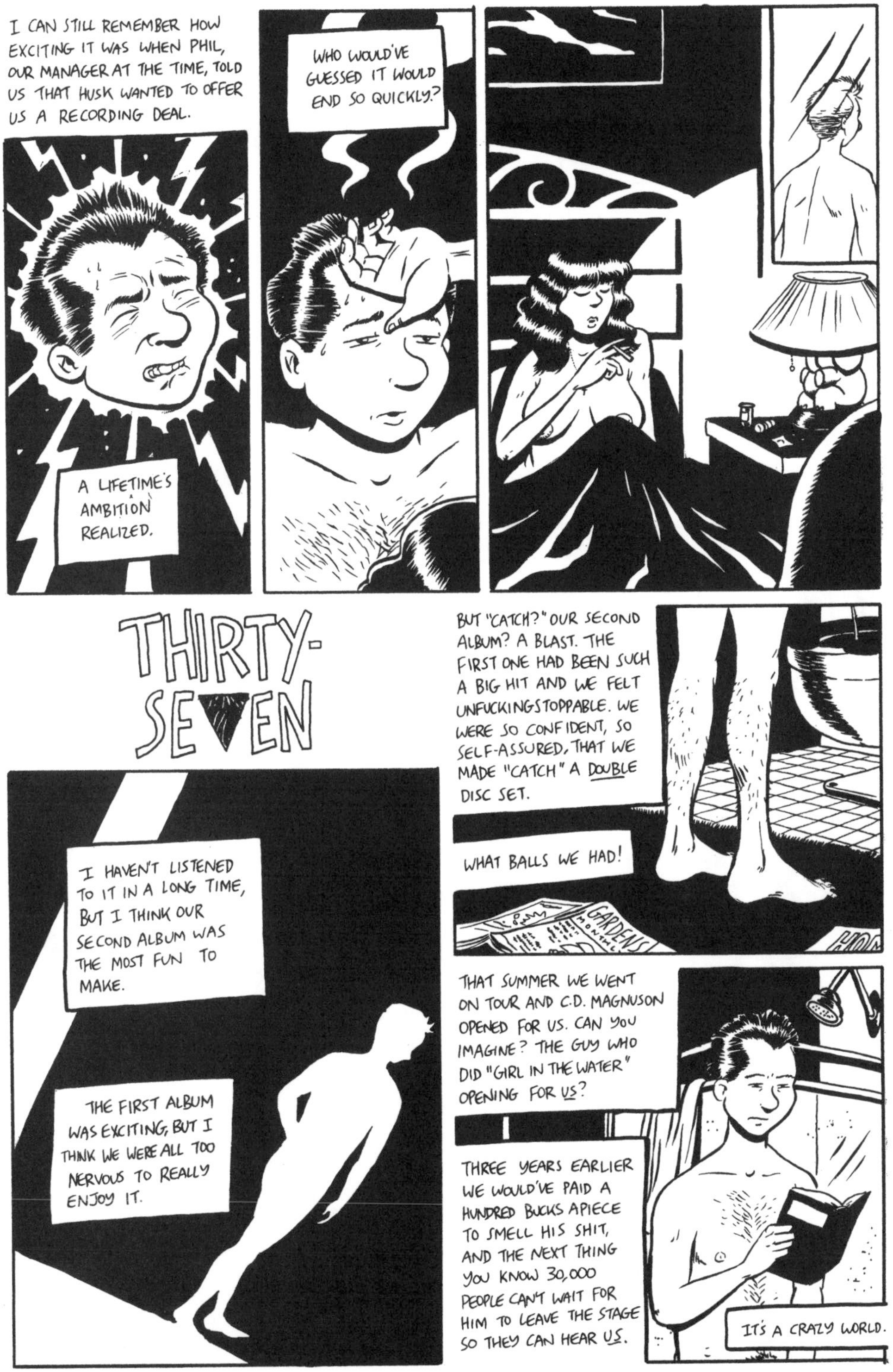
I CAN STILL REMEMBER HOW EXCITING IT WAS WHEN PHIL, OUR MANAGER AT THE TIME, TOLD US THAT HUSK WANTED TO OFFER US A RECORDING DEAL.
A LIFETIME'S AMBITION REALIZED.
WHO WOULD'VE GUESSED IT WOULD END SO QUICKLY?
THIRTY-SEVEN
BUT "CATCH?" OUR SECOND ALBUM? A BLAST. THE FIRST ONE HAD BEEN SUCH A BIG HIT AND WE FELT UNFUCKINGSTOPPABLE. WE WERE SO CONFIDENT, SO SELF-ASSURED, THAT WE MADE "CATCH" A DOUBLE DISC SET.
WHAT BALLS WE HAD!
GARDENS MONTHLY
I HAVEN'T LISTENED TO IT IN A LONG TIME, BUT I THINK OUR SECOND ALBUM WAS THE MOST FUN TO MAKE.
THE FIRST ALBUM WAS EXCITING, BUT I THINK WE WERE ALL TOO NERVOUS TO REALLY ENJOY IT.
THAT SUMMER WE WENT ON TOUR AND C.D. MAGNUSON OPENED FOR US. CAN YOU IMAGINE? THE GUY WHO DID "GIRL IN THE WATER" OPENING FOR US?
THREE YEARS EARLIER WE WOULD'VE PAID A HUNDRED BUCKS APIECE TO SMELL HIS SHIT, AND THE NEXT THING YOU KNOW 30,000 PEOPLE CAN'T WAIT FOR HIM TO LEAVE THE STAGE SO THEY CAN HEAR US.
IT'S A CRAZY WORLD.

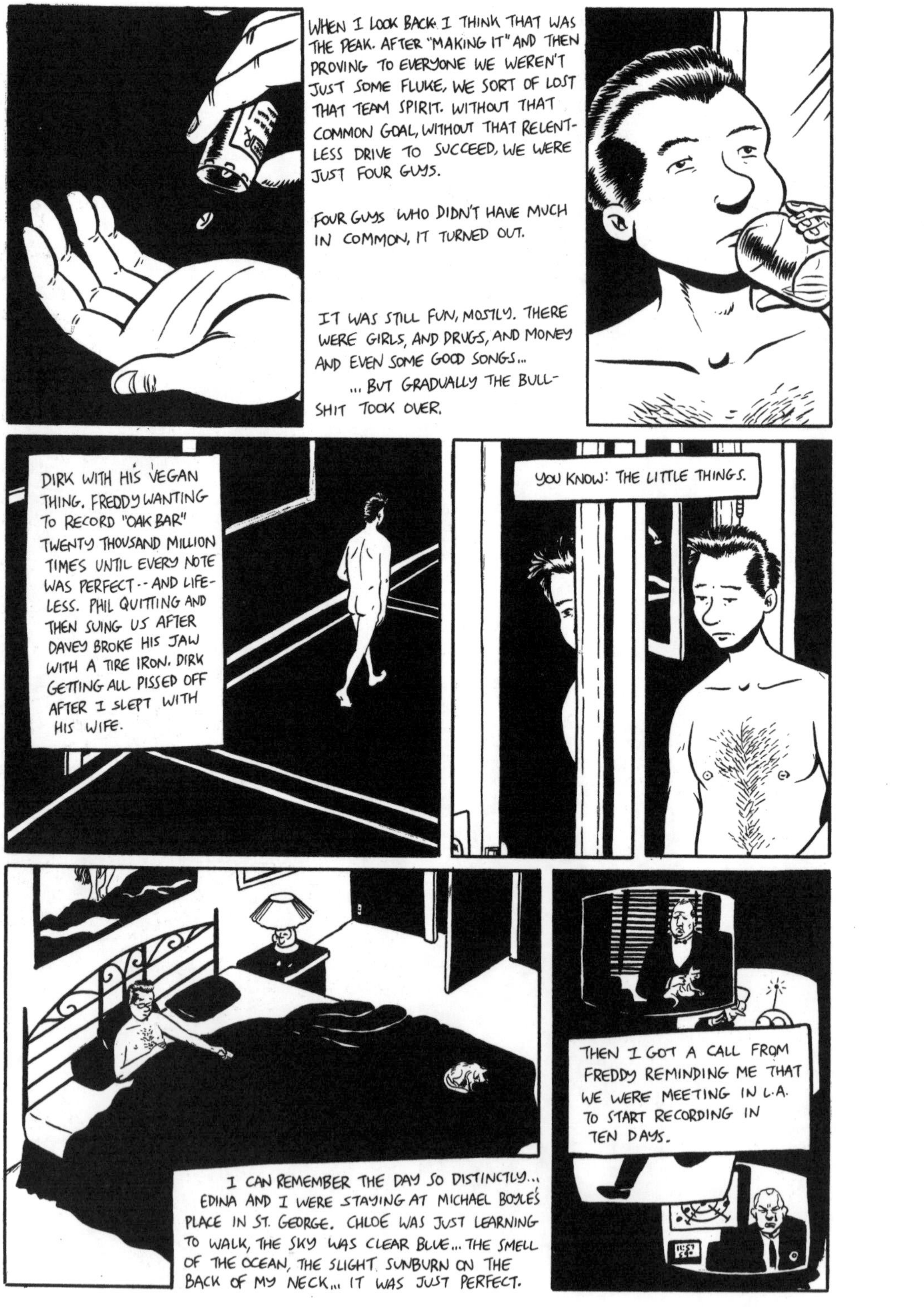
WHEN I LOOK BACK I THINK THAT WAS THE PEAK. AFTER "MAKING IT" AND THEN PROVING TO EVERYONE WE WEREN'T JUST SOME FLUKE, WE SORT OF LOST THAT TEAM SPIRIT. WITHOUT THAT COMMON GOAL, WITHOUT THAT RELENTLESS DRIVE TO SUCCEED, WE WERE JUST FOUR GUYS.
FOUR GUYS WHO DIDN'T HAVE MUCH IN COMMON, IT TURNED OUT.
IT WAS STILL FUN, MOSTLY. THERE WERE GIRLS, AND DRUGS, AND MONEY AND EVEN SOME GOOD SONGS...
... BUT GRADUALLY THE BULLSHIT TOOK OVER.
DIRK WITH HIS VEGAN THING. FREDDY WANTING TO RECORD "OAK BAR" TWENTY THOUSAND MILLION TIMES UNTIL EVERY NOTE WAS PERFECT -- AND LIFELESS. PHIL QUITTING AND THEN SUING US AFTER DAVEY BROKE HIS JAW WITH A TIRE IRON. DIRK GETTING ALL PISSED OFF AFTER I SLEPT WITH HIS WIFE.
YOU KNOW: THE LITTLE THINGS.
I CAN REMEMBER THE DAY SO DISTINCTLY... EDINA AND I WERE STAYING AT MICHAEL BOYLE'S PLACE IN ST. GEORGE. CHLOE WAS JUST LEARNING TO WALK, THE SKY WAS CLEAR BLUE... THE SMELL OF THE OCEAN, THE SLIGHT SUNBURN ON THE BACK OF MY NECK... IT WAS JUST PERFECT.
THEN I GOT A CALL FROM FREDDY REMINDING ME THAT WE WERE MEETING IN L.A. TO START RECORDING IN TEN DAYS.

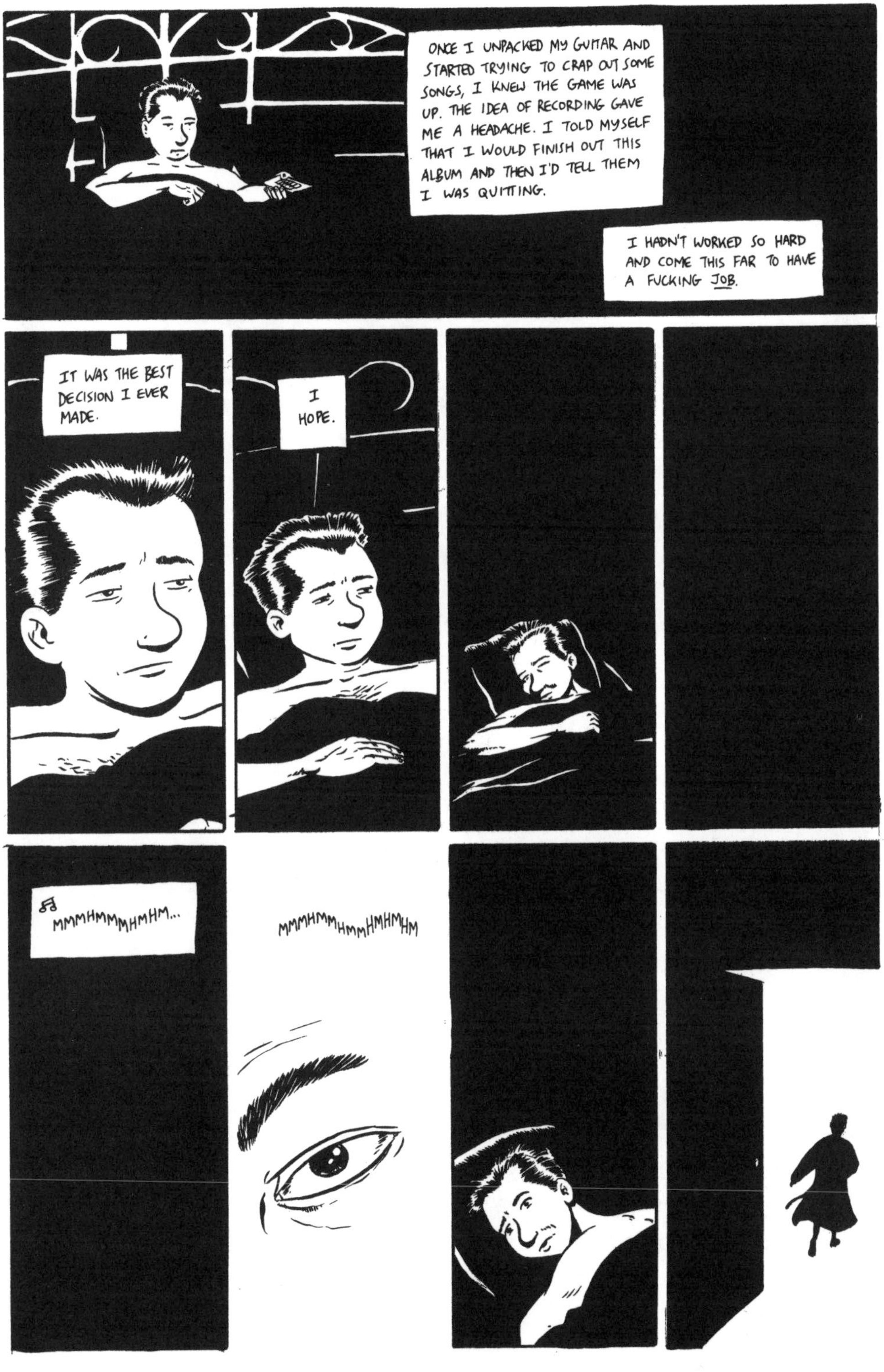
ONCE I UNPACKED MY GUITAR AND STARTED TRYING TO CRAP OUT SOME SONGS, I KNEW THE GAME WAS UP. THE IDEA OF RECORDING GAVE ME A HEADACHE. I TOLD MYSELF THAT I WOULD FINISH OUT THIS ALBUM AND THEN I'D TELL THEM I WAS QUITTING.
I HADN'T WORKED SO HARD AND COME THIS FAR TO HAVE A FUCKING JOB.
IT WAS THE BEST DECISION I EVER MADE.
I HOPE.
MMMHMMMHMHM...
MMMHMMHMMHMHMHM

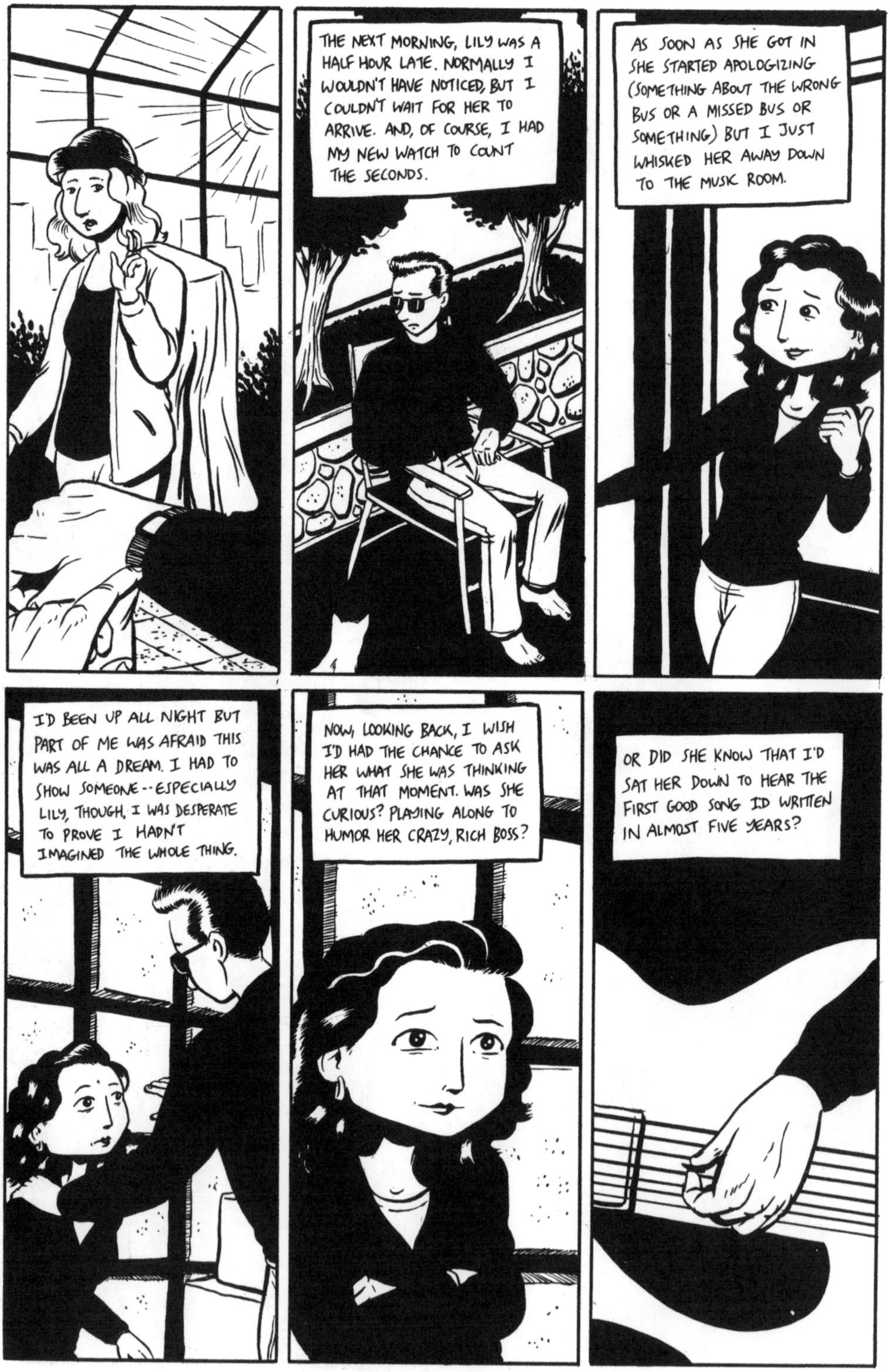
THE NEXT MORNING, LILY WAS A HALF HOUR LATE. NORMALLY I WOULDN'T HAVE NOTICED, BUT I COULDN'T WAIT FOR HER TO ARRIVE. AND, OF COURSE, I HAD MY NEW WATCH TO COUNT THE SECONDS.
AS SOON AS SHE GOT IN SHE STARTED APOLOGIZING (SOMETHING ABOUT THE WRONG BUS OR A MISSED BUS OR SOMETHING) BUT I JUST WHISKED HER AWAY DOWN TO THE MUSIC ROOM.
I'D BEEN UP ALL NIGHT BUT PART OF ME WAS AFRAID THIS WAS ALL A DREAM. I HAD TO SHOW SOMEONE--ESPECIALLY LILY, THOUGH. I WAS DESPERATE TO PROVE I HADN'T IMAGINED THE WHOLE THING.
NOW, LOOKING BACK, I WISH I'D HAD THE CHANCE TO ASK HER WHAT SHE WAS THINKING AT THAT MOMENT. WAS SHE CURIOUS? PLAYING ALONG TO HUMOR HER CRAZY, RICH BOSS?
OR DID SHE KNOW THAT I'D SAT HER DOWN TO HEAR THE FIRST GOOD SONG I'D WRITTEN IN ALMOST FIVE YEARS?

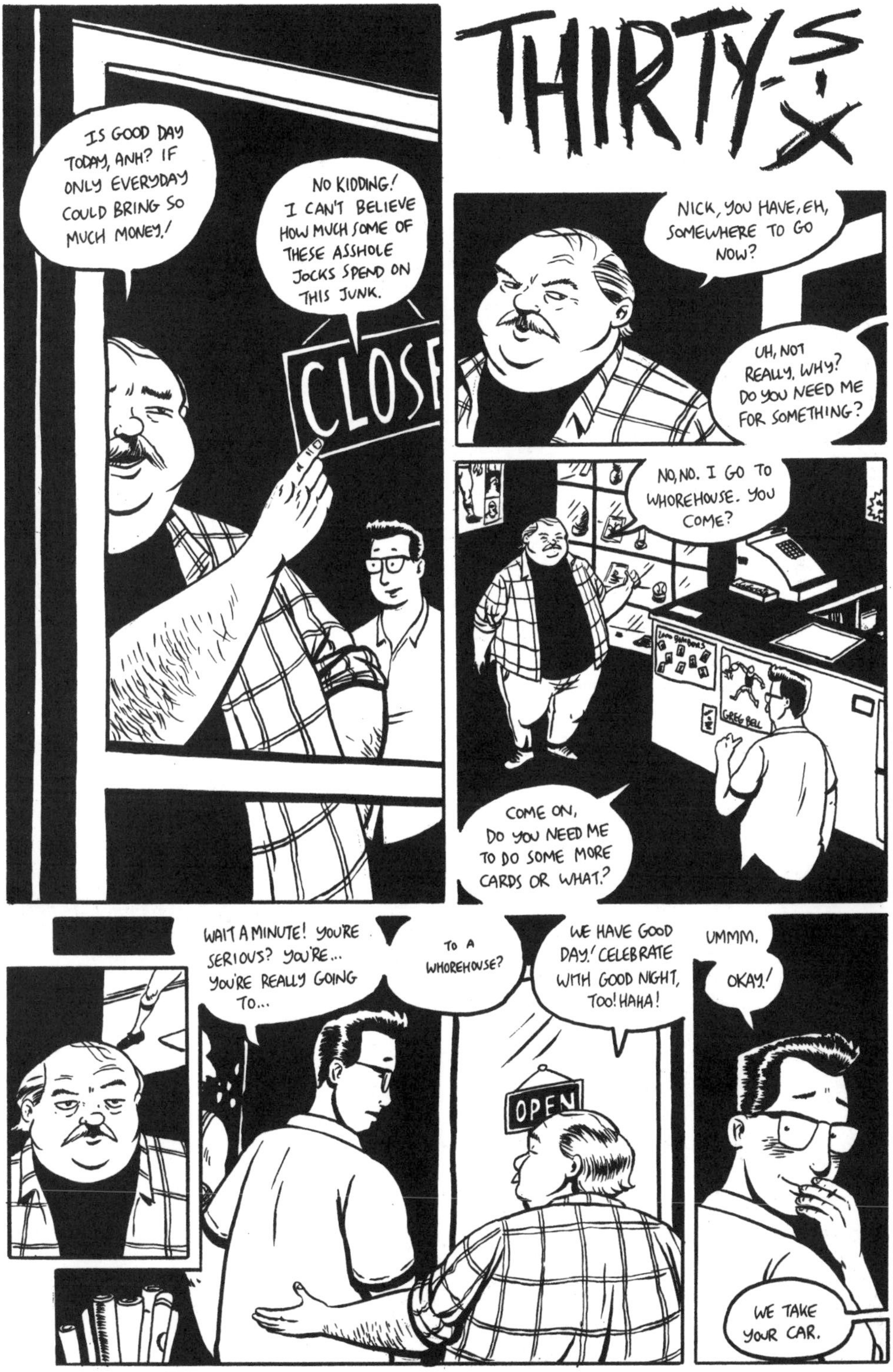
THIRTY-SIX
IS GOOD DAY TODAY, ANH? IF ONLY EVERYDAY COULD BRING SO MUCH MONEY!
NO KIDDING! I CAN'T BELIEVE HOW MUCH SOME OF THESE ASSHOLE JOCKS SPEND ON THIS JUNK.
CLOSE
NICK, YOU HAVE, EH, SOMEWHERE TO GO NOW?
UH, NOT REALLY. WHY? DO YOU NEED ME FOR SOMETHING?
NO, NO. I GO TO WHOREHOUSE. YOU COME?
GREG BELL
COME ON, DO YOU NEED ME TO DO SOME MORE CARDS OR WHAT?
WAIT A MINUTE! YOU'RE SERIOUS? YOU'RE... YOU'RE REALLY GOING TO...
TO A WHOREHOUSE?
WE HAVE GOOD DAY! CELEBRATE WITH GOOD NIGHT, TOO! HAHA!
OPEN
UMMM. OKAY!
WE TAKE YOUR CAR.

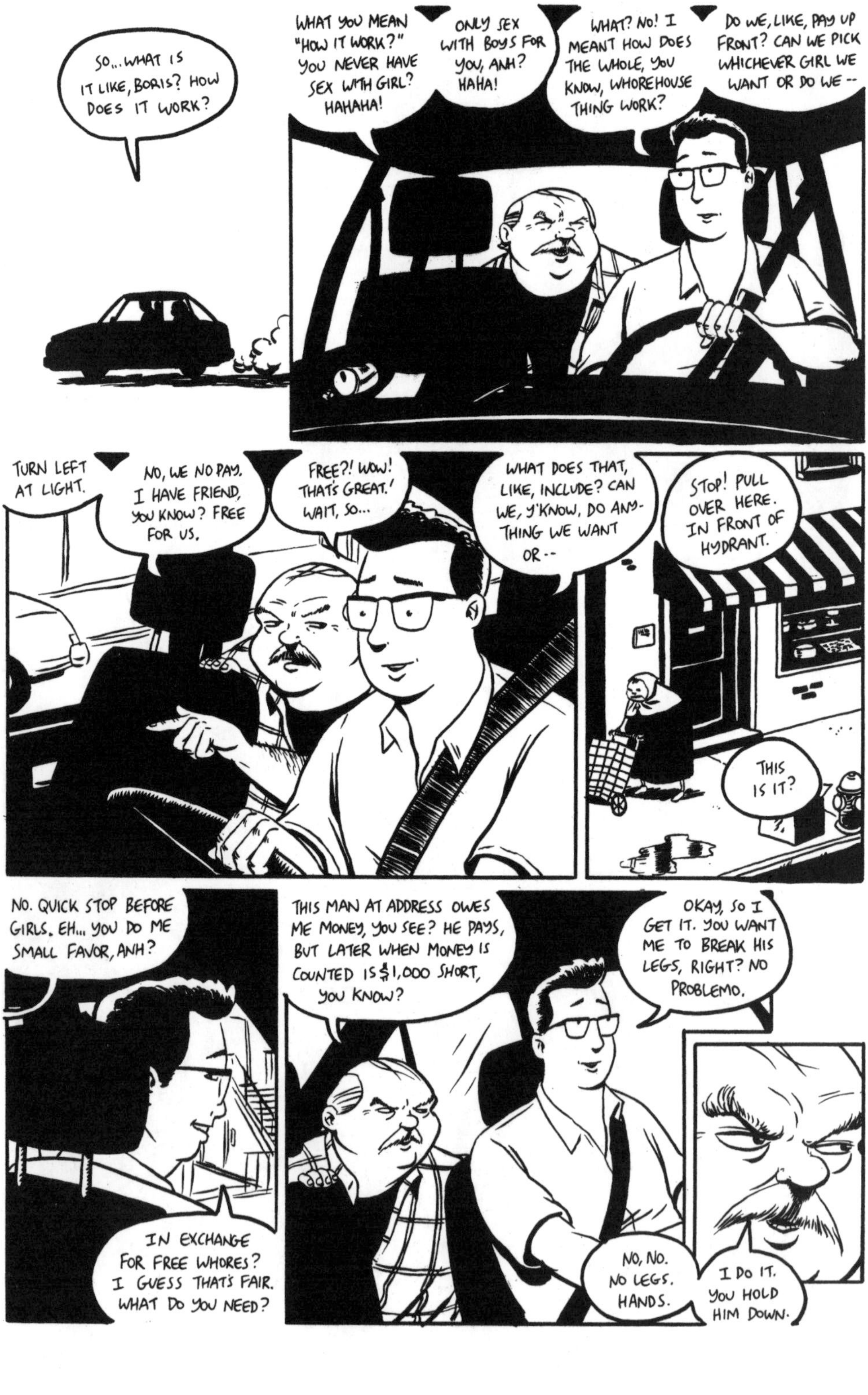
SO... WHAT IS IT LIKE, BORIS? HOW DOES IT WORK?
WHAT YOU MEAN "HOW IT WORK?" YOU NEVER HAVE SEX WITH GIRL? HAHAHA!
ONLY SEX WITH BOYS FOR YOU, ANH? HAHA!
WHAT? NO! I MEANT HOW DOES THE WHOLE, YOU KNOW, WHOREHOUSE THING WORK?
DO WE, LIKE, PAY UP FRONT? CAN WE PICK WHICHEVER GIRL WE WANT OR DO WE --
TURN LEFT AT LIGHT.
NO, WE NO PAY. I HAVE FRIEND, YOU KNOW? FREE FOR US.
FREE?! WOW! THAT'S GREAT! WAIT, SO...
WHAT DOES THAT, LIKE, INCLUDE? CAN WE, Y'KNOW, DO ANYTHING WE WANT OR --
STOP! PULL OVER HERE. IN FRONT OF HYDRANT.
THIS IS IT?
NO. QUICK STOP BEFORE GIRLS. EH... YOU DO ME SMALL FAVOR, ANH?
IN EXCHANGE FOR FREE WHORES? I GUESS THAT'S FAIR. WHAT DO YOU NEED?
THIS MAN AT ADDRESS OWES ME MONEY, YOU SEE? HE PAYS, BUT LATER WHEN MONEY IS COUNTED IS $1,000 SHORT, YOU KNOW?
OKAY, SO I GET IT. YOU WANT ME TO BREAK HIS LEGS, RIGHT? NO PROBLEMO.
NO, NO. NO LEGS. HANDS.
I DO IT. YOU HOLD HIM DOWN.

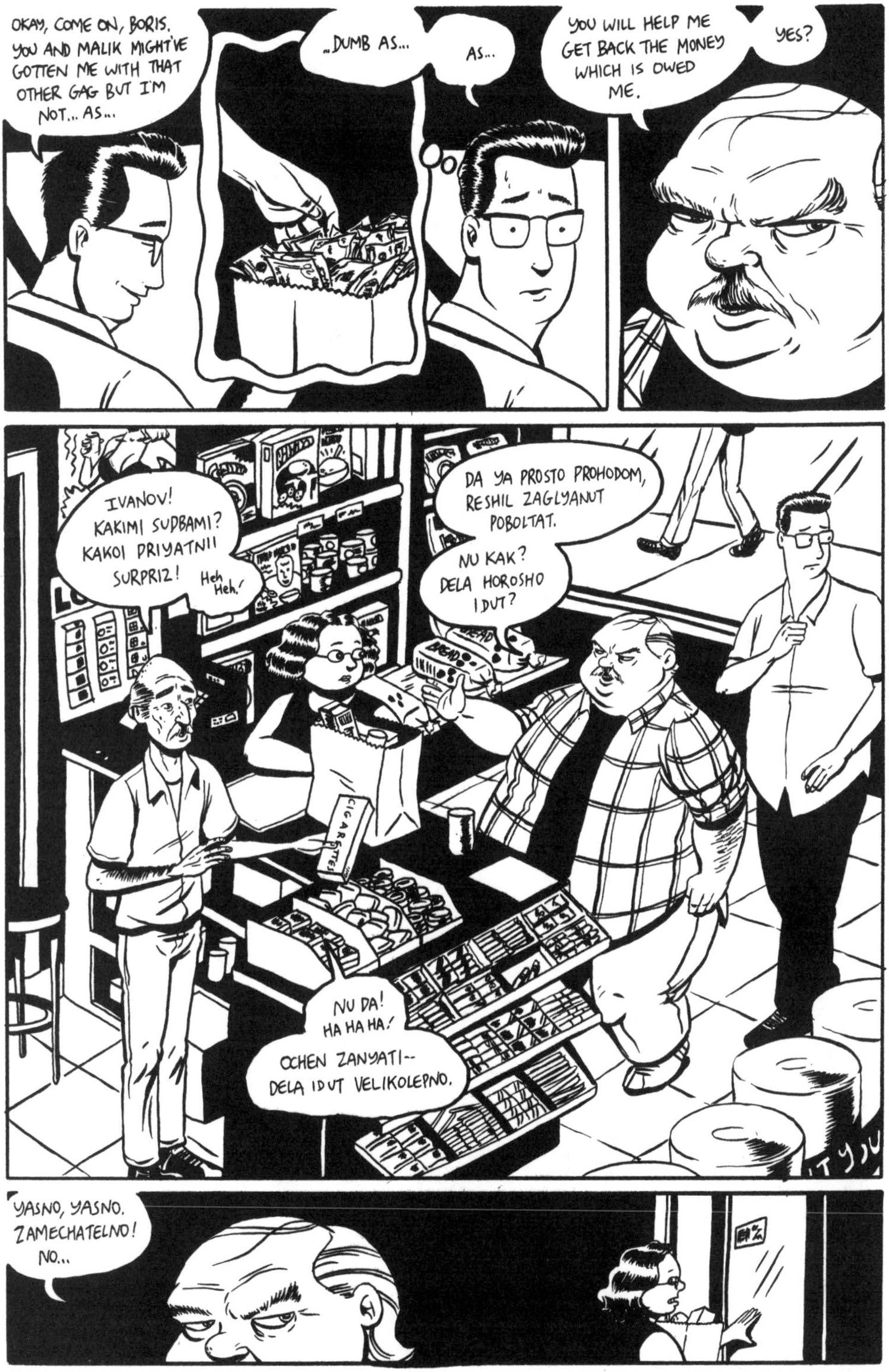
OKAY, COME ON, BORIS. YOU AND MALIK MIGHT'VE GOTTEN ME WITH THAT OTHER GAG BUT I'M NOT... AS...
...DUMB AS...
AS...
YOU WILL HELP ME GET BACK THE MONEY WHICH IS OWED ME.
YES?
IVANOV! KAKIMI SUDBAMI? KAKOI PRIYATNII SURPRIZ!
Heh Heh!
DA YA PROSTO PROHODOM, RESHIL ZAGLYANUT POBOLTAT.
NU KAK? DELA HOROSHO IDUT?
CIGARETTES
NU DA! HA HA HA!
OCHEN ZANYATI-- DELA IDUT VELIKOLEPNO.
YASNO, YASNO. ZAMECHATELNO! NO...

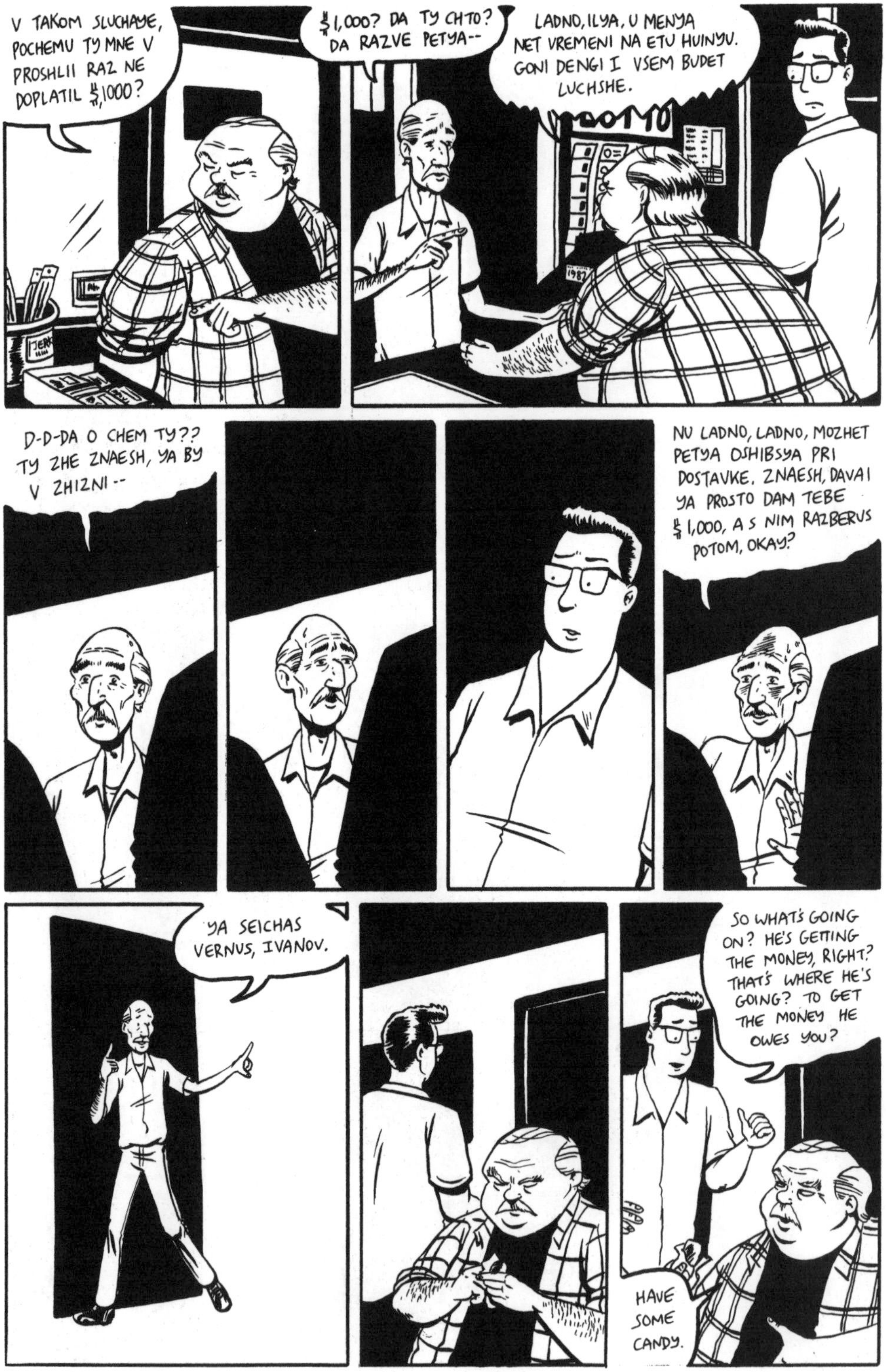
V TAKOM SLUCHAYE, POCHEMU TY MNE V PROSHLII RAZ NE DOPLATIL $1,000?
$1,000? DA TY CHTO? DA RAZVE PETYA--
LADNO, ILYA, U MENYA NET VREMENI NA ETU HUINYU. GONI DENGI I VSEM BUDET LUCHSHE.
D-D-DA O CHEM TY?? TY ZHE ZNAESH, YA BY V ZHIZNI--
NU LADNO, LADNO, MOZHET PETYA OSHIBSYA PRI DOSTAVKE. ZNAESH, DAVAI YA PROSTO DAM TEBE $1,000, A S NIM RAZBERUS POTOM, OKAY?
YA SEICHAS VERNUS, IVANOV.
SO WHAT'S GOING ON? HE'S GETTING THE MONEY, RIGHT? THAT'S WHERE HE'S GOING? TO GET THE MONEY HE OWES YOU?
HAVE SOME CANDY.

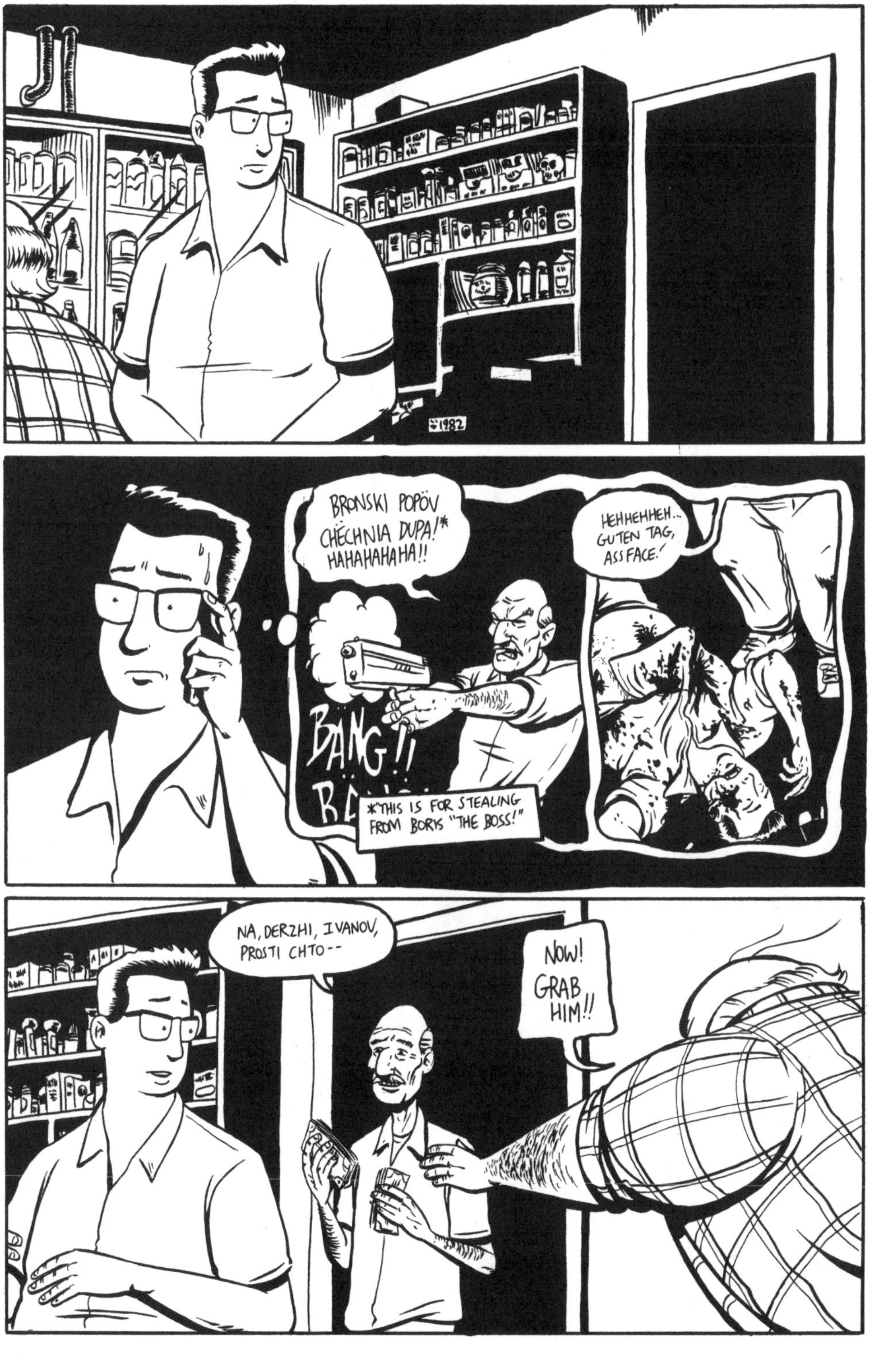
1982
BRONSKI POPÖV CHÉCHNIA DUPA!* HAHAHAHAHA!!
BANG!! BA
*THIS IS FOR STEALING FROM BORIS "THE BOSS!"
HEHHEHHEH.. GUTEN TAG, ASSFACE!
NA, DERZHI, IVANOV, PROSTI CHTO--
NOW! GRAB HIM!!

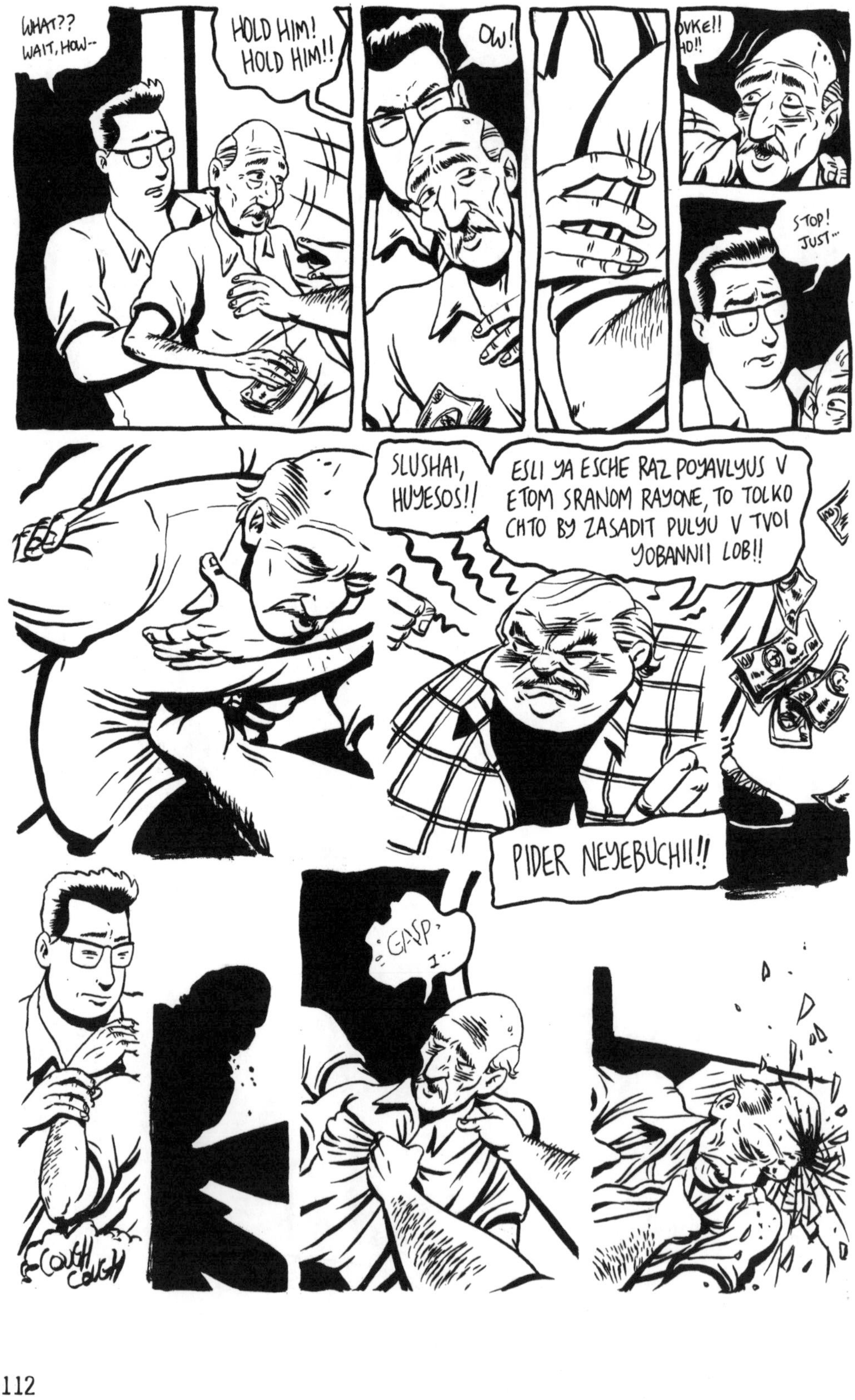
WHAT?? WAIT, HOW--
HOLD HIM! HOLD HIM!!
OW!
STOP! JUST...
SLUSHAI, HUYESOS!!
ESLI YA ESCHE RAZ POYAVLYUS V ETOM SRANOM RAYONE, TO TOLKO CHTO BY ZASADIT PULYU V TVOI YOBANNII LOB!!
PIDER NEYEBUCH!!!!
COUGH COUGH
GASP, I..

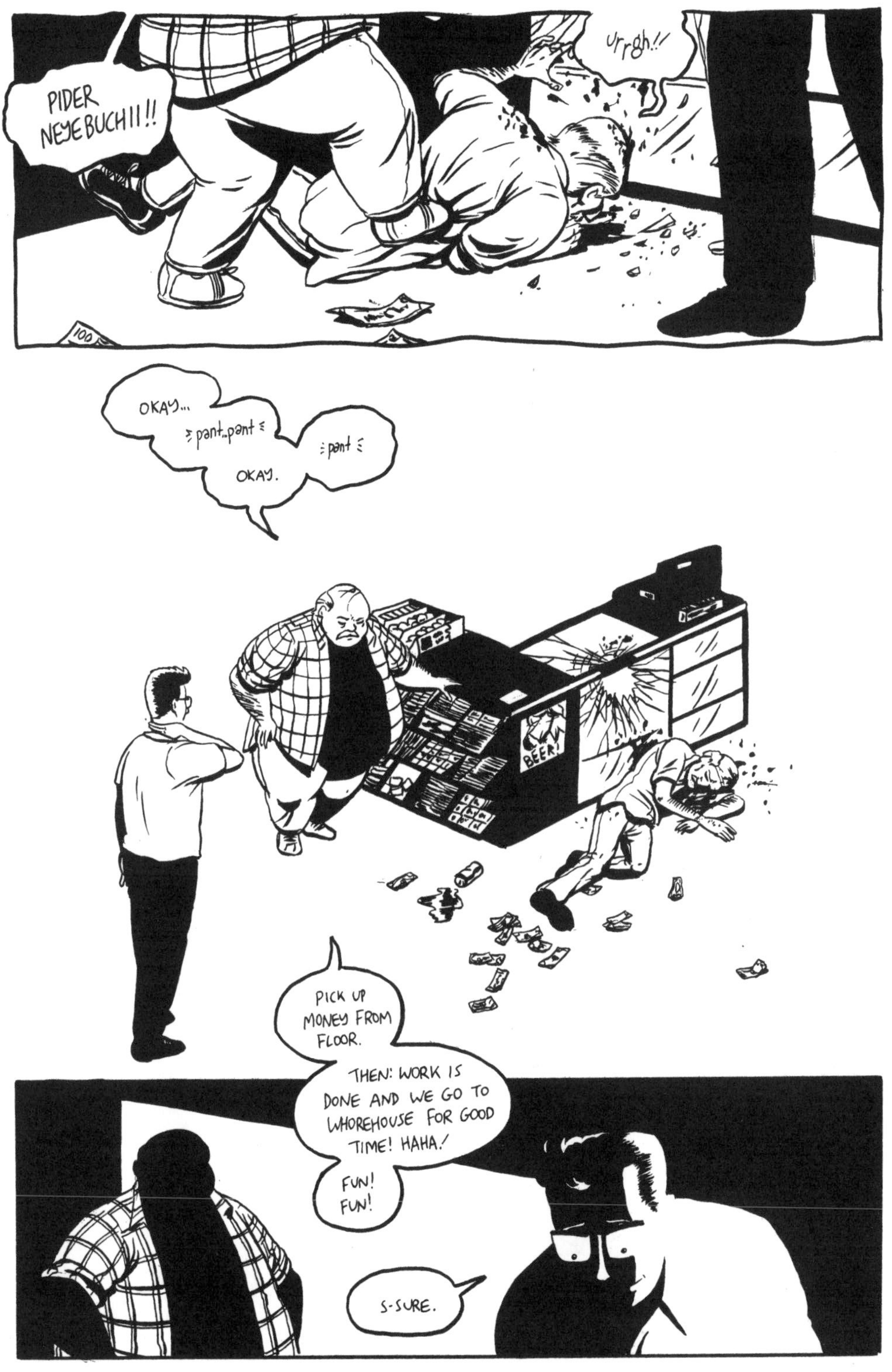
PIDER NEYEBUCH!!!!
urrgh!!
OKAY... pant..pant pant OKAY.
PICK UP MONEY FROM FLOOR.
THEN: WORK IS DONE AND WE GO TO WHOREHOUSE FOR GOOD TIME! HAHA!
FUN! FUN!
S-SURE.

THIRTY-FIVE

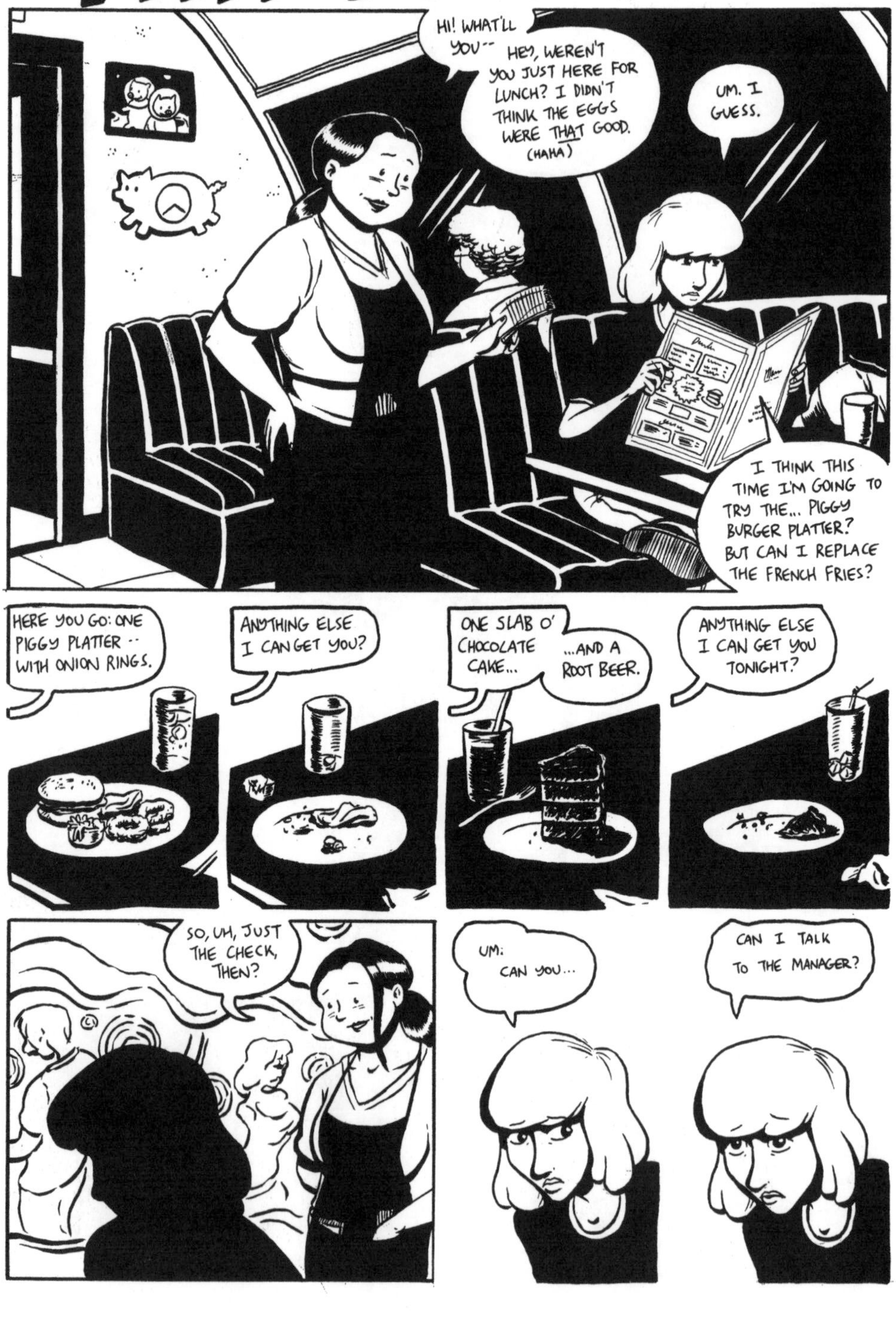
HI! WHAT'LL YOU--
HEY, WEREN'T YOU JUST HERE FOR LUNCH? I DIDN'T THINK THE EGGS WERE THAT GOOD. (HAHA)
UM. I GUESS.
I THINK THIS TIME I'M GOING TO TRY THE... PIGGY BURGER PLATTER? BUT CAN I REPLACE THE FRENCH FRIES?
HERE YOU GO: ONE PIGGY PLATTER -- WITH ONION RINGS.
ANYTHING ELSE I CAN GET YOU?
ONE SLAB O' CHOCOLATE CAKE...
...AND A ROOT BEER.
ANYTHING ELSE I CAN GET YOU TONIGHT?
SO, UH, JUST THE CHECK, THEN?
UM: CAN YOU...
CAN I TALK TO THE MANAGER?

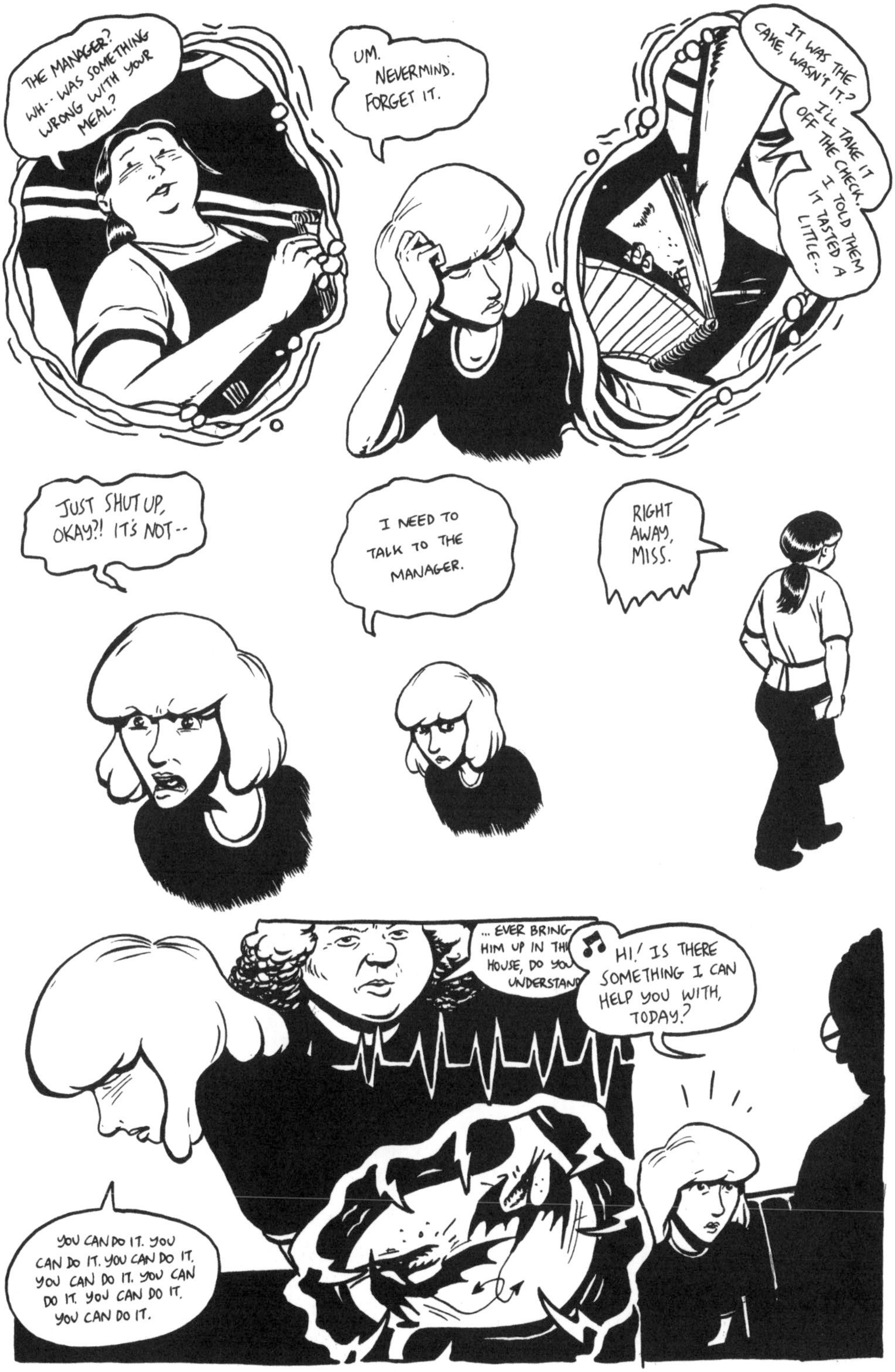
THE MANAGER? WH-- WAS SOMETHING WRONG WITH YOUR MEAL?
UM. NEVERMIND. FORGET IT.
IT WAS THE CAKE, WASN'T IT? I'LL TAKE IT OFF THE CHECK. I TOLD THEM IT TASTED A LITTLE..
JUST SHUT UP, OKAY?! IT'S NOT--
I NEED TO TALK TO THE MANAGER.
RIGHT AWAY, MISS.
... EVER BRING HIM UP IN THI HOUSE, DO YOU UNDERSTAND
HI! IS THERE SOMETHING I CAN HELP YOU WITH, TODAY?
YOU CAN DO IT. YOU CAN DO IT. YOU CAN DO IT. YOU CAN DO IT. YOU CAN DO IT. YOU CAN DO IT. YOU CAN DO IT.

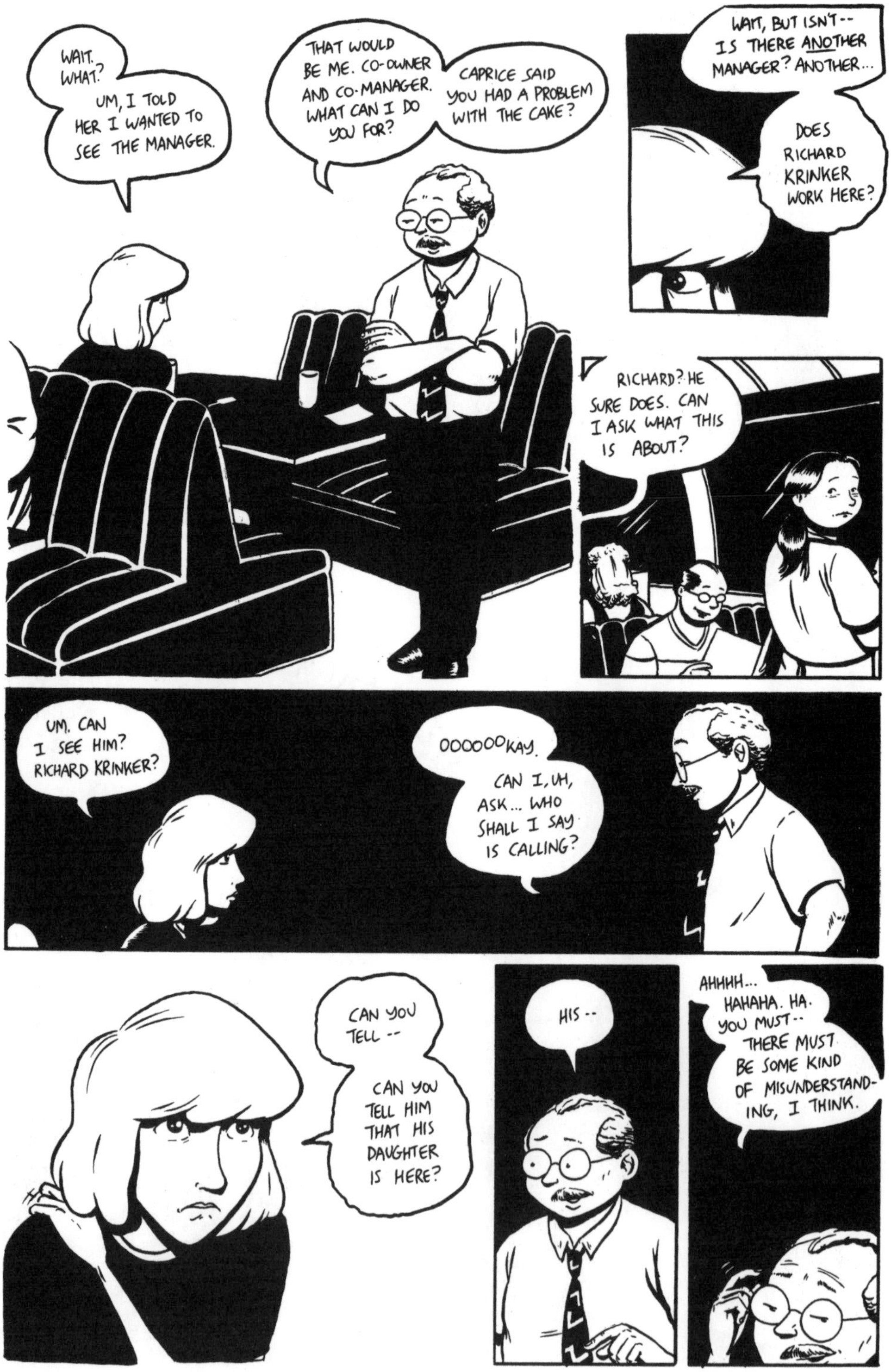
WAIT. WHAT?
UM, I TOLD HER I WANTED TO SEE THE MANAGER.
THAT WOULD BE ME. CO-OWNER AND CO-MANAGER. WHAT CAN I DO YOU FOR?
CAPRICE SAID YOU HAD A PROBLEM WITH THE CAKE?
WAIT, BUT ISN'T -- IS THERE ANOTHER MANAGER? ANOTHER...
DOES RICHARD KRINKER WORK HERE?
RICHARD? HE SURE DOES. CAN I ASK WHAT THIS IS ABOUT?
UM. CAN I SEE HIM? RICHARD KRINKER?
OOOOOOKAY.
CAN I, UH, ASK... WHO SHALL I SAY IS CALLING?
CAN YOU TELL --
CAN YOU TELL HIM THAT HIS DAUGHTER IS HERE?
HIS --
AHHHH... HAHAHA. HA. YOU MUST -- THERE MUST BE SOME KIND OF MISUNDERSTAND-ING, I THINK.

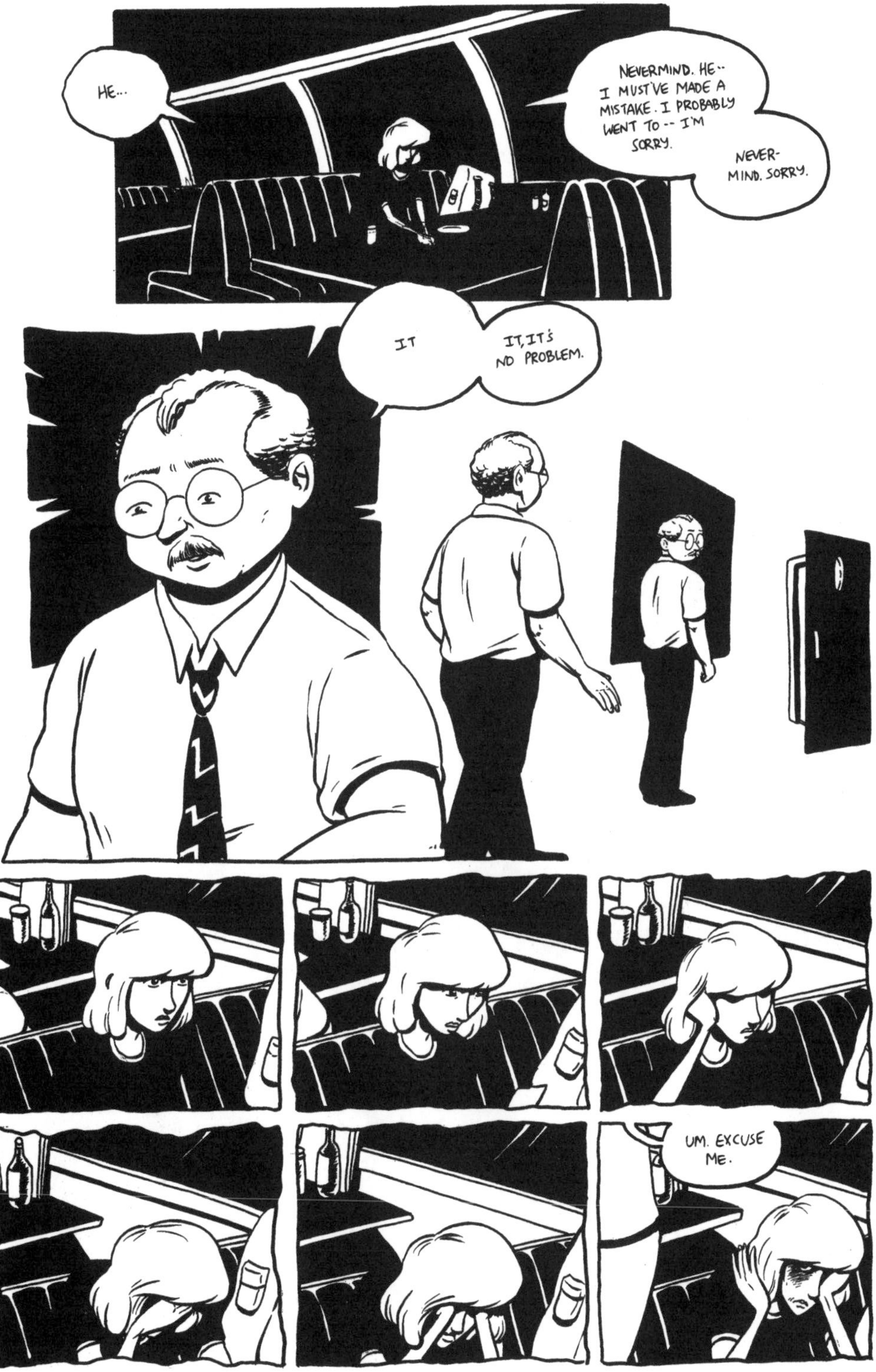
HE...
NEVERMIND. HE-- I MUST'VE MADE A MISTAKE. I PROBABLY WENT TO -- I'M SORRY.
NEVER-MIND. SORRY.
IT
IT, IT'S NO PROBLEM.
UM. EXCUSE ME.

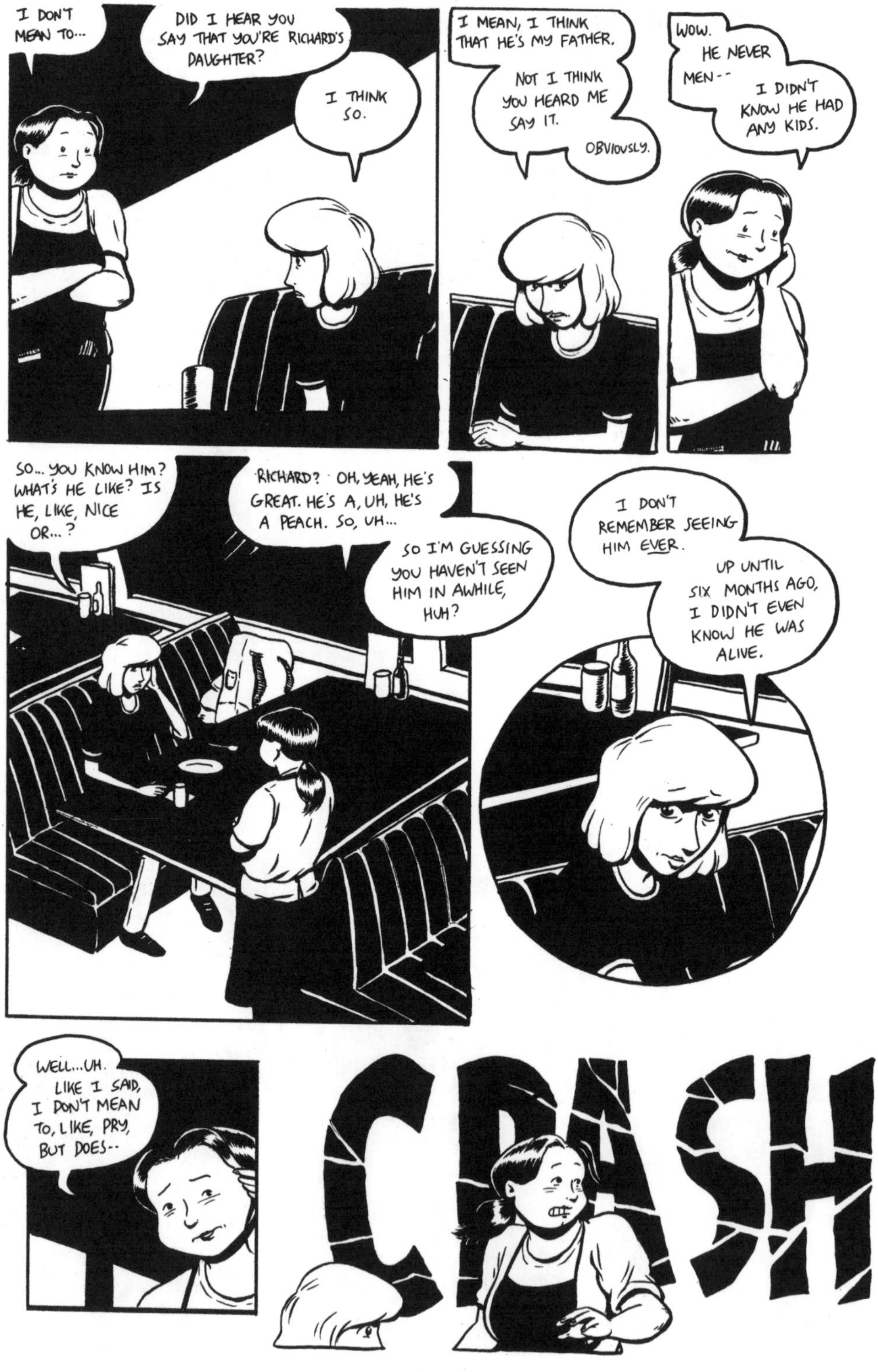

I DON'T MEAN TO...
DID I HEAR YOU SAY THAT YOU'RE RICHARD'S DAUGHTER?
I THINK SO.
I MEAN, I THINK THAT HE'S MY FATHER.
NOT I THINK YOU HEARD ME SAY IT.
OBVIOUSLY.
WOW.
HE NEVER MEN--
I DIDN'T KNOW HE HAD ANY KIDS.
SO... YOU KNOW HIM? WHAT'S HE LIKE? IS HE, LIKE, NICE OR...?
RICHARD? OH, YEAH, HE'S GREAT. HE'S A, UH, HE'S A PEACH. SO, UH...
SO I'M GUESSING YOU HAVEN'T SEEN HIM IN AWHILE, HUH?
I DON'T REMEMBER SEEING HIM EVER.
UP UNTIL SIX MONTHS AGO, I DIDN'T EVEN KNOW HE WAS ALIVE.
WELL...UH. LIKE I SAID, I DON'T MEAN TO, LIKE, PRY, BUT DOES--
CRASH

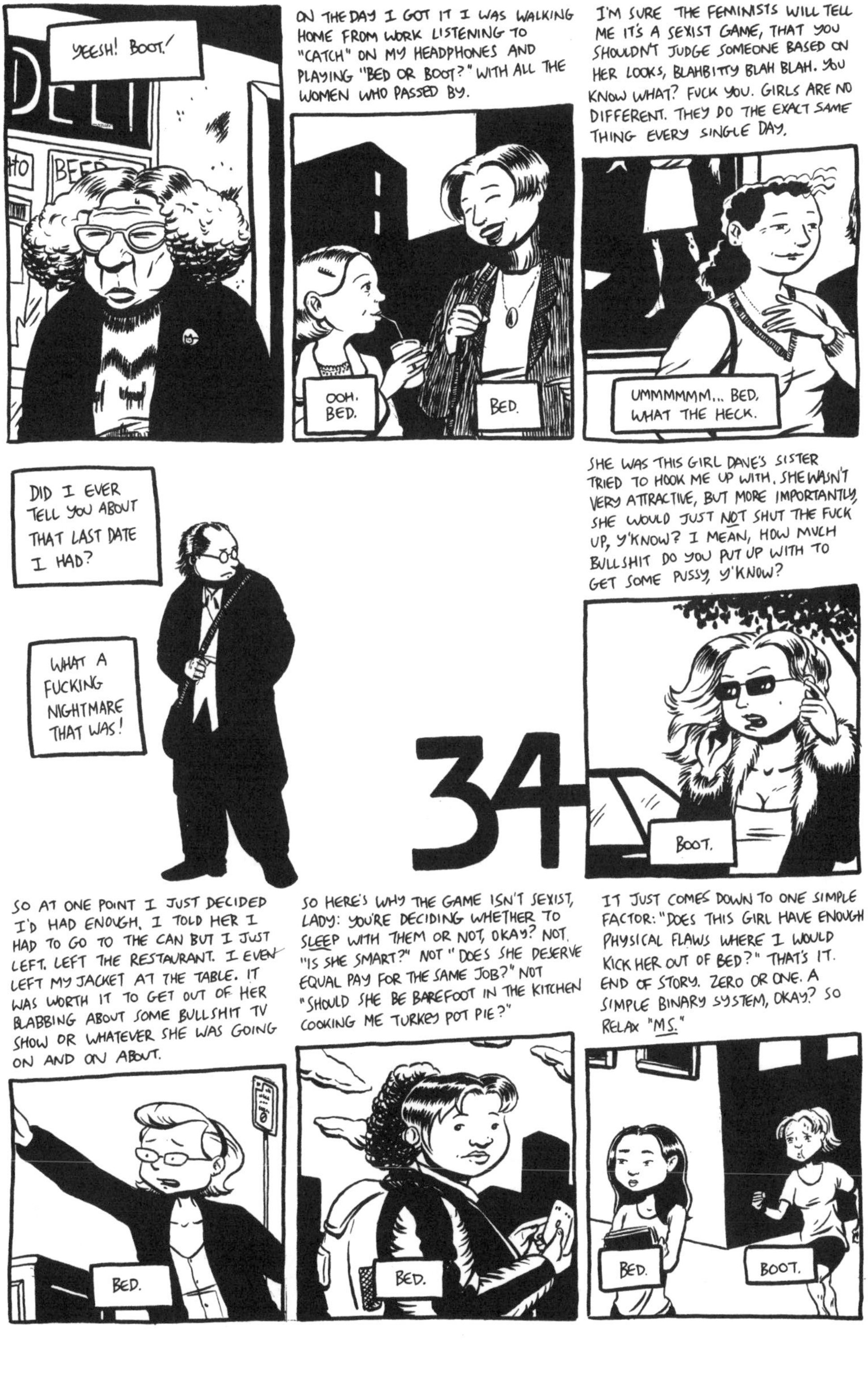
YEESH! BOOT!
DELI
BEER
ON THE DAY I GOT IT I WAS WALKING HOME FROM WORK LISTENING TO "CATCH" ON MY HEADPHONES AND PLAYING "BED OR BOOT?" WITH ALL THE WOMEN WHO PASSED BY.
OOH. BED.
BED.
I'M SURE THE FEMINISTS WILL TELL ME IT'S A SEXIST GAME, THAT YOU SHOULDN'T JUDGE SOMEONE BASED ON HER LOOKS, BLAHBITTY BLAH BLAH. YOU KNOW WHAT? FUCK YOU. GIRLS ARE NO DIFFERENT. THEY DO THE EXACT SAME THING EVERY SINGLE DAY.
UMMMMMM... BED. WHAT THE HECK.
DID I EVER TELL YOU ABOUT THAT LAST DATE I HAD?
WHAT A FUCKING NIGHTMARE THAT WAS!
34
SHE WAS THIS GIRL DAVE'S SISTER TRIED TO HOOK ME UP WITH. SHE WASN'T VERY ATTRACTIVE, BUT MORE IMPORTANTLY, SHE WOULD JUST NOT SHUT THE FUCK UP, Y'KNOW? I MEAN, HOW MUCH BULLSHIT DO YOU PUT UP WITH TO GET SOME PUSSY, Y'KNOW?
BOOT.
SO AT ONE POINT I JUST DECIDED I'D HAD ENOUGH. I TOLD HER I HAD TO GO TO THE CAN BUT I JUST LEFT. LEFT THE RESTAURANT. I EVEN LEFT MY JACKET AT THE TABLE. IT WAS WORTH IT TO GET OUT OF HER BLABBING ABOUT SOME BULLSHIT TV SHOW OR WHATEVER SHE WAS GOING ON AND ON ABOUT.
BED.
SO HERE'S WHY THE GAME ISN'T SEXIST, LADY: YOU'RE DECIDING WHETHER TO SLEEP WITH THEM OR NOT, OKAY? NOT "IS SHE SMART?" NOT "DOES SHE DESERVE EQUAL PAY FOR THE SAME JOB?" NOT "SHOULD SHE BE BAREFOOT IN THE KITCHEN COOKING ME TURKEY POT PIE?"
BED.
IT JUST COMES DOWN TO ONE SIMPLE FACTOR: "DOES THIS GIRL HAVE ENOUGH PHYSICAL FLAWS WHERE I WOULD KICK HER OUT OF BED?" THAT'S IT. END OF STORY. ZERO OR ONE. A SIMPLE BINARY SYSTEM, OKAY? SO RELAX "MS."
BED.
BOOT.

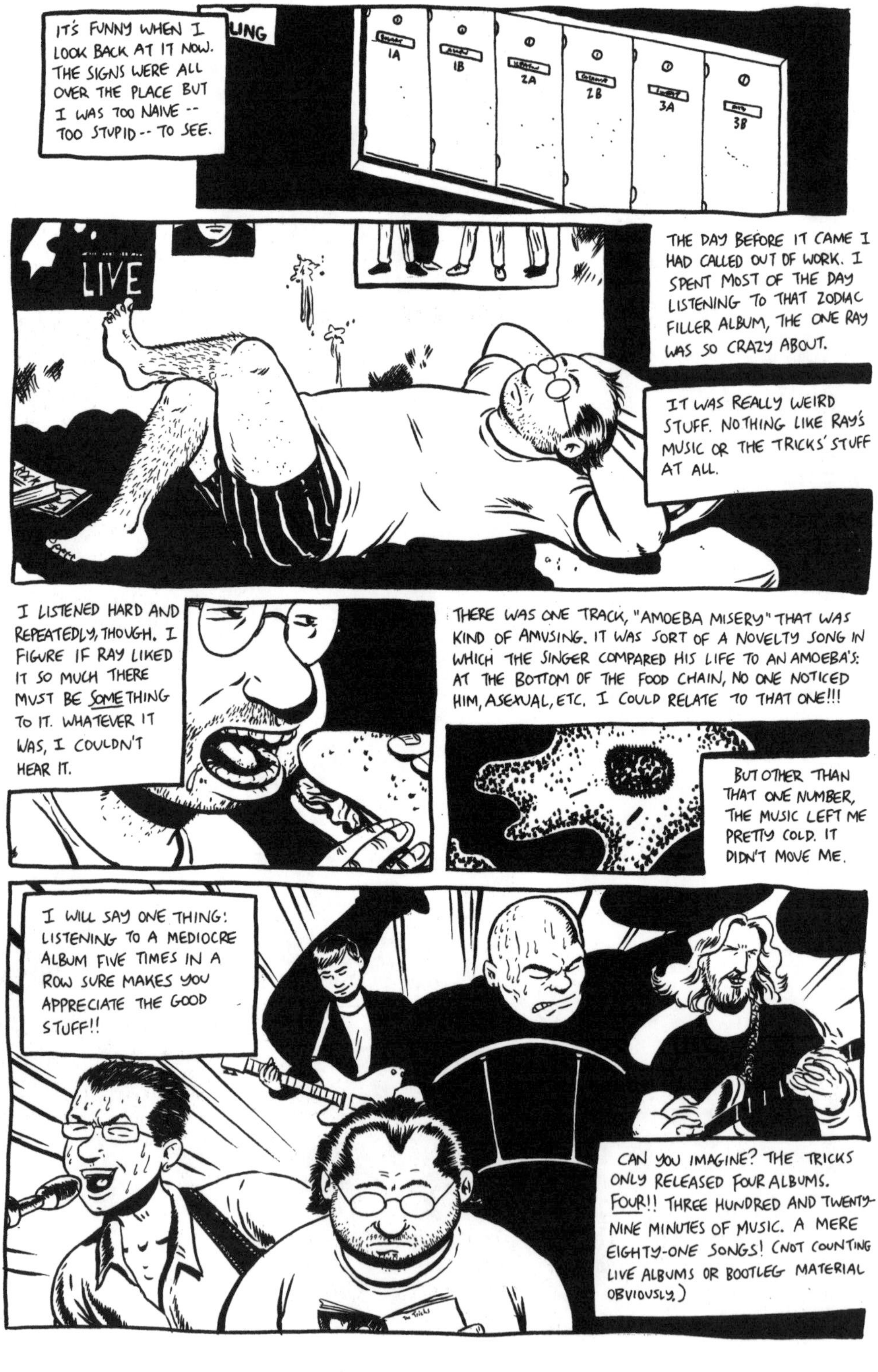
IT'S FUNNY WHEN I LOOK BACK AT IT NOW. THE SIGNS WERE ALL OVER THE PLACE BUT I WAS TOO NAIVE -- TOO STUPID -- TO SEE.
LING
1A
1B
2A
2B
3A
3B
THE DAY BEFORE IT CAME I HAD CALLED OUT OF WORK. I SPENT MOST OF THE DAY LISTENING TO THAT ZODIAC FILLER ALBUM, THE ONE RAY WAS SO CRAZY ABOUT.
LIVE
IT WAS REALLY WEIRD STUFF. NOTHING LIKE RAY'S MUSIC OR THE TRICKS' STUFF AT ALL.
I LISTENED HARD AND REPEATEDLY, THOUGH. I FIGURE IF RAY LIKED IT SO MUCH THERE MUST BE SOMETHING TO IT. WHATEVER IT WAS, I COULDN'T HEAR IT.
THERE WAS ONE TRACK, "AMOEBA MISERY" THAT WAS KIND OF AMUSING. IT WAS SORT OF A NOVELTY SONG IN WHICH THE SINGER COMPARED HIS LIFE TO AN AMOEBA'S: AT THE BOTTOM OF THE FOOD CHAIN, NO ONE NOTICED HIM, ASEXUAL, ETC. I COULD RELATE TO THAT ONE!!!
BUT OTHER THAN THAT ONE NUMBER, THE MUSIC LEFT ME PRETTY COLD. IT DIDN'T MOVE ME.
I WILL SAY ONE THING: LISTENING TO A MEDIOCRE ALBUM FIVE TIMES IN A ROW SURE MAKES YOU APPRECIATE THE GOOD STUFF!!
CAN YOU IMAGINE? THE TRICKS ONLY RELEASED FOUR ALBUMS. FOUR!! THREE HUNDRED AND TWENTY-NINE MINUTES OF MUSIC. A MERE EIGHTY-ONE SONGS! (NOT COUNTING LIVE ALBUMS OR BOOTLEG MATERIAL OBVIOUSLY.)

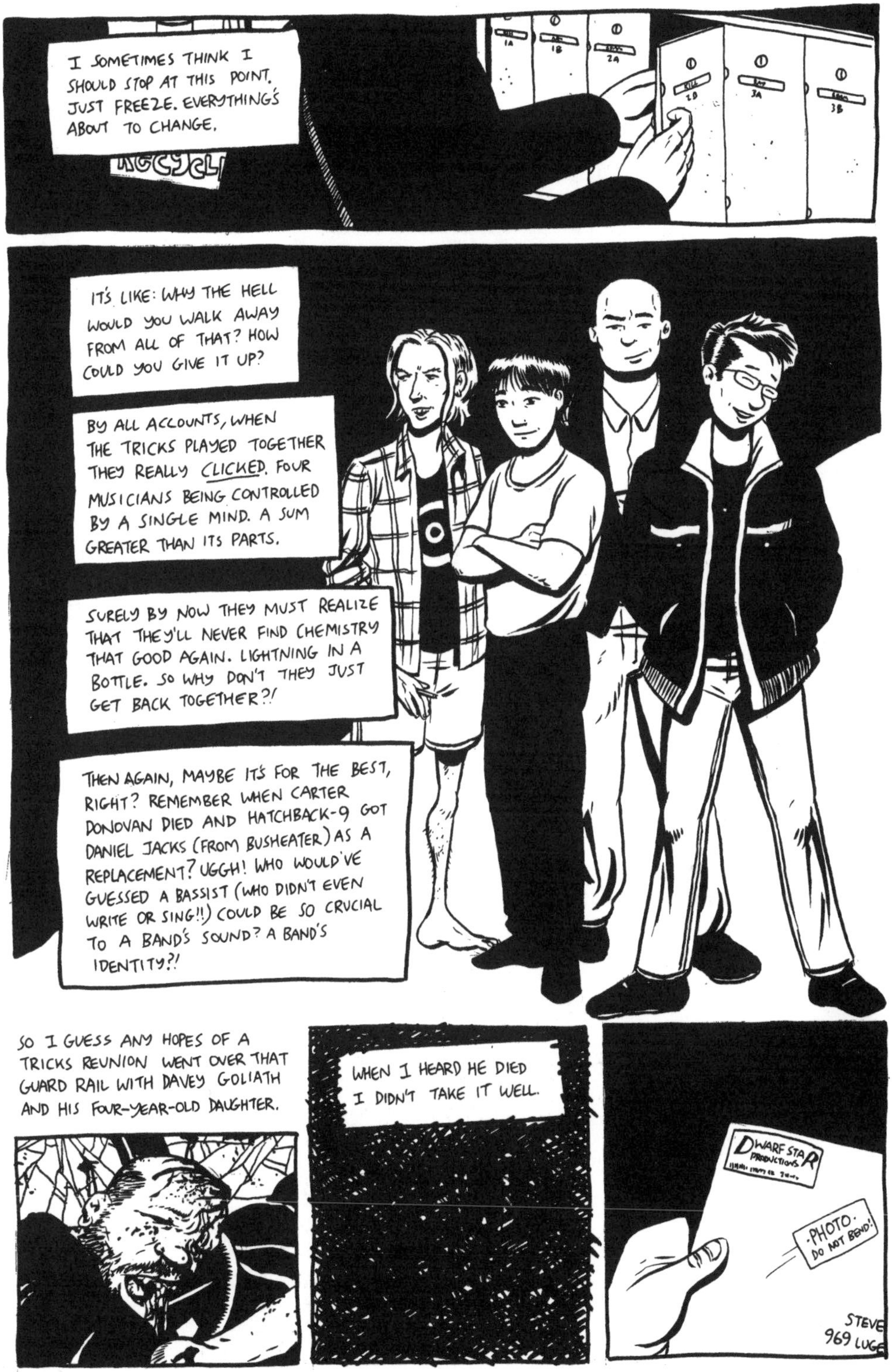
I SOMETIMES THINK I SHOULD STOP AT THIS POINT. JUST FREEZE. EVERYTHING'S ABOUT TO CHANGE.
IT'S LIKE: WHY THE HELL WOULD YOU WALK AWAY FROM ALL OF THAT? HOW COULD YOU GIVE IT UP?
BY ALL ACCOUNTS, WHEN THE TRICKS PLAYED TOGETHER THEY REALLY CLICKED. FOUR MUSICIANS BEING CONTROLLED BY A SINGLE MIND. A SUM GREATER THAN ITS PARTS.
SURELY BY NOW THEY MUST REALIZE THAT THEY'LL NEVER FIND CHEMISTRY THAT GOOD AGAIN. LIGHTNING IN A BOTTLE. SO WHY DON'T THEY JUST GET BACK TOGETHER?!
THEN AGAIN, MAYBE IT'S FOR THE BEST, RIGHT? REMEMBER WHEN CARTER DONOVAN DIED AND HATCHBACK-9 GOT DANIEL JACKS (FROM BUSHEATER) AS A REPLACEMENT? UGGH! WHO WOULD'VE GUESSED A BASSIST (WHO DIDN'T EVEN WRITE OR SING!!) COULD BE SO CRUCIAL TO A BAND'S SOUND? A BAND'S IDENTITY?!
SO I GUESS ANY HOPES OF A TRICKS REUNION WENT OVER THAT GUARD RAIL WITH DAVEY GOLIATH AND HIS FOUR-YEAR-OLD DAUGHTER.
WHEN I HEARD HE DIED I DIDN'T TAKE IT WELL.
DWARF STAR PRODUCTIONS
PHOTO
DO NOT BEND!
STEVE

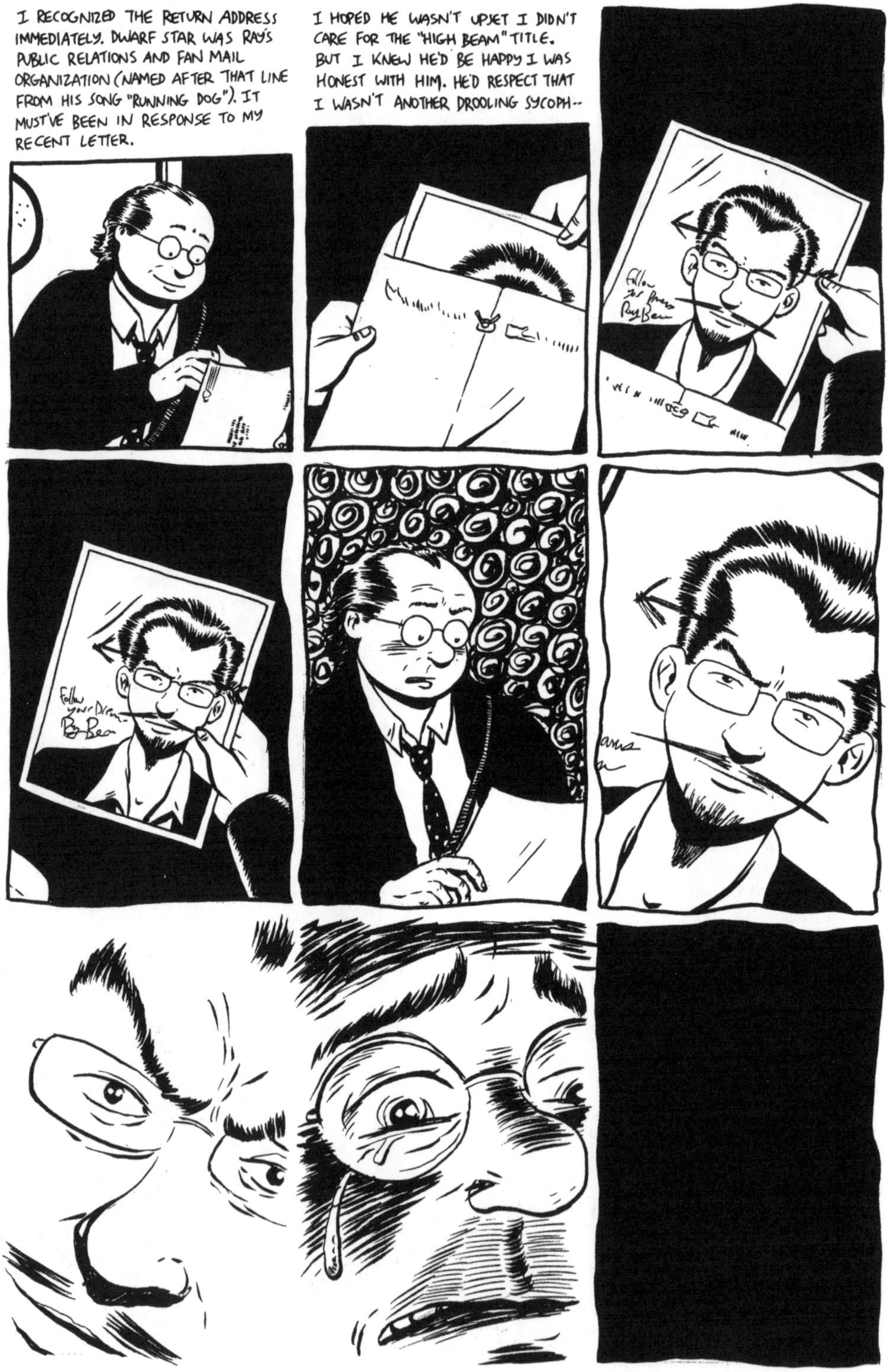
I RECOGNIZED THE RETURN ADDRESS IMMEDIATELY. DWARF STAR WAS RAY'S PUBLIC RELATIONS AND FAN MAIL ORGANIZATION (NAMED AFTER THAT LINE FROM HIS SONG "RUNNING DOG"). IT MUST'VE BEEN IN RESPONSE TO MY RECENT LETTER.
I HOPED HE WASN'T UPSET I DIDN'T CARE FOR THE "HIGH BEAM" TITLE. BUT I KNEW HE'D BE HAPPY I WAS HONEST WITH HIM. HE'D RESPECT THAT I WASN'T ANOTHER DROOLING SYCOPH--

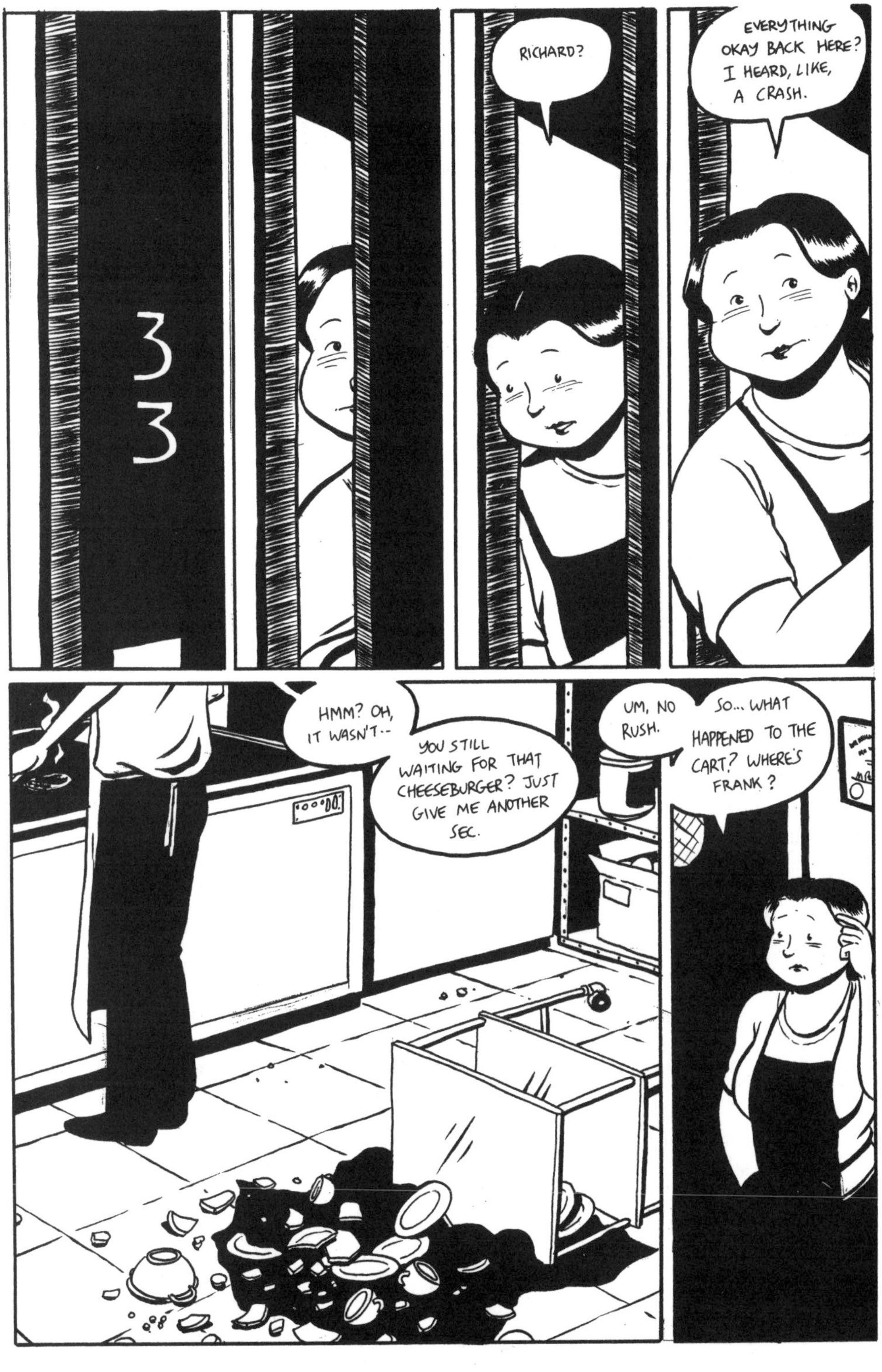
RICHARD?
EVERYTHING OKAY BACK HERE? I HEARD, LIKE, A CRASH.
HMM? OH, IT WASN'T.-
YOU STILL WAITING FOR THAT CHEESEBURGER? JUST GIVE ME ANOTHER SEC.
UM, NO RUSH.
SO... WHAT HAPPENED TO THE CART? WHERE'S FRANK?

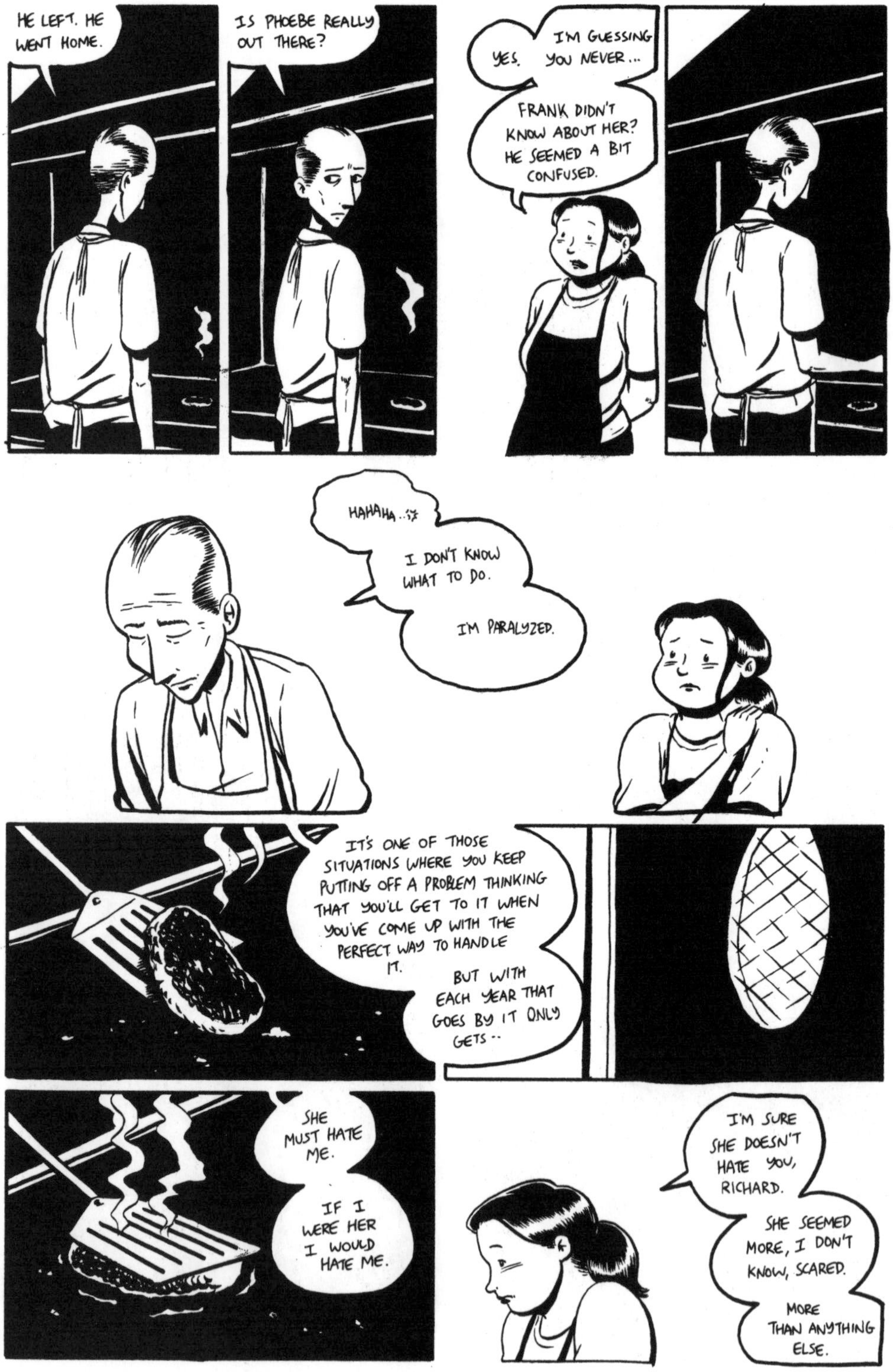

HE LEFT. HE WENT HOME.
IS PHOEBE REALLY OUT THERE?
YES.
I'M GUESSING YOU NEVER...
FRANK DIDN'T KNOW ABOUT HER? HE SEEMED A BIT CONFUSED.
HAHAHA..
I DON'T KNOW WHAT TO DO.
I'M PARALYZED.
IT'S ONE OF THOSE SITUATIONS WHERE YOU KEEP PUTTING OFF A PROBLEM THINKING THAT YOU'LL GET TO IT WHEN YOU'VE COME UP WITH THE PERFECT WAY TO HANDLE IT.
BUT WITH EACH YEAR THAT GOES BY IT ONLY GETS..
SHE MUST HATE ME.
IF I WERE HER I WOULD HATE ME.
I'M SURE SHE DOESN'T HATE YOU, RICHARD.
SHE SEEMED MORE, I DON'T KNOW, SCARED.
MORE THAN ANYTHING ELSE.

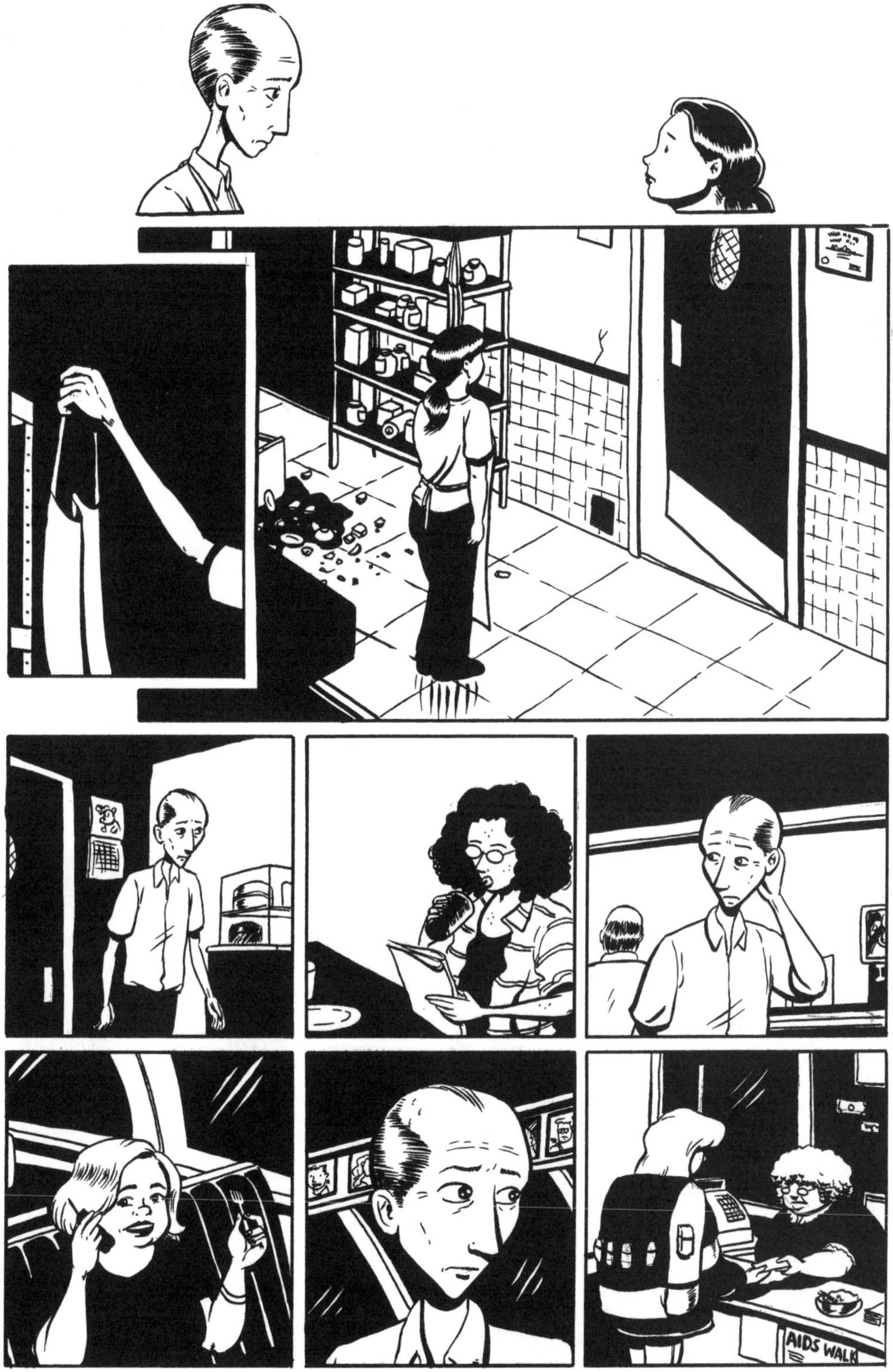
AIDS WALK

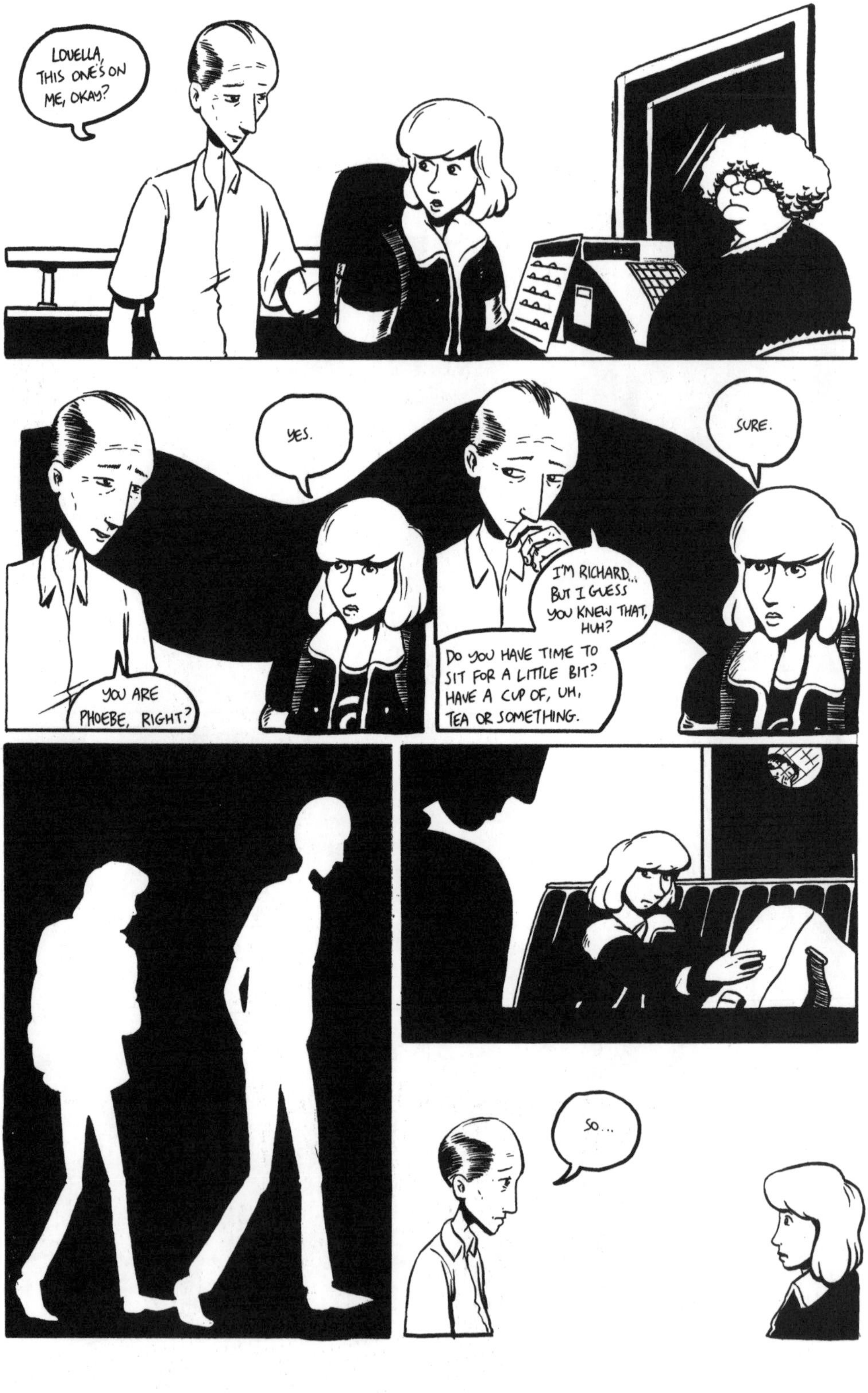
LOUELLA, THIS ONE'S ON ME, OKAY?
YOU ARE PHOEBE, RIGHT?
YES.
I'M RICHARD... BUT I GUESS YOU KNEW THAT, HUH?
DO YOU HAVE TIME TO SIT FOR A LITTLE BIT? HAVE A CUP OF, UH, TEA OR SOMETHING.
SURE.
SO...

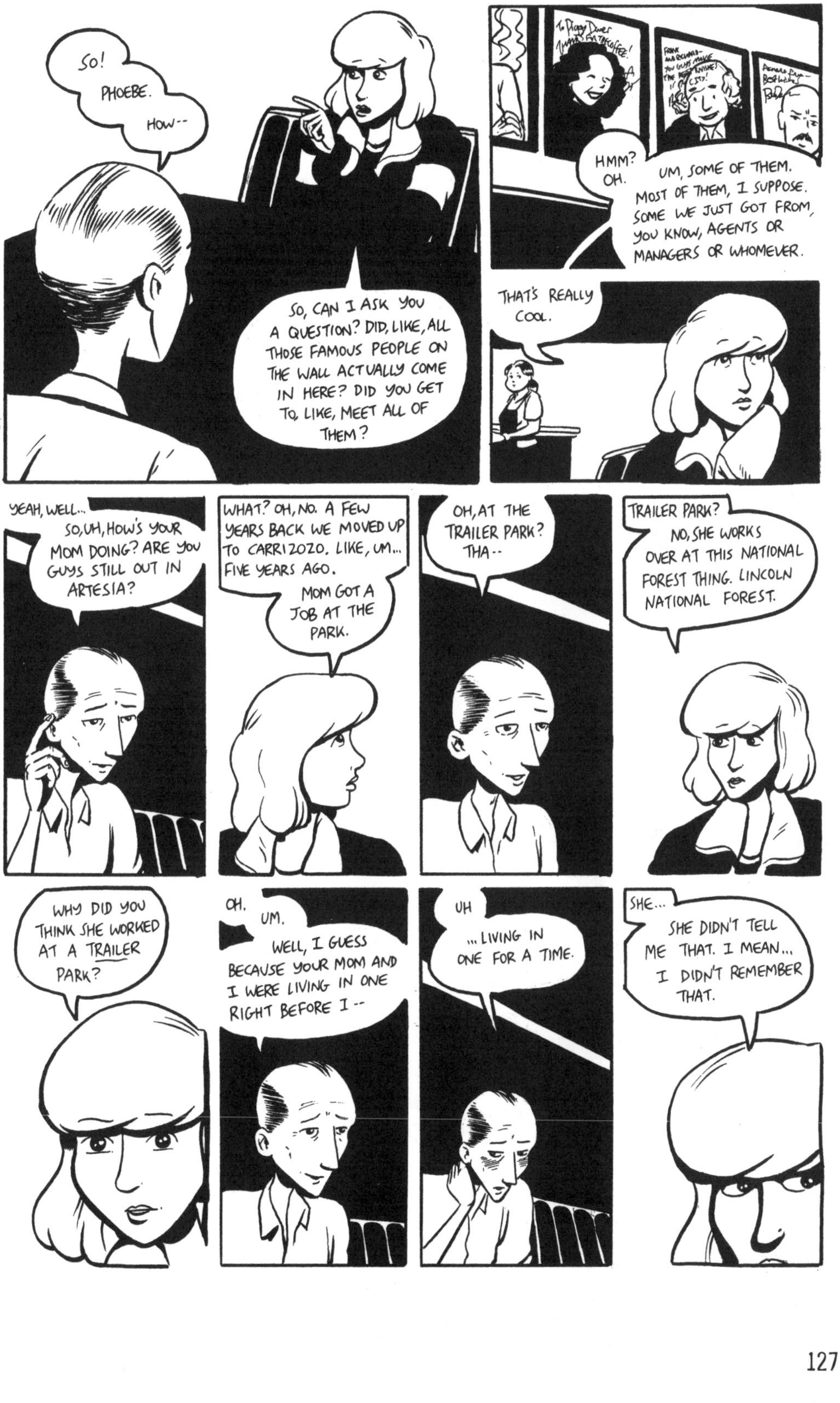
SO! PHOEBE. HOW--
SO, CAN I ASK YOU A QUESTION? DID, LIKE, ALL THOSE FAMOUS PEOPLE ON THE WALL ACTUALLY COME IN HERE? DID YOU GET TO, LIKE, MEET ALL OF THEM?
HMM? OH.
UM, SOME OF THEM. MOST OF THEM, I SUPPOSE. SOME WE JUST GOT FROM, YOU KNOW, AGENTS OR MANAGERS OR WHOMEVER.
THAT'S REALLY COOL.
YEAH, WELL...
SO, UH, HOW'S YOUR MOM DOING? ARE YOU GUYS STILL OUT IN ARTESIA?
WHAT? OH, NO. A FEW YEARS BACK WE MOVED UP TO CARRIZOZO. LIKE, UM... FIVE YEARS AGO.
MOM GOT A JOB AT THE PARK.
OH, AT THE TRAILER PARK? THA--
TRAILER PARK?
NO, SHE WORKS OVER AT THIS NATIONAL FOREST THING. LINCOLN NATIONAL FOREST.
WHY DID YOU THINK SHE WORKED AT A TRAILER PARK?
OH.
UM.
WELL, I GUESS BECAUSE YOUR MOM AND I WERE LIVING IN ONE RIGHT BEFORE I--
UH
...LIVING IN ONE FOR A TIME.
SHE...
SHE DIDN'T TELL ME THAT. I MEAN... I DIDN'T REMEMBER THAT.

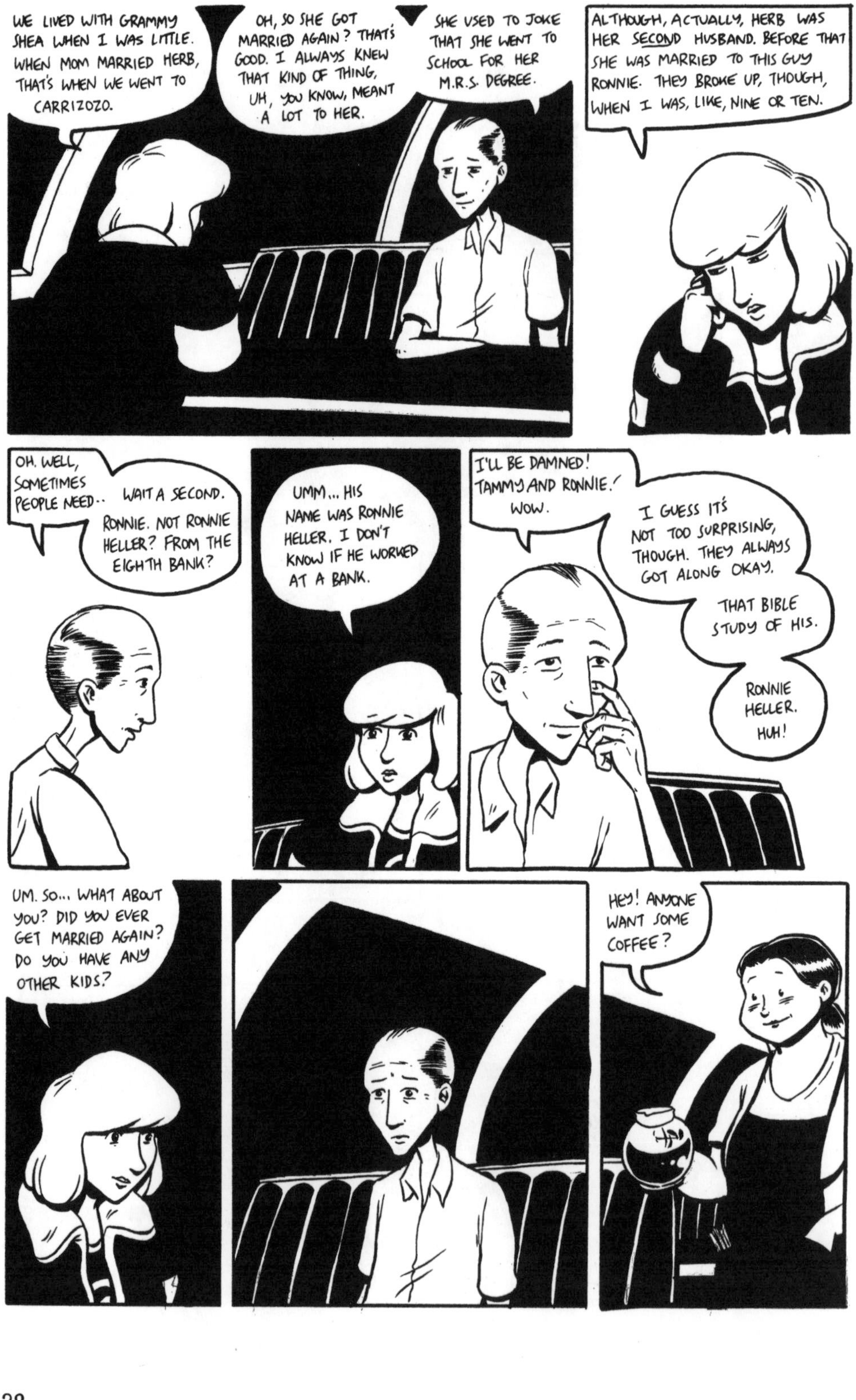
WE LIVED WITH GRAMMY SHEA WHEN I WAS LITTLE. WHEN MOM MARRIED HERB, THAT'S WHEN WE WENT TO CARRIZOZO.
OH, SO SHE GOT MARRIED AGAIN? THAT'S GOOD. I ALWAYS KNEW THAT KIND OF THING, UH, YOU KNOW, MEANT A LOT TO HER.
SHE USED TO JOKE THAT SHE WENT TO SCHOOL FOR HER M.R.S. DEGREE.
ALTHOUGH, ACTUALLY, HERB WAS HER SECOND HUSBAND. BEFORE THAT SHE WAS MARRIED TO THIS GUY RONNIE. THEY BROKE UP, THOUGH, WHEN I WAS, LIKE, NINE OR TEN.
OH. WELL, SOMETIMES PEOPLE NEED..
WAIT A SECOND. RONNIE. NOT RONNIE HELLER? FROM THE EIGHTH BANK?
UMM... HIS NAME WAS RONNIE HELLER. I DON'T KNOW IF HE WORKED AT A BANK.
I'LL BE DAMNED! TAMMY AND RONNIE! WOW.
I GUESS IT'S NOT TOO SURPRISING, THOUGH. THEY ALWAYS GOT ALONG OKAY.
THAT BIBLE STUDY OF HIS.
RONNIE HELLER. HUH!
UM. SO... WHAT ABOUT YOU? DID YOU EVER GET MARRIED AGAIN? DO YOU HAVE ANY OTHER KIDS?
HEY! ANYONE WANT SOME COFFEE?

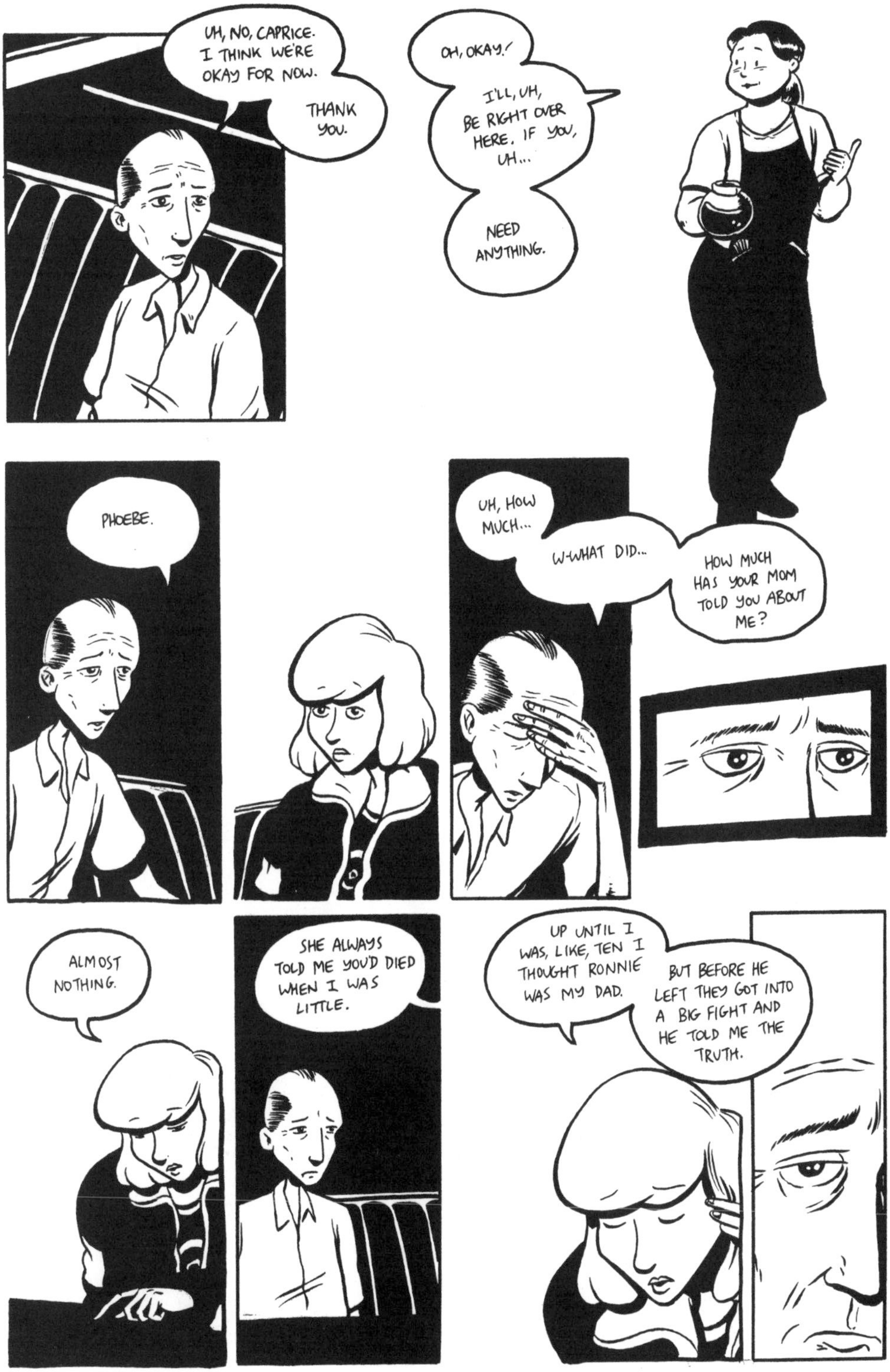
UH, NO, CAPRICE. I THINK WE'RE OKAY FOR NOW.
THANK YOU.
OH, OKAY!
I'LL, UH, BE RIGHT OVER HERE. IF YOU, UH...
NEED ANYTHING.
PHOEBE.
UH, HOW MUCH...
W-WHAT DID...
HOW MUCH HAS YOUR MOM TOLD YOU ABOUT ME?
ALMOST NOTHING.
SHE ALWAYS TOLD ME YOU'D DIED WHEN I WAS LITTLE.
UP UNTIL I WAS, LIKE, TEN I THOUGHT RONNIE WAS MY DAD.
BUT BEFORE HE LEFT THEY GOT INTO A BIG FIGHT AND HE TOLD ME THE TRUTH.

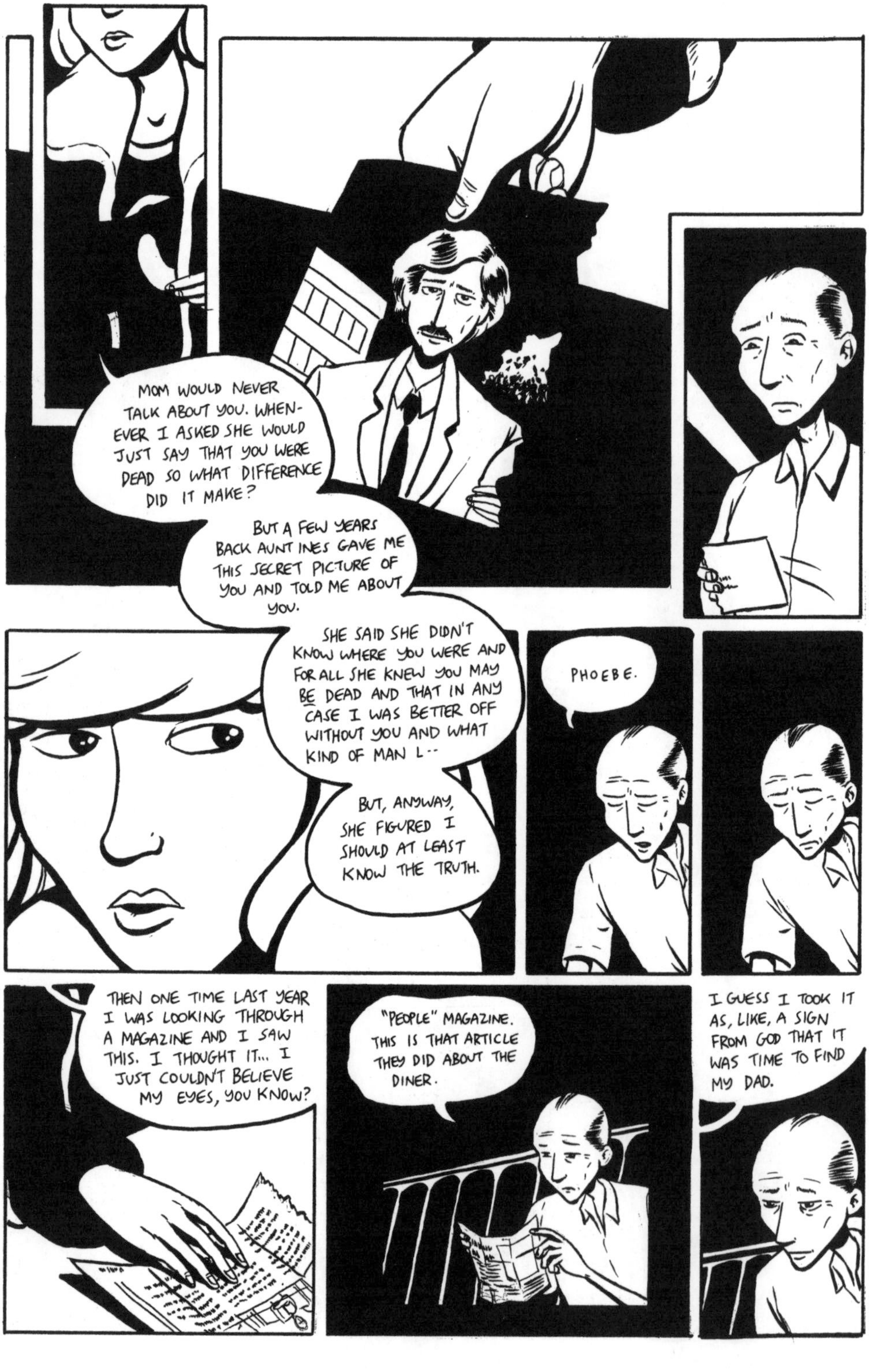
MOM WOULD NEVER TALK ABOUT YOU. WHEN-EVER I ASKED SHE WOULD JUST SAY THAT YOU WERE DEAD SO WHAT DIFFERENCE DID IT MAKE?
BUT A FEW YEARS BACK AUNT INES GAVE ME THIS SECRET PICTURE OF YOU AND TOLD ME ABOUT YOU.
SHE SAID SHE DIDN'T KNOW WHERE YOU WERE AND FOR ALL SHE KNEW YOU MAY BE DEAD AND THAT IN ANY CASE I WAS BETTER OFF WITHOUT YOU AND WHAT KIND OF MAN L--
BUT, ANYWAY, SHE FIGURED I SHOULD AT LEAST KNOW THE TRUTH.
PHOEBE.
THEN ONE TIME LAST YEAR I WAS LOOKING THROUGH A MAGAZINE AND I SAW THIS. I THOUGHT IT... I JUST COULDN'T BELIEVE MY EYES, YOU KNOW?
"PEOPLE" MAGAZINE. THIS IS THAT ARTICLE THEY DID ABOUT THE DINER.
I GUESS I TOOK IT AS, LIKE, A SIGN FROM GOD THAT IT WAS TIME TO FIND MY DAD.

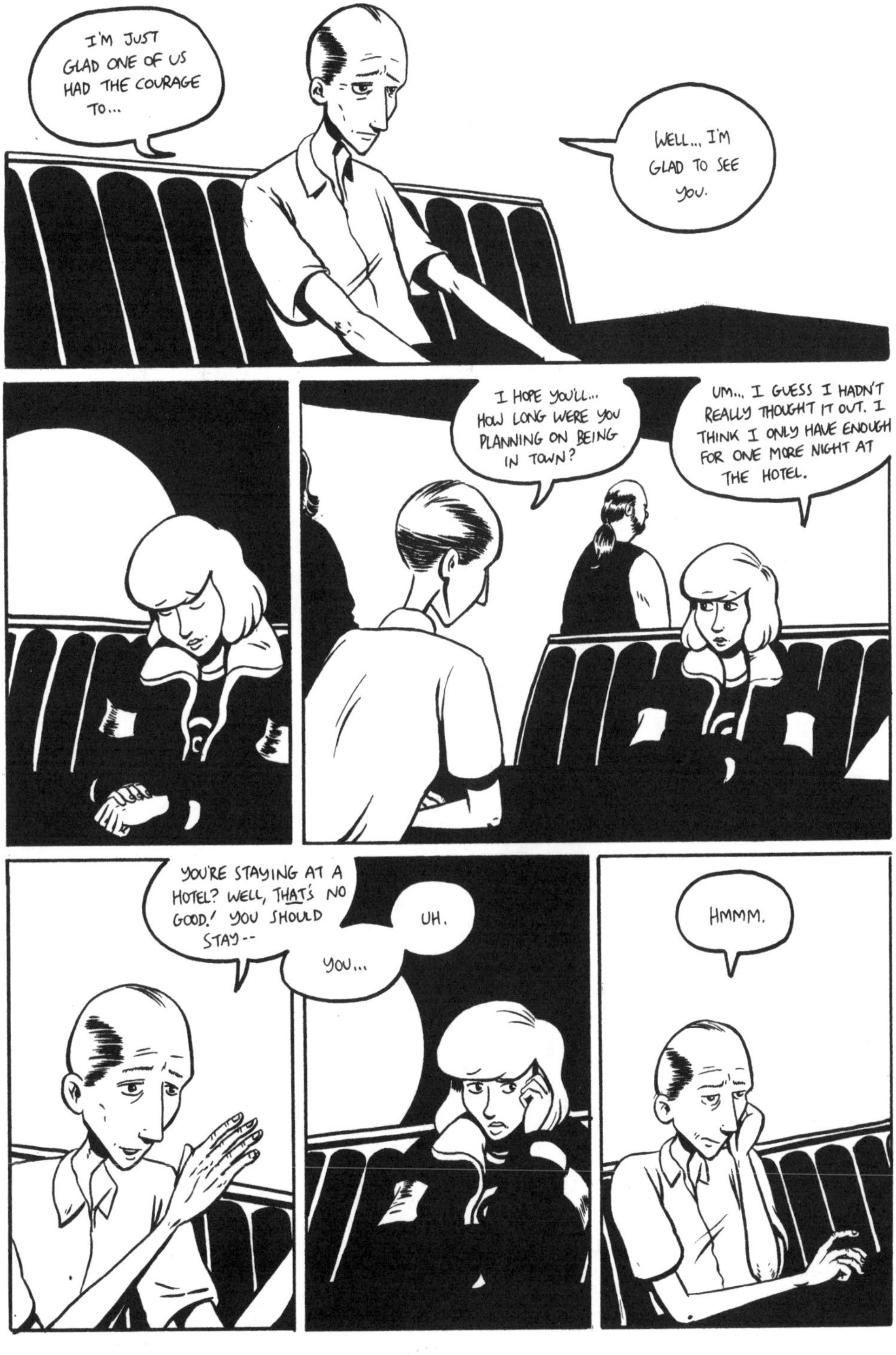
I'M JUST GLAD ONE OF US HAD THE COURAGE TO...
WELL... I'M GLAD TO SEE YOU.
I HOPE YOU'LL... HOW LONG WERE YOU PLANNING ON BEING IN TOWN?
UM... I GUESS I HADN'T REALLY THOUGHT IT OUT. I THINK I ONLY HAVE ENOUGH FOR ONE MORE NIGHT AT THE HOTEL.
YOU'RE STAYING AT A HOTEL? WELL, THAT'S NO GOOD! YOU SHOULD STAY--
UH.
YOU...
HMMM.

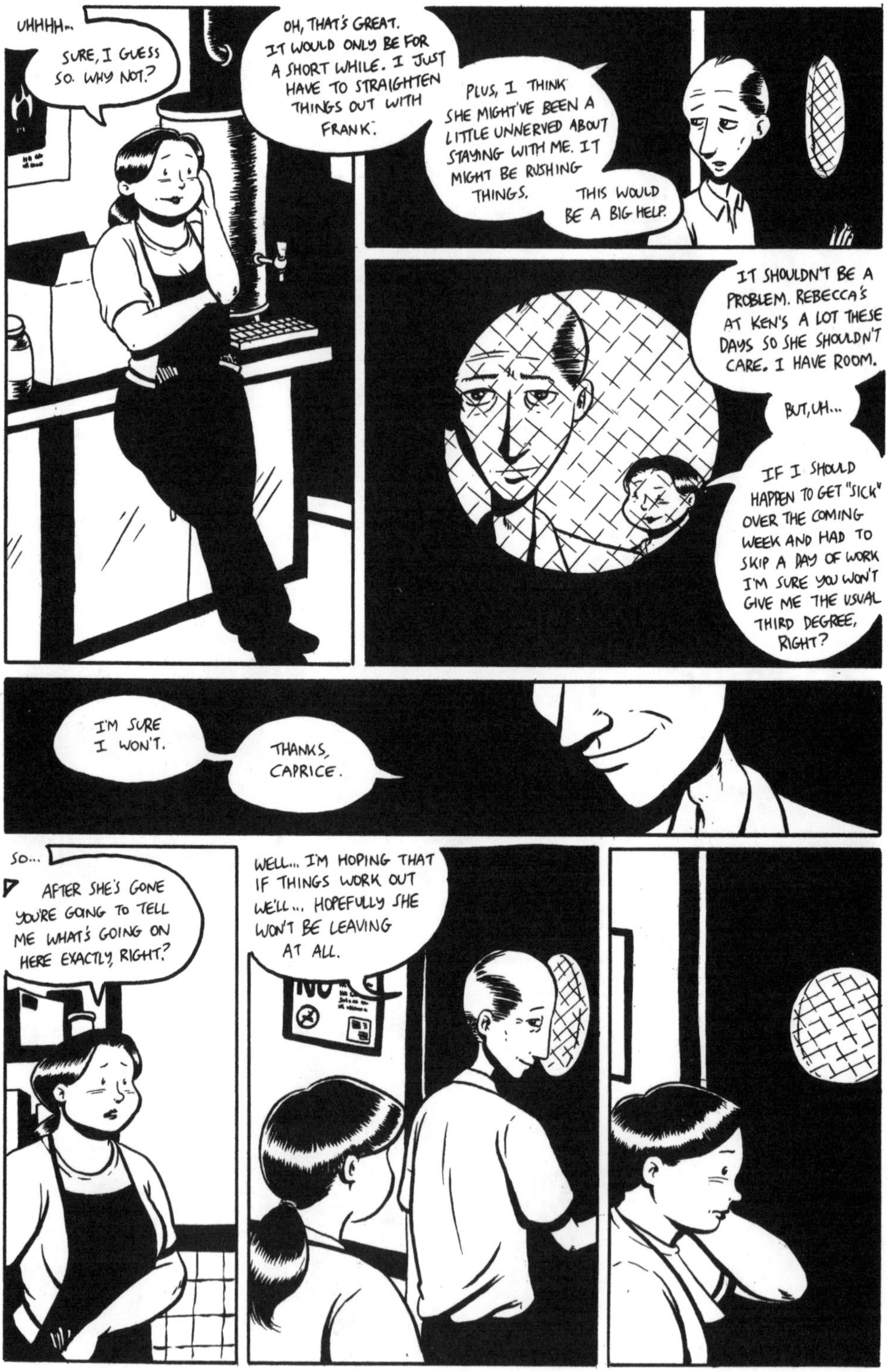
UHHHH...
SURE, I GUESS SO. WHY NOT?
OH, THAT'S GREAT. IT WOULD ONLY BE FOR A SHORT WHILE. I JUST HAVE TO STRAIGHTEN THINGS OUT WITH FRANK.
PLUS, I THINK SHE MIGHT'VE BEEN A LITTLE UNNERVED ABOUT STAYING WITH ME. IT MIGHT BE RUSHING THINGS.
THIS WOULD BE A BIG HELP.
IT SHOULDN'T BE A PROBLEM. REBECCA'S AT KEN'S A LOT THESE DAYS SO SHE SHOULDN'T CARE. I HAVE ROOM.
BUT, UH...
IF I SHOULD HAPPEN TO GET "SICK" OVER THE COMING WEEK AND HAD TO SKIP A DAY OF WORK I'M SURE YOU WON'T GIVE ME THE USUAL THIRD DEGREE, RIGHT?
I'M SURE I WON'T.
THANKS, CAPRICE.
SO...
AFTER SHE'S GONE YOU'RE GOING TO TELL ME WHAT'S GOING ON HERE EXACTLY, RIGHT?
WELL... I'M HOPING THAT IF THINGS WORK OUT WELL... HOPEFULLY SHE WON'T BE LEAVING AT ALL.

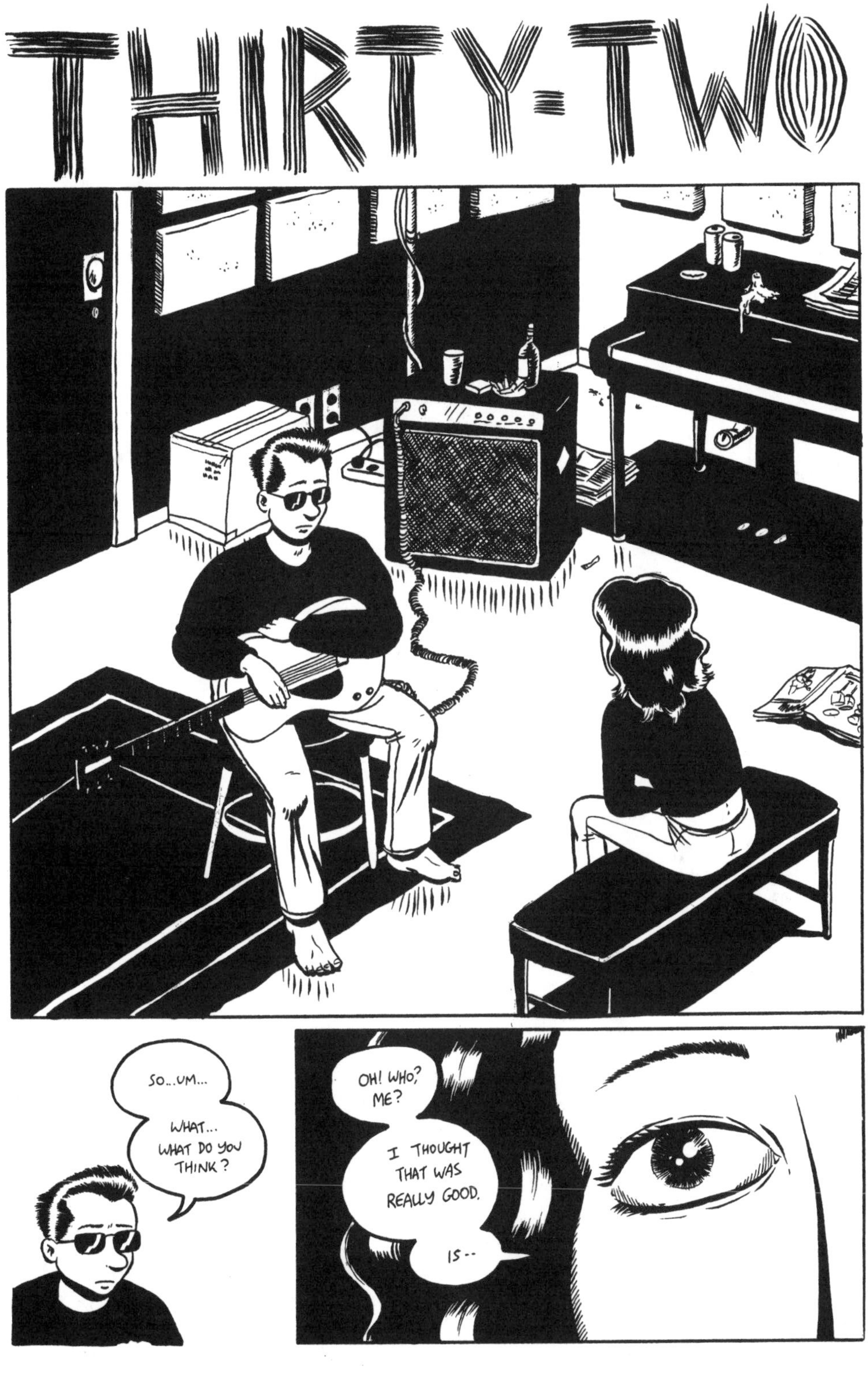
THIRTY-TWO
SO...UM...
WHAT... WHAT DO YOU THINK?
OH! WHO? ME?
I THOUGHT THAT WAS REALLY GOOD.
IS--

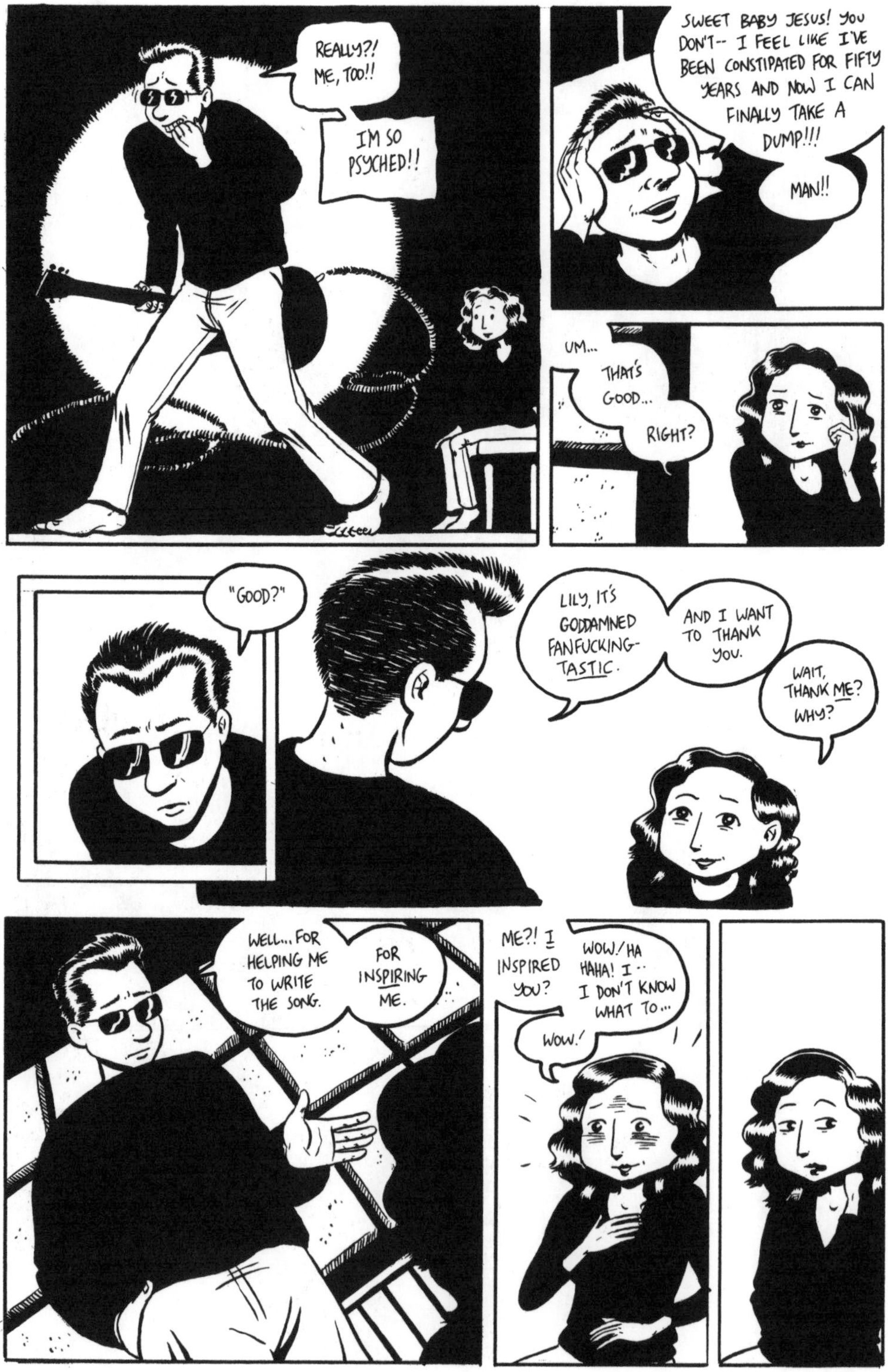
REALLY?! ME, TOO!!
I'M SO PSYCHED!!
SWEET BABY JESUS! YOU DON'T-- I FEEL LIKE I'VE BEEN CONSTIPATED FOR FIFTY YEARS AND NOW I CAN FINALLY TAKE A DUMP!!!
MAN!!
UM... THAT'S GOOD... RIGHT?
"GOOD?"
LILY, IT'S GODDAMNED FANFUCKING-TASTIC.
AND I WANT TO THANK YOU.
WAIT, THANK ME? WHY?
WELL... FOR HELPING ME TO WRITE THE SONG.
FOR INSPIRING ME.
ME?! I INSPIRED YOU?
WOW! HA HAHA! I-- I DON'T KNOW WHAT TO...
WOW!

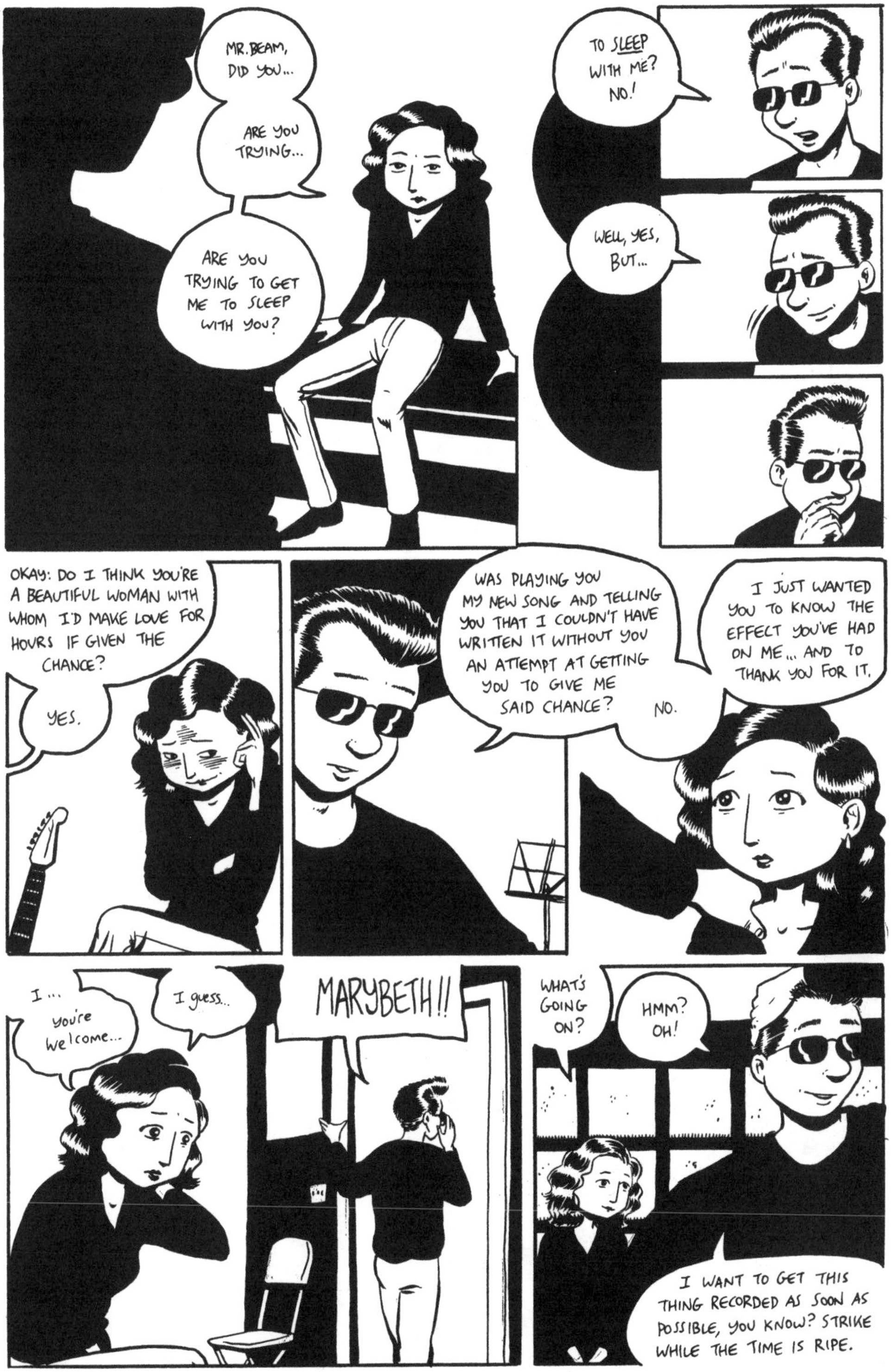
MR. BEAM, DID YOU...
ARE YOU TRYING...
ARE YOU TRYING TO GET ME TO SLEEP WITH YOU?
TO SLEEP WITH ME? NO!
WELL, YES, BUT...
OKAY: DO I THINK YOU'RE A BEAUTIFUL WOMAN WITH WHOM I'D MAKE LOVE FOR HOURS IF GIVEN THE CHANCE?
YES.
WAS PLAYING YOU MY NEW SONG AND TELLING YOU THAT I COULDN'T HAVE WRITTEN IT WITHOUT YOU AN ATTEMPT AT GETTING YOU TO GIVE ME SAID CHANCE?
NO.
I JUST WANTED YOU TO KNOW THE EFFECT YOU'VE HAD ON ME... AND TO THANK YOU FOR IT.
I... you're welcome...
I guess...
MARYBETH!!
WHAT'S GOING ON?
HMM? OH!
I WANT TO GET THIS THING RECORDED AS SOON AS POSSIBLE, YOU KNOW? STRIKE WHILE THE TIME IS RIPE.

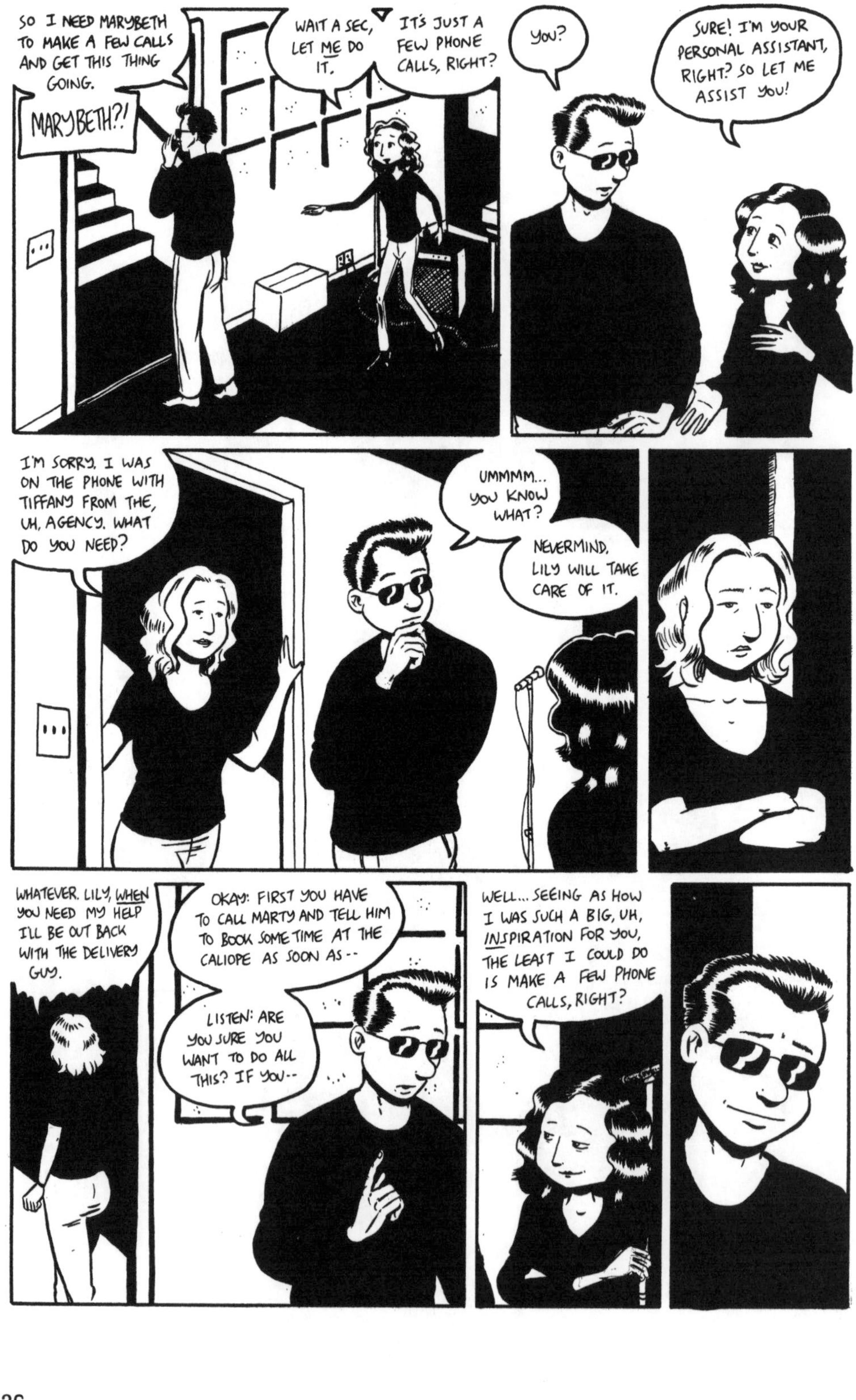
SO I NEED MARYBETH TO MAKE A FEW CALLS AND GET THIS THING GOING.
MARYBETH?!
WAIT A SEC, LET ME DO IT.
IT'S JUST A FEW PHONE CALLS, RIGHT?
YOU?
SURE! I'M YOUR PERSONAL ASSISTANT, RIGHT? SO LET ME ASSIST YOU!
I'M SORRY. I WAS ON THE PHONE WITH TIFFANY FROM THE, UH, AGENCY. WHAT DO YOU NEED?
UMMMM... YOU KNOW WHAT?
NEVERMIND. LILY WILL TAKE CARE OF IT.
WHATEVER. LILY, WHEN YOU NEED MY HELP I'LL BE OUT BACK WITH THE DELIVERY GUY.
OKAY: FIRST YOU HAVE TO CALL MARTY AND TELL HIM TO BOOK SOME TIME AT THE CALIOPE AS SOON AS--
LISTEN: ARE YOU SURE YOU WANT TO DO ALL THIS? IF YOU--
WELL... SEEING AS HOW I WAS SUCH A BIG, UH, INSPIRATION FOR YOU, THE LEAST I COULD DO IS MAKE A FEW PHONE CALLS, RIGHT?

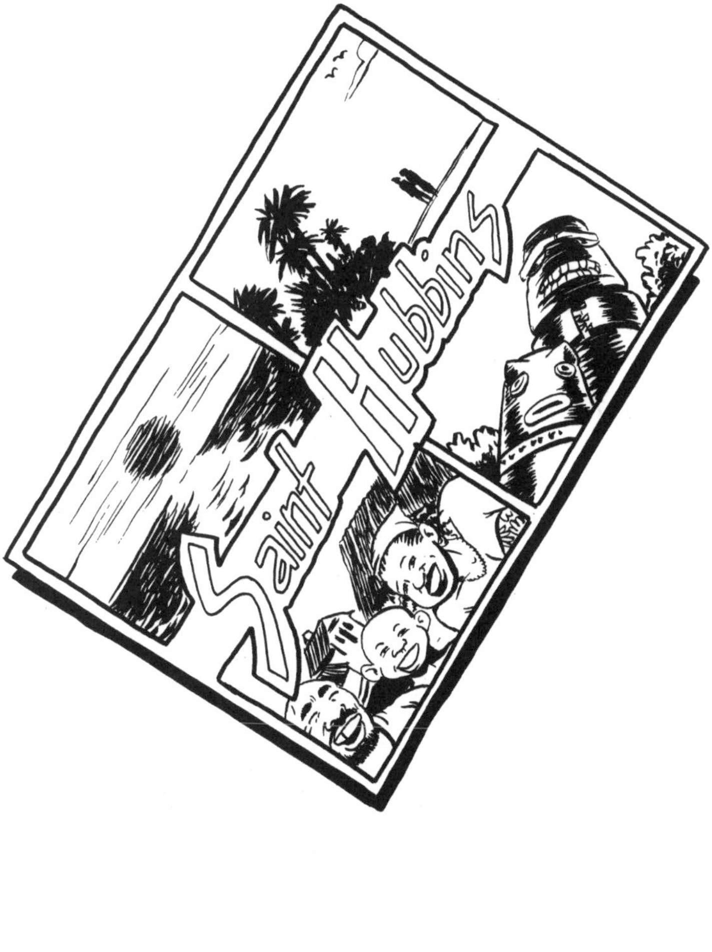
Saint Hubbins

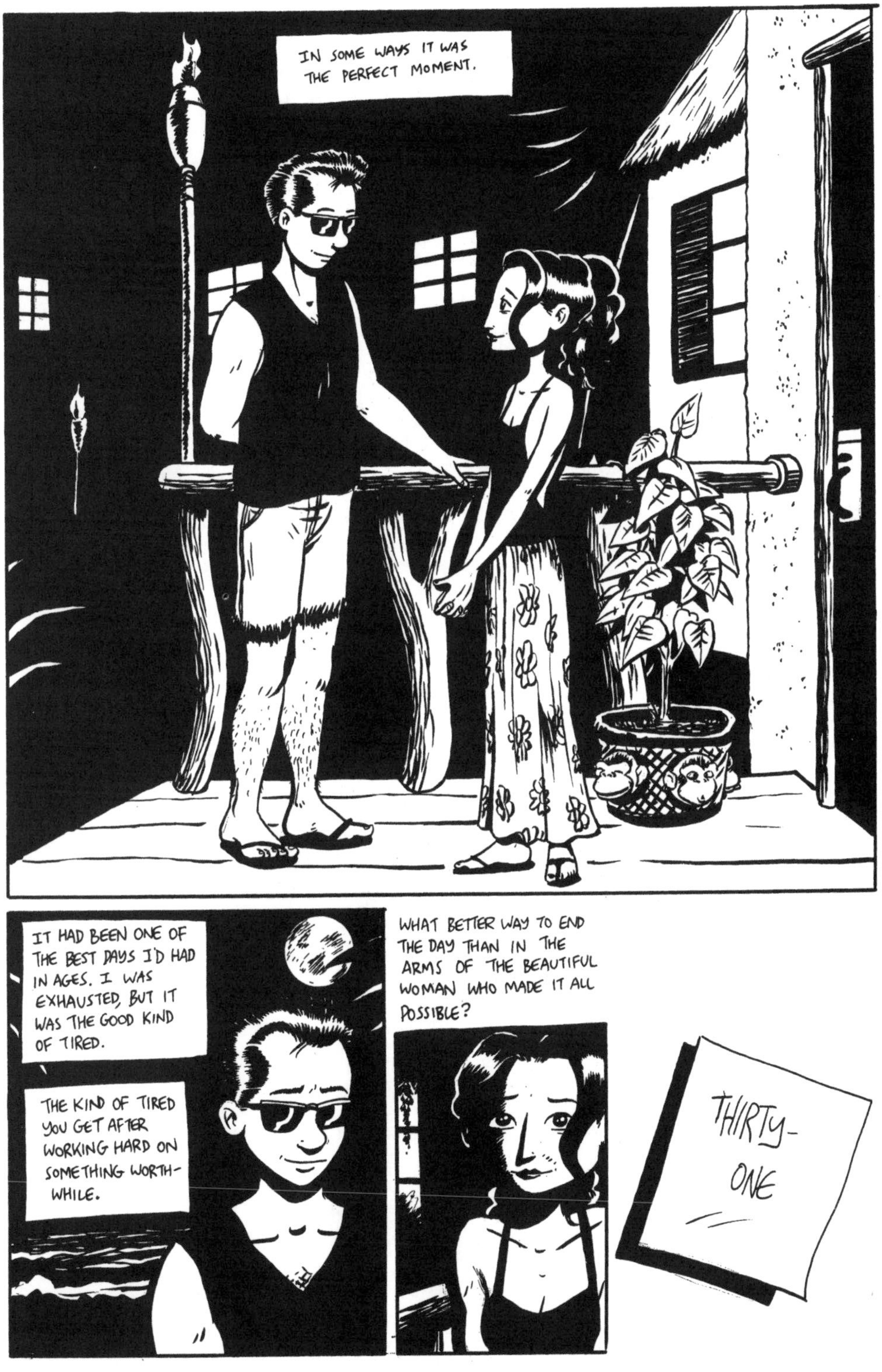
IN SOME WAYS IT WAS THE PERFECT MOMENT.
IT HAD BEEN ONE OF THE BEST DAYS I'D HAD IN AGES. I WAS EXHAUSTED, BUT IT WAS THE GOOD KIND OF TIRED.
THE KIND OF TIRED YOU GET AFTER WORKING HARD ON SOMETHING WORTH-WHILE.
WHAT BETTER WAY TO END THE DAY THAN IN THE ARMS OF THE BEAUTIFUL WOMAN WHO MADE IT ALL POSSIBLE?
THIRTY-ONE

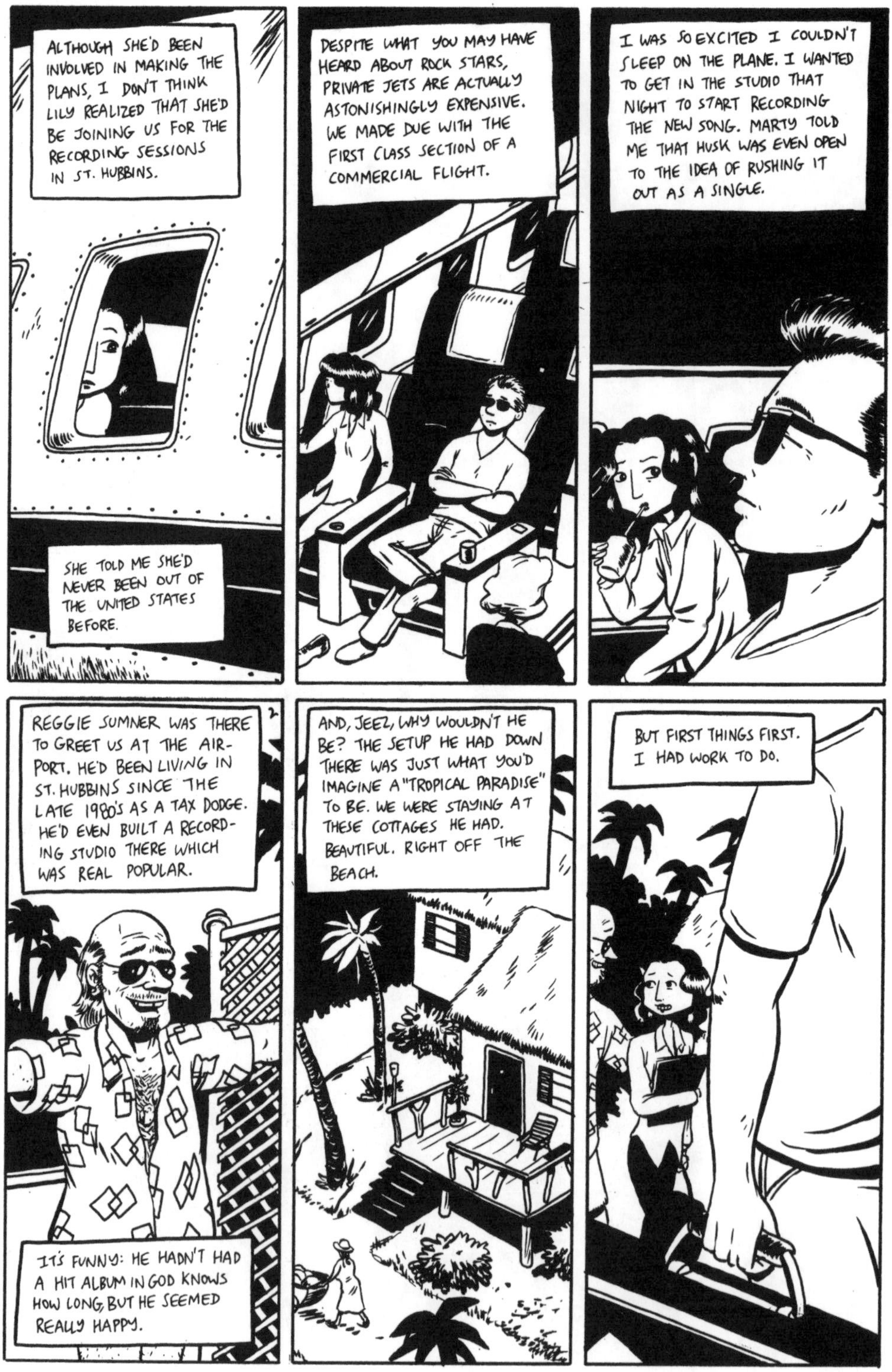
ALTHOUGH SHE'D BEEN INVOLVED IN MAKING THE PLANS, I DON'T THINK LILY REALIZED THAT SHE'D BE JOINING US FOR THE RECORDING SESSIONS IN ST. HUBBINS.
SHE TOLD ME SHE'D NEVER BEEN OUT OF THE UNITED STATES BEFORE.
DESPITE WHAT YOU MAY HAVE HEARD ABOUT ROCK STARS, PRIVATE JETS ARE ACTUALLY ASTONISHINGLY EXPENSIVE. WE MADE DUE WITH THE FIRST CLASS SECTION OF A COMMERCIAL FLIGHT.
I WAS SO EXCITED I COULDN'T SLEEP ON THE PLANE. I WANTED TO GET IN THE STUDIO THAT NIGHT TO START RECORDING THE NEW SONG. MARTY TOLD ME THAT HUSK WAS EVEN OPEN TO THE IDEA OF RUSHING IT OUT AS A SINGLE.
REGGIE SUMNER WAS THERE TO GREET US AT THE AIR-PORT. HE'D BEEN LIVING IN ST. HUBBINS SINCE THE LATE 1980'S AS A TAX DODGE. HE'D EVEN BUILT A RECORD-ING STUDIO THERE WHICH WAS REAL POPULAR.
IT'S FUNNY: HE HADN'T HAD A HIT ALBUM IN GOD KNOWS HOW LONG, BUT HE SEEMED REALLY HAPPY.
AND, JEEZ, WHY WOULDN'T HE BE? THE SETUP HE HAD DOWN THERE WAS JUST WHAT YOU'D IMAGINE A "TROPICAL PARADISE" TO BE. WE WERE STAYING AT THESE COTTAGES HE HAD. BEAUTIFUL. RIGHT OFF THE BEACH.
BUT FIRST THINGS FIRST. I HAD WORK TO DO.

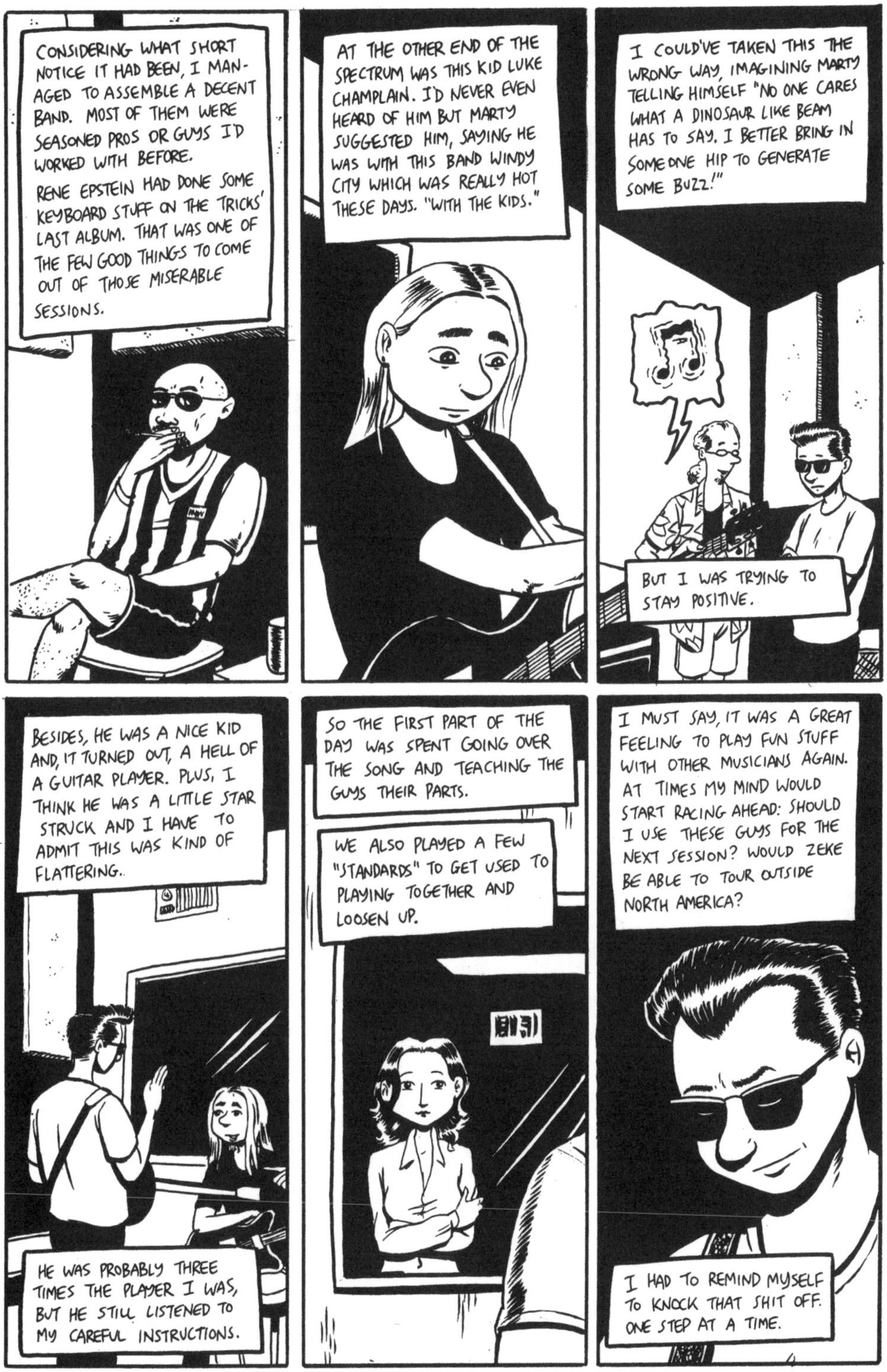
CONSIDERING WHAT SHORT NOTICE IT HAD BEEN, I MANAGED TO ASSEMBLE A DECENT BAND. MOST OF THEM WERE SEASONED PROS OR GUYS I'D WORKED WITH BEFORE.
RENE EPSTEIN HAD DONE SOME KEYBOARD STUFF ON THE TRICKS' LAST ALBUM. THAT WAS ONE OF THE FEW GOOD THINGS TO COME OUT OF THOSE MISERABLE SESSIONS.
AT THE OTHER END OF THE SPECTRUM WAS THIS KID LUKE CHAMPLAIN. I'D NEVER EVEN HEARD OF HIM BUT MARTY SUGGESTED HIM, SAYING HE WAS WITH THIS BAND WINDY CITY WHICH WAS REALLY HOT THESE DAYS. "WITH THE KIDS."
I COULD'VE TAKEN THIS THE WRONG WAY, IMAGINING MARTY TELLING HIMSELF "NO ONE CARES WHAT A DINOSAUR LIKE BEAM HAS TO SAY. I BETTER BRING IN SOMEONE HIP TO GENERATE SOME BUZZ!"
BUT I WAS TRYING TO STAY POSITIVE.
BESIDES, HE WAS A NICE KID AND, IT TURNED OUT, A HELL OF A GUITAR PLAYER. PLUS, I THINK HE WAS A LITTLE STAR STRUCK AND I HAVE TO ADMIT THIS WAS KIND OF FLATTERING.
HE WAS PROBABLY THREE TIMES THE PLAYER I WAS, BUT HE STILL LISTENED TO MY CAREFUL INSTRUCTIONS.
SO THE FIRST PART OF THE DAY WAS SPENT GOING OVER THE SONG AND TEACHING THE GUYS THEIR PARTS.
WE ALSO PLAYED A FEW "STANDARDS" TO GET USED TO PLAYING TOGETHER AND LOOSEN UP.
I MUST SAY, IT WAS A GREAT FEELING TO PLAY FUN STUFF WITH OTHER MUSICIANS AGAIN. AT TIMES MY MIND WOULD START RACING AHEAD: SHOULD I USE THESE GUYS FOR THE NEXT SESSION? WOULD ZEKE BE ABLE TO TOUR OUTSIDE NORTH AMERICA?
I HAD TO REMIND MYSELF TO KNOCK THAT SHIT OFF. ONE STEP AT A TIME.

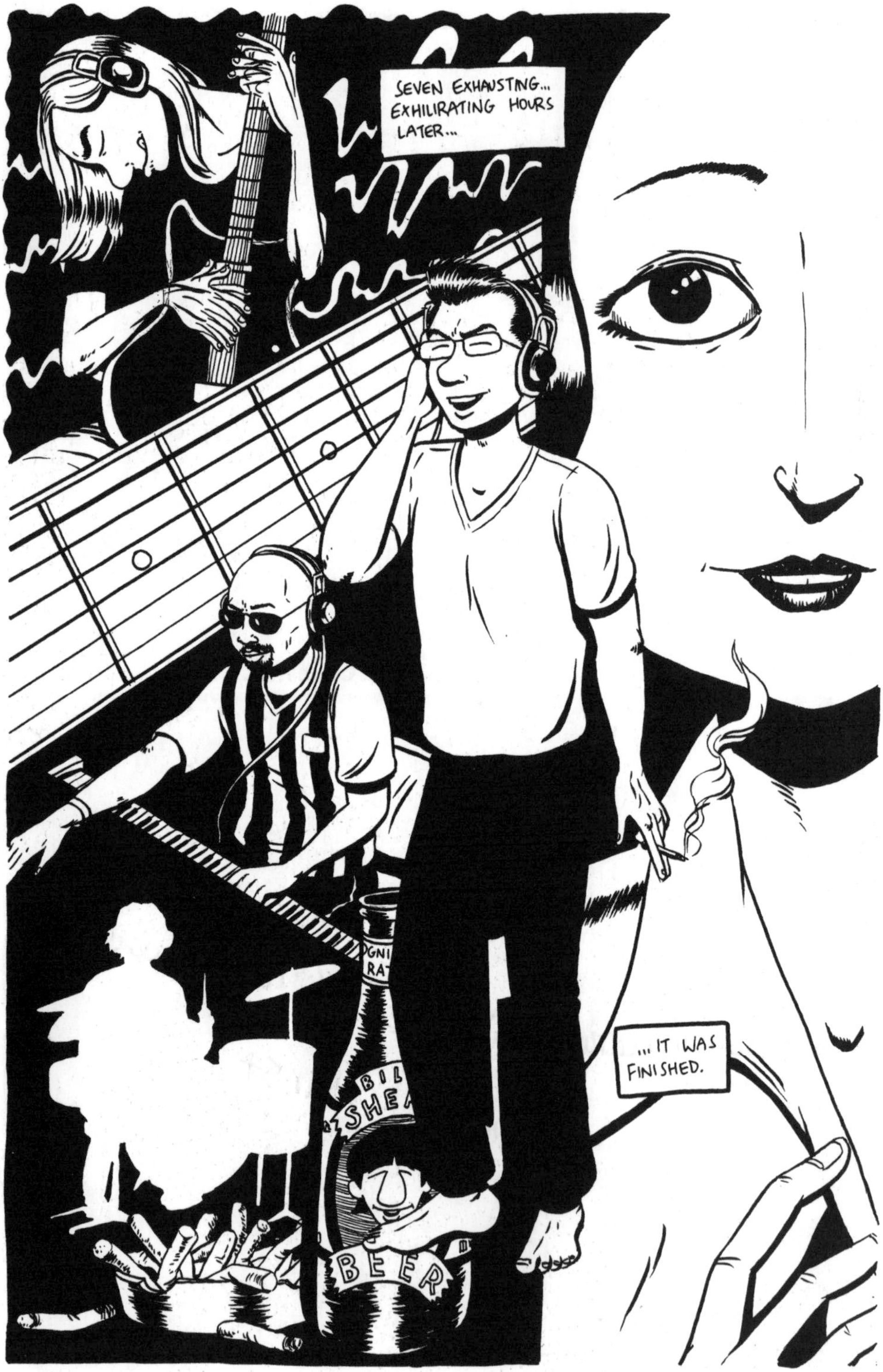
SEVEN EXHAUSTING... EXHILIRATING HOURS LATER...
BEER
...IT WAS FINISHED.

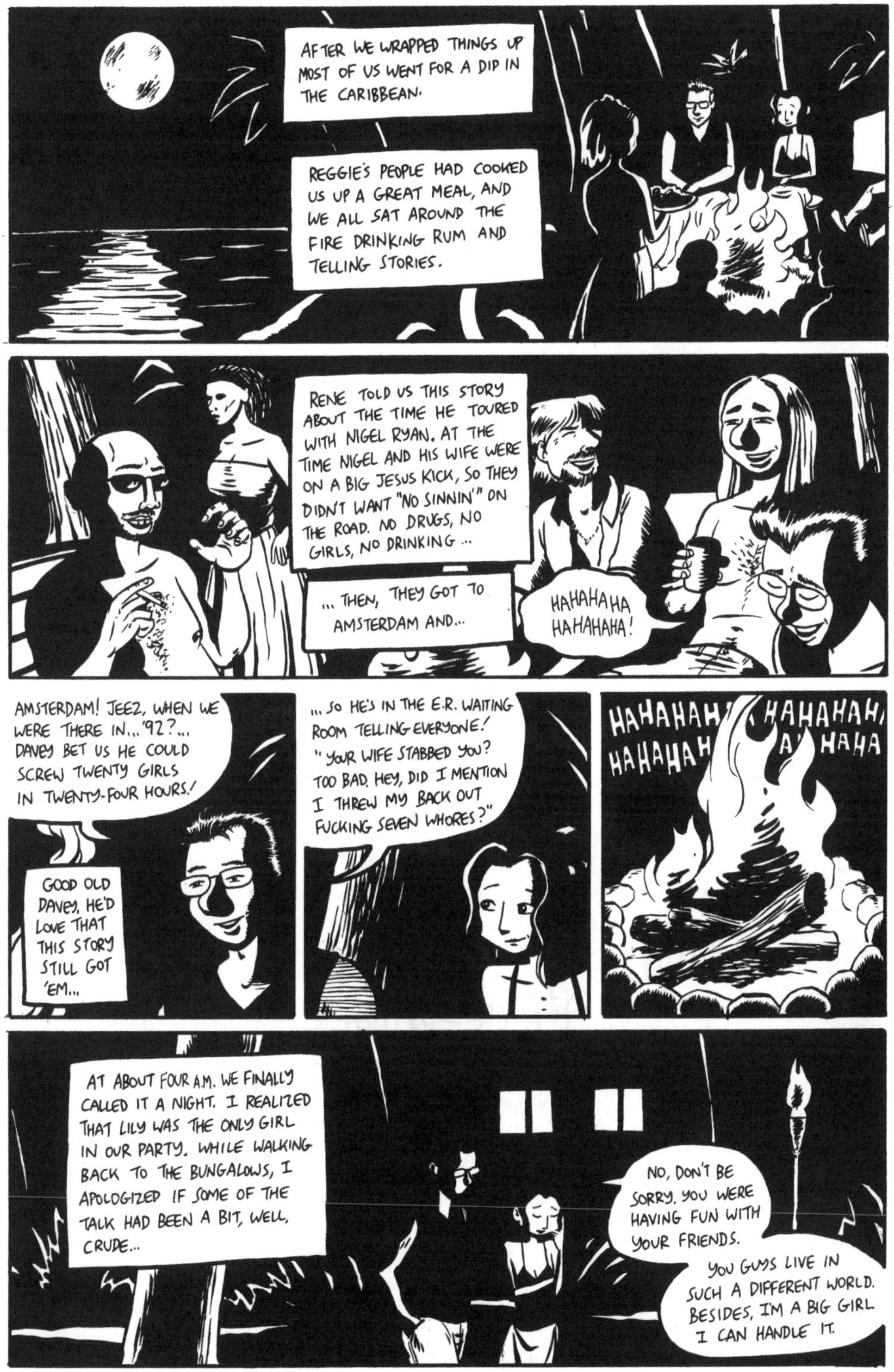

AFTER WE WRAPPED THINGS UP MOST OF US WENT FOR A DIP IN THE CARIBBEAN.
REGGIE'S PEOPLE HAD COOKED US UP A GREAT MEAL, AND WE ALL SAT AROUND THE FIRE DRINKING RUM AND TELLING STORIES.
RENE TOLD US THIS STORY ABOUT THE TIME HE TOURED WITH NIGEL RYAN. AT THE TIME NIGEL AND HIS WIFE WERE ON A BIG JESUS KICK, SO THEY DIDN'T WANT "NO SINNIN'" ON THE ROAD. NO DRUGS, NO GIRLS, NO DRINKING ...
... THEN, THEY GOT TO AMSTERDAM AND...
HAHAHAHA HAHAHAHA!
AMSTERDAM! JEEZ, WHEN WE WERE THERE IN... '92?... DAVEY BET US HE COULD SCREW TWENTY GIRLS IN TWENTY-FOUR HOURS!
GOOD OLD DAVEY. HE'D LOVE THAT THIS STORY STILL GOT 'EM...
... SO HE'S IN THE E.R. WAITING ROOM TELLING EVERYONE! "YOUR WIFE STABBED YOU? TOO BAD. HEY, DID I MENTION I THREW MY BACK OUT FUCKING SEVEN WHORES?"
HAHAHAH HAHAHAH HAHAHAH HAHA
AT ABOUT FOUR A.M. WE FINALLY CALLED IT A NIGHT. I REALIZED THAT LILY WAS THE ONLY GIRL IN OUR PARTY. WHILE WALKING BACK TO THE BUNGALOWS, I APOLOGIZED IF SOME OF THE TALK HAD BEEN A BIT, WELL, CRUDE...
NO, DON'T BE SORRY. YOU WERE HAVING FUN WITH YOUR FRIENDS.
YOU GUYS LIVE IN SUCH A DIFFERENT WORLD. BESIDES, I'M A BIG GIRL I CAN HANDLE IT.

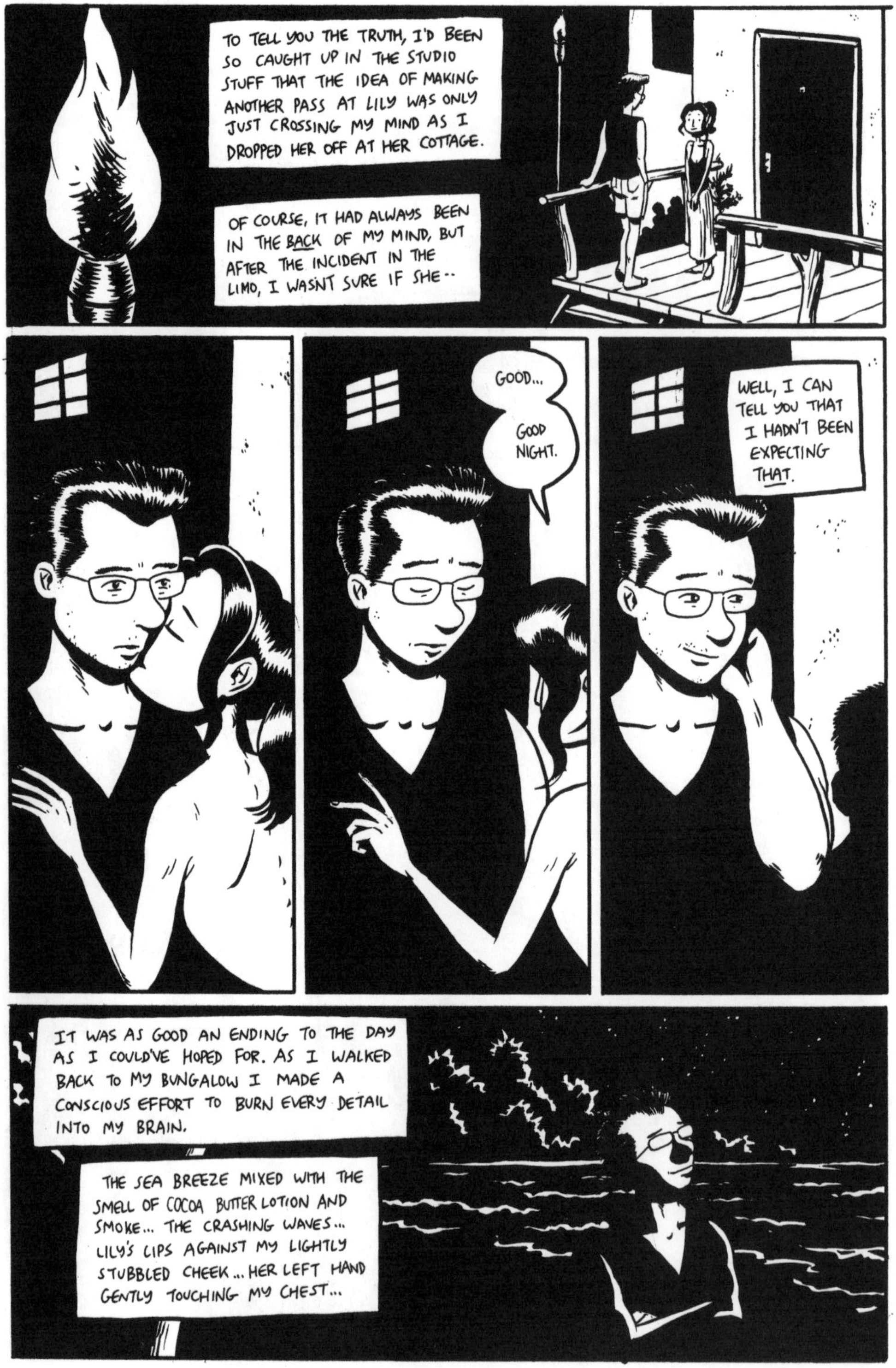

TO TELL YOU THE TRUTH, I'D BEEN SO CAUGHT UP IN THE STUDIO STUFF THAT THE IDEA OF MAKING ANOTHER PASS AT LILY WAS ONLY JUST CROSSING MY MIND AS I DROPPED HER OFF AT HER COTTAGE.
OF COURSE, IT HAD ALWAYS BEEN IN THE BACK OF MY MIND, BUT AFTER THE INCIDENT IN THE LIMO, I WASN'T SURE IF SHE--
GOOD...
GOOD NIGHT.
WELL, I CAN TELL YOU THAT I HADN'T BEEN EXPECTING THAT.
IT WAS AS GOOD AN ENDING TO THE DAY AS I COULD'VE HOPED FOR. AS I WALKED BACK TO MY BUNGALOW I MADE A CONSCIOUS EFFORT TO BURN EVERY DETAIL INTO MY BRAIN.
THE SEA BREEZE MIXED WITH THE SMELL OF COCOA BUTTER LOTION AND SMOKE... THE CRASHING WAVES... LILY'S LIPS AGAINST MY LIGHTLY STUBBLED CHEEK... HER LEFT HAND GENTLY TOUCHING MY CHEST...

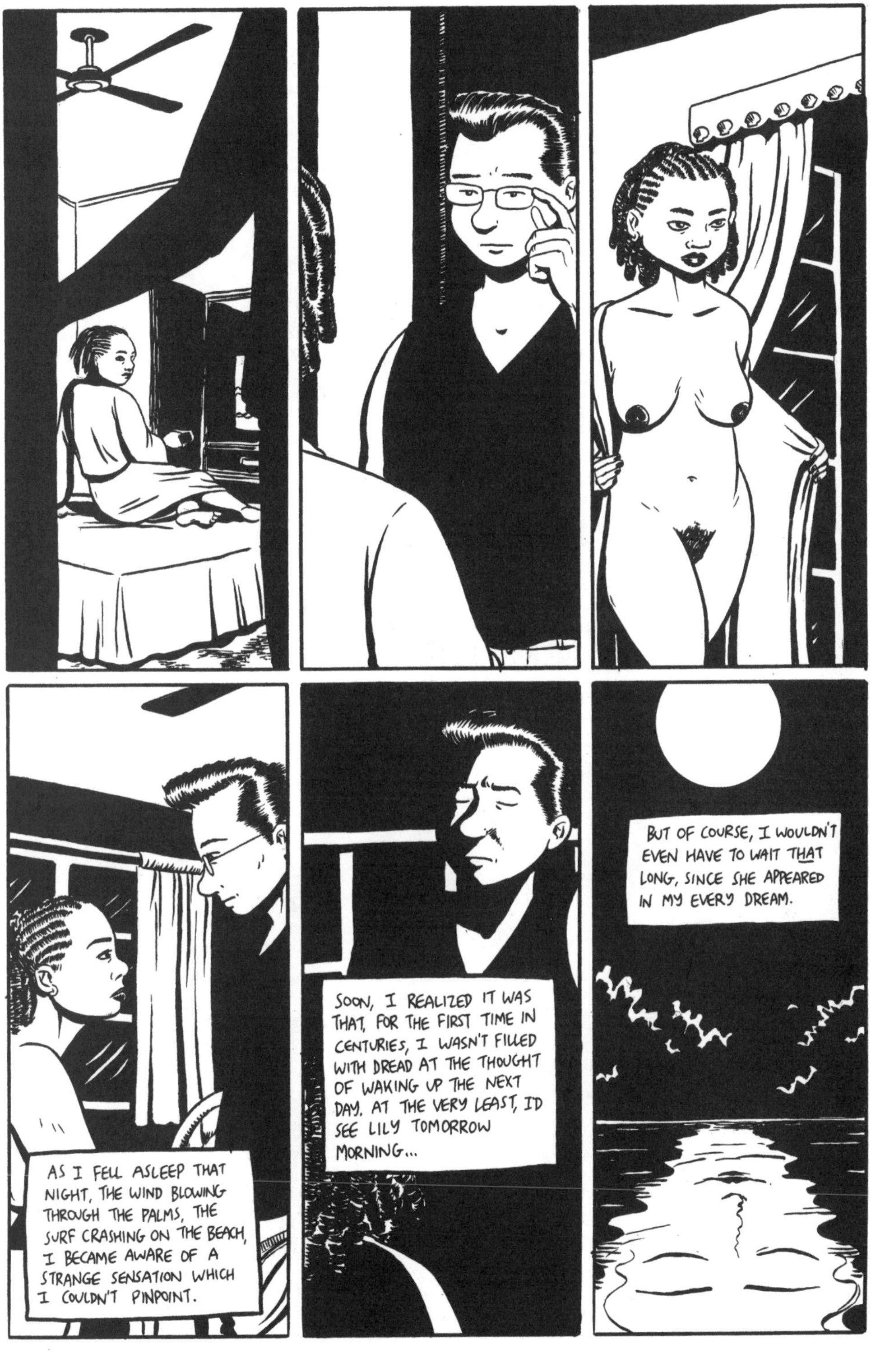
AS I FELL ASLEEP THAT NIGHT, THE WIND BLOWING THROUGH THE PALMS, THE SURF CRASHING ON THE BEACH, I BECAME AWARE OF A STRANGE SENSATION WHICH I COULDN'T PINPOINT.
SOON, I REALIZED IT WAS THAT, FOR THE FIRST TIME IN CENTURIES, I WASN'T FILLED WITH DREAD AT THE THOUGHT OF WAKING UP THE NEXT DAY. AT THE VERY LEAST, I'D SEE LILY TOMORROW MORNING...
BUT OF COURSE, I WOULDN'T EVEN HAVE TO WAIT THAT LONG, SINCE SHE APPEARED IN MY EVERY DREAM.

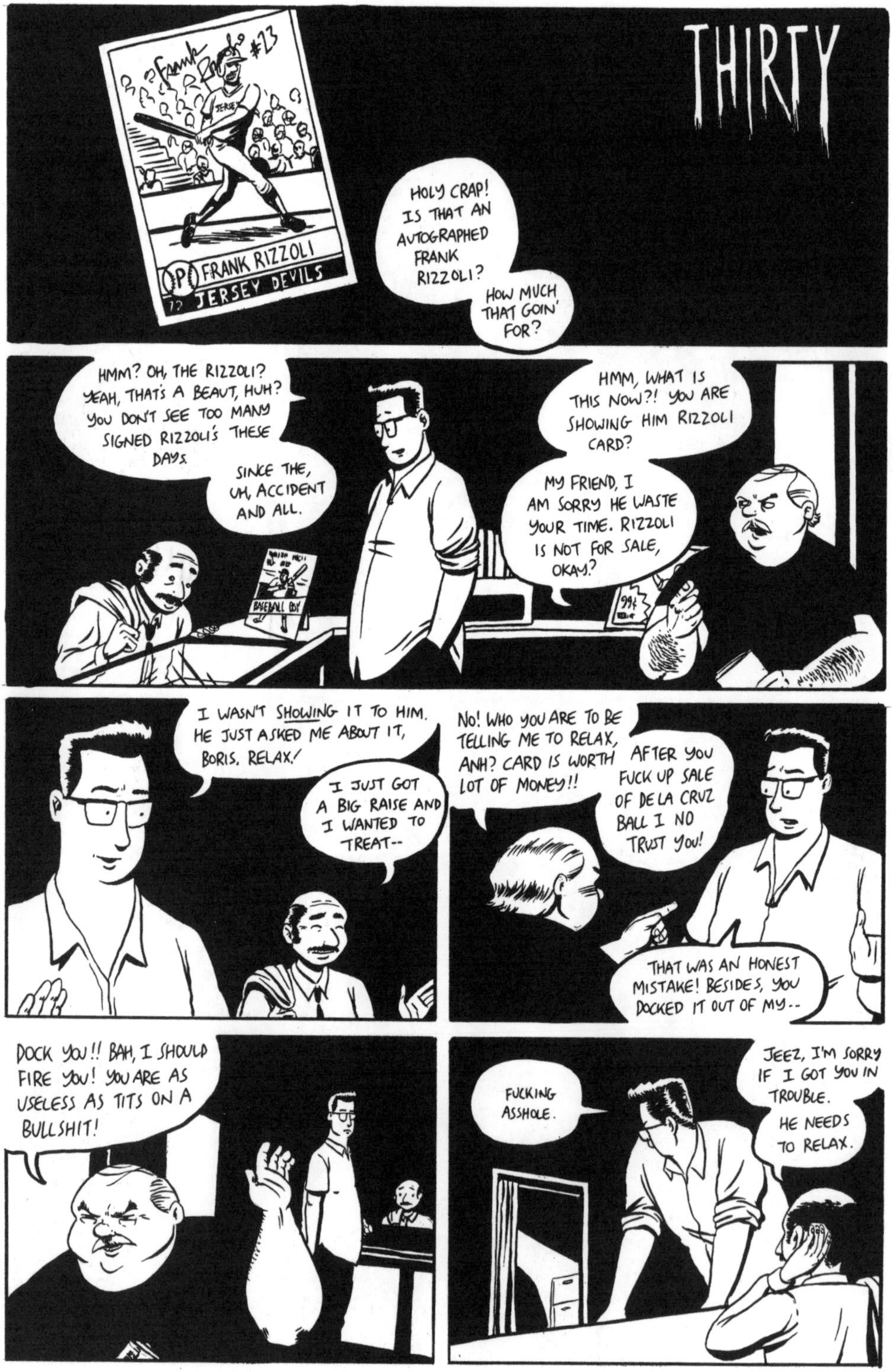
THIRTY
FRANK RIZZOLI
JERSEY DEVILS
HOLY CRAP! IS THAT AN AUTOGRAPHED FRANK RIZZOLI?
HOW MUCH THAT GOIN' FOR?
HMM? OH, THE RIZZOLI? YEAH, THAT'S A BEAUT, HUH? YOU DON'T SEE TOO MANY SIGNED RIZZOLI'S THESE DAYS.
SINCE THE, UH, ACCIDENT AND ALL.
BASEBALL BOY
HMM, WHAT IS THIS NOW?! YOU ARE SHOWING HIM RIZZOLI CARD?
MY FRIEND, I AM SORRY HE WASTE YOUR TIME. RIZZOLI IS NOT FOR SALE, OKAY?
99¢
I WASN'T SHOWING IT TO HIM. HE JUST ASKED ME ABOUT IT, BORIS. RELAX!
I JUST GOT A BIG RAISE AND I WANTED TO TREAT--
NO! WHO YOU ARE TO BE TELLING ME TO RELAX, ANH? CARD IS WORTH LOT OF MONEY!!
AFTER YOU FUCK UP SALE OF DE LA CRUZ BALL I NO TRUST YOU!
THAT WAS AN HONEST MISTAKE! BESIDES, YOU DOCKED IT OUT OF MY..
DOCK YOU!! BAH, I SHOULD FIRE YOU! YOU ARE AS USELESS AS TITS ON A BULLSHIT!
FUCKING ASSHOLE.
JEEZ, I'M SORRY IF I GOT YOU IN TROUBLE.
HE NEEDS TO RELAX.

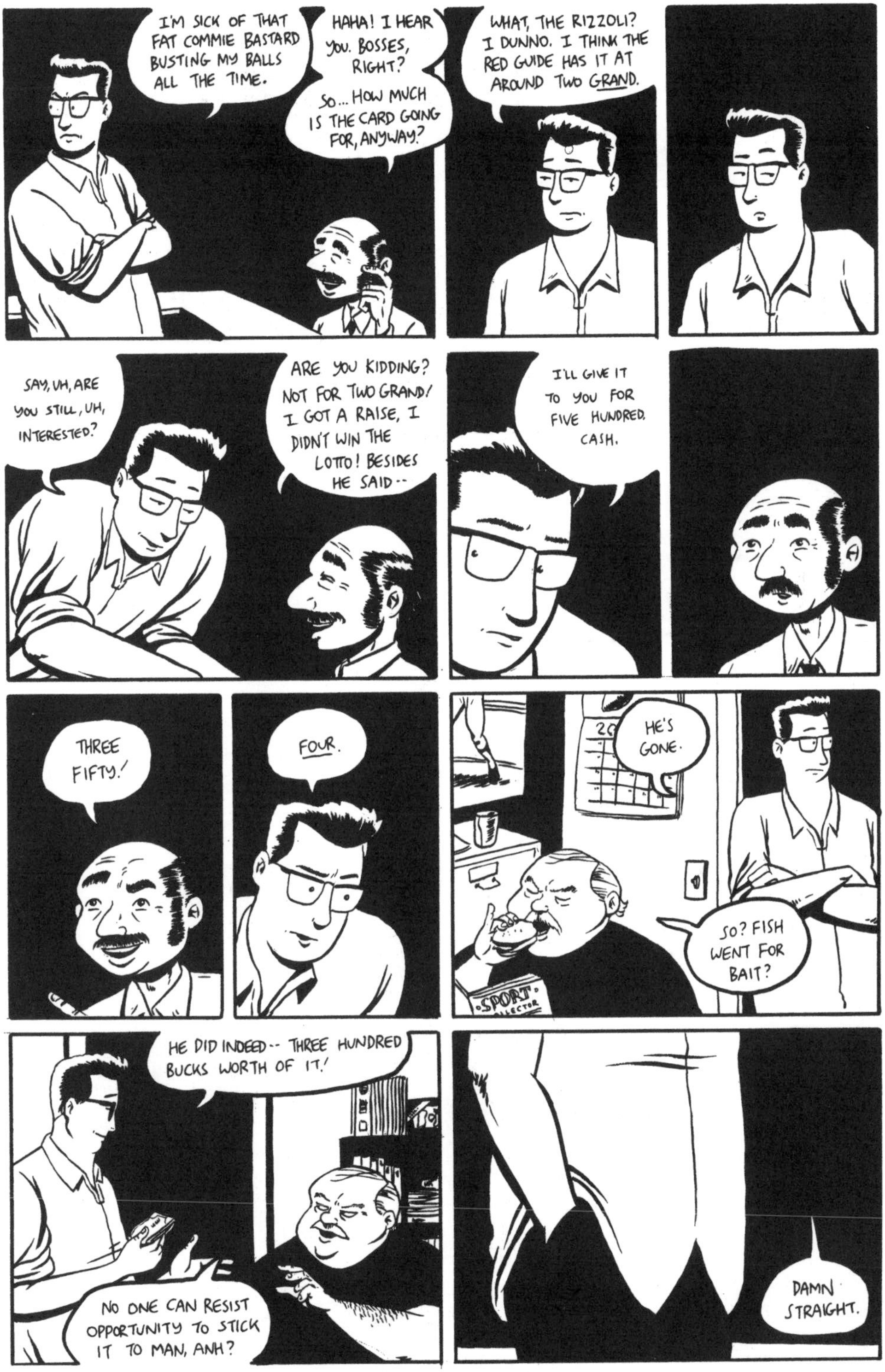
I'M SICK OF THAT FAT COMMIE BASTARD BUSTING MY BALLS ALL THE TIME.
HAHA! I HEAR YOU. BOSSES, RIGHT?
SO... HOW MUCH IS THE CARD GOING FOR, ANYWAY?
WHAT, THE RIZZOLI? I DUNNO. I THINK THE RED GUIDE HAS IT AT AROUND TWO GRAND.
SAY, UH, ARE YOU STILL, UH, INTERESTED?
ARE YOU KIDDING? NOT FOR TWO GRAND! I GOT A RAISE, I DIDN'T WIN THE LOTTO! BESIDES HE SAID--
I'LL GIVE IT TO YOU FOR FIVE HUNDRED. CASH.
THREE FIFTY!
FOUR.
HE'S GONE.
SO? FISH WENT FOR BAIT?
SPORT
HE DID INDEED-- THREE HUNDRED BUCKS WORTH OF IT!
NO ONE CAN RESIST OPPORTUNITY TO STICK IT TO MAN, ANH?
DAMN STRAIGHT.

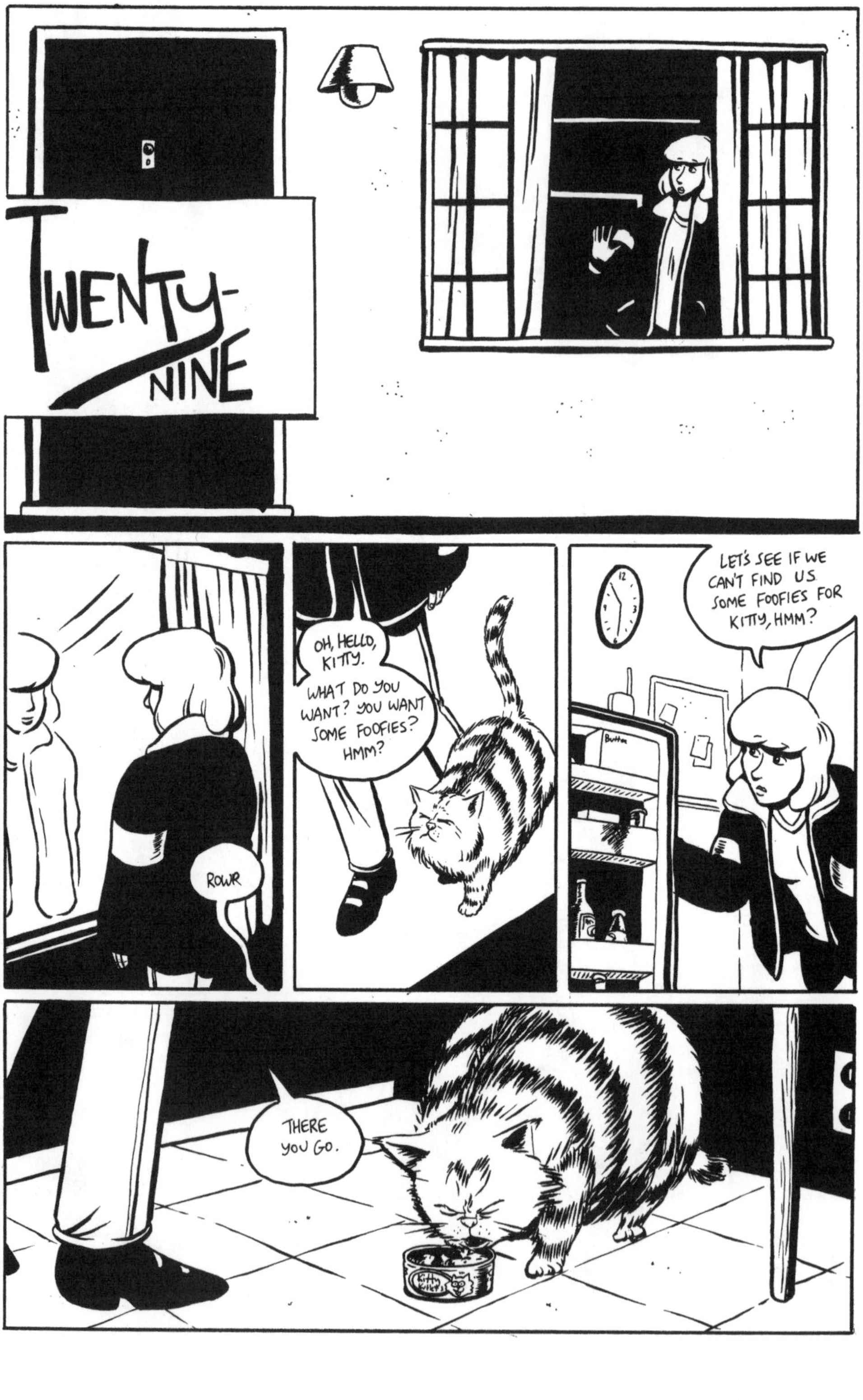
TWENTY-NINE
ROWR
OH, HELLO, KITTY.
WHAT DO YOU WANT? YOU WANT SOME FOOFIES? HMM?
LET'S SEE IF WE CAN'T FIND US SOME FOOFIES FOR KITTY, HMM?
THERE YOU GO.

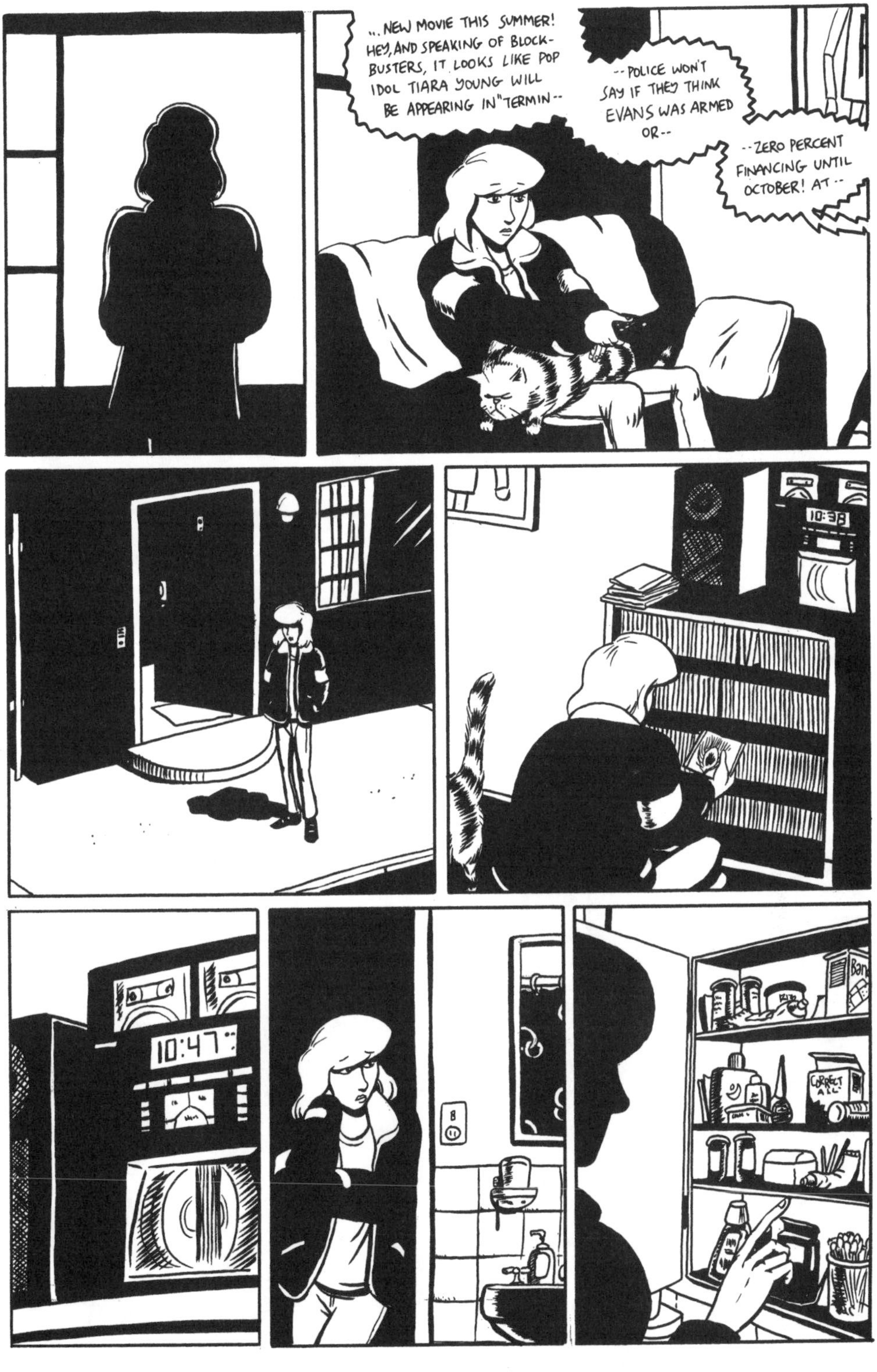
..NEW MOVIE THIS SUMMER! HEY, AND SPEAKING OF BLOCK-BUSTERS, IT LOOKS LIKE POP IDOL TIARA YOUNG WILL BE APPEARING IN "TERMIN--
--POLICE WON'T SAY IF THEY THINK EVANS WAS ARMED OR--
--ZERO PERCENT FINANCING UNTIL OCTOBER! AT--
10:38
10:47
CORRECT ALL

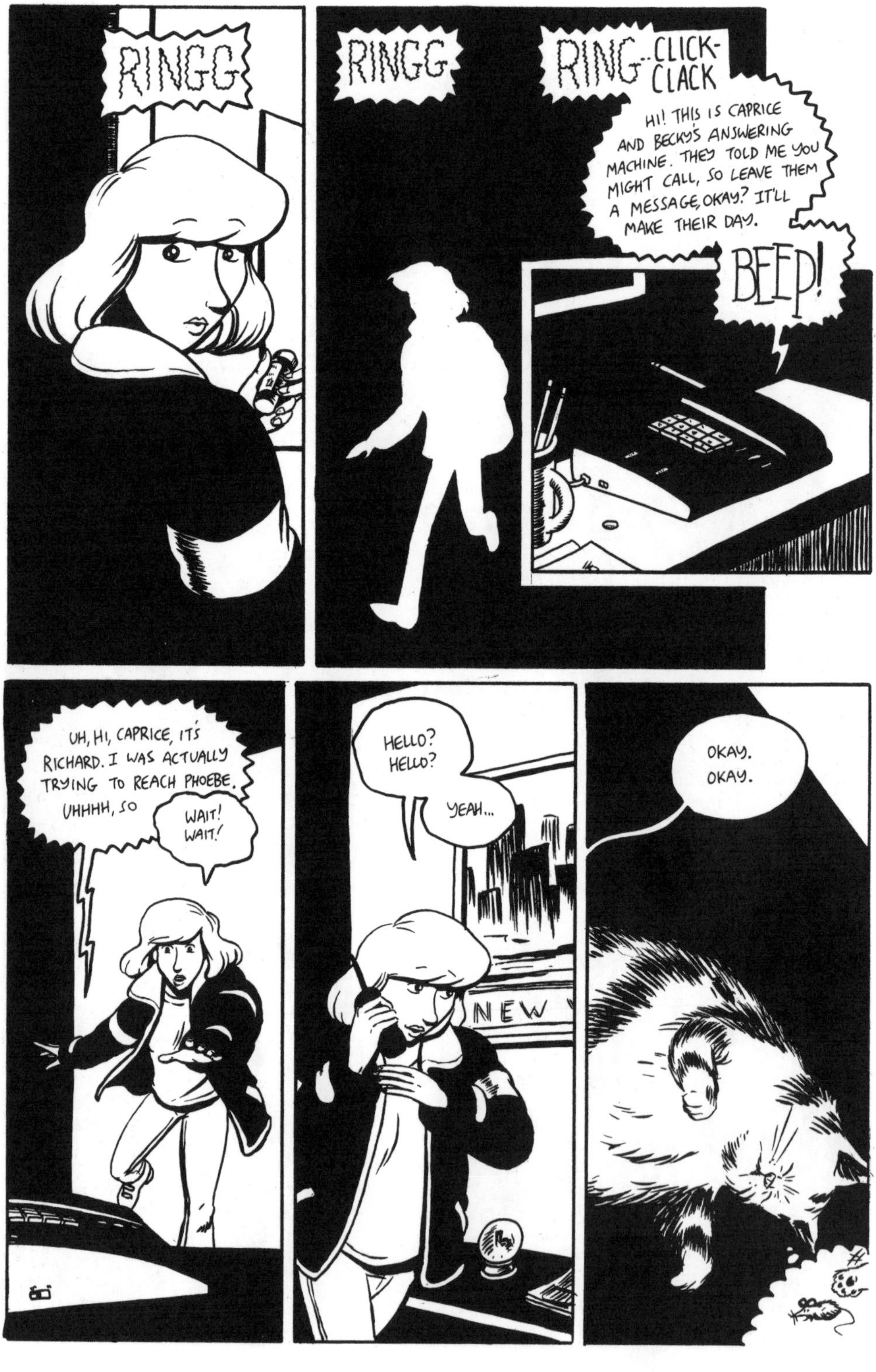
RINGG
RINGG
RING..CLICK-CLACK
HI! THIS IS CAPRICE AND BECKY'S ANSWERING MACHINE. THEY TOLD ME YOU MIGHT CALL, SO LEAVE THEM A MESSAGE, OKAY? IT'LL MAKE THEIR DAY.
BEEP!
UH, HI, CAPRICE, IT'S RICHARD. I WAS ACTUALLY TRYING TO REACH PHOEBE. UHHHH, SO
WAIT! WAIT!
HELLO? HELLO?
YEAH...
NEW
OKAY. OKAY.

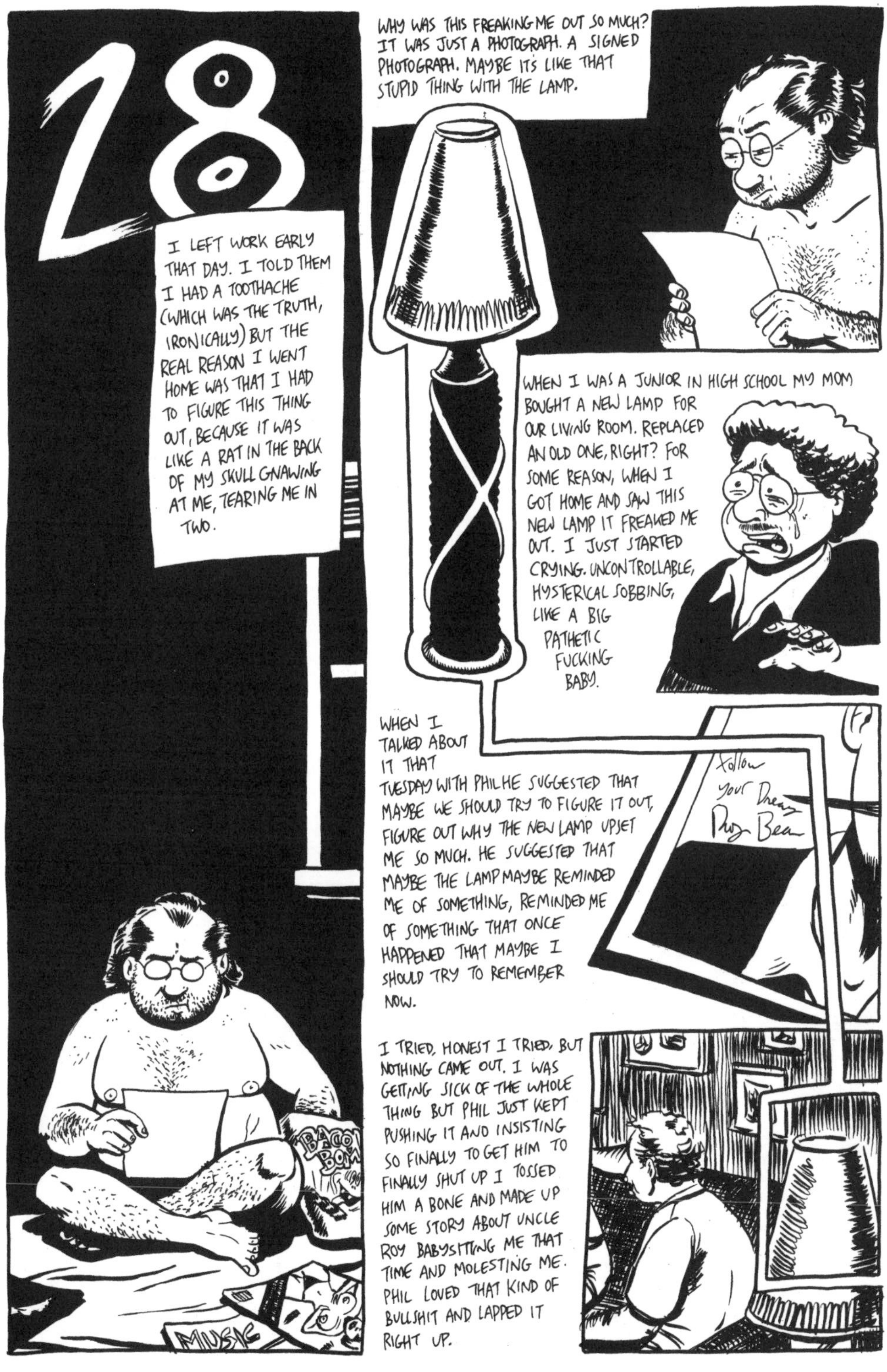
28
I LEFT WORK EARLY THAT DAY. I TOLD THEM I HAD A TOOTHACHE (WHICH WAS THE TRUTH, IRONICALLY) BUT THE REAL REASON I WENT HOME WAS THAT I HAD TO FIGURE THIS THING OUT, BECAUSE IT WAS LIKE A RAT IN THE BACK OF MY SKULL GNAWING AT ME, TEARING ME IN TWO.
WHY WAS THIS FREAKING ME OUT SO MUCH? IT WAS JUST A PHOTOGRAPH. A SIGNED PHOTOGRAPH. MAYBE IT'S LIKE THAT STUPID THING WITH THE LAMP.
WHEN I WAS A JUNIOR IN HIGH SCHOOL MY MOM BOUGHT A NEW LAMP FOR OUR LIVING ROOM. REPLACED AN OLD ONE, RIGHT? FOR SOME REASON, WHEN I GOT HOME AND SAW THIS NEW LAMP IT FREAKED ME OUT. I JUST STARTED CRYING. UNCONTROLLABLE, HYSTERICAL SOBBING, LIKE A BIG PATHETIC FUCKING BABY.
WHEN I TALKED ABOUT IT THAT TUESDAY WITH PHIL HE SUGGESTED THAT MAYBE WE SHOULD TRY TO FIGURE IT OUT, FIGURE OUT WHY THE NEW LAMP UPSET ME SO MUCH. HE SUGGESTED THAT MAYBE THE LAMP MAYBE REMINDED ME OF SOMETHING, REMINDED ME OF SOMETHING THAT ONCE HAPPENED THAT MAYBE I SHOULD TRY TO REMEMBER NOW.
Follow your Dreams
I TRIED, HONEST I TRIED, BUT NOTHING CAME OUT. I WAS GETTING SICK OF THE WHOLE THING BUT PHIL JUST KEPT PUSHING IT AND INSISTING SO FINALLY TO GET HIM TO FINALLY SHUT UP I TOSSED HIM A BONE AND MADE UP SOME STORY ABOUT UNCLE ROY BABYSITTING ME THAT TIME AND MOLESTING ME. PHIL LOVED THAT KIND OF BULLSHIT AND LAPPED IT RIGHT UP.
MUSIC

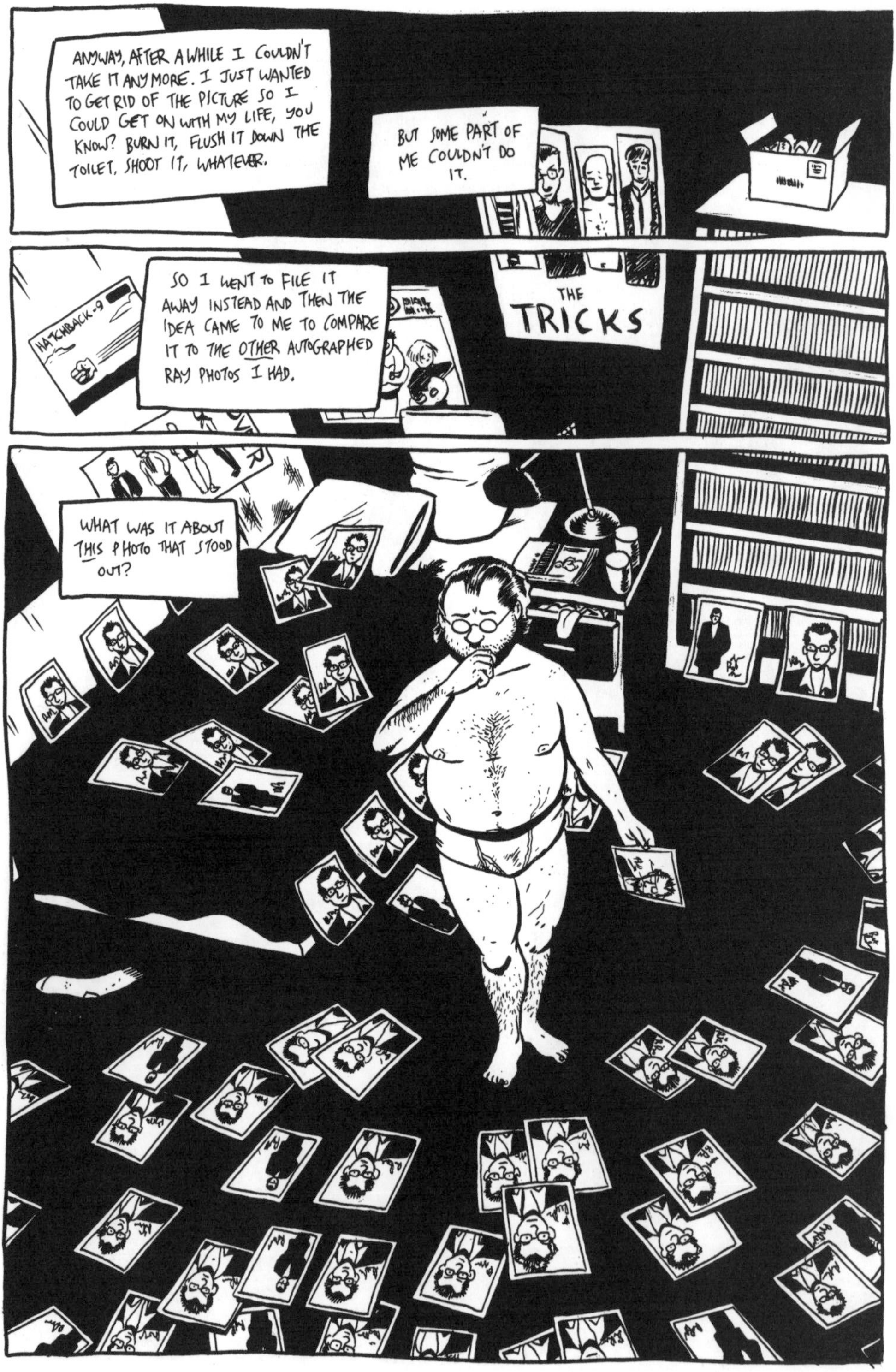
ANYWAY, AFTER A WHILE I COULDN'T TAKE IT ANYMORE. I JUST WANTED TO GET RID OF THE PICTURE SO I COULD GET ON WITH MY LIFE, YOU KNOW? BURN IT, FLUSH IT DOWN THE TOILET, SHOOT IT, WHATEVER.
BUT SOME PART OF ME COULDN'T DO IT.
SO I WENT TO FILE IT AWAY INSTEAD AND THEN THE IDEA CAME TO ME TO COMPARE IT TO THE OTHER AUTOGRAPHED RAY PHOTOS I HAD.
HATCHBACK-9
THE TRICKS
WHAT WAS IT ABOUT THIS PHOTO THAT STOOD OUT?

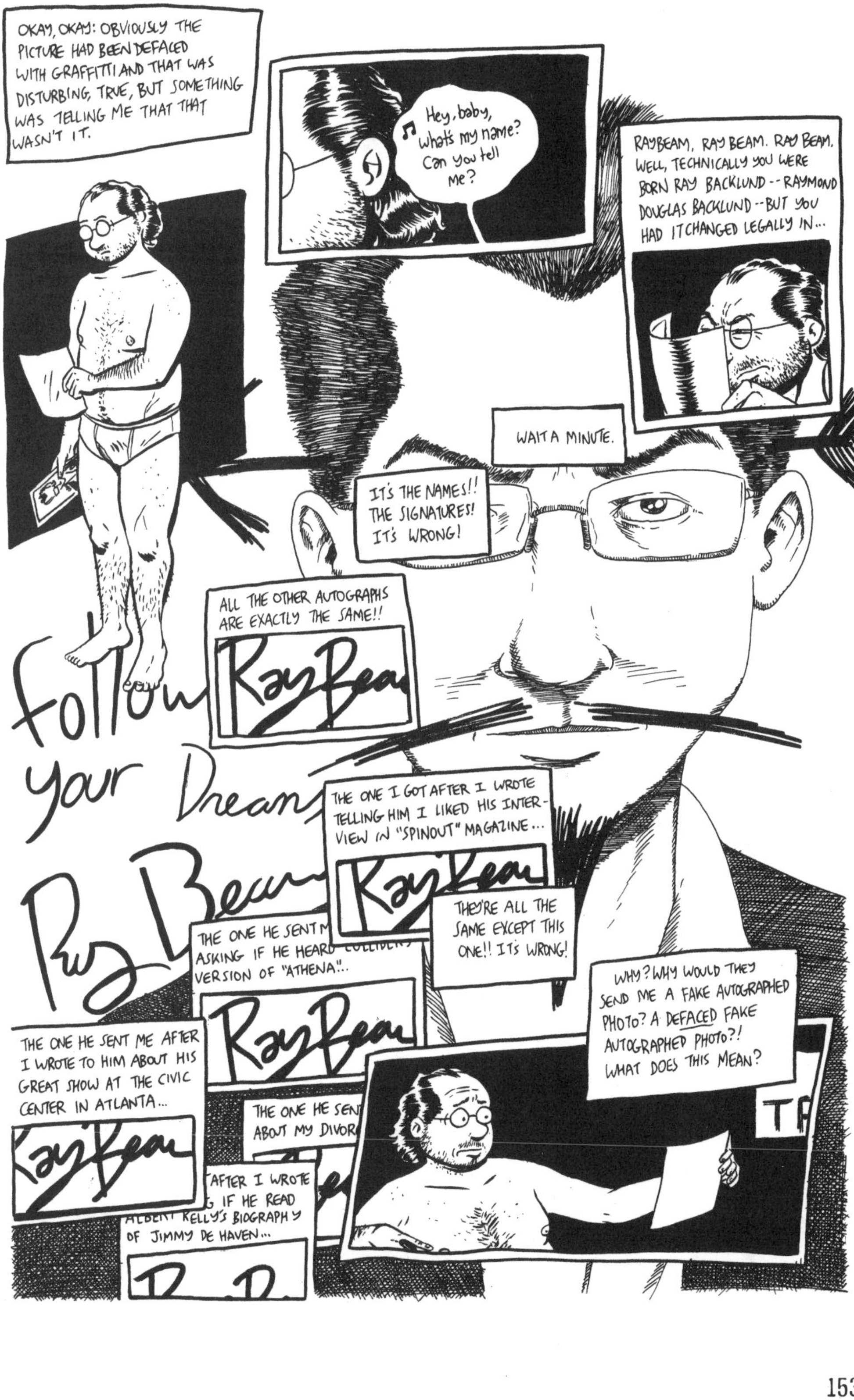

OKAY, OKAY: OBVIOUSLY THE PICTURE HAD BEEN DEFACED WITH GRAFFITTI AND THAT WAS DISTURBING, TRUE, BUT SOMETHING WAS TELLING ME THAT THAT WASN'T IT.
Hey, baby, what's my name? Can you tell me?
RAYBEAM, RAY BEAM. RAY BEAM. WELL, TECHNICALLY YOU WERE BORN RAY BACKLUND -- RAYMOND DOUGLAS BACKLUND -- BUT YOU HAD IT CHANGED LEGALLY IN...
WAIT A MINUTE.
IT'S THE NAMES!! THE SIGNATURES! IT'S WRONG!
ALL THE OTHER AUTOGRAPHS ARE EXACTLY THE SAME!!
Ray Bea
Follow your Dream
Ray Bea
THE ONE I GOT AFTER I WROTE TELLING HIM I LIKED HIS INTER-VIEW IN "SPINOUT" MAGAZINE...
Ray Bea
THEY'RE ALL THE SAME EXCEPT THIS ONE!! IT'S WRONG!
VERSION OF "ATHENA"...
Ray Bea
WHY? WHY WOULD THEY SEND ME A FAKE AUTOGRAPHED PHOTO? A DEFACED FAKE AUTOGRAPHED PHOTO?! WHAT DOES THIS MEAN?
THE ONE HE SENT ME AFTER I WROTE TO HIM ABOUT HIS GREAT SHOW AT THE CIVIC CENTER IN ATLANTA...
Ray Bea
ABOUT MY DIVOR
AFTER I WROTE
IF HE READ
KELLY'S BIOGRAPHY OF JIMMY DE HAVEN...

TWENTYSEVEN

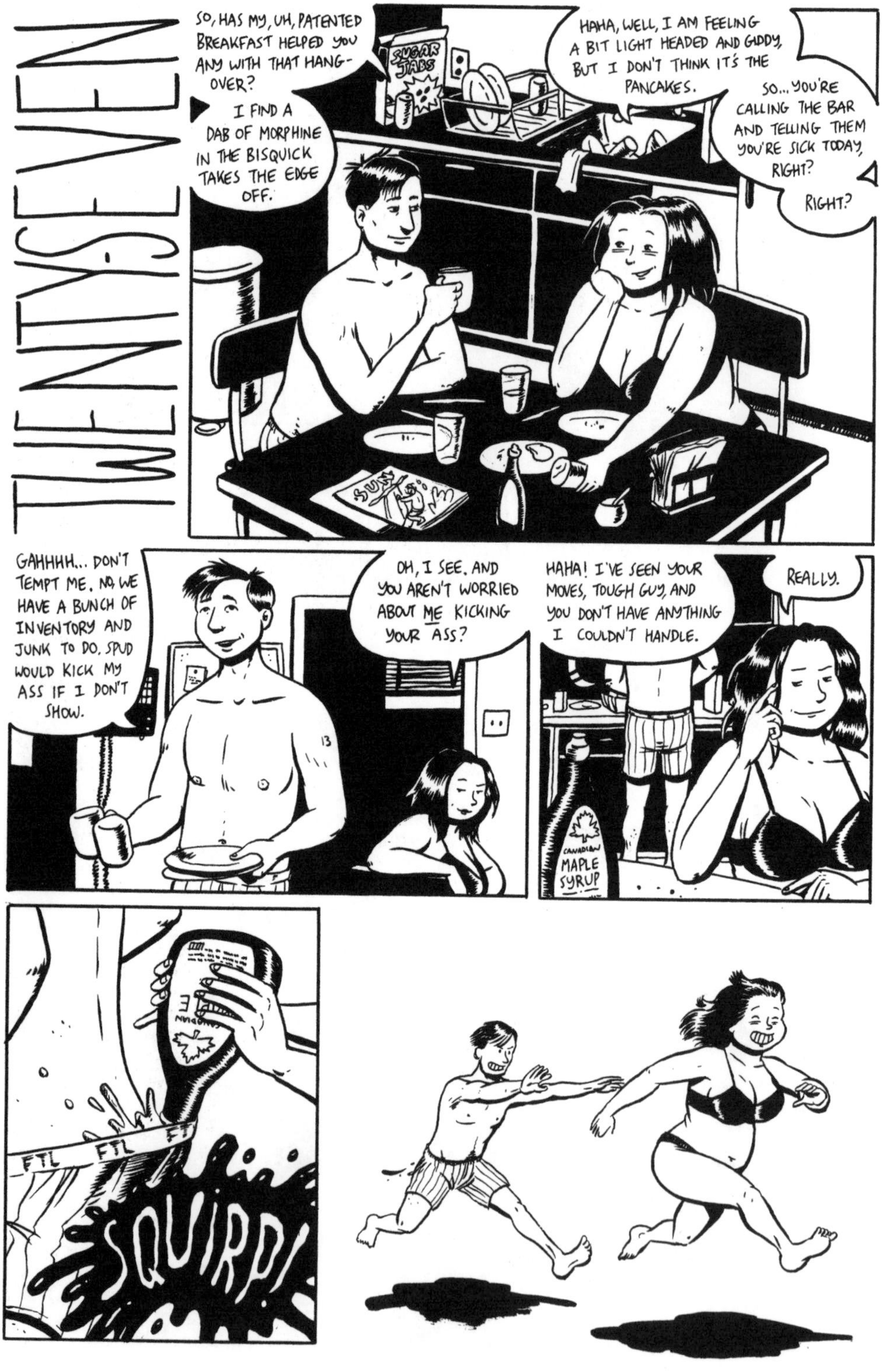
SO, HAS MY, UH, PATENTED BREAKFAST HELPED YOU ANY WITH THAT HANG-OVER?
I FIND A DAB OF MORPHINE IN THE BISQUICK TAKES THE EDGE OFF.
SUGAR JABS
HAHA, WELL, I AM FEELING A BIT LIGHT HEADED AND GIDDY, BUT I DON'T THINK IT'S THE PANCAKES.
SO... YOU'RE CALLING THE BAR AND TELLING THEM YOU'RE SICK TODAY, RIGHT?
RIGHT?
SUN
GAHHHH... DON'T TEMPT ME. NO, WE HAVE A BUNCH OF INVENTORY AND JUNK TO DO. SPUD WOULD KICK MY ASS IF I DON'T SHOW.
OH, I SEE. AND YOU AREN'T WORRIED ABOUT ME KICKING YOUR ASS?
HAHA! I'VE SEEN YOUR MOVES, TOUGH GUY, AND YOU DON'T HAVE ANYTHING I COULDN'T HANDLE.
REALLY.
CANADIAN MAPLE SYRUP
FTL FTL FT
SQUIRP!

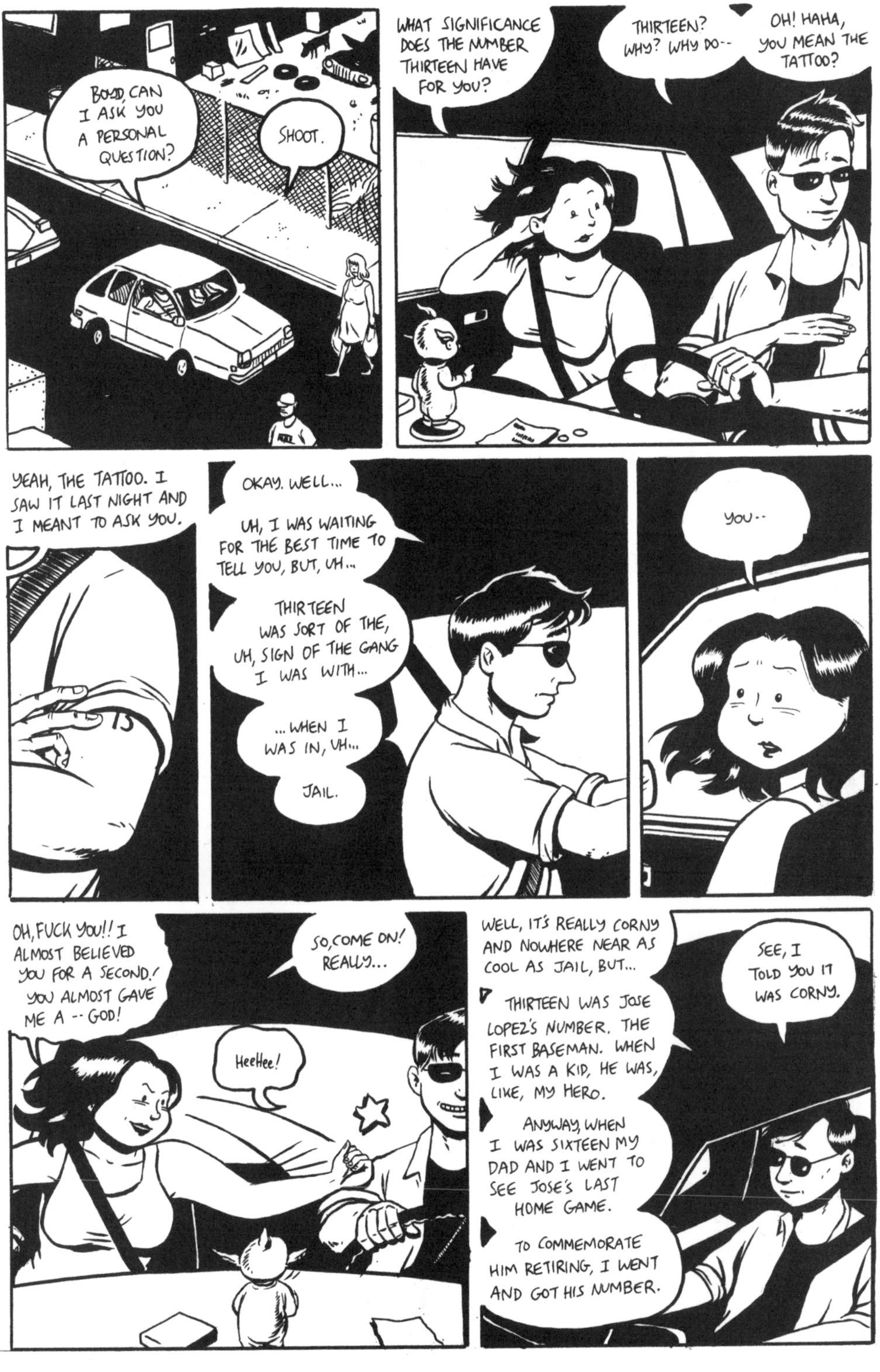
BOYD, CAN I ASK YOU A PERSONAL QUESTION?
SHOOT.
WHAT SIGNIFICANCE DOES THE NUMBER THIRTEEN HAVE FOR YOU?
THIRTEEN? WHY? WHY DO--
OH! HAHA, YOU MEAN THE TATTOO?
YEAH, THE TATTOO. I SAW IT LAST NIGHT AND I MEANT TO ASK YOU.
OKAY. WELL...
UH, I WAS WAITING FOR THE BEST TIME TO TELL YOU, BUT, UH...
THIRTEEN WAS SORT OF THE, UH, SIGN OF THE GANG I WAS WITH...
...WHEN I WAS IN, UH...
JAIL.
YOU--
OH, FUCK YOU!! I ALMOST BELIEVED YOU FOR A SECOND! YOU ALMOST GAVE ME A -- GOD!
SO, COME ON! REALLY...
HeeHee!
WELL, IT'S REALLY CORNY AND NOWHERE NEAR AS COOL AS JAIL, BUT...
THIRTEEN WAS JOSE LOPEZ'S NUMBER. THE FIRST BASEMAN. WHEN I WAS A KID, HE WAS, LIKE, MY HERO.
ANYWAY, WHEN I WAS SIXTEEN MY DAD AND I WENT TO SEE JOSE'S LAST HOME GAME.
TO COMMEMORATE HIM RETIRING, I WENT AND GOT HIS NUMBER.
SEE, I TOLD YOU IT WAS CORNY.

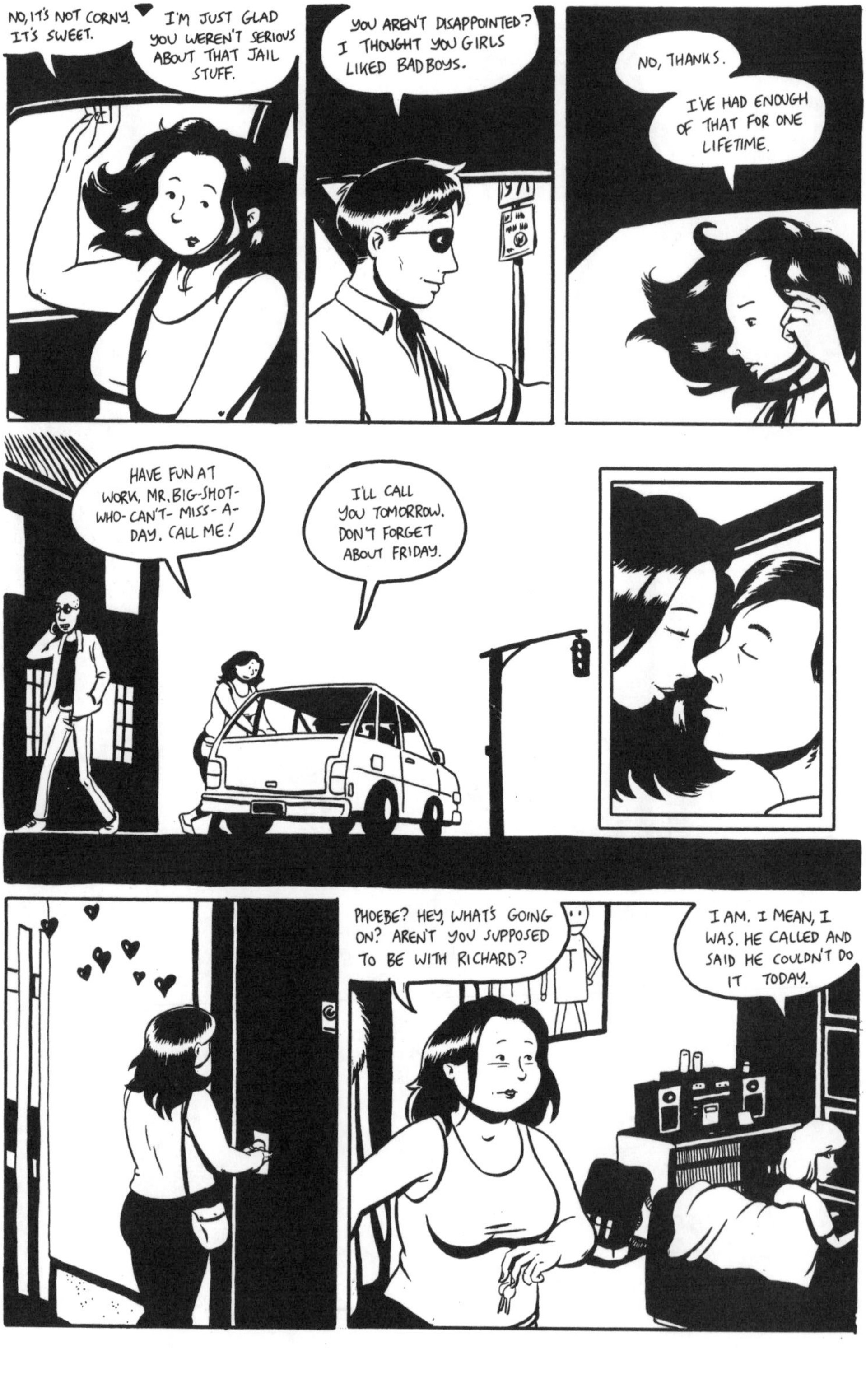
NO, IT'S NOT CORNY. IT'S SWEET.
I'M JUST GLAD YOU WEREN'T SERIOUS ABOUT THAT JAIL STUFF.
YOU AREN'T DISAPPOINTED? I THOUGHT YOU GIRLS LIKED BAD BOYS.
NO, THANKS.
I'VE HAD ENOUGH OF THAT FOR ONE LIFETIME.
HAVE FUN AT WORK, MR. BIG-SHOT-WHO-CAN'T-MISS-A-DAY. CALL ME!
I'LL CALL YOU TOMORROW. DON'T FORGET ABOUT FRIDAY.
PHOEBE? HEY, WHAT'S GOING ON? AREN'T YOU SUPPOSED TO BE WITH RICHARD?
I AM. I MEAN, I WAS. HE CALLED AND SAID HE COULDN'T DO IT TODAY.

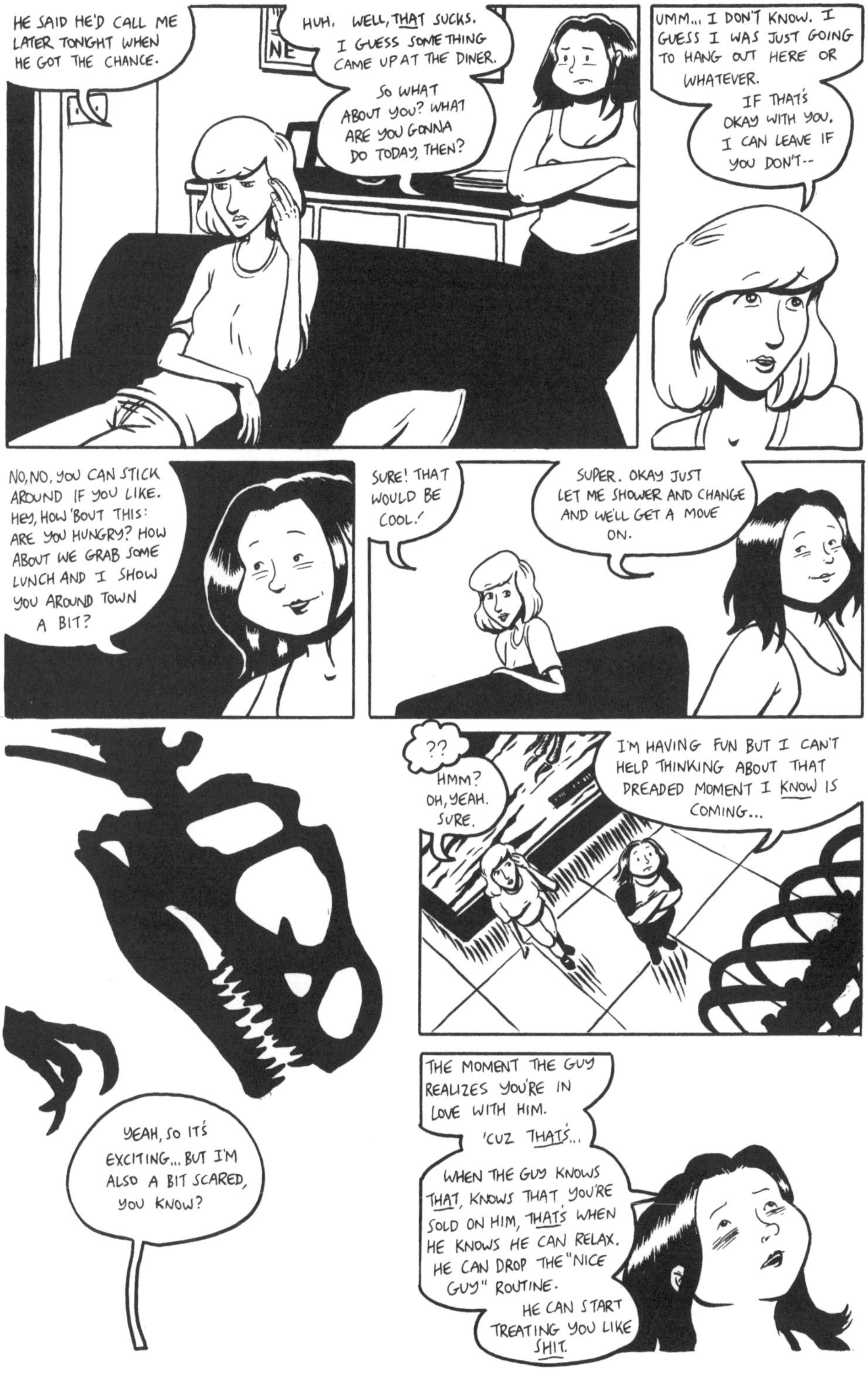
HE SAID HE'D CALL ME LATER TONIGHT WHEN HE GOT THE CHANCE.
HUH. WELL, THAT SUCKS. I GUESS SOMETHING CAME UP AT THE DINER.
SO WHAT ABOUT YOU? WHAT ARE YOU GONNA DO TODAY, THEN?
UMM... I DON'T KNOW. I GUESS I WAS JUST GOING TO HANG OUT HERE OR WHATEVER.
IF THAT'S OKAY WITH YOU. I CAN LEAVE IF YOU DON'T--
NO, NO, YOU CAN STICK AROUND IF YOU LIKE. HEY, HOW 'BOUT THIS: ARE YOU HUNGRY? HOW ABOUT WE GRAB SOME LUNCH AND I SHOW YOU AROUND TOWN A BIT?
SURE! THAT WOULD BE COOL!
SUPER. OKAY JUST LET ME SHOWER AND CHANGE AND WE'LL GET A MOVE ON.
YEAH, SO IT'S EXCITING... BUT I'M ALSO A BIT SCARED, YOU KNOW?
??
HMM? OH, YEAH. SURE.
I'M HAVING FUN BUT I CAN'T HELP THINKING ABOUT THAT DREADED MOMENT I KNOW IS COMING...
THE MOMENT THE GUY REALIZES YOU'RE IN LOVE WITH HIM.
'CUZ THAT'S...
WHEN THE GUY KNOWS THAT, KNOWS THAT YOU'RE SOLD ON HIM, THAT'S WHEN HE KNOWS HE CAN RELAX. HE CAN DROP THE "NICE GUY" ROUTINE.
HE CAN START TREATING YOU LIKE SHIT.

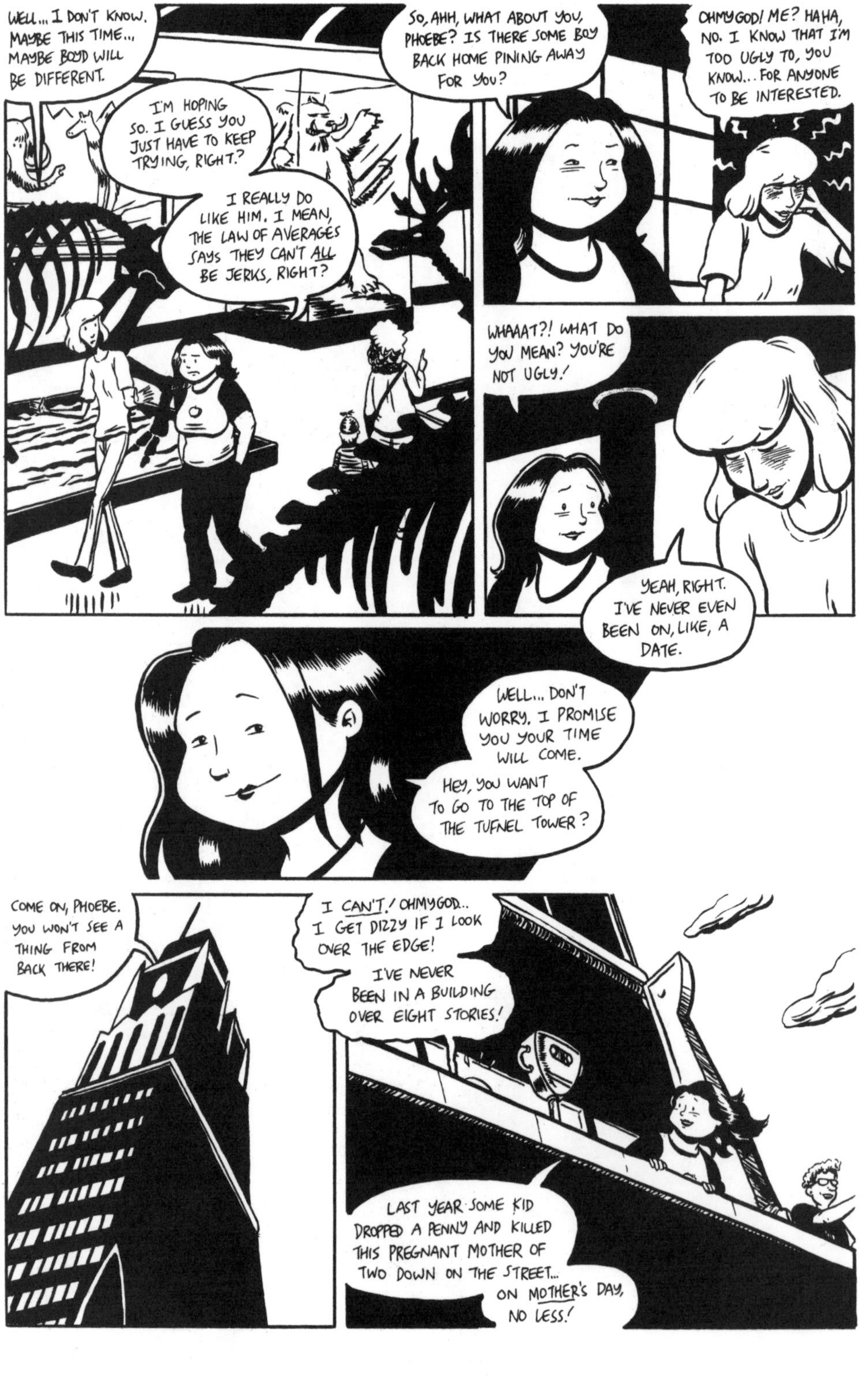
WELL... I DON'T KNOW. MAYBE THIS TIME... MAYBE BOYD WILL BE DIFFERENT.
I'M HOPING SO. I GUESS YOU JUST HAVE TO KEEP TRYING, RIGHT?
I REALLY DO LIKE HIM. I MEAN, THE LAW OF AVERAGES SAYS THEY CAN'T ALL BE JERKS, RIGHT?
SO, AHH, WHAT ABOUT YOU, PHOEBE? IS THERE SOME BOY BACK HOME PINING AWAY FOR YOU?
OHMYGOD! ME? HAHA, NO. I KNOW THAT I'M TOO UGLY TO, YOU KNOW... FOR ANYONE TO BE INTERESTED.
WHAAAT?! WHAT DO YOU MEAN? YOU'RE NOT UGLY!
YEAH, RIGHT. I'VE NEVER EVEN BEEN ON, LIKE, A DATE.
WELL... DON'T WORRY. I PROMISE YOU YOUR TIME WILL COME.
HEY, YOU WANT TO GO TO THE TOP OF THE TUFNEL TOWER?
COME ON, PHOEBE. YOU WON'T SEE A THING FROM BACK THERE!
I CAN'T! OHMYGOD... I GET DIZZY IF I LOOK OVER THE EDGE!
I'VE NEVER BEEN IN A BUILDING OVER EIGHT STORIES!
LAST YEAR SOME KID DROPPED A PENNY AND KILLED THIS PREGNANT MOTHER OF TWO DOWN ON THE STREET...
ON MOTHER'S DAY, NO LESS!

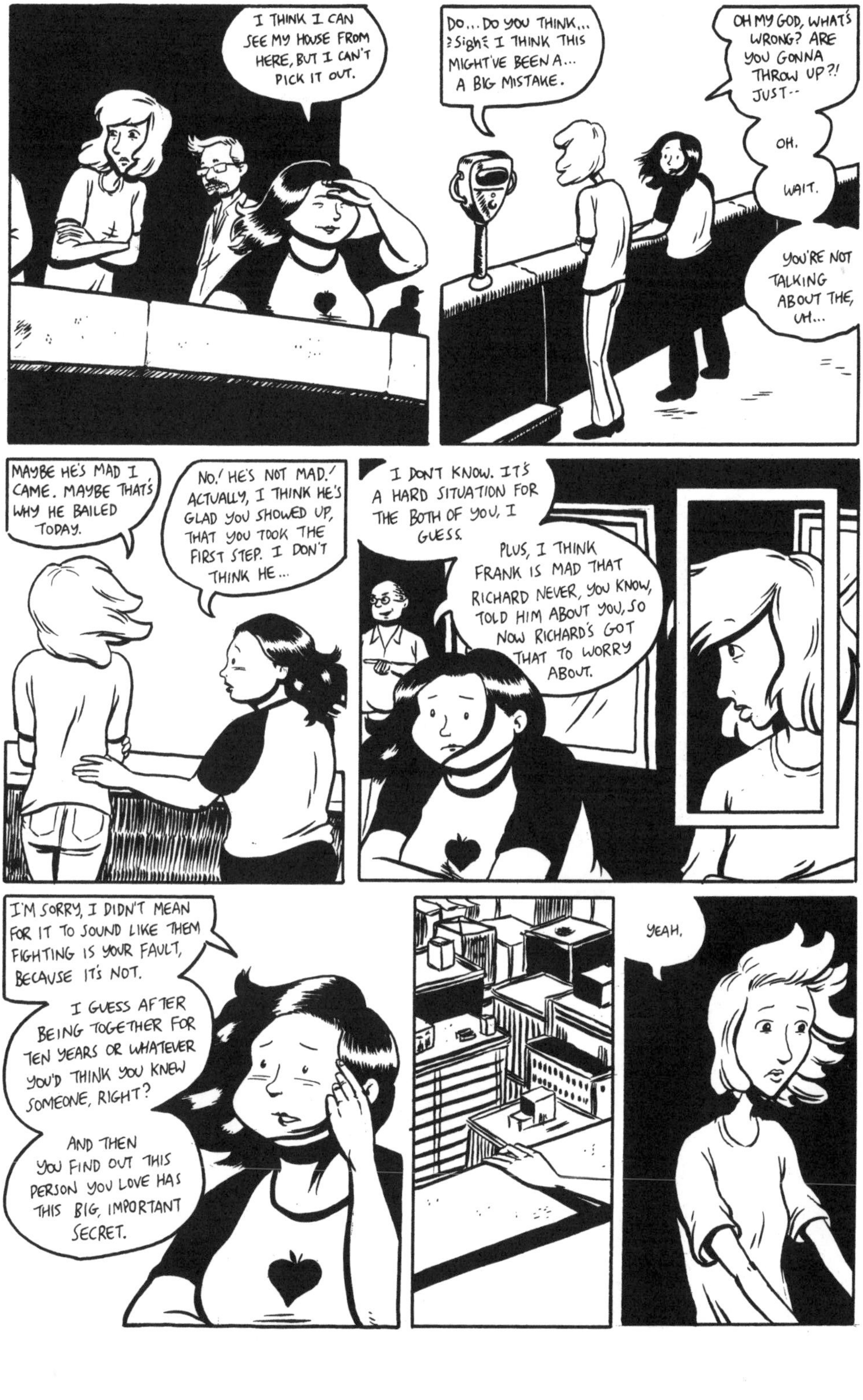
I THINK I CAN SEE MY HOUSE FROM HERE, BUT I CAN'T PICK IT OUT.
DO... DO YOU THINK... ≷SIGH≶ I THINK THIS MIGHT'VE BEEN A... A BIG MISTAKE.
OH MY GOD, WHAT'S WRONG? ARE YOU GONNA THROW UP?! JUST--
OH.
WAIT.
YOU'RE NOT TALKING ABOUT THE, UH...
MAYBE HE'S MAD I CAME. MAYBE THAT'S WHY HE BAILED TODAY.
NO! HE'S NOT MAD! ACTUALLY, I THINK HE'S GLAD YOU SHOWED UP, THAT YOU TOOK THE FIRST STEP. I DON'T THINK HE...
I DON'T KNOW. IT'S A HARD SITUATION FOR THE BOTH OF YOU, I GUESS.
PLUS, I THINK FRANK IS MAD THAT RICHARD NEVER, YOU KNOW, TOLD HIM ABOUT YOU, SO NOW RICHARD'S GOT THAT TO WORRY ABOUT.
I'M SORRY, I DIDN'T MEAN FOR IT TO SOUND LIKE THEM FIGHTING IS YOUR FAULT, BECAUSE IT'S NOT.
I GUESS AFTER BEING TOGETHER FOR TEN YEARS OR WHATEVER YOU'D THINK YOU KNEW SOMEONE, RIGHT?
AND THEN YOU FIND OUT THIS PERSON YOU LOVE HAS THIS BIG, IMPORTANT SECRET.
YEAH.

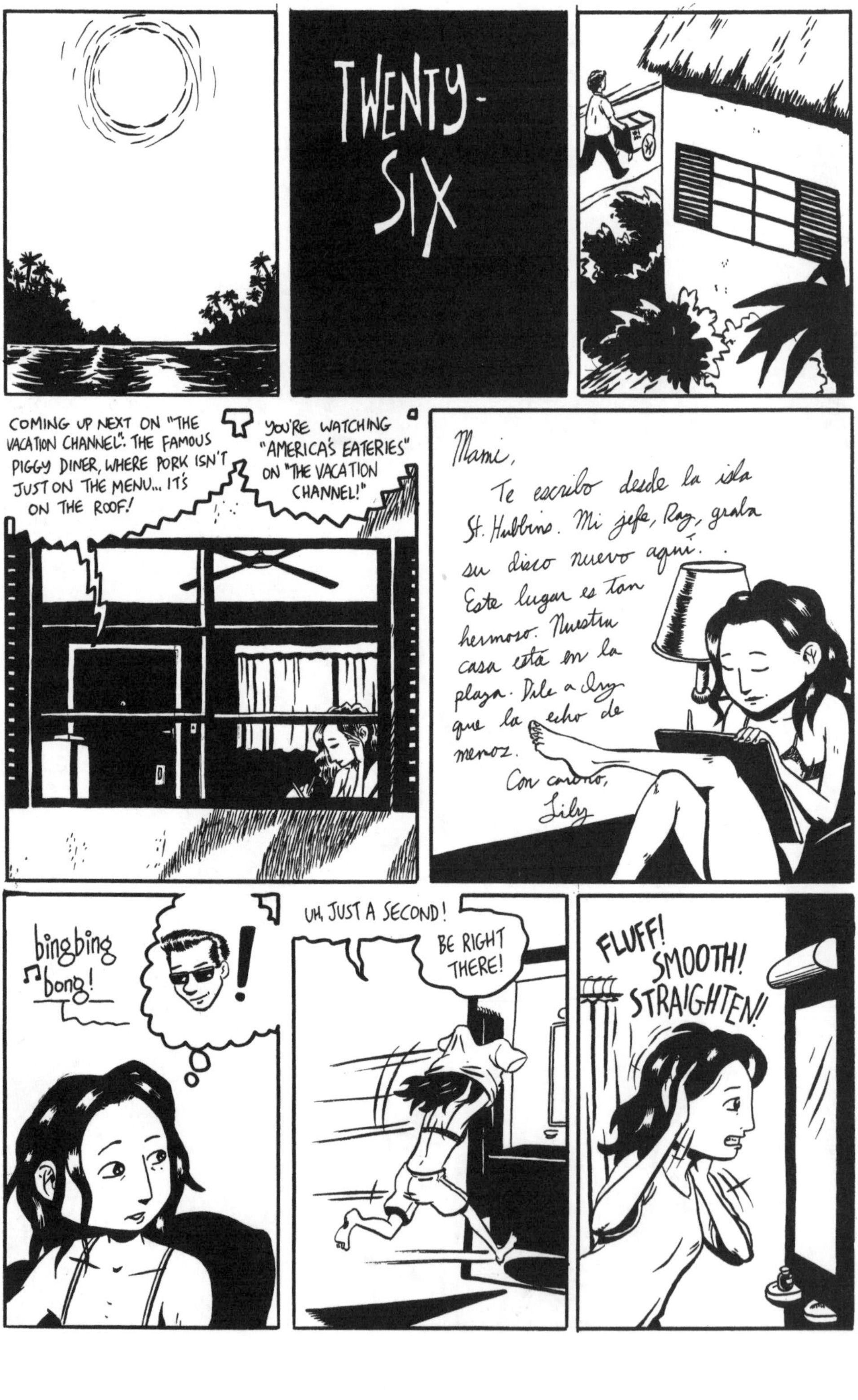
TWENTY-SIX
COMING UP NEXT ON "THE VACATION CHANNEL": THE FAMOUS PIGGY DINER, WHERE PORK ISN'T JUST ON THE MENU... IT'S ON THE ROOF!
YOU'RE WATCHING "AMERICA'S EATERIES" ON "THE VACATION CHANNEL!"
Mami,
Te escribo desde la isla St. Hubbins. Mi jefe, Ray, graba su disco nuevo aquí. Este lugar es tan hermoso. Nuestra casa está en la playa. Dile a Ivy que la echo de menoz.
Con cariño,
Lily
bingbing bong!
!
UH, JUST A SECOND!
BE RIGHT THERE!
FLUFF! SMOOTH! STRAIGHTEN!

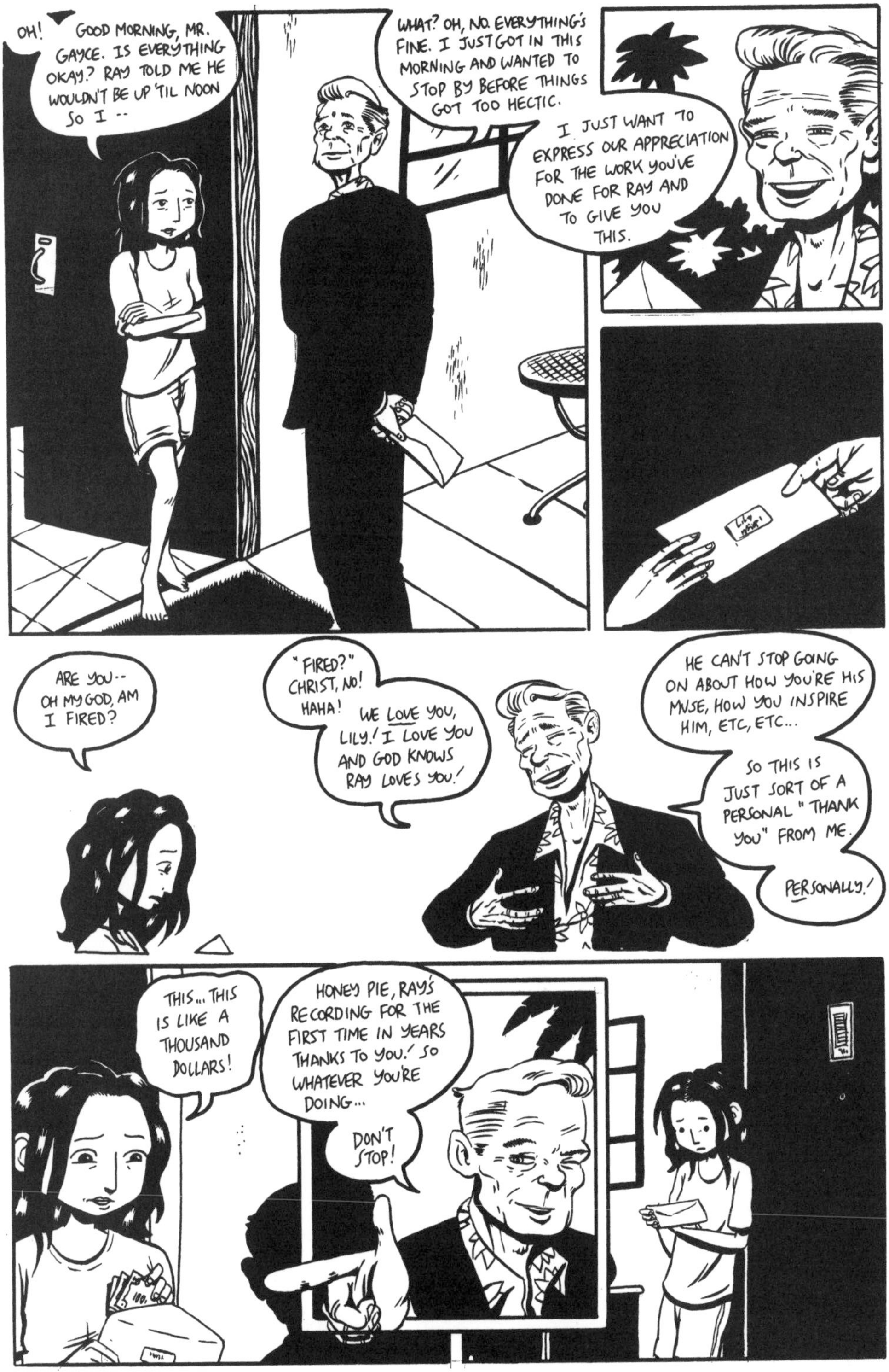
OH!
GOOD MORNING, MR. GAYCE. IS EVERYTHING OKAY? RAY TOLD ME HE WOULDN'T BE UP 'TIL NOON SO I --
WHAT? OH, NO. EVERYTHING'S FINE. I JUST GOT IN THIS MORNING AND WANTED TO STOP BY BEFORE THINGS GOT TOO HECTIC.
I JUST WANT TO EXPRESS OUR APPRECIATION FOR THE WORK YOU'VE DONE FOR RAY AND TO GIVE YOU THIS.
ARE YOU-- OH MY GOD, AM I FIRED?
"FIRED?" CHRIST, NO! HAHA!
WE LOVE YOU, LILY! I LOVE YOU AND GOD KNOWS RAY LOVES YOU!
HE CAN'T STOP GOING ON ABOUT HOW YOU'RE HIS MUSE, HOW YOU INSPIRE HIM, ETC, ETC...
SO THIS IS JUST SORT OF A PERSONAL "THANK YOU" FROM ME.
PERSONALLY!
THIS... THIS IS LIKE A THOUSAND DOLLARS!
HONEY PIE, RAY'S RECORDING FOR THE FIRST TIME IN YEARS THANKS TO YOU! SO WHATEVER YOU'RE DOING...
DON'T STOP!

1) BE MINDFUL OF PLAYERS BEHIND YOU
2) STEP OFF PUTTING GREENS BEFORE MARKING SCORE.
3) OBSCENE LANGUAGE, GESTURES, ATTIRE OR BEHAVIOR WILL NOT BE TOLERATED.
HOLE NO.
PAR
NAME
NAME
NAME
NAME
NAME

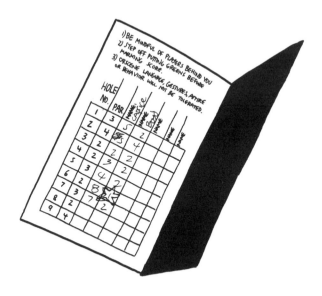

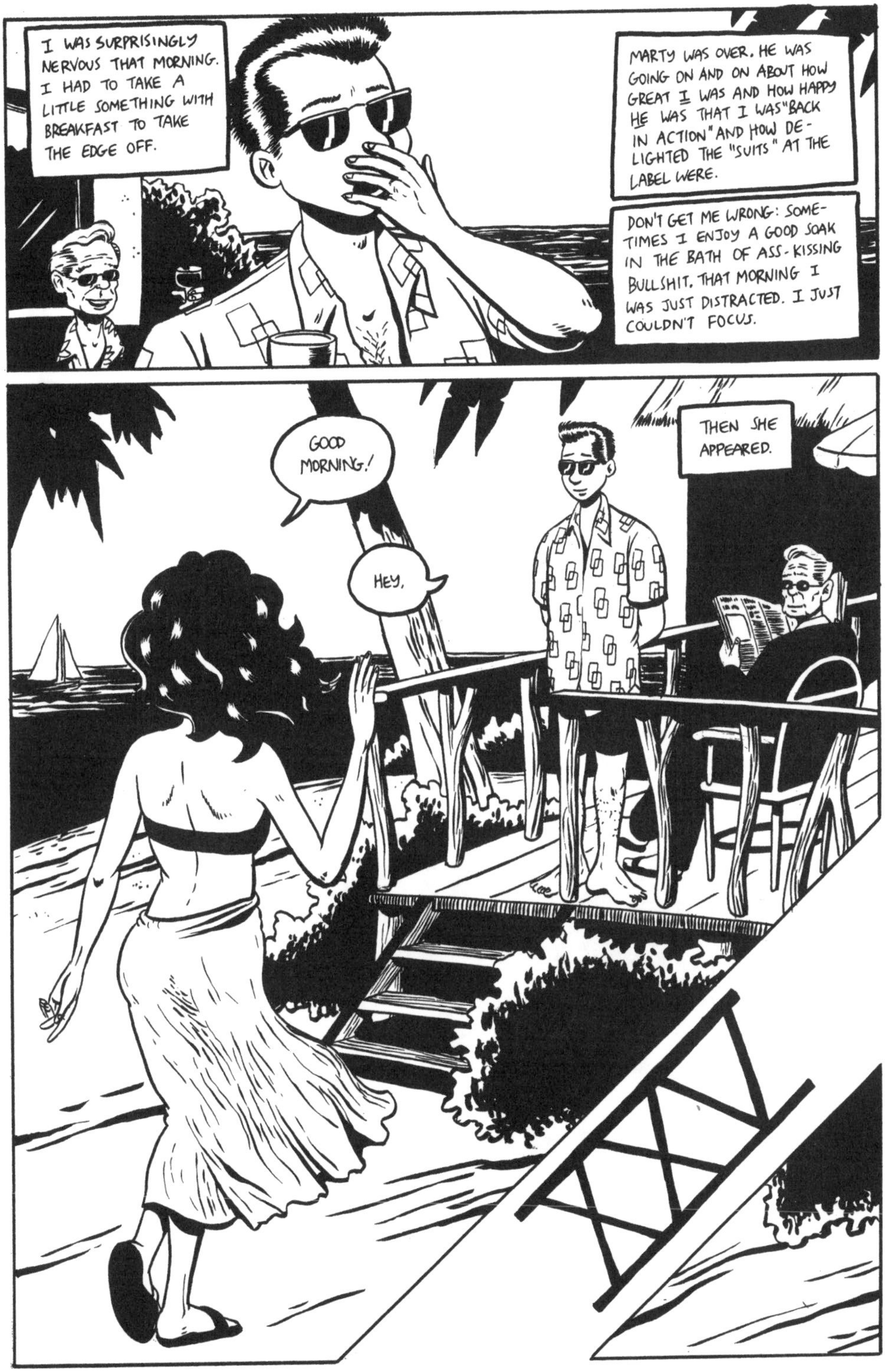
I WAS SURPRISINGLY NERVOUS THAT MORNING. I HAD TO TAKE A LITTLE SOMETHING WITH BREAKFAST TO TAKE THE EDGE OFF.
MARTY WAS OVER. HE WAS GOING ON AND ON ABOUT HOW GREAT I WAS AND HOW HAPPY HE WAS THAT I WAS "BACK IN ACTION" AND HOW DELIGHTED THE "SUITS" AT THE LABEL WERE.
DON'T GET ME WRONG: SOMETIMES I ENJOY A GOOD SOAK IN THE BATH OF ASS-KISSING BULLSHIT. THAT MORNING I WAS JUST DISTRACTED. I JUST COULDN'T FOCUS.
THEN SHE APPEARED.
GOOD MORNING!
HEY.

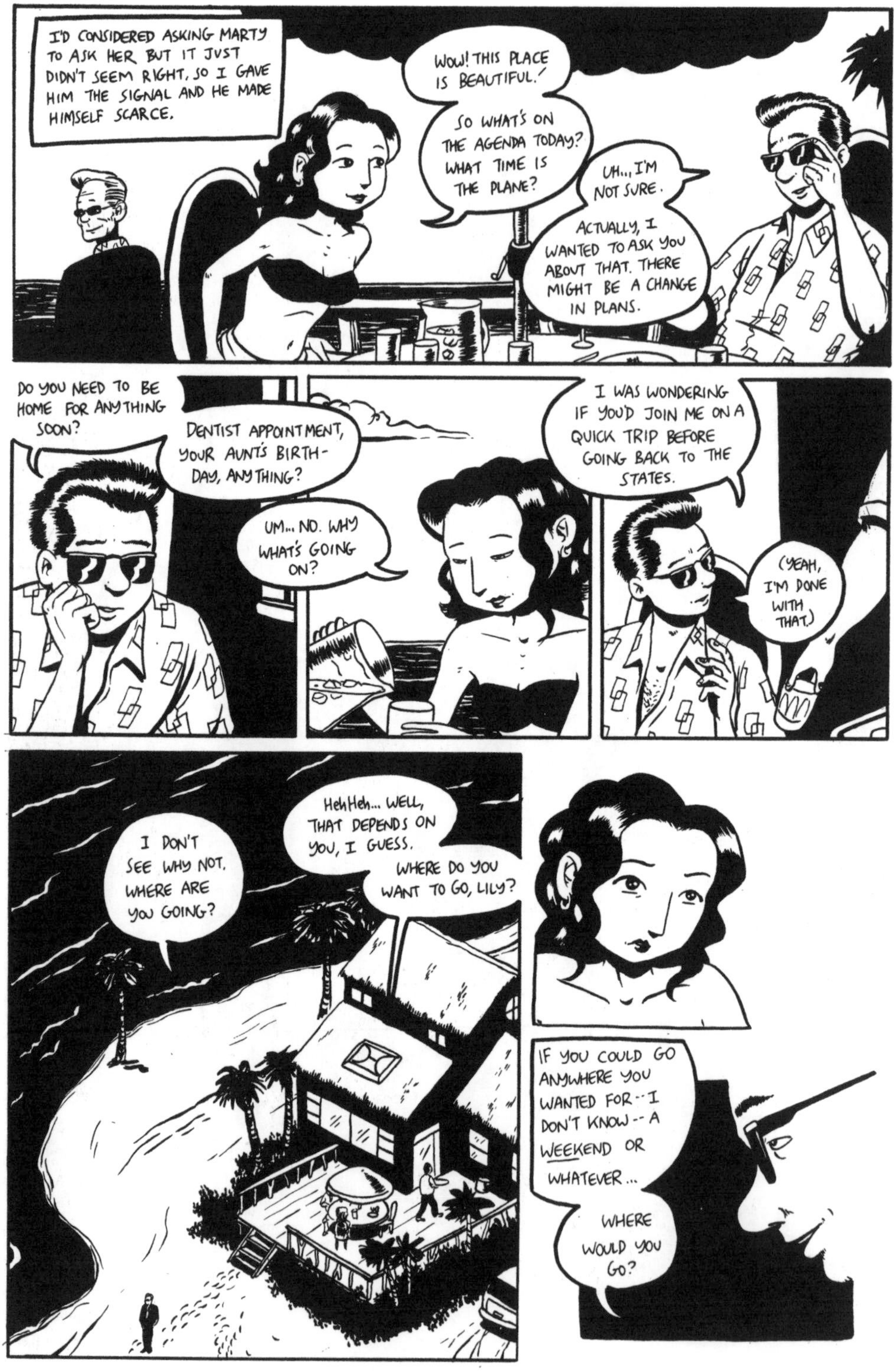
I'D CONSIDERED ASKING MARTY TO ASK HER BUT IT JUST DIDN'T SEEM RIGHT, SO I GAVE HIM THE SIGNAL AND HE MADE HIMSELF SCARCE.
WOW! THIS PLACE IS BEAUTIFUL!
SO WHAT'S ON THE AGENDA TODAY? WHAT TIME IS THE PLANE?
UH..., I'M NOT SURE.
ACTUALLY, I WANTED TO ASK YOU ABOUT THAT. THERE MIGHT BE A CHANGE IN PLANS.
DO YOU NEED TO BE HOME FOR ANYTHING SOON?
DENTIST APPOINTMENT, YOUR AUNT'S BIRTH-DAY, ANYTHING?
UM... NO. WHY WHAT'S GOING ON?
I WAS WONDERING IF YOU'D JOIN ME ON A QUICK TRIP BEFORE GOING BACK TO THE STATES.
(YEAH, I'M DONE WITH THAT.)
I DON'T SEE WHY NOT. WHERE ARE YOU GOING?
HehHeh... WELL, THAT DEPENDS ON YOU, I GUESS.
WHERE DO YOU WANT TO GO, LILY?
IF YOU COULD GO ANYWHERE YOU WANTED FOR -- I DON'T KNOW -- A WEEKEND OR WHATEVER...
WHERE WOULD YOU GO?

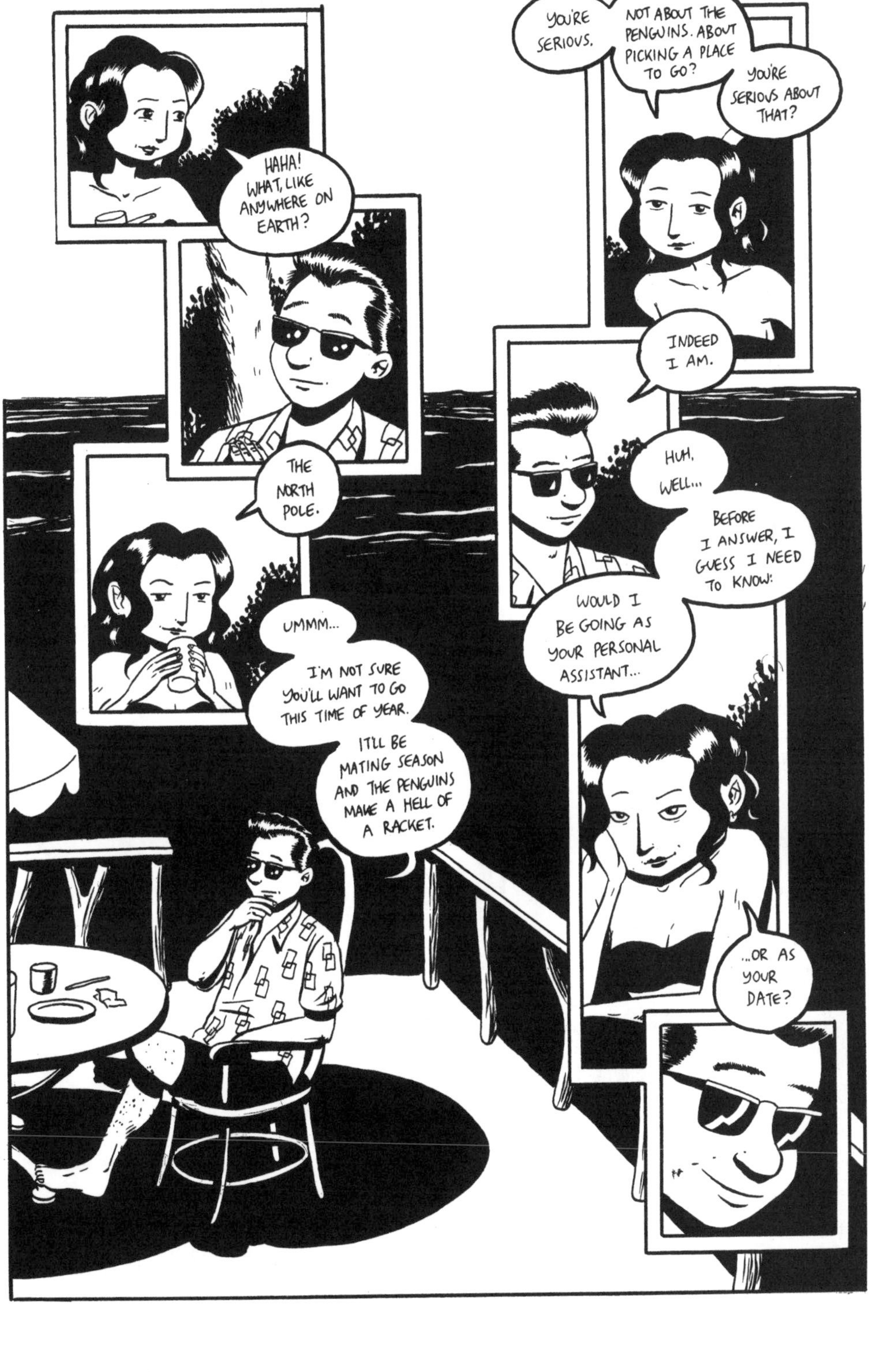
HAHA! WHAT, LIKE ANYWHERE ON EARTH?
THE NORTH POLE.
UMMM...
I'M NOT SURE YOU'LL WANT TO GO THIS TIME OF YEAR.
IT'LL BE MATING SEASON AND THE PENGUINS MAKE A HELL OF A RACKET.
YOU'RE SERIOUS.
NOT ABOUT THE PENGUINS. ABOUT PICKING A PLACE TO GO?
YOU'RE SERIOUS ABOUT THAT?
INDEED I AM.
HUH. WELL...
BEFORE I ANSWER, I GUESS I NEED TO KNOW:
WOULD I BE GOING AS YOUR PERSONAL ASSISTANT...
...OR AS YOUR DATE?

TWENTY-FOUR

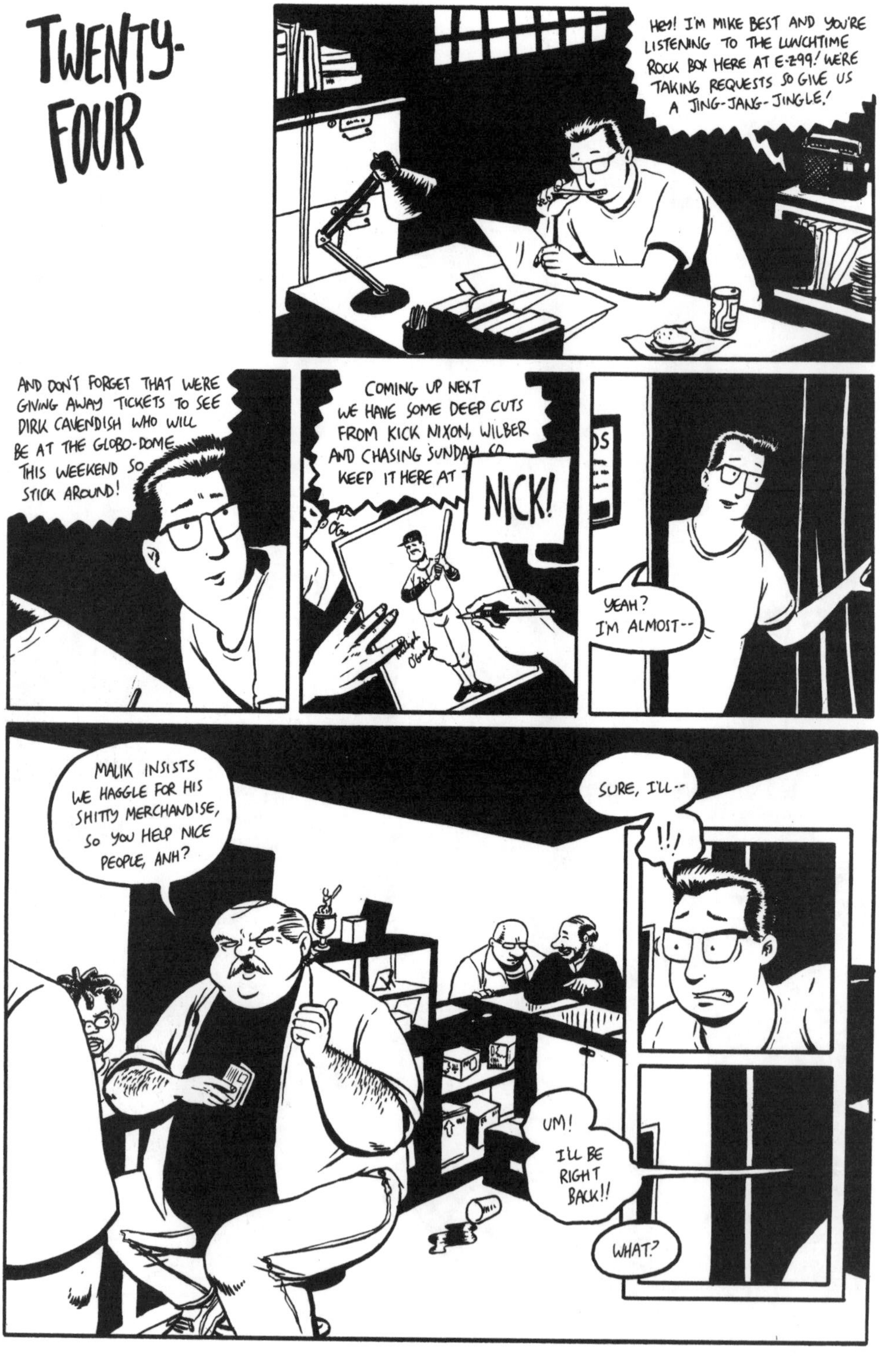
HEY! I'M MIKE BEST AND YOU'RE LISTENING TO THE LUNCHTIME ROCK BOX HERE AT E-Z99! WE'RE TAKING REQUESTS SO GIVE US A JING-JANG-JINGLE!
AND DON'T FORGET THAT WE'RE GIVING AWAY TICKETS TO SEE DIRK CAVENDISH WHO WILL BE AT THE GLOBO-DOME THIS WEEKEND SO STICK AROUND!
COMING UP NEXT WE HAVE SOME DEEP CUTS FROM KICK NIXON, WILBER AND CHASING SUNDAY
KEEP IT HERE AT
NICK!
YEAH? I'M ALMOST--
MALIK INSISTS WE HAGGLE FOR HIS SHITTY MERCHANDISE, SO YOU HELP NICE PEOPLE, ANH?
SURE, I'LL--
!!
UM!
I'LL BE RIGHT BACK!!
WHAT?

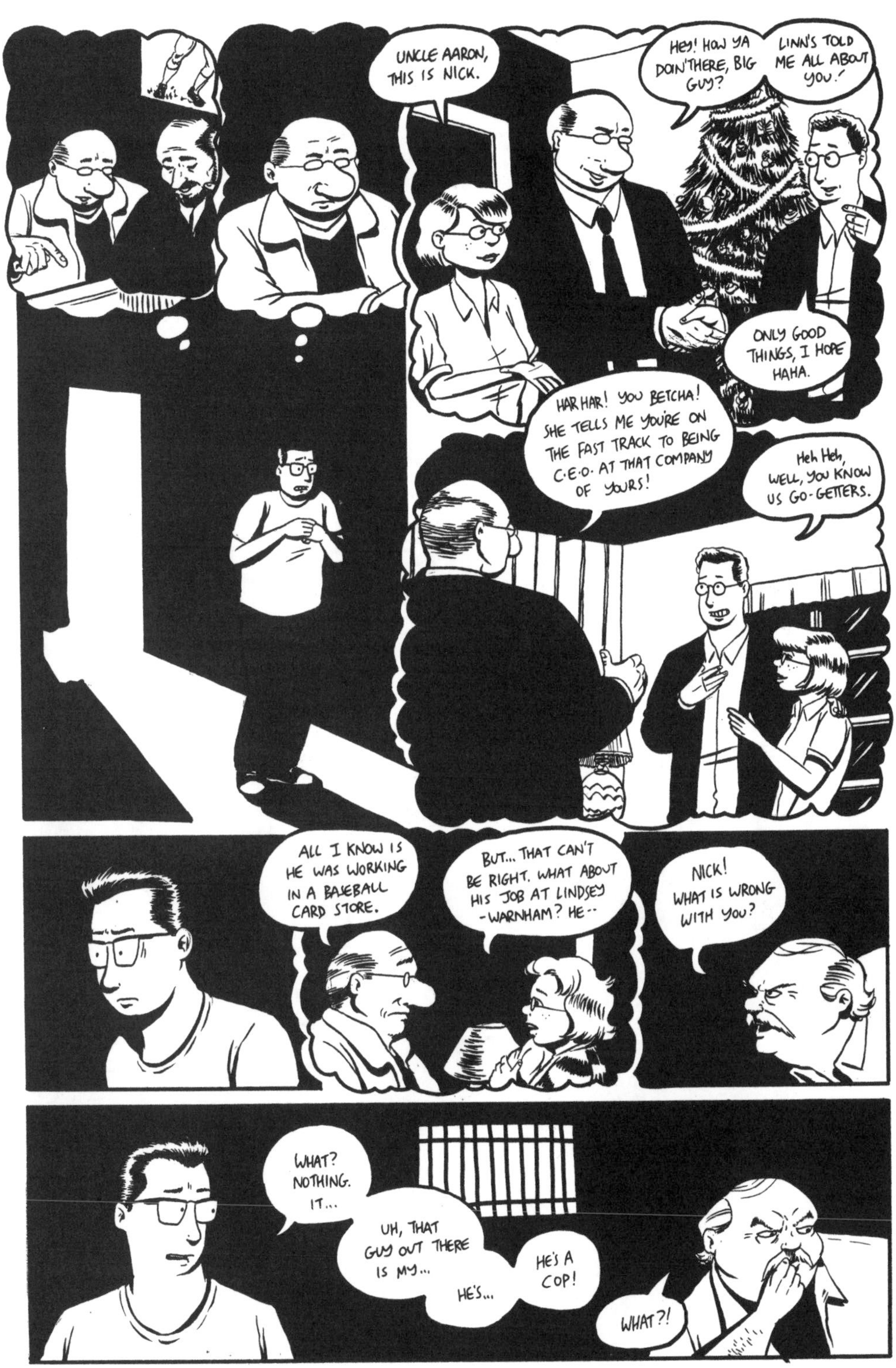
UNCLE AARON, THIS IS NICK.
HEY! HOW YA DOIN' THERE, BIG GUY?
LINN'S TOLD ME ALL ABOUT YOU.
ONLY GOOD THINGS, I HOPE HAHA.
HAR HAR! YOU BETCHA! SHE TELLS ME YOU'RE ON THE FAST TRACK TO BEING C.E.O. AT THAT COMPANY OF YOURS!
Heh Heh, WELL, YOU KNOW US GO-GETTERS.
ALL I KNOW IS HE WAS WORKING IN A BASEBALL CARD STORE.
BUT... THAT CAN'T BE RIGHT. WHAT ABOUT HIS JOB AT LINDSEY-WARNHAM? HE--
NICK! WHAT IS WRONG WITH YOU?
WHAT? NOTHING. IT...
UH, THAT GUY OUT THERE IS MY...
HE'S...
HE'S A COP!
WHAT?!

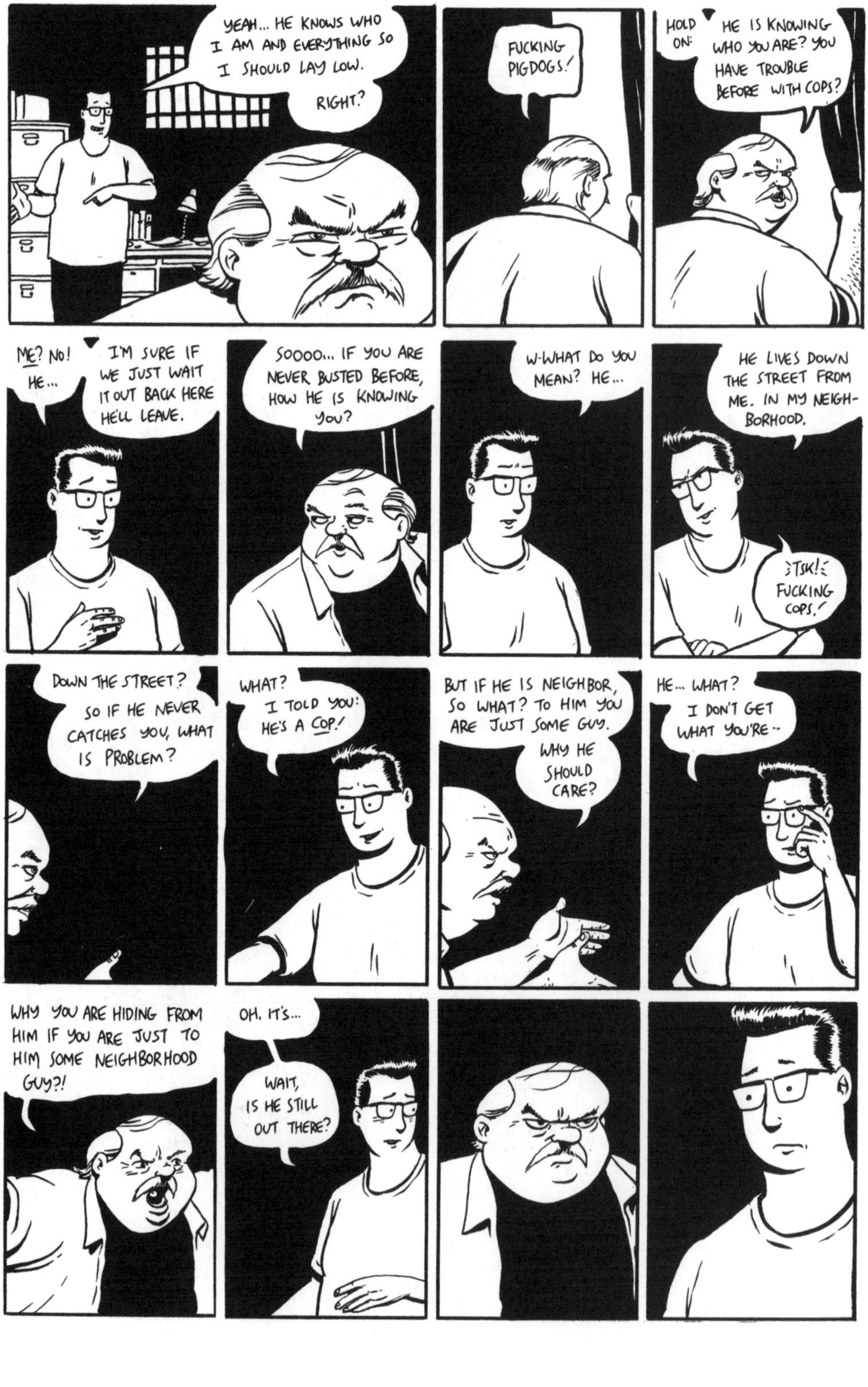
YEAH... HE KNOWS WHO I AM AND EVERYTHING SO I SHOULD LAY LOW.
RIGHT?
FUCKING PIGDOGS!
HOLD ON:
HE IS KNOWING WHO YOU ARE? YOU HAVE TROUBLE BEFORE WITH COPS?
ME? NO! HE...
I'M SURE IF WE JUST WAIT IT OUT BACK HERE HE'LL LEAVE.
SOOOO... IF YOU ARE NEVER BUSTED BEFORE, HOW HE IS KNOWING YOU?
W-WHAT DO YOU MEAN? HE...
HE LIVES DOWN THE STREET FROM ME. IN MY NEIGHBORHOOD.
TSK! FUCKING COPS.
DOWN THE STREET?
SO IF HE NEVER CATCHES YOU, WHAT IS PROBLEM?
WHAT?
I TOLD YOU: HE'S A COP!
BUT IF HE IS NEIGHBOR, SO WHAT? TO HIM YOU ARE JUST SOME GUY.
WHY HE SHOULD CARE?
HE... WHAT?
I DON'T GET WHAT YOU'RE--
WHY YOU ARE HIDING FROM HIM IF YOU ARE JUST TO HIM SOME NEIGHBORHOOD GUY?!
OH. IT'S...
WAIT, IS HE STILL OUT THERE?

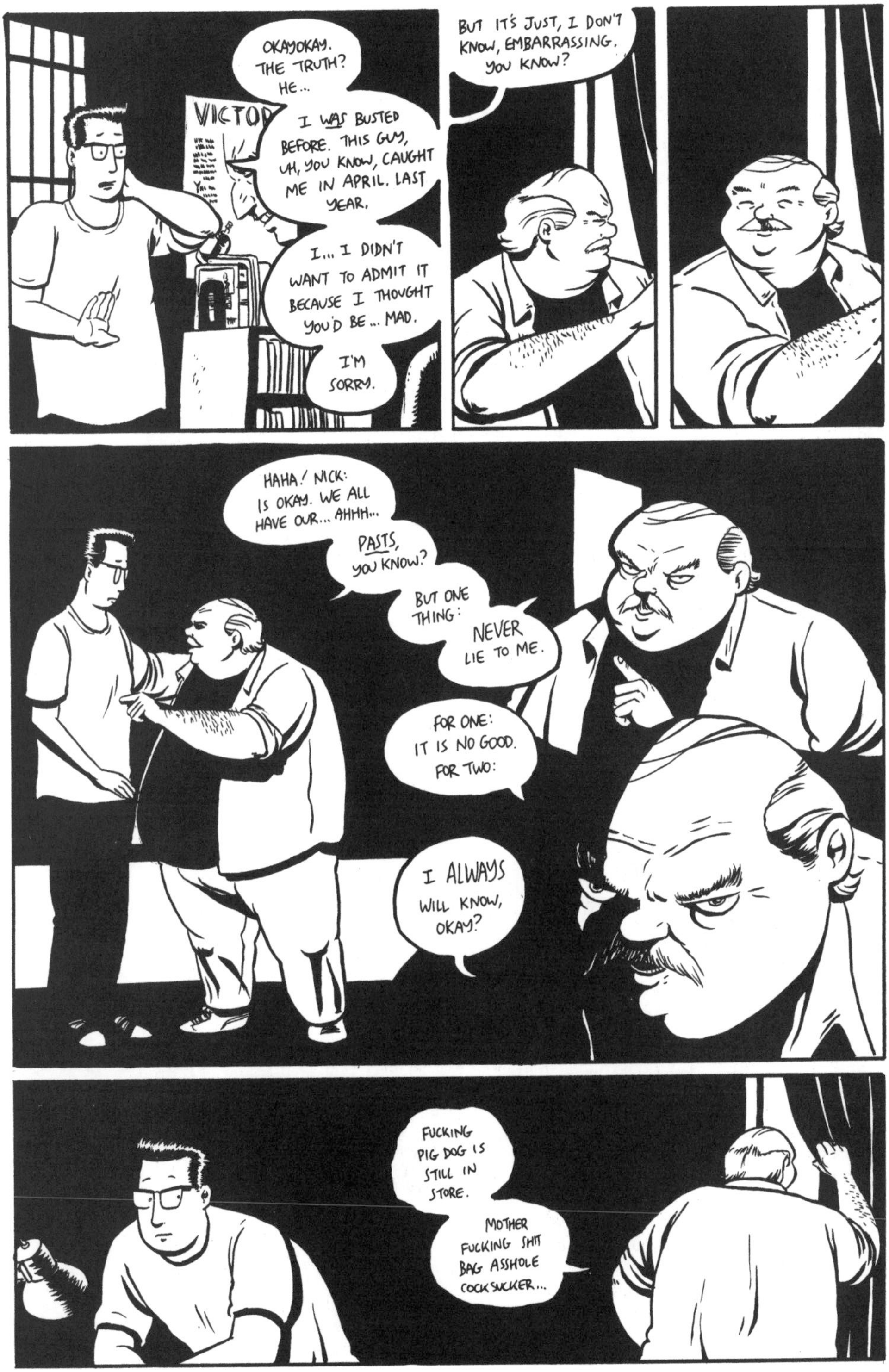
OKAYOKAY. THE TRUTH? HE...
I WAS BUSTED BEFORE. THIS GUY, UH, YOU KNOW, CAUGHT ME IN APRIL. LAST YEAR.
I... I DIDN'T WANT TO ADMIT IT BECAUSE I THOUGHT YOU'D BE... MAD.
I'M SORRY.
BUT IT'S JUST, I DON'T KNOW, EMBARRASSING. YOU KNOW?
HAHA! NICK: IS OKAY. WE ALL HAVE OUR... AHHH...
PASTS, YOU KNOW?
BUT ONE THING: NEVER LIE TO ME.
FOR ONE: IT IS NO GOOD. FOR TWO:
I ALWAYS WILL KNOW, OKAY?
FUCKING PIG DOG IS STILL IN STORE.
MOTHER FUCKING SHIT BAG ASSHOLE COCKSUCKER...

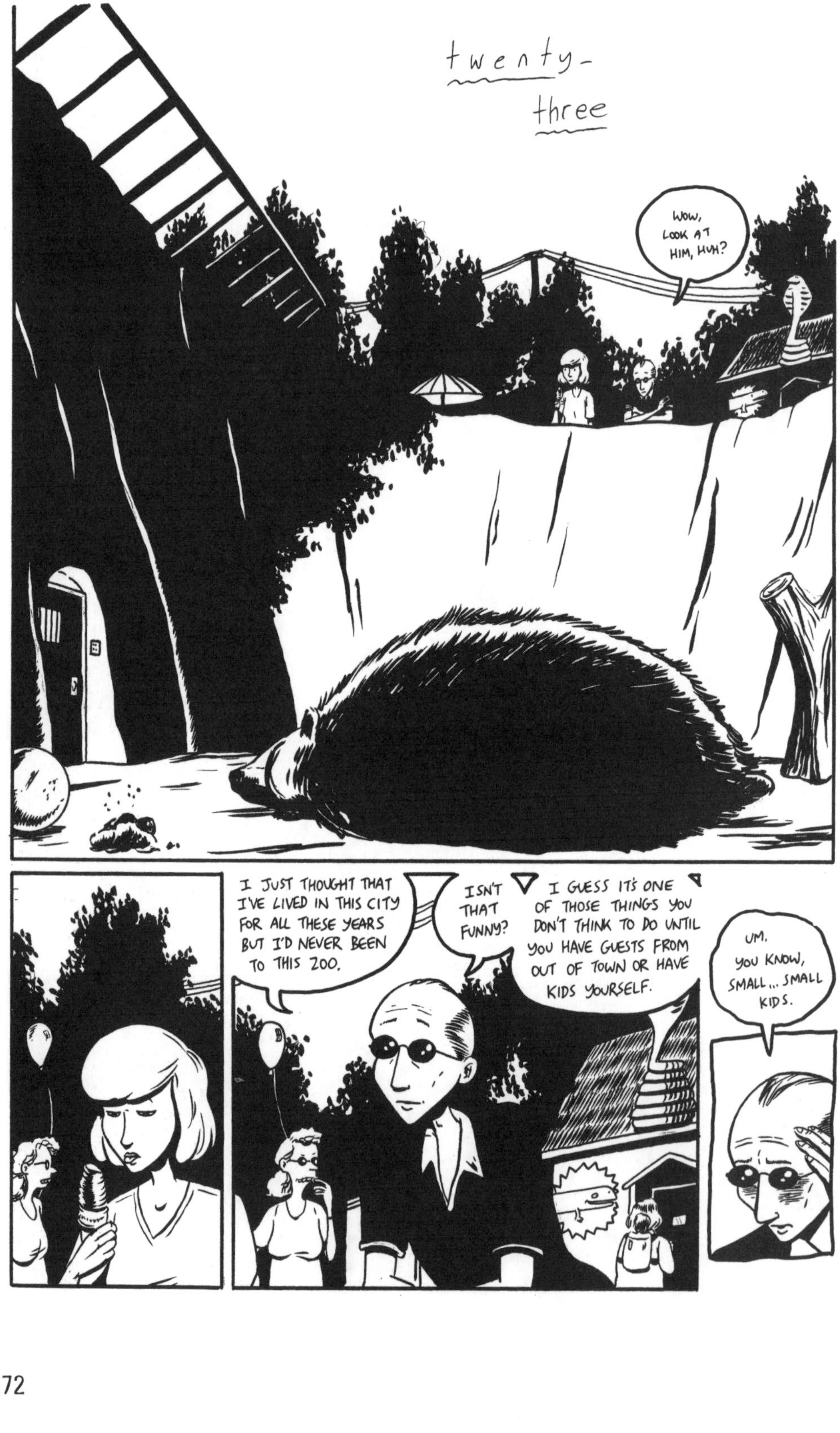
twenty-three
WOW, LOOK AT HIM, HUH?
I JUST THOUGHT THAT I'VE LIVED IN THIS CITY FOR ALL THESE YEARS BUT I'D NEVER BEEN TO THIS ZOO.
ISN'T THAT FUNNY?
I GUESS IT'S ONE OF THOSE THINGS YOU DON'T THINK TO DO UNTIL YOU HAVE GUESTS FROM OUT OF TOWN OR HAVE KIDS YOURSELF.
UM. YOU KNOW, SMALL... SMALL KIDS.

WHERE TO NOW? IF I SEE ANOTHER BROWN ANIMAL WITH HOOVES AND ANTLERS I'LL SCREAM.

OOH, HOW ABOUT ASIA? THEY HAVE ELEPHANTS AND A TIGER EXHIBIT.

OKAY.

SO... I'M REALLY SORRY ABOUT CANCELLING THE OTHER DAY. THINGS HAVE BEEN REALLY HECTIC AT THE DINER.

IT'S OKAY.

FRANK, THE OTHER OWNER (WHO I THINK YOU MET THE OTHER DAY) HAS BEEN OUT FOR A FEW DAYS SO IT'S BEEN CRAZY.

IS HE ANGRY ABOUT ME?

"ANGRY?" NO!! WHY WOULD HE BE ANGRY?? NO, HE JUST... HE HAS SOME, YOU KNOW, DENTAL, UH..., NO, HE'S NOT ANGRY.

TIGERS: OUR VANISHING FRIENDS

BUT CAPRICE TOLD ME YOU GUYS HAD FUN. WHAT DID YOU DO?

UM... WE WENT TO A MUSEUM... AND ATE... AND WENT TO THAT TEFLON TOWER THING.

AND SHE TALKED ABOUT HER NEW BOYFRIEND, BOYD.

AH! YES, SHE'S MENTIONED HIM. I'M GLAD THAT'S WORKING OUT.

SO, UH, HOW ABOUT YOU?

HOW ABOUT ME WHAT?

EXIT

DO YOU HAVE A BOYF--

IS THERE ANYONE "SPECIAL" BACK HOME?

173

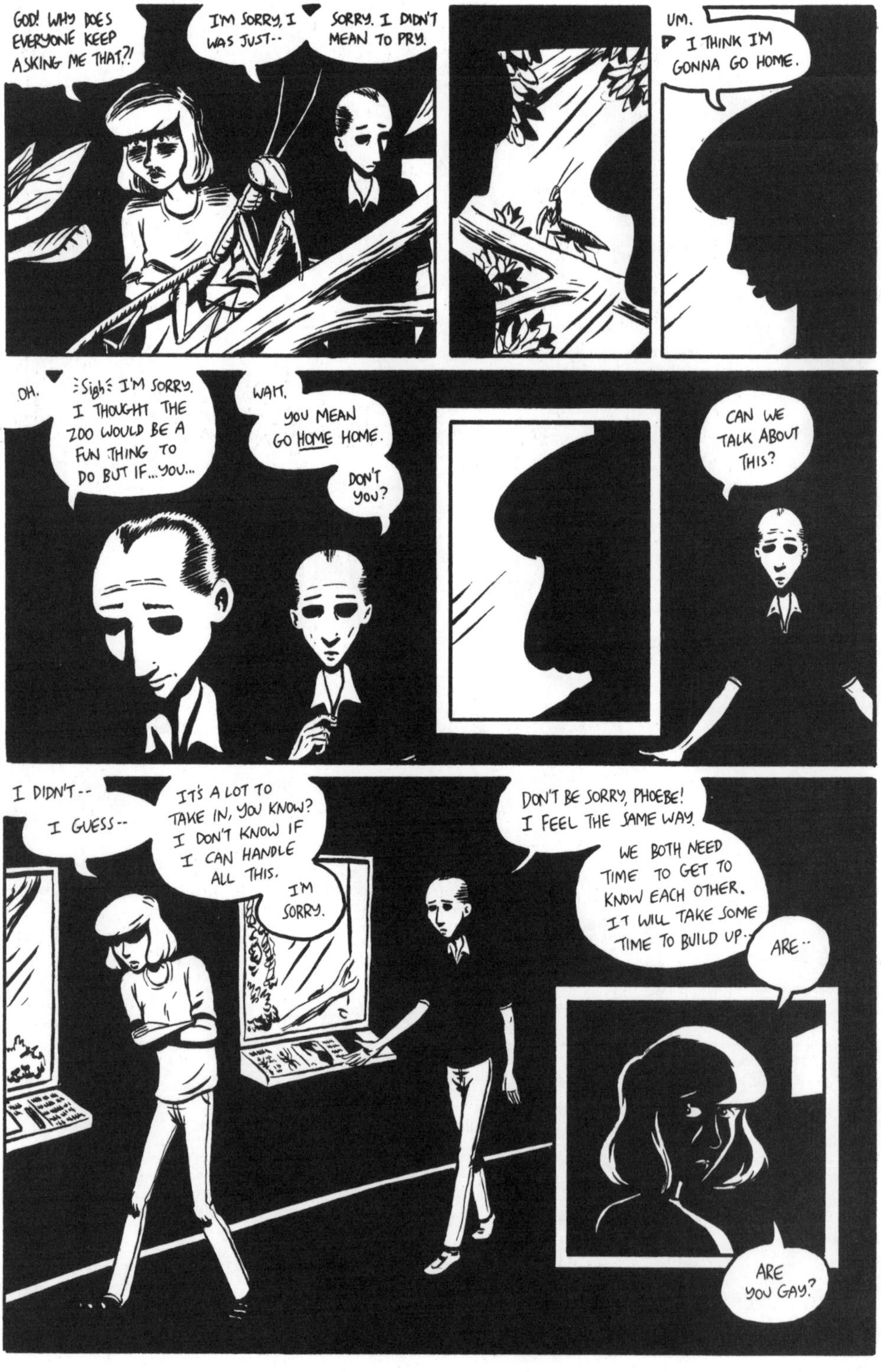
GOD! WHY DOES EVERYONE KEEP ASKING ME THAT?!
I'M SORRY, I WAS JUST--
SORRY. I DIDN'T MEAN TO PRY.
UM.
I THINK I'M GONNA GO HOME.
OH.
Sigh I'M SORRY. I THOUGHT THE ZOO WOULD BE A FUN THING TO DO BUT IF...YOU...
WAIT. YOU MEAN GO HOME HOME.
DON'T YOU?
CAN WE TALK ABOUT THIS?
I DIDN'T--
I GUESS--
IT'S A LOT TO TAKE IN, YOU KNOW? I DON'T KNOW IF I CAN HANDLE ALL THIS.
I'M SORRY.
DON'T BE SORRY, PHOEBE! I FEEL THE SAME WAY.
WE BOTH NEED TIME TO GET TO KNOW EACH OTHER. IT WILL TAKE SOME TIME TO BUILD UP...
ARE--
ARE YOU GAY?

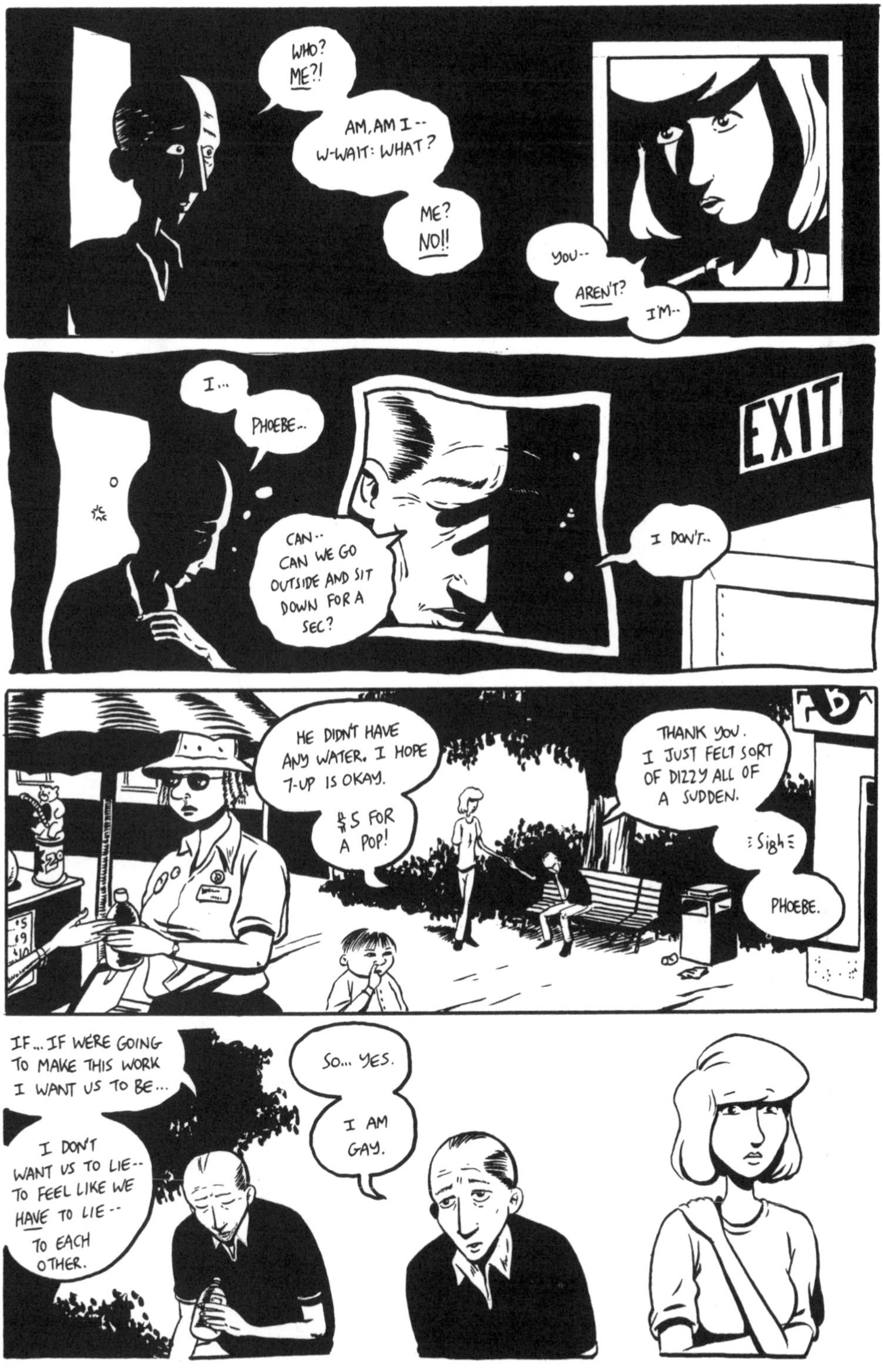
WHO? ME?!
AM, AM I -- W-WAIT: WHAT?
ME? NO!!
YOU-- AREN'T? I'M..
I... PHOEBE..
CAN.. CAN WE GO OUTSIDE AND SIT DOWN FOR A SEC?
I DON'T..
EXIT
HE DIDN'T HAVE ANY WATER. I HOPE 7-UP IS OKAY.
$5 FOR A POP!
THANK YOU. I JUST FELT SORT OF DIZZY ALL OF A SUDDEN.
Sigh
PHOEBE.
IF... IF WE'RE GOING TO MAKE THIS WORK I WANT US TO BE...
I DON'T WANT US TO LIE-- TO FEEL LIKE WE HAVE TO LIE-- TO EACH OTHER.
SO... YES.
I AM GAY.

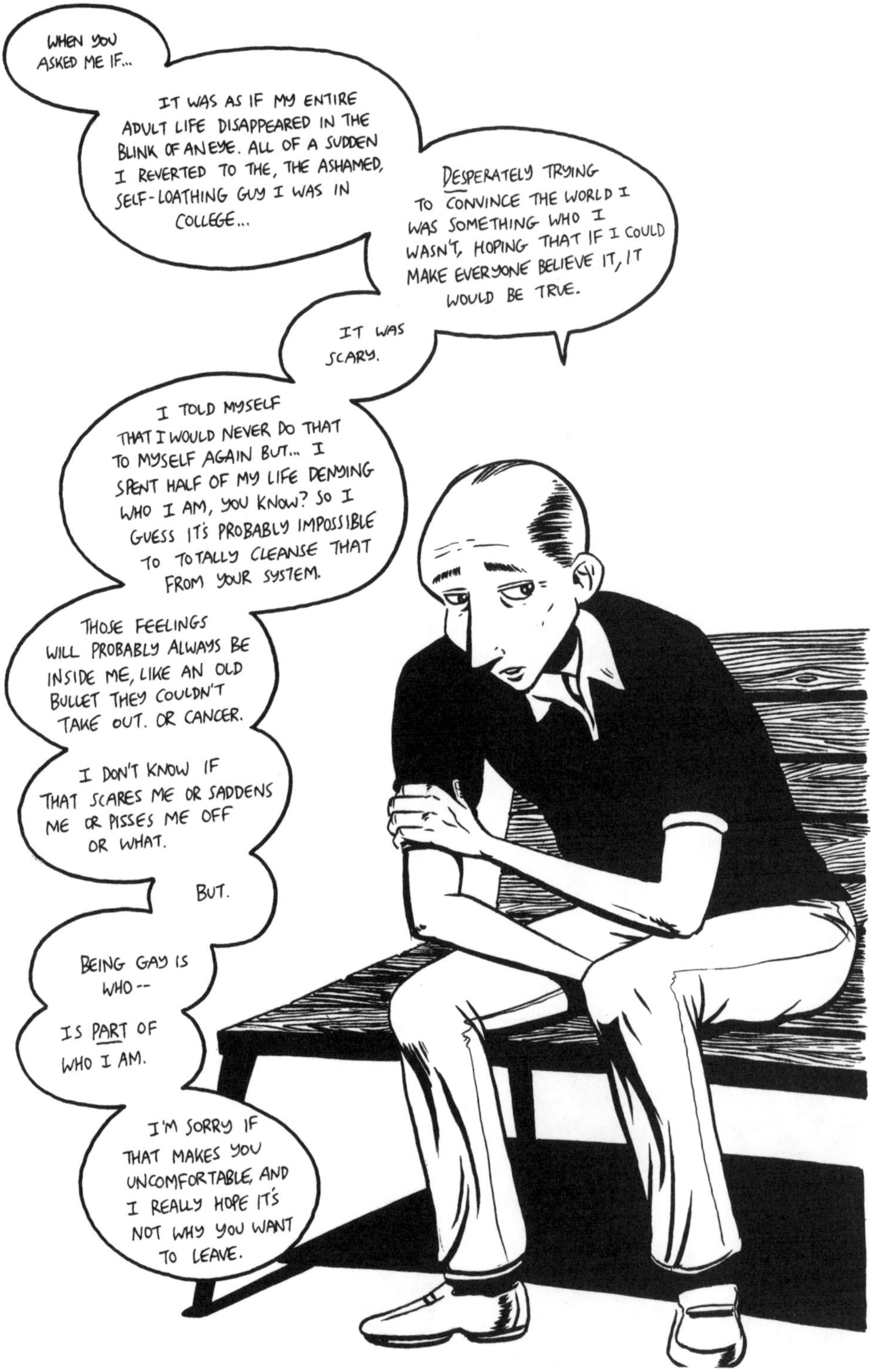
WHEN YOU ASKED ME IF...
IT WAS AS IF MY ENTIRE ADULT LIFE DISAPPEARED IN THE BLINK OF AN EYE. ALL OF A SUDDEN I REVERTED TO THE, THE ASHAMED, SELF-LOATHING GUY I WAS IN COLLEGE...
DESPERATELY TRYING TO CONVINCE THE WORLD I WAS SOMETHING WHO I WASN'T, HOPING THAT IF I COULD MAKE EVERYONE BELIEVE IT, IT WOULD BE TRUE.
IT WAS SCARY.
I TOLD MYSELF THAT I WOULD NEVER DO THAT TO MYSELF AGAIN BUT... I SPENT HALF OF MY LIFE DENYING WHO I AM, YOU KNOW? SO I GUESS IT'S PROBABLY IMPOSSIBLE TO TOTALLY CLEANSE THAT FROM YOUR SYSTEM.
THOSE FEELINGS WILL PROBABLY ALWAYS BE INSIDE ME, LIKE AN OLD BULLET THEY COULDN'T TAKE OUT. OR CANCER.
I DON'T KNOW IF THAT SCARES ME OR SADDENS ME OR PISSES ME OFF OR WHAT.
BUT.
BEING GAY IS WHO--
IS PART OF WHO I AM.
I'M SORRY IF THAT MAKES YOU UNCOMFORTABLE, AND I REALLY HOPE IT'S NOT WHY YOU WANT TO LEAVE.

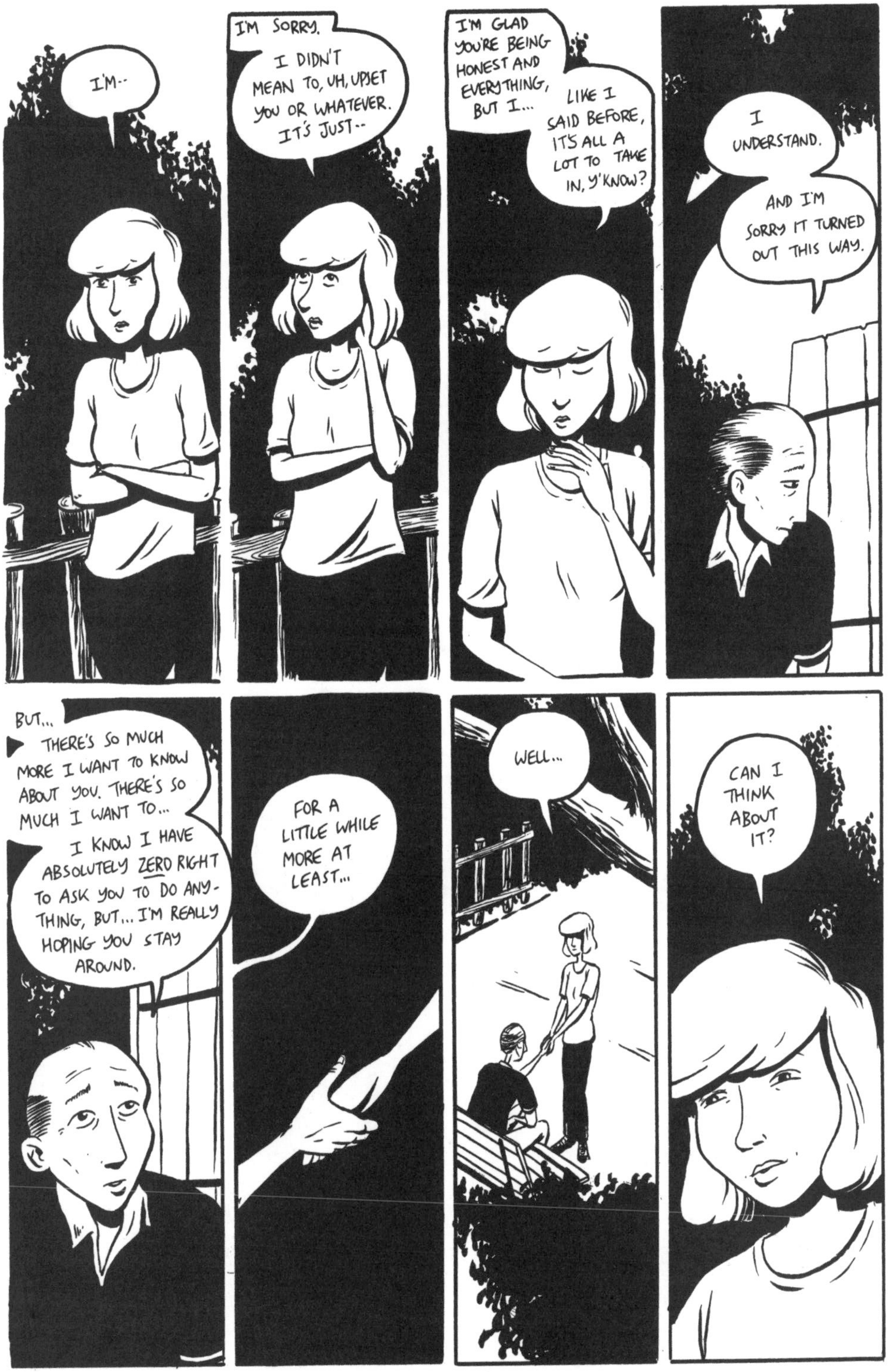
I'M--
I'M SORRY.
I DIDN'T MEAN TO, UH, UPSET YOU OR WHATEVER. IT'S JUST--
I'M GLAD YOU'RE BEING HONEST AND EVERYTHING, BUT I...
LIKE I SAID BEFORE, IT'S ALL A LOT TO TAKE IN, Y'KNOW?
I UNDERSTAND.
AND I'M SORRY IT TURNED OUT THIS WAY.
BUT...
THERE'S SO MUCH MORE I WANT TO KNOW ABOUT YOU. THERE'S SO MUCH I WANT TO...
I KNOW I HAVE ABSOLUTELY ZERO RIGHT TO ASK YOU TO DO ANY-THING, BUT... I'M REALLY HOPING YOU STAY AROUND.
FOR A LITTLE WHILE MORE AT LEAST...
WELL...
CAN I THINK ABOUT IT?

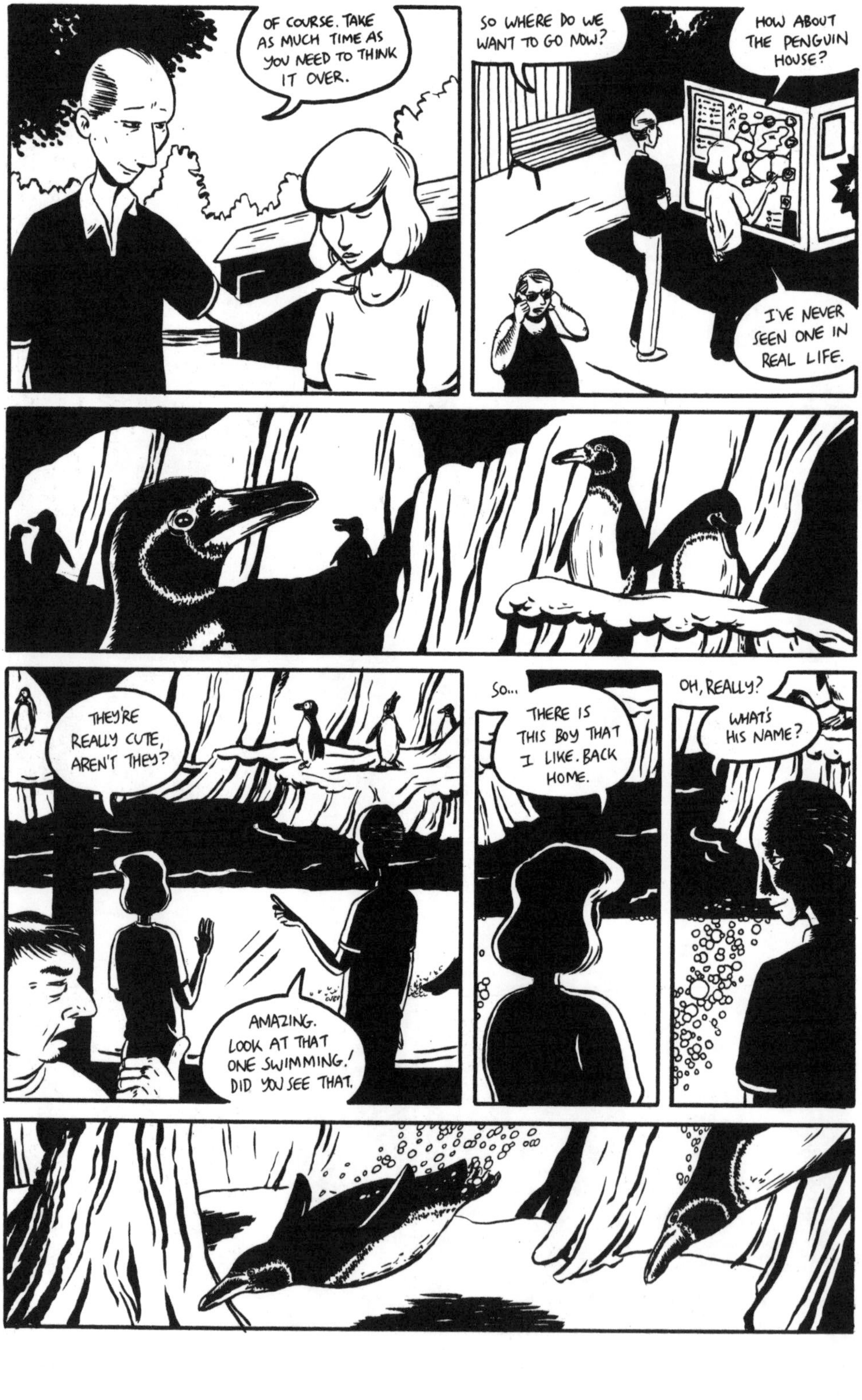
OF COURSE. TAKE AS MUCH TIME AS YOU NEED TO THINK IT OVER.
SO WHERE DO WE WANT TO GO NOW?
HOW ABOUT THE PENGUIN HOUSE?
I'VE NEVER SEEN ONE IN REAL LIFE.
THEY'RE REALLY CUTE, AREN'T THEY?
AMAZING. LOOK AT THAT ONE SWIMMING! DID YOU SEE THAT.
SO...
THERE IS THIS BOY THAT I LIKE. BACK HOME.
OH, REALLY?
WHAT'S HIS NAME?

THAT NIGHT I HAD A VIVID DREAM THAT I WAS BEING CONSUMED BY A HUGE AMOEBA.

Z Z Z Z
Z Z Z Z Z
Z Z Z Z
Z Z Z Z
Z Z Z Z
Z Z Z 22

AND THE VERY NEXT DAY THEY FIRED ME.

31

JED HAD CALLED ME INTO HIS OFFICE AND I JUST FIGURED HE WAS HAVING ANOTHER PROBLEM WITH HIS SYSTEM BECAUSE HE'S SUCH A RETARD HE PROBABLY HAS TO CALL TECHNICAL SUPPORT WHEN HE WANTS TO WIPE HIS ASS.

HE'S ONE OF THESE CORPORATE FUCKS YOU SEE ALL THE TIME WITH THEIR GOURMET COFFEE AND THEIR LITTLE CUTIE KNICK-KNACKS TRYING TO TRICK YOU INTO THINKING THEY'RE "REGULAR GUYS" INSTEAD OF THE SOULLESS WHITE-COLLAR GHOULS THEY ARE.

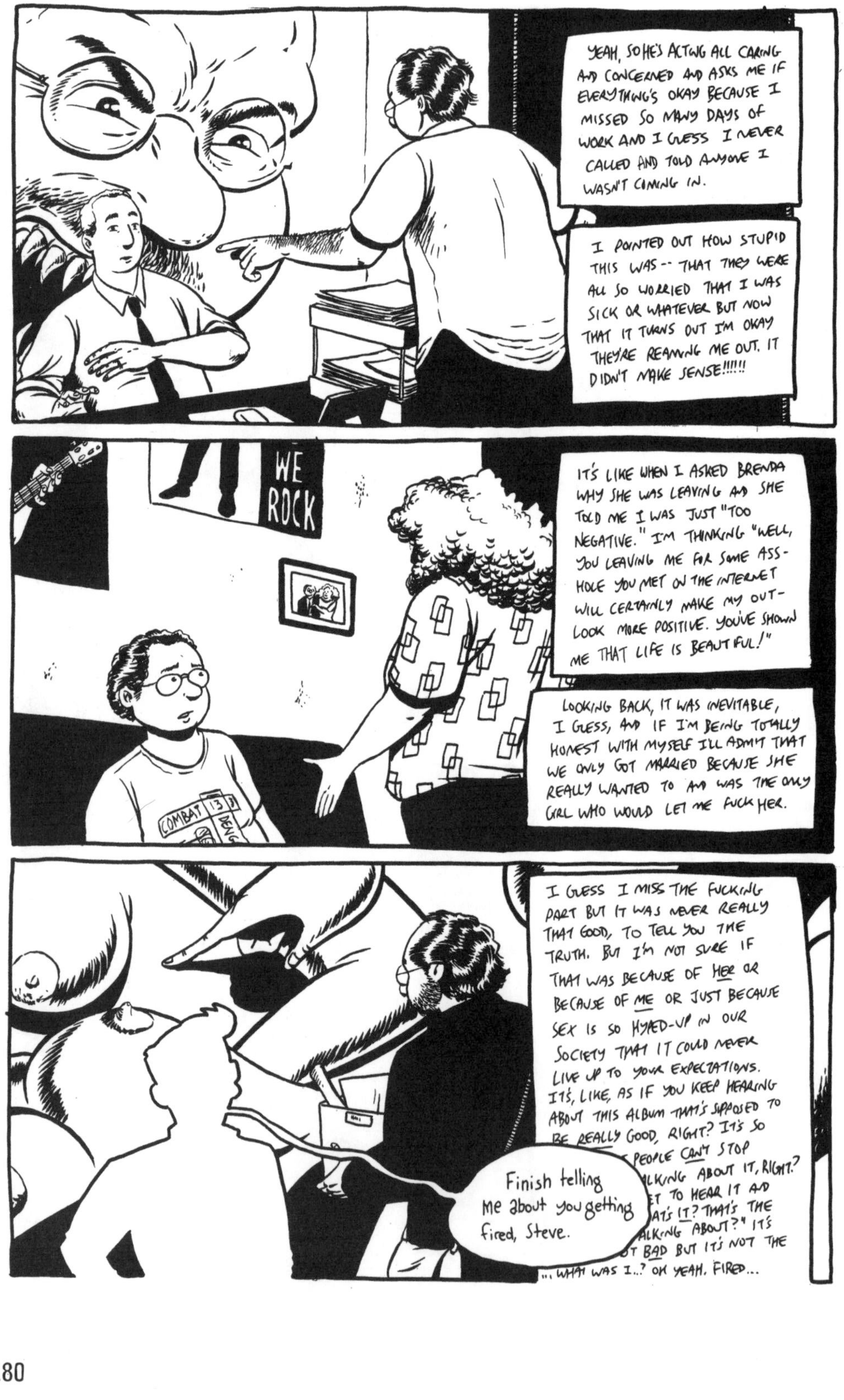

YEAH, SO HE'S ACTING ALL CARING AND CONCERNED AND ASKS ME IF EVERYTHING'S OKAY BECAUSE I MISSED SO MANY DAYS OF WORK AND I GUESS I NEVER CALLED AND TOLD ANYONE I WASN'T COMING IN.
I POINTED OUT HOW STUPID THIS WAS -- THAT THEY WERE ALL SO WORRIED THAT I WAS SICK OR WHATEVER BUT NOW THAT IT TURNS OUT I'M OKAY THEY'RE REAMING ME OUT. IT DIDN'T MAKE SENSE!!!!!!
WE ROCK
IT'S LIKE WHEN I ASKED BRENDA WHY SHE WAS LEAVING AND SHE TOLD ME I WAS JUST "TOO NEGATIVE." I'M THINKING "WELL, YOU LEAVING ME FOR SOME ASS-HOLE YOU MET ON THE INTERNET WILL CERTAINLY MAKE MY OUT-LOOK MORE POSITIVE. YOU'VE SHOWN ME THAT LIFE IS BEAUTIFUL!"
LOOKING BACK, IT WAS INEVITABLE, I GUESS, AND IF I'M BEING TOTALLY HONEST WITH MYSELF I'LL ADMIT THAT WE ONLY GOT MARRIED BECAUSE SHE REALLY WANTED TO AND WAS THE ONLY GIRL WHO WOULD LET ME FUCK HER.
COMBAT 13
I GUESS I MISS THE FUCKING PART BUT IT WAS NEVER REALLY THAT GOOD, TO TELL YOU THE TRUTH. BUT I'M NOT SURE IF THAT WAS BECAUSE OF HER OR BECAUSE OF ME OR JUST BECAUSE SEX IS SO HYPED-UP IN OUR SOCIETY THAT IT COULD NEVER LIVE UP TO YOUR EXPECTATIONS. IT'S, LIKE, AS IF YOU KEEP HEARING ABOUT THIS ALBUM THAT'S SUPPOSED TO BE REALLY GOOD, RIGHT? IT'S SO
PEOPLE CAN'T STOP
ALKING ABOUT IT, RIGHT?
ET TO HEAR IT AND
AT'S IT? THAT'S THE
ALKING ABOUT?" IT'S
T BAD BUT IT'S NOT THE
... WHAT WAS I...? OH YEAH. FIRED...
Finish telling me about you getting fired, Steve.

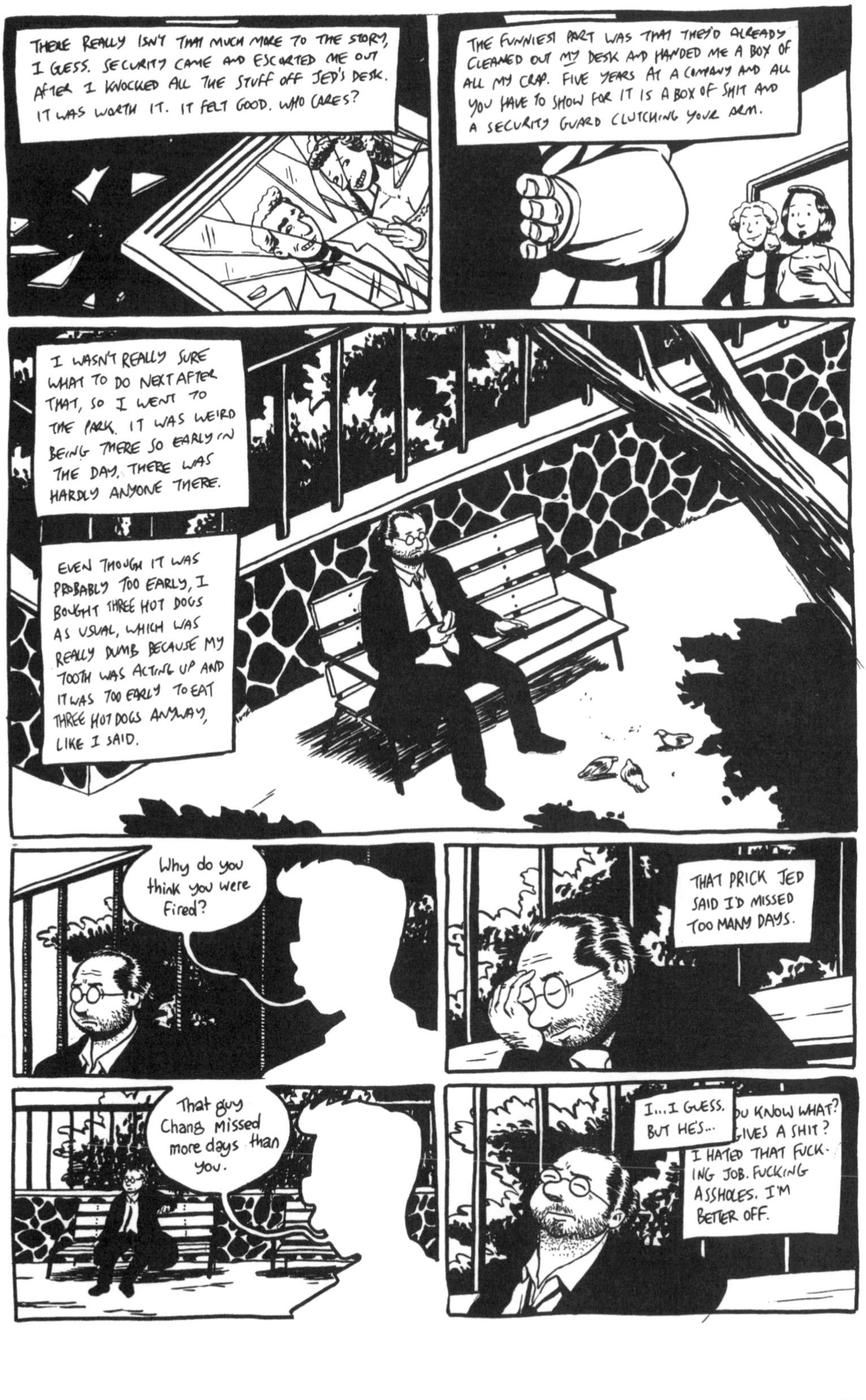
THERE REALLY ISN'T THAT MUCH MORE TO THE STORY, I GUESS. SECURITY CAME AND ESCORTED ME OUT AFTER I KNOCKED ALL THE STUFF OFF JED'S DESK. IT WAS WORTH IT. IT FELT GOOD. WHO CARES?
THE FUNNIEST PART WAS THAT THEY'D ALREADY CLEANED OUT MY DESK AND HANDED ME A BOX OF ALL MY CRAP. FIVE YEARS AT A COMPANY AND ALL YOU HAVE TO SHOW FOR IT IS A BOX OF SHIT AND A SECURITY GUARD CLUTCHING YOUR ARM.
I WASN'T REALLY SURE WHAT TO DO NEXT AFTER THAT, SO I WENT TO THE PARK. IT WAS WEIRD BEING THERE SO EARLY IN THE DAY, THERE WAS HARDLY ANYONE THERE.
EVEN THOUGH IT WAS PROBABLY TOO EARLY, I BOUGHT THREE HOT DOGS AS USUAL, WHICH WAS REALLY DUMB BECAUSE MY TOOTH WAS ACTING UP AND IT WAS TOO EARLY TO EAT THREE HOT DOGS ANYWAY, LIKE I SAID.
Why do you think you were fired?
THAT PRICK JED SAID I'D MISSED TOO MANY DAYS.
That guy Chang missed more days than you.
I...I GUESS. BUT HE'S...
OU KNOW WHAT? GIVES A SHIT? I HATED THAT FUCK-ING JOB. FUCKING ASSHOLES. I'M BETTER OFF.

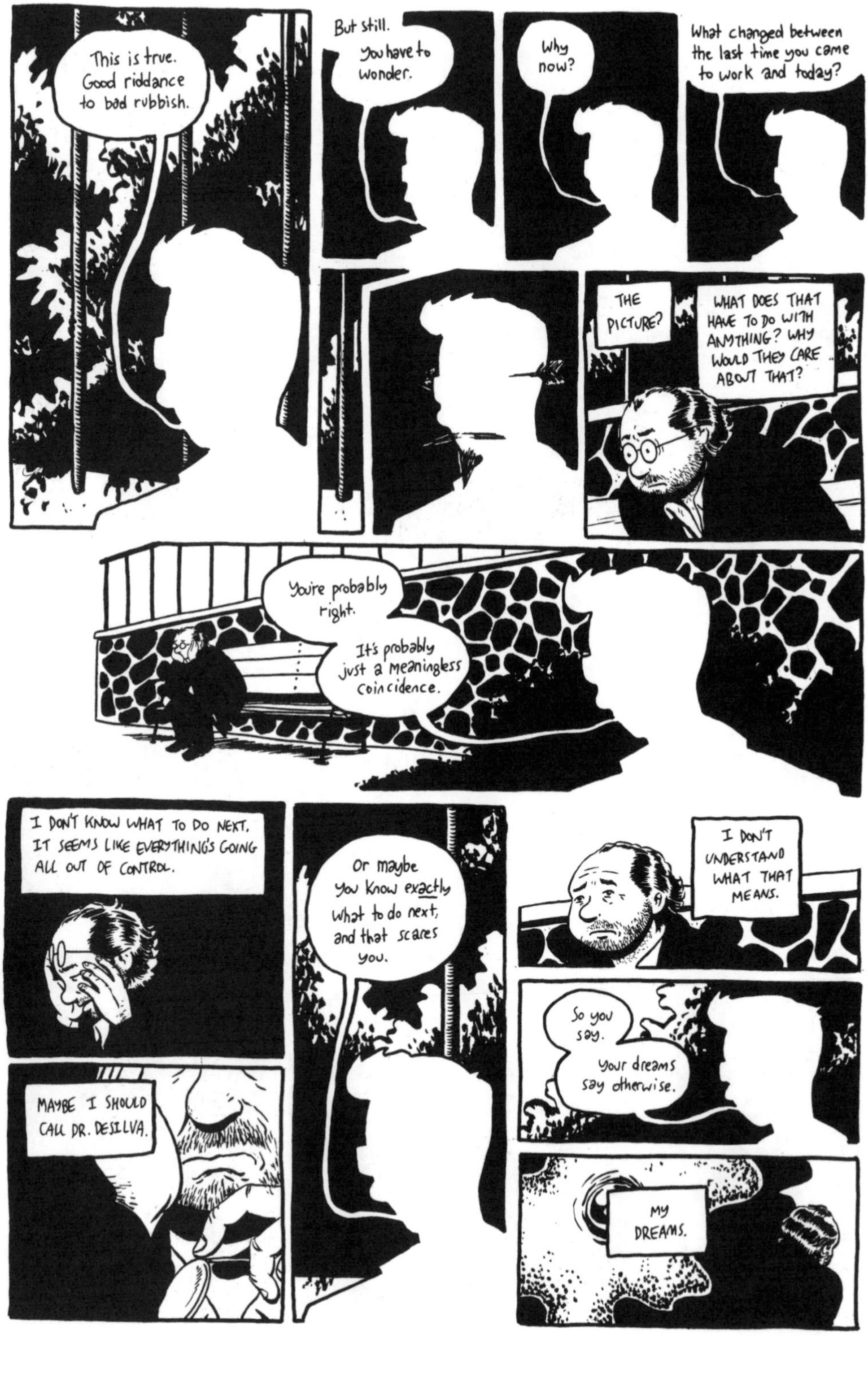
This is true. Good riddance to bad rubbish.
But still.
You have to wonder.
Why now?
What changed between the last time you came to work and today?
THE PICTURE?
WHAT DOES THAT HAVE TO DO WITH ANYTHING? WHY WOULD THEY CARE ABOUT THAT?
You're probably right.
It's probably just a meaningless coincidence.
I DON'T KNOW WHAT TO DO NEXT. IT SEEMS LIKE EVERYTHING'S GOING ALL OUT OF CONTROL.
MAYBE I SHOULD CALL DR. DESILVA.
Or maybe you know exactly what to do next, and that scares you.
I DON'T UNDERSTAND WHAT THAT MEANS.
So you say.
Your dreams say otherwise.
MY DREAMS.

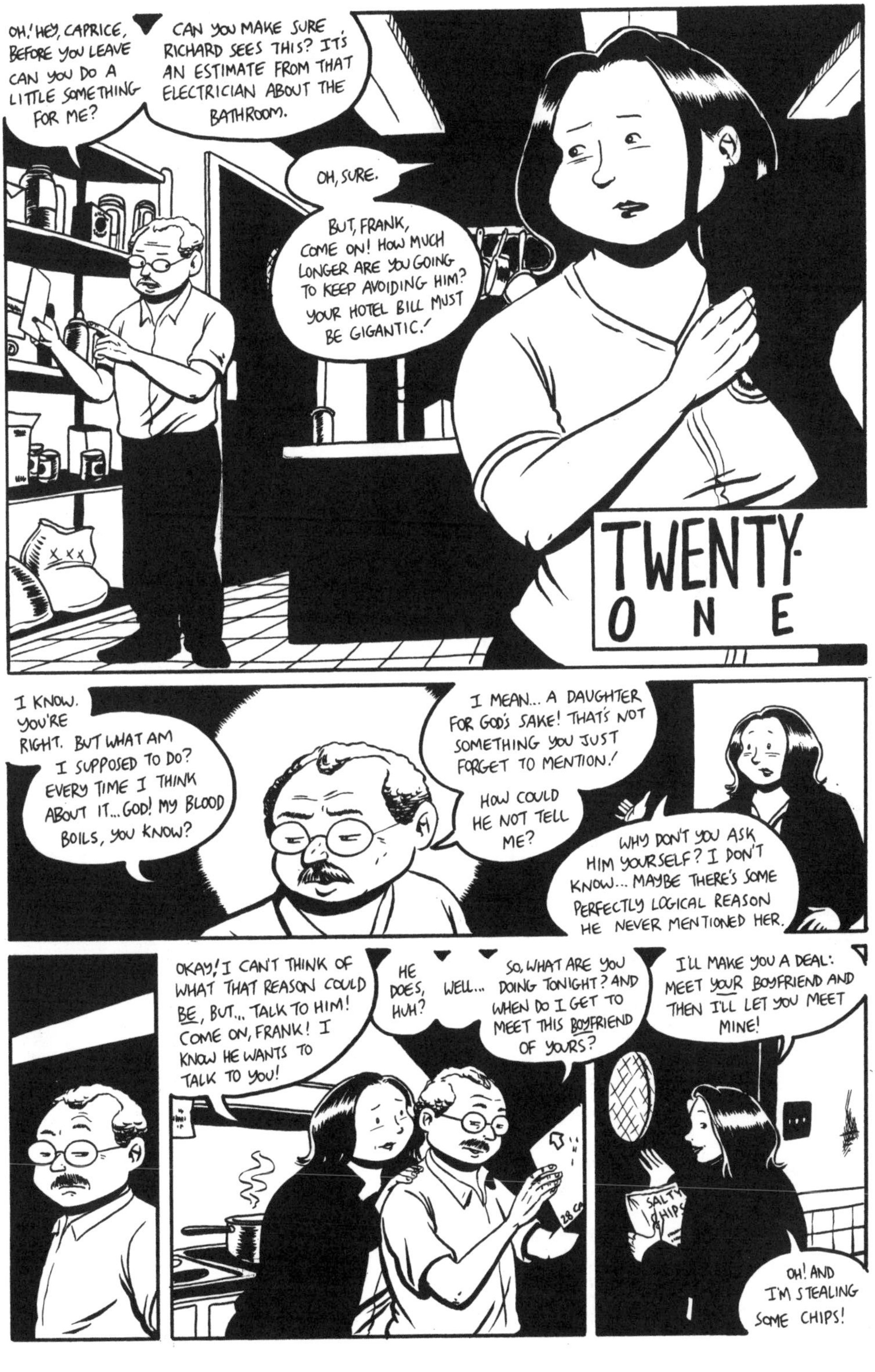
OH! HEY, CAPRICE, BEFORE YOU LEAVE CAN YOU DO A LITTLE SOMETHING FOR ME?
CAN YOU MAKE SURE RICHARD SEES THIS? IT'S AN ESTIMATE FROM THAT ELECTRICIAN ABOUT THE BATHROOM.
OH, SURE.
BUT, FRANK, COME ON! HOW MUCH LONGER ARE YOU GOING TO KEEP AVOIDING HIM? YOUR HOTEL BILL MUST BE GIGANTIC!
TWENTY-ONE
I KNOW. YOU'RE RIGHT. BUT WHAT AM I SUPPOSED TO DO? EVERY TIME I THINK ABOUT IT... GOD! MY BLOOD BOILS, YOU KNOW?
I MEAN... A DAUGHTER FOR GOD'S SAKE! THAT'S NOT SOMETHING YOU JUST FORGET TO MENTION!
HOW COULD HE NOT TELL ME?
WHY DON'T YOU ASK HIM YOURSELF? I DON'T KNOW... MAYBE THERE'S SOME PERFECTLY LOGICAL REASON HE NEVER MENTIONED HER.
OKAY! I CAN'T THINK OF WHAT THAT REASON COULD BE, BUT... TALK TO HIM! COME ON, FRANK! I KNOW HE WANTS TO TALK TO YOU!
HE DOES, HUH?
WELL...
SO, WHAT ARE YOU DOING TONIGHT? AND WHEN DO I GET TO MEET THIS BOYFRIEND OF YOURS?
I'LL MAKE YOU A DEAL: MEET YOUR BOYFRIEND AND THEN I'LL LET YOU MEET MINE!
SALTY CHIPS
OH! AND I'M STEALING SOME CHIPS!

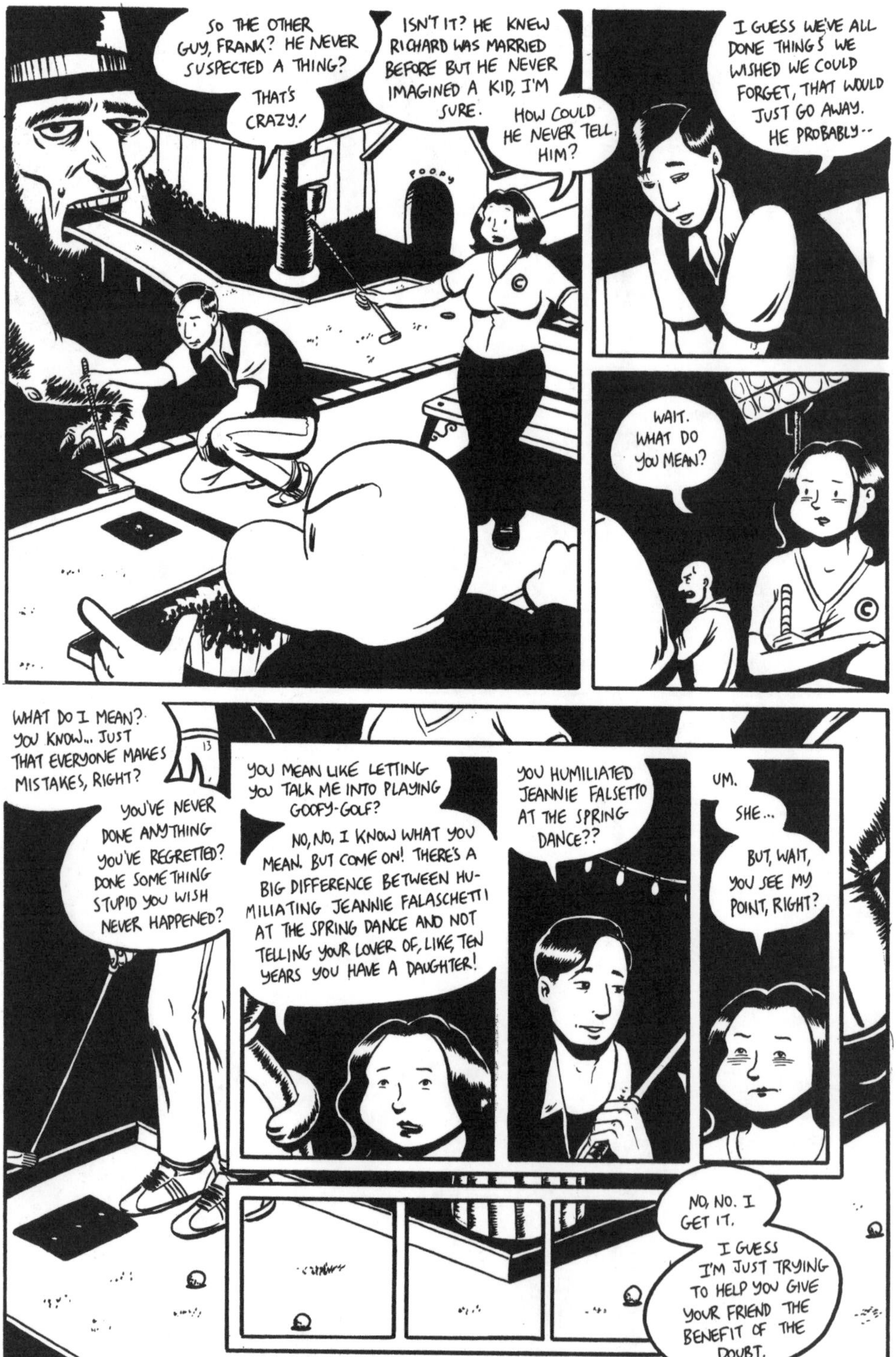
SO THE OTHER GUY, FRANK? HE NEVER SUSPECTED A THING?
THAT'S CRAZY!
ISN'T IT? HE KNEW RICHARD WAS MARRIED BEFORE BUT HE NEVER IMAGINED A KID, I'M SURE.
HOW COULD HE NEVER TELL HIM?
POOPY
I GUESS WE'VE ALL DONE THINGS WE WISHED WE COULD FORGET, THAT WOULD JUST GO AWAY. HE PROBABLY--
WAIT. WHAT DO YOU MEAN?
WHAT DO I MEAN? YOU KNOW... JUST THAT EVERYONE MAKES MISTAKES, RIGHT?
YOU'VE NEVER DONE ANYTHING YOU'VE REGRETTED? DONE SOMETHING STUPID YOU WISH NEVER HAPPENED?
YOU MEAN LIKE LETTING YOU TALK ME INTO PLAYING GOOFY-GOLF?
NO, NO, I KNOW WHAT YOU MEAN. BUT COME ON! THERE'S A BIG DIFFERENCE BETWEEN HUMILIATING JEANNIE FALASCHETTI AT THE SPRING DANCE AND NOT TELLING YOUR LOVER OF, LIKE, TEN YEARS YOU HAVE A DAUGHTER!
YOU HUMILIATED JEANNIE FALSETTO AT THE SPRING DANCE??
UM.
SHE...
BUT, WAIT, YOU SEE MY POINT, RIGHT?
NO, NO. I GET IT.
I GUESS I'M JUST TRYING TO HELP YOU GIVE YOUR FRIEND THE BENEFIT OF THE DOUBT.

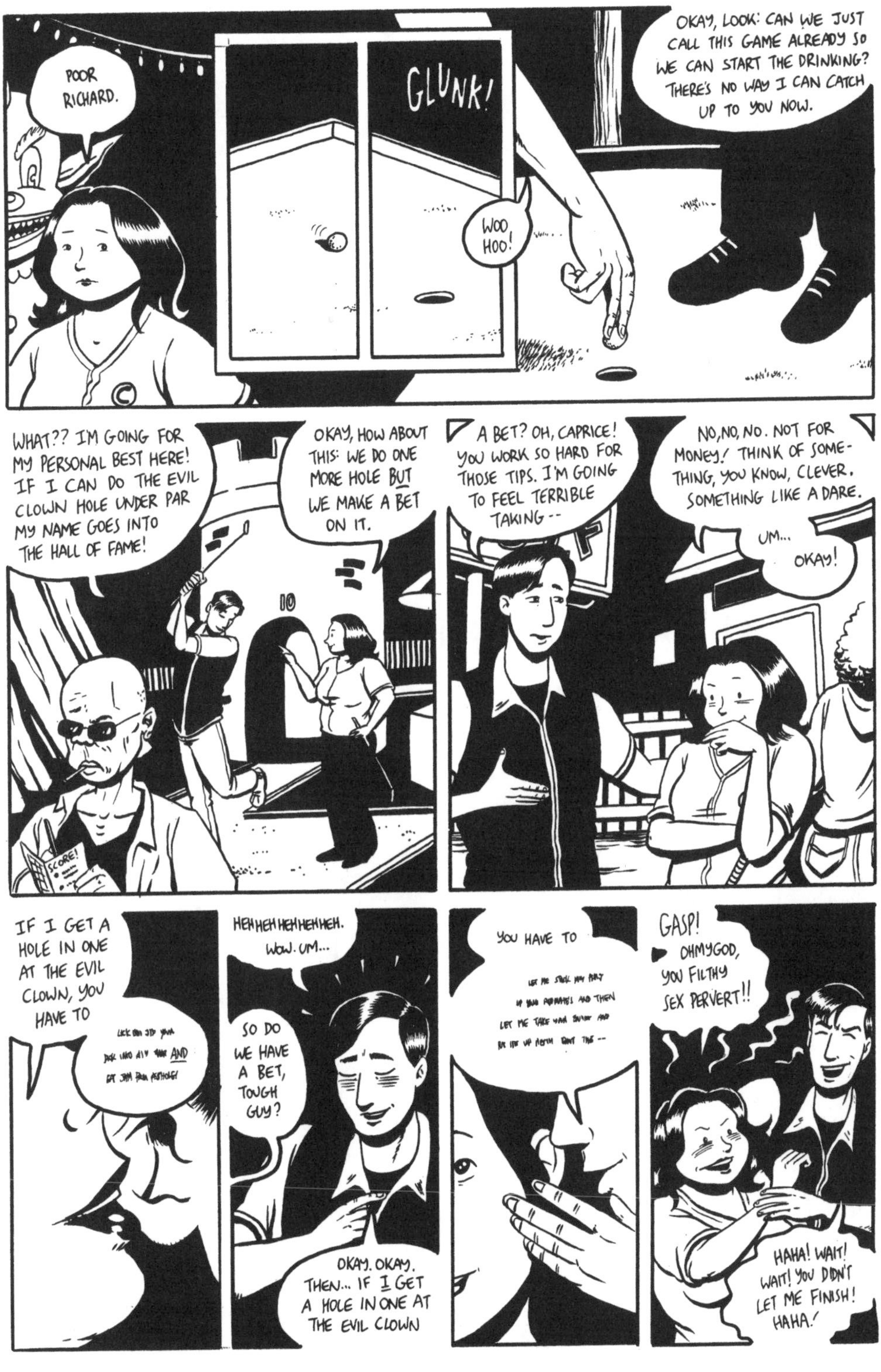
POOR RICHARD.
GLUNK!
WOO HOO!
OKAY, LOOK: CAN WE JUST CALL THIS GAME ALREADY SO WE CAN START THE DRINKING? THERE'S NO WAY I CAN CATCH UP TO YOU NOW.
WHAT?? I'M GOING FOR MY PERSONAL BEST HERE! IF I CAN DO THE EVIL CLOWN HOLE UNDER PAR MY NAME GOES INTO THE HALL OF FAME!
OKAY, HOW ABOUT THIS: WE DO ONE MORE HOLE BUT WE MAKE A BET ON IT.
SCORE!
10
A BET? OH, CAPRICE! YOU WORK SO HARD FOR THOSE TIPS. I'M GOING TO FEEL TERRIBLE TAKING --
NO, NO, NO. NOT FOR MONEY! THINK OF SOMETHING, YOU KNOW, CLEVER. SOMETHING LIKE A DARE.
UM... OKAY!
IF I GET A HOLE IN ONE AT THE EVIL CLOWN, YOU HAVE TO
HEHHEHHEHHEHHEH. WOW. UM...
SO DO WE HAVE A BET, TOUGH GUY?
OKAY. OKAY. THEN... IF I GET A HOLE IN ONE AT THE EVIL CLOWN
YOU HAVE TO
GASP! OHMYGOD, YOU FILTHY SEX PERVERT!!
HAHA! WAIT! WAIT! YOU DIDN'T LET ME FINISH! HAHA!

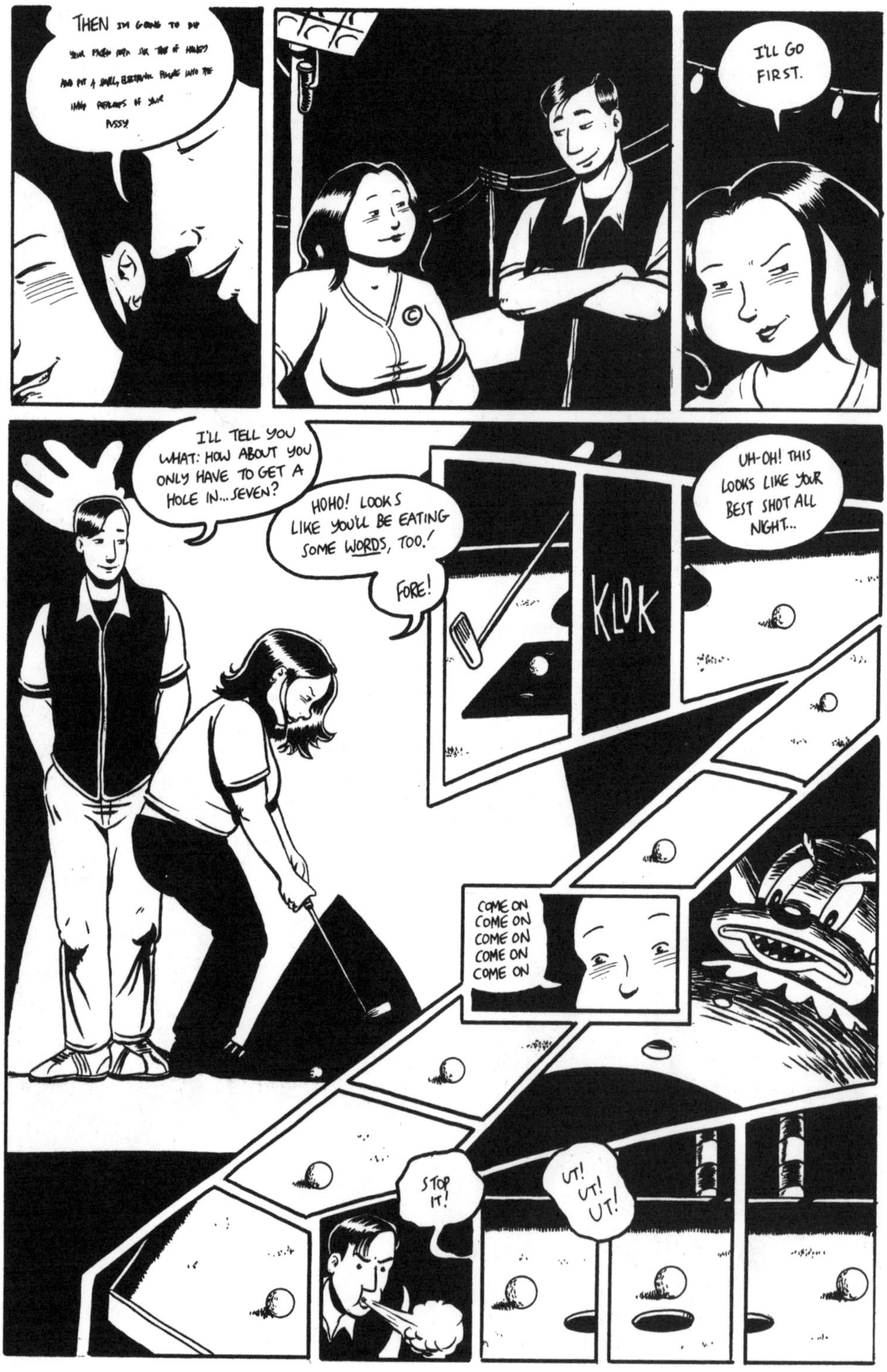
THEN I'M GOING TO DIP
I'LL GO FIRST.
I'LL TELL YOU WHAT: HOW ABOUT YOU ONLY HAVE TO GET A HOLE IN... SEVEN?
HOHO! LOOKS LIKE YOU'LL BE EATING SOME WORDS, TOO!
FORE!
KLOK
UH-OH! THIS LOOKS LIKE YOUR BEST SHOT ALL NIGHT...
COME ON COME ON COME ON COME ON COME ON
STOP IT!
UT! UT! UT!

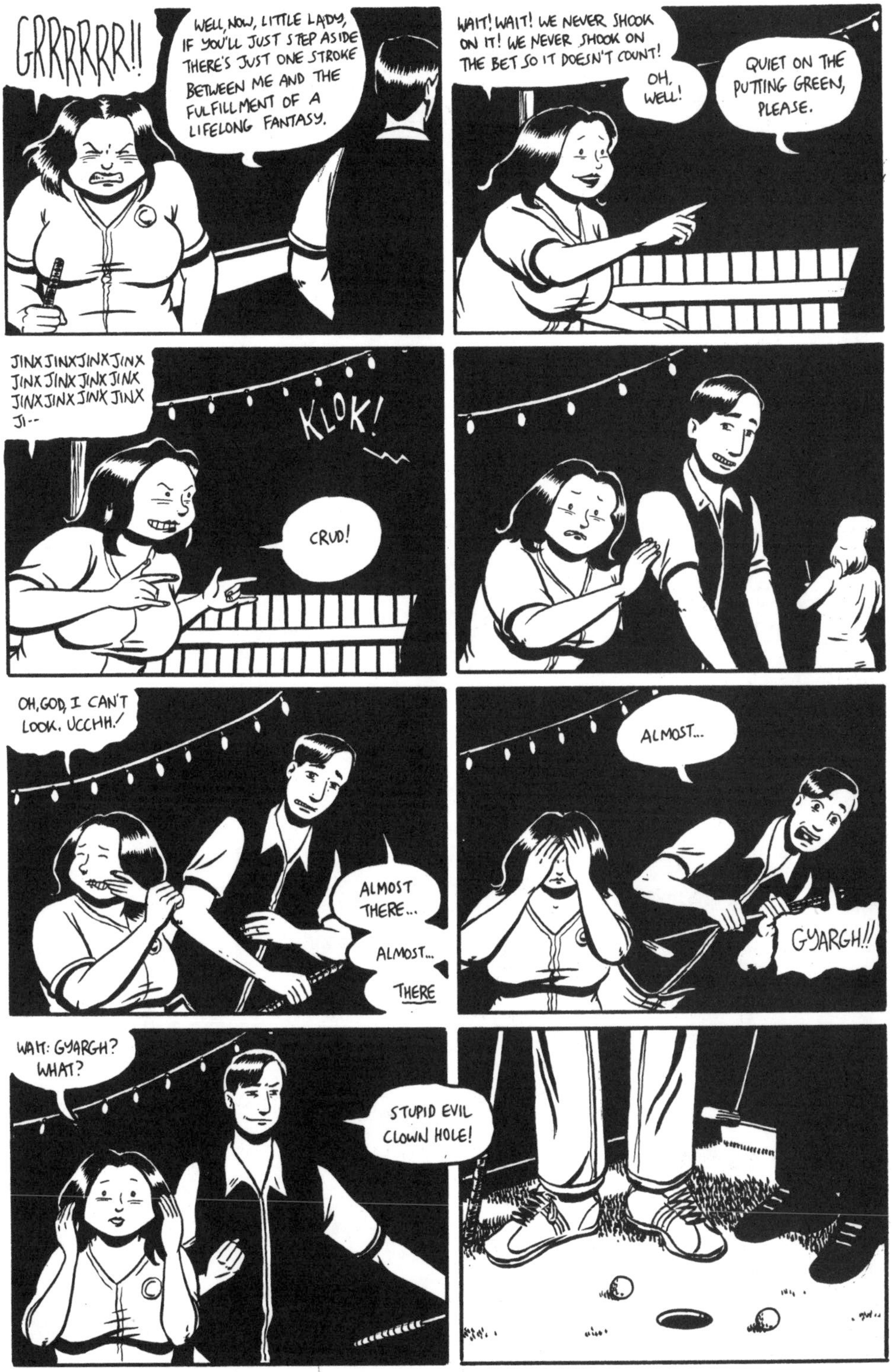
GRRRRRR!!
WELL, NOW, LITTLE LADY, IF YOU'LL JUST STEP ASIDE THERE'S JUST ONE STROKE BETWEEN ME AND THE FULFILLMENT OF A LIFELONG FANTASY.
WAIT! WAIT! WE NEVER SHOOK ON IT! WE NEVER SHOOK ON THE BET SO IT DOESN'T COUNT!
OH, WELL!
QUIET ON THE PUTTING GREEN, PLEASE.
JINX JINX JINX JINX JINX JINX JINX JINX JINX JINX JINX JINX JI--
KLOK!
CRUD!
OH, GOD, I CAN'T LOOK. UCCHH.!
ALMOST THERE...
ALMOST...
THERE
ALMOST...
GYARGH!!
WAIT: GYARGH? WHAT?
STUPID EVIL CLOWN HOLE!

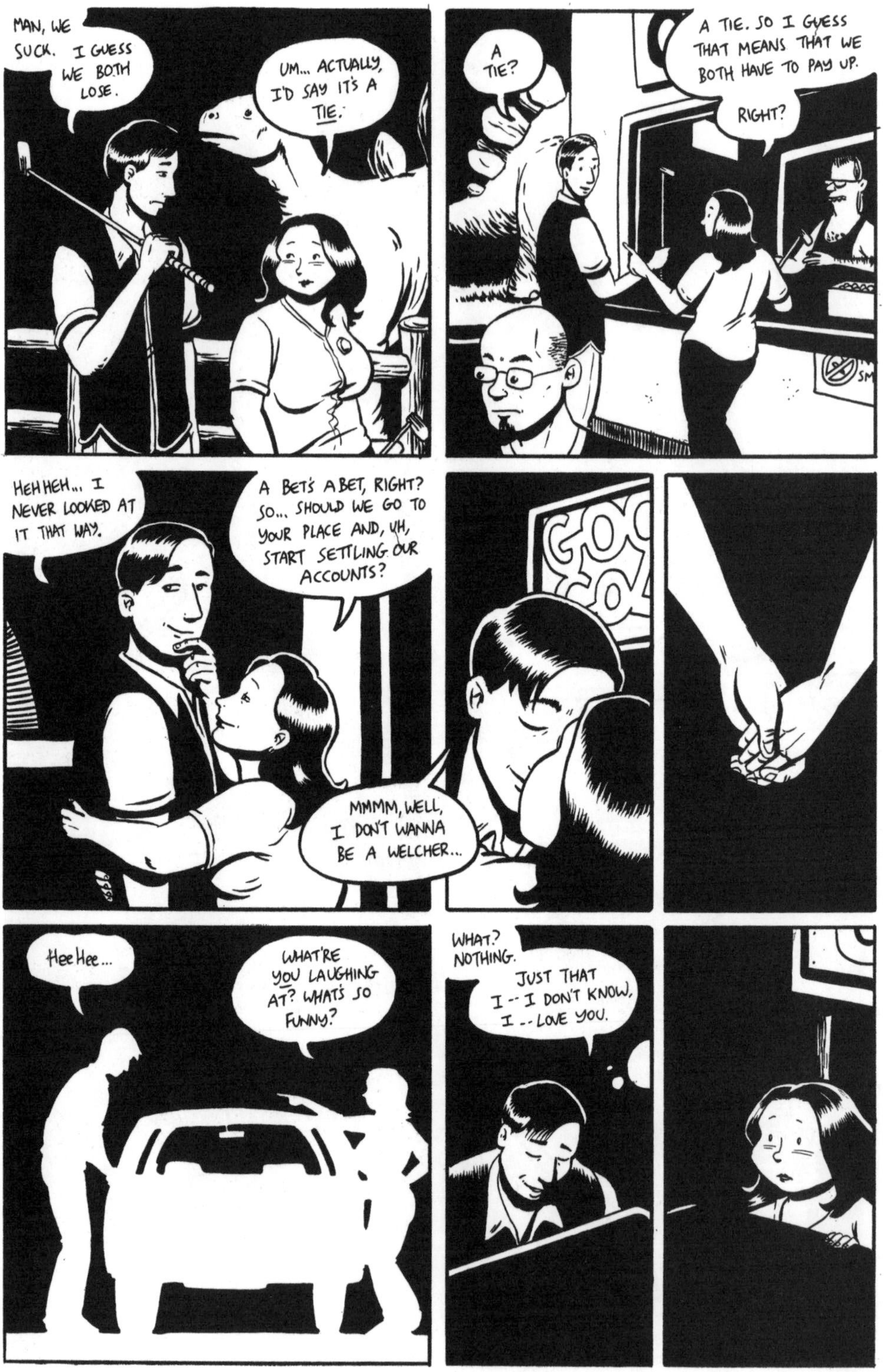
MAN, WE SUCK. I GUESS WE BOTH LOSE.
UM... ACTUALLY, I'D SAY IT'S A TIE.
A TIE?
A TIE. SO I GUESS THAT MEANS THAT WE BOTH HAVE TO PAY UP.
RIGHT?
HEHHEH... I NEVER LOOKED AT IT THAT WAY.
A BET'S A BET, RIGHT? SO... SHOULD WE GO TO YOUR PLACE AND, UH, START SETTLING OUR ACCOUNTS?
MMMM, WELL, I DON'T WANNA BE A WELCHER...
HeeHee...
WHAT'RE YOU LAUGHING AT? WHAT'S SO FUNNY?
WHAT? NOTHING.
JUST THAT I-- I DON'T KNOW. I--LOVE YOU.

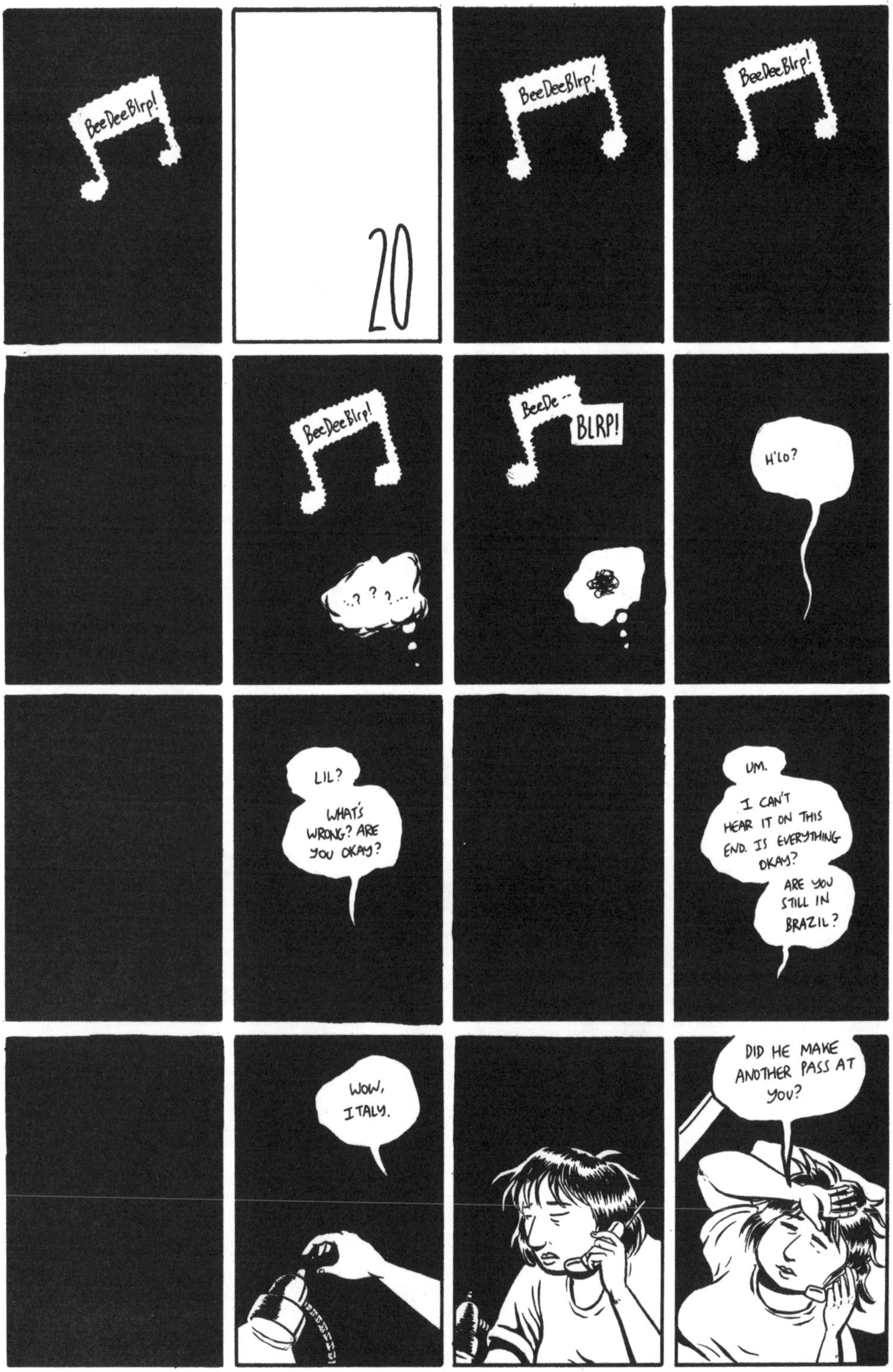
BeeDeeBlrp!
20
BeeDeeBlrp!
BeeDeeBlrp!
BeeDeeBlrp!
..? ? ?...
BeeDe--
BLRP!
H'LO?
LIL?
WHAT'S WRONG? ARE YOU OKAY?
UM.
I CAN'T HEAR IT ON THIS END. IS EVERYTHING OKAY?
ARE YOU STILL IN BRAZIL?
WOW, ITALY.
DID HE MAKE ANOTHER PASS AT YOU?

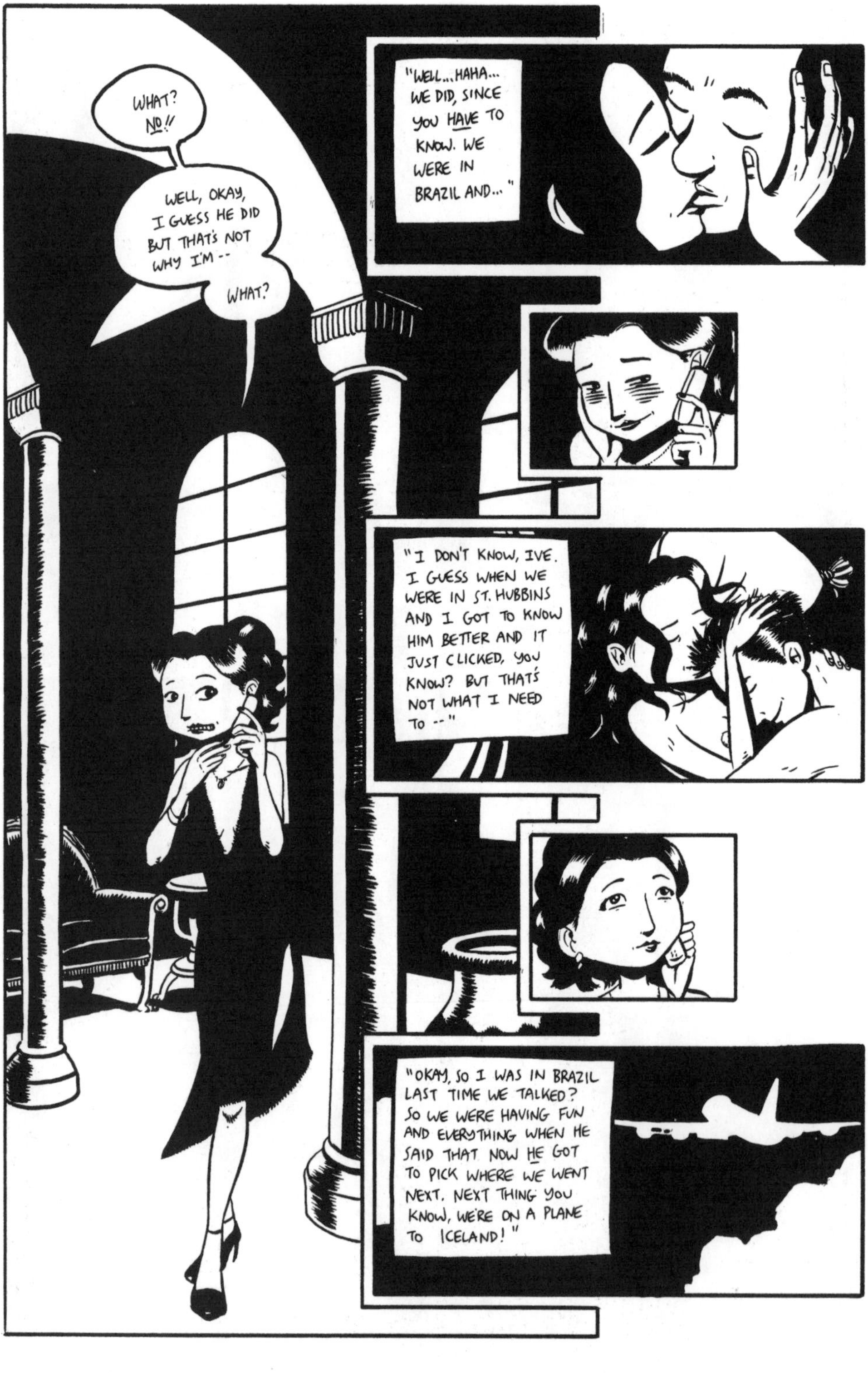

WHAT? NO!!
WELL, OKAY, I GUESS HE DID BUT THAT'S NOT WHY I'M --
WHAT?
"WELL...HAHA... WE DID, SINCE YOU HAVE TO KNOW. WE WERE IN BRAZIL AND..."
"I DON'T KNOW, IVE. I GUESS WHEN WE WERE IN ST. HUBBINS AND I GOT TO KNOW HIM BETTER AND IT JUST CLICKED, YOU KNOW? BUT THAT'S NOT WHAT I NEED TO --"
"OKAY, SO I WAS IN BRAZIL LAST TIME WE TALKED? SO WE WERE HAVING FUN AND EVERYTHING WHEN HE SAID THAT NOW HE GOT TO PICK WHERE WE WENT NEXT. NEXT THING YOU KNOW, WE'RE ON A PLANE TO ICELAND!"

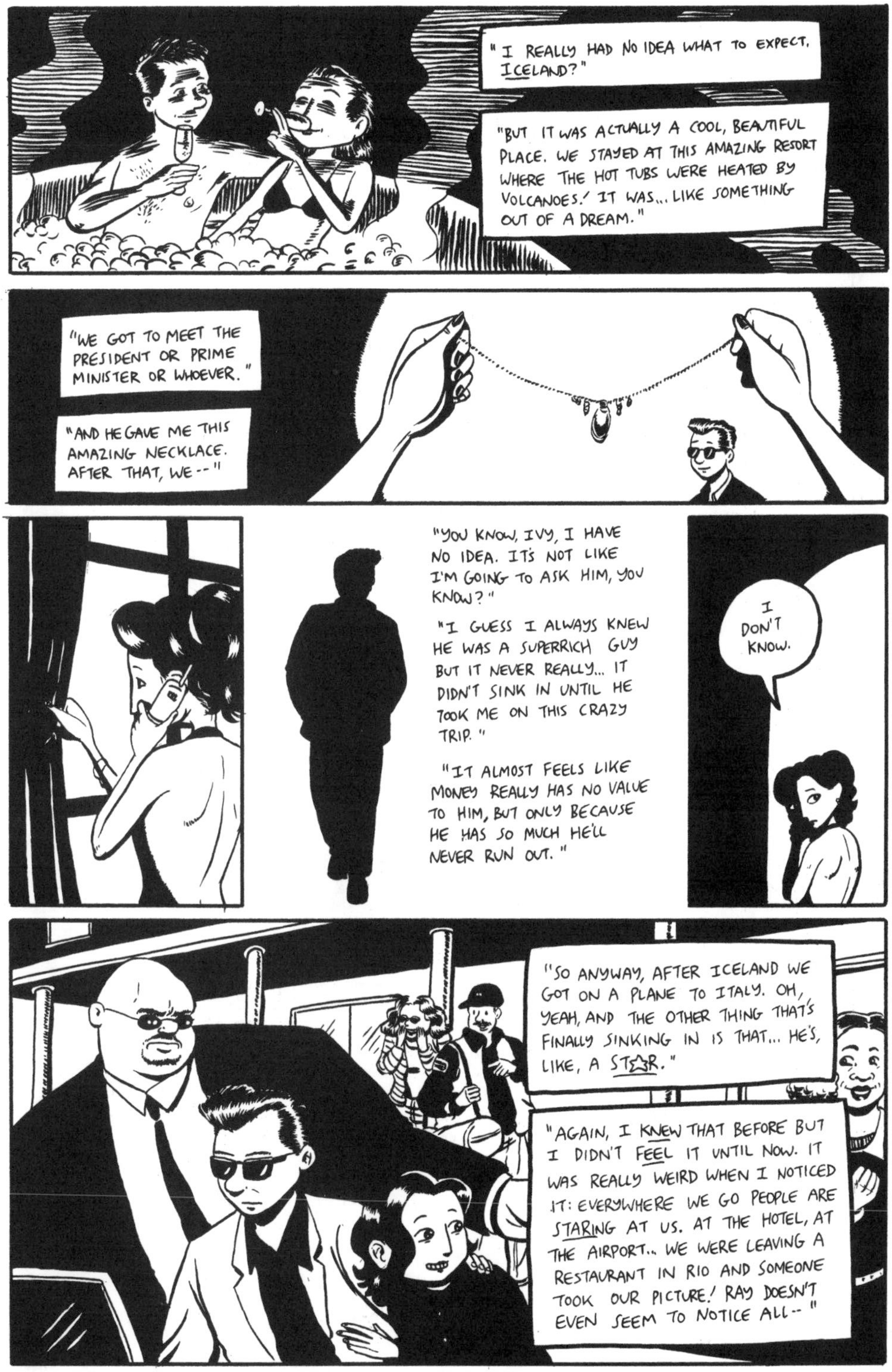
"I REALLY HAD NO IDEA WHAT TO EXPECT. ICELAND?"
"BUT IT WAS ACTUALLY A COOL, BEAUTIFUL PLACE. WE STAYED AT THIS AMAZING RESORT WHERE THE HOT TUBS WERE HEATED BY VOLCANOES! IT WAS... LIKE SOMETHING OUT OF A DREAM."
"WE GOT TO MEET THE PRESIDENT OR PRIME MINISTER OR WHOEVER."
"AND HE GAVE ME THIS AMAZING NECKLACE. AFTER THAT, WE--"
"YOU KNOW, IVY, I HAVE NO IDEA. IT'S NOT LIKE I'M GOING TO ASK HIM, YOU KNOW?"
"I GUESS I ALWAYS KNEW HE WAS A SUPERRICH GUY BUT IT NEVER REALLY... IT DIDN'T SINK IN UNTIL HE TOOK ME ON THIS CRAZY TRIP."
"IT ALMOST FEELS LIKE MONEY REALLY HAS NO VALUE TO HIM, BUT ONLY BECAUSE HE HAS SO MUCH HE'LL NEVER RUN OUT."
I DON'T KNOW.
"SO ANYWAY, AFTER ICELAND WE GOT ON A PLANE TO ITALY. OH, YEAH, AND THE OTHER THING THAT'S FINALLY SINKING IN IS THAT... HE'S, LIKE, A STAR."
"AGAIN, I KNEW THAT BEFORE BUT I DIDN'T FEEL IT UNTIL NOW. IT WAS REALLY WEIRD WHEN I NOTICED IT: EVERYWHERE WE GO PEOPLE ARE STARING AT US. AT THE HOTEL, AT THE AIRPORT.. WE WERE LEAVING A RESTAURANT IN RIO AND SOMEONE TOOK OUR PICTURE! RAY DOESN'T EVEN SEEM TO NOTICE ALL--"

HE'S REALLY A SWEET GUY, YOU KNOW? HE EVEN SEEMS KIND OF, I DON'T KNOW, LONELY.

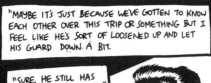

"MAYBE IT'S JUST BECAUSE WE'VE GOTTEN TO KNOW EACH OTHER OVER THIS TRIP OR SOMETHING BUT I FEEL LIKE HE'S SORT OF LOOSENED UP AND LET HIS GUARD DOWN A BIT."

"SURE, HE STILL HAS HIS QUIRKS BUT DEEP--"

WAIT A MINUTE: "QUIRKS?" WHAT DO YOU MEAN?

LIKE HE WANTS YOU TO SPANK HIM OR DRESS UP LIKE A NUN OR SOMETHING?

HeeHee! NO, NOTHING LIKE THAT (AT LEAST NOT YET.)

▷ IT'S MORE ᵢ LITTLE THINGS. LIKE... UM...

"I DON'T KNOW, THE... OH! HERE'S ONE: WHENEVER WE GO OUT TO EAT SOMEWHERE, EVEN IF IT'S A REAL FANCY PLACE, HE ALWAYS BRINGS A SET OF UTENSILS WITH HIM TO EAT WITH."

WOW! HOW STRANGE. ARE THEY MADE OUT OF GOLD OR SOMETHING? IS IT LIKE AN OBSESSIVE- COMPULSIVE THING?

I DON'T KNOW, I'VE. I DON'T WANT TO EMBARASS HIM BY ASKING. IT'S--

"OH, SHOOT! I HAVE TO GET BACK. BUT, LISTEN, I HAVE TO TELL WHAT HAPPENED!"

"FOR DINNER HE TOOK ME TO THIS AMAZING RESTAURANT, RIGHT? SO AFTERWARDS WE'RE OUT ON THIS, UH, LIKE, VERANDA?"

"AND THEN HE, LIKE, ASKS ME TO... TO MARRY HIM!"

WAIT, WHAT?

HAHA, I THOUGHT YOU SAID HE ASKED YOU TO MARRY HIM.

·nineteen·

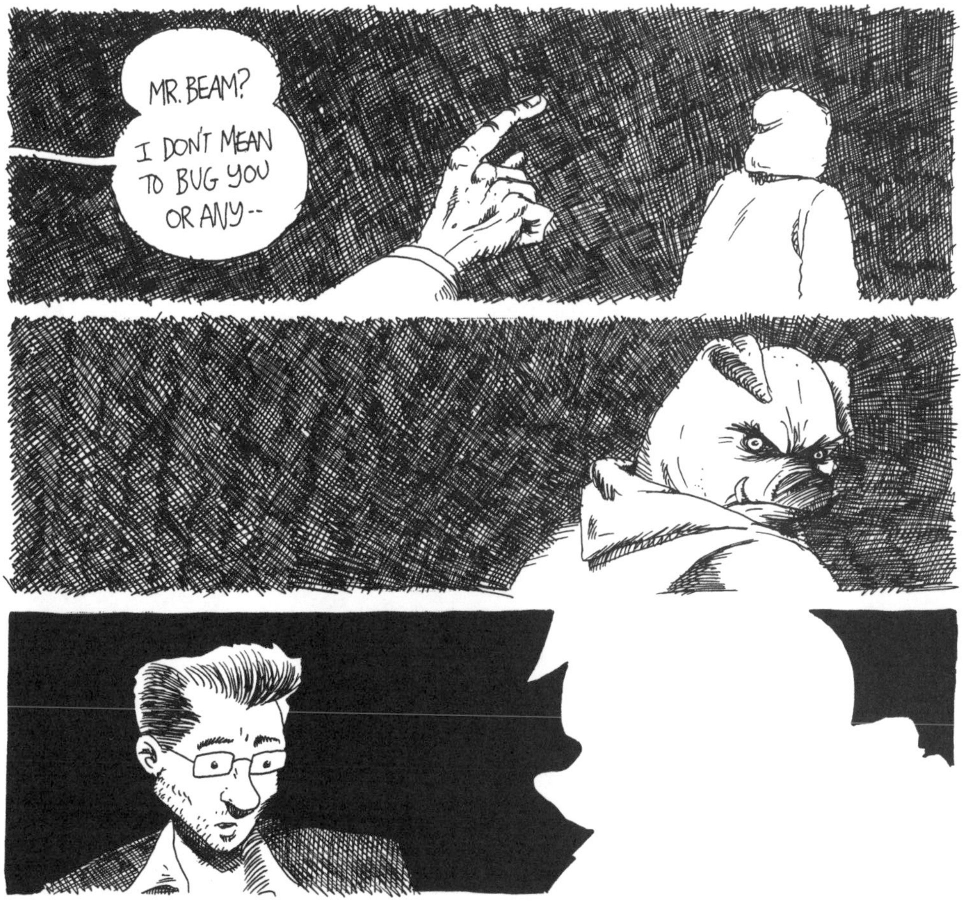
MR. BEAM?
I DON'T MEAN TO BUG YOU OR ANY--

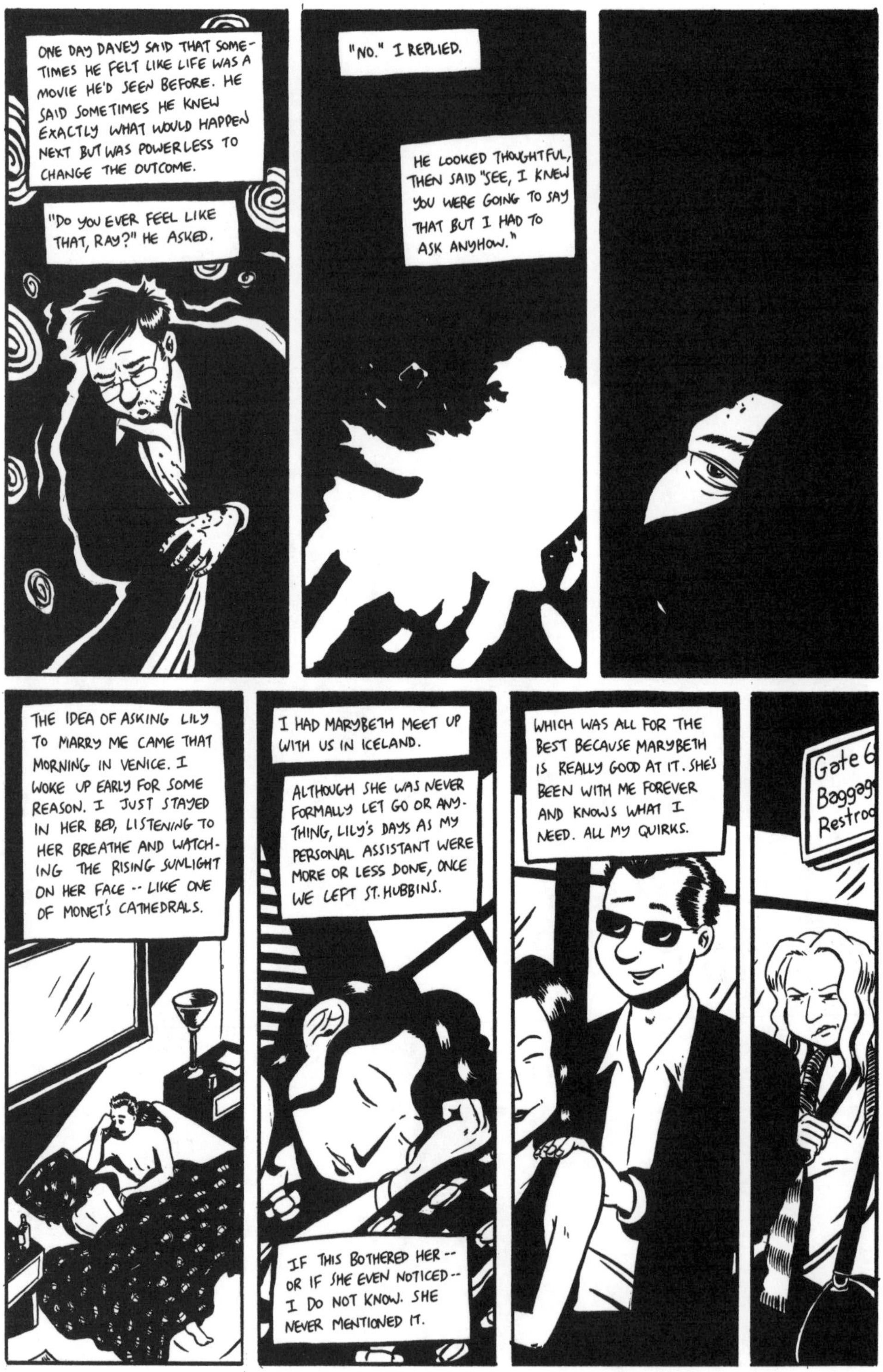
ONE DAY DAVEY SAID THAT SOMETIMES HE FELT LIKE LIFE WAS A MOVIE HE'D SEEN BEFORE. HE SAID SOMETIMES HE KNEW EXACTLY WHAT WOULD HAPPEN NEXT BUT WAS POWERLESS TO CHANGE THE OUTCOME.
"DO YOU EVER FEEL LIKE THAT, RAY?" HE ASKED.
"NO." I REPLIED.
HE LOOKED THOUGHTFUL, THEN SAID "SEE, I KNEW YOU WERE GOING TO SAY THAT BUT I HAD TO ASK ANYHOW."
THE IDEA OF ASKING LILY TO MARRY ME CAME THAT MORNING IN VENICE. I WOKE UP EARLY FOR SOME REASON. I JUST STAYED IN HER BED, LISTENING TO HER BREATHE AND WATCHING THE RISING SUNLIGHT ON HER FACE -- LIKE ONE OF MONET'S CATHEDRALS.
I HAD MARYBETH MEET UP WITH US IN ICELAND.
ALTHOUGH SHE WAS NEVER FORMALLY LET GO OR ANYTHING, LILY'S DAYS AS MY PERSONAL ASSISTANT WERE MORE OR LESS DONE, ONCE WE LEFT ST. HUBBINS.
IF THIS BOTHERED HER -- OR IF SHE EVEN NOTICED -- I DO NOT KNOW. SHE NEVER MENTIONED IT.
WHICH WAS ALL FOR THE BEST BECAUSE MARYBETH IS REALLY GOOD AT IT. SHE'S BEEN WITH ME FOREVER AND KNOWS WHAT I NEED. ALL MY QUIRKS.
Gate 6
Baggag
Restroo

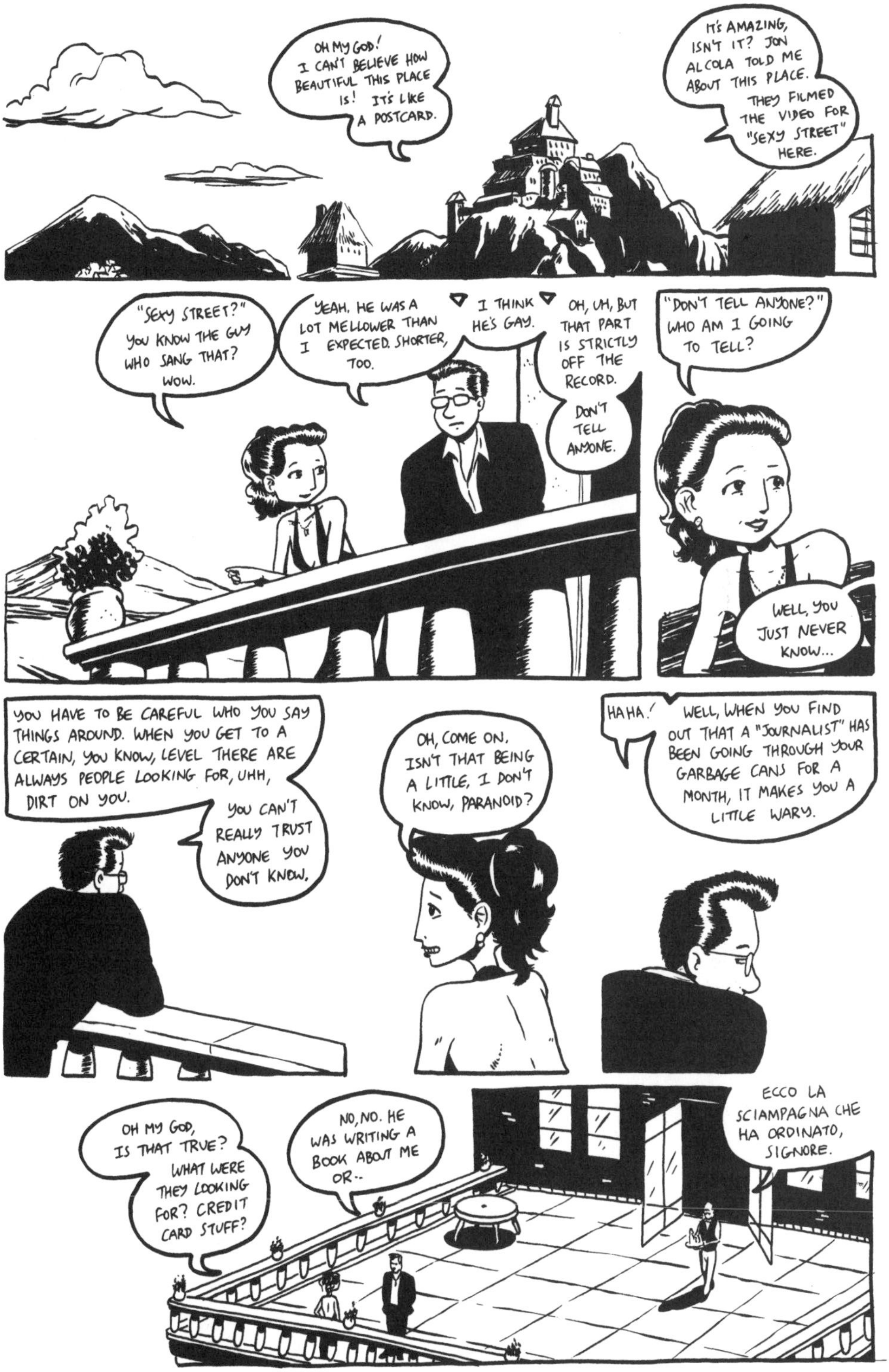
OH MY GOD! I CAN'T BELIEVE HOW BEAUTIFUL THIS PLACE IS! IT'S LIKE A POSTCARD.
IT'S AMAZING, ISN'T IT? JON ALCOLA TOLD ME ABOUT THIS PLACE.
THEY FILMED THE VIDEO FOR "SEXY STREET" HERE.
"SEXY STREET?" YOU KNOW THE GUY WHO SANG THAT? WOW.
YEAH. HE WAS A LOT MELLOWER THAN I EXPECTED. SHORTER, TOO.
I THINK HE'S GAY.
OH, UH, BUT THAT PART IS STRICTLY OFF THE RECORD.
DON'T TELL ANYONE.
"DON'T TELL ANYONE?" WHO AM I GOING TO TELL?
WELL, YOU JUST NEVER KNOW...
YOU HAVE TO BE CAREFUL WHO YOU SAY THINGS AROUND. WHEN YOU GET TO A CERTAIN, YOU KNOW, LEVEL THERE ARE ALWAYS PEOPLE LOOKING FOR, UHH, DIRT ON YOU.
YOU CAN'T REALLY TRUST ANYONE YOU DON'T KNOW.
OH, COME ON. ISN'T THAT BEING A LITTLE, I DON'T KNOW, PARANOID?
HAHA!
WELL, WHEN YOU FIND OUT THAT A "JOURNALIST" HAS BEEN GOING THROUGH YOUR GARBAGE CANS FOR A MONTH, IT MAKES YOU A LITTLE WARY.
OH MY GOD, IS THAT TRUE?
WHAT WERE THEY LOOKING FOR? CREDIT CARD STUFF?
NO, NO. HE WAS WRITING A BOOK ABOUT ME OR--
ECCO LA SCIAMPAGNA CHE HA ORDINATO, SIGNORE.

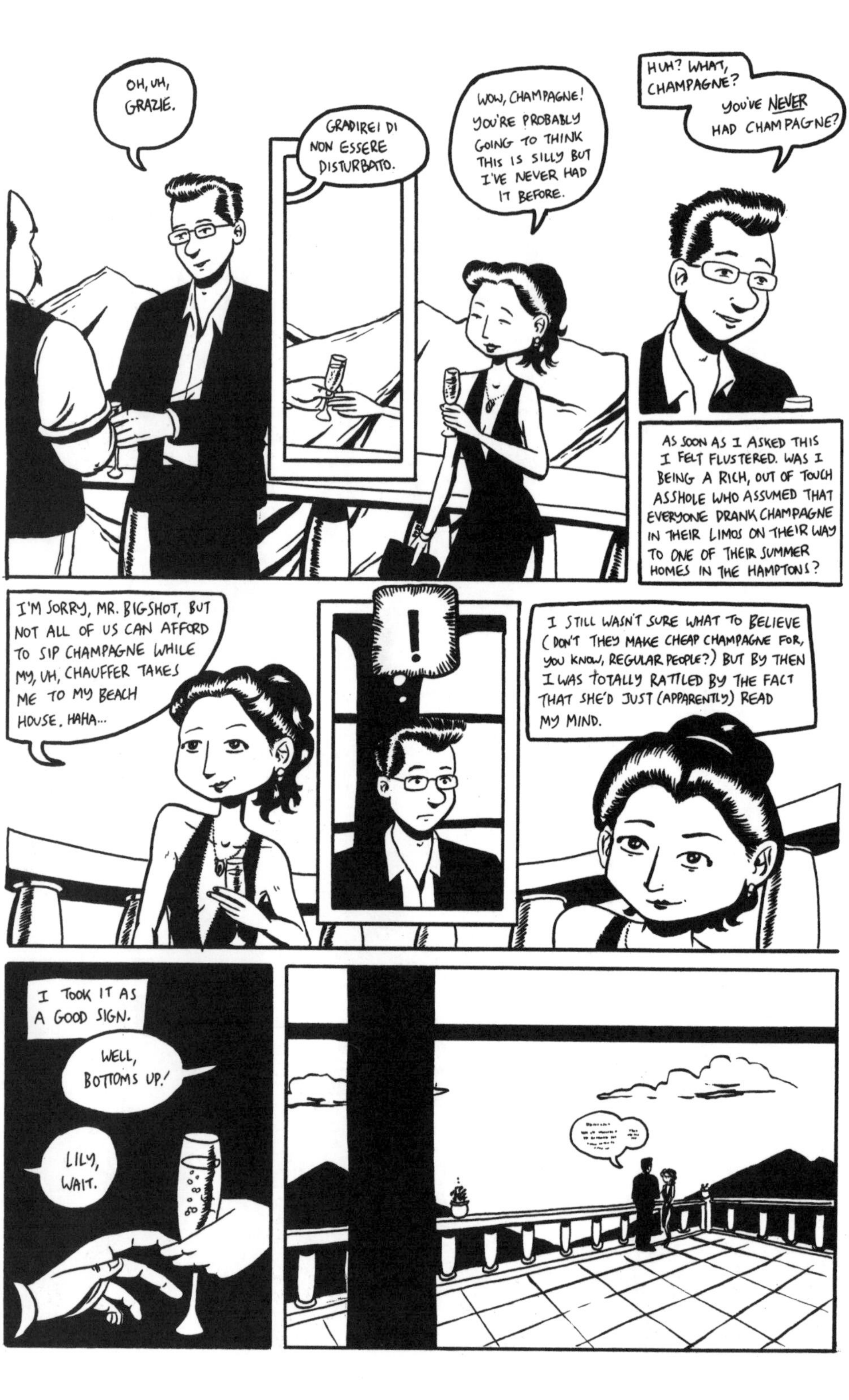
OH, UH, GRAZIE.
GRADIREI DI NON ESSERE DISTURBATO.
WOW, CHAMPAGNE! YOU'RE PROBABLY GOING TO THINK THIS IS SILLY BUT I'VE NEVER HAD IT BEFORE.
HUH? WHAT, CHAMPAGNE?
YOU'VE NEVER HAD CHAMPAGNE?
AS SOON AS I ASKED THIS I FELT FLUSTERED. WAS I BEING A RICH, OUT OF TOUCH ASSHOLE WHO ASSUMED THAT EVERYONE DRANK CHAMPAGNE IN THEIR LIMOS ON THEIR WAY TO ONE OF THEIR SUMMER HOMES IN THE HAMPTONS?
I'M SORRY, MR. BIGSHOT, BUT NOT ALL OF US CAN AFFORD TO SIP CHAMPAGNE WHILE MY, UH, CHAUFFER TAKES ME TO MY BEACH HOUSE. HAHA...
!
I STILL WASN'T SURE WHAT TO BELIEVE (DON'T THEY MAKE CHEAP CHAMPAGNE FOR, YOU KNOW, REGULAR PEOPLE?) BUT BY THEN I WAS TOTALLY RATTLED BY THE FACT THAT SHE'D JUST (APPARENTLY) READ MY MIND.
I TOOK IT AS A GOOD SIGN.
WELL, BOTTOMS UP!
LILY, WAIT.

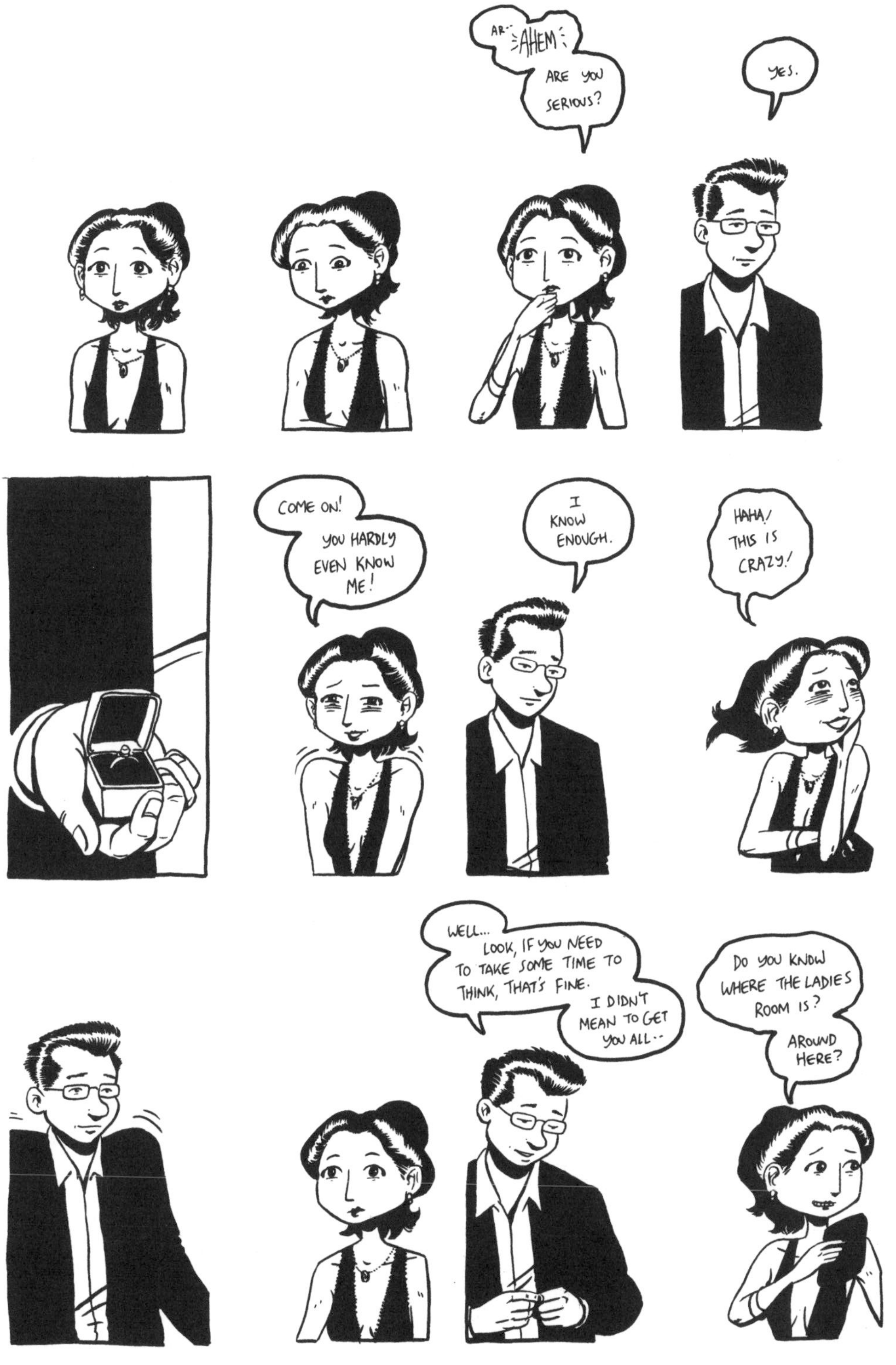
AR-- AHEM
ARE YOU SERIOUS?
YES.
COME ON! YOU HARDLY EVEN KNOW ME!
I KNOW ENOUGH.
HAHA! THIS IS CRAZY!
WELL... LOOK, IF YOU NEED TO TAKE SOME TIME TO THINK, THAT'S FINE. I DIDN'T MEAN TO GET YOU ALL--
DO YOU KNOW WHERE THE LADIES ROOM IS? AROUND HERE?

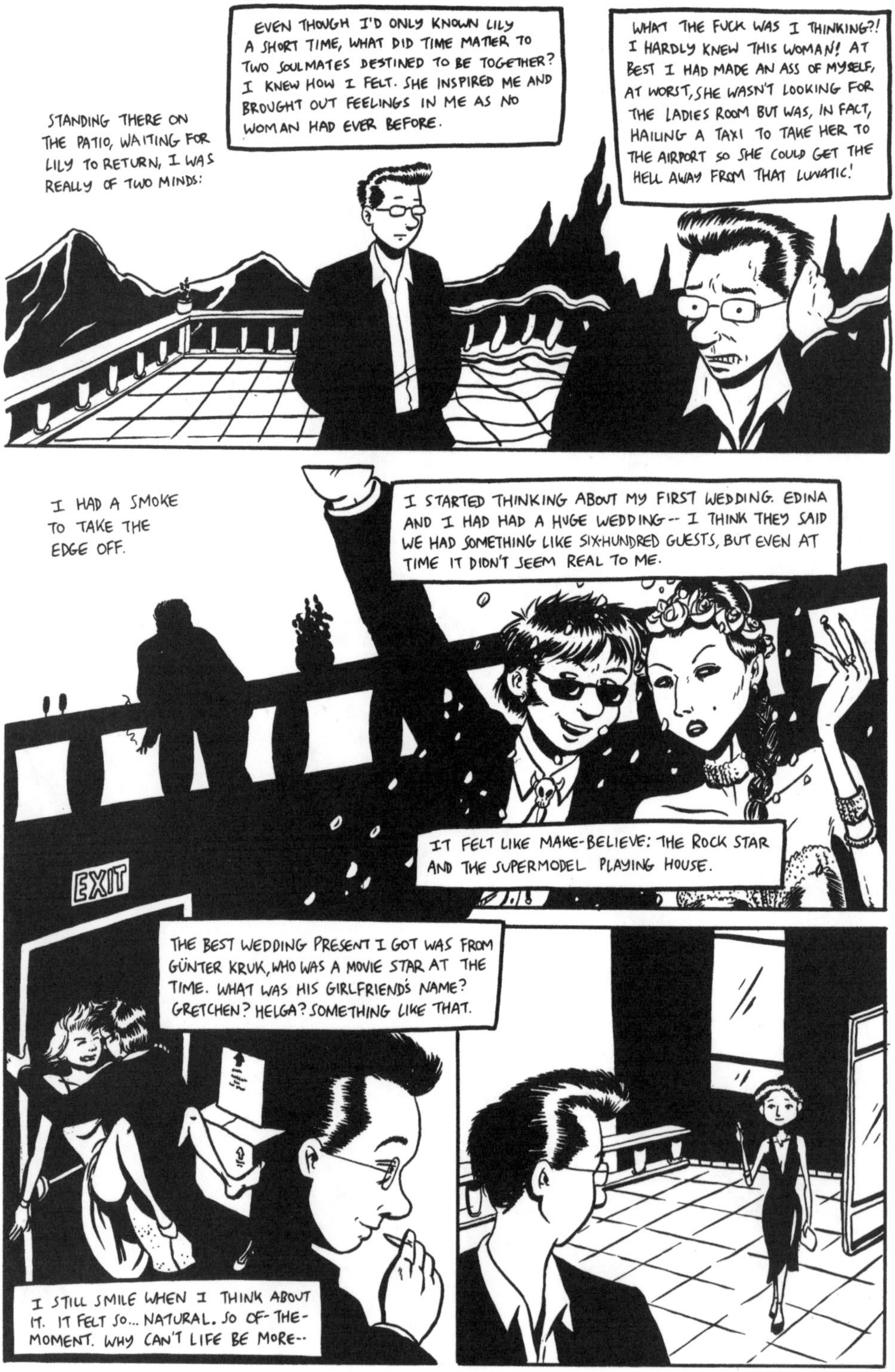
STANDING THERE ON THE PATIO, WAITING FOR LILY TO RETURN, I WAS REALLY OF TWO MINDS:
EVEN THOUGH I'D ONLY KNOWN LILY A SHORT TIME, WHAT DID TIME MATTER TO TWO SOULMATES DESTINED TO BE TOGETHER? I KNEW HOW I FELT. SHE INSPIRED ME AND BROUGHT OUT FEELINGS IN ME AS NO WOMAN HAD EVER BEFORE.
WHAT THE FUCK WAS I THINKING?! I HARDLY KNEW THIS WOMAN! AT BEST I HAD MADE AN ASS OF MYSELF, AT WORST, SHE WASN'T LOOKING FOR THE LADIES ROOM BUT WAS, IN FACT, HAILING A TAXI TO TAKE HER TO THE AIRPORT SO SHE COULD GET THE HELL AWAY FROM THAT LUNATIC!
I HAD A SMOKE TO TAKE THE EDGE OFF.
I STARTED THINKING ABOUT MY FIRST WEDDING. EDINA AND I HAD HAD A HUGE WEDDING -- I THINK THEY SAID WE HAD SOMETHING LIKE SIX-HUNDRED GUESTS, BUT EVEN AT TIME IT DIDN'T SEEM REAL TO ME.
IT FELT LIKE MAKE-BELIEVE: THE ROCK STAR AND THE SUPERMODEL PLAYING HOUSE.
EXIT
THE BEST WEDDING PRESENT I GOT WAS FROM GÜNTER KRUK, WHO WAS A MOVIE STAR AT THE TIME. WHAT WAS HIS GIRLFRIEND'S NAME? GRETCHEN? HELGA? SOMETHING LIKE THAT.
I STILL SMILE WHEN I THINK ABOUT IT. IT FELT SO... NATURAL. SO OF-THE-MOMENT. WHY CAN'T LIFE BE MORE--

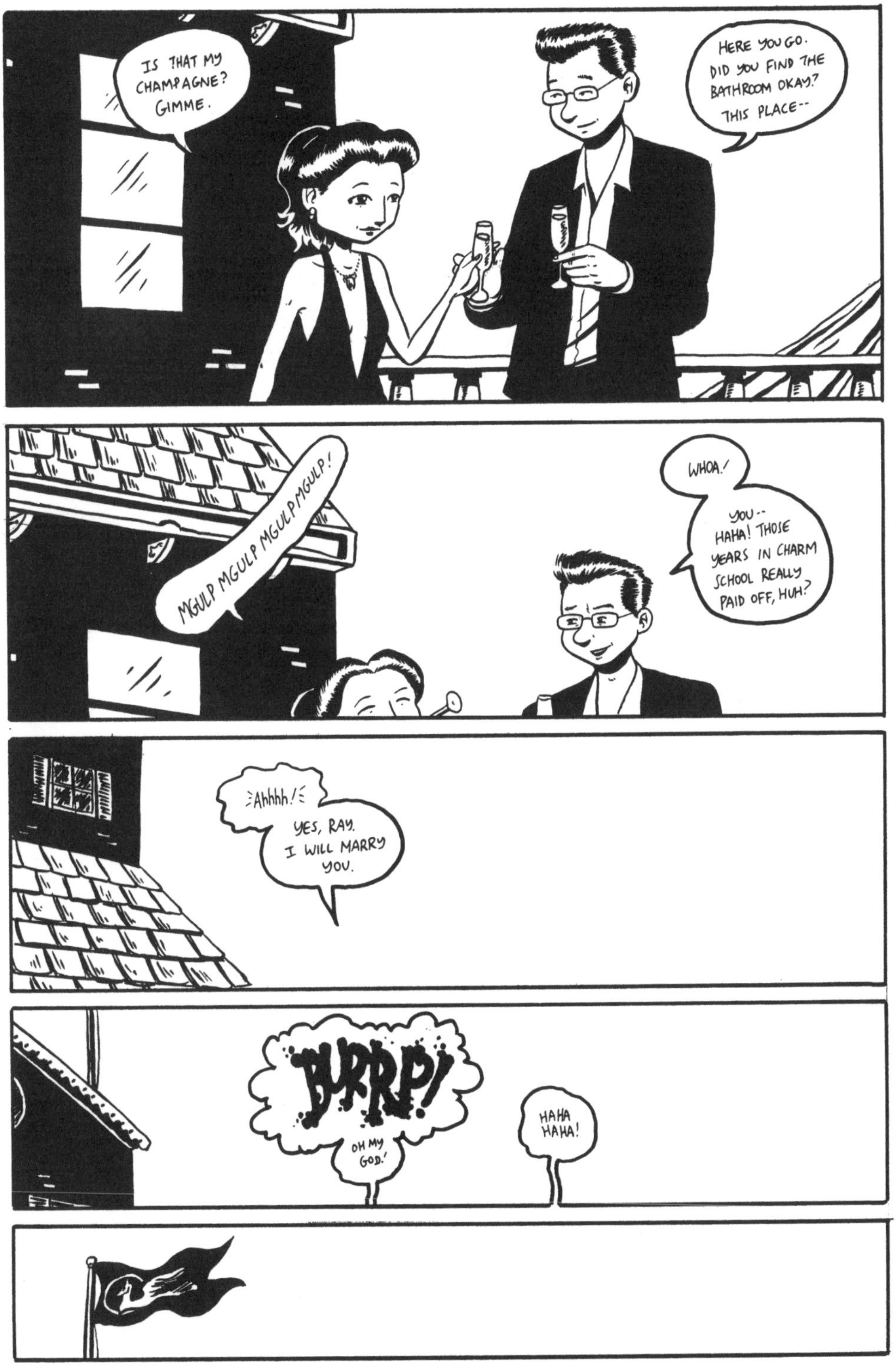
IS THAT MY CHAMPAGNE? GIMME.
HERE YOU GO. DID YOU FIND THE BATHROOM OKAY? THIS PLACE--
MGULP MGULP MGULP MGULP MGULP!
WHOA!
YOU-- HAHA! THOSE YEARS IN CHARM SCHOOL REALLY PAID OFF, HUH?
Ahhhh!
YES, RAY. I WILL MARRY YOU.
BURRP!
OH MY GOD!
HAHA HAHA!

EIGHTEEN

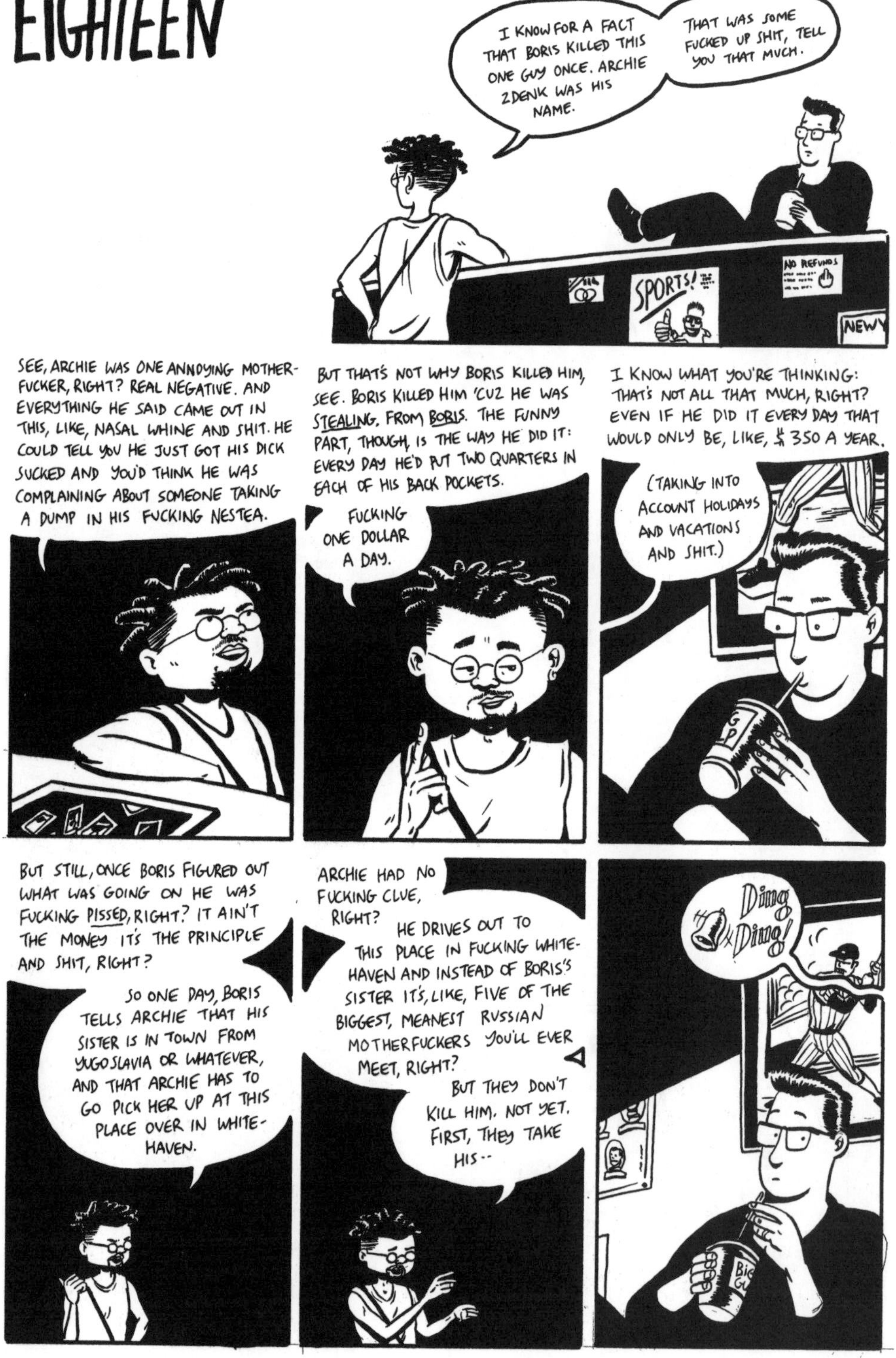
I KNOW FOR A FACT THAT BORIS KILLED THIS ONE GUY ONCE. ARCHIE ZDENK WAS HIS NAME.
THAT WAS SOME FUCKED UP SHIT, TELL YOU THAT MUCH.
SPORTS!
NO REFUNDS
NEWY
SEE, ARCHIE WAS ONE ANNOYING MOTHER-FUCKER, RIGHT? REAL NEGATIVE. AND EVERYTHING HE SAID CAME OUT IN THIS, LIKE, NASAL WHINE AND SHIT. HE COULD TELL YOU HE JUST GOT HIS DICK SUCKED AND YOU'D THINK HE WAS COMPLAINING ABOUT SOMEONE TAKING A DUMP IN HIS FUCKING NESTEA.
BUT THAT'S NOT WHY BORIS KILLED HIM, SEE. BORIS KILLED HIM 'CUZ HE WAS STEALING. FROM BORIS. THE FUNNY PART, THOUGH, IS THE WAY HE DID IT: EVERY DAY HE'D PUT TWO QUARTERS IN EACH OF HIS BACK POCKETS.
FUCKING ONE DOLLAR A DAY.
I KNOW WHAT YOU'RE THINKING: THAT'S NOT ALL THAT MUCH, RIGHT? EVEN IF HE DID IT EVERY DAY THAT WOULD ONLY BE, LIKE, $350 A YEAR.
(TAKING INTO ACCOUNT HOLIDAYS AND VACATIONS AND SHIT.)
BUT STILL, ONCE BORIS FIGURED OUT WHAT WAS GOING ON HE WAS FUCKING PISSED, RIGHT? IT AIN'T THE MONEY IT'S THE PRINCIPLE AND SHIT, RIGHT?
SO ONE DAY, BORIS TELLS ARCHIE THAT HIS SISTER IS IN TOWN FROM YUGOSLAVIA OR WHATEVER, AND THAT ARCHIE HAS TO GO PICK HER UP AT THIS PLACE OVER IN WHITE-HAVEN.
ARCHIE HAD NO FUCKING CLUE, RIGHT?
HE DRIVES OUT TO THIS PLACE IN FUCKING WHITE-HAVEN AND INSTEAD OF BORIS'S SISTER IT'S, LIKE, FIVE OF THE BIGGEST, MEANEST RUSSIAN MOTHERFUCKERS YOU'LL EVER MEET, RIGHT?
BUT THEY DON'T KILL HIM. NOT YET. FIRST, THEY TAKE HIS--
Ding Ding!

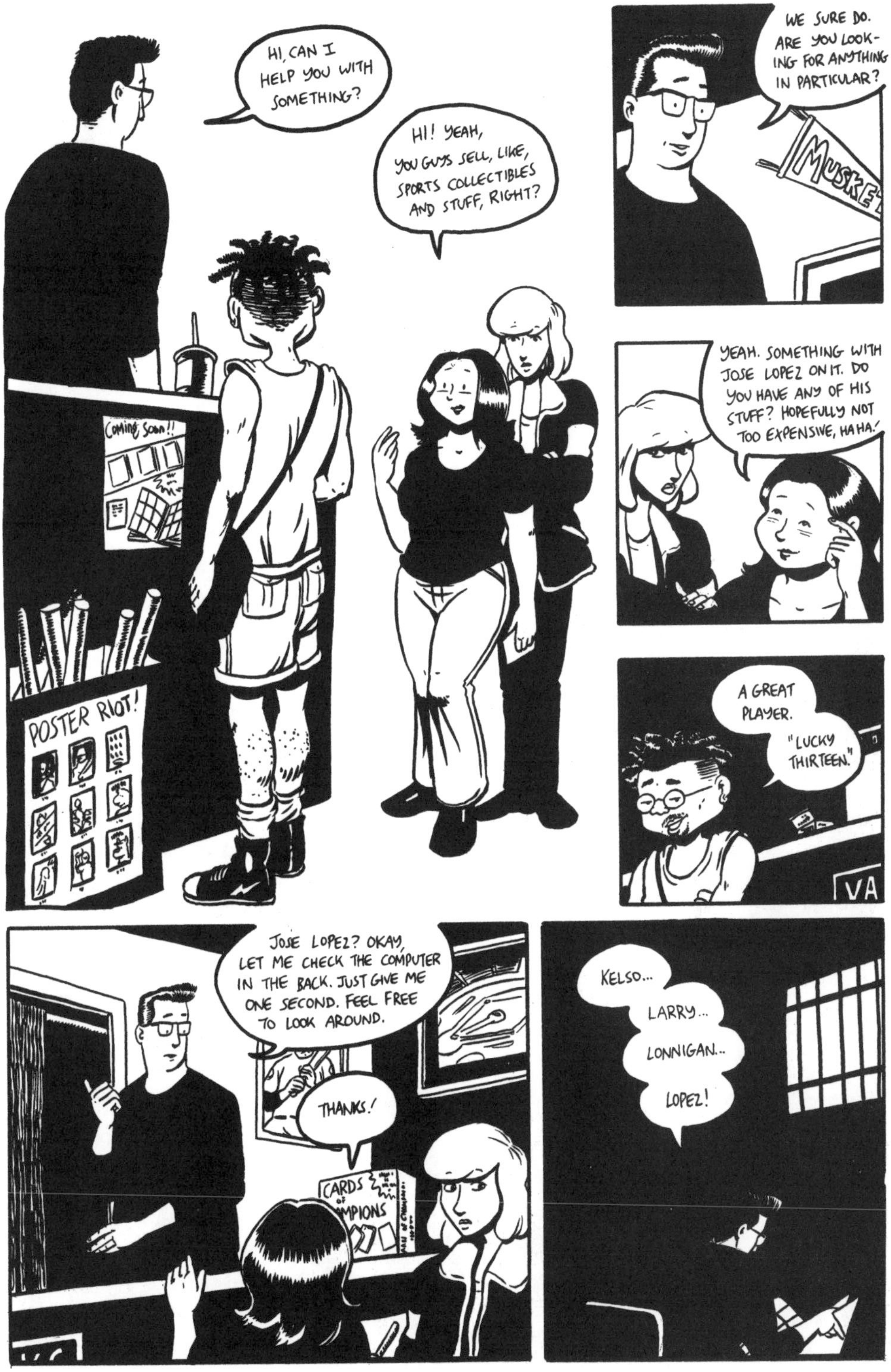
HI, CAN I HELP YOU WITH SOMETHING?
HI! YEAH, YOU GUYS SELL, LIKE, SPORTS COLLECTIBLES AND STUFF, RIGHT?
Coming Soon!!
POSTER RIOT!
WE SURE DO. ARE YOU LOOKING FOR ANYTHING IN PARTICULAR?
MUSKE
YEAH. SOMETHING WITH JOSE LOPEZ ON IT. DO YOU HAVE ANY OF HIS STUFF? HOPEFULLY NOT TOO EXPENSIVE, HAHA!
A GREAT PLAYER.
"LUCKY THIRTEEN."
JOSE LOPEZ? OKAY, LET ME CHECK THE COMPUTER IN THE BACK. JUST GIVE ME ONE SECOND. FEEL FREE TO LOOK AROUND.
THANKS!
CARDS OF CHAMPIONS
KELSO...
LARRY...
LONNIGAN...
LOPEZ!

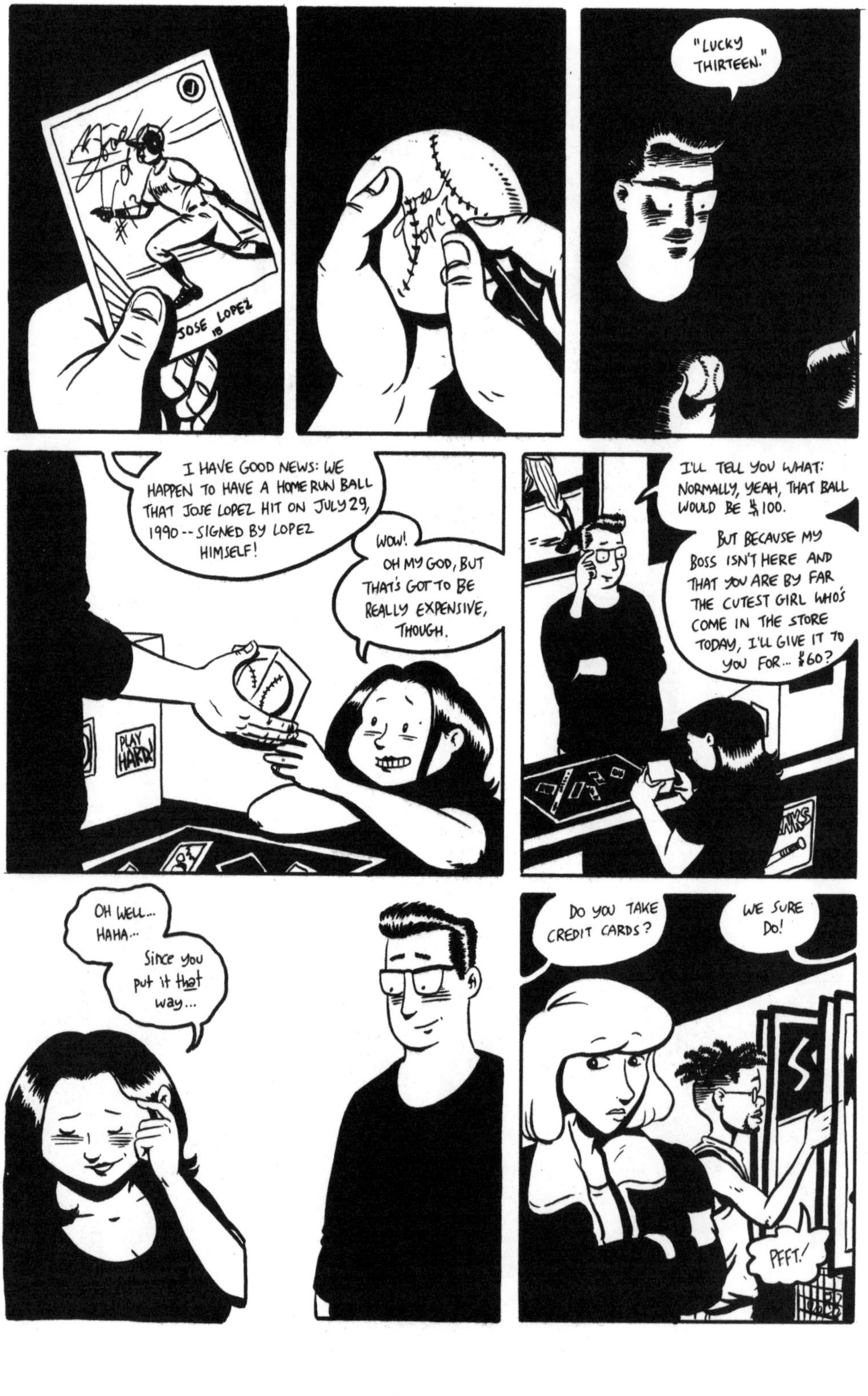
JOSE LOPEZ
1B
"LUCKY THIRTEEN."
I HAVE GOOD NEWS: WE HAPPEN TO HAVE A HOME RUN BALL THAT JOSE LOPEZ HIT ON JULY 29, 1990 -- SIGNED BY LOPEZ HIMSELF!
WOW! OH MY GOD, BUT THAT'S GOT TO BE REALLY EXPENSIVE, THOUGH.
PLAY HARD!
I'LL TELL YOU WHAT: NORMALLY, YEAH, THAT BALL WOULD BE $100.
BUT BECAUSE MY BOSS ISN'T HERE AND THAT YOU ARE BY FAR THE CUTEST GIRL WHO'S COME IN THE STORE TODAY, I'LL GIVE IT TO YOU FOR... $60?
OH WELL... HAHA...
Since you put it that way...
DO YOU TAKE CREDIT CARDS?
WE SURE DO!
PFFT!

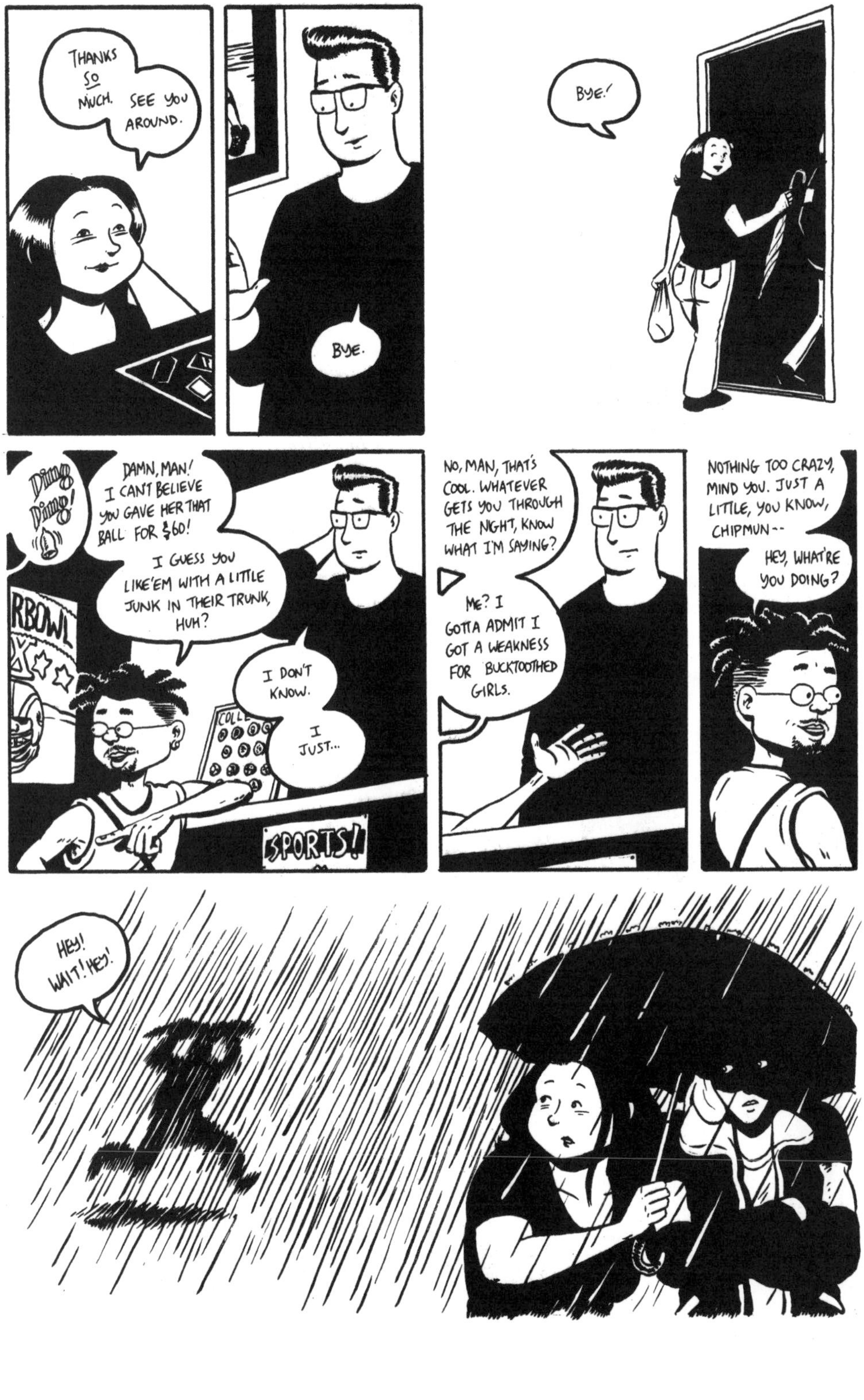
THANKS SO MUCH. SEE YOU AROUND.
BYE.
BYE!
DING DING!
DAMN, MAN! I CAN'T BELIEVE YOU GAVE HER THAT BALL FOR $60!
I GUESS YOU LIKE'EM WITH A LITTLE JUNK IN THEIR TRUNK, HUH?
I DON'T KNOW.
I JUST...
SPORTS!
NO, MAN, THAT'S COOL. WHATEVER GETS YOU THROUGH THE NIGHT, KNOW WHAT I'M SAYING?
ME? I GOTTA ADMIT I GOT A WEAKNESS FOR BUCKTOOTHED GIRLS.
NOTHING TOO CRAZY, MIND YOU. JUST A LITTLE, YOU KNOW, CHIPMUN--
HEY, WHAT'RE YOU DOING?
HEY! WAIT! HEY!

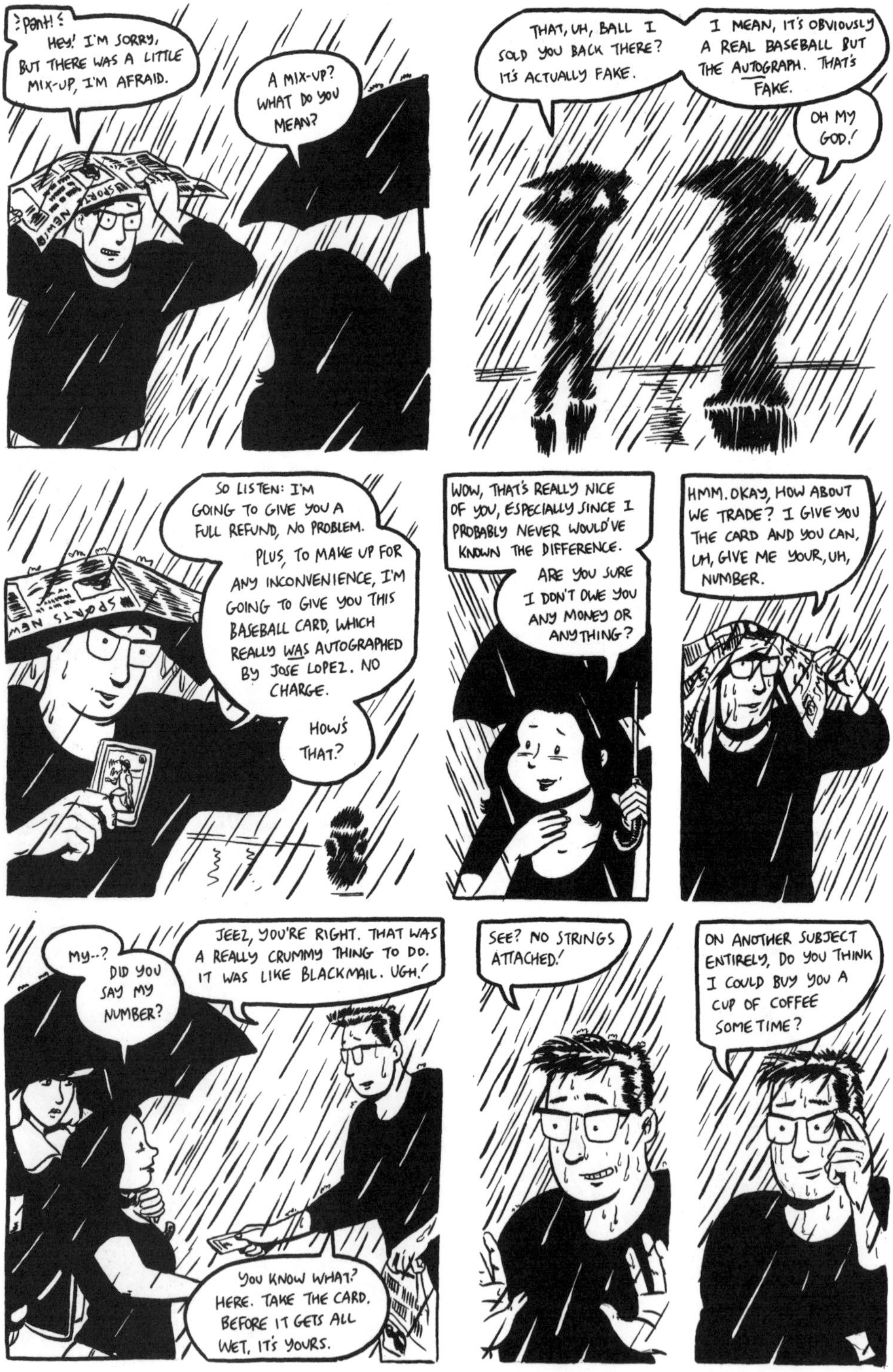

PANT! HEY! I'M SORRY, BUT THERE WAS A LITTLE MIX-UP, I'M AFRAID.
A MIX-UP? WHAT DO YOU MEAN?
THAT, UH, BALL I SOLD YOU BACK THERE? IT'S ACTUALLY FAKE.
I MEAN, IT'S OBVIOUSLY A REAL BASEBALL BUT THE AUTOGRAPH. THAT'S FAKE.
OH MY GOD!
SO LISTEN: I'M GOING TO GIVE YOU A FULL REFUND, NO PROBLEM.
PLUS, TO MAKE UP FOR ANY INCONVENIENCE, I'M GOING TO GIVE YOU THIS BASEBALL CARD, WHICH REALLY WAS AUTOGRAPHED BY JOSE LOPEZ. NO CHARGE.
HOW'S THAT?
WOW, THAT'S REALLY NICE OF YOU, ESPECIALLY SINCE I PROBABLY NEVER WOULD'VE KNOWN THE DIFFERENCE.
ARE YOU SURE I DON'T OWE YOU ANY MONEY OR ANYTHING?
HMM. OKAY, HOW ABOUT WE TRADE? I GIVE YOU THE CARD AND YOU CAN, UH, GIVE ME YOUR, UH, NUMBER.
MY--? DID YOU SAY MY NUMBER?
JEEZ, YOU'RE RIGHT. THAT WAS A REALLY CRUMMY THING TO DO. IT WAS LIKE BLACKMAIL. UGH!
YOU KNOW WHAT? HERE. TAKE THE CARD. BEFORE IT GETS ALL WET. IT'S YOURS.
SEE? NO STRINGS ATTACHED!
ON ANOTHER SUBJECT ENTIRELY, DO YOU THINK I COULD BUY YOU A CUP OF COFFEE SOMETIME?

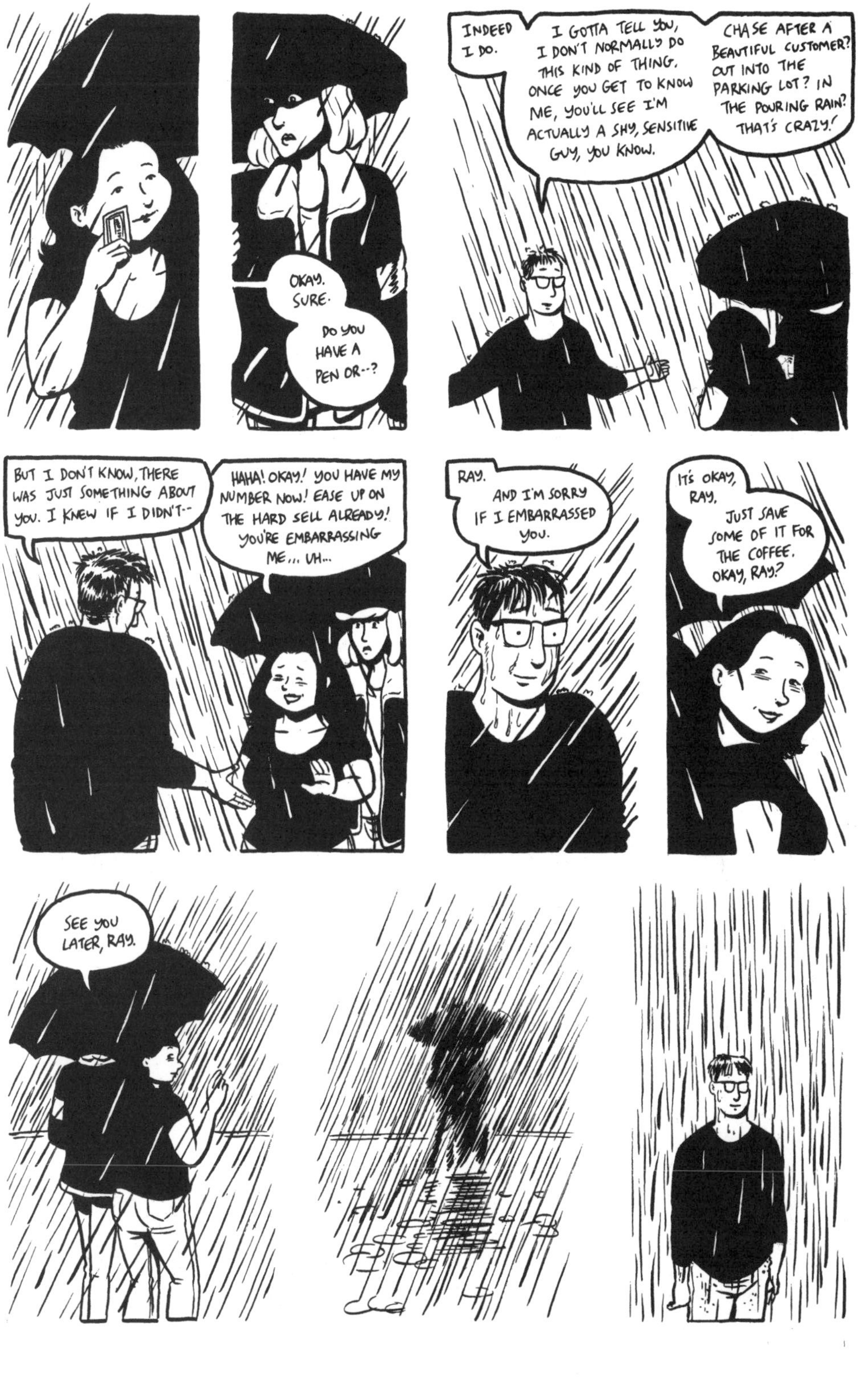
OKAY. SURE.
DO YOU HAVE A PEN OR--?
INDEED I DO.
I GOTTA TELL YOU, I DON'T NORMALLY DO THIS KIND OF THING. ONCE YOU GET TO KNOW ME, YOU'LL SEE I'M ACTUALLY A SHY, SENSITIVE GUY, YOU KNOW.
CHASE AFTER A BEAUTIFUL CUSTOMER? OUT INTO THE PARKING LOT? IN THE POURING RAIN? THAT'S CRAZY!
BUT I DON'T KNOW, THERE WAS JUST SOMETHING ABOUT YOU. I KNEW IF I DIDN'T--
HAHA! OKAY! YOU HAVE MY NUMBER NOW! EASE UP ON THE HARD SELL ALREADY! YOU'RE EMBARRASSING ME... UH...
RAY.
AND I'M SORRY IF I EMBARRASSED YOU.
IT'S OKAY, RAY.
JUST SAVE SOME OF IT FOR THE COFFEE. OKAY, RAY?
SEE YOU LATER, RAY.

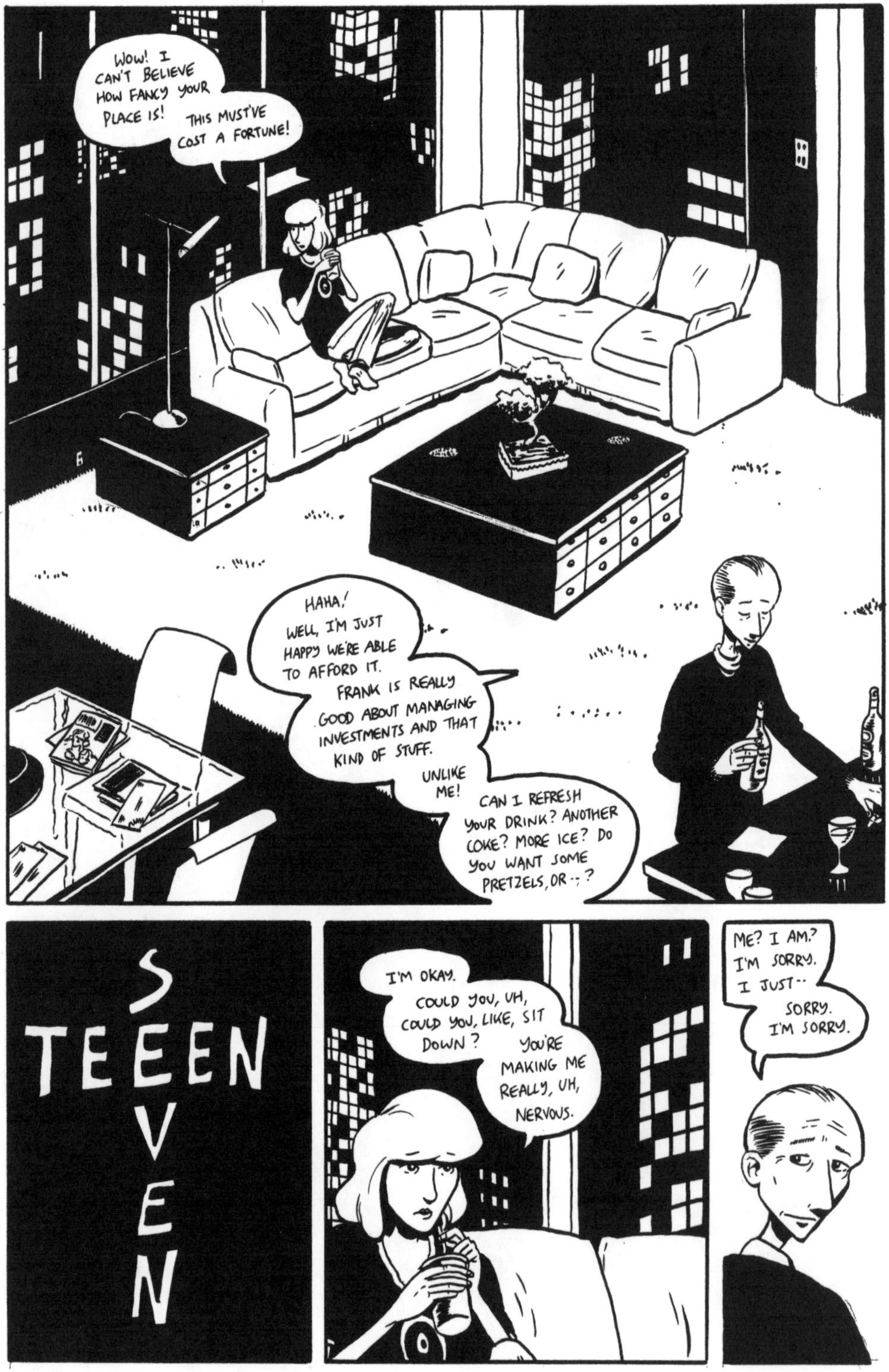
WOW! I CAN'T BELIEVE HOW FANCY YOUR PLACE IS!
THIS MUST'VE COST A FORTUNE!
HAHA! WELL, I'M JUST HAPPY WE'RE ABLE TO AFFORD IT.
FRANK IS REALLY GOOD ABOUT MANAGING INVESTMENTS AND THAT KIND OF STUFF.
UNLIKE ME!
CAN I REFRESH YOUR DRINK? ANOTHER COKE? MORE ICE? DO YOU WANT SOME PRETZELS, OR--?
SEVEN
TEEN
I'M OKAY.
COULD YOU, UH, COULD YOU, LIKE, SIT DOWN?
YOU'RE MAKING ME REALLY, UH, NERVOUS.
ME? I AM? I'M SORRY. I JUST--
SORRY. I'M SORRY.

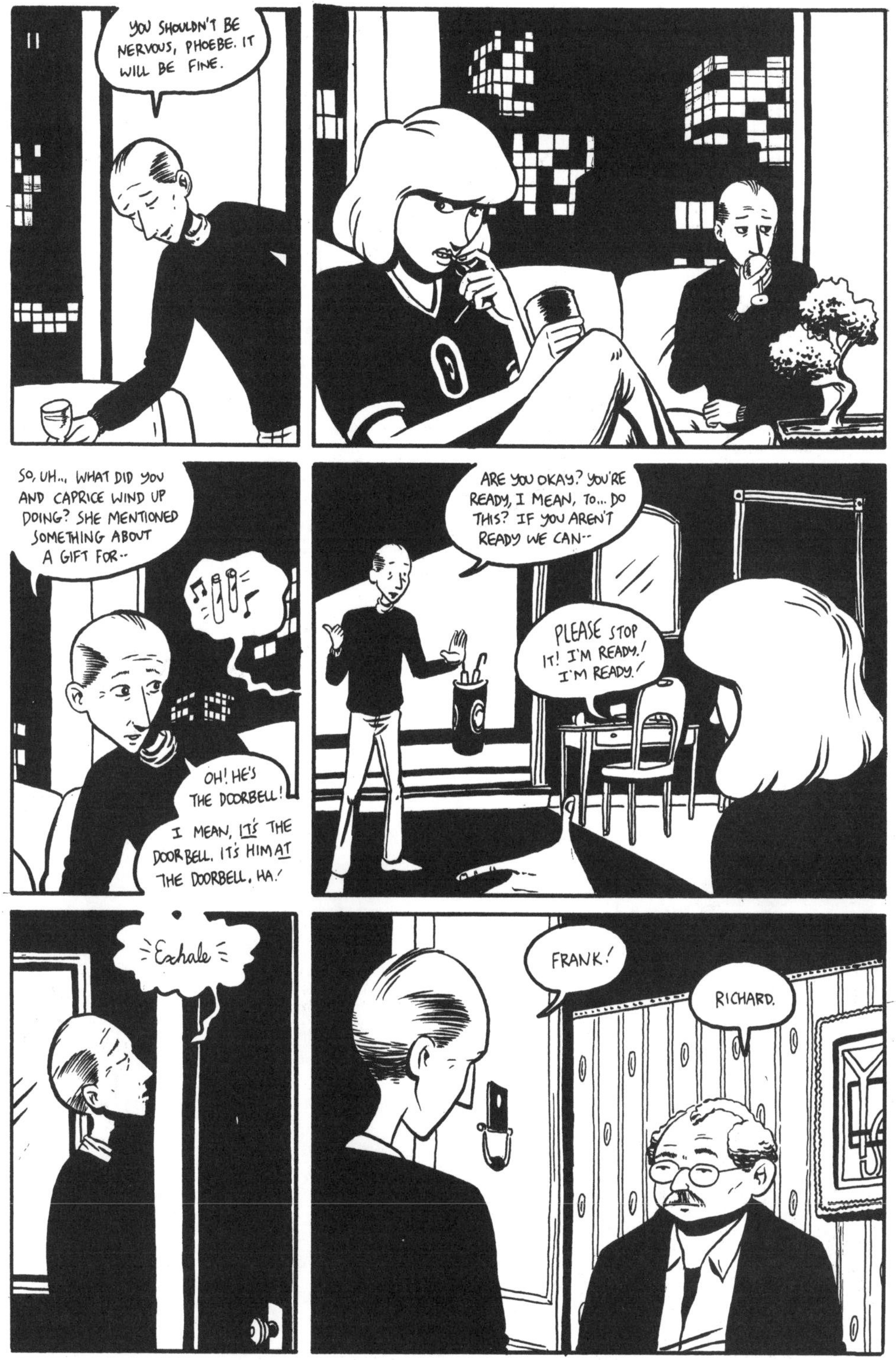
YOU SHOULDN'T BE NERVOUS, PHOEBE. IT WILL BE FINE.
SO, UH... WHAT DID YOU AND CAPRICE WIND UP DOING? SHE MENTIONED SOMETHING ABOUT A GIFT FOR--
OH! HE'S THE DOORBELL!
I MEAN, IT'S THE DOORBELL. IT'S HIM AT THE DOORBELL. HA!
ARE YOU OKAY? YOU'RE READY, I MEAN, TO... DO THIS? IF YOU AREN'T READY WE CAN--
PLEASE STOP IT! I'M READY! I'M READY!
Exhale
FRANK!
RICHARD.

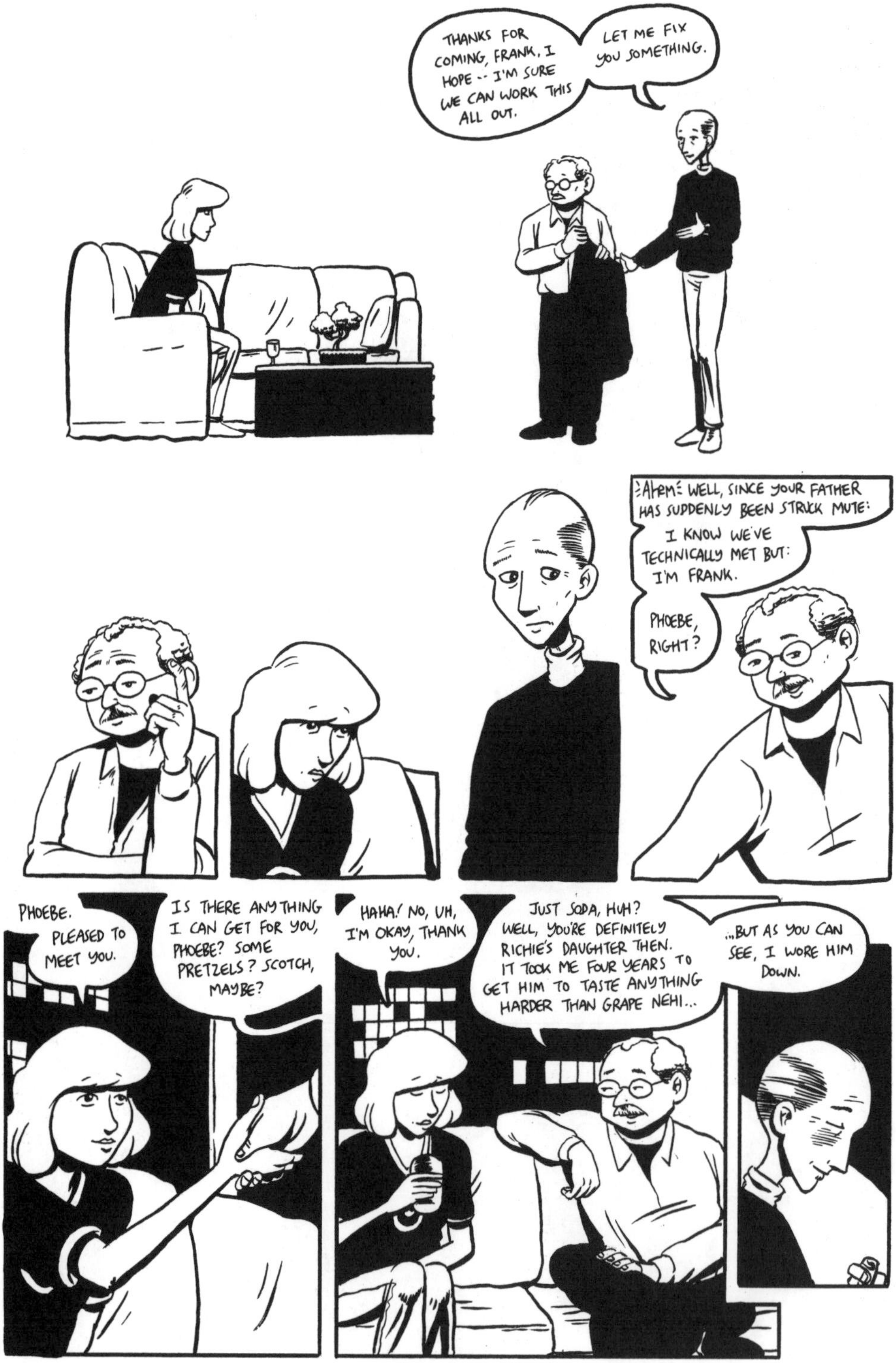
THANKS FOR COMING, FRANK, I HOPE -- I'M SURE WE CAN WORK THIS ALL OUT.
LET ME FIX YOU SOMETHING.
:AHEM: WELL, SINCE YOUR FATHER HAS SUDDENLY BEEN STRUCK MUTE:
I KNOW WE'VE TECHNICALLY MET BUT: I'M FRANK.
PHOEBE, RIGHT?
PHOEBE.
PLEASED TO MEET YOU.
IS THERE ANYTHING I CAN GET FOR YOU, PHOEBE? SOME PRETZELS? SCOTCH, MAYBE?
HAHA! NO, UH, I'M OKAY, THANK YOU.
JUST SODA, HUH? WELL, YOU'RE DEFINITELY RICHIE'S DAUGHTER THEN. IT TOOK ME FOUR YEARS TO GET HIM TO TASTE ANYTHING HARDER THAN GRAPE NEHI...
...BUT AS YOU CAN SEE, I WORE HIM DOWN.

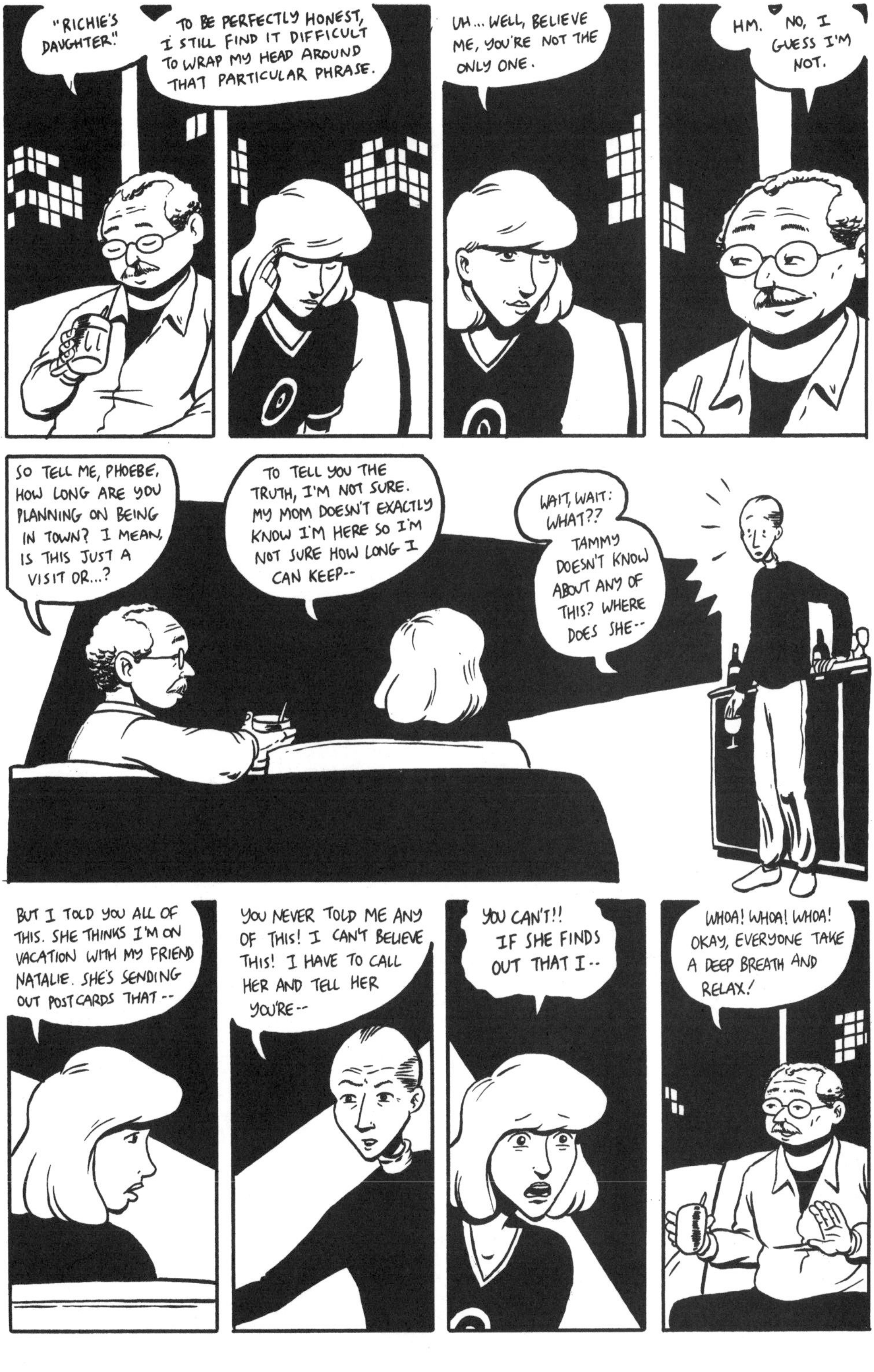
"RICHIE'S DAUGHTER."
TO BE PERFECTLY HONEST, I STILL FIND IT DIFFICULT TO WRAP MY HEAD AROUND THAT PARTICULAR PHRASE.
UH... WELL, BELIEVE ME, YOU'RE NOT THE ONLY ONE.
HM. NO, I GUESS I'M NOT.
SO TELL ME, PHOEBE, HOW LONG ARE YOU PLANNING ON BEING IN TOWN? I MEAN, IS THIS JUST A VISIT OR...?
TO TELL YOU THE TRUTH, I'M NOT SURE. MY MOM DOESN'T EXACTLY KNOW I'M HERE SO I'M NOT SURE HOW LONG I CAN KEEP--
WAIT, WAIT: WHAT??
TAMMY DOESN'T KNOW ABOUT ANY OF THIS? WHERE DOES SHE--
BUT I TOLD YOU ALL OF THIS. SHE THINKS I'M ON VACATION WITH MY FRIEND NATALIE. SHE'S SENDING OUT POSTCARDS THAT--
YOU NEVER TOLD ME ANY OF THIS! I CAN'T BELIEVE THIS! I HAVE TO CALL HER AND TELL HER YOU'RE--
YOU CAN'T!! IF SHE FINDS OUT THAT I--
WHOA! WHOA! WHOA! OKAY, EVERYONE TAKE A DEEP BREATH AND RELAX!

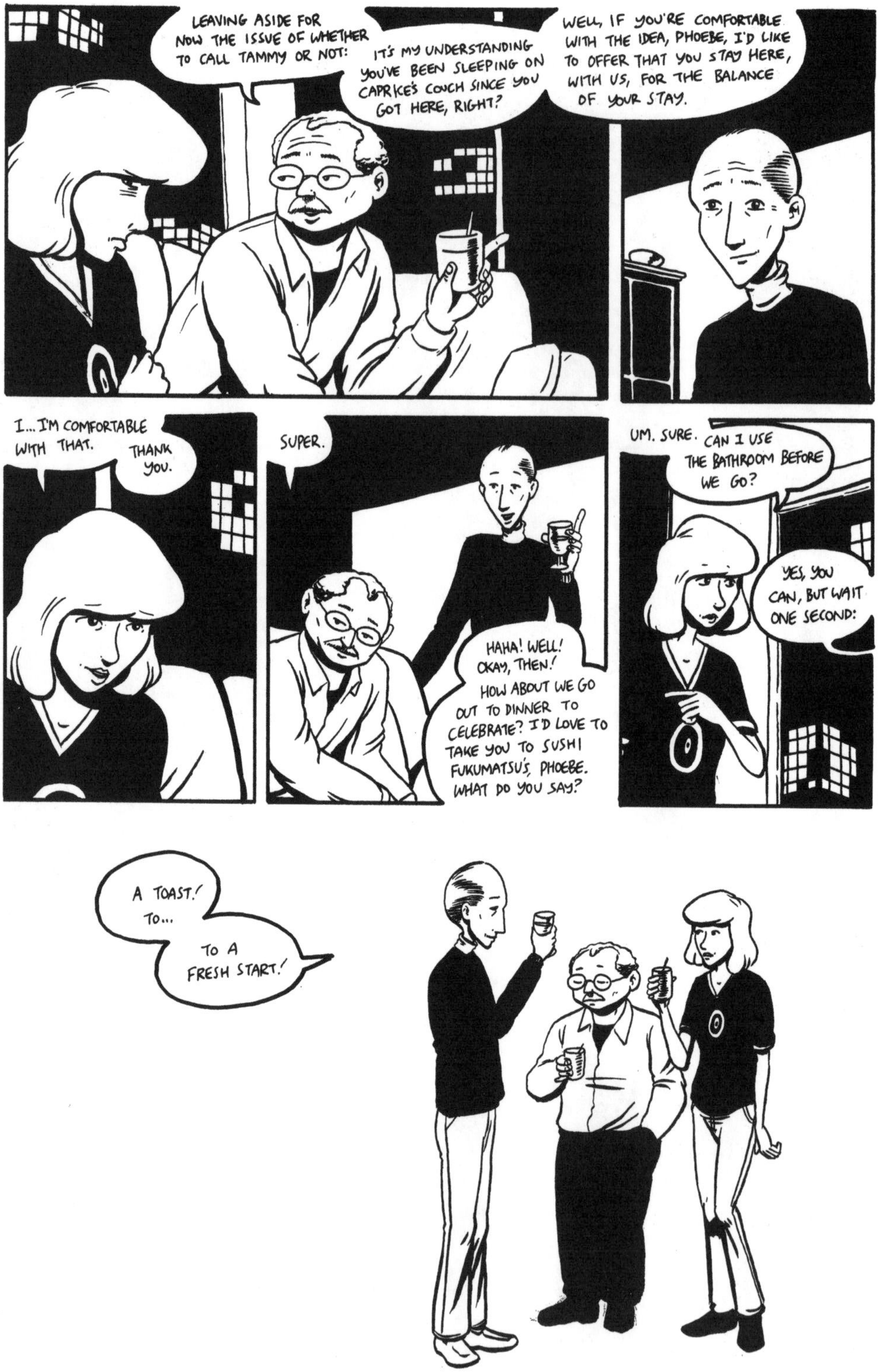
LEAVING ASIDE FOR NOW THE ISSUE OF WHETHER TO CALL TAMMY OR NOT:
IT'S MY UNDERSTANDING YOU'VE BEEN SLEEPING ON CAPRICE'S COUCH SINCE YOU GOT HERE, RIGHT?
WELL, IF YOU'RE COMFORTABLE WITH THE IDEA, PHOEBE, I'D LIKE TO OFFER THAT YOU STAY HERE, WITH US, FOR THE BALANCE OF YOUR STAY.
I... I'M COMFORTABLE WITH THAT.
THANK YOU.
SUPER.
HAHA! WELL! OKAY, THEN!
HOW ABOUT WE GO OUT TO DINNER TO CELEBRATE? I'D LOVE TO TAKE YOU TO SUSHI FUKUMATSU'S, PHOEBE. WHAT DO YOU SAY?
UM. SURE.
CAN I USE THE BATHROOM BEFORE WE GO?
YES, YOU CAN, BUT WAIT ONE SECOND:
A TOAST! TO...
TO A FRESH START!

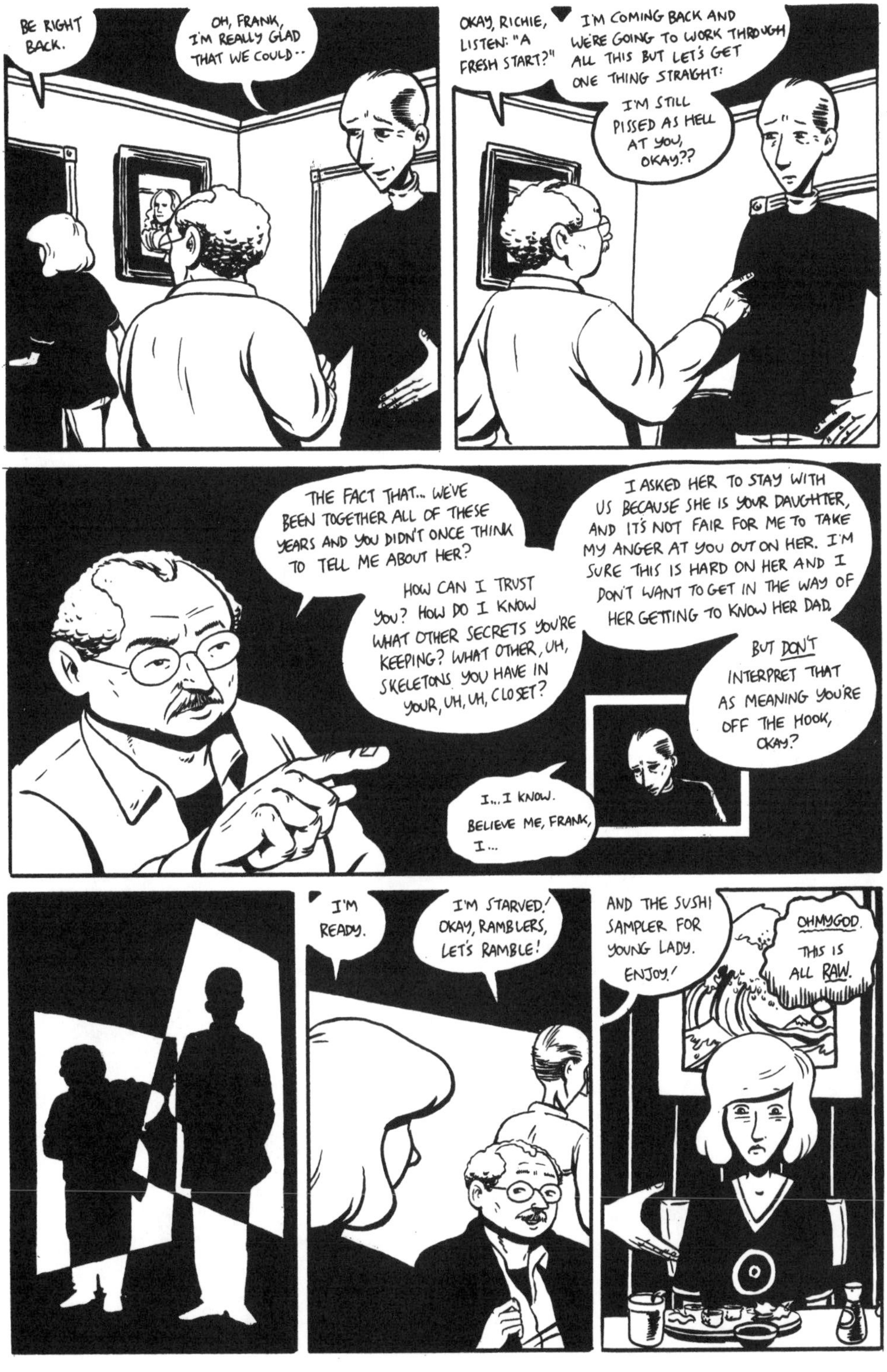
BE RIGHT BACK.
OH, FRANK, I'M REALLY GLAD THAT WE COULD..
OKAY, RICHIE, LISTEN: "A FRESH START?"
I'M COMING BACK AND WE'RE GOING TO WORK THROUGH ALL THIS BUT LET'S GET ONE THING STRAIGHT:
I'M STILL PISSED AS HELL AT YOU, OKAY??
THE FACT THAT.. WE'VE BEEN TOGETHER ALL OF THESE YEARS AND YOU DIDN'T ONCE THINK TO TELL ME ABOUT HER?
HOW CAN I TRUST YOU? HOW DO I KNOW WHAT OTHER SECRETS YOU'RE KEEPING? WHAT OTHER, UH, SKELETONS YOU HAVE IN YOUR, UH, UH, CLOSET?
I ASKED HER TO STAY WITH US BECAUSE SHE IS YOUR DAUGHTER, AND IT'S NOT FAIR FOR ME TO TAKE MY ANGER AT YOU OUT ON HER. I'M SURE THIS IS HARD ON HER AND I DON'T WANT TO GET IN THE WAY OF HER GETTING TO KNOW HER DAD.
BUT DON'T INTERPRET THAT AS MEANING YOU'RE OFF THE HOOK, OKAY?
I.. I KNOW. BELIEVE ME, FRANK, I...
I'M READY.
I'M STARVED! OKAY, RAMBLERS, LET'S RAMBLE!
AND THE SUSHI SAMPLER FOR YOUNG LADY. ENJOY!
OHMYGOD. THIS IS ALL RAW.

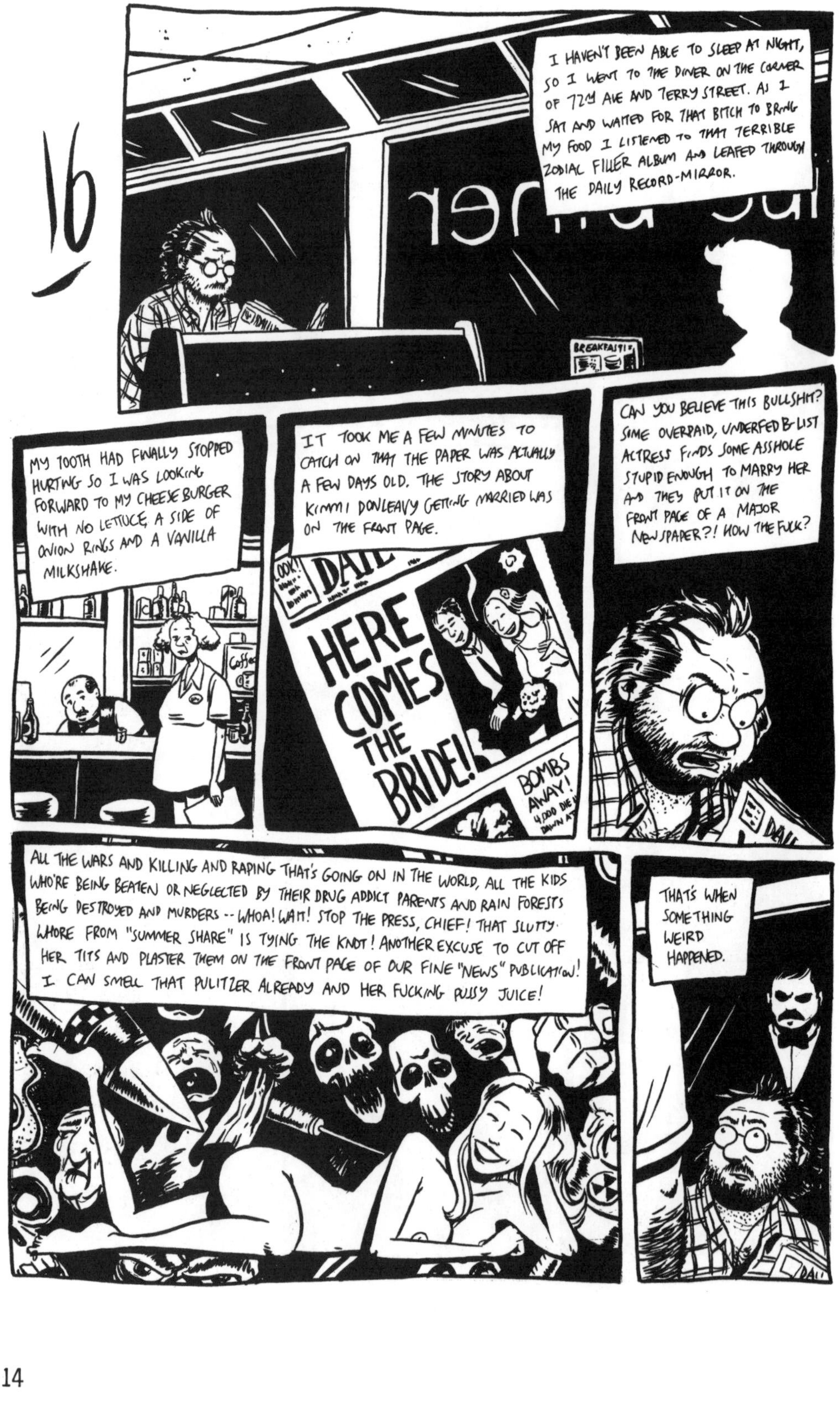
16
I HAVEN'T BEEN ABLE TO SLEEP AT NIGHT, SO I WENT TO THE DINER ON THE CORNER OF 72ND AVE AND TERRY STREET. AS I SAT AND WAITED FOR THAT BITCH TO BRING MY FOOD I LISTENED TO THAT TERRIBLE ZODIAC FILLER ALBUM AND LEAFED THROUGH THE DAILY RECORD-MIRROR.
BREAKFAST
MY TOOTH HAD FINALLY STOPPED HURTING SO I WAS LOOKING FORWARD TO MY CHEESEBURGER WITH NO LETTUCE, A SIDE OF ONION RINGS AND A VANILLA MILKSHAKE.
IT TOOK ME A FEW MINUTES TO CATCH ON THAT THE PAPER WAS ACTUALLY A FEW DAYS OLD. THE STORY ABOUT KIMMI DONLEAVY GETTING MARRIED WAS ON THE FRONT PAGE.
HERE COMES THE BRIDE!
BOMBS AWAY!
CAN YOU BELIEVE THIS BULLSHIT? SOME OVERPAID, UNDERFED B-LIST ACTRESS FINDS SOME ASSHOLE STUPID ENOUGH TO MARRY HER AND THEY PUT IT ON THE FRONT PAGE OF A MAJOR NEWSPAPER?! HOW THE FUCK?
ALL THE WARS AND KILLING AND RAPING THAT'S GOING ON IN THE WORLD, ALL THE KIDS WHO'RE BEING BEATEN OR NEGLECTED BY THEIR DRUG ADDICT PARENTS AND RAIN FORESTS BEING DESTROYED AND MURDERS -- WHOA! WAIT! STOP THE PRESS, CHIEF! THAT SLUTTY WHORE FROM "SUMMER SHARE" IS TYING THE KNOT! ANOTHER EXCUSE TO CUT OFF HER TITS AND PLASTER THEM ON THE FRONT PAGE OF OUR FINE "NEWS" PUBLICATION! I CAN SMELL THAT PULITZER ALREADY AND HER FUCKING PUSSY JUICE!
THAT'S WHEN SOMETHING WEIRD HAPPENED.

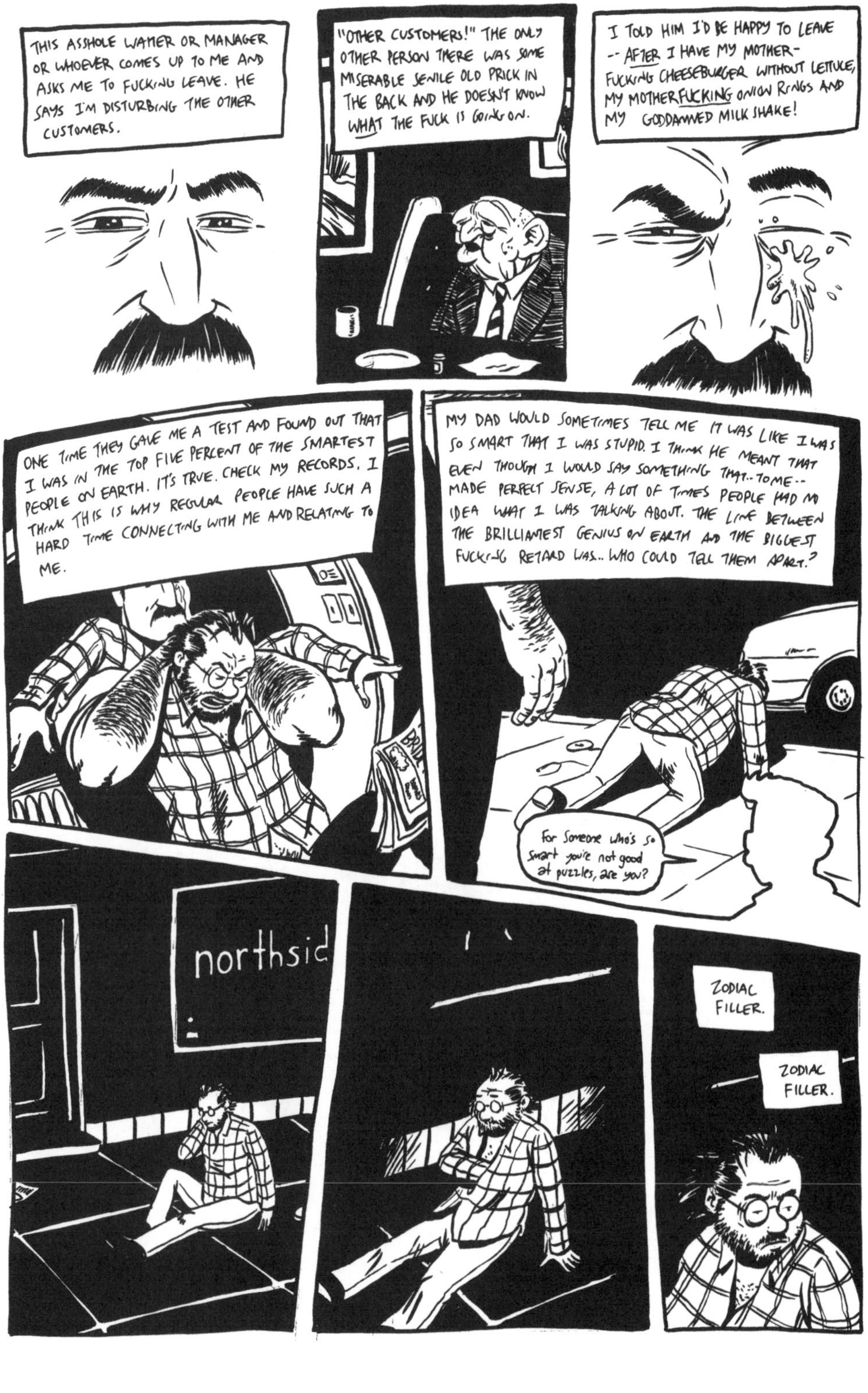
THIS ASSHOLE WAITER OR MANAGER OR WHOEVER COMES UP TO ME AND ASKS ME TO FUCKING LEAVE. HE SAYS I'M DISTURBING THE OTHER CUSTOMERS.
"OTHER CUSTOMERS!" THE ONLY OTHER PERSON THERE WAS SOME MISERABLE SENILE OLD PRICK IN THE BACK AND HE DOESN'T KNOW WHAT THE FUCK IS GOING ON.
I TOLD HIM I'D BE HAPPY TO LEAVE -- AFTER I HAVE MY MOTHER-FUCKING CHEESEBURGER WITHOUT LETTUCE, MY MOTHERFUCKING ONION RINGS AND MY GODDAMNED MILK SHAKE!
ONE TIME THEY GAVE ME A TEST AND FOUND OUT THAT I WAS IN THE TOP FIVE PERCENT OF THE SMARTEST PEOPLE ON EARTH. IT'S TRUE. CHECK MY RECORDS. I THINK THIS IS WHY REGULAR PEOPLE HAVE SUCH A HARD TIME CONNECTING WITH ME AND RELATING TO ME.
MY DAD WOULD SOMETIMES TELL ME IT WAS LIKE I WAS SO SMART THAT I WAS STUPID. I THINK HE MEANT THAT EVEN THOUGH I WOULD SAY SOMETHING THAT.. TO ME-- MADE PERFECT SENSE, A LOT OF TIMES PEOPLE HAD NO IDEA WHAT I WAS TALKING ABOUT. THE LINE BETWEEN THE BRILLIANTEST GENIUS ON EARTH AND THE BIGGEST FUCKING RETARD WAS.. WHO COULD TELL THEM APART?
For someone who's so smart you're not good at puzzles, are you?
northsid
ZODIAC FILLER.
ZODIAC FILLER.

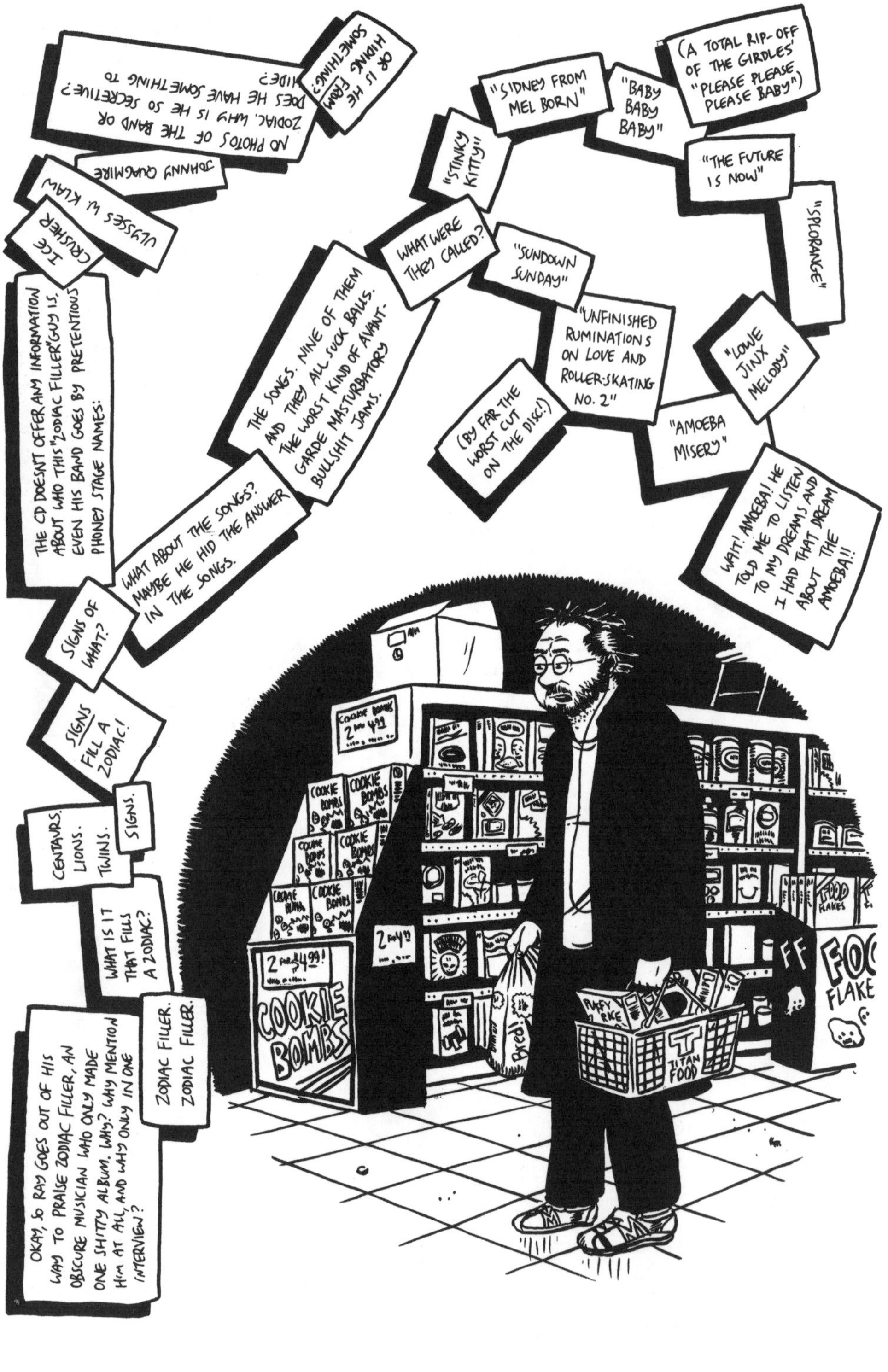
OKAY, SO RAY GOES OUT OF HIS WAY TO PRAISE ZODIAC FILLER, AN OBSCURE MUSICIAN WHO ONLY MADE ONE SHITTY ALBUM. WHY? WHY MENTION HIM AT ALL, AND WHY ONLY IN ONE INTERVIEW?
ZODIAC FILLER. ZODIAC FILLER.
WHAT IS IT THAT FILLS A ZODIAC?
CENTAURS. LIONS. TWINS.
SIGNS.
SIGNS FILL A ZODIAC!
SIGNS OF WHAT?
THE CD DOESN'T OFFER ANY INFORMATION ABOUT WHO THIS "ZODIAC FILLER" GUY IS. EVEN HIS BAND GOES BY PRETENTIOUS PHONEY STAGE NAMES:
ICE CRUSHER
ULYSSES W. KLAW
JOHNNY QUAGMIRE
NO PHOTOS OF THE BAND OR ZODIAC. WHY IS HE SO SECRETIVE? DOES HE HAVE SOMETHING TO HIDE?
OR IS HE HIDING FROM SOMETHING?
WHAT ABOUT THE SONGS? MAYBE HE HID THE ANSWER IN THE SONGS.
THE SONGS. NINE OF THEM AND THEY ALL SUCK BALLS. THE WORST KIND OF AVANT-GARDE MASTURBATORY BULLSHIT JAMS.
WHAT WERE THEY CALLED?
"STINKY KITTY"
"SIDNEY FROM MEL BORN"
"BABY BABY BABY"
(A TOTAL RIP-OFF OF THE GIRDLES' "PLEASE PLEASE PLEASE BABY")
"THE FUTURE IS NOW"
"SPLORANGE"
"LOWE JINX MELODY"
"SUNDOWN SUNDAY"
"UNFINISHED RUMINATIONS ON LOVE AND ROLLER-SKATING NO. 2"
(BY FAR THE WORST CUT ON THE DISC!)
"AMOEBA MISERY"
WAIT! AMOEBA! HE TOLD ME TO LISTEN TO MY DREAMS AND I HAD THAT DREAM ABOUT THE AMOEBA!!
COOKIE BOMBS
2 FOR $4.99!
FOOD FLAKES
TITAN FOOD
Bread

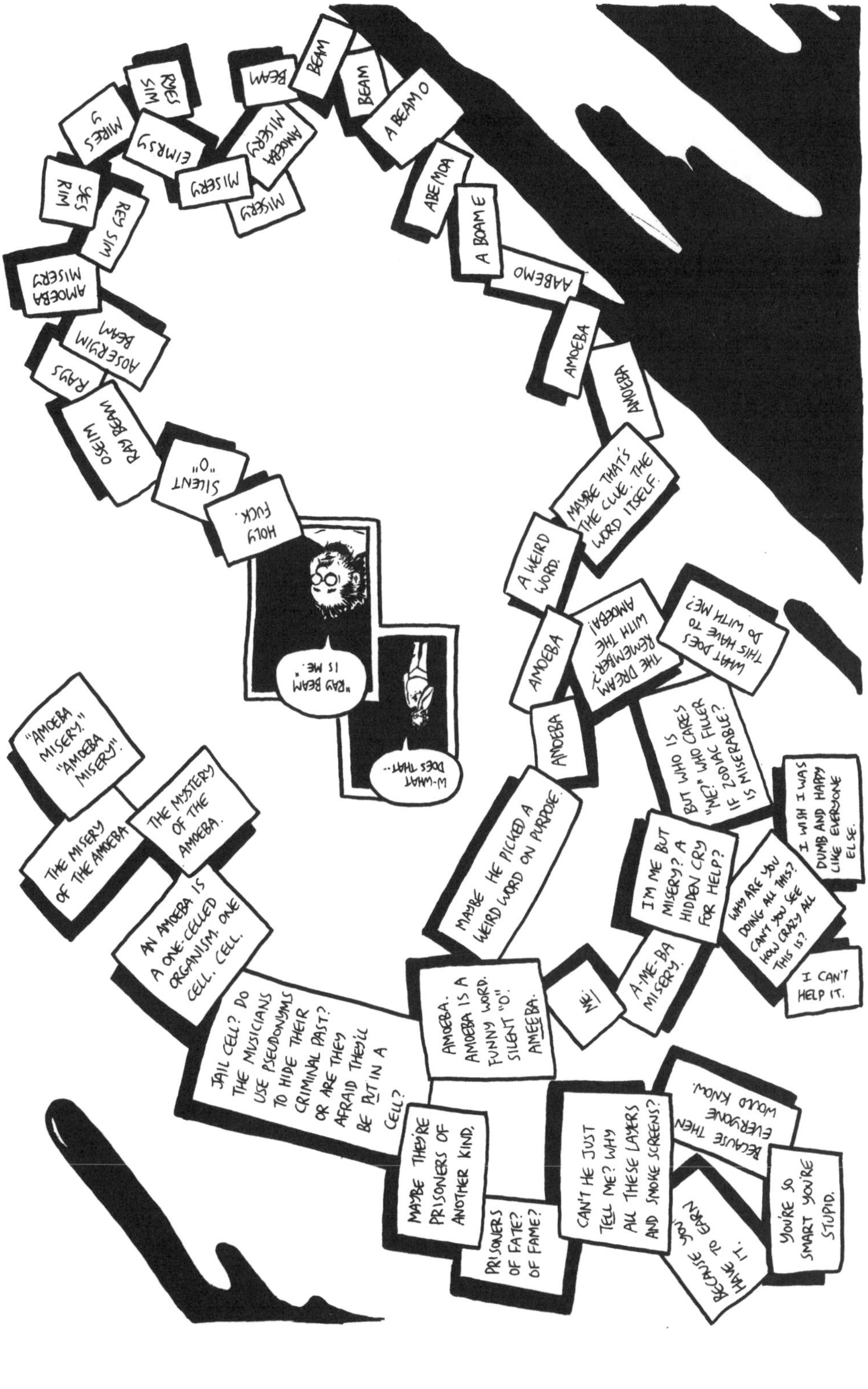
"AMOEBA MISERY." "AMOEBA MISERY."
THE MISERY OF THE AMOEBA
THE MYSTERY OF THE AMOEBA.
AN AMOEBA IS A ONE-CELLED ORGANISM. ONE CELL. CELL.
JAIL CELL? DO THE MUSICIANS USE PSEUDONYMS TO HIDE THEIR CRIMINAL PAST? OR ARE THEY AFRAID THEY'LL BE PUT IN A CELL?
MAYBE THEY'RE PRISONERS OF ANOTHER KIND.
PRISONERS OF FATE? OF FAME?
CAN'T HE JUST TELL ME? WHY ALL THESE LAYERS AND SMOKE SCREENS?
BECAUSE YOU HAVE TO EARN IT.
BECAUSE THEN EVERYONE WOULD KNOW.
YOU'RE SO SMART YOU'RE STUPID.
AMOEBA. AMOEBA IS A FUNNY WORD. SILENT "O". AMEEBA.
ME!
A-ME-BA MISERY.
I'M ME BUT MISERY? A HIDDEN CRY FOR HELP?
WHY ARE YOU DOING ALL THIS? CAN'T YOU SEE HOW CRAZY ALL THIS IS?
I CAN'T HELP IT.
I WISH I WAS DUMB AND HAPPY LIKE EVERYONE ELSE.
BUT WHO IS "ME?" WHO CARES IF ZODIAC FILLER IS MISERABLE?
WHAT DOES THIS HAVE TO DO WITH ME?
THE DREAM? REMEMBER WITH THE AMOEBA!
MAYBE HE PICKED A WEIRD WORD ON PURPOSE.
AMOEBA
AMOEBA
A WEIRD WORD.
MAYBE THAT'S THE CLUE. THE WORD ITSELF.
AMOEBA
AMOEBA
AABEMO
A BOAM E
ABE MOA
A BEAM O
BEAM
BEAM
BEAM
RYES SIM
MIRES O
EIMRSY
AMOEBA MISERY
MISERY
MISERY
YES RIM
REY SIM
AMOEBA MISERY
AOSERYM BEAM
RAYS
RAY BEAM
OSEIM
SILENT "O"
HOLY FUCK.
"RAY BEAM" IS ME.
W-WHAT DOES THAT--

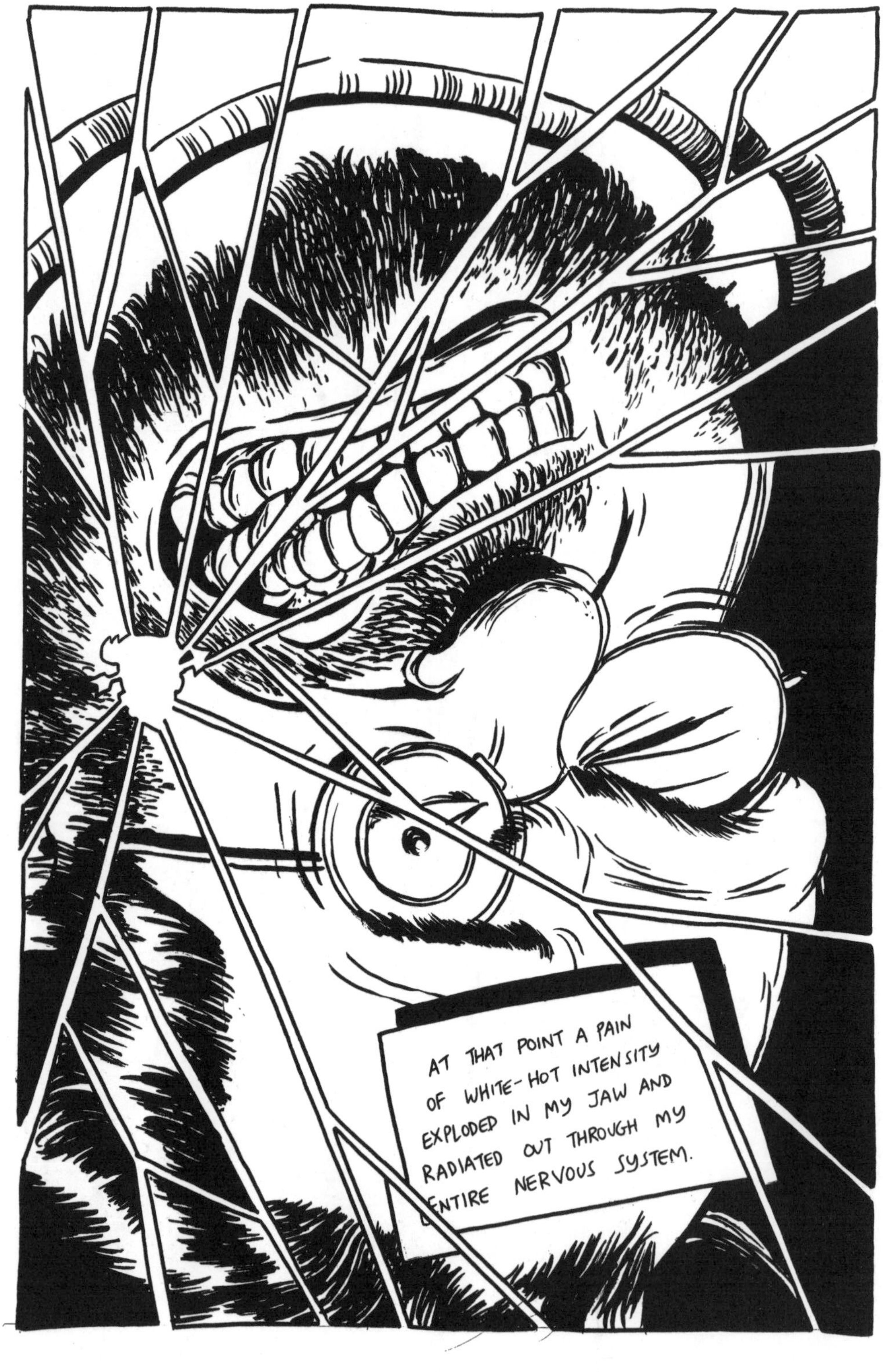
AT THAT POINT A PAIN OF WHITE-HOT INTENSITY EXPLODED IN MY JAW AND RADIATED OUT THROUGH MY ENTIRE NERVOUS SYSTEM.

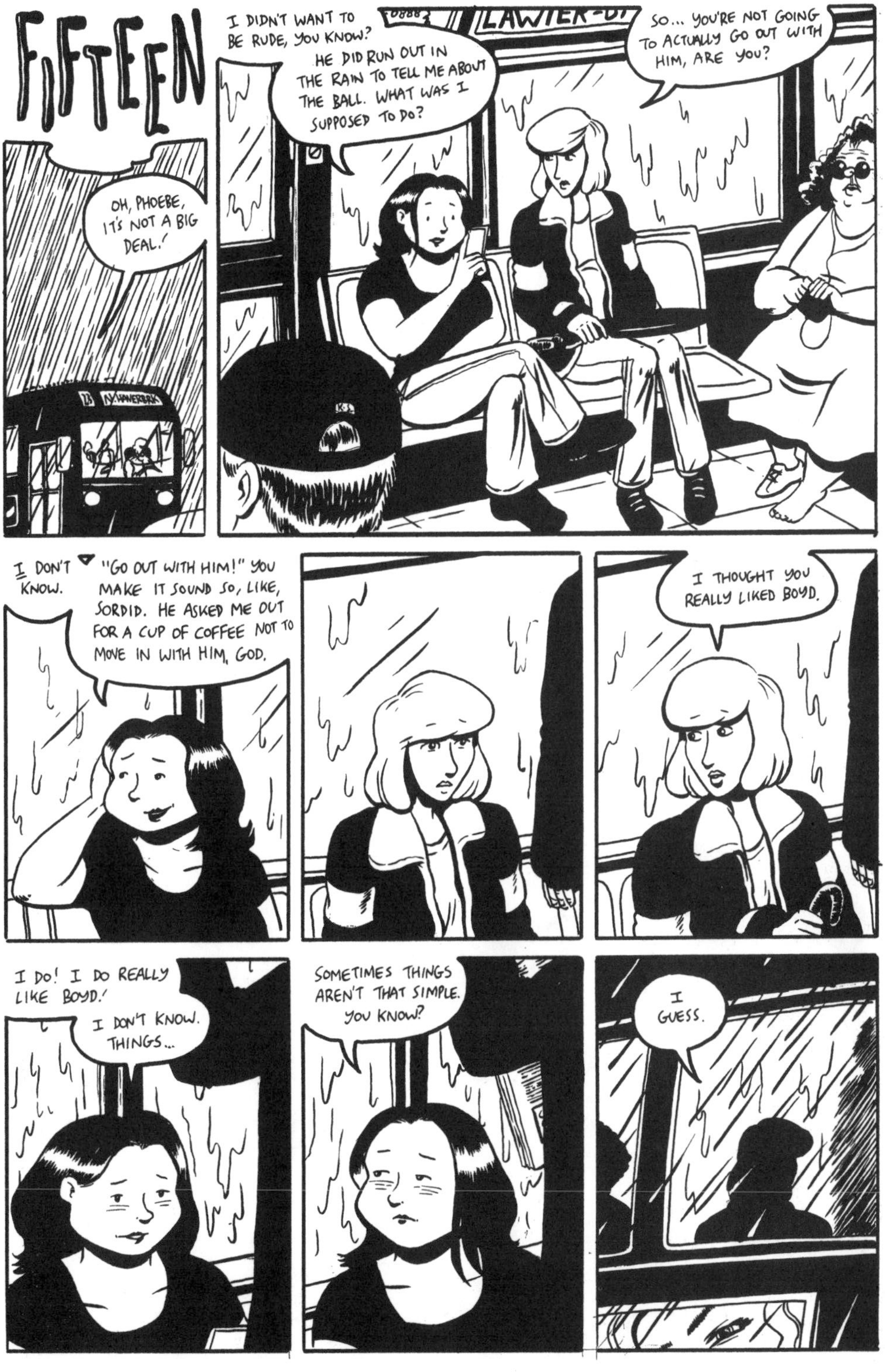
FIFTEEN
OH, PHOEBE, IT'S NOT A BIG DEAL!
I DIDN'T WANT TO BE RUDE, YOU KNOW?
HE DID RUN OUT IN THE RAIN TO TELL ME ABOUT THE BALL. WHAT WAS I SUPPOSED TO DO?
SO... YOU'RE NOT GOING TO ACTUALLY GO OUT WITH HIM, ARE YOU?
I DON'T KNOW.
"GO OUT WITH HIM!" YOU MAKE IT SOUND SO, LIKE, SORDID. HE ASKED ME OUT FOR A CUP OF COFFEE NOT TO MOVE IN WITH HIM, GOD.
I THOUGHT YOU REALLY LIKED BOYD.
I DO! I DO REALLY LIKE BOYD!
I DON'T KNOW. THINGS...
SOMETIMES THINGS AREN'T THAT SIMPLE. YOU KNOW?
I GUESS.

SURPRISE!!

OH, MAN. I WAS WONDERING WHY YOU HAD ME GO TO THAT LIQUOR STORE ALL THE WAY OUT IN VANDERBILT.

HeeHee! YOUR FRIENDS FROM WORK SET IT ALL UP! I JUST HELPED!

HAPPY TWENTY-FIFTH!

ONE TIME I WENT TO THIS PARTY, RIGHT?

I TOLD THOSE GUYS "DON'T YOU HAVE ANY PRIDE?"

I CAN'T BELIEVE I PASSED OUT GETTING STONED—ASS—

WHAT'S THAT SONG CALLED?

HAHA!

NO WAY!

LAST WEEK WE SAW DIRK CAVENDISH. HE FUCKIN' ROCKED!

"WHAT DO YOUR ELF SEE?"

DUDE, THAT'S THE MOST AWESOMEST LAMP EVER!!

I ALMOST BOUGHT HIM SOCKS.

WHAT DO YOU THINK?

DID YOU EVER ASK HER OUT? THE ONE FROM WORK?

GOD, I'M SO FUCKIN' DRUNK.

THE BEST ONE IS WHERE NICK AUDITIONS FOR THE BAND!

HAH!

I THINK HE'S KINDA HOT, Y'KNOW?

I SAID TO HIM "WHEN THE FUCK DID EVER ASK YOU FOR PERMISSION TO COME HERE?!"

LET'S GET GOIN'

GETTING LATE...

'NIGHT!

'NIGHT! DRIVE SAFE!

NIGH

HAPPY BIRTHDAY, BRO!

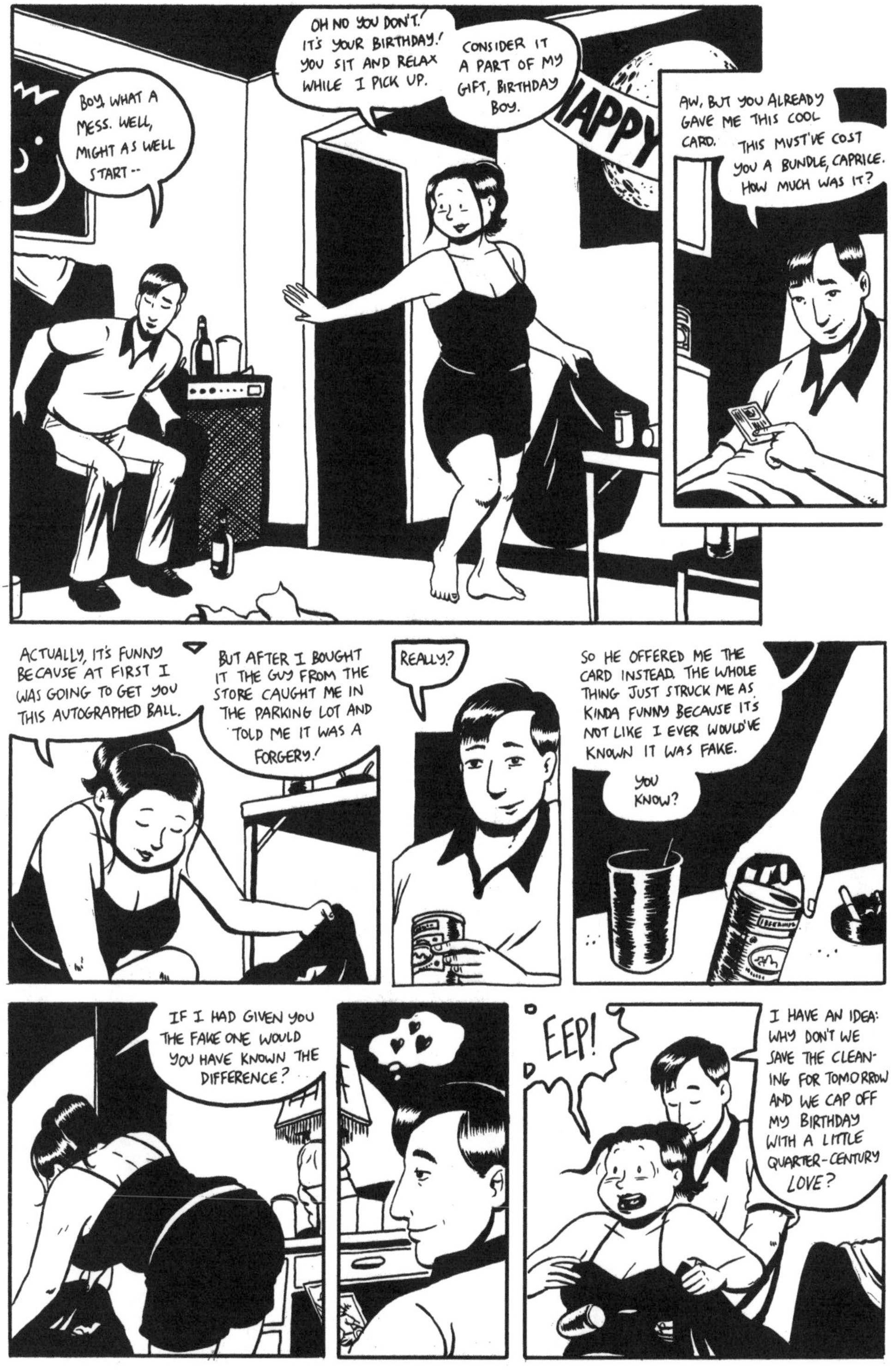
BOY, WHAT A MESS. WELL, MIGHT AS WELL START --
OH NO YOU DON'T! IT'S YOUR BIRTHDAY! YOU SIT AND RELAX WHILE I PICK UP.
CONSIDER IT A PART OF MY GIFT, BIRTHDAY BOY.
HAPPY
AW, BUT YOU ALREADY GAVE ME THIS COOL CARD.
THIS MUST'VE COST YOU A BUNDLE, CAPRICE. HOW MUCH WAS IT?
ACTUALLY, IT'S FUNNY BECAUSE AT FIRST I WAS GOING TO GET YOU THIS AUTOGRAPHED BALL.
BUT AFTER I BOUGHT IT THE GUY FROM THE STORE CAUGHT ME IN THE PARKING LOT AND TOLD ME IT WAS A FORGERY!
REALLY?
SO HE OFFERED ME THE CARD INSTEAD. THE WHOLE THING JUST STRUCK ME AS KINDA FUNNY BECAUSE ITS NOT LIKE I EVER WOULD'VE KNOWN IT WAS FAKE.
YOU KNOW?
IF I HAD GIVEN YOU THE FAKE ONE WOULD YOU HAVE KNOWN THE DIFFERENCE?
EEP!
I HAVE AN IDEA: WHY DON'T WE SAVE THE CLEANING FOR TOMORROW AND WE CAP OFF MY BIRTHDAY WITH A LITTLE QUARTER-CENTURY LOVE?

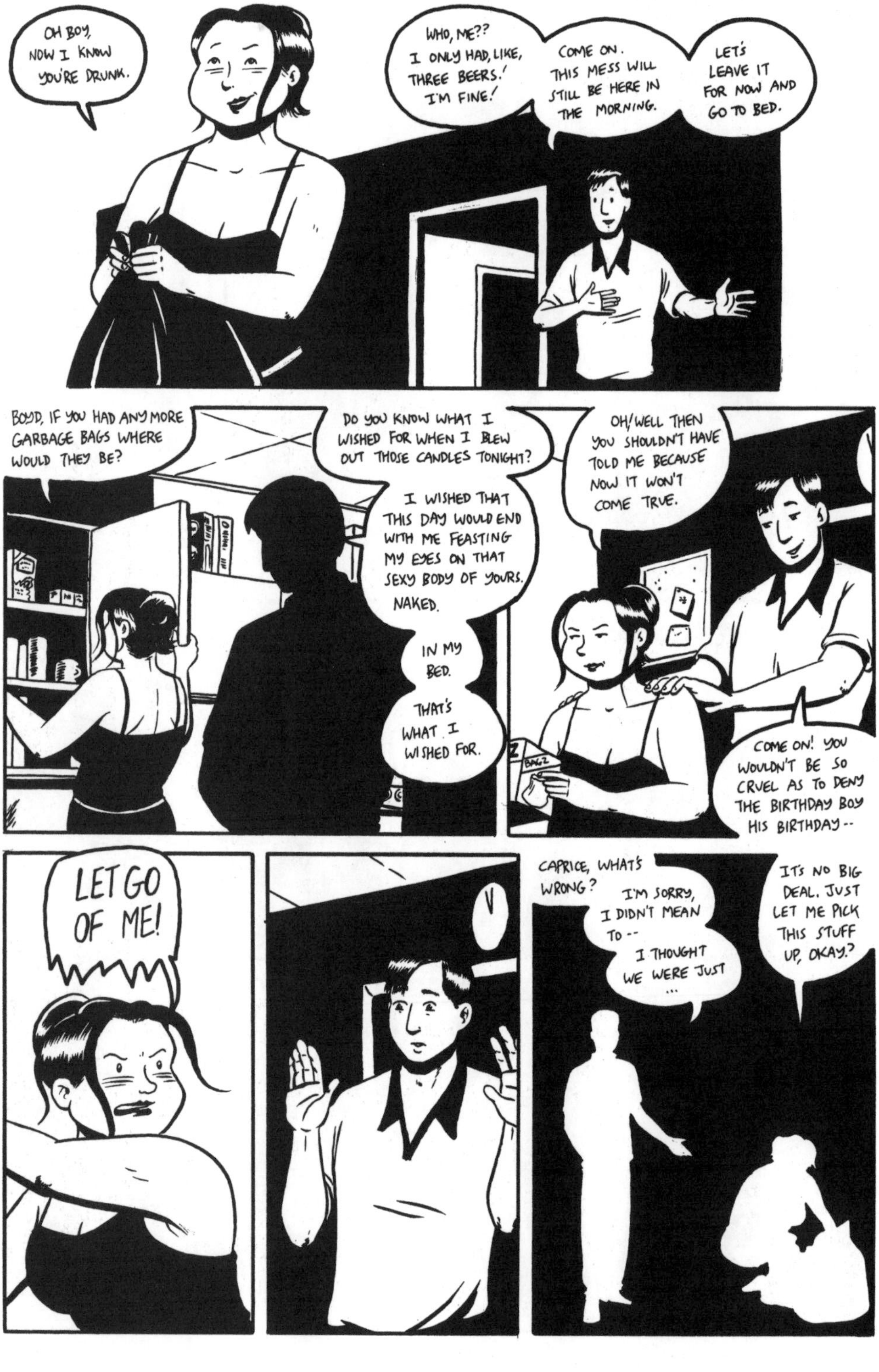

OH BOY, NOW I KNOW YOU'RE DRUNK.
WHO, ME?? I ONLY HAD, LIKE, THREE BEERS.! I'M FINE!
COME ON. THIS MESS WILL STILL BE HERE IN THE MORNING.
LET'S LEAVE IT FOR NOW AND GO TO BED.
BOYD, IF YOU HAD ANY MORE GARBAGE BAGS WHERE WOULD THEY BE?
DO YOU KNOW WHAT I WISHED FOR WHEN I BLEW OUT THOSE CANDLES TONIGHT?
I WISHED THAT THIS DAY WOULD END WITH ME FEASTING MY EYES ON THAT SEXY BODY OF YOURS. NAKED.
IN MY BED.
THAT'S WHAT I WISHED FOR.
OH! WELL THEN YOU SHOULDN'T HAVE TOLD ME BECAUSE NOW IT WON'T COME TRUE.
COME ON! YOU WOULDN'T BE SO CRUEL AS TO DENY THE BIRTHDAY BOY HIS BIRTHDAY--
LET GO OF ME!
CAPRICE, WHAT'S WRONG?
I'M SORRY, I DIDN'T MEAN TO --
I THOUGHT WE WERE JUST ...
IT'S NO BIG DEAL. JUST LET ME PICK THIS STUFF UP, OKAY?

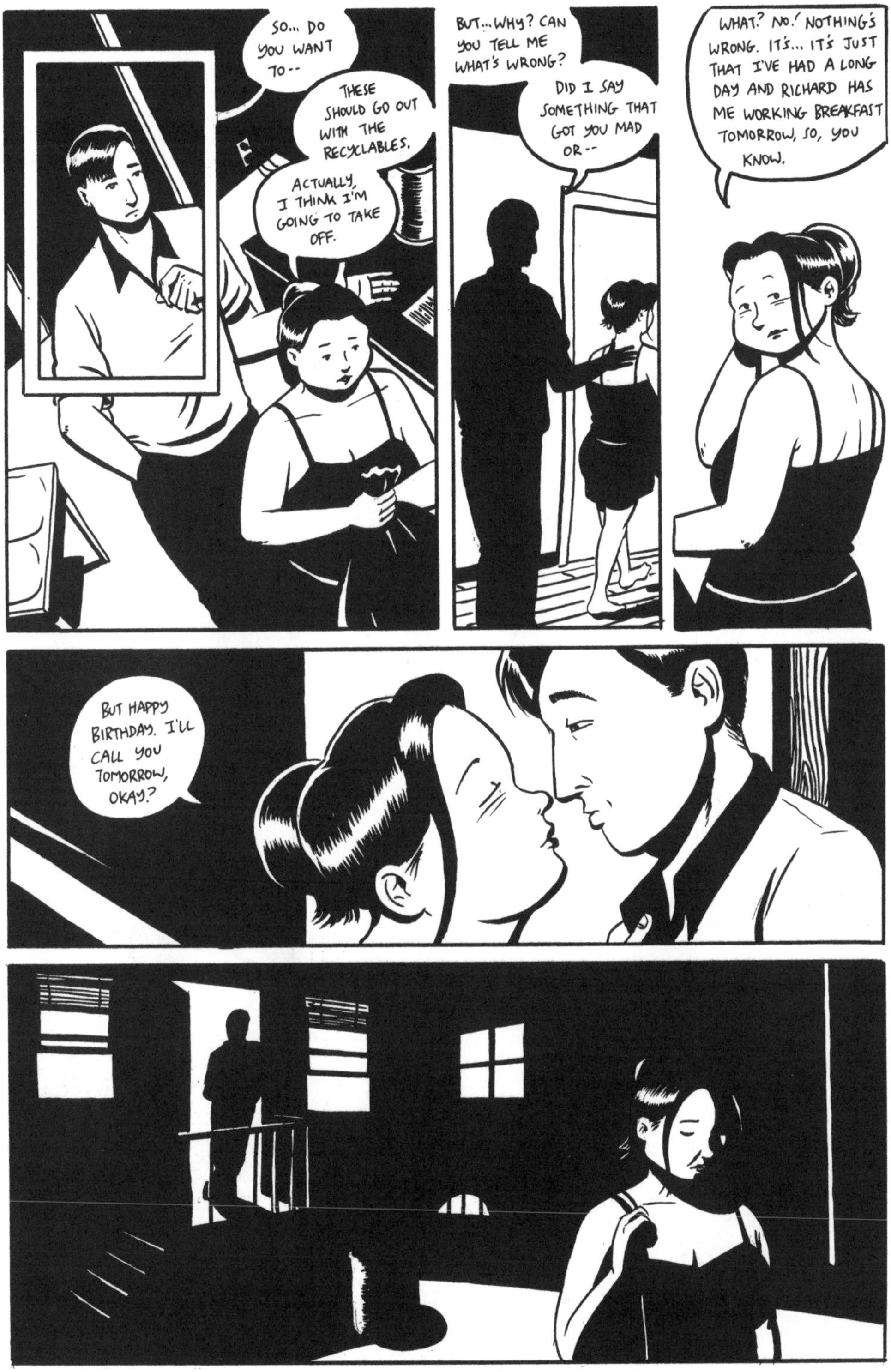
SO... DO YOU WANT TO--
THESE SHOULD GO OUT WITH THE RECYCLABLES.
ACTUALLY, I THINK I'M GOING TO TAKE OFF.
BUT... WHY? CAN YOU TELL ME WHAT'S WRONG?
DID I SAY SOMETHING THAT GOT YOU MAD OR--
WHAT? NO! NOTHING'S WRONG. IT'S... IT'S JUST THAT I'VE HAD A LONG DAY AND RICHARD HAS ME WORKING BREAKFAST TOMORROW, SO, YOU KNOW.
BUT HAPPY BIRTHDAY. I'LL CALL YOU TOMORROW, OKAY?

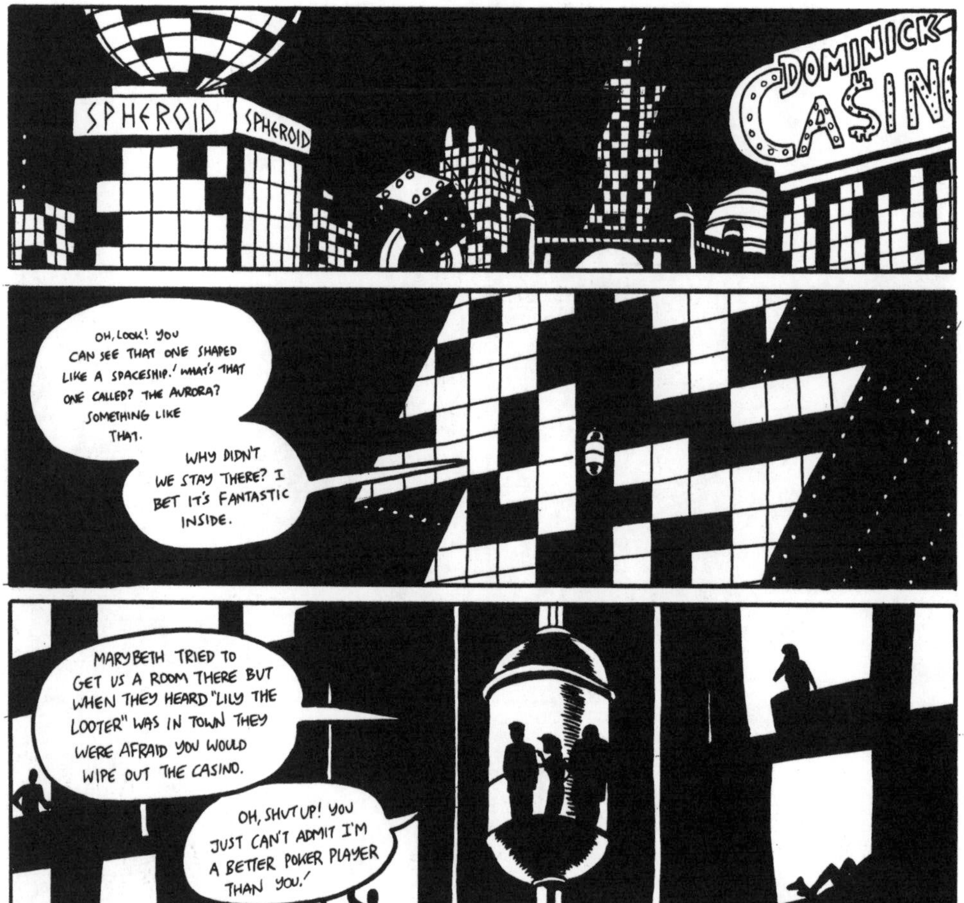
SPHEROID
SPHEROID
DOMINICK CA$INO
OH, LOOK! YOU CAN SEE THAT ONE SHAPED LIKE A SPACESHIP! WHAT'S THAT ONE CALLED? THE AURORA? SOMETHING LIKE THAT.
WHY DIDN'T WE STAY THERE? I BET IT'S FANTASTIC INSIDE.
MARYBETH TRIED TO GET US A ROOM THERE BUT WHEN THEY HEARD "LILY THE LOOTER" WAS IN TOWN THEY WERE AFRAID YOU WOULD WIPE OUT THE CASINO.
OH, SHUT UP! YOU JUST CAN'T ADMIT I'M A BETTER POKER PLAYER THAN YOU!

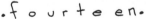

.fourteen.

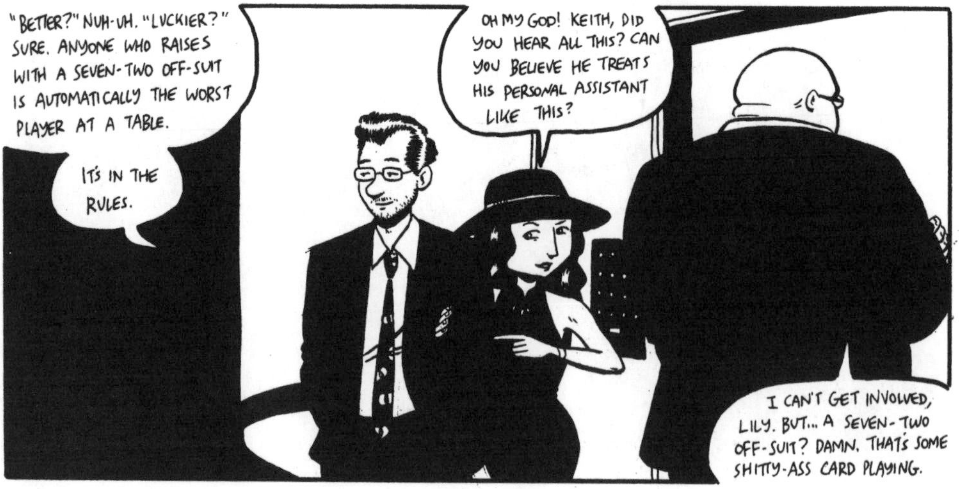
"BETTER?" NUH-UH. "LUCKIER?" SURE. ANYONE WHO RAISES WITH A SEVEN-TWO OFF-SUIT IS AUTOMATICALLY THE WORST PLAYER AT A TABLE.
IT'S IN THE RULES.
OH MY GOD! KEITH, DID YOU HEAR ALL THIS? CAN YOU BELIEVE HE TREATS HIS PERSONAL ASSISTANT LIKE THIS?
I CAN'T GET INVOLVED, LILY. BUT... A SEVEN-TWO OFF-SUIT? DAMN. THAT'S SOME SHITTY-ASS CARD PLAYING.

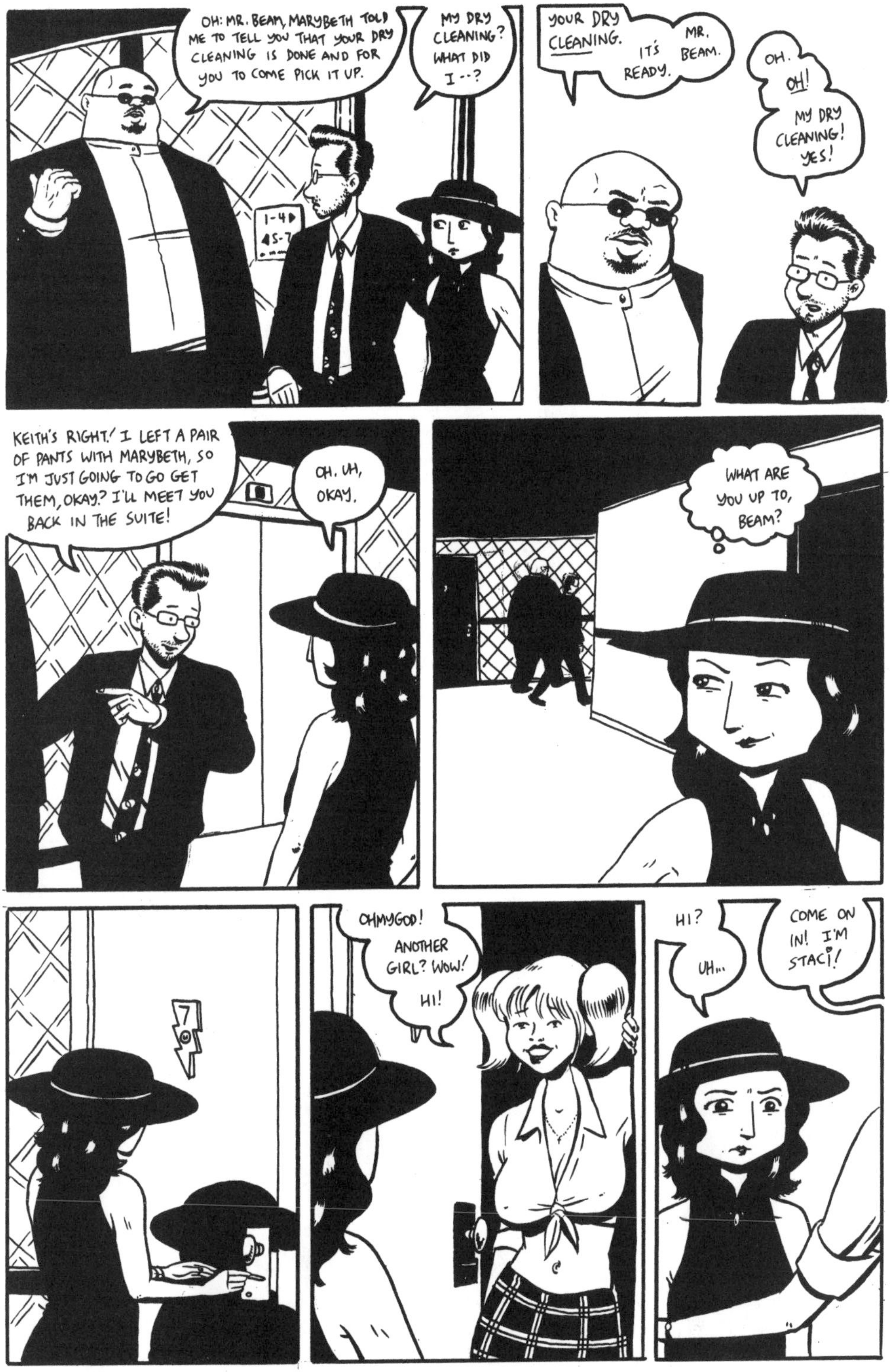
OH: MR. BEAM, MARYBETH TOLD ME TO TELL YOU THAT YOUR DRY CLEANING IS DONE AND FOR YOU TO COME PICK IT UP.
MY DRY CLEANING? WHAT DID I --?
YOUR DRY CLEANING.
IT'S READY.
MR. BEAM.
OH.
OH!
MY DRY CLEANING! YES!
KEITH'S RIGHT! I LEFT A PAIR OF PANTS WITH MARYBETH, SO I'M JUST GOING TO GO GET THEM, OKAY? I'LL MEET YOU BACK IN THE SUITE!
OH. UH, OKAY.
WHAT ARE YOU UP TO, BEAM?
7
OHMYGOD!
ANOTHER GIRL? WOW!
HI!
HI?
UH...
COME ON IN! I'M STACI!

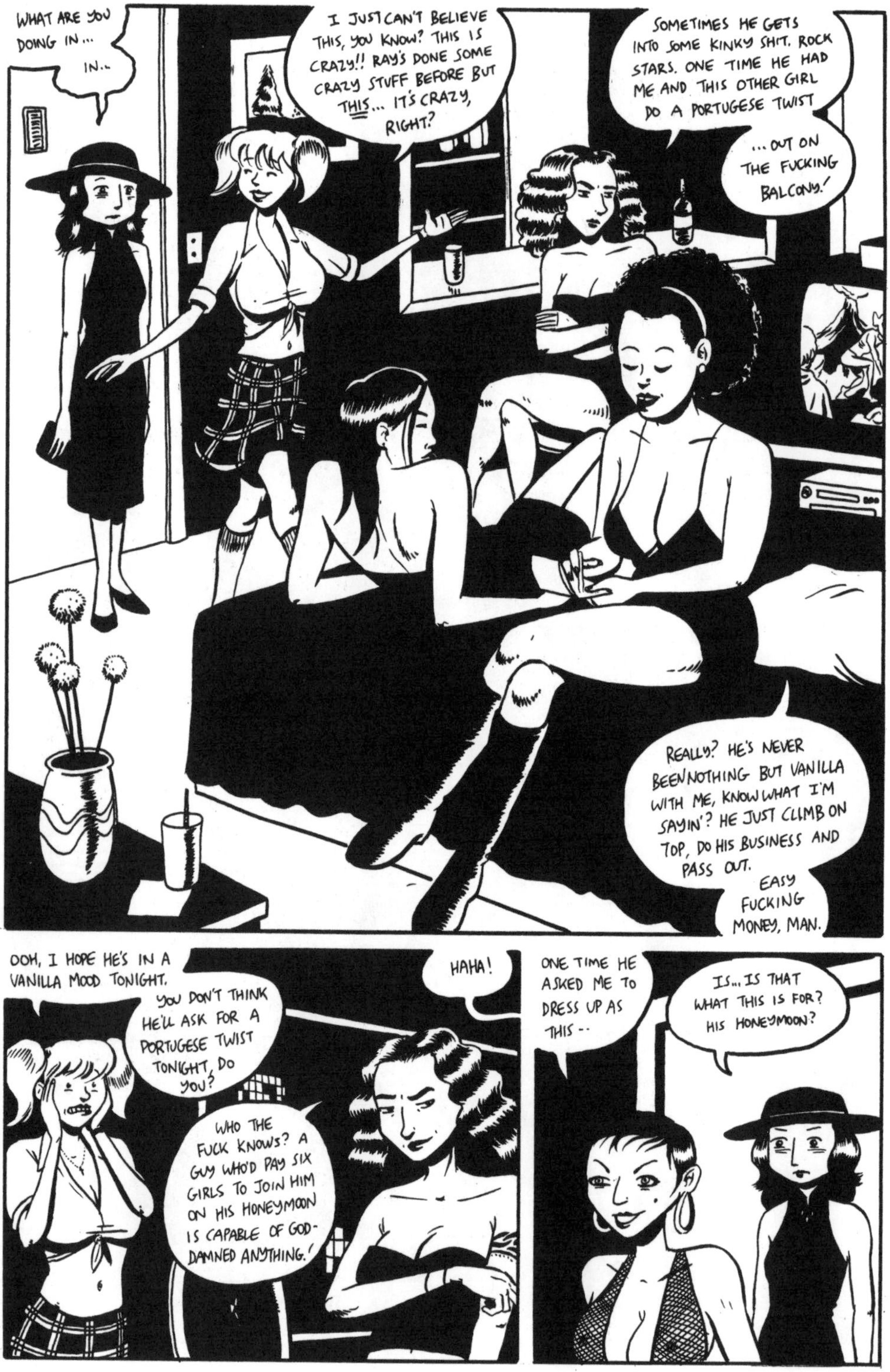
WHAT ARE YOU DOING IN... IN..
I JUST CAN'T BELIEVE THIS, YOU KNOW? THIS IS CRAZY!! RAY'S DONE SOME CRAZY STUFF BEFORE BUT THIS... IT'S CRAZY, RIGHT?
SOMETIMES HE GETS INTO SOME KINKY SHIT. ROCK STARS. ONE TIME HE HAD ME AND THIS OTHER GIRL DO A PORTUGESE TWIST
...OUT ON THE FUCKING BALCONY!
REALLY? HE'S NEVER BEEN NOTHING BUT VANILLA WITH ME, KNOW WHAT I'M SAYIN'? HE JUST CLIMB ON TOP, DO HIS BUSINESS AND PASS OUT.
EASY FUCKING MONEY, MAN.
OOH, I HOPE HE'S IN A VANILLA MOOD TONIGHT.
HAHA!
YOU DON'T THINK HE'LL ASK FOR A PORTUGESE TWIST TONIGHT, DO YOU?
WHO THE FUCK KNOWS? A GUY WHO'D PAY SIX GIRLS TO JOIN HIM ON HIS HONEYMOON IS CAPABLE OF GOD-DAMNED ANYTHING!
ONE TIME HE ASKED ME TO DRESS UP AS THIS --
IS... IS THAT WHAT THIS IS FOR? HIS HONEYMOON?

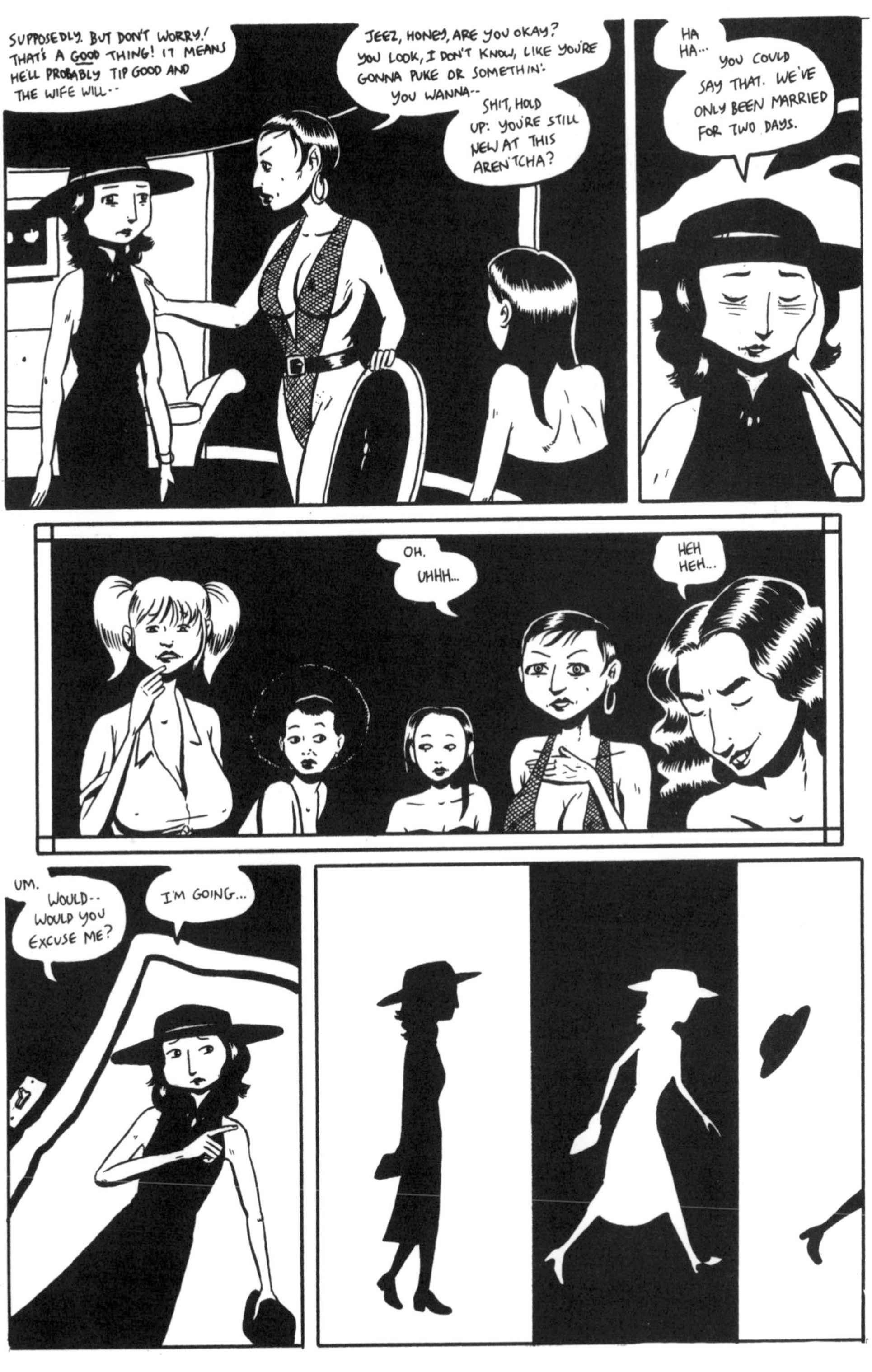
SUPPOSEDLY. BUT DON'T WORRY! THAT'S A GOOD THING! IT MEANS HE'LL PROBABLY TIP GOOD AND THE WIFE WILL--
JEEZ, HONEY, ARE YOU OKAY? YOU LOOK, I DON'T KNOW, LIKE YOU'RE GONNA PUKE OR SOMETHIN'. YOU WANNA--
SHIT, HOLD UP: YOU'RE STILL NEW AT THIS AREN'TCHA?
HA HA...
YOU COULD SAY THAT. WE'VE ONLY BEEN MARRIED FOR TWO DAYS.
OH. UHHH...
HEH HEH...
UM. WOULD-- WOULD YOU EXCUSE ME?
I'M GOING...

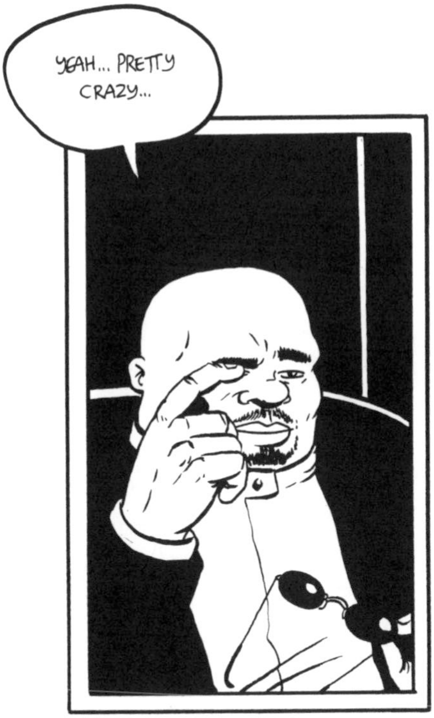
YEAH... PRETTY CRAZY...

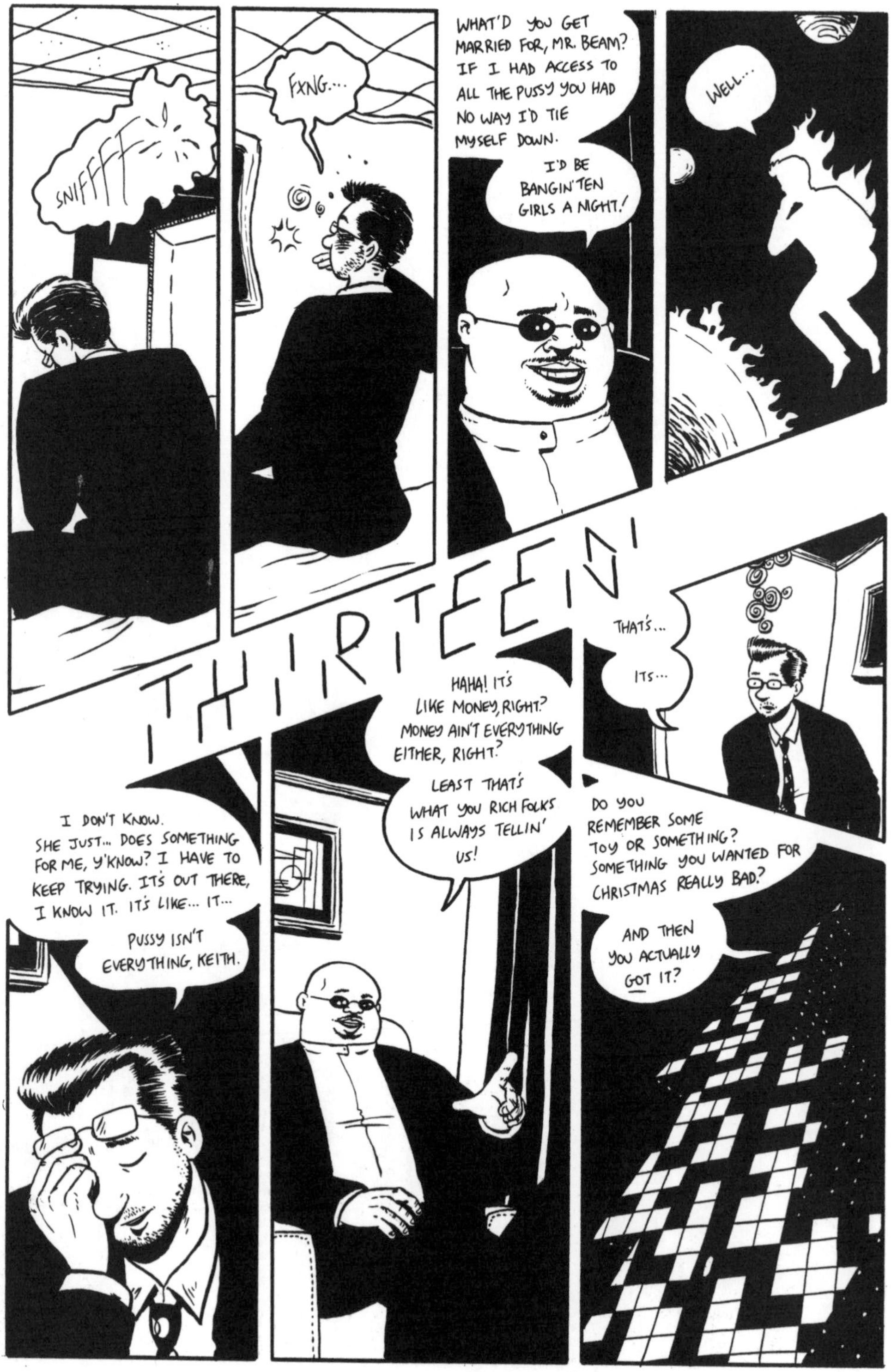
SNIFFFF
FXNG...
WHAT'D YOU GET MARRIED FOR, MR. BEAM? IF I HAD ACCESS TO ALL THE PUSSY YOU HAD NO WAY I'D TIE MYSELF DOWN.
I'D BE BANGIN' TEN GIRLS A NIGHT!
WELL...
THIRTEEN
THAT'S...
ITS...
I DON'T KNOW. SHE JUST... DOES SOMETHING FOR ME, Y'KNOW? I HAVE TO KEEP TRYING. IT'S OUT THERE, I KNOW IT. IT'S LIKE... IT...
PUSSY ISN'T EVERYTHING, KEITH.
HAHA! IT'S LIKE MONEY, RIGHT? MONEY AIN'T EVERYTHING EITHER, RIGHT?
LEAST THAT'S WHAT YOU RICH FOLKS IS ALWAYS TELLIN' US!
DO YOU REMEMBER SOME TOY OR SOMETHING? SOMETHING YOU WANTED FOR CHRISTMAS REALLY BAD?
AND THEN YOU ACTUALLY GOT IT?

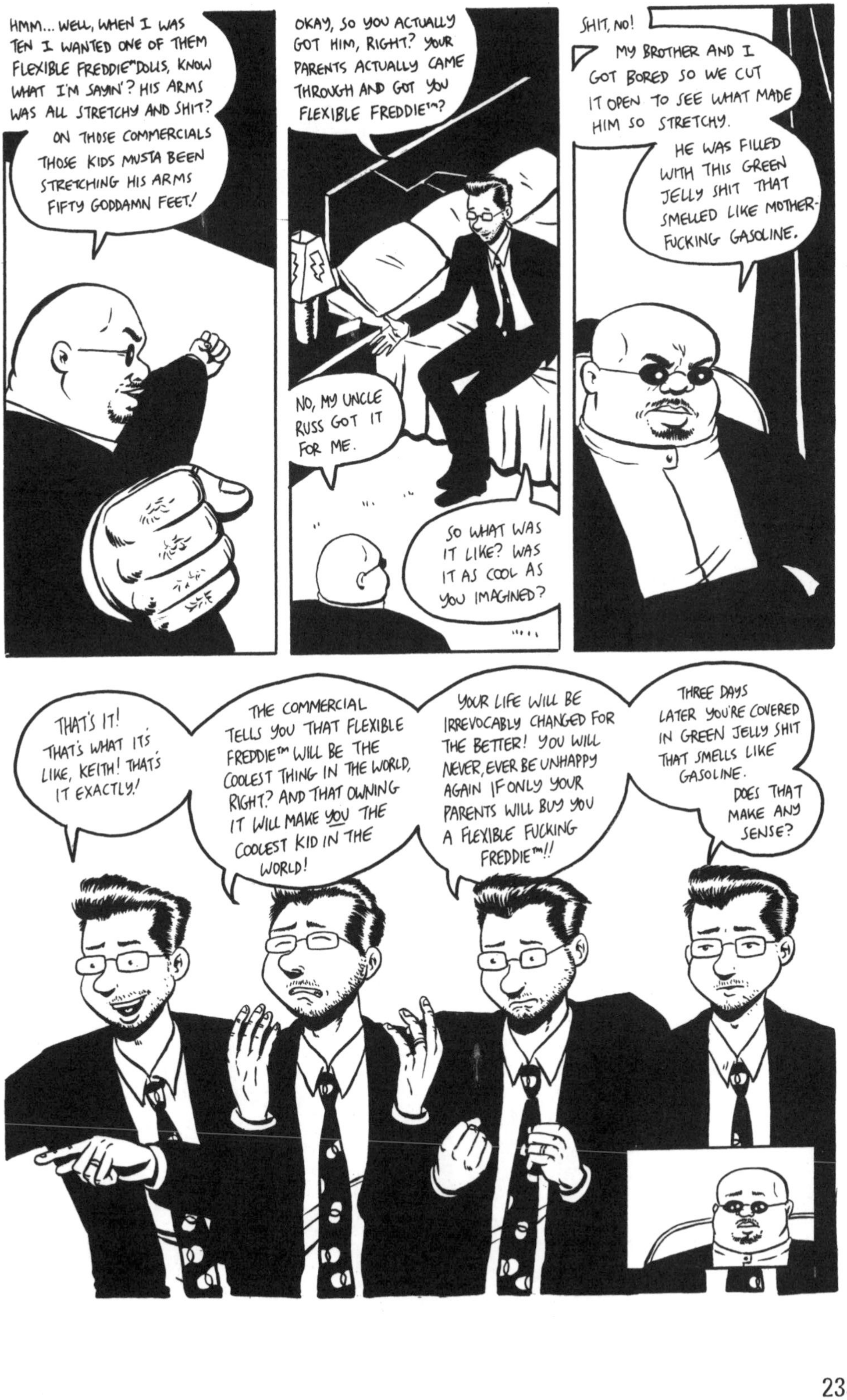
HMM... WELL, WHEN I WAS TEN I WANTED ONE OF THEM FLEXIBLE FREDDIE™ DOLLS, KNOW WHAT I'M SAYIN'? HIS ARMS WAS ALL STRETCHY AND SHIT?
ON THOSE COMMERCIALS THOSE KIDS MUSTA BEEN STRETCHING HIS ARMS FIFTY GODDAMN FEET!
OKAY, SO YOU ACTUALLY GOT HIM, RIGHT? YOUR PARENTS ACTUALLY CAME THROUGH AND GOT YOU FLEXIBLE FREDDIE™?
NO, MY UNCLE RUSS GOT IT FOR ME.
SO WHAT WAS IT LIKE? WAS IT AS COOL AS YOU IMAGINED?
SHIT, NO!
MY BROTHER AND I GOT BORED SO WE CUT IT OPEN TO SEE WHAT MADE HIM SO STRETCHY.
HE WAS FILLED WITH THIS GREEN JELLY SHIT THAT SMELLED LIKE MOTHER-FUCKING GASOLINE.
THAT'S IT! THAT'S WHAT IT'S LIKE, KEITH! THAT'S IT EXACTLY!
THE COMMERCIAL TELLS YOU THAT FLEXIBLE FREDDIE™ WILL BE THE COOLEST THING IN THE WORLD, RIGHT? AND THAT OWNING IT WILL MAKE YOU THE COOLEST KID IN THE WORLD!
YOUR LIFE WILL BE IRREVOCABLY CHANGED FOR THE BETTER! YOU WILL NEVER, EVER BE UNHAPPY AGAIN IF ONLY YOUR PARENTS WILL BUY YOU A FLEXIBLE FUCKING FREDDIE™!!
THREE DAYS LATER YOU'RE COVERED IN GREEN JELLY SHIT THAT SMELLS LIKE GASOLINE.
DOES THAT MAKE ANY SENSE?

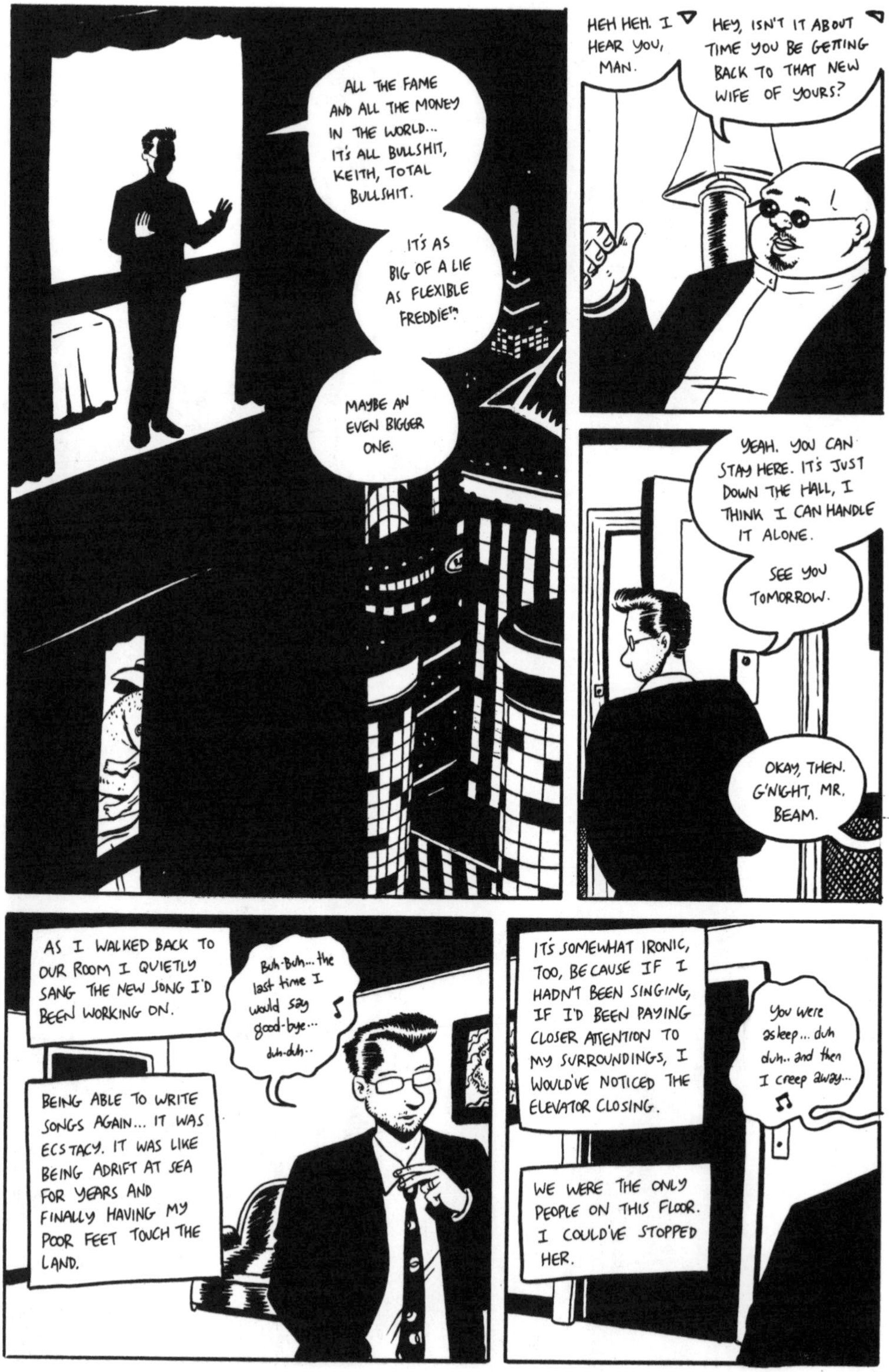

ALL THE FAME AND ALL THE MONEY IN THE WORLD... IT'S ALL BULLSHIT, KEITH, TOTAL BULLSHIT.
IT'S AS BIG OF A LIE AS FLEXIBLE FREDDIE™
MAYBE AN EVEN BIGGER ONE.
HEH HEH. I HEAR YOU, MAN.
HEY, ISN'T IT ABOUT TIME YOU BE GETTING BACK TO THAT NEW WIFE OF YOURS?
YEAH. YOU CAN STAY HERE. IT'S JUST DOWN THE HALL, I THINK I CAN HANDLE IT ALONE.
SEE YOU TOMORROW.
OKAY, THEN. G'NIGHT, MR. BEAM.
AS I WALKED BACK TO OUR ROOM I QUIETLY SANG THE NEW SONG I'D BEEN WORKING ON.
Buh-Buh... the last time I would say good-bye... duh-duh..
BEING ABLE TO WRITE SONGS AGAIN... IT WAS ECSTACY. IT WAS LIKE BEING ADRIFT AT SEA FOR YEARS AND FINALLY HAVING MY POOR FEET TOUCH THE LAND.
IT'S SOMEWHAT IRONIC, TOO, BECAUSE IF I HADN'T BEEN SINGING, IF I'D BEEN PAYING CLOSER ATTENTION TO MY SURROUNDINGS, I WOULD'VE NOTICED THE ELEVATOR CLOSING.
You were asleep... duh duh.. and then I creep away...
WE WERE THE ONLY PEOPLE ON THIS FLOOR. I COULD'VE STOPPED HER.

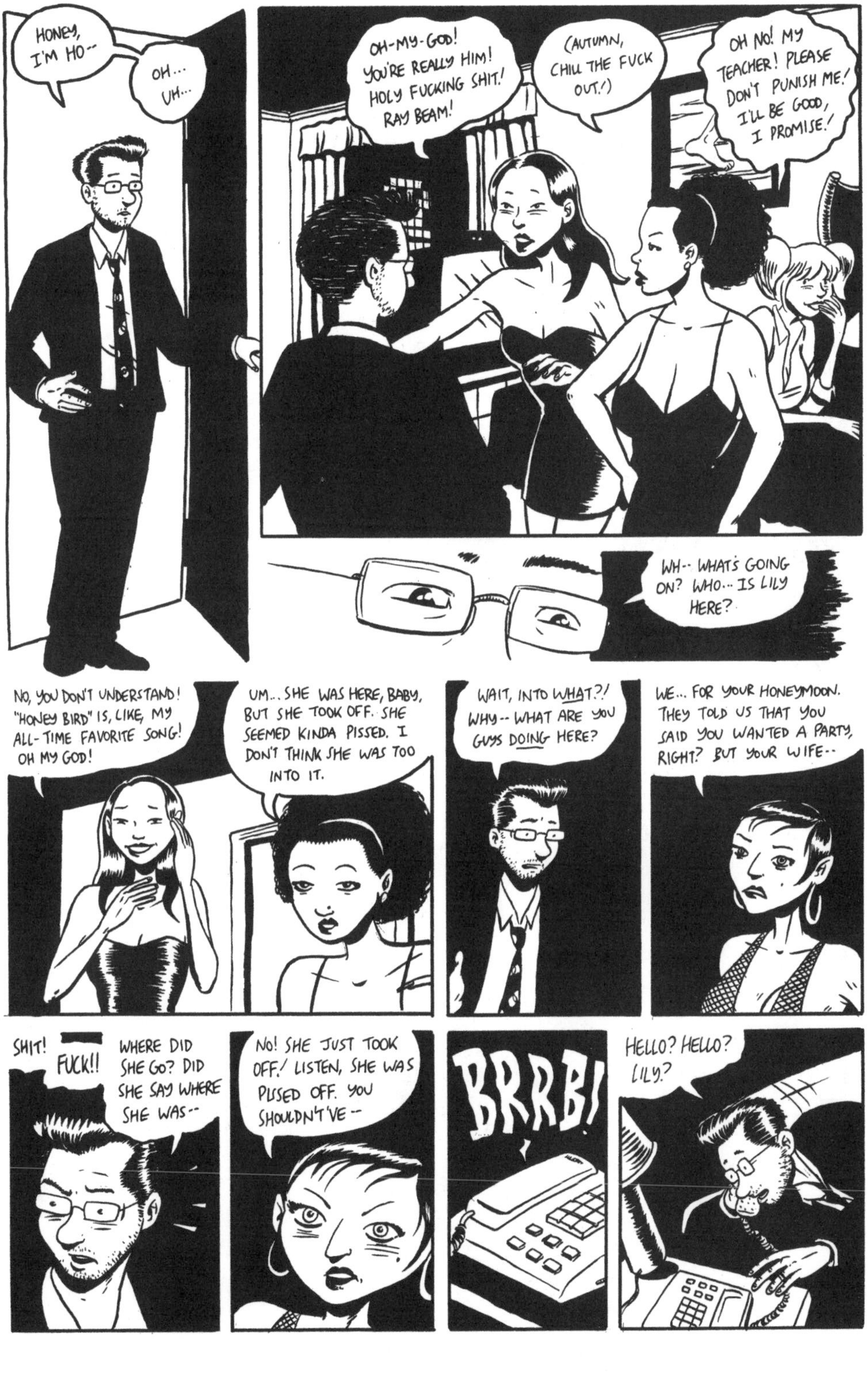

HONEY, I'M HO--
OH... UH...
OH-MY-GOD! YOU'RE REALLY HIM! HOLY FUCKING SHIT! RAY BEAM!
(AUTUMN, CHILL THE FUCK OUT!)
OH NO! MY TEACHER! PLEASE DON'T PUNISH ME! I'LL BE GOOD, I PROMISE!
WH-- WHAT'S GOING ON? WHO... IS LILY HERE?
NO, YOU DON'T UNDERSTAND! "HONEY BIRD" IS, LIKE, MY ALL-TIME FAVORITE SONG! OH MY GOD!
UM... SHE WAS HERE, BABY, BUT SHE TOOK OFF. SHE SEEMED KINDA PISSED. I DON'T THINK SHE WAS TOO INTO IT.
WAIT, INTO WHAT?! WHY-- WHAT ARE YOU GUYS DOING HERE?
WE... FOR YOUR HONEYMOON. THEY TOLD US THAT YOU SAID YOU WANTED A PARTY, RIGHT? BUT YOUR WIFE--
SHIT! [redacted] FUCK!!
WHERE DID SHE GO? DID SHE SAY WHERE SHE WAS--
NO! SHE JUST TOOK OFF! LISTEN, SHE WAS PISSED OFF. YOU SHOULDN'T'VE --
BRRB!
HELLO? HELLO? LILY?

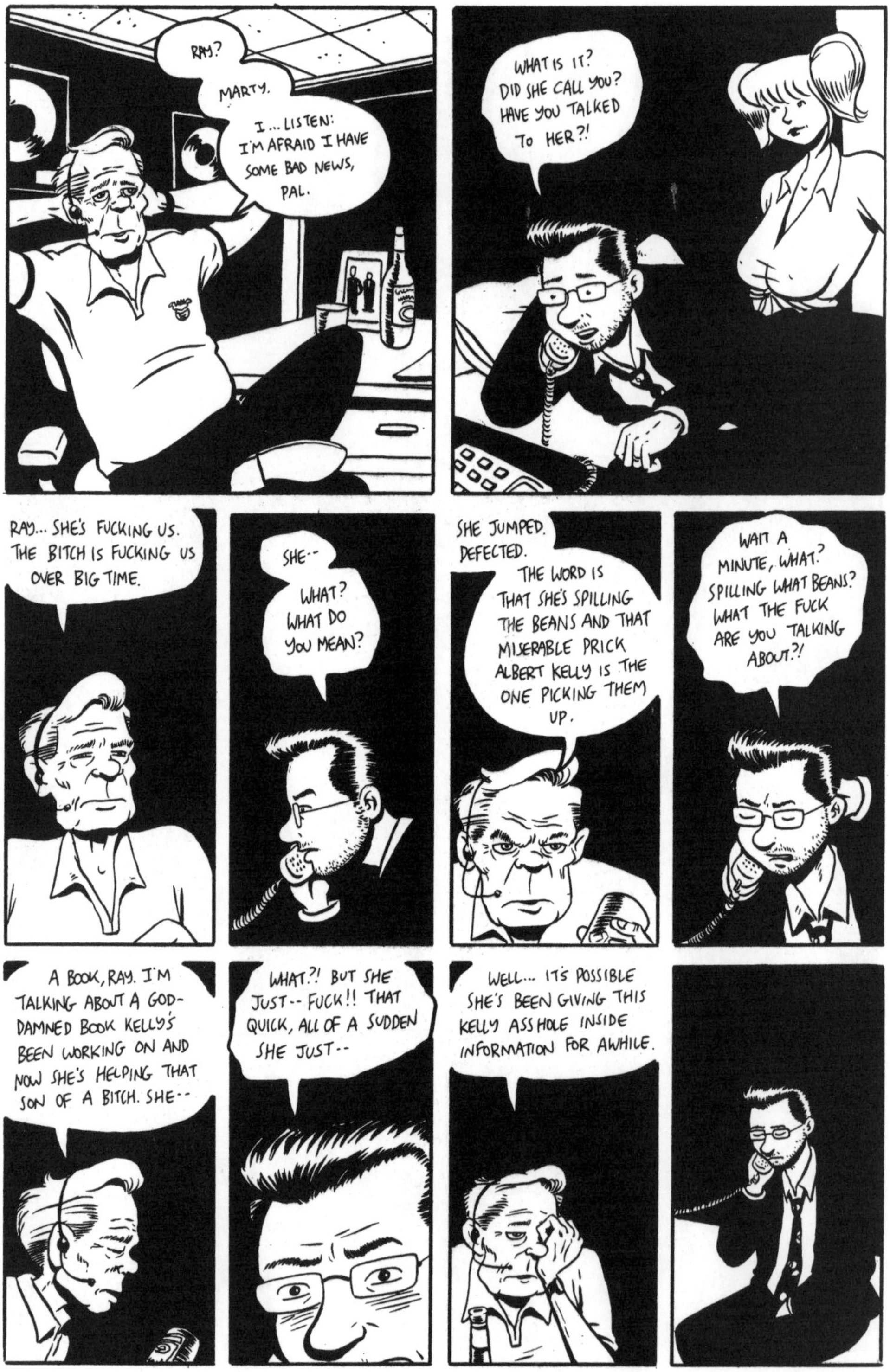
RAY?
MARTY.
I... LISTEN: I'M AFRAID I HAVE SOME BAD NEWS, PAL.
WHAT IS IT? DID SHE CALL YOU? HAVE YOU TALKED TO HER?!
RAY... SHE'S FUCKING US. THE BITCH IS FUCKING US OVER BIG TIME.
SHE--
WHAT? WHAT DO YOU MEAN?
SHE JUMPED. DEFECTED.
THE WORD IS THAT SHE'S SPILLING THE BEANS AND THAT MISERABLE PRICK ALBERT KELLY IS THE ONE PICKING THEM UP.
WAIT A MINUTE, WHAT? SPILLING WHAT BEANS? WHAT THE FUCK ARE YOU TALKING ABOUT?!
A BOOK, RAY. I'M TALKING ABOUT A GOD-DAMNED BOOK KELLY'S BEEN WORKING ON AND NOW SHE'S HELPING THAT SON OF A BITCH. SHE--
WHAT?! BUT SHE JUST-- FUCK!! THAT QUICK, ALL OF A SUDDEN SHE JUST--
WELL... IT'S POSSIBLE SHE'S BEEN GIVING THIS KELLY ASSHOLE INSIDE INFORMATION FOR AWHILE.

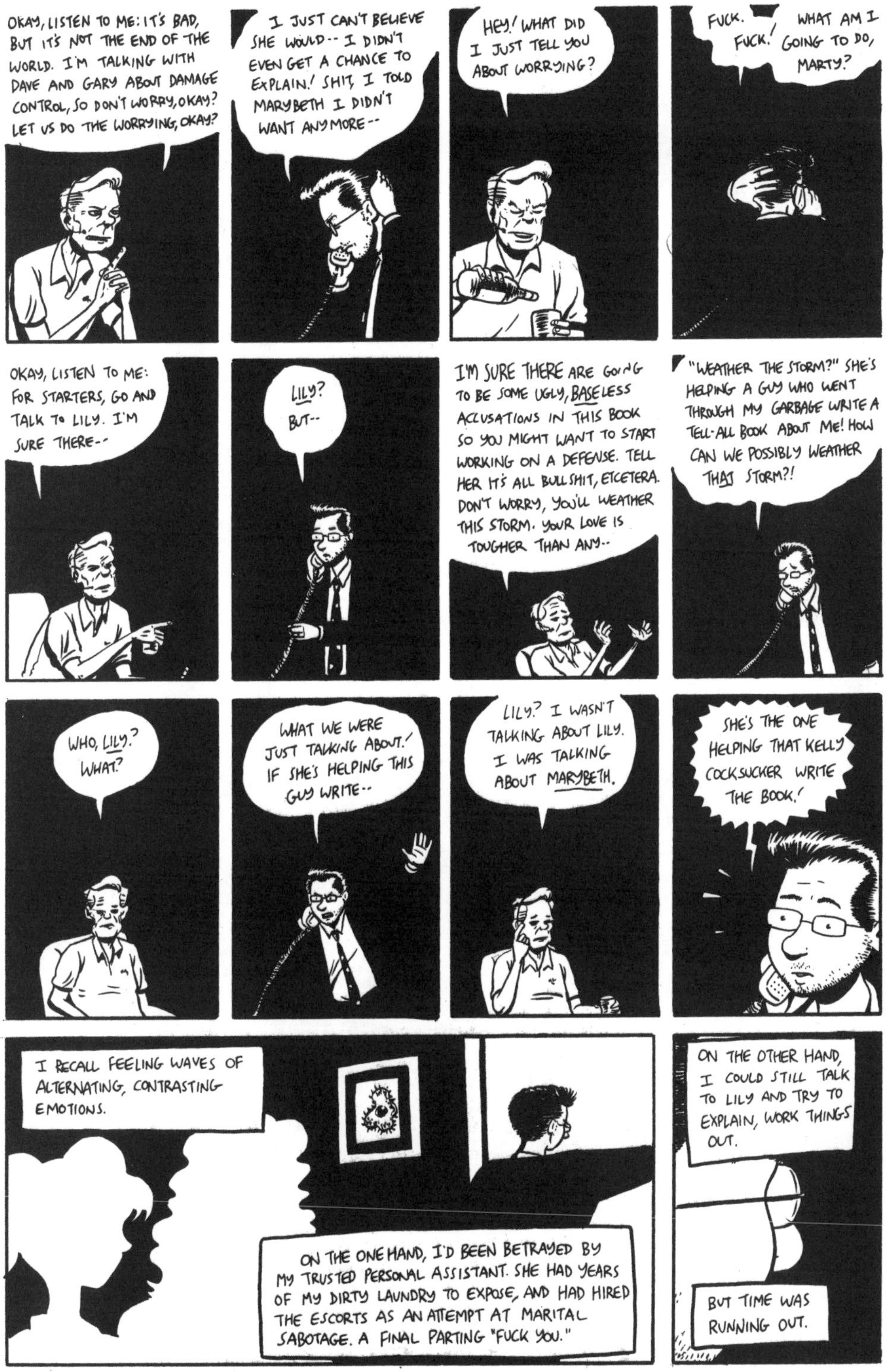
OKAY, LISTEN TO ME: IT'S BAD, BUT IT'S NOT THE END OF THE WORLD. I'M TALKING WITH DAVE AND GARY ABOUT DAMAGE CONTROL, SO DON'T WORRY, OKAY? LET US DO THE WORRYING, OKAY?
I JUST CAN'T BELIEVE SHE WOULD-- I DIDN'T EVEN GET A CHANCE TO EXPLAIN! SHIT, I TOLD MARYBETH I DIDN'T WANT ANYMORE--
HEY! WHAT DID I JUST TELL YOU ABOUT WORRYING?
FUCK.
FUCK!
WHAT AM I GOING TO DO, MARTY?
OKAY, LISTEN TO ME: FOR STARTERS, GO AND TALK TO LILY. I'M SURE THERE--
LILY? BUT--
I'M SURE THERE ARE GOING TO BE SOME UGLY, BASELESS ACCUSATIONS IN THIS BOOK SO YOU MIGHT WANT TO START WORKING ON A DEFENSE. TELL HER IT'S ALL BULLSHIT, ETCETERA. DON'T WORRY, YOU'LL WEATHER THIS STORM. YOUR LOVE IS TOUGHER THAN ANY--
"WEATHER THE STORM?" SHE'S HELPING A GUY WHO WENT THROUGH MY GARBAGE WRITE A TELL-ALL BOOK ABOUT ME! HOW CAN WE POSSIBLY WEATHER THAT STORM?!
WHO, LILY? WHAT?
WHAT WE WERE JUST TALKING ABOUT! IF SHE'S HELPING THIS GUY WRITE--
LILY? I WASN'T TALKING ABOUT LILY. I WAS TALKING ABOUT MARYBETH.
SHE'S THE ONE HELPING THAT KELLY COCKSUCKER WRITE THE BOOK!
I RECALL FEELING WAVES OF ALTERNATING, CONTRASTING EMOTIONS.
ON THE ONE HAND, I'D BEEN BETRAYED BY MY TRUSTED PERSONAL ASSISTANT. SHE HAD YEARS OF MY DIRTY LAUNDRY TO EXPOSE, AND HAD HIRED THE ESCORTS AS AN ATTEMPT AT MARITAL SABOTAGE. A FINAL PARTING "FUCK YOU."
ON THE OTHER HAND, I COULD STILL TALK TO LILY AND TRY TO EXPLAIN, WORK THINGS OUT.
BUT TIME WAS RUNNING OUT.

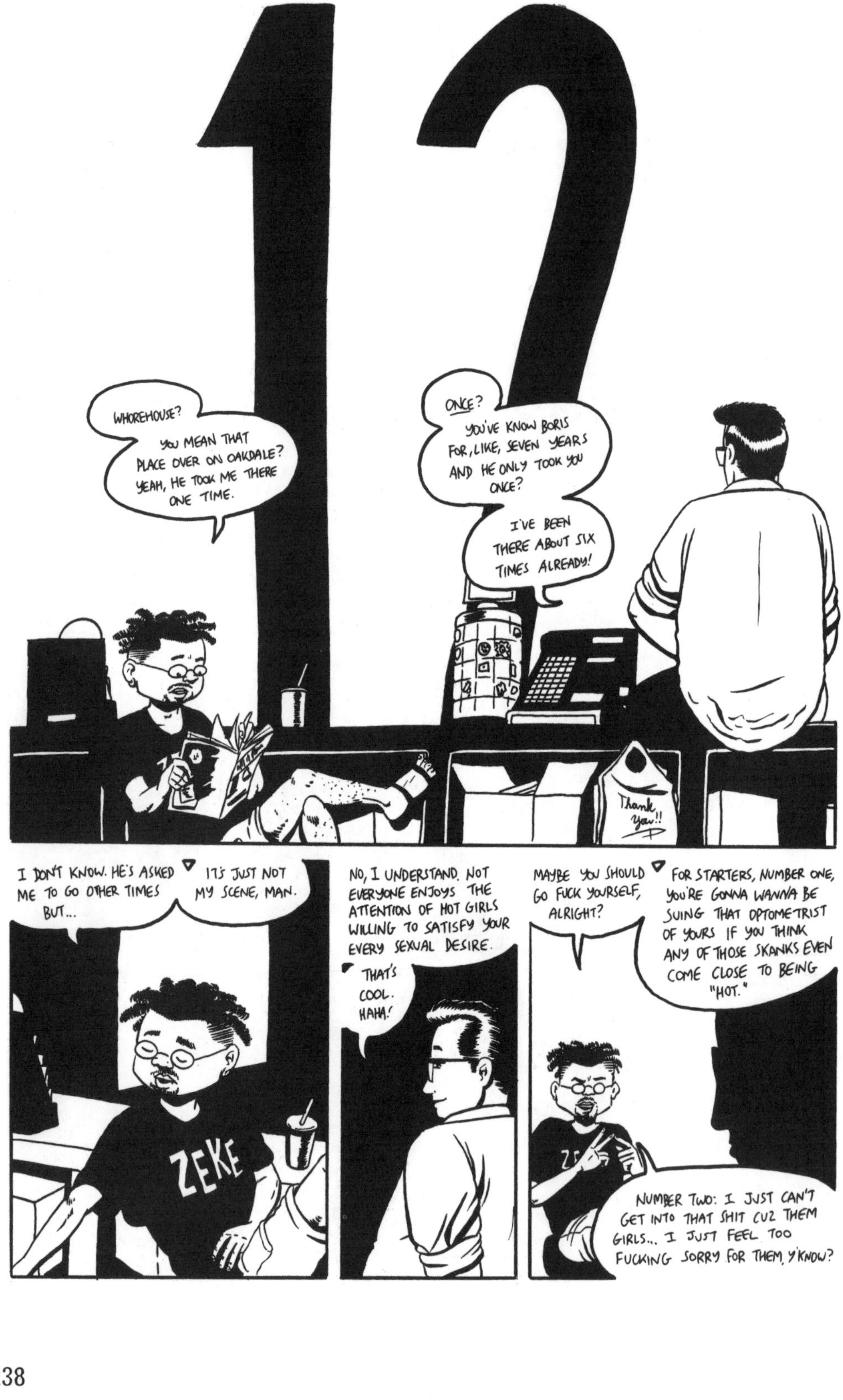
12
WHOREHOUSE? YOU MEAN THAT PLACE OVER ON OAKDALE? YEAH, HE TOOK ME THERE ONE TIME.
ONCE? YOU'VE KNOW BORIS FOR, LIKE, SEVEN YEARS AND HE ONLY TOOK YOU ONCE?
I'VE BEEN THERE ABOUT SIX TIMES ALREADY!
Thank you!!
I DON'T KNOW. HE'S ASKED ME TO GO OTHER TIMES BUT...
IT'S JUST NOT MY SCENE, MAN.
ZEKE
NO, I UNDERSTAND. NOT EVERYONE ENJOYS THE ATTENTION OF HOT GIRLS WILLING TO SATISFY YOUR EVERY SEXUAL DESIRE.
THAT'S COOL. HAHA!
MAYBE YOU SHOULD GO FUCK YOURSELF, ALRIGHT?
FOR STARTERS, NUMBER ONE, YOU'RE GONNA WANNA BE SUING THAT OPTOMETRIST OF YOURS IF YOU THINK ANY OF THOSE SKANKS EVEN COME CLOSE TO BEING "HOT."
NUMBER TWO: I JUST CAN'T GET INTO THAT SHIT CUZ THEM GIRLS... I JUST FEEL TOO FUCKING SORRY FOR THEM, Y'KNOW?

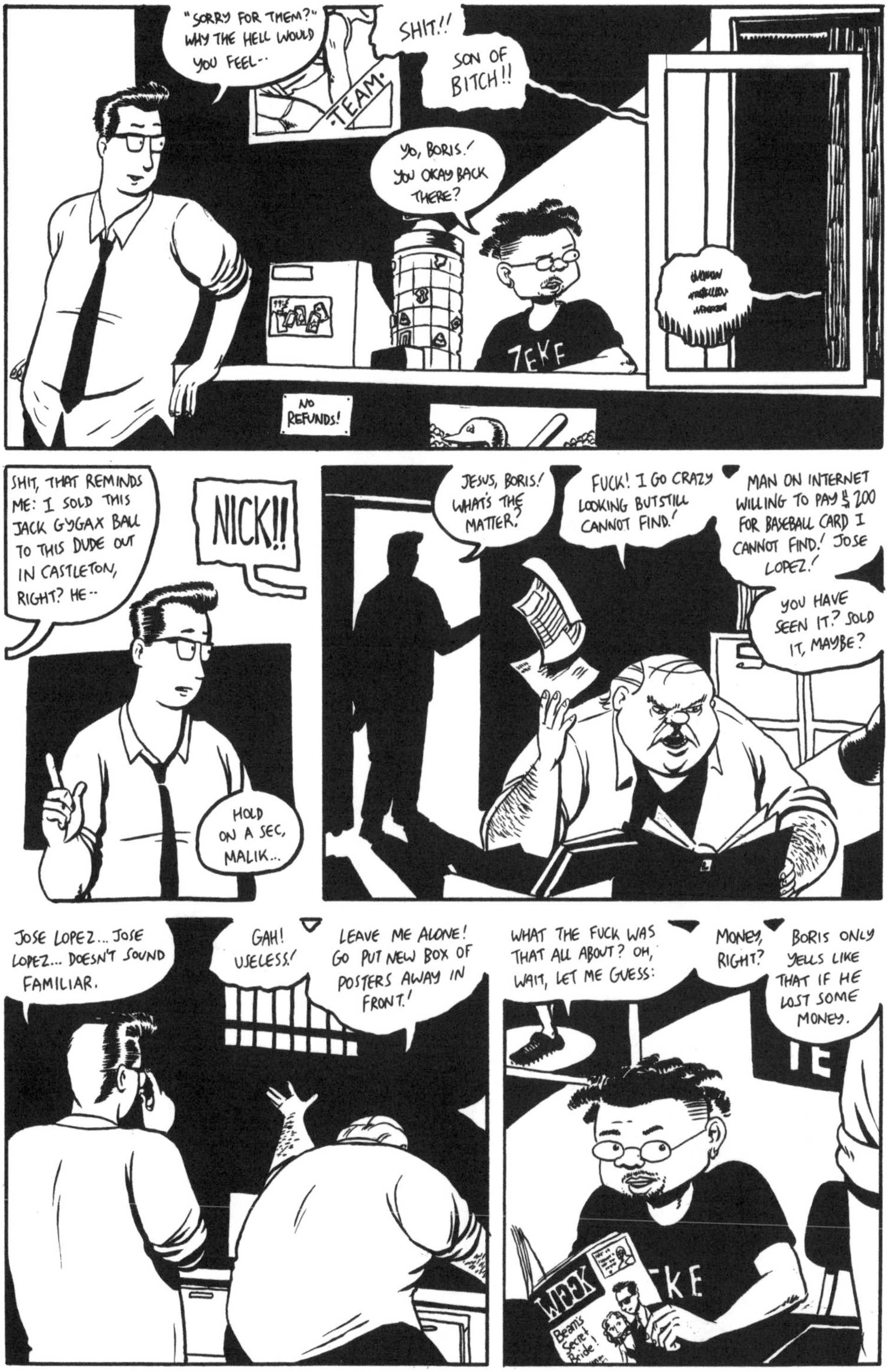
"SORRY FOR THEM?" WHY THE HELL WOULD YOU FEEL--
SHIT!!
SON OF BITCH!!
TEAM
YO, BORIS! YOU OKAY BACK THERE?
ZEKE
NO REFUNDS!
SHIT, THAT REMINDS ME: I SOLD THIS JACK GYGAX BALL TO THIS DUDE OUT IN CASTLETON, RIGHT? HE--
NICK!!
HOLD ON A SEC, MALIK...
JESUS, BORIS! WHAT'S THE MATTER?
FUCK! I GO CRAZY LOOKING BUT STILL CANNOT FIND!
MAN ON INTERNET WILLING TO PAY $200 FOR BASEBALL CARD I CANNOT FIND! JOSE LOPEZ!
YOU HAVE SEEN IT? SOLD IT, MAYBE?
JOSE LOPEZ... JOSE LOPEZ... DOESN'T SOUND FAMILIAR.
GAH! USELESS!
LEAVE ME ALONE! GO PUT NEW BOX OF POSTERS AWAY IN FRONT!
WHAT THE FUCK WAS THAT ALL ABOUT? OH, WAIT, LET ME GUESS:
MONEY, RIGHT?
BORIS ONLY YELLS LIKE THAT IF HE LOST SOME MONEY.
WEEK
Bean's Secret Bride!
ZEKE

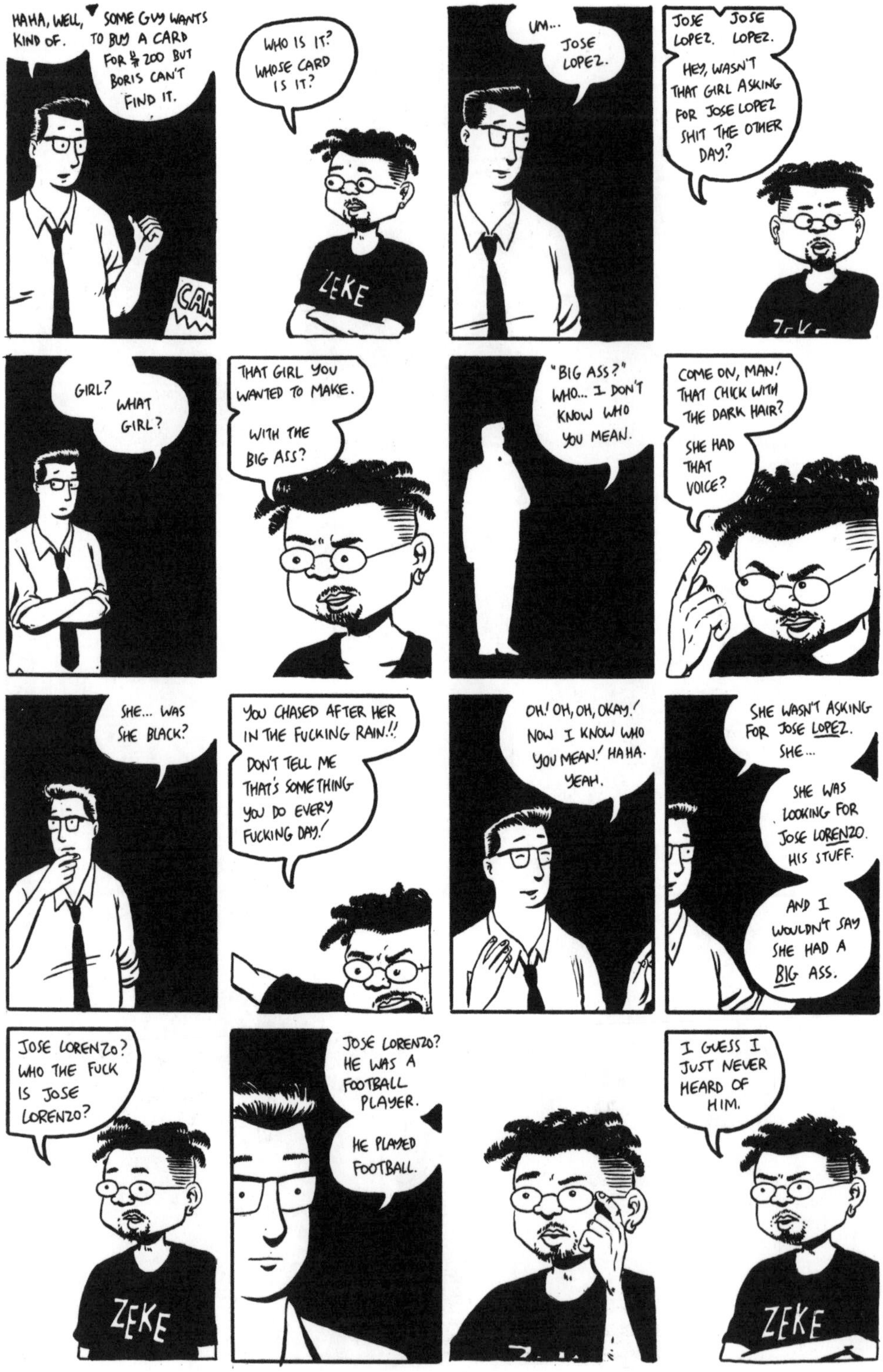
HAHA, WELL, KIND OF.
SOME GUY WANTS TO BUY A CARD FOR 원200 BUT BORIS CAN'T FIND IT.
WHO IS IT? WHOSE CARD IS IT?
UM... JOSE LOPEZ.
JOSE LOPEZ. JOSE LOPEZ.
HEY, WASN'T THAT GIRL ASKING FOR JOSE LOPEZ SHIT THE OTHER DAY?
GIRL? WHAT GIRL?
THAT GIRL YOU WANTED TO MAKE.
WITH THE BIG ASS?
"BIG ASS?" WHO... I DON'T KNOW WHO YOU MEAN.
COME ON, MAN! THAT CHICK WITH THE DARK HAIR?
SHE HAD THAT VOICE?
SHE... WAS SHE BLACK?
YOU CHASED AFTER HER IN THE FUCKING RAIN!!
DON'T TELL ME THAT'S SOMETHING YOU DO EVERY FUCKING DAY!
OH! OH, OH, OKAY! NOW I KNOW WHO YOU MEAN! HAHA. YEAH.
SHE WASN'T ASKING FOR JOSE LOPEZ. SHE...
SHE WAS LOOKING FOR JOSE LORENZO. HIS STUFF.
AND I WOULDN'T SAY SHE HAD A BIG ASS.
JOSE LORENZO? WHO THE FUCK IS JOSE LORENZO?
JOSE LORENZO? HE WAS A FOOTBALL PLAYER.
HE PLAYED FOOTBALL.
I GUESS I JUST NEVER HEARD OF HIM.

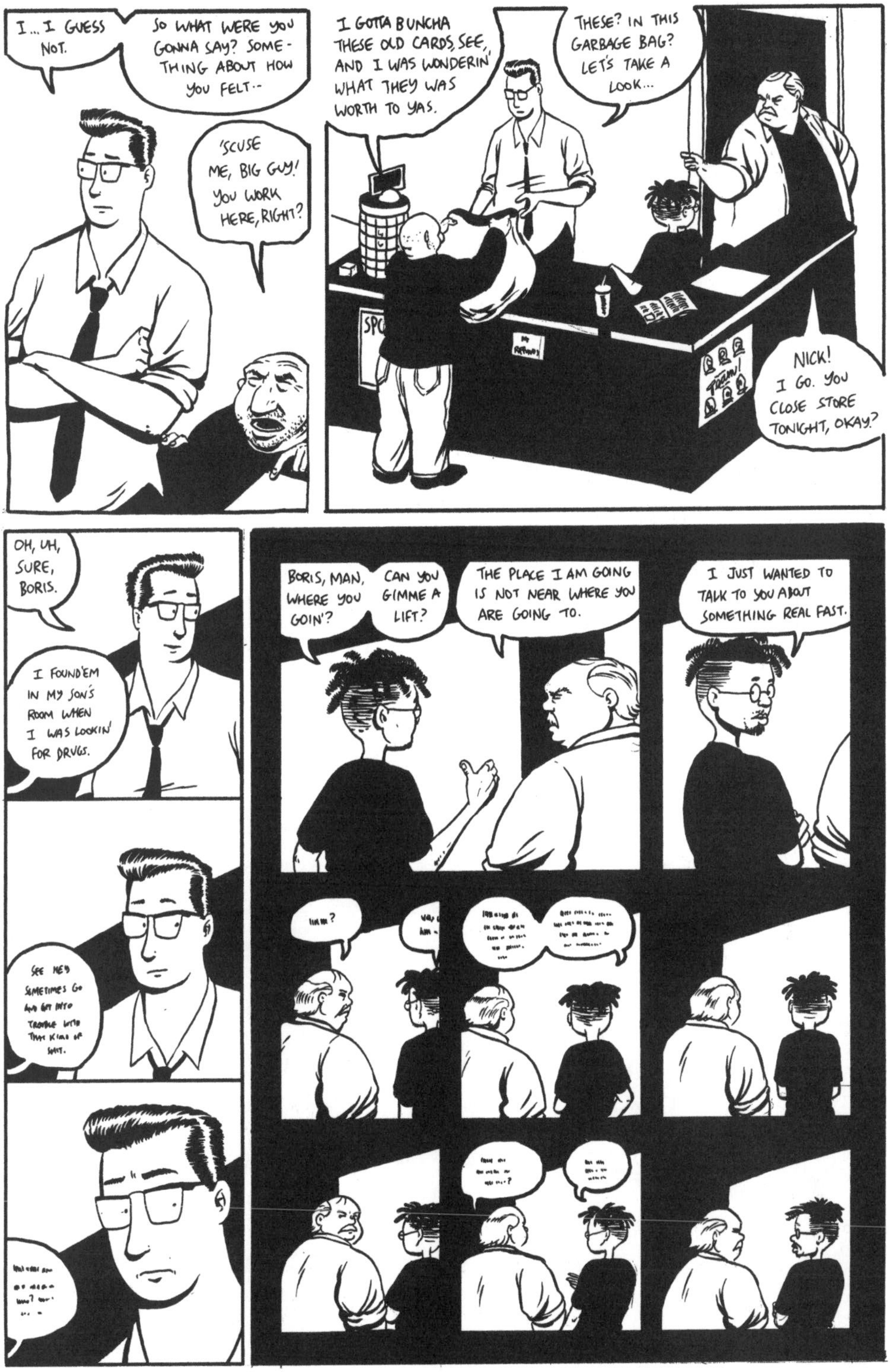
I... I GUESS NOT.
SO WHAT WERE YOU GONNA SAY? SOMETHING ABOUT HOW YOU FELT--
'SCUSE ME, BIG GUY! YOU WORK HERE, RIGHT?
I GOTTA BUNCHA THESE OLD CARDS, SEE, AND I WAS WONDERIN' WHAT THEY WAS WORTH TO YAS.
THESE? IN THIS GARBAGE BAG? LET'S TAKE A LOOK...
NICK! I GO. YOU CLOSE STORE TONIGHT, OKAY?
OH, UH, SURE, BORIS.
I FOUND 'EM IN MY SON'S ROOM WHEN I WAS LOOKIN' FOR DRUGS.
BORIS, MAN, WHERE YOU GOIN'?
CAN YOU GIMME A LIFT?
THE PLACE I AM GOING IS NOT NEAR WHERE YOU ARE GOING TO.
I JUST WANTED TO TALK TO YOU ABOUT SOMETHING REAL FAST.
SEE HE'S SOMETIMES GO AND GET INTO TROUBLE WITH THAT KIND OF SHIT.

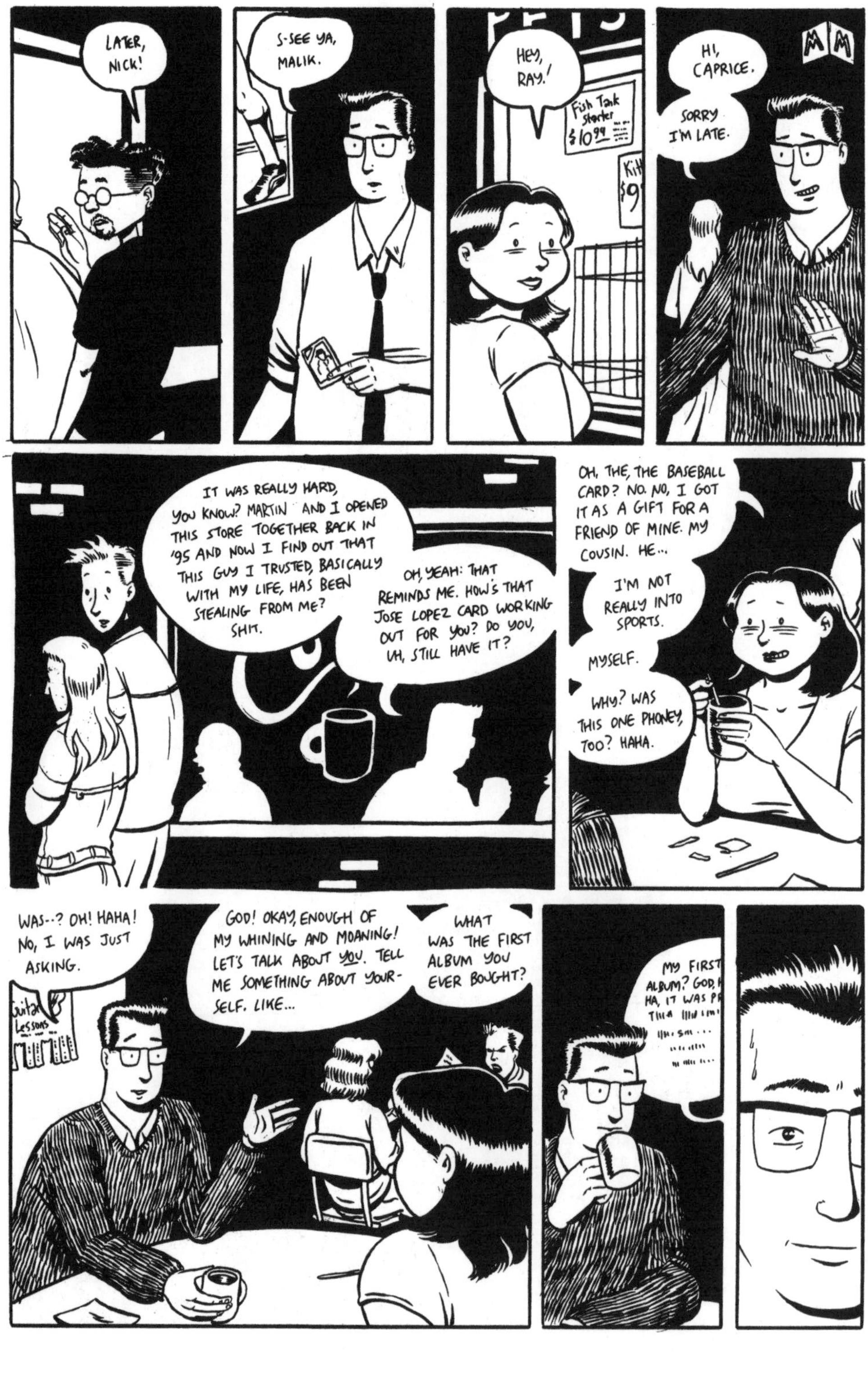
LATER, NICK!
S-SEE YA, MALIK.
HEY, RAY!
Fish Tank Starter $10.99
HI, CAPRICE.
SORRY I'M LATE.
IT WAS REALLY HARD, YOU KNOW? MARTIN AND I OPENED THIS STORE TOGETHER BACK IN '95 AND NOW I FIND OUT THAT THIS GUY I TRUSTED, BASICALLY WITH MY LIFE, HAS BEEN STEALING FROM ME? SHIT.
OH, YEAH: THAT REMINDS ME. HOW'S THAT JOSE LOPEZ CARD WORKING OUT FOR YOU? DO YOU, UH, STILL HAVE IT?
OH, THE, THE BASEBALL CARD? NO. NO, I GOT IT AS A GIFT FOR A FRIEND OF MINE. MY COUSIN. HE...
I'M NOT REALLY INTO SPORTS.
MYSELF.
WHY? WAS THIS ONE PHONEY, TOO? HAHA.
WAS--? OH! HAHA! NO, I WAS JUST ASKING.
Guitar Lessons
GOD! OKAY, ENOUGH OF MY WHINING AND MOANING! LET'S TALK ABOUT YOU. TELL ME SOMETHING ABOUT YOURSELF. LIKE...
WHAT WAS THE FIRST ALBUM YOU EVER BOUGHT?
MY FIRST ALBUM? GOD, HA, IT WAS P

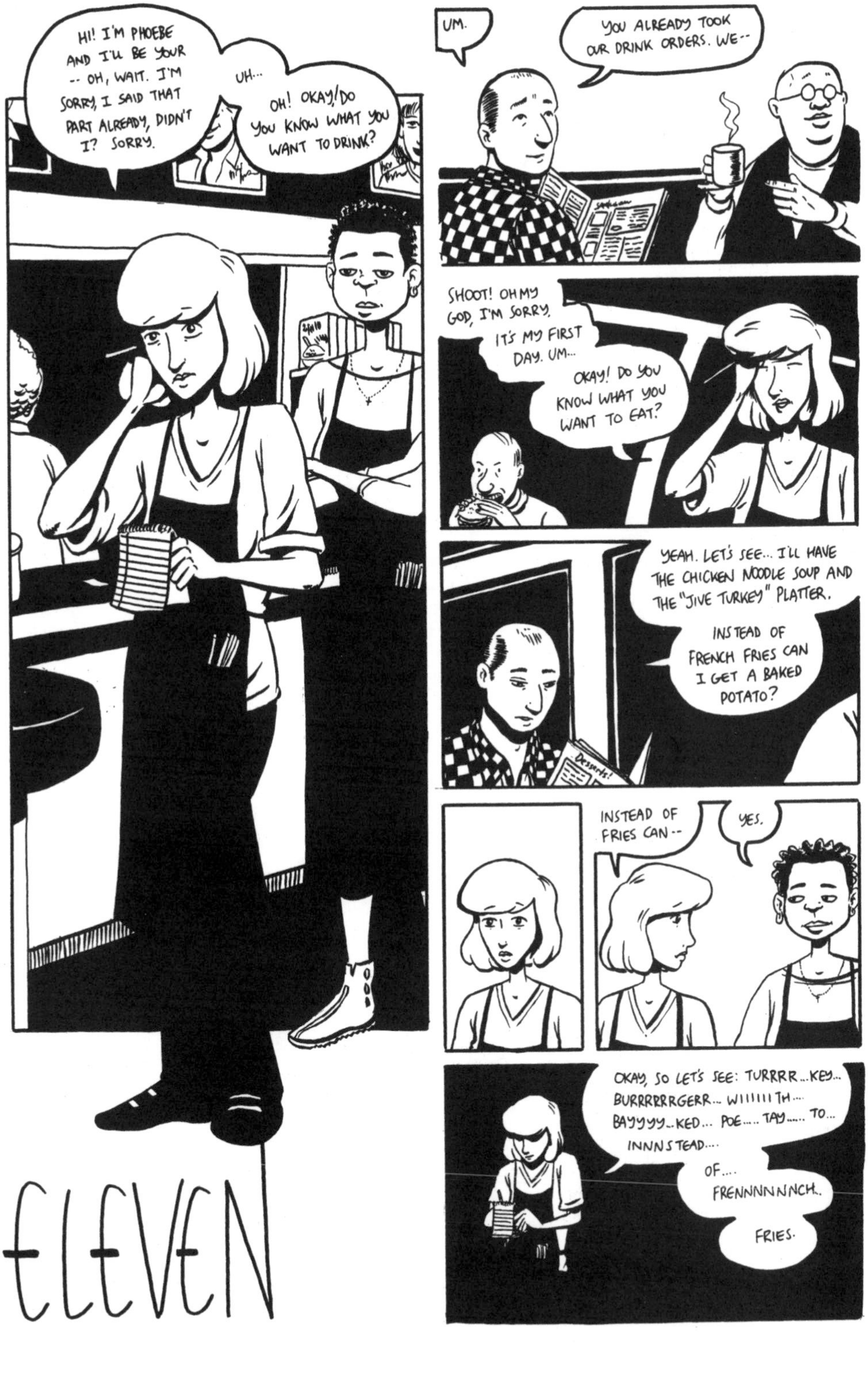
HI! I'M PHOEBE AND I'LL BE YOUR -- OH, WAIT. I'M SORRY, I SAID THAT PART ALREADY, DIDN'T I? SORRY.
UH...
OH! OKAY! DO YOU KNOW WHAT YOU WANT TO DRINK?
ELEVEN
UM.
YOU ALREADY TOOK OUR DRINK ORDERS. WE--
SHOOT! OH MY GOD, I'M SORRY.
IT'S MY FIRST DAY. UM...
OKAY! DO YOU KNOW WHAT YOU WANT TO EAT?
YEAH. LET'S SEE... I'LL HAVE THE CHICKEN NOODLE SOUP AND THE "JIVE TURKEY" PLATTER.
INSTEAD OF FRENCH FRIES CAN I GET A BAKED POTATO?
Desserts!
INSTEAD OF FRIES CAN--
YES.
OKAY, SO LET'S SEE: TURRRR...KEY... BURRRRRRGERR... WIIIIIITH... BAYYYY...KED... POE..... TAY...... TO... INNNSTEAD....
OF....
FRENNNNNNCH..
FRIES.

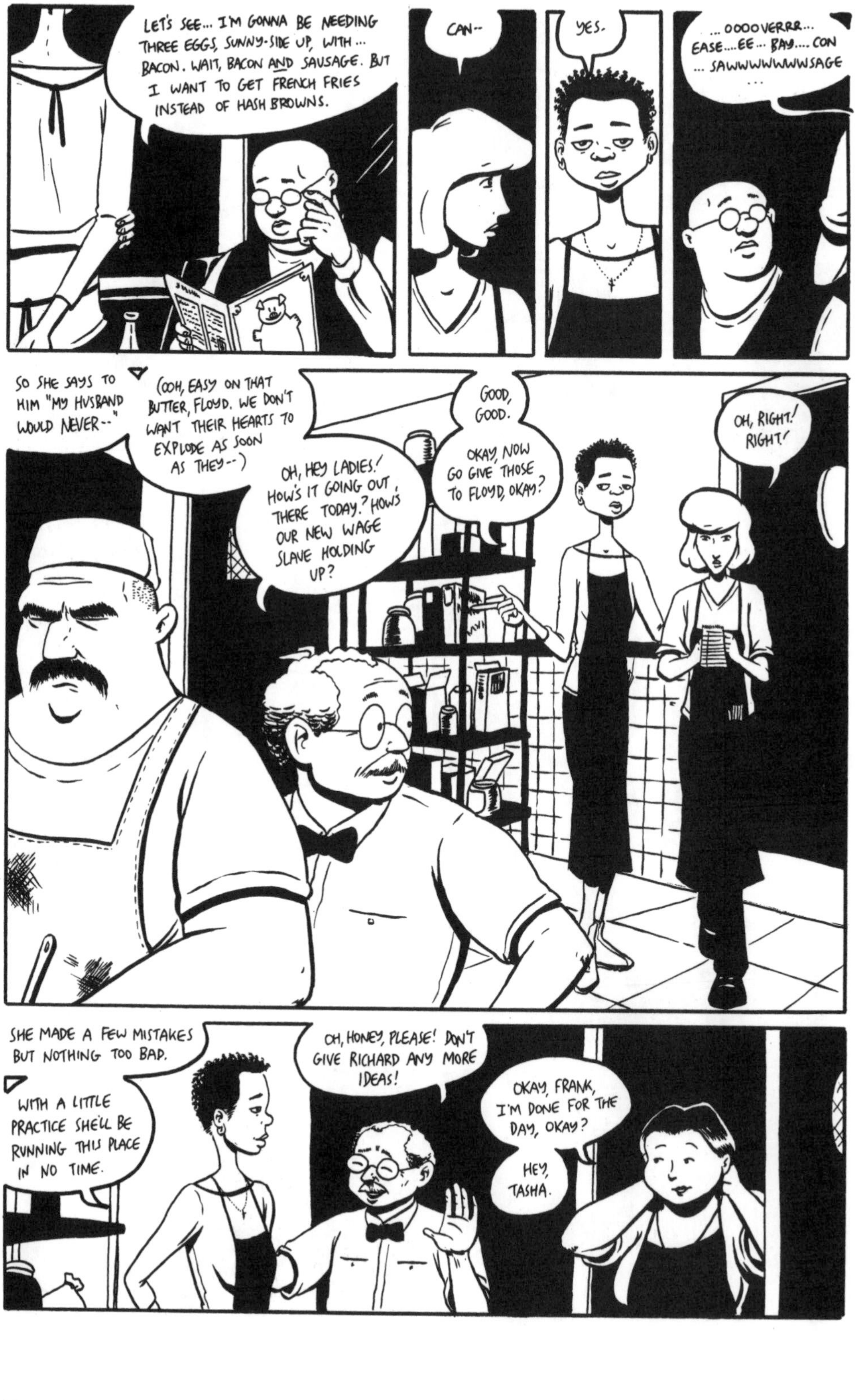
LET'S SEE... I'M GONNA BE NEEDING THREE EGGS, SUNNY-SIDE UP, WITH... BACON. WAIT, BACON AND SAUSAGE. BUT I WANT TO GET FRENCH FRIES INSTEAD OF HASH BROWNS.
CAN--
YES.
...OOOOVERRR... EASE....EE... BAY.... CON ... SAWWWWWWWSAGE ...
SO SHE SAYS TO HIM "MY HUSBAND WOULD NEVER--"
(OOH, EASY ON THAT BUTTER, FLOYD. WE DON'T WANT THEIR HEARTS TO EXPLODE AS SOON AS THEY--)
OH, HEY LADIES! HOW'S IT GOING OUT THERE TODAY? HOW'S OUR NEW WAGE SLAVE HOLDING UP?
GOOD, GOOD.
OKAY, NOW GO GIVE THOSE TO FLOYD, OKAY?
OH, RIGHT! RIGHT!
SHE MADE A FEW MISTAKES BUT NOTHING TOO BAD.
WITH A LITTLE PRACTICE SHE'LL BE RUNNING THIS PLACE IN NO TIME.
OH, HONEY, PLEASE! DON'T GIVE RICHARD ANY MORE IDEAS!
OKAY, FRANK, I'M DONE FOR THE DAY, OKAY?
HEY, TASHA.

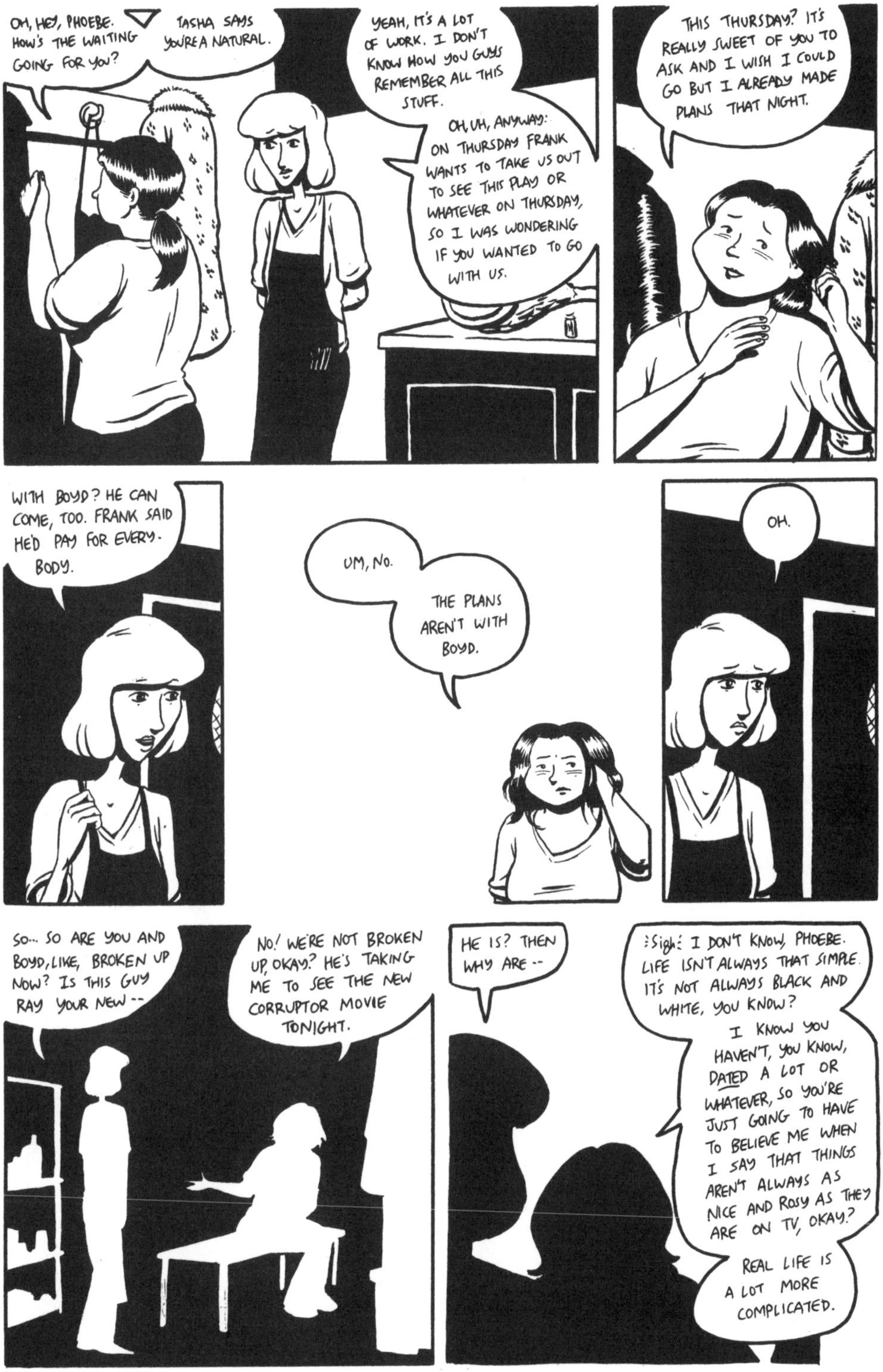
OH, HEY, PHOEBE. HOW'S THE WAITING GOING FOR YOU?
TASHA SAYS YOU'RE A NATURAL.
YEAH, IT'S A LOT OF WORK. I DON'T KNOW HOW YOU GUYS REMEMBER ALL THIS STUFF.
OH, UH, ANYWAY: ON THURSDAY FRANK WANTS TO TAKE US OUT TO SEE THIS PLAY OR WHATEVER ON THURSDAY, SO I WAS WONDERING IF YOU WANTED TO GO WITH US.
THIS THURSDAY? IT'S REALLY SWEET OF YOU TO ASK AND I WISH I COULD GO BUT I ALREADY MADE PLANS THAT NIGHT.
WITH BOYD? HE CAN COME, TOO. FRANK SAID HE'D PAY FOR EVERY-BODY.
UM, NO.
THE PLANS AREN'T WITH BOYD.
OH.
SO... SO ARE YOU AND BOYD, LIKE, BROKEN UP NOW? IS THIS GUY RAY YOUR NEW --
NO! WE'RE NOT BROKEN UP, OKAY? HE'S TAKING ME TO SEE THE NEW CORRUPTOR MOVIE TONIGHT.
HE IS? THEN WHY ARE --
:SIGH: I DON'T KNOW, PHOEBE. LIFE ISN'T ALWAYS THAT SIMPLE. IT'S NOT ALWAYS BLACK AND WHITE, YOU KNOW?
I KNOW YOU HAVEN'T, YOU KNOW, DATED A LOT OR WHATEVER, SO YOU'RE JUST GOING TO HAVE TO BELIEVE ME WHEN I SAY THAT THINGS AREN'T ALWAYS AS NICE AND ROSY AS THEY ARE ON TV, OKAY?
REAL LIFE IS A LOT MORE COMPLICATED.

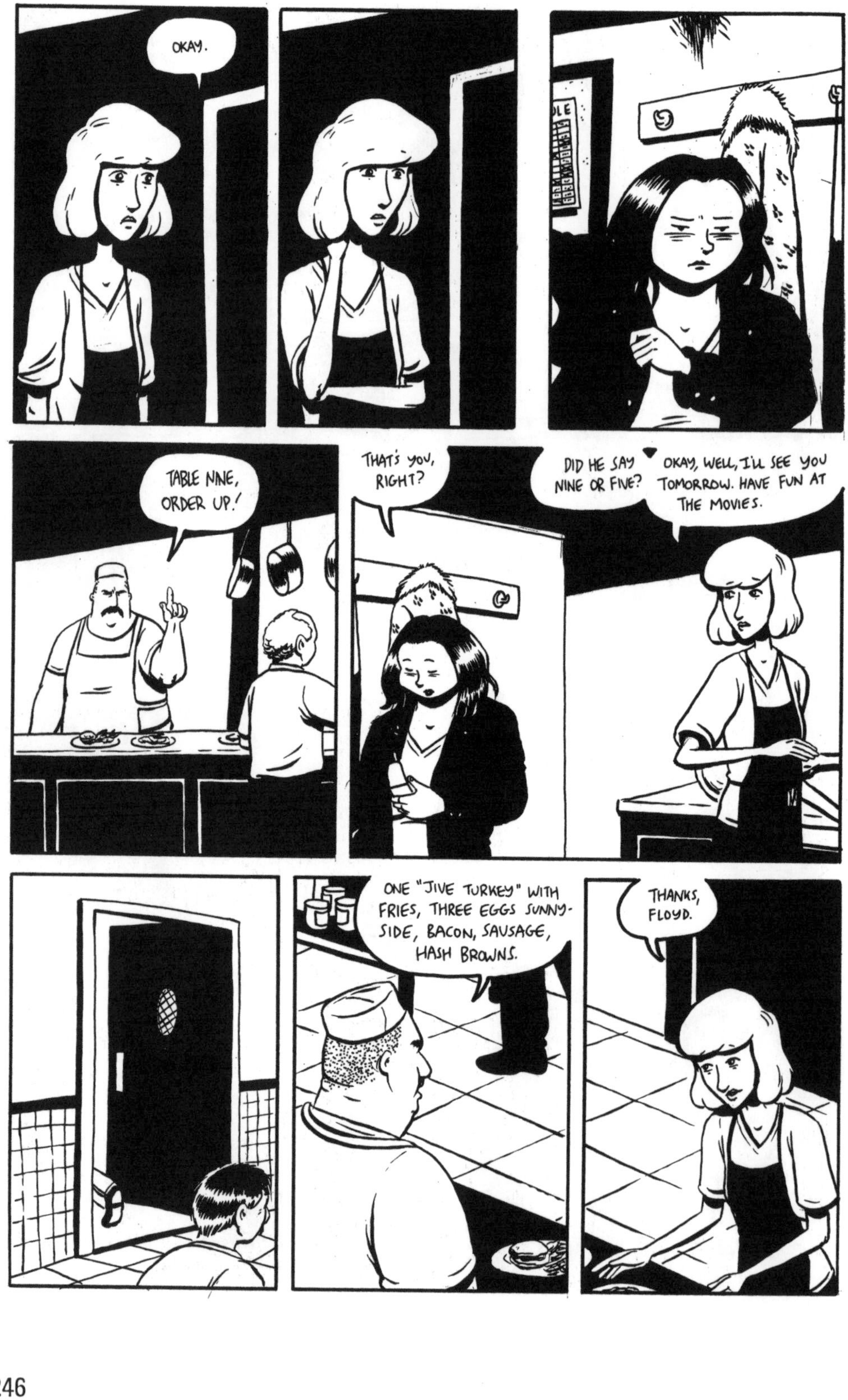
OKAY.
TABLE NINE, ORDER UP!
THAT'S YOU, RIGHT?
DID HE SAY NINE OR FIVE?
OKAY, WELL, I'LL SEE YOU TOMORROW. HAVE FUN AT THE MOVIES.
ONE "JIVE TURKEY" WITH FRIES, THREE EGGS SUNNY-SIDE, BACON, SAUSAGE, HASH BROWNS.
THANKS, FLOYD.

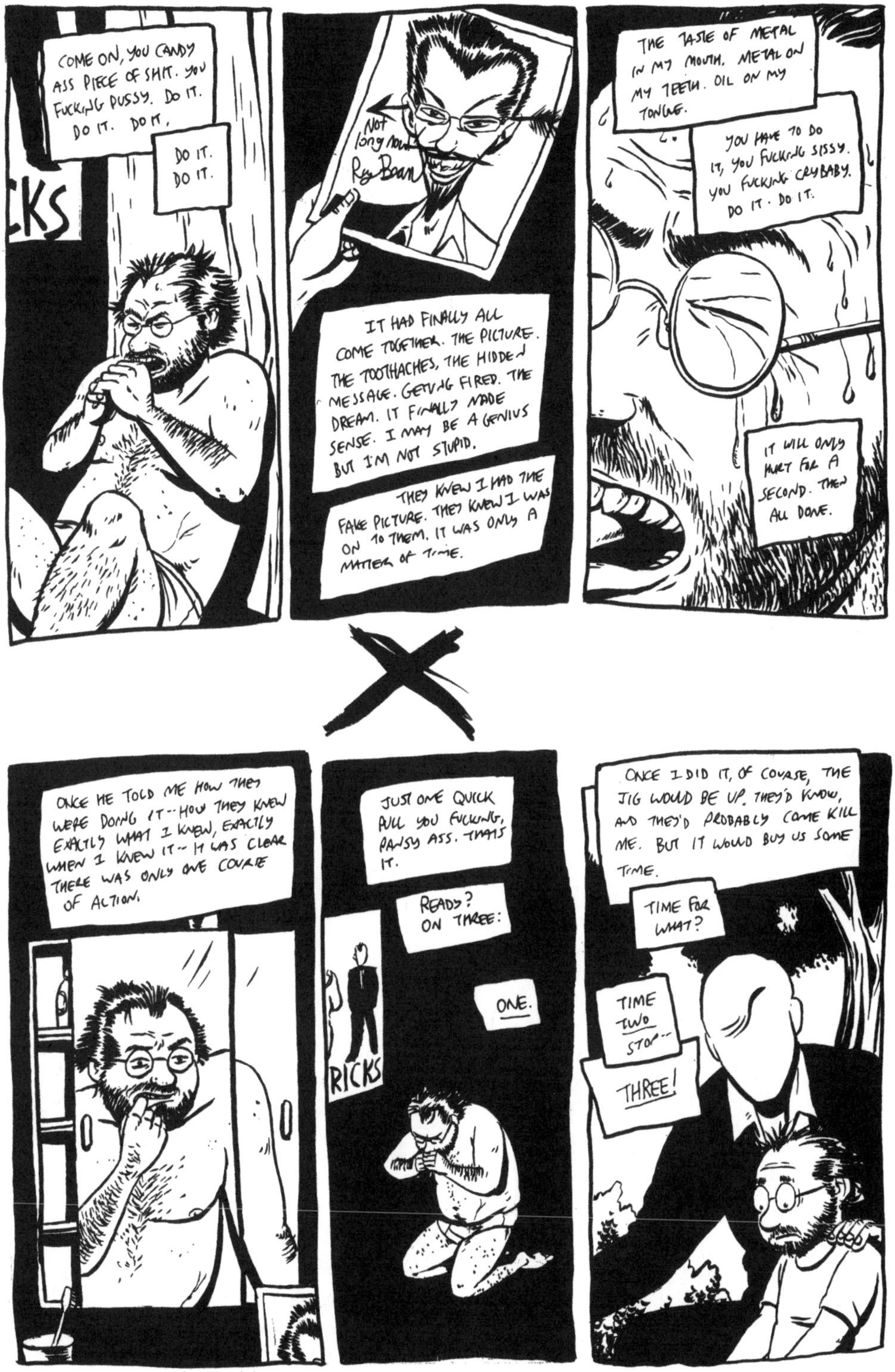
COME ON, YOU CANDY ASS PIECE OF SHIT. YOU FUCKING PUSSY. DO IT. DO IT. DO IT.
DO IT. DO IT.
CKS
IT HAD FINALLY ALL COME TOGETHER. THE PICTURE. THE TOOTHACHES, THE HIDDEN MESSAGE. GETTING FIRED. THE DREAM. IT FINALLY MADE SENSE. I MAY BE A GENIUS BUT I'M NOT STUPID.
THEY KNEW I HAD THE FAKE PICTURE. THEY KNEW I WAS ON TO THEM. IT WAS ONLY A MATTER OF TIME.
THE TASTE OF METAL IN MY MOUTH. METAL ON MY TEETH. OIL ON MY TONGUE.
YOU HAVE TO DO IT, YOU FUCKING SISSY. YOU FUCKING CRYBABY. DO IT. DO IT.
IT WILL ONLY HURT FOR A SECOND. THEN ALL DONE.
ONCE HE TOLD ME HOW THEY WERE DOING IT -- HOW THEY KNEW EXACTLY WHAT I KNEW, EXACTLY WHEN I KNEW IT -- IT WAS CLEAR THERE WAS ONLY ONE COURSE OF ACTION.
JUST ONE QUICK PULL YOU FUCKING, PANSY ASS. THAT'S IT.
READY? ON THREE:
ONE.
RICKS
ONCE I DID IT, OF COURSE, THE JIG WOULD BE UP. THEY'D KNOW, AND THEY'D PROBABLY COME KILL ME. BUT IT WOULD BUY US SOME TIME.
TIME FOR WHAT?
TIME TWO STOP--
THREE!

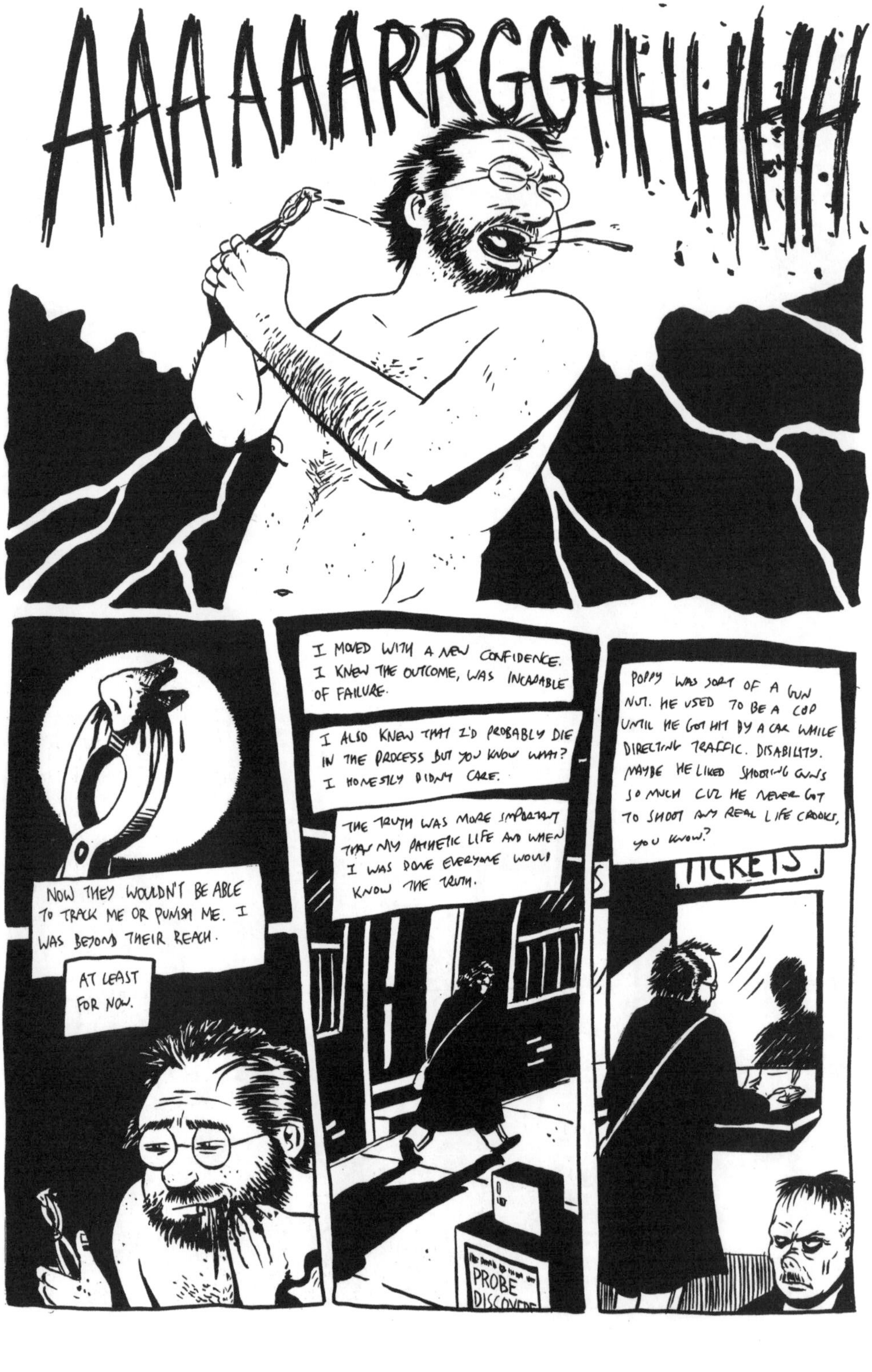
AAAAAARRGGHHHHH
NOW THEY WOULDN'T BE ABLE TO TRACK ME OR PUNISH ME. I WAS BEYOND THEIR REACH.
AT LEAST FOR NOW.
I MOVED WITH A NEW CONFIDENCE. I KNEW THE OUTCOME, WAS INCAPABLE OF FAILURE.
I ALSO KNEW THAT I'D PROBABLY DIE IN THE PROCESS BUT YOU KNOW WHAT? I HONESTLY DIDN'T CARE.
THE TRUTH WAS MORE IMPORTANT THAN MY PATHETIC LIFE AND WHEN I WAS DONE EVERYONE WOULD KNOW THE TRUTH.
PROBE
POPPY WAS SORT OF A GUN NUT. HE USED TO BE A COP UNTIL HE GOT HIT BY A CAR WHILE DIRECTING TRAFFIC. DISABILITY. MAYBE HE LIKED SHOOTING GUNS SO MUCH CUZ HE NEVER GOT TO SHOOT ANY REAL LIFE CROOKS, YOU KNOW?
TICKETS

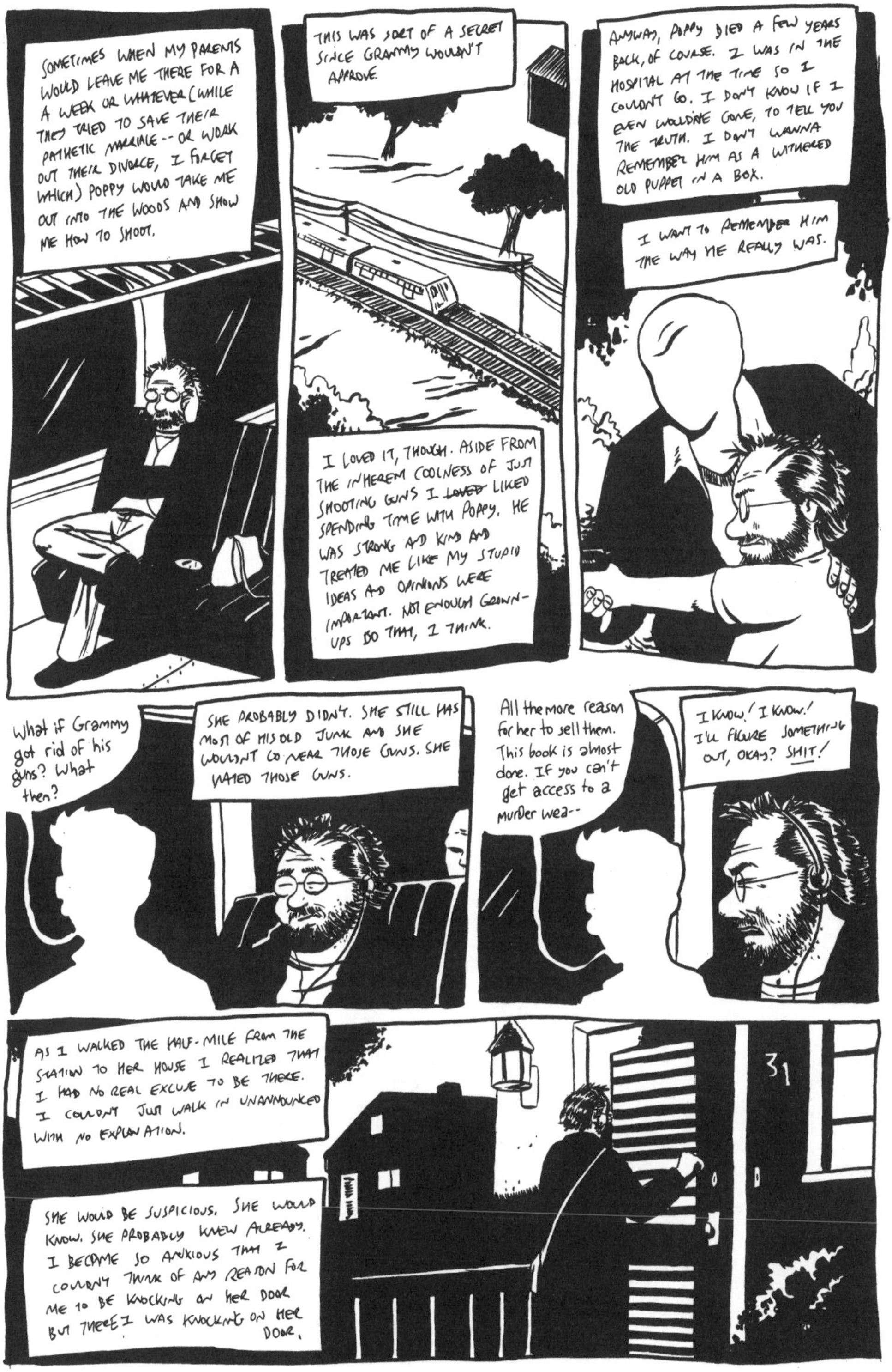
SOMETIMES WHEN MY PARENTS WOULD LEAVE ME THERE FOR A WEEK OR WHATEVER (WHILE THEY TRIED TO SAVE THEIR PATHETIC MARRIAGE -- OR WORK OUT THEIR DIVORCE, I FORGET WHICH) POPPY WOULD TAKE ME OUT INTO THE WOODS AND SHOW ME HOW TO SHOOT.
THIS WAS SORT OF A SECRET SINCE GRAMMY WOULDN'T APPROVE.
I LOVED IT, THOUGH. ASIDE FROM THE INHERENT COOLNESS OF JUST SHOOTING GUNS I ~~LOVED~~ LIKED SPENDING TIME WITH POPPY. HE WAS STRONG AND KIND AND TREATED ME LIKE MY STUPID IDEAS AND OPINIONS WERE IMPORTANT. NOT ENOUGH GROWN-UPS DO THAT, I THINK.
ANYWAY, POPPY DIED A FEW YEARS BACK, OF COURSE. I WAS IN THE HOSPITAL AT THE TIME SO I COULDN'T GO. I DON'T KNOW IF I EVEN WOULD'VE GONE, TO TELL YOU THE TRUTH. I DON'T WANNA REMEMBER HIM AS A WITHERED OLD PUPPET IN A BOX.
I WANT TO REMEMBER HIM THE WAY HE REALLY WAS.
What if Grammy got rid of his guns? What then?
SHE PROBABLY DIDN'T. SHE STILL HAS MOST OF HIS OLD JUNK AND SHE WOULDN'T GO NEAR THOSE GUNS. SHE HATED THOSE GUNS.
All the more reason for her to sell them. This book is almost done. If you can't get access to a murder wea--
I KNOW! I KNOW! I'LL FIGURE SOMETHING OUT, OKAY? SHIT!
AS I WALKED THE HALF-MILE FROM THE STATION TO HER HOUSE I REALIZED THAT I HAD NO REAL EXCUSE TO BE THERE. I COULDN'T JUST WALK IN UNANNOUNCED WITH NO EXPLANATION.
31
SHE WOULD BE SUSPICIOUS. SHE WOULD KNOW. SHE PROBABLY KNEW ALREADY. I BECAME SO ANXIOUS THAT I COULDN'T THINK OF ANY REASON FOR ME TO BE KNOCKING ON HER DOOR BUT THERE I WAS KNOCKING ON HER DOOR.

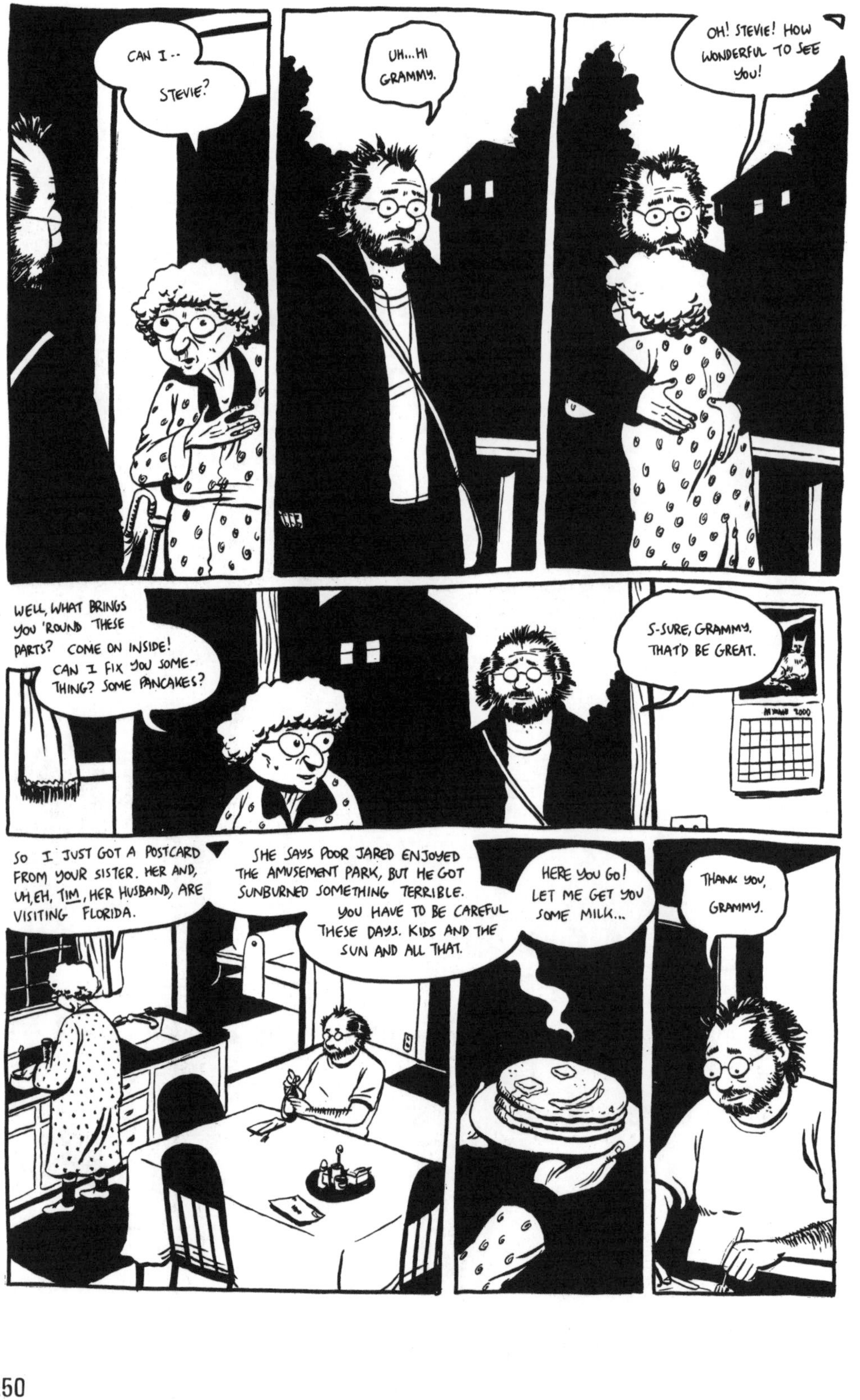
CAN I -- STEVIE?
UH... HI GRAMMY.
OH! STEVIE! HOW WONDERFUL TO SEE YOU!
WELL, WHAT BRINGS YOU 'ROUND THESE PARTS? COME ON INSIDE! CAN I FIX YOU SOMETHING? SOME PANCAKES?
S-SURE, GRAMMY. THAT'D BE GREAT.
SO I JUST GOT A POSTCARD FROM YOUR SISTER. HER AND, UH, EH, TIM, HER HUSBAND, ARE VISITING FLORIDA.
SHE SAYS POOR JARED ENJOYED THE AMUSEMENT PARK, BUT HE GOT SUNBURNED SOMETHING TERRIBLE. YOU HAVE TO BE CAREFUL THESE DAYS. KIDS AND THE SUN AND ALL THAT.
HERE YOU GO! LET ME GET YOU SOME MILK...
THANK YOU, GRAMMY.

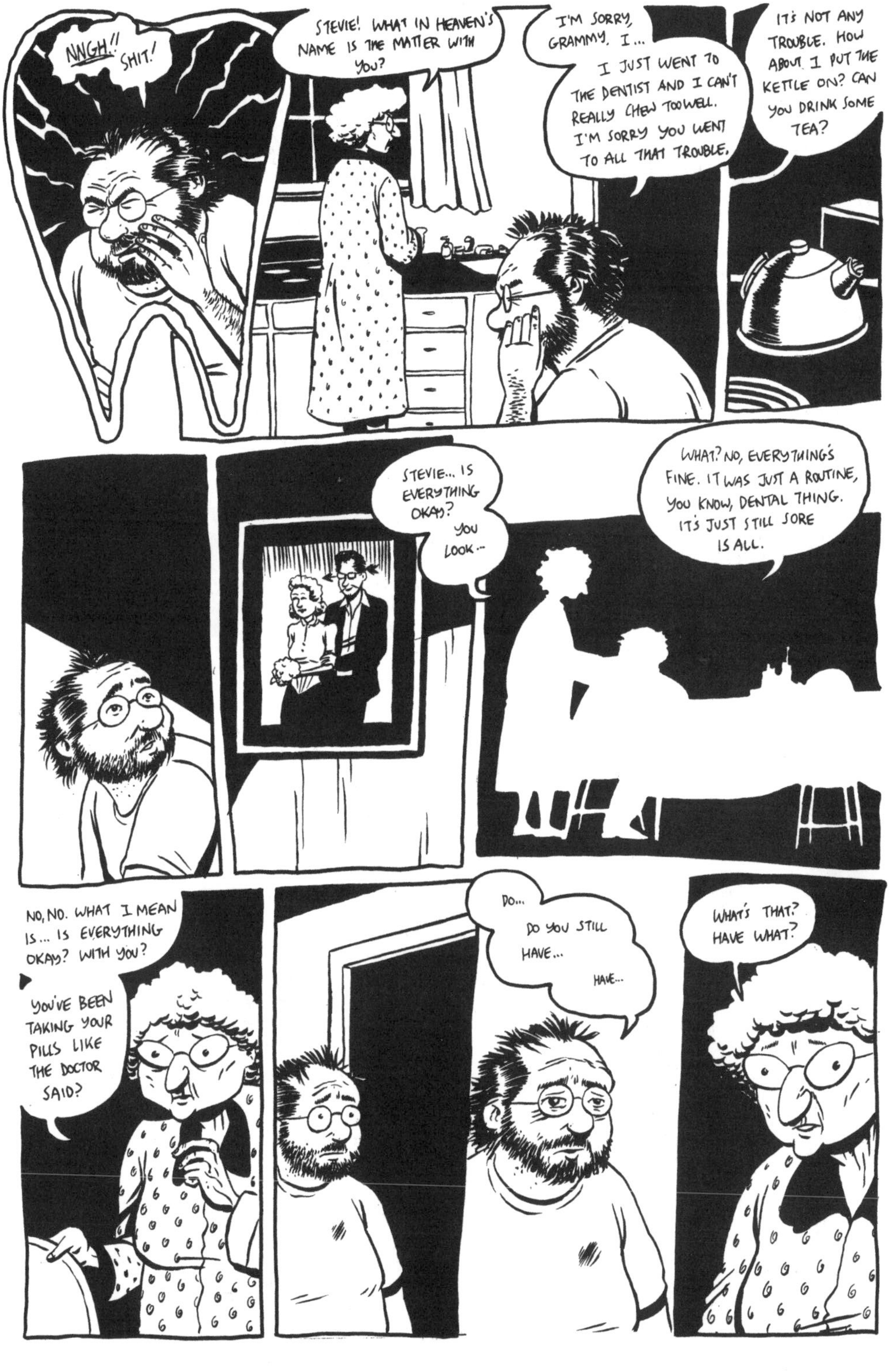
NNGH!! SHIT!
STEVIE! WHAT IN HEAVEN'S NAME IS THE MATTER WITH YOU?
I'M SORRY, GRAMMY, I...
I JUST WENT TO THE DENTIST AND I CAN'T REALLY CHEW TOO WELL. I'M SORRY YOU WENT TO ALL THAT TROUBLE.
IT'S NOT ANY TROUBLE. HOW ABOUT I PUT THE KETTLE ON? CAN YOU DRINK SOME TEA?
STEVIE... IS EVERYTHING OKAY? YOU LOOK...
WHAT? NO, EVERYTHING'S FINE. IT WAS JUST A ROUTINE, YOU KNOW, DENTAL THING. IT'S JUST STILL SORE IS ALL.
NO, NO. WHAT I MEAN IS... IS EVERYTHING OKAY? WITH YOU?
YOU'VE BEEN TAKING YOUR PILLS LIKE THE DOCTOR SAID?
DO...
DO YOU STILL HAVE...
HAVE...
WHAT'S THAT? HAVE WHAT?

I ALMOST TOLD HER. I WANTED TO
TELL HER. SO BADLY. TELL HER THAT I
WASN'T TAKING MY PILLS ANYMORE
BECAUSE IT DIDN'T MATTER BECAUSE I
DIDN'T NEED THEM ANYMORE. I ALMOST
TOLD HER ABOUT THE FAKE RAY PICTURE
THEY SENT ME AND HOW THE REAL RAY WAS
HIDING BUT SENDING ME MESSAGES ~~XXXX~~ HE RECORDED
UNDER A FAKE NAME AND HOW ONCE THEY REALIZED
I WAS STARTING TO FIGURE THIS ALL OUT THEY
STARTED MAKING MY TOOTH HURT, AND THEY EVEN
HAD ME FIRED FROM MY JOB, BUT I STILL WOULDN'T
BACK DOWN SO THEY HAD MY TOOTH GO NUCLEAR SO
I HAD TO PULL IT OUT AND NOW I WAS HERE TO
STEAL ONE OF POPPA'S GUNS SO I COULD GO BACK TO
THE CITY AND FIND THIS FAKE RAY SO I COULD SHOOT
THIS FAKE RAY TO PUT ~~YES~~ AN END TO ALL THIS AND
WHEN I SAY IT ALL OUT LOUD IT MAY SOUND LIKE
I'M CRAZY AND MAYBE I DO NEED THOSE PILLS, AND
HOW I WASN'T SURE IF EVERYTHING WAS FINALLY
CRYSTAL CLEAR OR SPINNING OUT OF CONTROL.

I'M SCARED, GRAMMY.
I'M REAL TERRIFIED, GRAMMY.

IT'S LIKE FIRE. NO, IT'S LIKE BEING ON FIRE.
IMAGINE IF SOMEONE CAME UP TO YOU AND POURED
GASOLINE ON YOU. JUST DOUSED YOU WITH IT SO
MUCH YOU COULD SMELL IT. AND THEN THEY TAKE
OUT A MATCH AND ACTUALLY LIGHT YOU ON FIRE. ON
FIRE. YOU FEEL YOUR SKIN BURNING, SEERING, AND
YOU CAN SMELL YOUR OWN FLESH COOKING LIKE
YOU WERE A PIG. YOU ARE ON FUCKING FIRE,
GODDAMN IT.
BUT THEN SOME JERKBAG TELLS YOU THAT YOU
AREN'T ON FIRE, THAT YOU'RE JUST ~~IMAGING~~
IMAGINING ALL THAT. IT'S ALL IN YOUR HEAD.
YOUR BODY, YOUR SENSES, YOUR NERVES, ARE
ALL LYING TO YOU.
FUCK YOU! CAN'T YOU SEE?! CAN'T YOU FEEL THE
FUCKING HEAT GENERATED AS THE FLAMES
CONSUME MY FUCKING BODY--MY FUCKING BODY.!!
CHRIST, CAN'T YOU SMELL MY BURNING HAIR?
LOOK!! GET ME SOME WATER, QUICK! PLEASE, I'M
BEGGING YOU TO STOP ME BURNING!!
NO.
I WILL NOT GET YOU WATER FOR THE SIMPLE REASON THAT YOU ARE NOT ON FIRE.

I WANTED TO TELL GRAMMY THAT I'M ON FIRE. THIS KIND OLD WOMAN WHO BOUGHT ME COLORING BOOKS ON RAINY
DAYS AND TOOK ME TO SEE "THE MAGIC GOOSE" AT THAT MOVIE THEATRE WITH THE BALCONY AND TOLD THAT BULLY DEREK
RENAN TO STOP PICKING ON ME.
I WANTED TO TELL HER AND HAVE HER TAKE ME IN HER ARMS AND SAY "OH! MY POOR LITTLE STEVE!" AND HUG ME
AND TELL ME THAT EVERYTHING WILL BE OKAY. I WANTED HER TO TELL ME THAT SHE COULD SEE THE FLAMES, TOO,
BUT THAT SHE WAS THERE TO HELP AND THAT EVERYTHING WOULD BE OKAY.

I WANTED TO TELL HER.

I ALMOST TOLD HER.

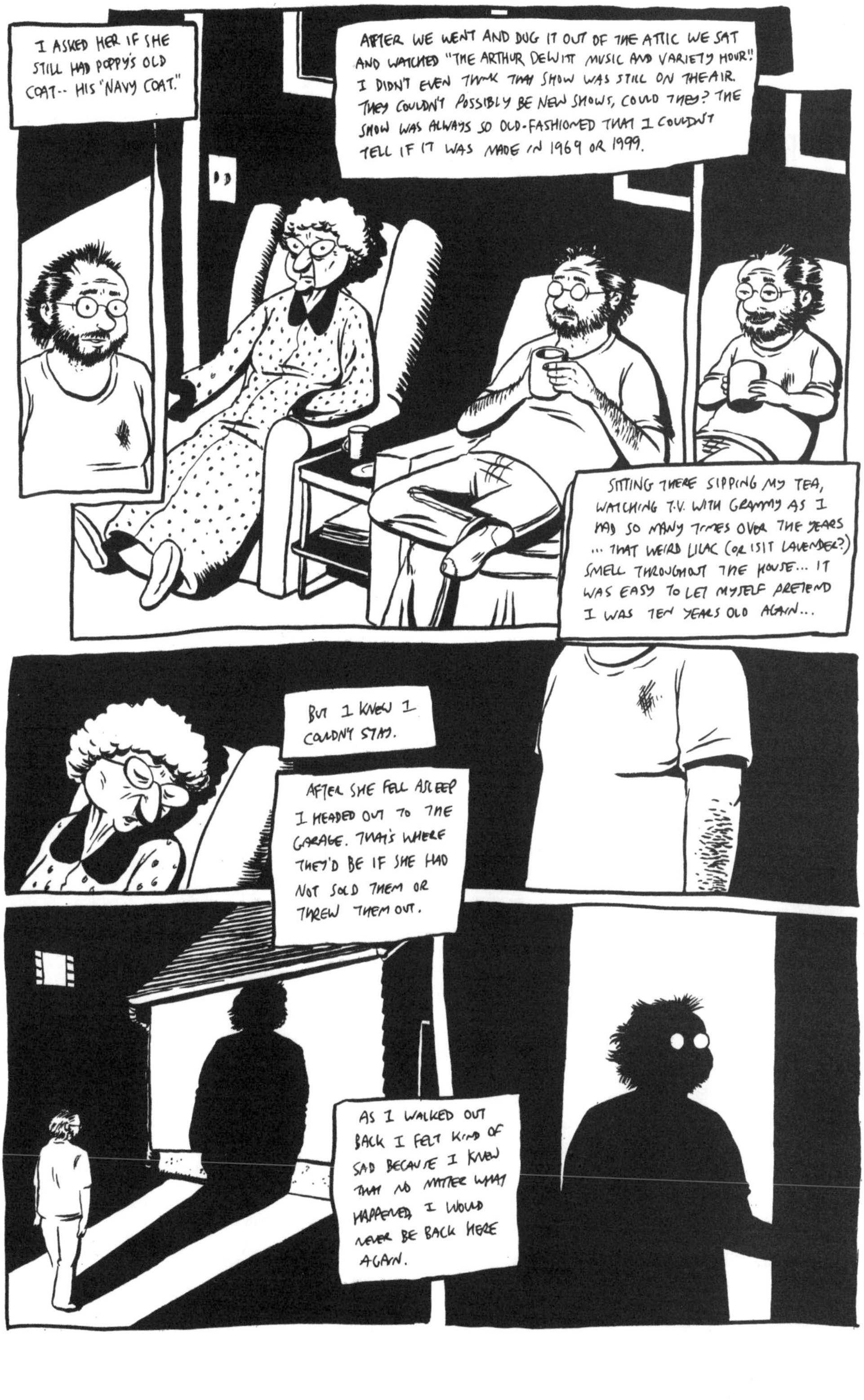
I ASKED HER IF SHE STILL HAD POPPY'S OLD COAT-- HIS "NAVY COAT."
AFTER WE WENT AND DUG IT OUT OF THE ATTIC WE SAT AND WATCHED "THE ARTHUR DEWITT MUSIC AND VARIETY HOUR"! I DIDN'T EVEN THINK THAT SHOW WAS STILL ON THE AIR. THEY COULDN'T POSSIBLY BE NEW SHOWS, COULD THEY? THE SHOW WAS ALWAYS SO OLD-FASHIONED THAT I COULDN'T TELL IF IT WAS MADE IN 1969 OR 1999.
SITTING THERE SIPPING MY TEA, WATCHING T.V. WITH GRAMMY AS I HAD SO MANY TIMES OVER THE YEARS ... THAT WEIRD LILAC (OR IS IT LAVENDER?) SMELL THROUGHOUT THE HOUSE... IT WAS EASY TO LET MYSELF PRETEND I WAS TEN YEARS OLD AGAIN...
BUT I KNEW I COULDN'T STAY.
AFTER SHE FELL ASLEEP I HEADED OUT TO THE GARAGE. THAT'S WHERE THEY'D BE IF SHE HAD NOT SOLD THEM OR THREW THEM OUT.
AS I WALKED OUT BACK I FELT KIND OF SAD BECAUSE I KNEW THAT NO MATTER WHAT HAPPENED, I WOULD NEVER BE BACK HERE AGAIN.

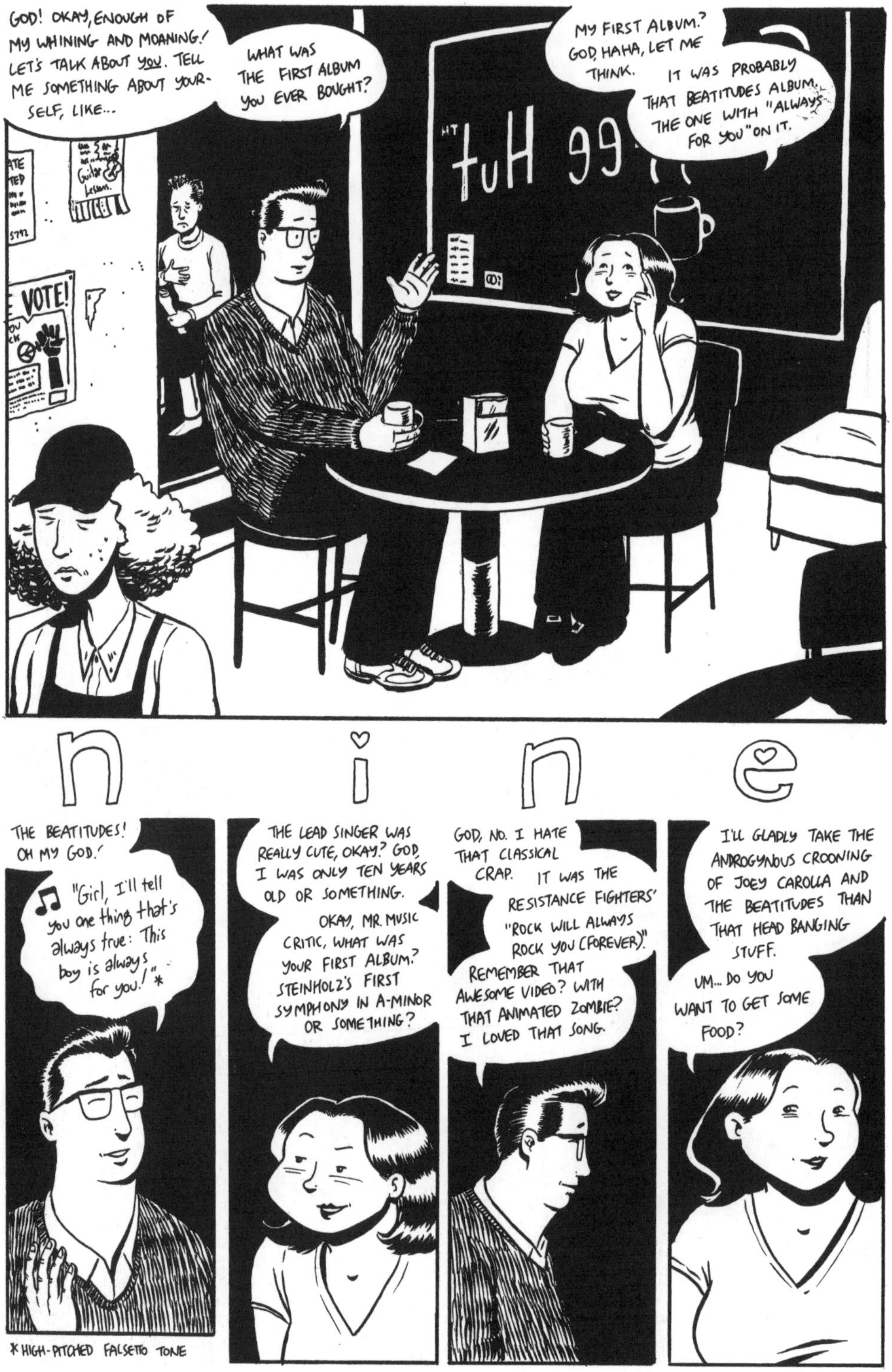
GOD! OKAY, ENOUGH OF MY WHINING AND MOANING! LET'S TALK ABOUT YOU. TELL ME SOMETHING ABOUT YOURSELF, LIKE...
WHAT WAS THE FIRST ALBUM YOU EVER BOUGHT?
MY FIRST ALBUM? GOD, HAHA, LET ME THINK.
IT WAS PROBABLY THAT BEATITUDES ALBUM. THE ONE WITH "ALWAYS FOR YOU" ON IT.
VOTE!
Guitar Lessons
nine
THE BEATITUDES! OH MY GOD!
♫ "Girl, I'll tell you one thing that's always true: This boy is always for you!" *
THE LEAD SINGER WAS REALLY CUTE, OKAY? GOD, I WAS ONLY TEN YEARS OLD OR SOMETHING.
OKAY, MR. MUSIC CRITIC, WHAT WAS YOUR FIRST ALBUM? STEINHOLZ'S FIRST SYMPHONY IN A-MINOR OR SOMETHING?
GOD, NO. I HATE THAT CLASSICAL CRAP.
IT WAS THE RESISTANCE FIGHTERS' "ROCK WILL ALWAYS ROCK YOU (FOREVER)."
REMEMBER THAT AWESOME VIDEO? WITH THAT ANIMATED ZOMBIE? I LOVED THAT SONG.
I'LL GLADLY TAKE THE ANDROGYNOUS CROONING OF JOEY CAROLLA AND THE BEATITUDES THAN THAT HEAD BANGING STUFF.
UM... DO YOU WANT TO GET SOME FOOD?
* HIGH-PITCHED FALSETTO TONE

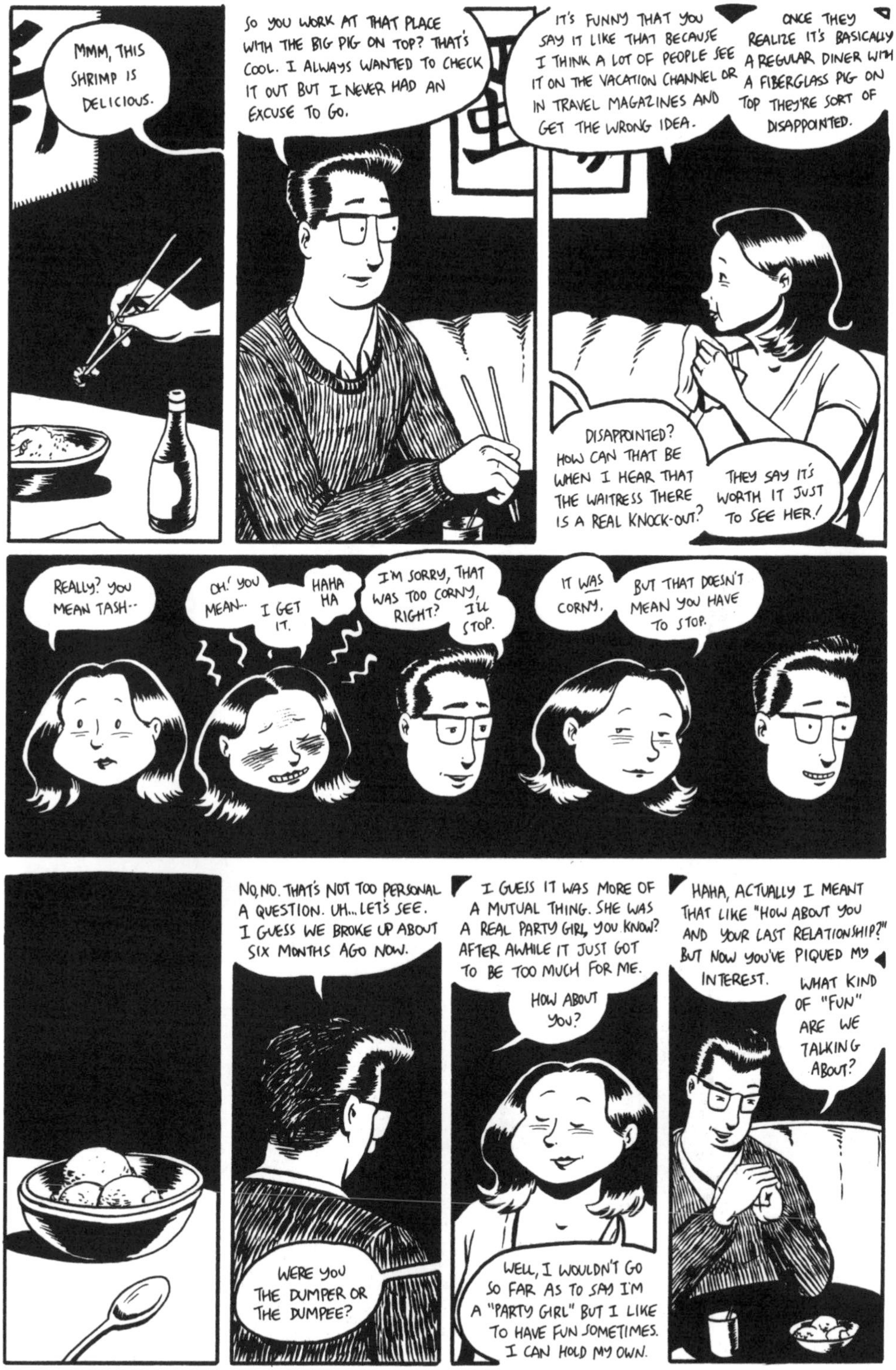
MMM, THIS SHRIMP IS DELICIOUS.
SO YOU WORK AT THAT PLACE WITH THE BIG PIG ON TOP? THAT'S COOL. I ALWAYS WANTED TO CHECK IT OUT BUT I NEVER HAD AN EXCUSE TO GO.
IT'S FUNNY THAT YOU SAY IT LIKE THAT BECAUSE I THINK A LOT OF PEOPLE SEE IT ON THE VACATION CHANNEL OR IN TRAVEL MAGAZINES AND GET THE WRONG IDEA.
ONCE THEY REALIZE IT'S BASICALLY A REGULAR DINER WITH A FIBERGLASS PIG ON TOP THEY'RE SORT OF DISAPPOINTED.
DISAPPOINTED? HOW CAN THAT BE WHEN I HEAR THAT THE WAITRESS THERE IS A REAL KNOCK-OUT?
THEY SAY IT'S WORTH IT JUST TO SEE HER!
REALLY? YOU MEAN TASH--
OH! YOU MEAN..
I GET IT.
HAHA HA
I'M SORRY, THAT WAS TOO CORNY, RIGHT?
I'LL STOP.
IT WAS CORNY.
BUT THAT DOESN'T MEAN YOU HAVE TO STOP.
NO, NO. THAT'S NOT TOO PERSONAL A QUESTION. UH... LET'S SEE. I GUESS WE BROKE UP ABOUT SIX MONTHS AGO NOW.
WERE YOU THE DUMPER OR THE DUMPEE?
I GUESS IT WAS MORE OF A MUTUAL THING. SHE WAS A REAL PARTY GIRL, YOU KNOW? AFTER AWHILE IT JUST GOT TO BE TOO MUCH FOR ME.
HOW ABOUT YOU?
WELL, I WOULDN'T GO SO FAR AS TO SAY I'M A "PARTY GIRL" BUT I LIKE TO HAVE FUN SOMETIMES. I CAN HOLD MY OWN.
HAHA, ACTUALLY I MEANT THAT LIKE "HOW ABOUT YOU AND YOUR LAST RELATIONSHIP?" BUT NOW YOU'VE PIQUED MY INTEREST.
WHAT KIND OF "FUN" ARE WE TALKING ABOUT?

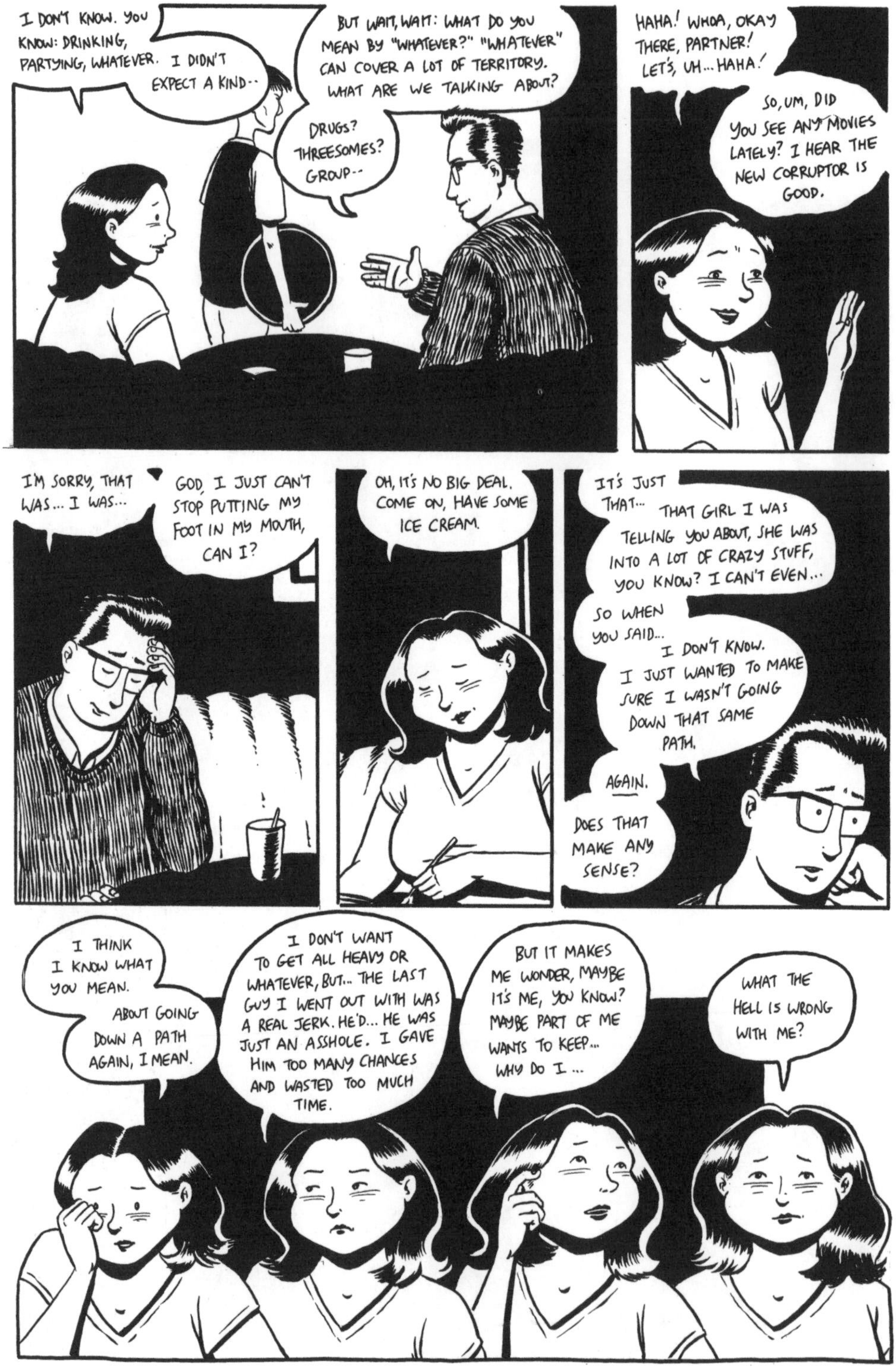
I DON'T KNOW. YOU KNOW: DRINKING, PARTYING, WHATEVER.
I DIDN'T EXPECT A KIND--
BUT WAIT, WAIT: WHAT DO YOU MEAN BY "WHATEVER?" "WHATEVER" CAN COVER A LOT OF TERRITORY. WHAT ARE WE TALKING ABOUT?
DRUGS? THREESOMES? GROUP--
HAHA! WHOA, OKAY THERE, PARTNER! LET'S, UH... HAHA!
SO, UM, DID YOU SEE ANY MOVIES LATELY? I HEAR THE NEW CORRUPTOR IS GOOD.
I'M SORRY, THAT WAS... I WAS...
GOD, I JUST CAN'T STOP PUTTING MY FOOT IN MY MOUTH, CAN I?
OH, IT'S NO BIG DEAL. COME ON, HAVE SOME ICE CREAM.
IT'S JUST THAT...
THAT GIRL I WAS TELLING YOU ABOUT, SHE WAS INTO A LOT OF CRAZY STUFF, YOU KNOW? I CAN'T EVEN...
SO WHEN YOU SAID...
I DON'T KNOW. I JUST WANTED TO MAKE SURE I WASN'T GOING DOWN THAT SAME PATH.
AGAIN.
DOES THAT MAKE ANY SENSE?
I THINK I KNOW WHAT YOU MEAN.
ABOUT GOING DOWN A PATH AGAIN, I MEAN.
I DON'T WANT TO GET ALL HEAVY OR WHATEVER, BUT... THE LAST GUY I WENT OUT WITH WAS A REAL JERK. HE'D... HE WAS JUST AN ASSHOLE. I GAVE HIM TOO MANY CHANCES AND WASTED TOO MUCH TIME.
BUT IT MAKES ME WONDER, MAYBE IT'S ME, YOU KNOW? MAYBE PART OF ME WANTS TO KEEP... WHY DO I ...
WHAT THE HELL IS WRONG WITH ME?

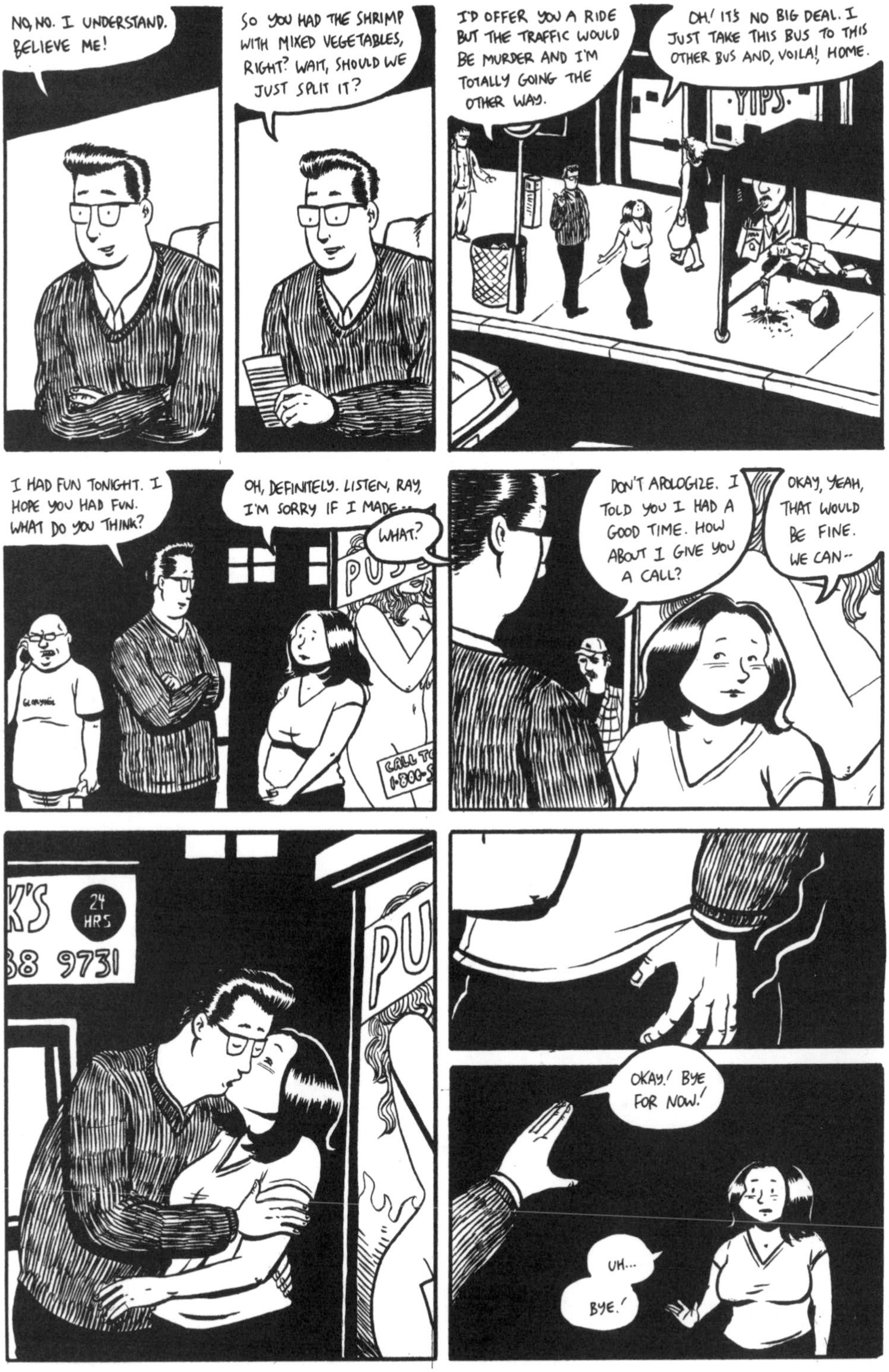
NO, NO. I UNDERSTAND. BELIEVE ME!
SO YOU HAD THE SHRIMP WITH MIXED VEGETABLES, RIGHT? WAIT, SHOULD WE JUST SPLIT IT?
I'D OFFER YOU A RIDE BUT THE TRAFFIC WOULD BE MURDER AND I'M TOTALLY GOING THE OTHER WAY.
OH! IT'S NO BIG DEAL. I JUST TAKE THIS BUS TO THIS OTHER BUS AND, VOILA!, HOME.
YIPS
I HAD FUN TONIGHT. I HOPE YOU HAD FUN. WHAT DO YOU THINK?
OH, DEFINITELY. LISTEN, RAY, I'M SORRY IF I MADE--
WHAT?
DON'T APOLOGIZE. I TOLD YOU I HAD A GOOD TIME. HOW ABOUT I GIVE YOU A CALL?
OKAY, YEAH, THAT WOULD BE FINE. WE CAN--
K'S
24 HRS
38 9731
PU
OKAY! BYE FOR NOW!
UH...
BYE!

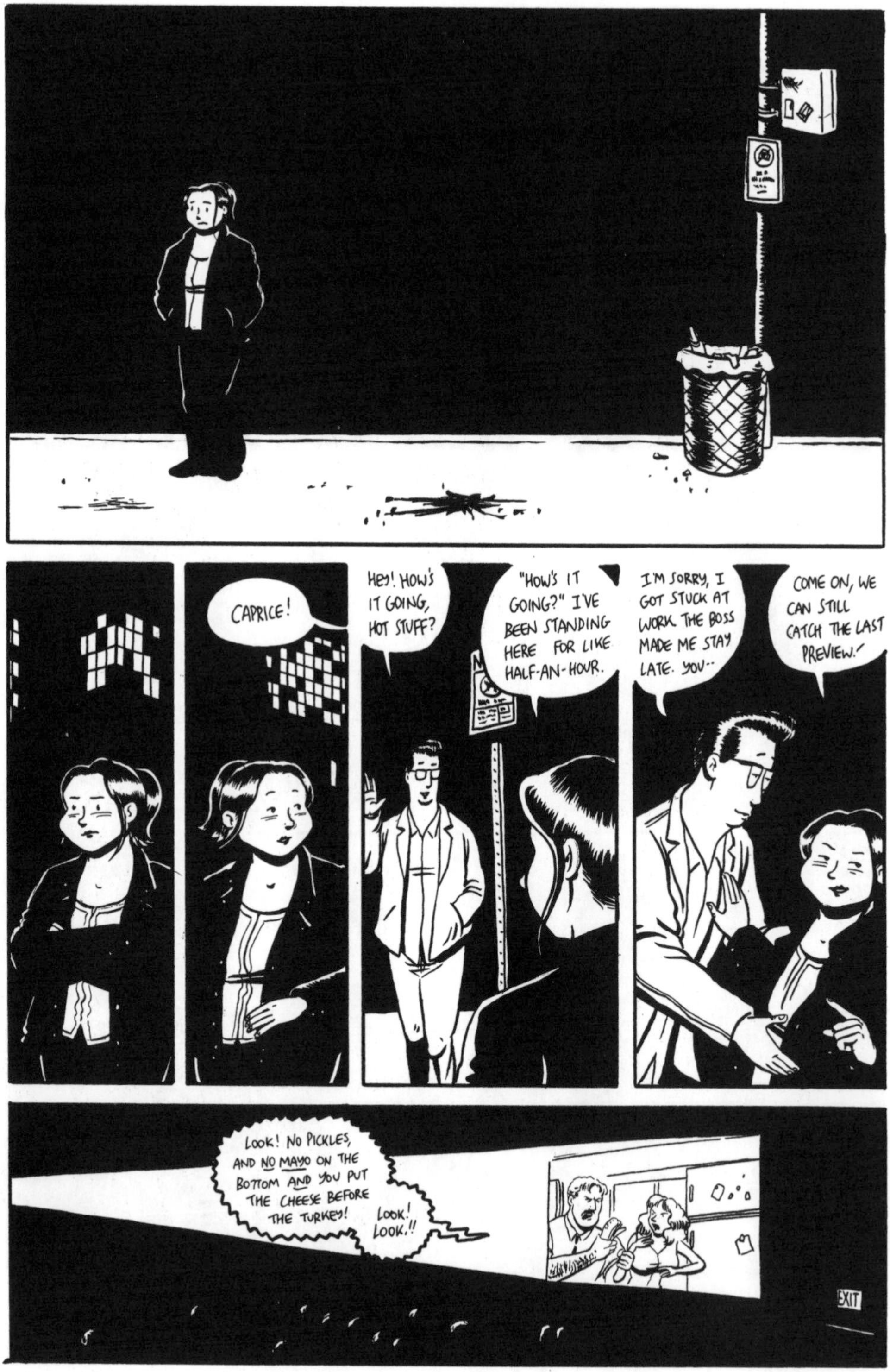
CAPRICE!
HEY! HOW'S IT GOING, HOT STUFF?
"HOW'S IT GOING?" I'VE BEEN STANDING HERE FOR LIKE HALF-AN-HOUR.
I'M SORRY, I GOT STUCK AT WORK. THE BOSS MADE ME STAY LATE. YOU--
COME ON, WE CAN STILL CATCH THE LAST PREVIEW!
LOOK! NO PICKLES, AND NO MAYO ON THE BOTTOM AND YOU PUT THE CHEESE BEFORE THE TURKEY!
LOOK! LOOK!!
EXIT

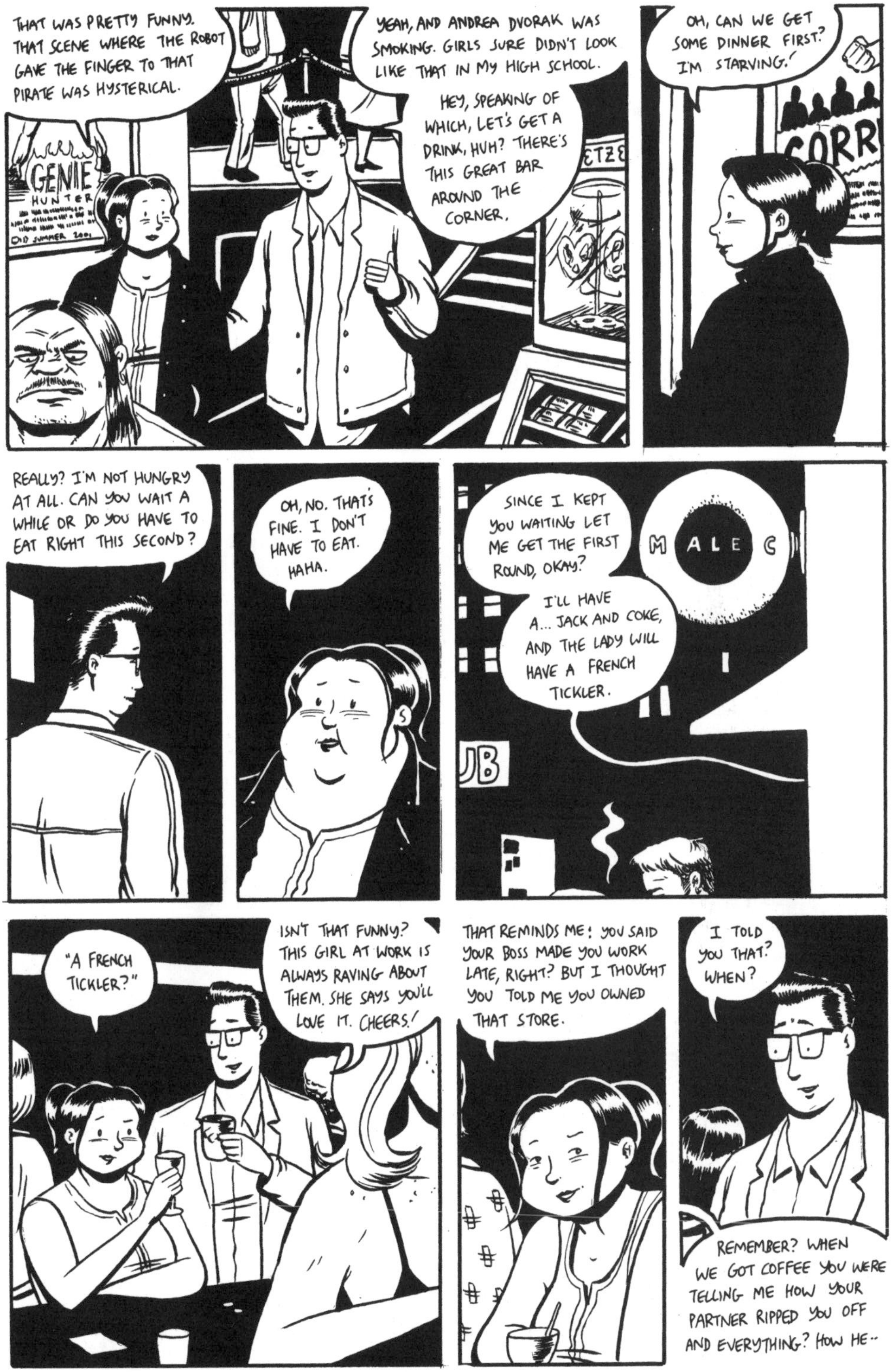
THAT WAS PRETTY FUNNY. THAT SCENE WHERE THE ROBOT GAVE THE FINGER TO THAT PIRATE WAS HYSTERICAL.
GENIE HUNTER
SUMMER 2001
YEAH, AND ANDREA DVORAK WAS SMOKING. GIRLS SURE DIDN'T LOOK LIKE THAT IN MY HIGH SCHOOL.
HEY, SPEAKING OF WHICH, LET'S GET A DRINK, HUH? THERE'S THIS GREAT BAR AROUND THE CORNER.
OH, CAN WE GET SOME DINNER FIRST? I'M STARVING!
REALLY? I'M NOT HUNGRY AT ALL. CAN YOU WAIT A WHILE OR DO YOU HAVE TO EAT RIGHT THIS SECOND?
OH, NO. THAT'S FINE. I DON'T HAVE TO EAT. HAHA.
SINCE I KEPT YOU WAITING LET ME GET THE FIRST ROUND, OKAY?
M ALE C
I'LL HAVE A... JACK AND COKE, AND THE LADY WILL HAVE A FRENCH TICKLER.
"A FRENCH TICKLER?"
ISN'T THAT FUNNY? THIS GIRL AT WORK IS ALWAYS RAVING ABOUT THEM. SHE SAYS YOU'LL LOVE IT. CHEERS!
THAT REMINDS ME: YOU SAID YOUR BOSS MADE YOU WORK LATE, RIGHT? BUT I THOUGHT YOU TOLD ME YOU OWNED THAT STORE.
I TOLD YOU THAT? WHEN?
REMEMBER? WHEN WE GOT COFFEE YOU WERE TELLING ME HOW YOUR PARTNER RIPPED YOU OFF AND EVERYTHING? HOW HE..

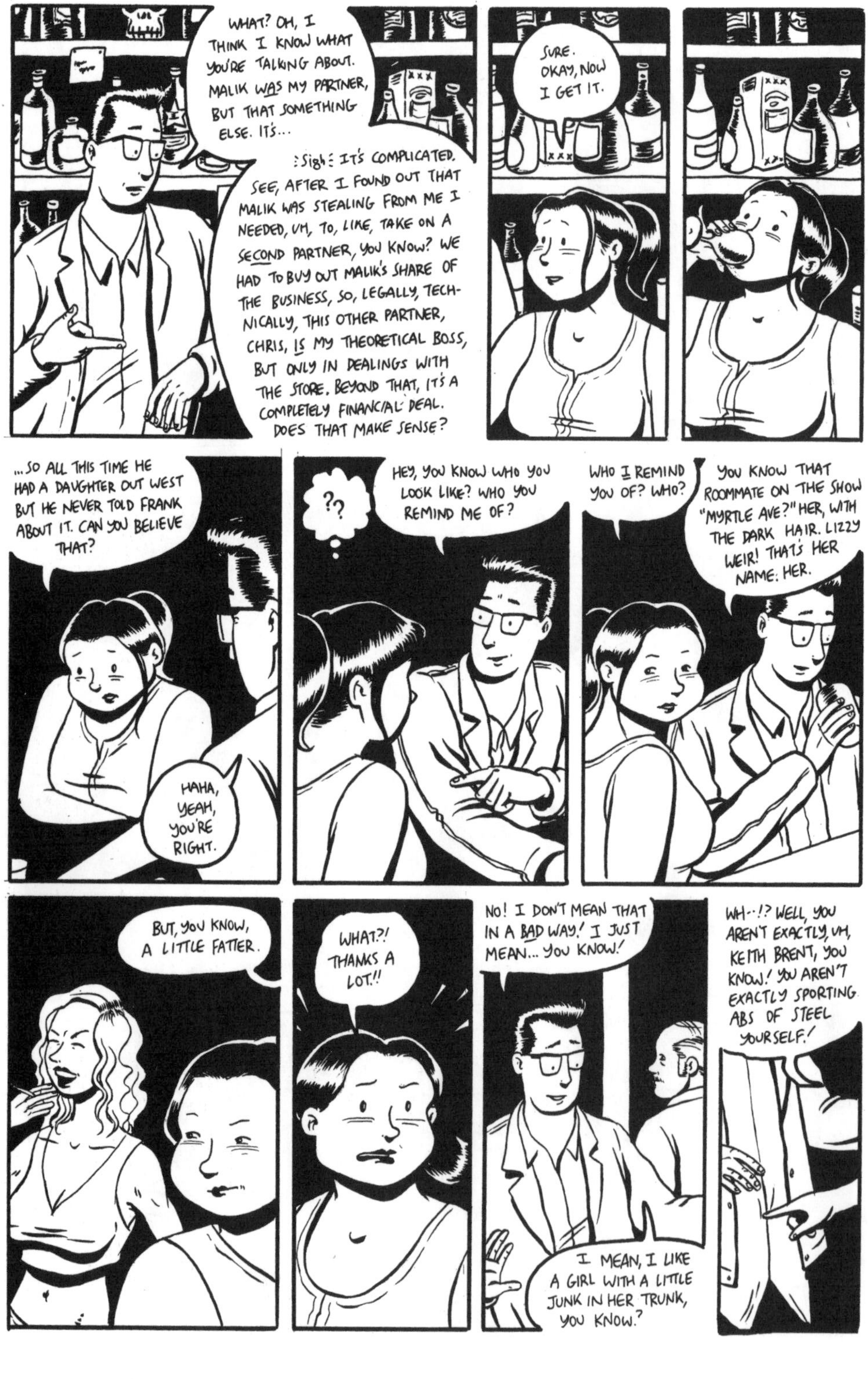
WHAT? OH, I THINK I KNOW WHAT YOU'RE TALKING ABOUT. MALIK WAS MY PARTNER, BUT THAT SOMETHING ELSE. IT'S...
:SIGH: IT'S COMPLICATED. SEE, AFTER I FOUND OUT THAT MALIK WAS STEALING FROM ME I NEEDED, UH, TO, LIKE, TAKE ON A SECOND PARTNER, YOU KNOW? WE HAD TO BUY OUT MALIK'S SHARE OF THE BUSINESS, SO, LEGALLY, TECHNICALLY, THIS OTHER PARTNER, CHRIS, IS MY THEORETICAL BOSS, BUT ONLY IN DEALINGS WITH THE STORE. BEYOND THAT, IT'S A COMPLETELY FINANCIAL DEAL. DOES THAT MAKE SENSE?
SURE. OKAY, NOW I GET IT.
...SO ALL THIS TIME HE HAD A DAUGHTER OUT WEST BUT HE NEVER TOLD FRANK ABOUT IT. CAN YOU BELIEVE THAT?
HAHA, YEAH, YOU'RE RIGHT.
??
HEY, YOU KNOW WHO YOU LOOK LIKE? WHO YOU REMIND ME OF?
WHO I REMIND YOU OF? WHO?
YOU KNOW THAT ROOMMATE ON THE SHOW "MYRTLE AVE?" HER, WITH THE DARK HAIR. LIZZY WEIR! THAT'S HER NAME. HER.
BUT, YOU KNOW, A LITTLE FATTER.
WHAT?! THANKS A LOT!!
NO! I DON'T MEAN THAT IN A BAD WAY! I JUST MEAN... YOU KNOW!
I MEAN, I LIKE A GIRL WITH A LITTLE JUNK IN HER TRUNK, YOU KNOW?
WH--!? WELL, YOU AREN'T EXACTLY, UH, KEITH BRENT, YOU KNOW! YOU AREN'T EXACTLY SPORTING ABS OF STEEL YOURSELF!

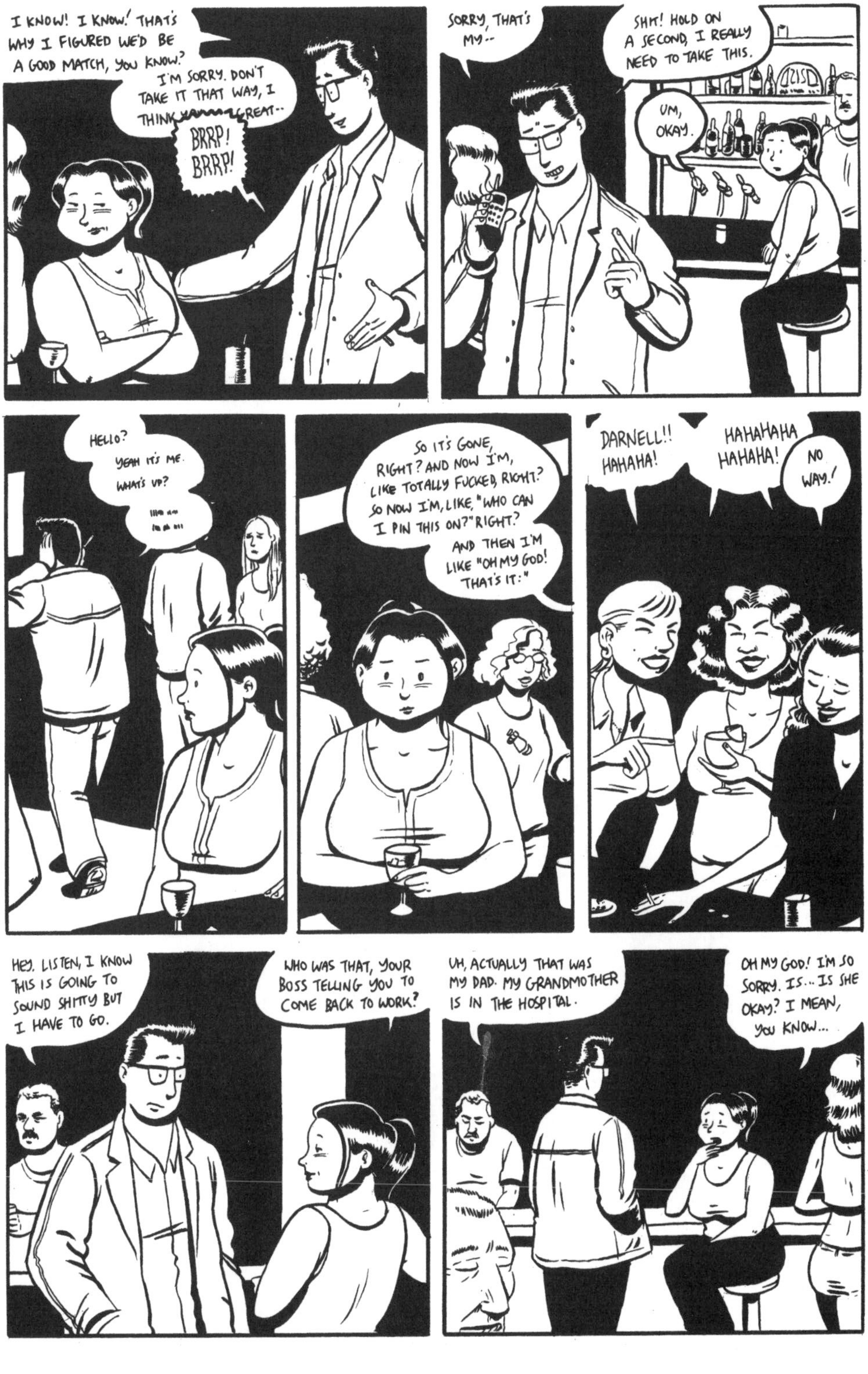
I KNOW! I KNOW! THAT'S WHY I FIGURED WE'D BE A GOOD MATCH, YOU KNOW?
I'M SORRY. DON'T TAKE IT THAT WAY, I THINK GREAT..
BRRP! BRRP!
SORRY, THAT'S MY..
SHIT! HOLD ON A SECOND, I REALLY NEED TO TAKE THIS.
UM, OKAY.
HELLO? YEAH IT'S ME. WHAT'S UP?
SO IT'S GONE, RIGHT? AND NOW I'M, LIKE TOTALLY FUCKED, RIGHT? SO NOW I'M, LIKE, "WHO CAN I PIN THIS ON?" RIGHT?
AND THEN I'M LIKE "OH MY GOD! THAT'S IT:"
DARNELL!! HAHAHA!
HAHAHAHA HAHAHA!
NO WAY!
HEY. LISTEN, I KNOW THIS IS GOING TO SOUND SHITTY BUT I HAVE TO GO.
WHO WAS THAT, YOUR BOSS TELLING YOU TO COME BACK TO WORK?
UH, ACTUALLY THAT WAS MY DAD. MY GRANDMOTHER IS IN THE HOSPITAL.
OH MY GOD! I'M SO SORRY. IS.. IS SHE OKAY? I MEAN, YOU KNOW...

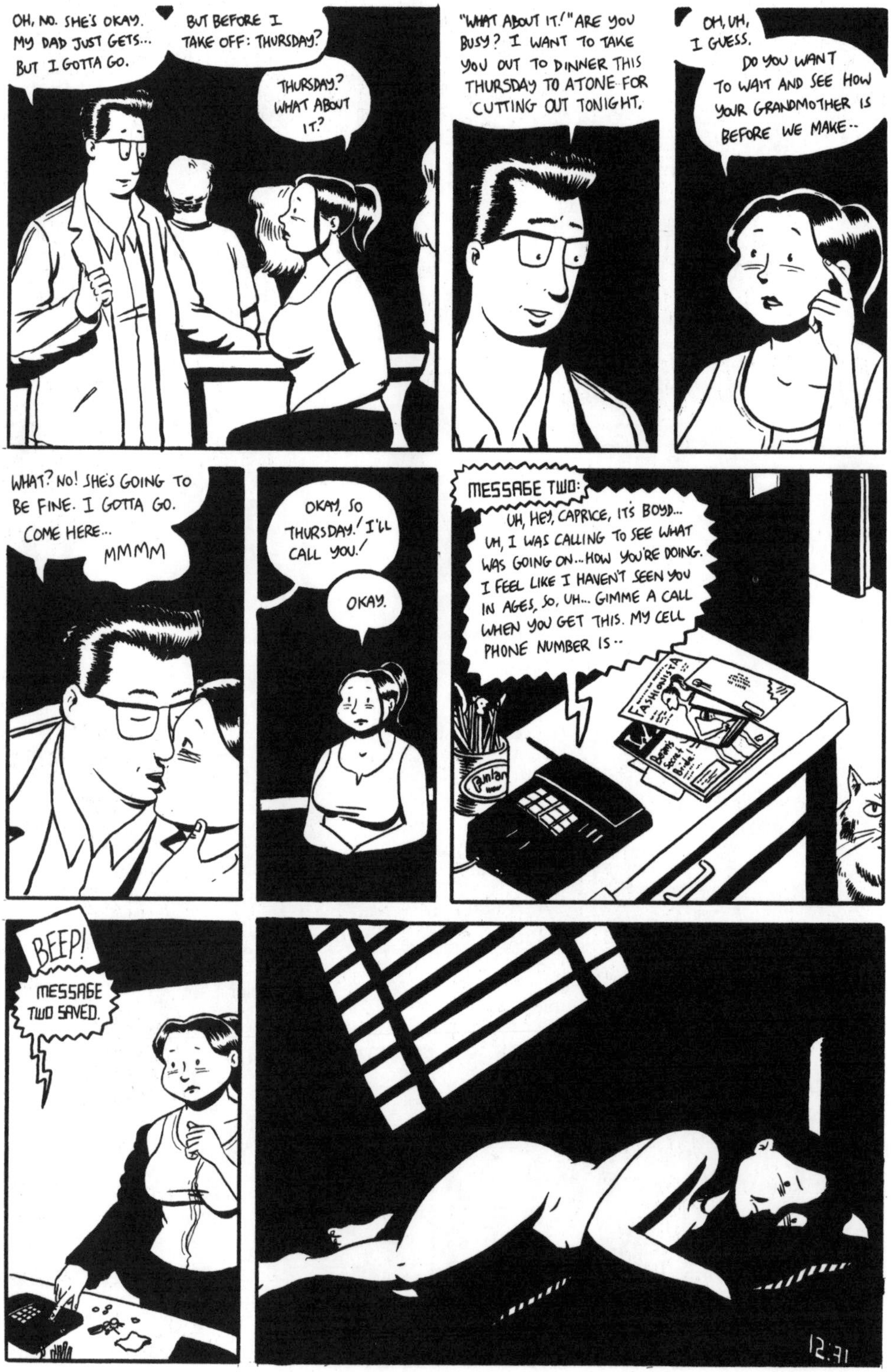
OH, NO. SHE'S OKAY. MY DAD JUST GETS... BUT I GOTTA GO.
BUT BEFORE I TAKE OFF: THURSDAY?
THURSDAY? WHAT ABOUT IT?
"WHAT ABOUT IT!" ARE YOU BUSY? I WANT TO TAKE YOU OUT TO DINNER THIS THURSDAY TO ATONE FOR CUTTING OUT TONIGHT.
OH, UH, I GUESS.
DO YOU WANT TO WAIT AND SEE HOW YOUR GRANDMOTHER IS BEFORE WE MAKE..
WHAT? NO! SHE'S GOING TO BE FINE. I GOTTA GO. COME HERE...
MMMM
OKAY, SO THURSDAY! I'LL CALL YOU!
OKAY.
MESSAGE TWO:
UH, HEY, CAPRICE, IT'S BOYD... UH, I WAS CALLING TO SEE WHAT WAS GOING ON... HOW YOU'RE DOING. I FEEL LIKE I HAVEN'T SEEN YOU IN AGES, SO, UH... GIMME A CALL WHEN YOU GET THIS. MY CELL PHONE NUMBER IS..
FASHIONISTA
BEEP!
MESSAGE TWO SAVED.
12:31

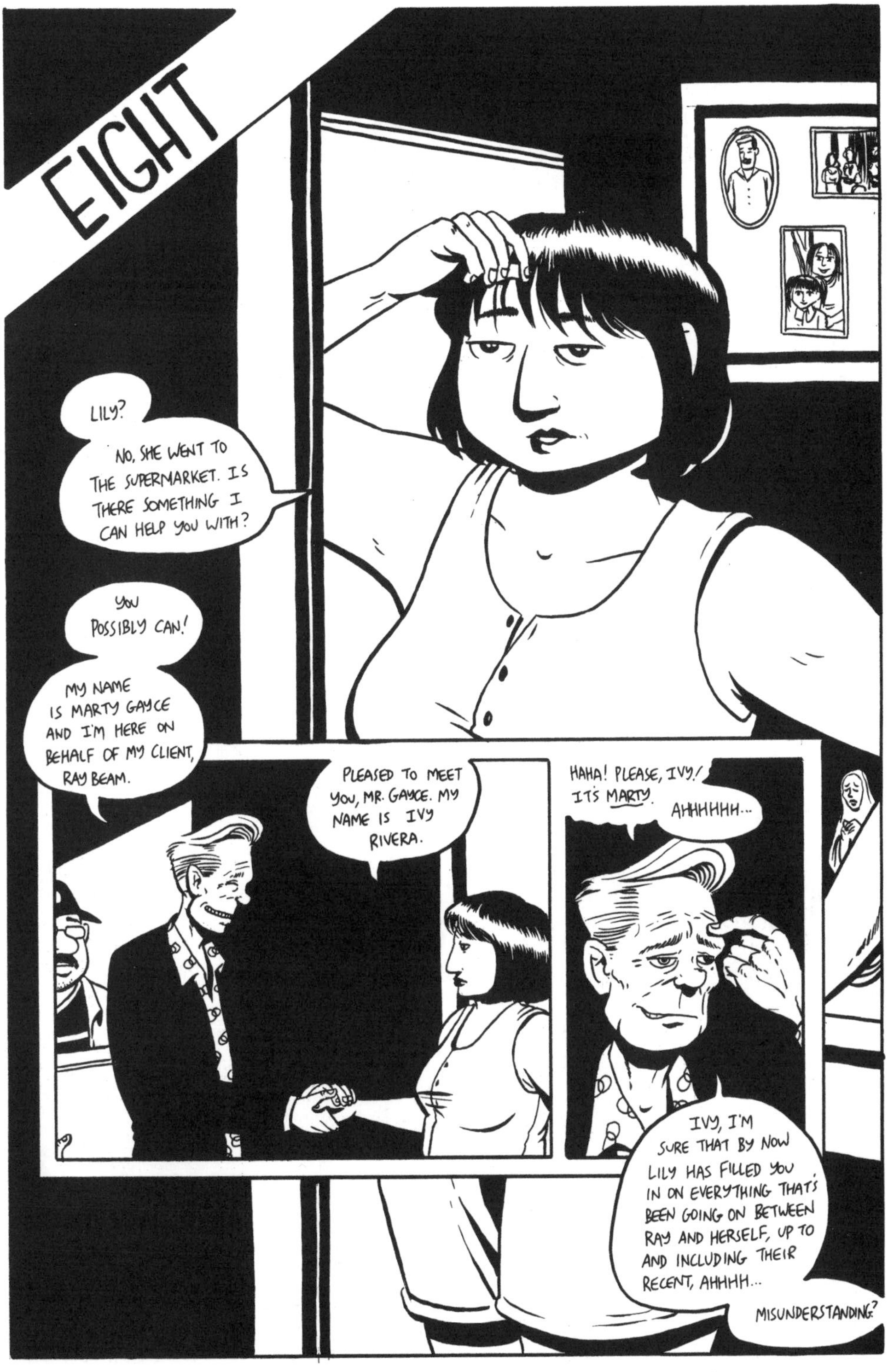
EIGHT
LILY?
NO, SHE WENT TO THE SUPERMARKET. IS THERE SOMETHING I CAN HELP YOU WITH?
YOU POSSIBLY CAN!
MY NAME IS MARTY GAYCE AND I'M HERE ON BEHALF OF MY CLIENT, RAY BEAM.
PLEASED TO MEET YOU, MR. GAYCE. MY NAME IS IVY RIVERA.
HAHA! PLEASE, IVY! IT'S MARTY.
AHHHHHH...
IVY, I'M SURE THAT BY NOW LILY HAS FILLED YOU IN ON EVERYTHING THAT'S BEEN GOING ON BETWEEN RAY AND HERSELF, UP TO AND INCLUDING THEIR RECENT, AHHHH...
MISUNDERSTANDING?

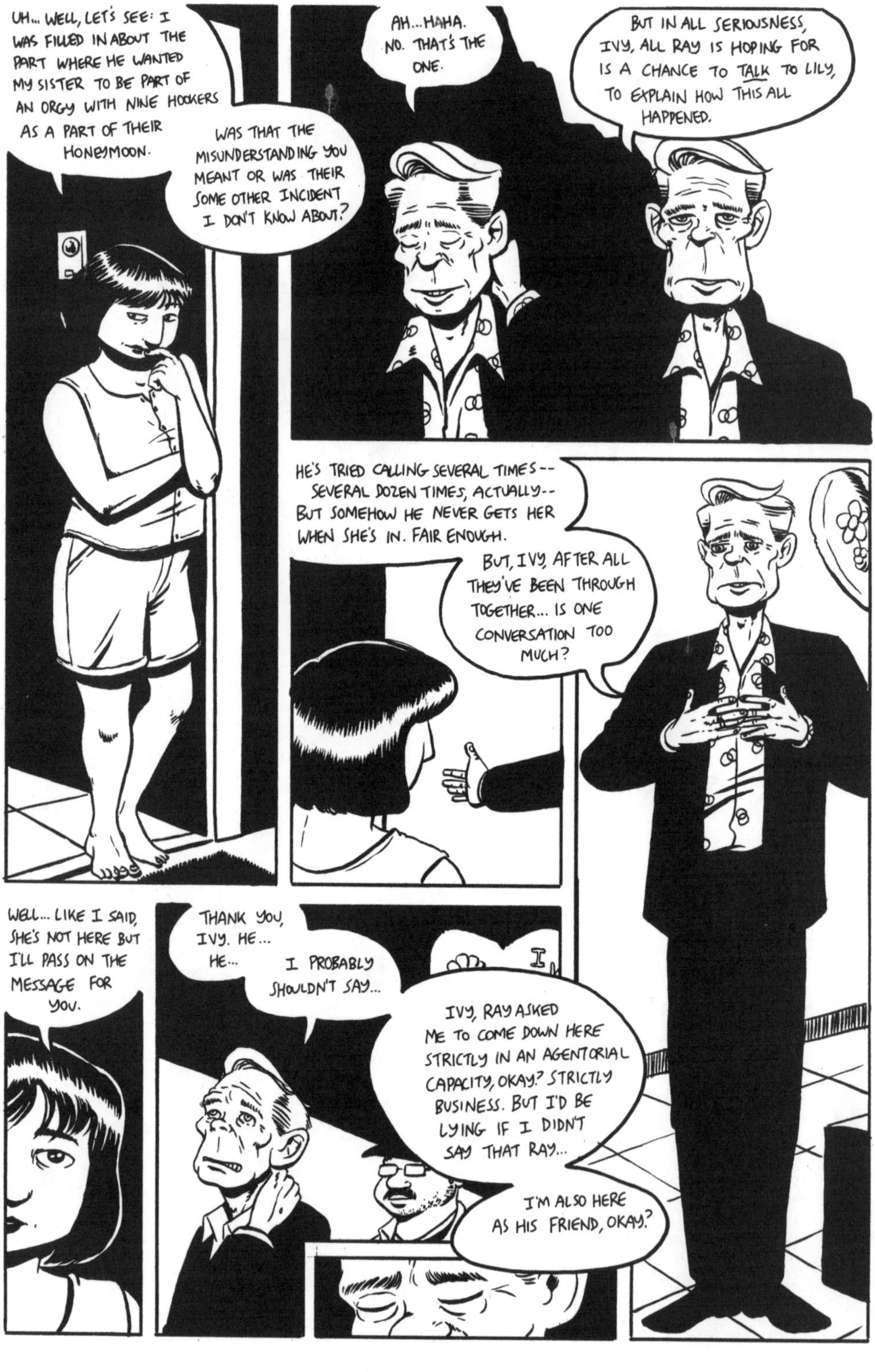
UH... WELL, LET'S SEE: I WAS FILLED IN ABOUT THE PART WHERE HE WANTED MY SISTER TO BE PART OF AN ORGY WITH NINE HOOKERS AS A PART OF THEIR HONEYMOON.
WAS THAT THE MISUNDERSTANDING YOU MEANT OR WAS THEIR SOME OTHER INCIDENT I DON'T KNOW ABOUT?
AH... HAHA. NO. THAT'S THE ONE.
BUT IN ALL SERIOUSNESS, IVY, ALL RAY IS HOPING FOR IS A CHANCE TO TALK TO LILY, TO EXPLAIN HOW THIS ALL HAPPENED.
HE'S TRIED CALLING SEVERAL TIMES -- SEVERAL DOZEN TIMES, ACTUALLY -- BUT SOMEHOW HE NEVER GETS HER WHEN SHE'S IN. FAIR ENOUGH.
BUT, IVY, AFTER ALL THEY'VE BEEN THROUGH TOGETHER... IS ONE CONVERSATION TOO MUCH?
WELL... LIKE I SAID, SHE'S NOT HERE BUT I'LL PASS ON THE MESSAGE FOR YOU.
THANK YOU, IVY. HE... HE...
I PROBABLY SHOULDN'T SAY...
IVY, RAY ASKED ME TO COME DOWN HERE STRICTLY IN AN AGENTORIAL CAPACITY, OKAY? STRICTLY BUSINESS. BUT I'D BE LYING IF I DIDN'T SAY THAT RAY...
I'M ALSO HERE AS HIS FRIEND, OKAY?

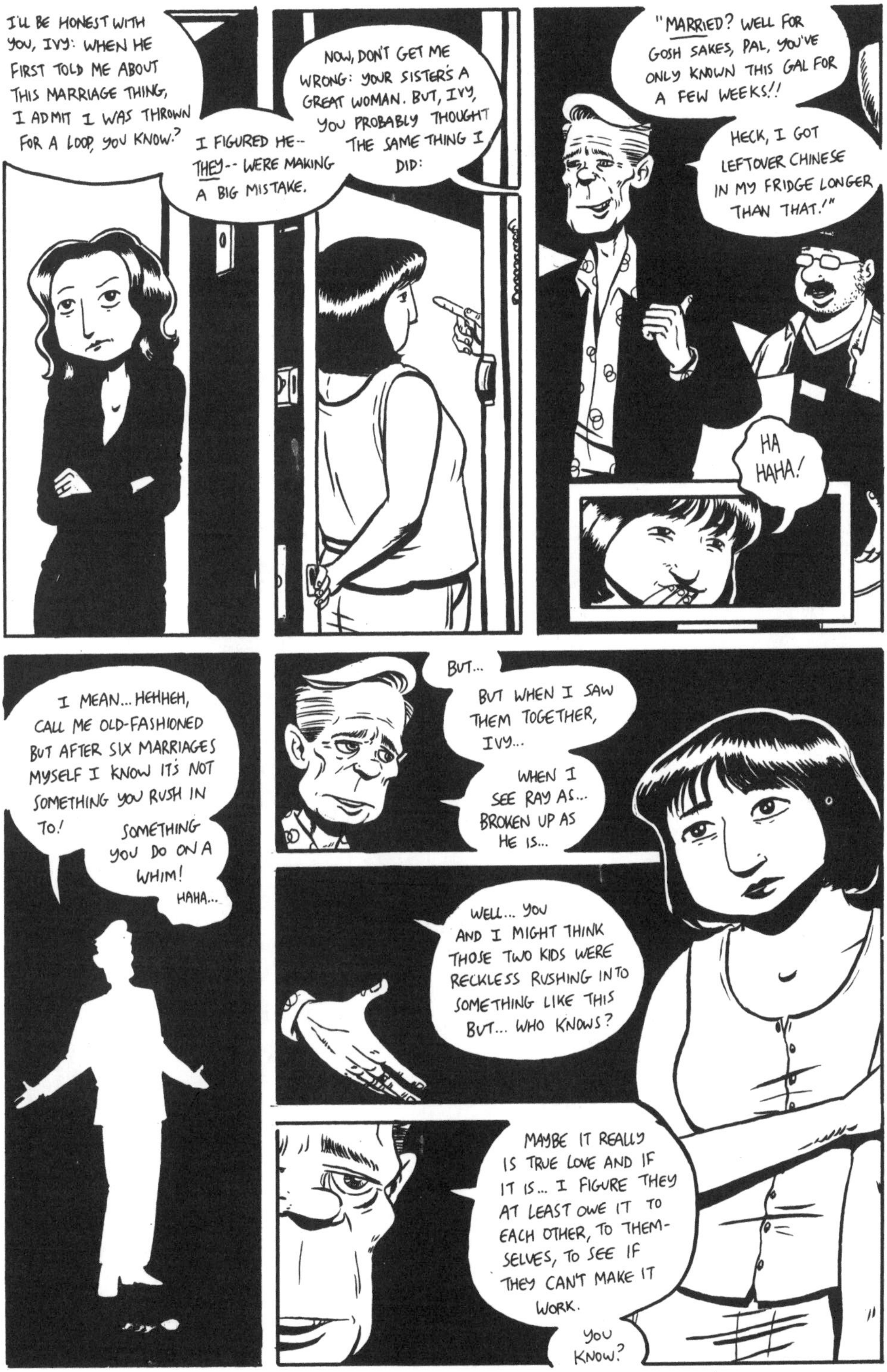
I'LL BE HONEST WITH YOU, IVY: WHEN HE FIRST TOLD ME ABOUT THIS MARRIAGE THING, I ADMIT I WAS THROWN FOR A LOOP, YOU KNOW?
I FIGURED HE-- THEY-- WERE MAKING A BIG MISTAKE.
NOW, DON'T GET ME WRONG: YOUR SISTER'S A GREAT WOMAN. BUT, IVY, YOU PROBABLY THOUGHT THE SAME THING I DID:
"MARRIED? WELL FOR GOSH SAKES, PAL, YOU'VE ONLY KNOWN THIS GAL FOR A FEW WEEKS!!
HECK, I GOT LEFTOVER CHINESE IN MY FRIDGE LONGER THAN THAT!"
HA HAHA!
I MEAN... HEHHEH, CALL ME OLD-FASHIONED BUT AFTER SIX MARRIAGES MYSELF I KNOW IT'S NOT SOMETHING YOU RUSH IN TO!
SOMETHING YOU DO ON A WHIM! HAHA...
BUT...
BUT WHEN I SAW THEM TOGETHER, IVY...
WHEN I SEE RAY AS... BROKEN UP AS HE IS...
WELL... YOU AND I MIGHT THINK THOSE TWO KIDS WERE RECKLESS RUSHING INTO SOMETHING LIKE THIS BUT... WHO KNOWS?
MAYBE IT REALLY IS TRUE LOVE AND IF IT IS... I FIGURE THEY AT LEAST OWE IT TO EACH OTHER, TO THEM-SELVES, TO SEE IF THEY CAN'T MAKE IT WORK.
YOU KNOW?

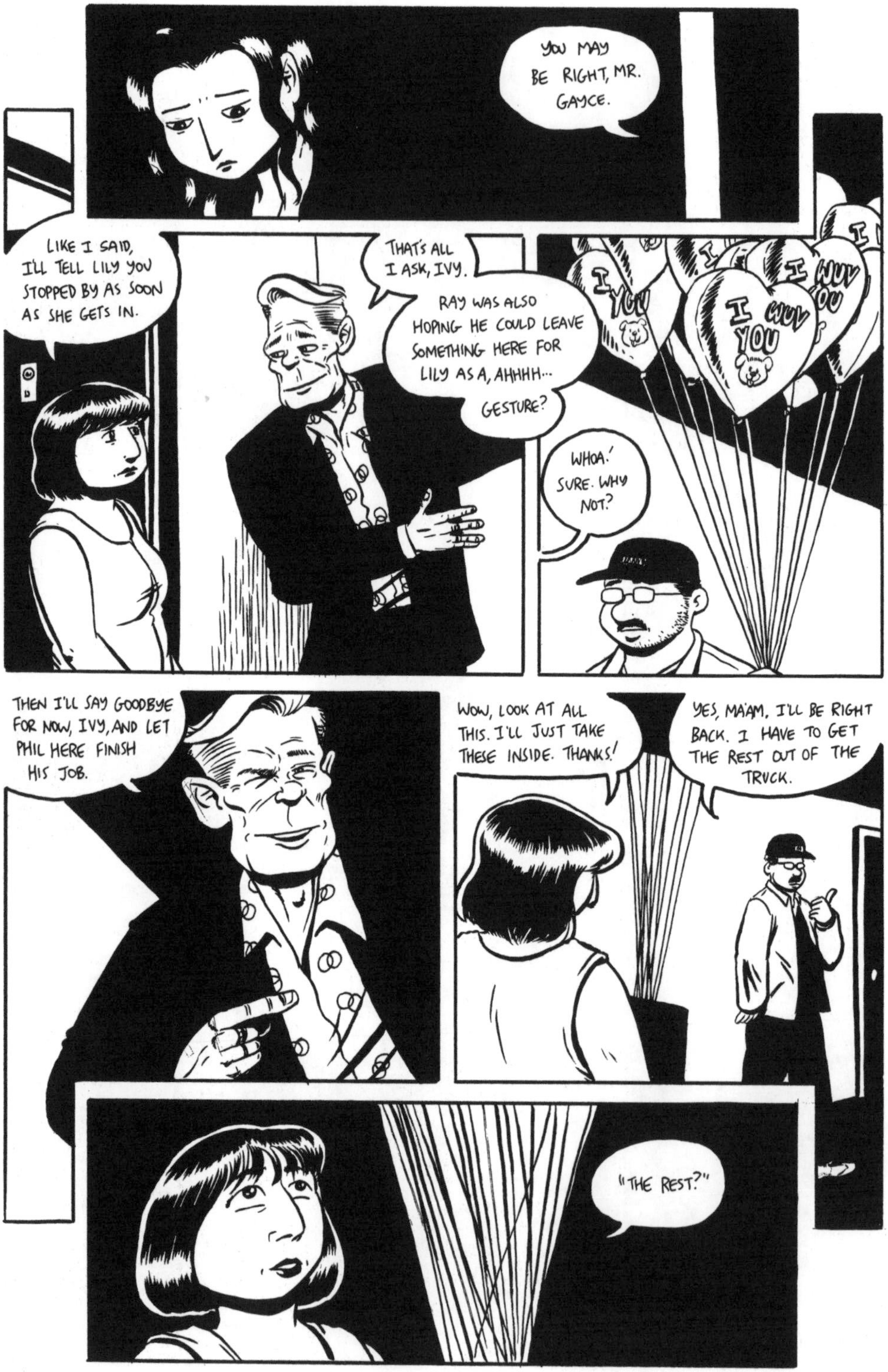
YOU MAY BE RIGHT, MR. GAYCE.
LIKE I SAID, I'LL TELL LILY YOU STOPPED BY AS SOON AS SHE GETS IN.
THAT'S ALL I ASK, IVY.
RAY WAS ALSO HOPING HE COULD LEAVE SOMETHING HERE FOR LILY AS A, AHHHH...
GESTURE?
I WUV YOU
WHOA! SURE. WHY NOT?
THEN I'LL SAY GOODBYE FOR NOW, IVY, AND LET PHIL HERE FINISH HIS JOB.
WOW, LOOK AT ALL THIS. I'LL JUST TAKE THESE INSIDE. THANKS!
YES, MA'AM. I'LL BE RIGHT BACK. I HAVE TO GET THE REST OUT OF THE TRUCK.
"THE REST?"

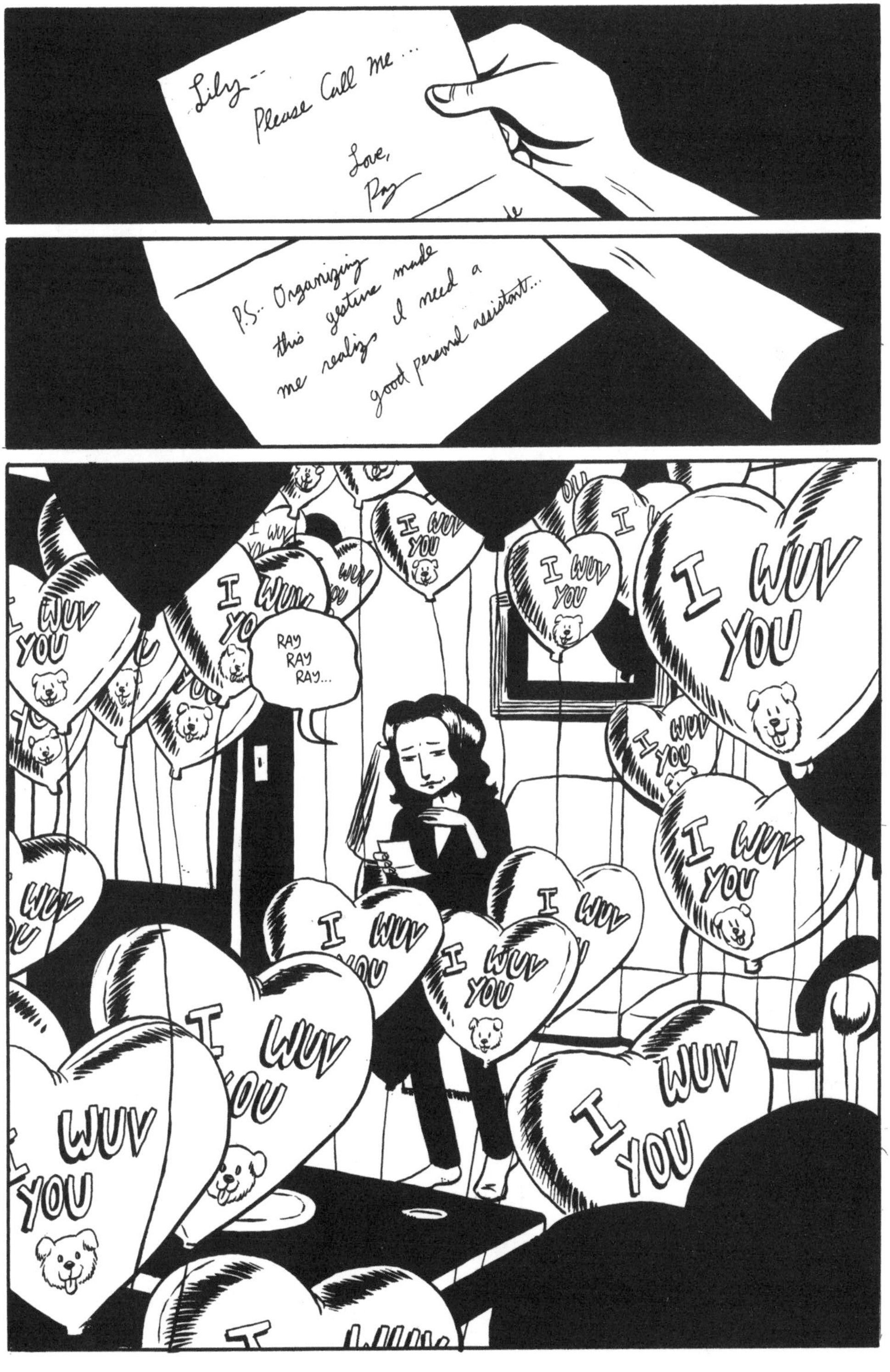
Lily--
Please Call me...
Love,
Ray
P.S.. Organizing this gesture made me realize I need a good personal assistant...
RAY RAY RAY...
I WUV YOU

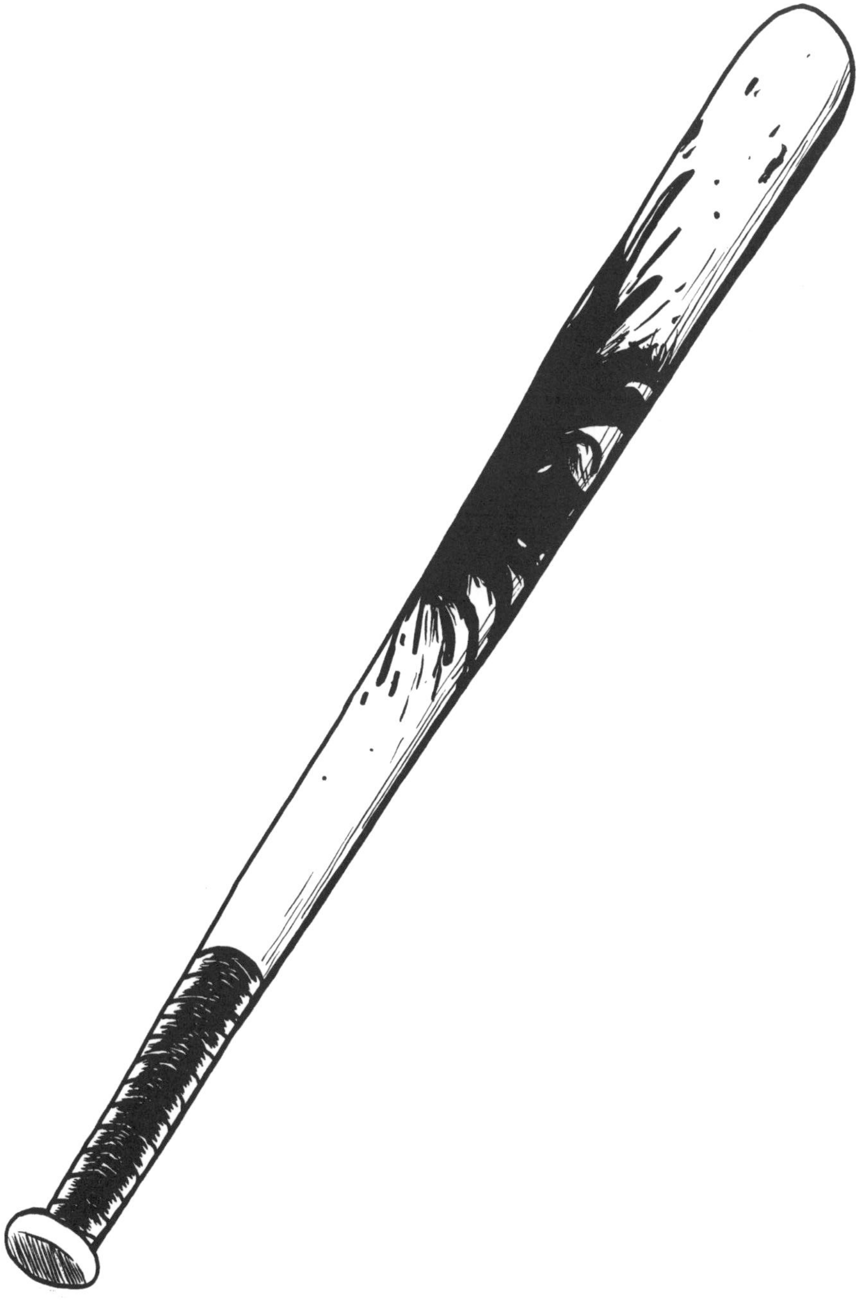

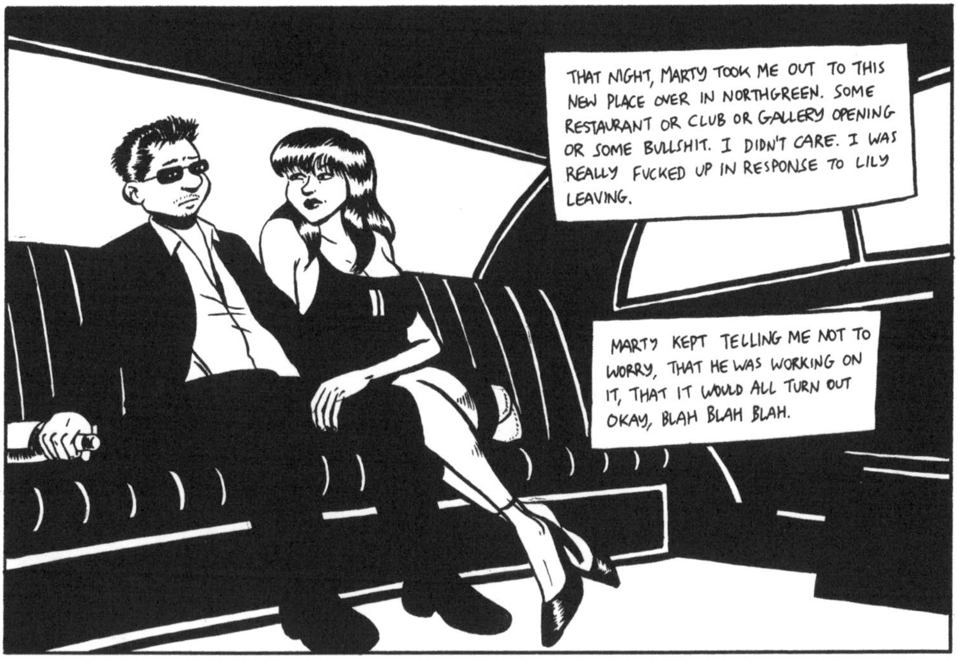
THAT NIGHT, MARTY TOOK ME OUT TO THIS NEW PLACE OVER IN NORTHGREEN. SOME RESTAURANT OR CLUB OR GALLERY OPENING OR SOME BULLSHIT. I DIDN'T CARE. I WAS REALLY FUCKED UP IN RESPONSE TO LILY LEAVING.
MARTY KEPT TELLING ME NOT TO WORRY, THAT HE WAS WORKING ON IT, THAT IT WOULD ALL TURN OUT OKAY, BLAH BLAH BLAH.

S E V E N

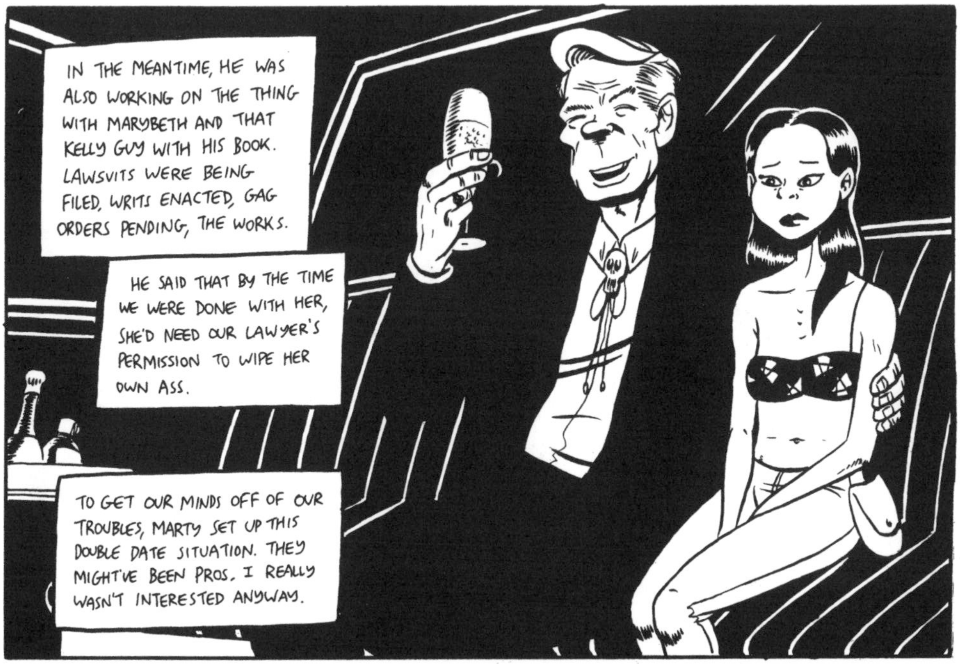
IN THE MEANTIME, HE WAS ALSO WORKING ON THE THING WITH MARYBETH AND THAT KELLY GUY WITH HIS BOOK. LAWSUITS WERE BEING FILED, WRITS ENACTED, GAG ORDERS PENDING, THE WORKS.
HE SAID THAT BY THE TIME WE WERE DONE WITH HER, SHE'D NEED OUR LAWYER'S PERMISSION TO WIPE HER OWN ASS.
TO GET OUR MINDS OFF OF OUR TROUBLES, MARTY SET UP THIS DOUBLE DATE SITUATION. THEY MIGHT'VE BEEN PROS. I REALLY WASN'T INTERESTED ANYWAY.

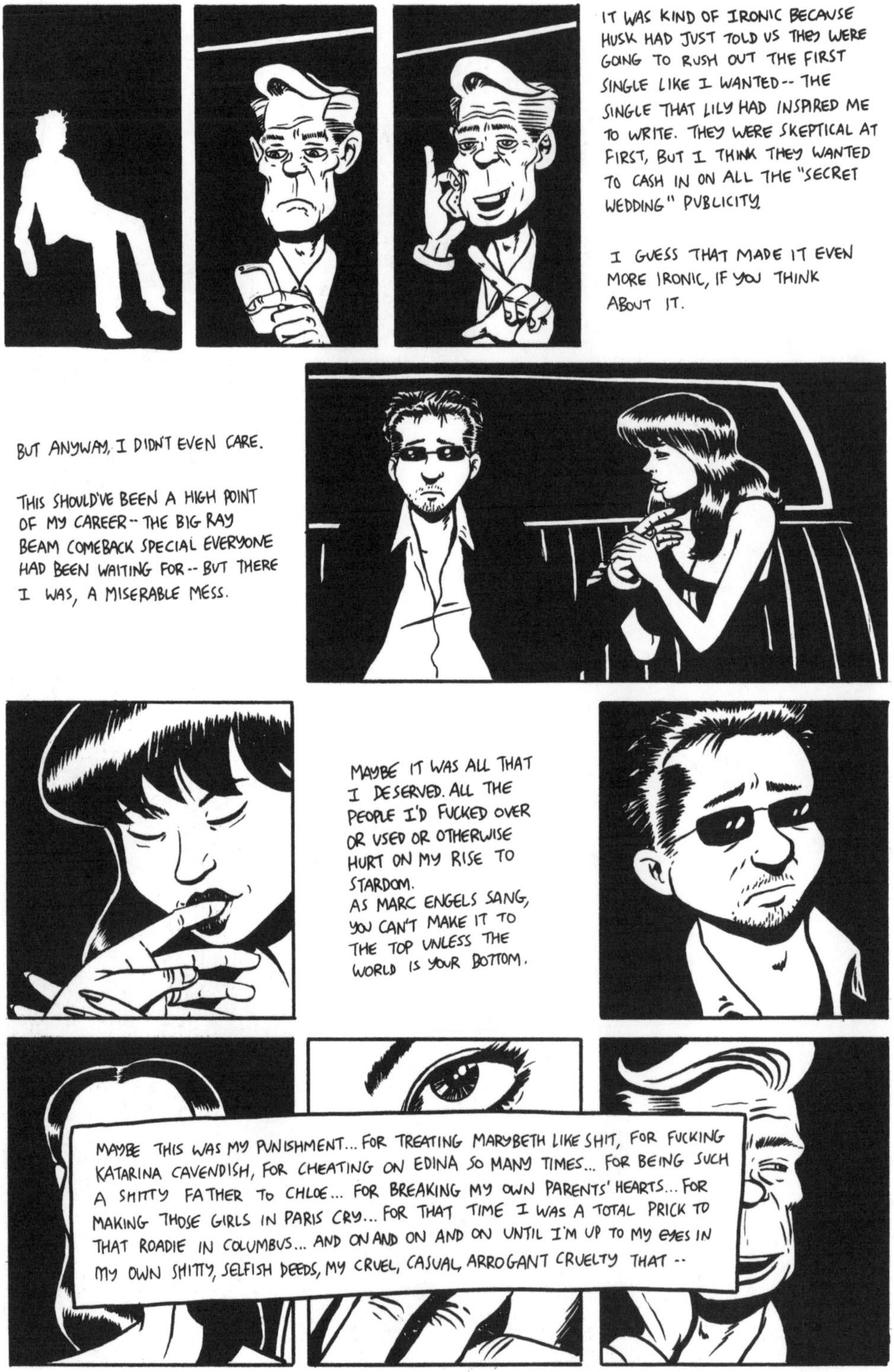
IT WAS KIND OF IRONIC BECAUSE HUSK HAD JUST TOLD US THEY WERE GOING TO RUSH OUT THE FIRST SINGLE LIKE I WANTED-- THE SINGLE THAT LILY HAD INSPIRED ME TO WRITE. THEY WERE SKEPTICAL AT FIRST, BUT I THINK THEY WANTED TO CASH IN ON ALL THE "SECRET WEDDING" PUBLICITY.
I GUESS THAT MADE IT EVEN MORE IRONIC, IF YOU THINK ABOUT IT.
BUT ANYWAY, I DIDN'T EVEN CARE.
THIS SHOULD'VE BEEN A HIGH POINT OF MY CAREER-- THE BIG RAY BEAM COMEBACK SPECIAL EVERYONE HAD BEEN WAITING FOR-- BUT THERE I WAS, A MISERABLE MESS.
MAYBE IT WAS ALL THAT I DESERVED. ALL THE PEOPLE I'D FUCKED OVER OR USED OR OTHERWISE HURT ON MY RISE TO STARDOM.
AS MARC ENGELS SANG, YOU CAN'T MAKE IT TO THE TOP UNLESS THE WORLD IS YOUR BOTTOM.
MAYBE THIS WAS MY PUNISHMENT... FOR TREATING MARYBETH LIKE SHIT, FOR FUCKING KATARINA CAVENDISH, FOR CHEATING ON EDINA SO MANY TIMES... FOR BEING SUCH A SHITTY FATHER TO CHLOE... FOR BREAKING MY OWN PARENTS' HEARTS... FOR MAKING THOSE GIRLS IN PARIS CRY... FOR THAT TIME I WAS A TOTAL PRICK TO THAT ROADIE IN COLUMBUS... AND ON AND ON AND ON UNTIL I'M UP TO MY EYES IN MY OWN SHITTY, SELFISH DEEDS, MY CRUEL, CASUAL, ARROGANT CRUELTY THAT --

RAY.

RAY?

RAY!

HUH? WHAT?

HAHA, LISTEN, PAL, WE NEED YOU BACK HERE ON EARTH FOR A SECOND. I'VE GOT SOME GREAT NEWS.

THAT CALL I JUST TOOK? LILY'S SISTER. IT SEEMS THAT LILY'S AGREED TO TAKE A MEETING WITH YOU!

WHAT? REALLY? SHE DID? SHE WILL?

MARTY, THAT'S EXCELLENT!

FAN-FUCKING-TASTIC!

OKAY, SO YOU GUYS WILL BE GOING TO DINNER ON FRIDAY! SEE? SHE TOLD ME WHERE SHE WANTS TO DO IT AND I'LL HAVE ELSIE AT THE OFFICE MAKE THE ARRANGEMENTS.

SEE? WHAT DID I TELL YOU, BUDDY? YOU JUST HAVE TO TRUST ME FROM NOW ON!

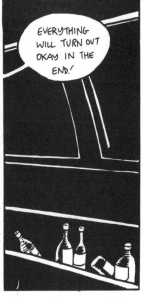

EVERYTHING WILL TURN OUT OKAY IN THE END!

273

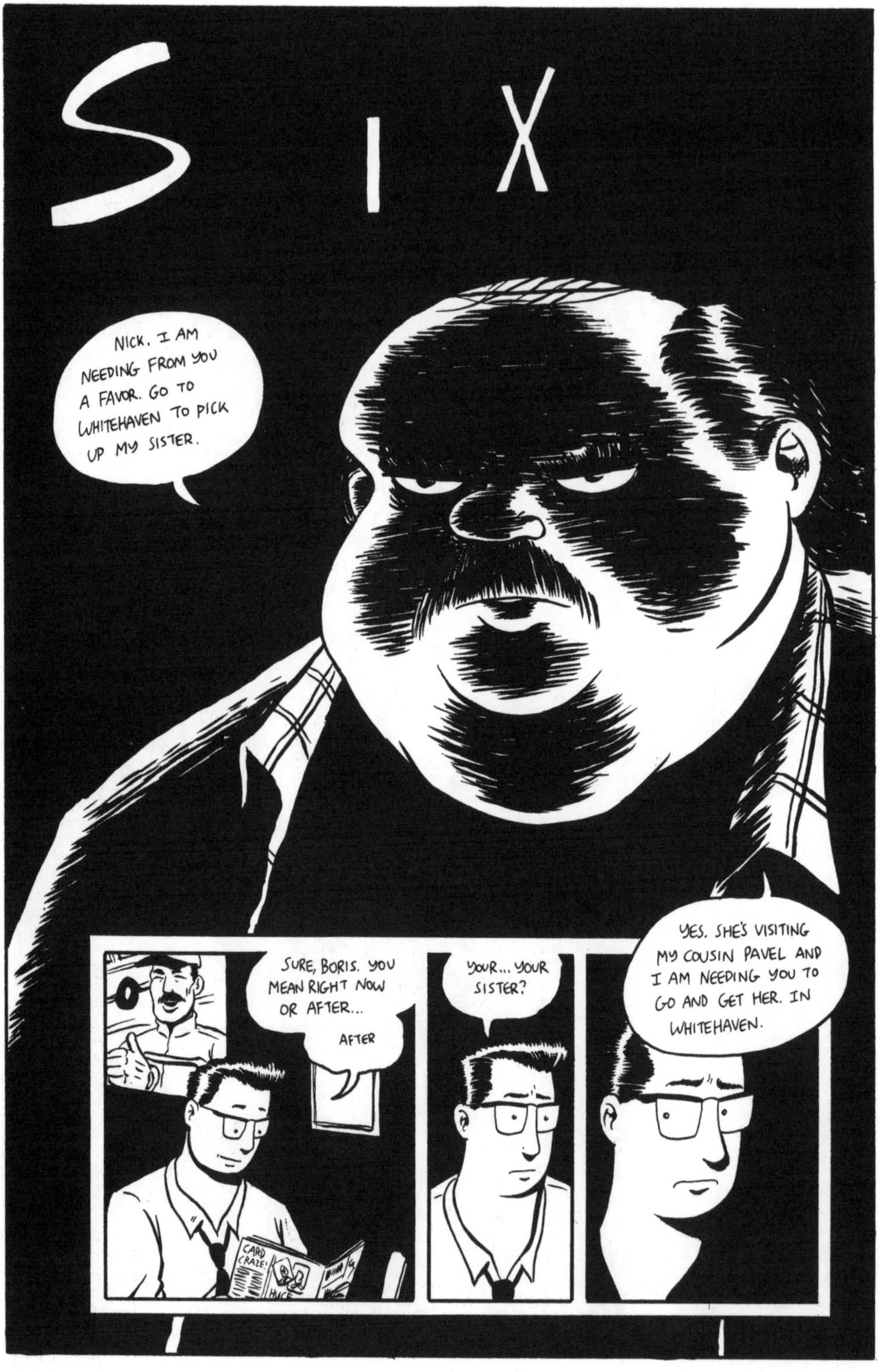
SIX
NICK. I AM NEEDING FROM YOU A FAVOR. GO TO WHITEHAVEN TO PICK UP MY SISTER.
SURE, BORIS. YOU MEAN RIGHT NOW OR AFTER...
AFTER
YOUR... YOUR SISTER?
YES. SHE'S VISITING MY COUSIN PAVEL AND I AM NEEDING YOU TO GO AND GET HER. IN WHITEHAVEN.
CARD CRAZE!

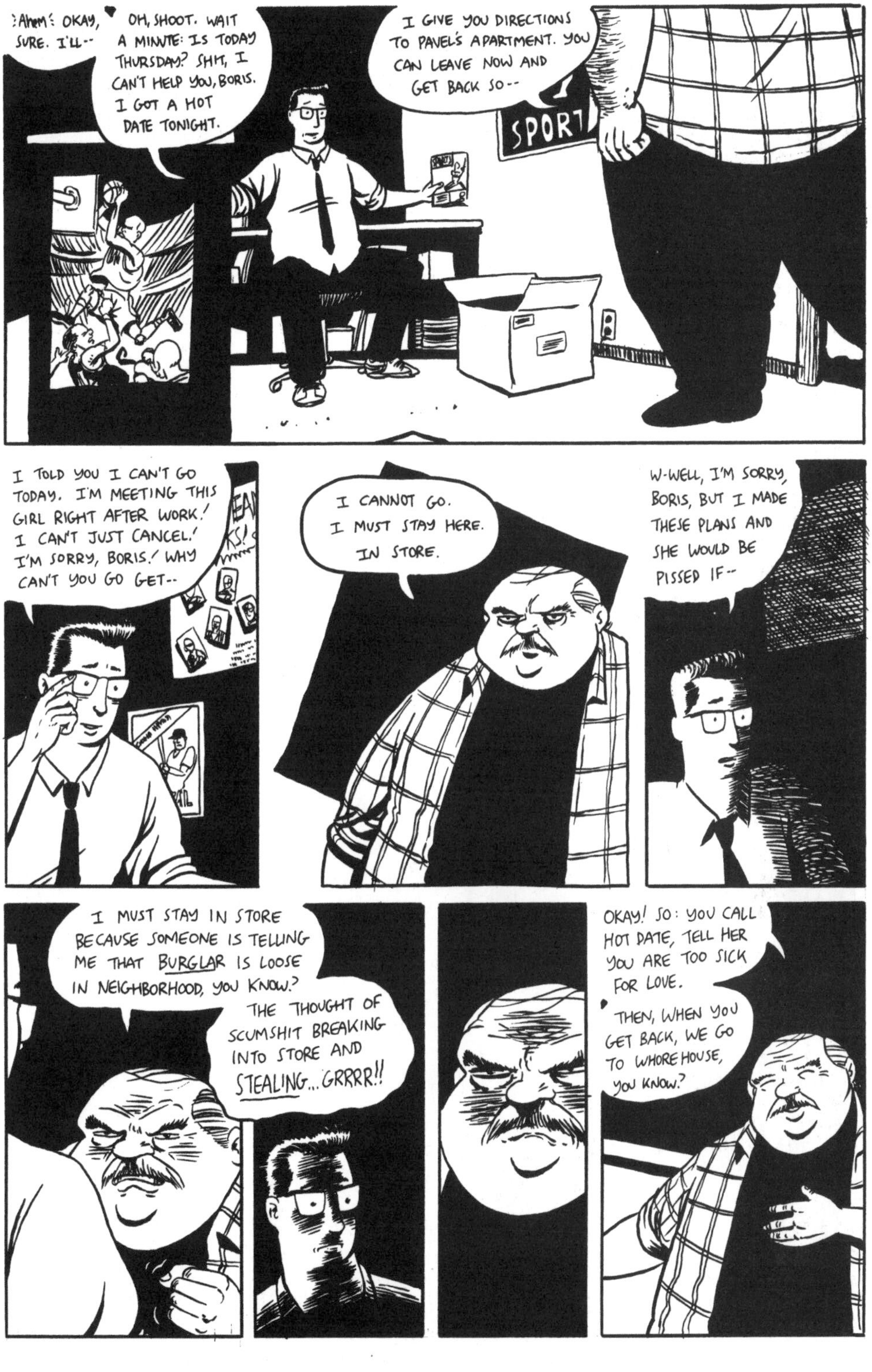
:AHEM: OKAY, SURE. I'LL--
OH, SHOOT. WAIT A MINUTE: IS TODAY THURSDAY? SHIT, I CAN'T HELP YOU, BORIS. I GOT A HOT DATE TONIGHT.
I GIVE YOU DIRECTIONS TO PAVEL'S APARTMENT. YOU CAN LEAVE NOW AND GET BACK SO--
SPORT
I TOLD YOU I CAN'T GO TODAY. I'M MEETING THIS GIRL RIGHT AFTER WORK! I CAN'T JUST CANCEL! I'M SORRY, BORIS! WHY CAN'T YOU GO GET--
I CANNOT GO. I MUST STAY HERE. IN STORE.
W-WELL, I'M SORRY, BORIS, BUT I MADE THESE PLANS AND SHE WOULD BE PISSED IF--
I MUST STAY IN STORE BECAUSE SOMEONE IS TELLING ME THAT BURGLAR IS LOOSE IN NEIGHBORHOOD, YOU KNOW?
THE THOUGHT OF SCUMSHIT BREAKING INTO STORE AND STEALING... GRRRR!!
OKAY! SO: YOU CALL HOT DATE, TELL HER YOU ARE TOO SICK FOR LOVE.
THEN, WHEN YOU GET BACK, WE GO TO WHOREHOUSE, YOU KNOW?

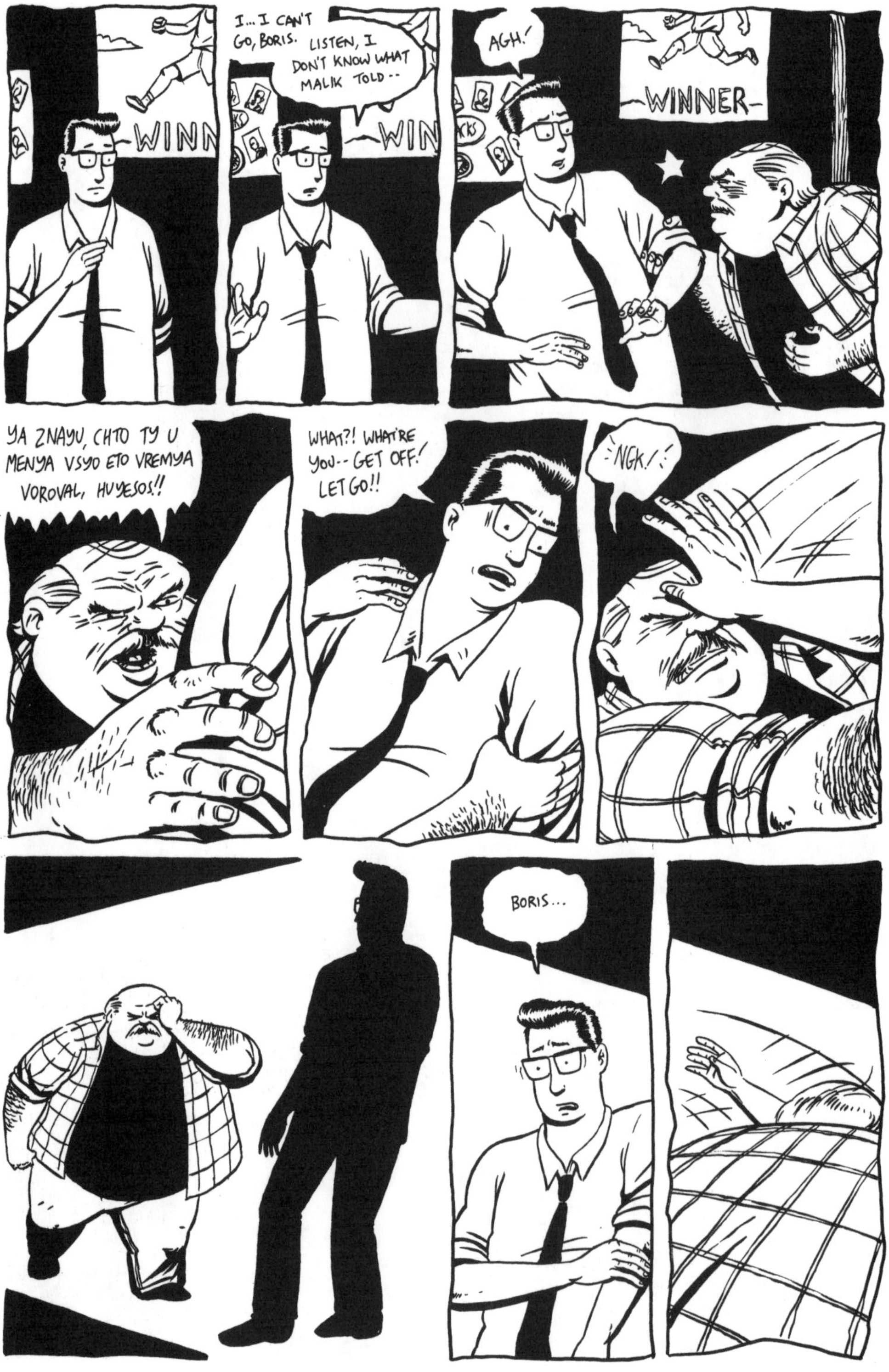
WINN
I... I CAN'T GO, BORIS.
LISTEN, I DON'T KNOW WHAT MALIK TOLD--
AGH!
WINNER
YA ZNAYU, CHTO TY U MENYA VSYO ETO VREMYA VOROVAL, HUYESOS!!
WHAT?! WHAT'RE YOU-- GET OFF! LET GO!!
NGK!
BORIS...

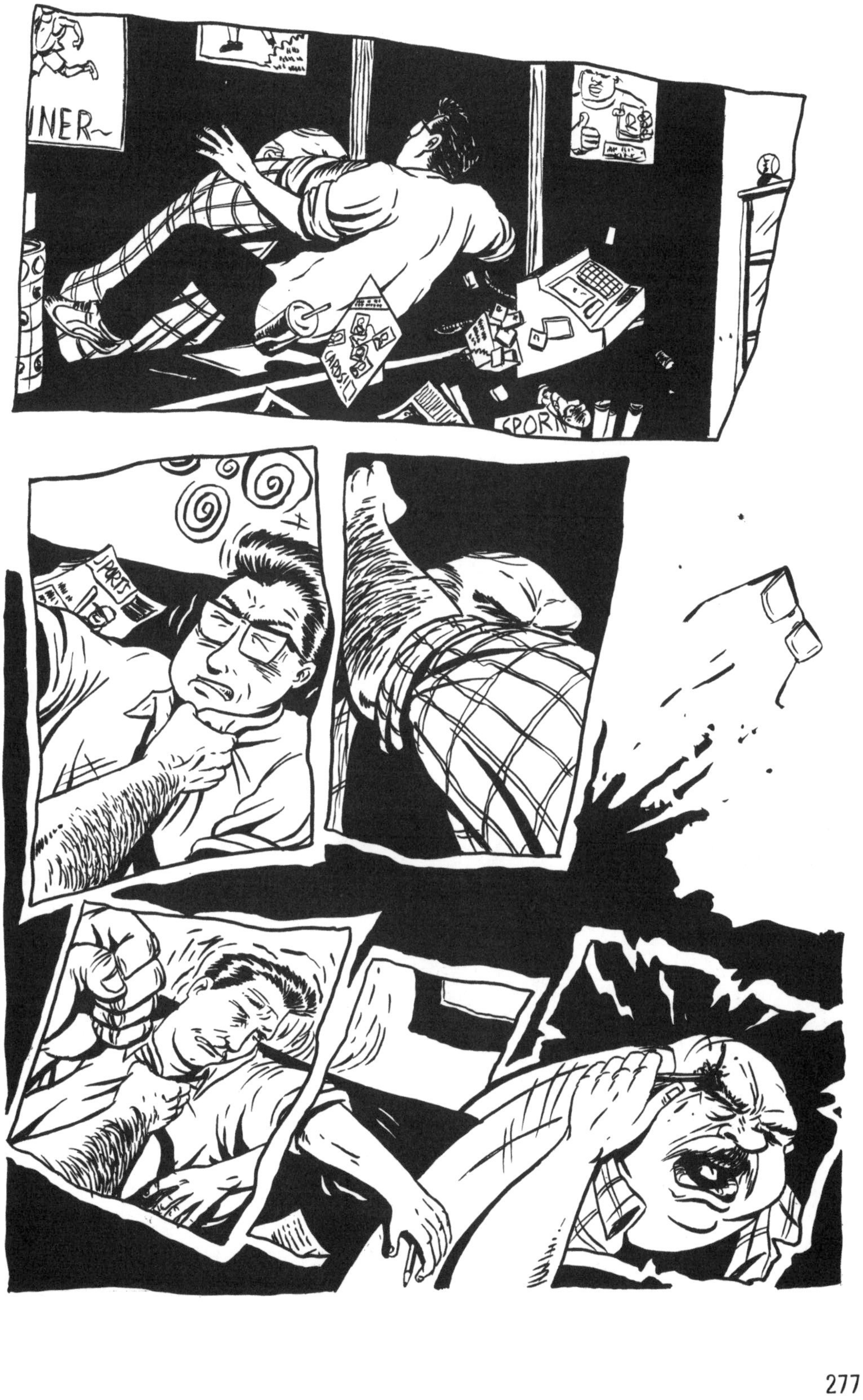
CARDS!
SPORTS

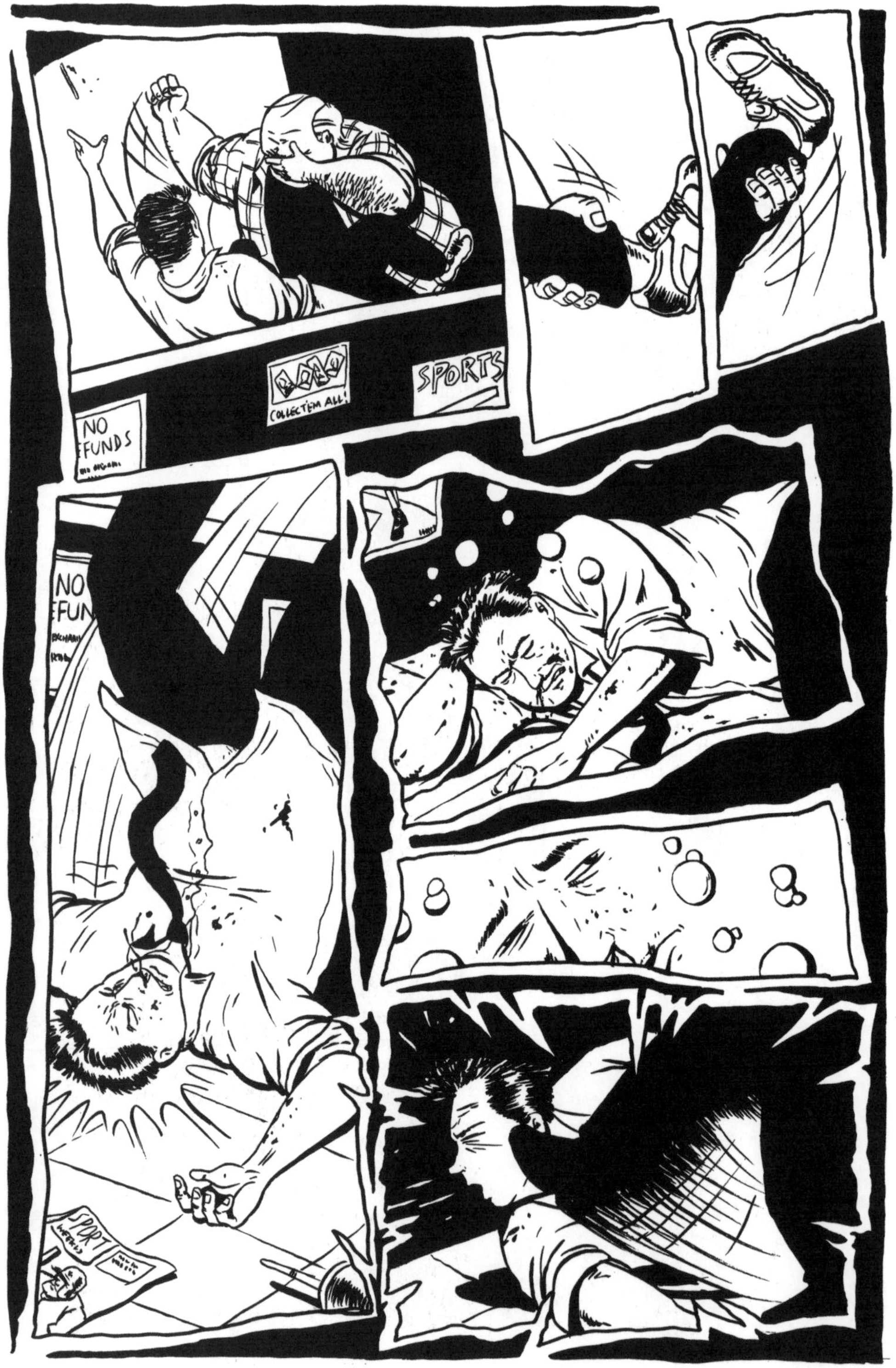
NO
FUNDS
COLLECT'EM ALL!
SPORTS

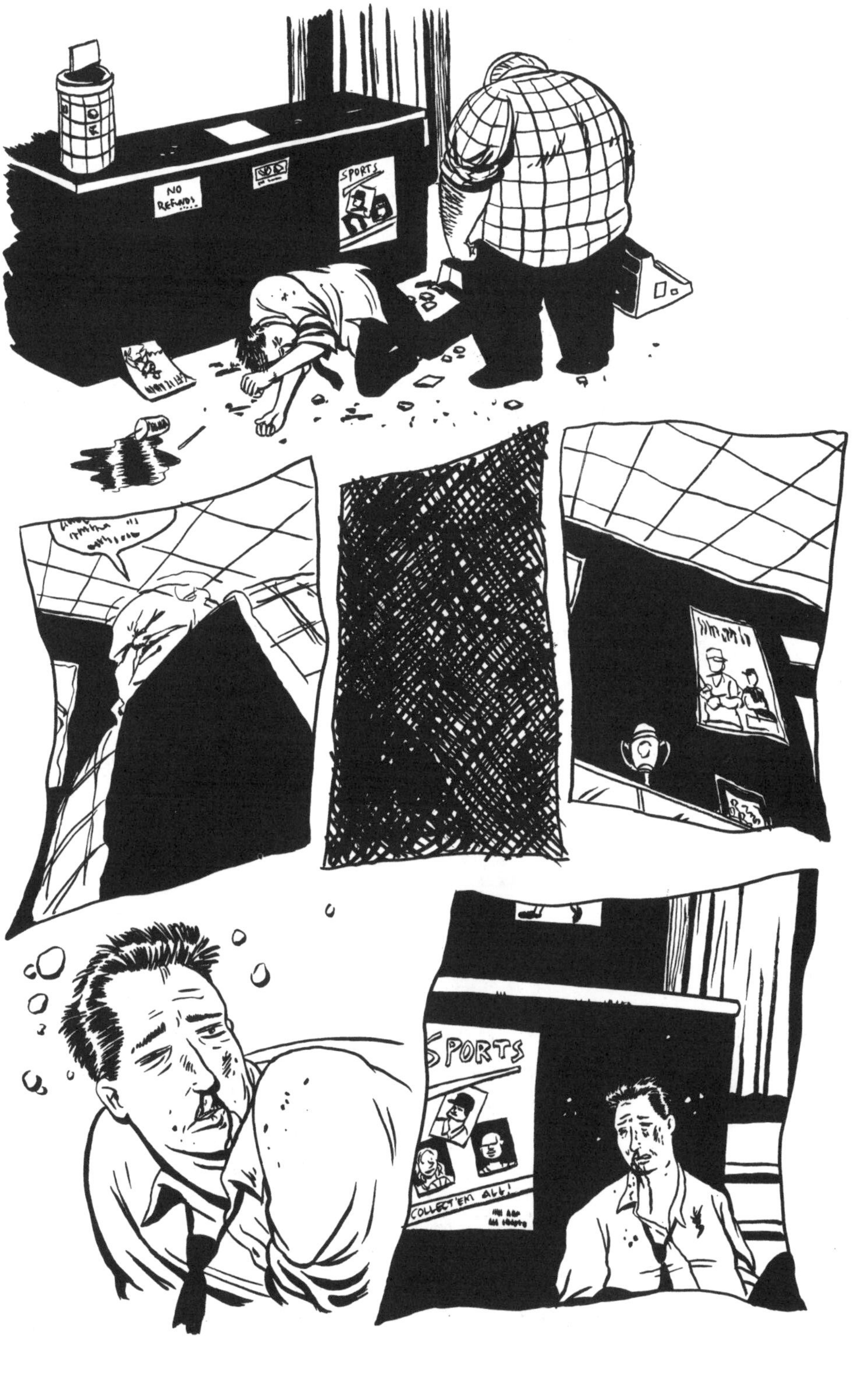
NO REFUNDS
SPORTS
SPORTS
COLLECT 'EM ALL!

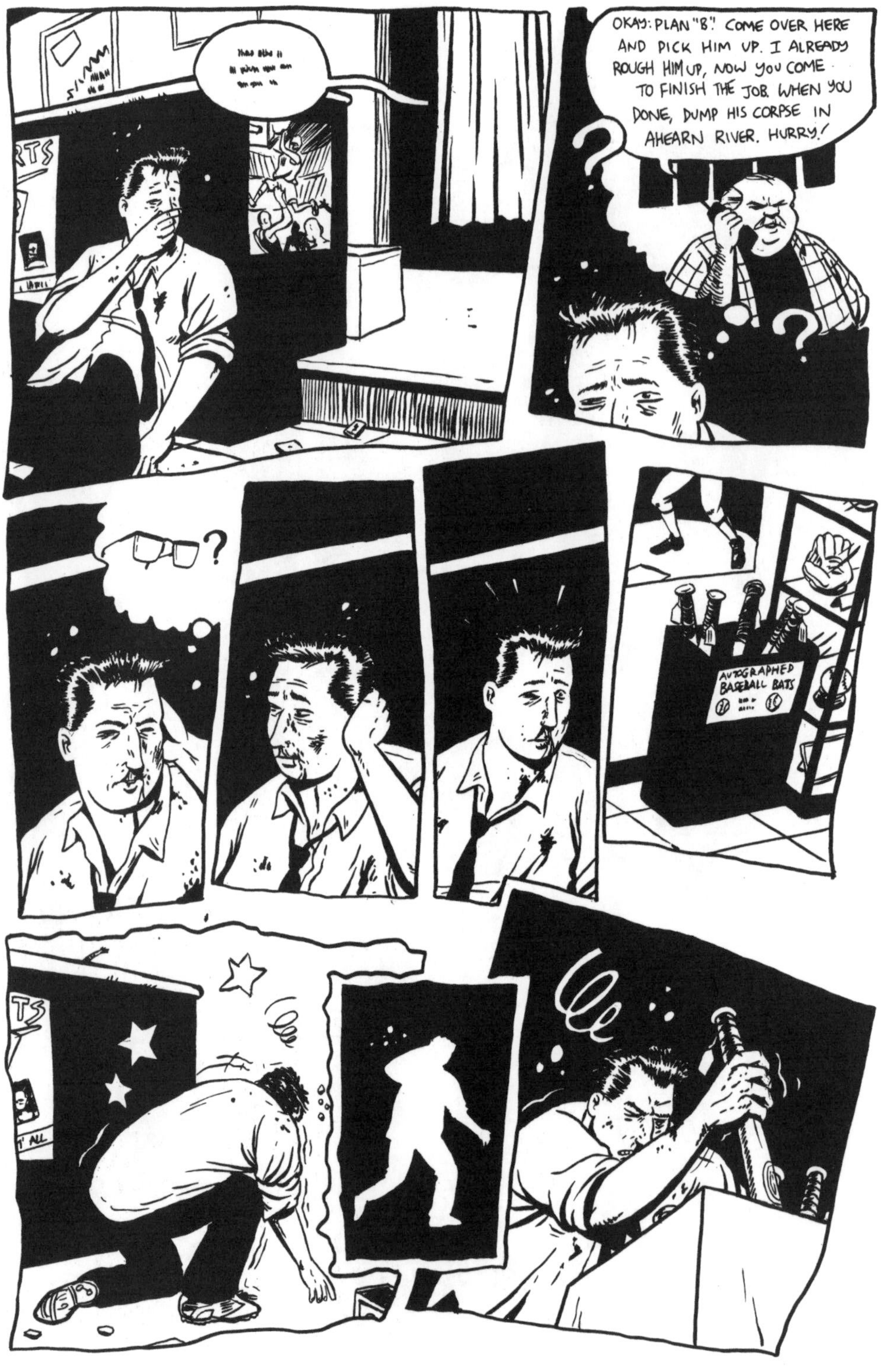
OKAY: PLAN "B". COME OVER HERE AND PICK HIM UP. I ALREADY ROUGH HIM UP, NOW YOU COME TO FINISH THE JOB. WHEN YOU DONE, DUMP HIS CORPSE IN AHEARN RIVER. HURRY!
AUTOGRAPHED BASEBALL BATS

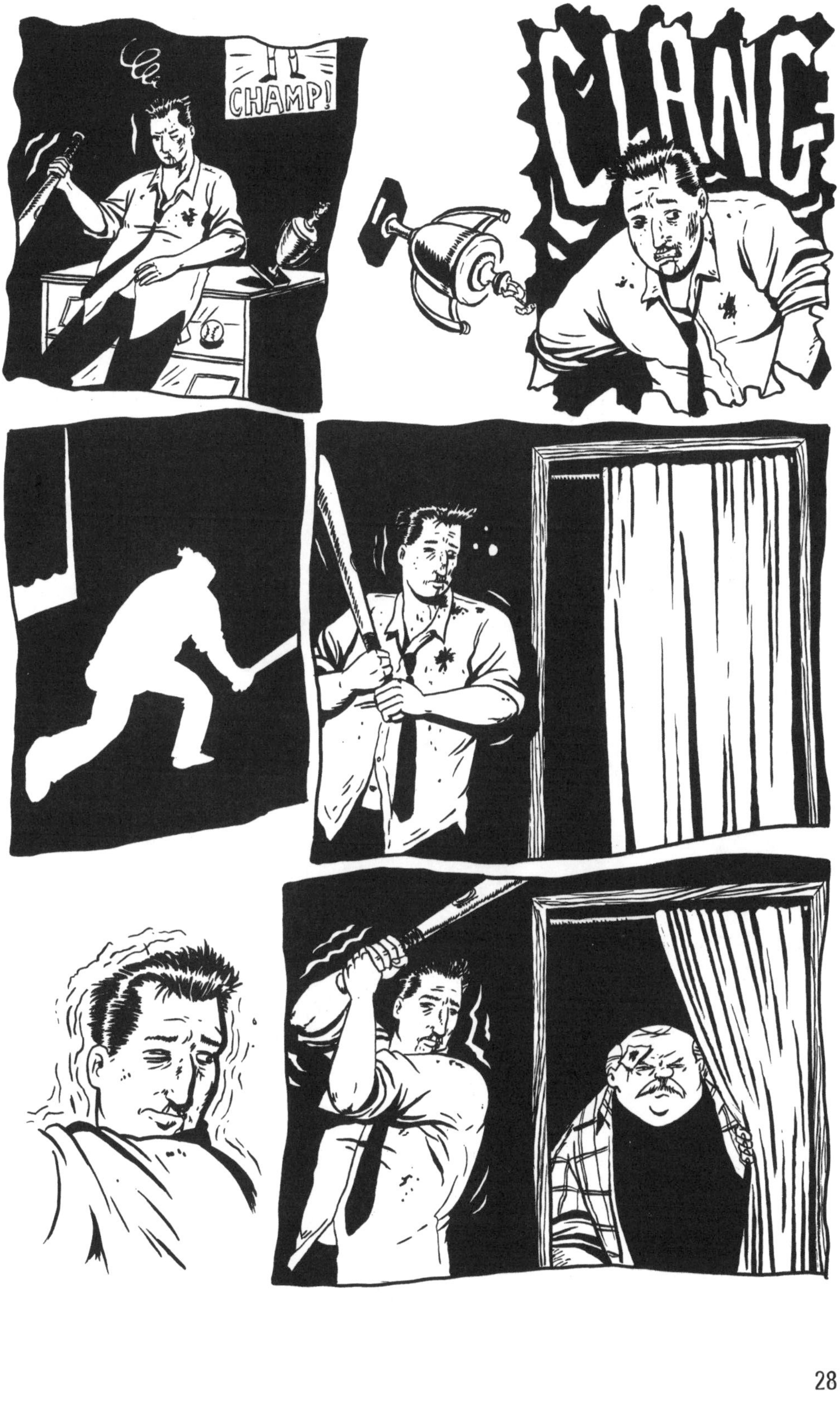
CHAMP!
CLANG

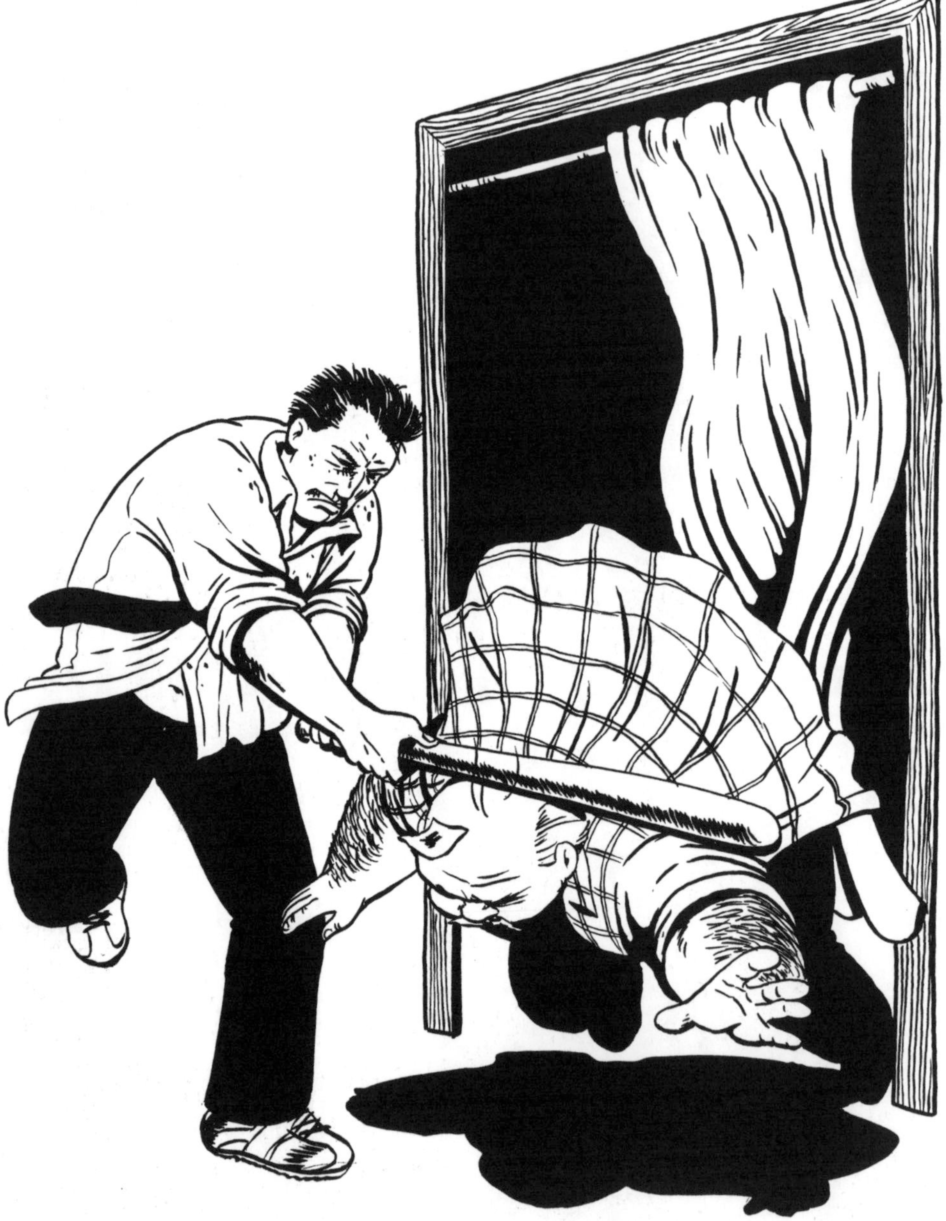

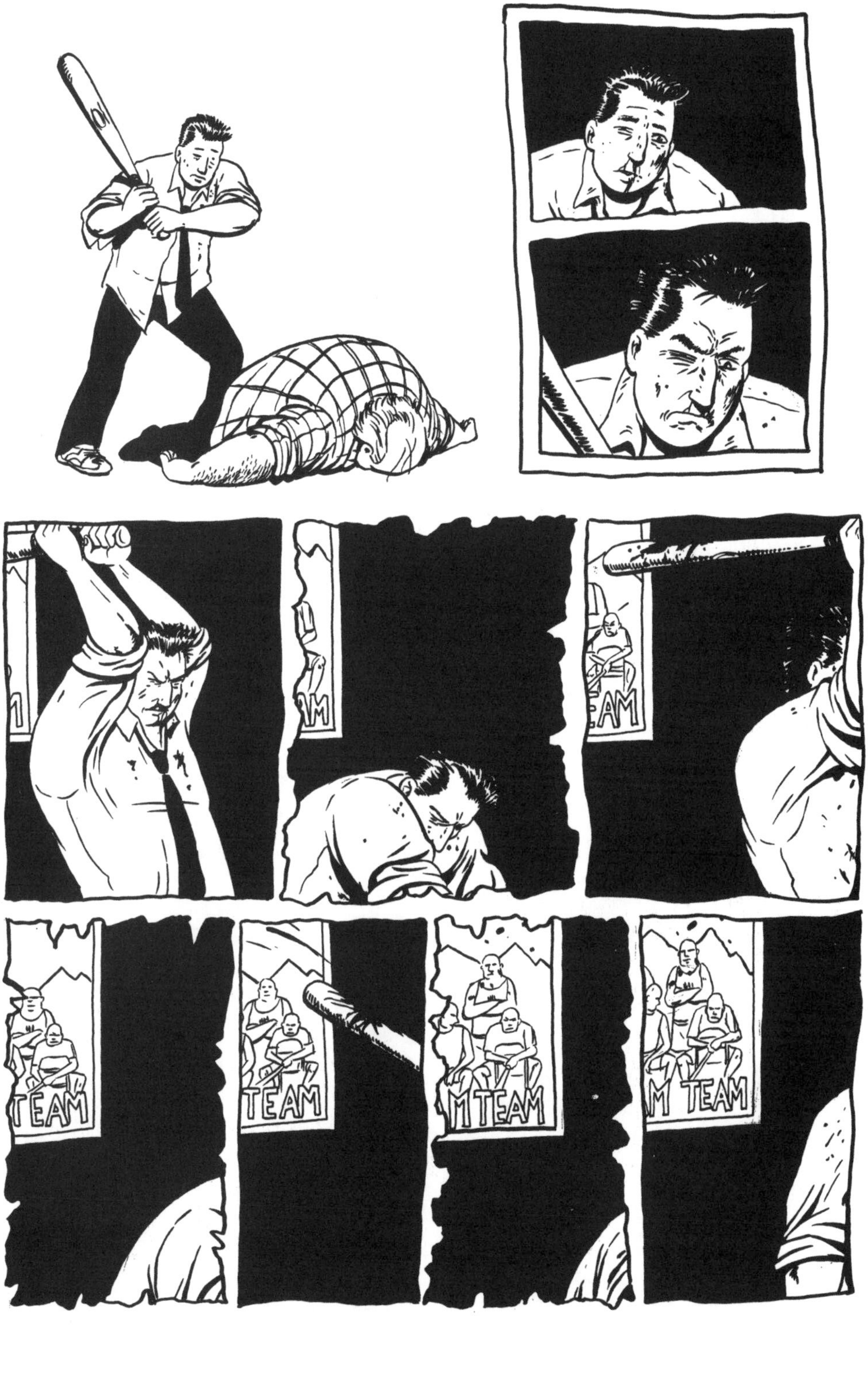
AM
AM
EAM
TEAM
TEAM
M TEAM
M TEAM

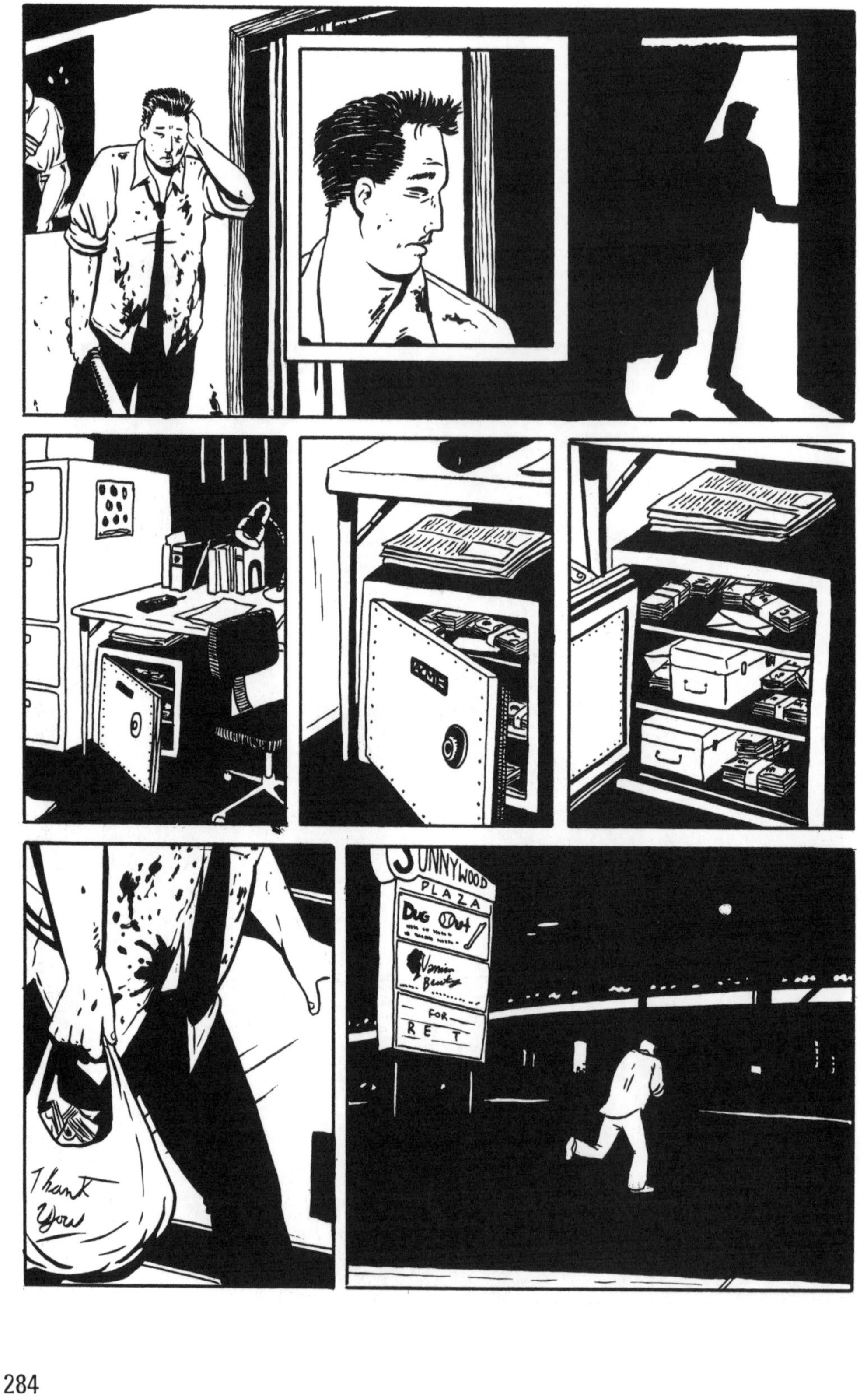
SUNNYWOOD
PLAZA
DUG Out
FOR
RE T
Thank You

five

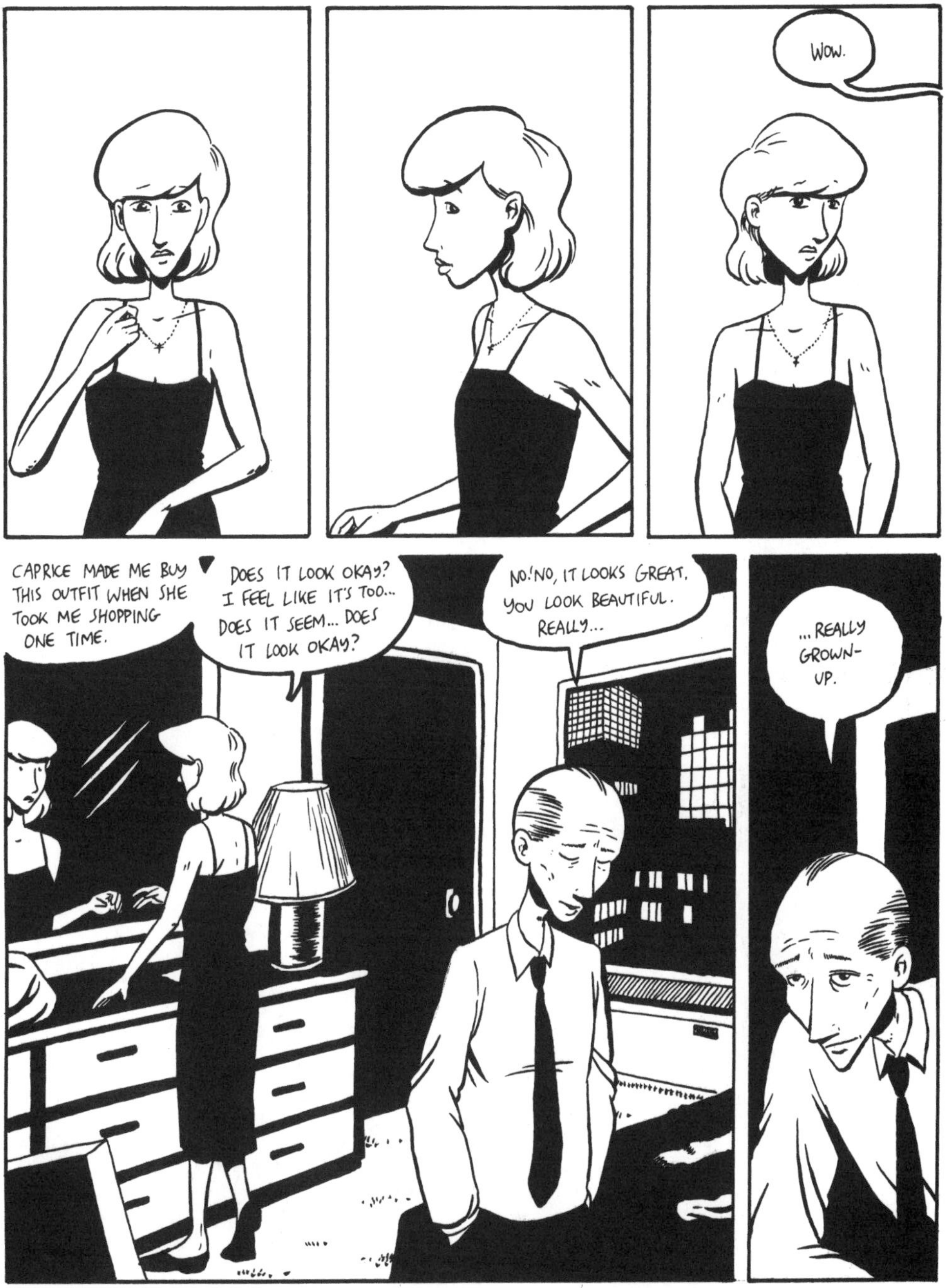
WOW.
CAPRICE MADE ME BUY THIS OUTFIT WHEN SHE TOOK ME SHOPPING ONE TIME.
DOES IT LOOK OKAY? I FEEL LIKE IT'S TOO... DOES IT SEEM... DOES IT LOOK OKAY?
NO! NO, IT LOOKS GREAT. YOU LOOK BEAUTIFUL. REALLY...
...REALLY GROWN-UP.

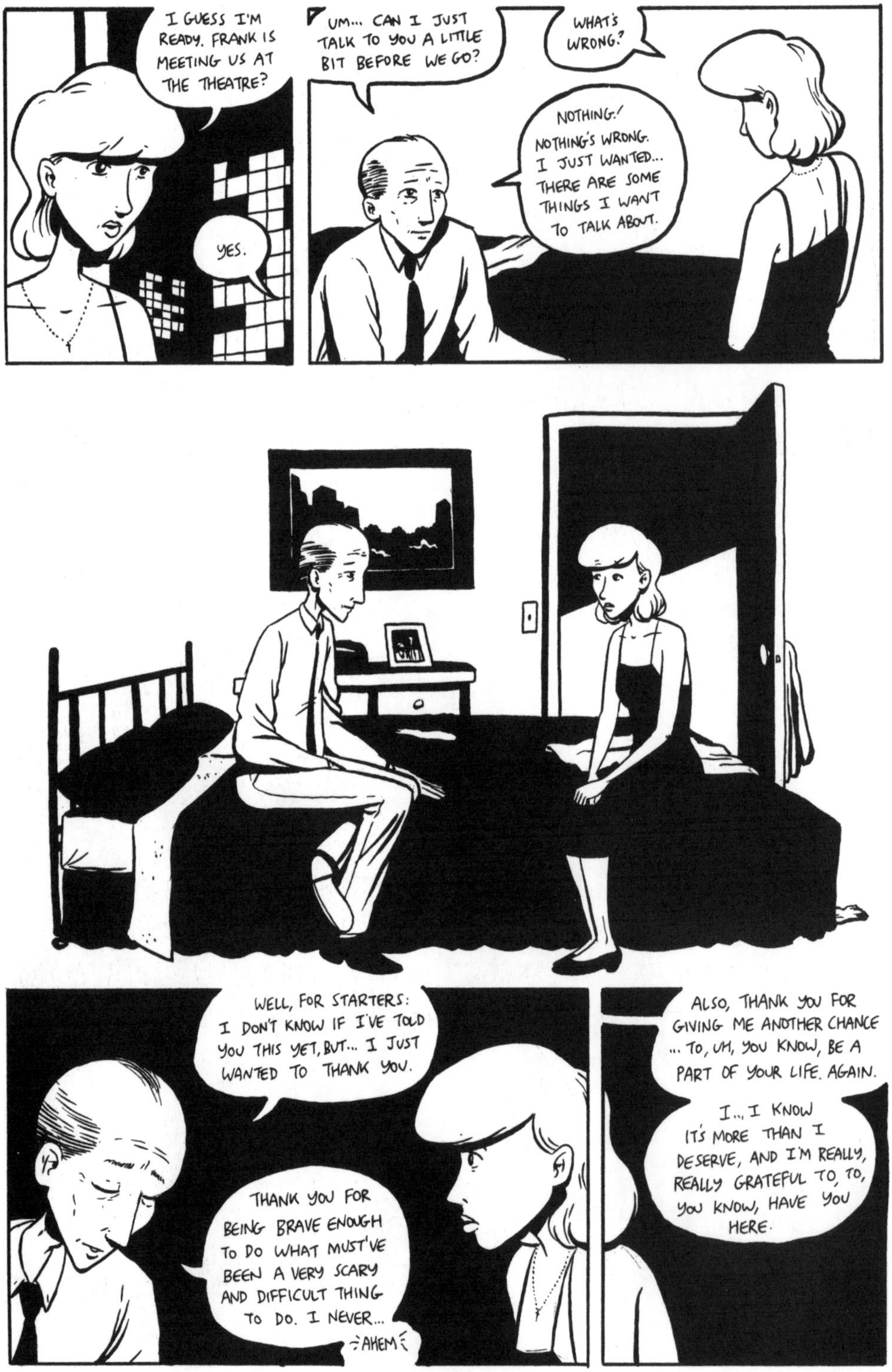
I GUESS I'M READY. FRANK IS MEETING US AT THE THEATRE?
YES.
UM... CAN I JUST TALK TO YOU A LITTLE BIT BEFORE WE GO?
WHAT'S WRONG?
NOTHING! NOTHING'S WRONG. I JUST WANTED... THERE ARE SOME THINGS I WANT TO TALK ABOUT.
WELL, FOR STARTERS: I DON'T KNOW IF I'VE TOLD YOU THIS YET, BUT... I JUST WANTED TO THANK YOU.
THANK YOU FOR BEING BRAVE ENOUGH TO DO WHAT MUST'VE BEEN A VERY SCARY AND DIFFICULT THING TO DO. I NEVER...
AHEM
ALSO, THANK YOU FOR GIVING ME ANOTHER CHANCE ... TO, UM, YOU KNOW, BE A PART OF YOUR LIFE. AGAIN.
I... I KNOW IT'S MORE THAN I DESERVE, AND I'M REALLY, REALLY GRATEFUL TO, TO, YOU KNOW, HAVE YOU HERE.

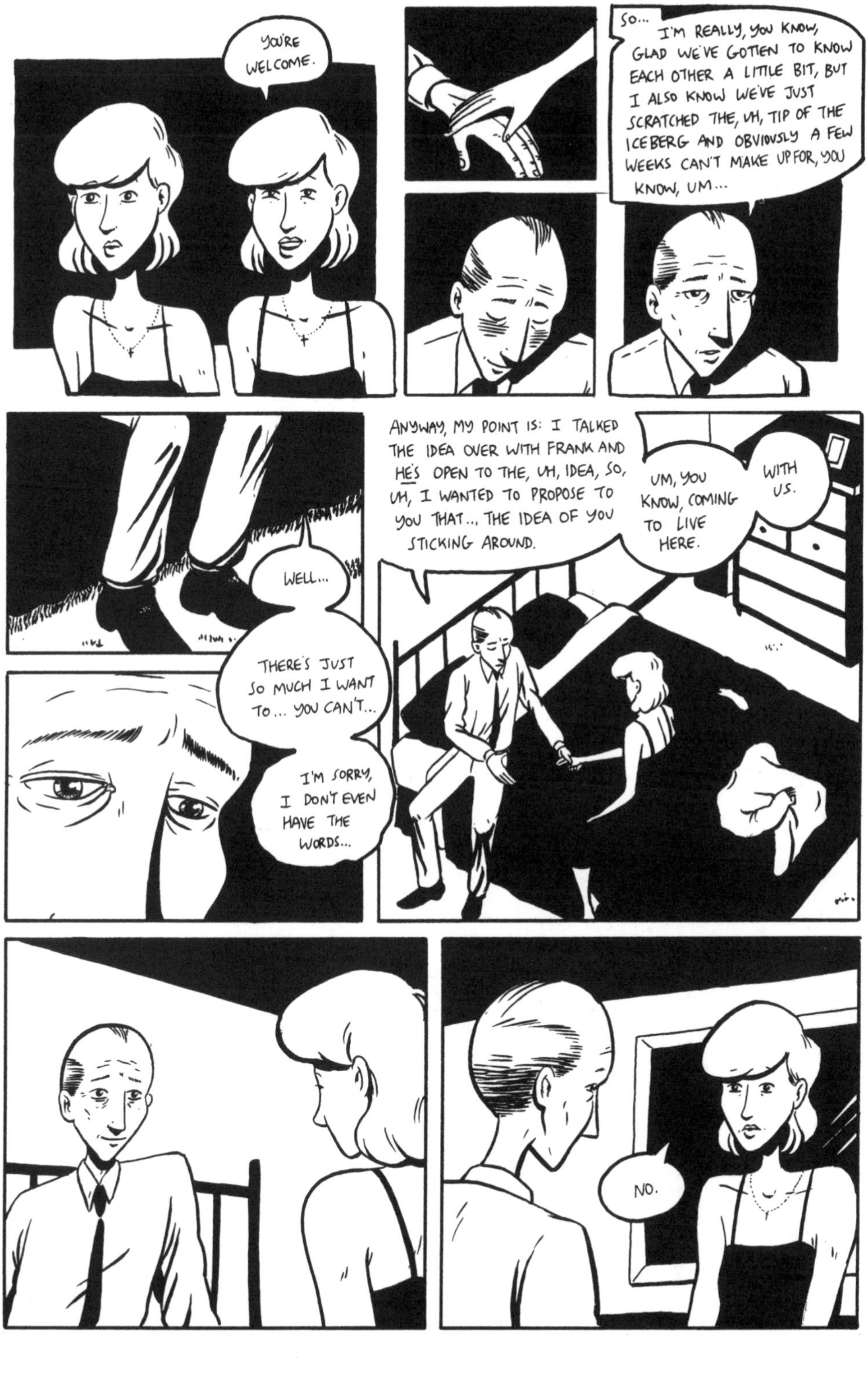
YOU'RE WELCOME.
SO... I'M REALLY, YOU KNOW, GLAD WE'VE GOTTEN TO KNOW EACH OTHER A LITTLE BIT, BUT I ALSO KNOW WE'VE JUST SCRATCHED THE, UH, TIP OF THE ICEBERG AND OBVIOUSLY A FEW WEEKS CAN'T MAKE UP FOR, YOU KNOW, UM...
WELL...
THERE'S JUST SO MUCH I WANT TO... YOU CAN'T...
I'M SORRY, I DON'T EVEN HAVE THE WORDS...
ANYWAY, MY POINT IS: I TALKED THE IDEA OVER WITH FRANK AND HE'S OPEN TO THE, UH, IDEA, SO, UH, I WANTED TO PROPOSE TO YOU THAT... THE IDEA OF YOU STICKING AROUND.
UM, YOU KNOW, COMING TO LIVE HERE.
WITH US.
NO.

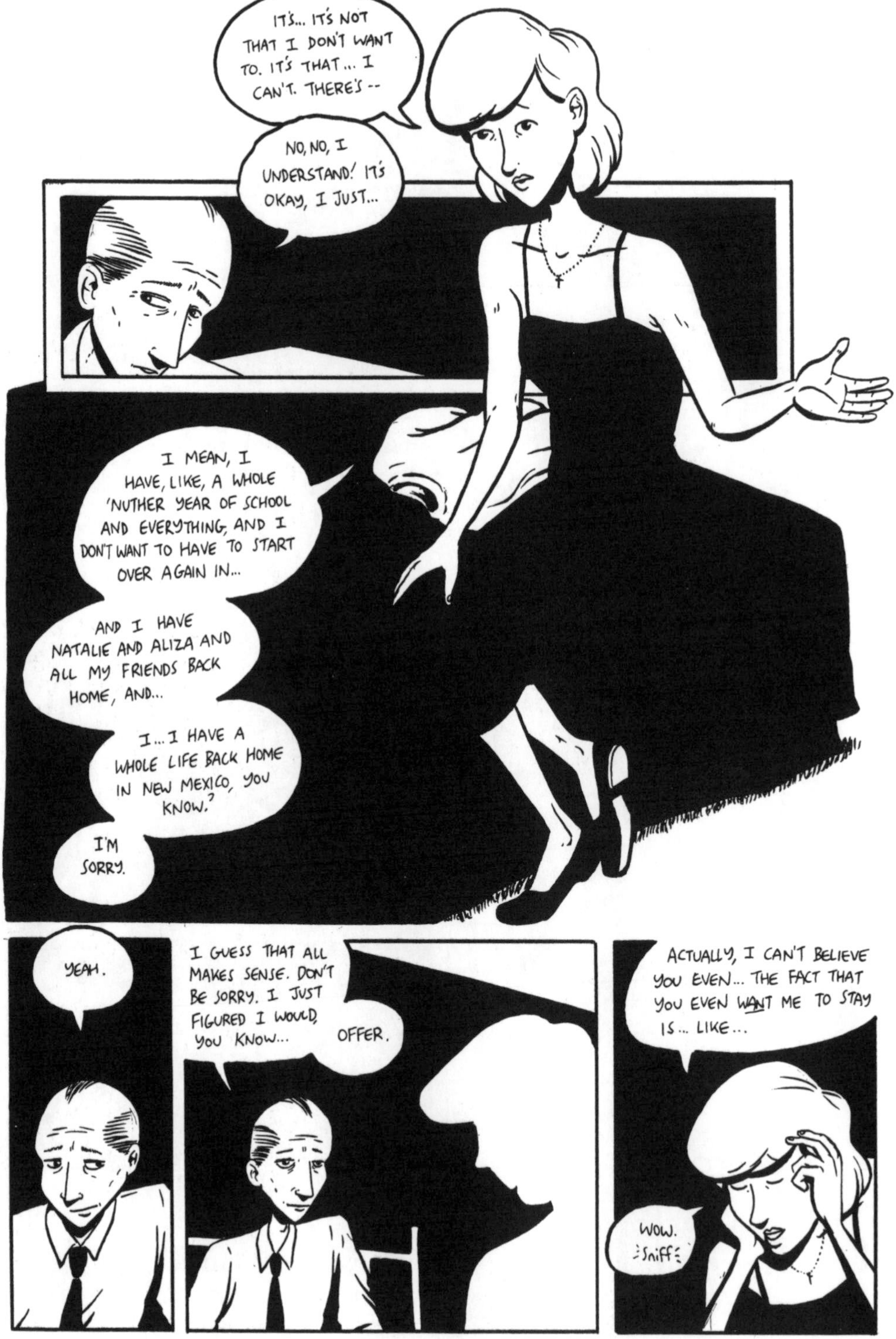
IT'S... IT'S NOT THAT I DON'T WANT TO. IT'S THAT... I CAN'T. THERE'S --
NO, NO, I UNDERSTAND! IT'S OKAY, I JUST...
I MEAN, I HAVE, LIKE, A WHOLE 'NUTHER YEAR OF SCHOOL AND EVERYTHING, AND I DON'T WANT TO HAVE TO START OVER AGAIN IN...
AND I HAVE NATALIE AND ALIZA AND ALL MY FRIENDS BACK HOME, AND...
I... I HAVE A WHOLE LIFE BACK HOME IN NEW MEXICO, YOU KNOW?
I'M SORRY.
YEAH.
I GUESS THAT ALL MAKES SENSE. DON'T BE SORRY. I JUST FIGURED I WOULD, YOU KNOW...
OFFER.
ACTUALLY, I CAN'T BELIEVE YOU EVEN... THE FACT THAT YOU EVEN WANT ME TO STAY IS... LIKE...
WOW.
SNIFF

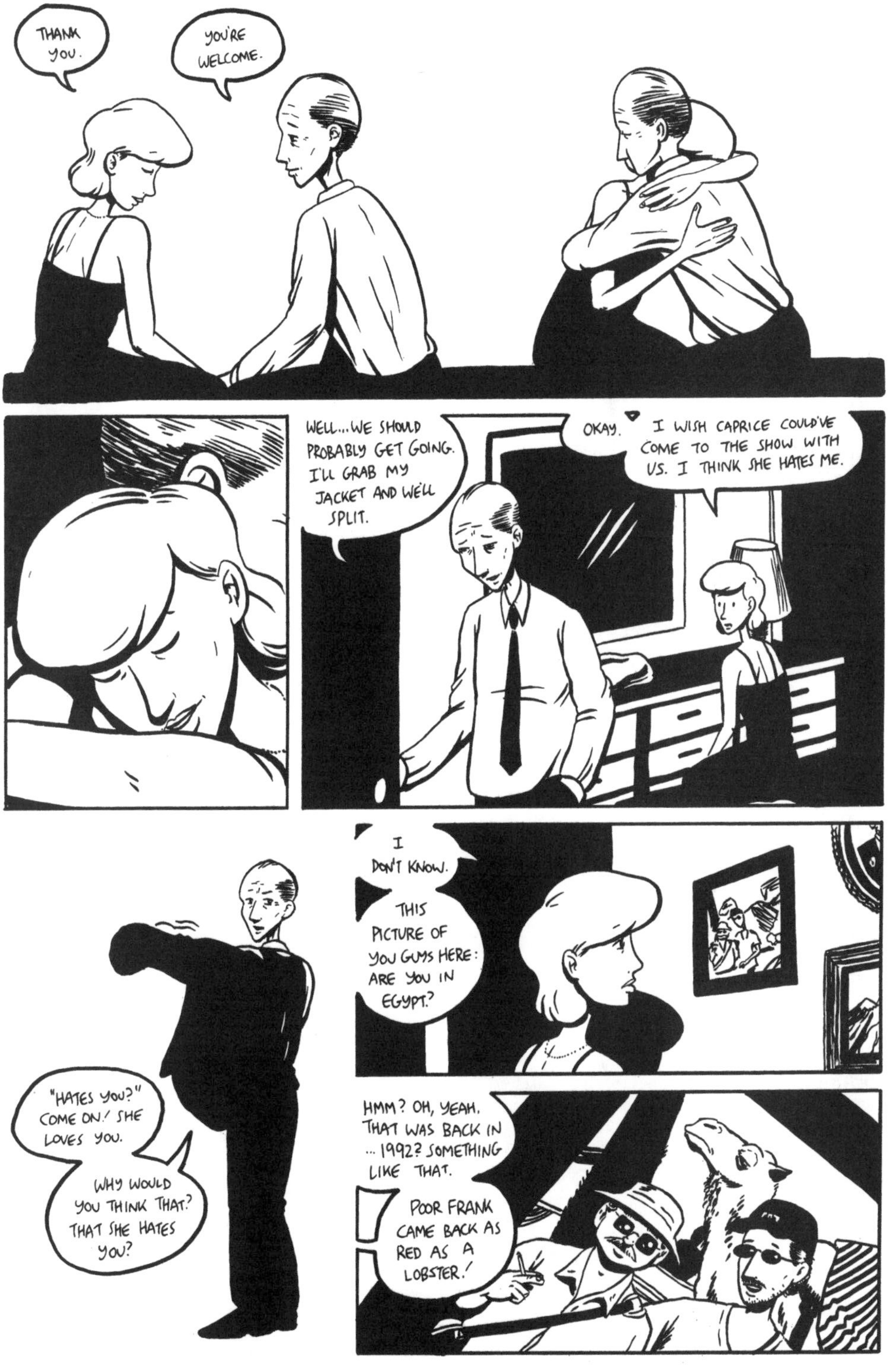
THANK YOU.
YOU'RE WELCOME.
WELL...WE SHOULD PROBABLY GET GOING. I'LL GRAB MY JACKET AND WE'LL SPLIT.
OKAY.
I WISH CAPRICE COULD'VE COME TO THE SHOW WITH US. I THINK SHE HATES ME.
"HATES YOU?" COME ON! SHE LOVES YOU.
WHY WOULD YOU THINK THAT? THAT SHE HATES YOU?
I DON'T KNOW.
THIS PICTURE OF YOU GUYS HERE: ARE YOU IN EGYPT?
HMM? OH, YEAH. THAT WAS BACK IN ...1992? SOMETHING LIKE THAT.
POOR FRANK CAME BACK AS RED AS A LOBSTER!

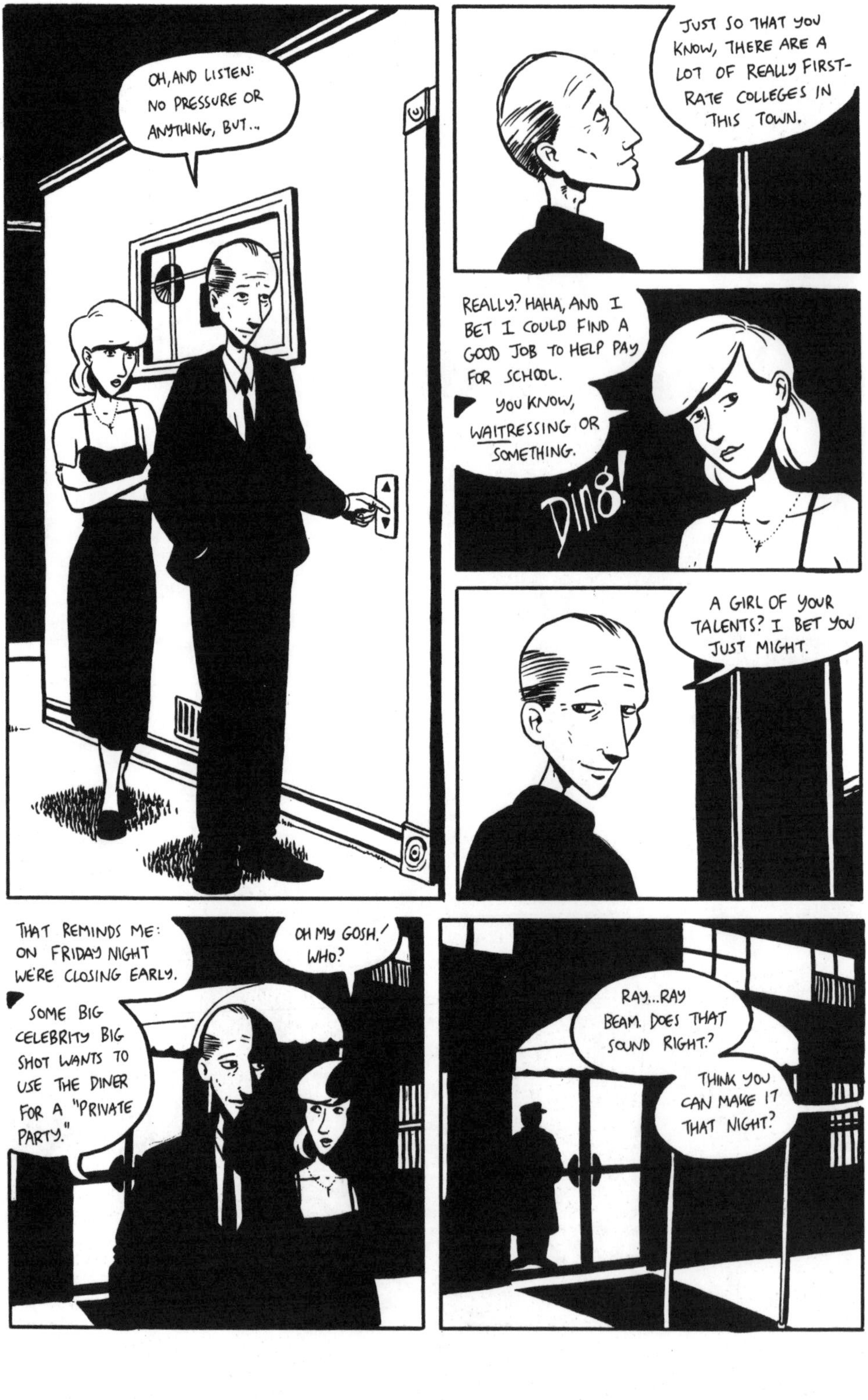
OH, AND LISTEN: NO PRESSURE OR ANYTHING, BUT...
JUST SO THAT YOU KNOW, THERE ARE A LOT OF REALLY FIRST-RATE COLLEGES IN THIS TOWN.
REALLY? HAHA, AND I BET I COULD FIND A GOOD JOB TO HELP PAY FOR SCHOOL.
YOU KNOW, WAITRESSING OR SOMETHING.
DING!
A GIRL OF YOUR TALENTS? I BET YOU JUST MIGHT.
THAT REMINDS ME: ON FRIDAY NIGHT WE'RE CLOSING EARLY.
SOME BIG CELEBRITY BIG SHOT WANTS TO USE THE DINER FOR A "PRIVATE PARTY."
OH MY GOSH! WHO?
RAY...RAY BEAM. DOES THAT SOUND RIGHT?
THINK YOU CAN MAKE IT THAT NIGHT?

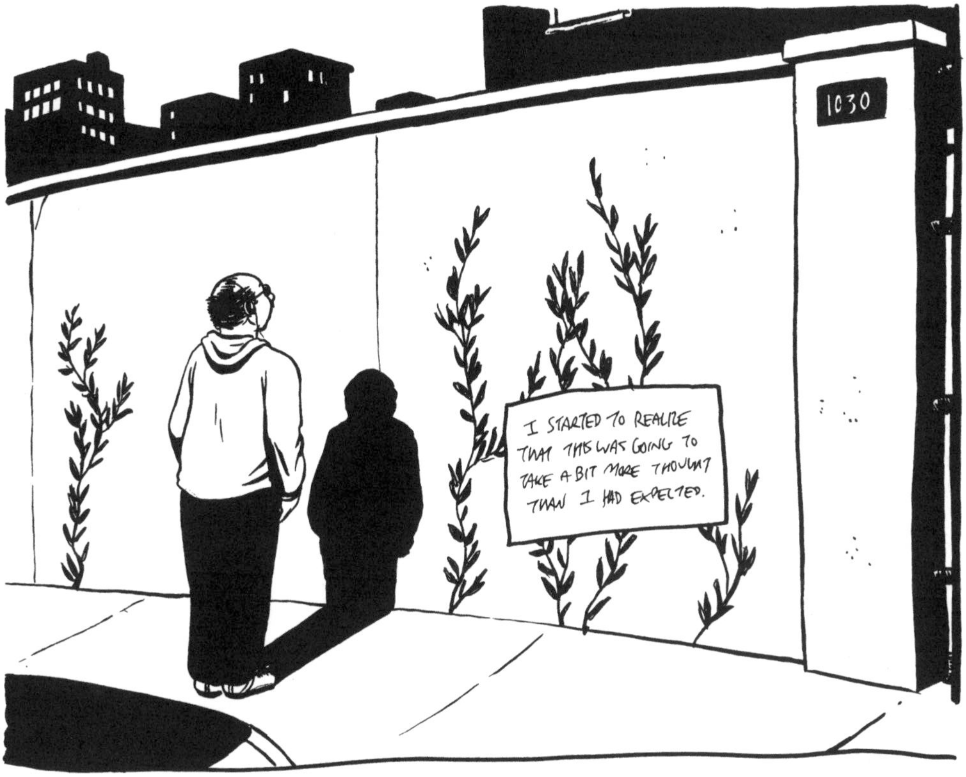
1030
I STARTED TO REALIZE THAT THIS WAS GOING TO TAKE A BIT MORE THOUGHT THAN I HAD EXPECTED.

FOUR

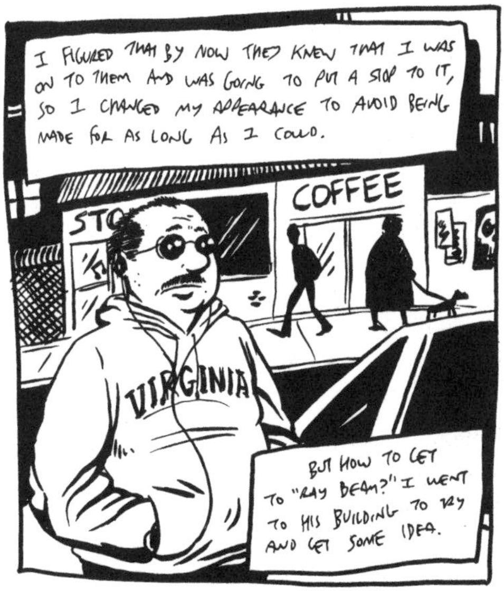
I FIGURED THAT BY NOW THEY KNEW THAT I WAS ON TO THEM AND WAS GOING TO PUT A STOP TO IT, SO I CHANGED MY APPEARANCE TO AVOID BEING MADE FOR AS LONG AS I COULD.
COFFEE
VIRGINIA
BUT HOW TO GET TO "RAY BEAM?" I WENT TO HIS BUILDING TO TRY AND GET SOME IDEA.

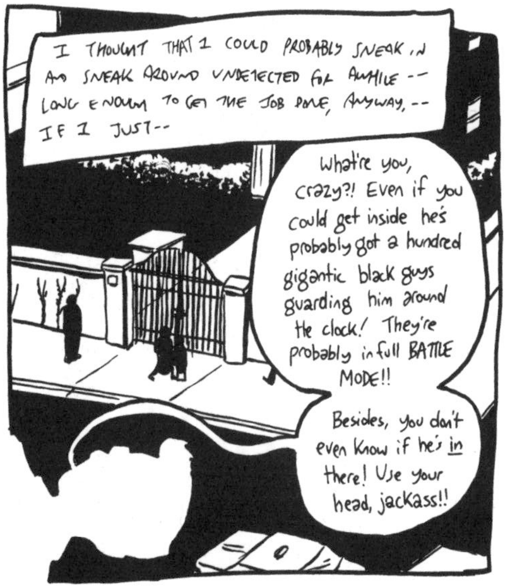
I THOUGHT THAT I COULD PROBABLY SNEAK IN AND SNEAK AROUND UNDETECTED FOR AWHILE -- LONG ENOUGH TO GET THE JOB DONE, ANYWAY, -- IF I JUST--
What're you, crazy?! Even if you could get inside he's probably got a hundred gigantic black guys guarding him around the clock! They're probably in full BATTLE MODE!!
Besides, you don't even know if he's in there! Use your head, jackass!!

AFTER A FEW HOURS I SAW A BIG BLACK LIMO GO THROUGH THE GATE. FOR A SECOND I THOUGHT ABOUT JUST SHOOTING INTO THE CAR AND HOPING FOR THE BEST BUT I COULDN'T BE SURE HE WAS IN THE CAR. IT MIGHT'VE BEEN SOMEONE ELSE ENTIRELY. HE'S FRIENDS WITH A LOT OF FAMOUS STARS. I WOULD HATE TO SHOOT INTO THE CAR AND FIND OUT I KILLED PHIL MONTY OR TERRI GOLD!

I ALSO FIGURED I WOULD PROBABLY ONLY HAVE ONE CHANCE AT THIS SO I HAD TO GET IT RIGHT.

I WENT BACK THE NEXT DAY AND HUNG AROUND SOMEMORE. WALKED AROUND THE NEIGHBORHOOD. TO TELL YOU THE TRUTH, I DIDN'T KNOW WHAT TO DO NEXT. I KNEW WHAT I HAD TO DO, WHAT MY MISSION WAS, OF COURSE, BUT I WAS EITHER TOO DUMB OR TOO SCARED TO FIGURE OUT MY NEXT STEP. IT WAS KIND OF FUNNY, IF YOU THINK ABOUT IT.

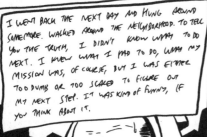

ON FRIDAY AFTERNOON THERE'S THIS BIG FAT GUY HANGING AROUND THE GATE. HE WAS TALKING TO THE DUMB GUARD WHO HANGS OUT IN THE LITTLE BOOTH INSIDE. EVERY NOW AND THEN HE WOULD GLANCE MY WAY.

IT MADE ME A LITTLE NERVOUS.

THEN HE STOPS TALKING TO THE GUARD. THEN HE TURNED AND STARTED WALKING TOWARDS ME.

HE WAS ABOUT SEVEN OR EIGHT FEET AWAY FROM ME WHEN HE SMILED AND SAID "YOU LOOK LIKE I COULD USE A DRINK MY TIRED FRIEND!"

IT'S A LINE, OF COURSE, FROM THE TALKS' SONG "TRAVELLER."

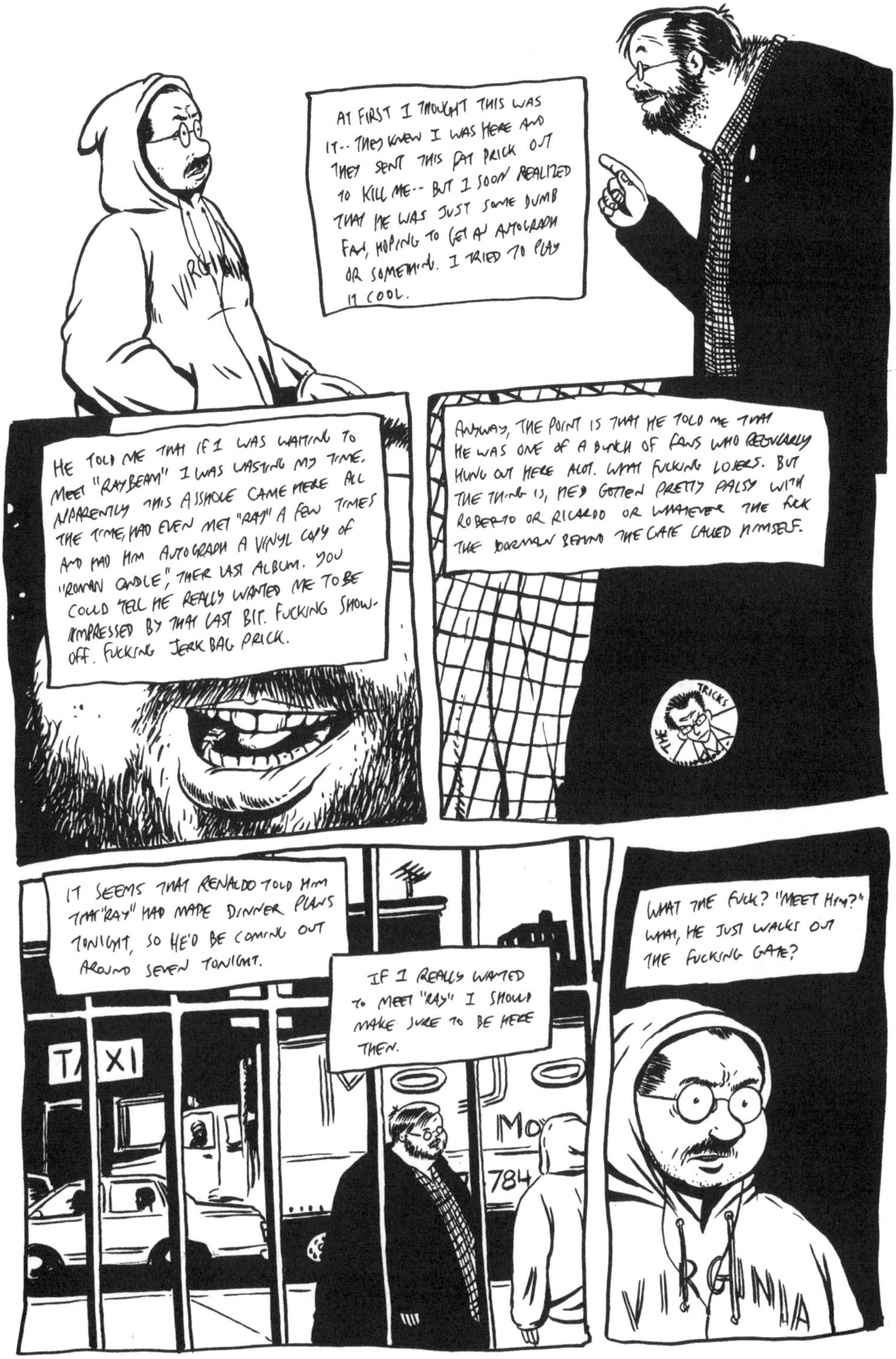
VIRGINIA
AT FIRST I THOUGHT THIS WAS IT-- THEY KNEW I WAS HERE AND THEY SENT THIS FAT PRICK OUT TO KILL ME-- BUT I SOON REALIZED THAT HE WAS JUST SOME DUMB FAN, HOPING TO GET AN AUTOGRAPH OR SOMETHING. I TRIED TO PLAY IT COOL.
HE TOLD ME THAT IF I WAS WAITING TO MEET "RAYBEAM" I WAS WASTING MY TIME. APPARENTLY THIS ASSHOLE CAME HERE ALL THE TIME, HAD EVEN MET "RAY" A FEW TIMES AND HAD HIM AUTOGRAPH A VINYL COPY OF "ROMAN CANDLE", THEIR LAST ALBUM. YOU COULD TELL HE REALLY WANTED ME TO BE IMPRESSED BY THAT LAST BIT. FUCKING SHOW-OFF. FUCKING JERK BAG PRICK.
ANYWAY, THE POINT IS THAT HE TOLD ME THAT HE WAS ONE OF A BUNCH OF FANS WHO REGULARLY HUNG OUT HERE ALOT. WHAT FUCKING LOSERS. BUT THE THING IS, HE'D GOTTEN PRETTY PALSY WITH ROBERTO OR RICARDO OR WHATEVER THE FUCK THE DOORMAN BEHIND THE GATE CALLED HIMSELF.
THE TRICKS
IT SEEMS THAT RENALDO TOLD HIM THAT "RAY" HAD MADE DINNER PLANS TONIGHT, SO HE'D BE COMING OUT AROUND SEVEN TONIGHT.
IF I REALLY WANTED TO MEET "RAY" I SHOULD MAKE SURE TO BE HERE THEN.
TAXI
784
WHAT THE FUCK? "MEET HIM?" WHAT, HE JUST WALKS OUT THE FUCKING GATE?
VIRGINIA

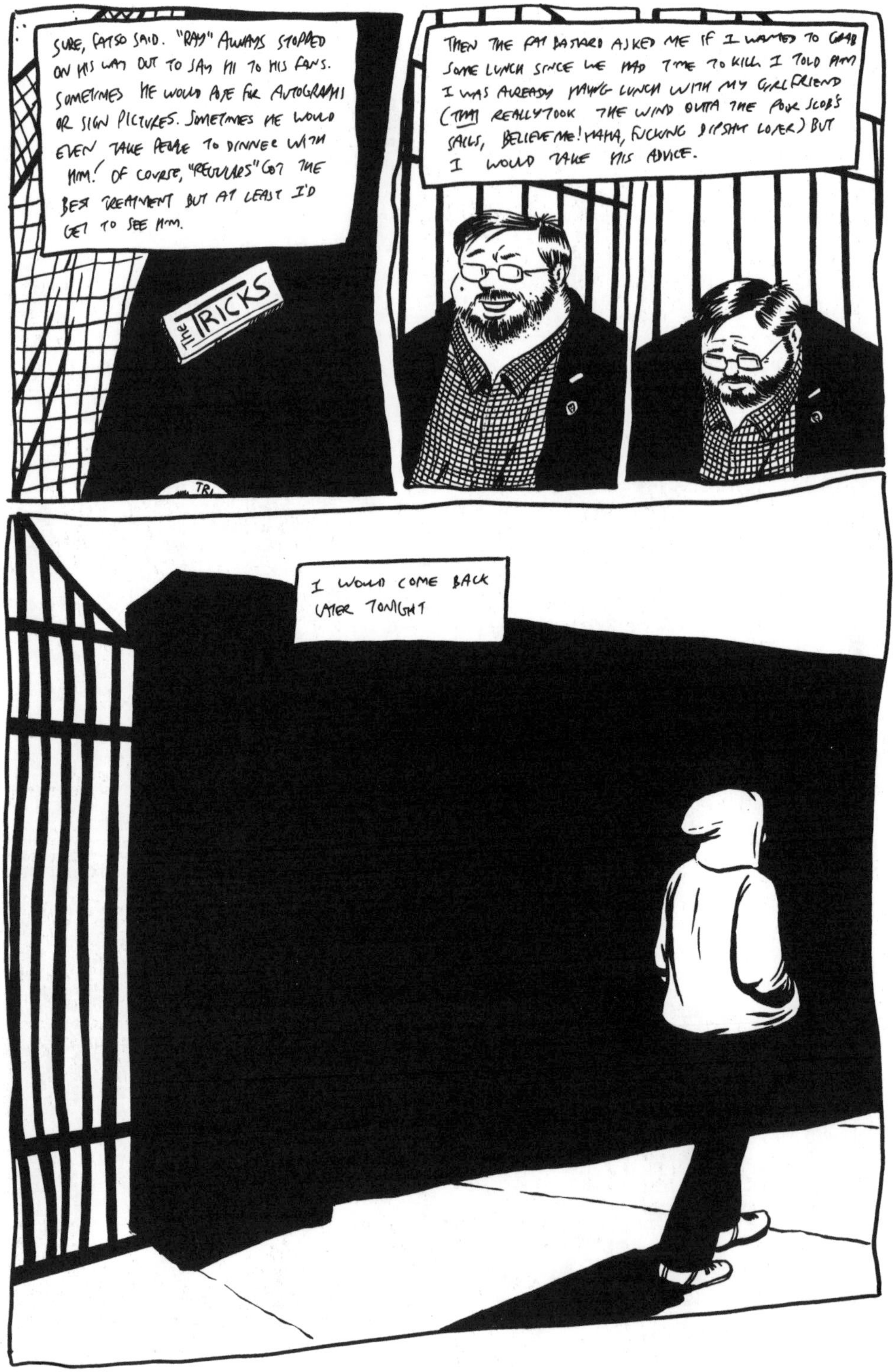
SURE, FATSO SAID. "RAY" ALWAYS STOPPED ON HIS WAY OUT TO SAY HI TO HIS FANS. SOMETIMES HE WOULD POSE FOR AUTOGRAPHS OR SIGN PICTURES. SOMETIMES HE WOULD EVEN TAKE PEOPLE TO DINNER WITH HIM! OF COURSE, "REGULARS" GOT THE BEST TREATMENT BUT AT LEAST I'D GET TO SEE HIM.
The TRICKS
THEN THE FAT BASTARD ASKED ME IF I WANTED TO GRAB SOME LUNCH SINCE WE HAD TIME TO KILL. I TOLD HIM I WAS ALREADY HAVING LUNCH WITH MY GIRLFRIEND (THAT REALLY TOOK THE WIND OUTTA THE POOR SLOB'S SAILS, BELIEVE ME! HAHA, FUCKING DIPSHIT LOSER) BUT I WOULD TAKE HIS ADVICE.
I WOULD COME BACK LATER TONIGHT

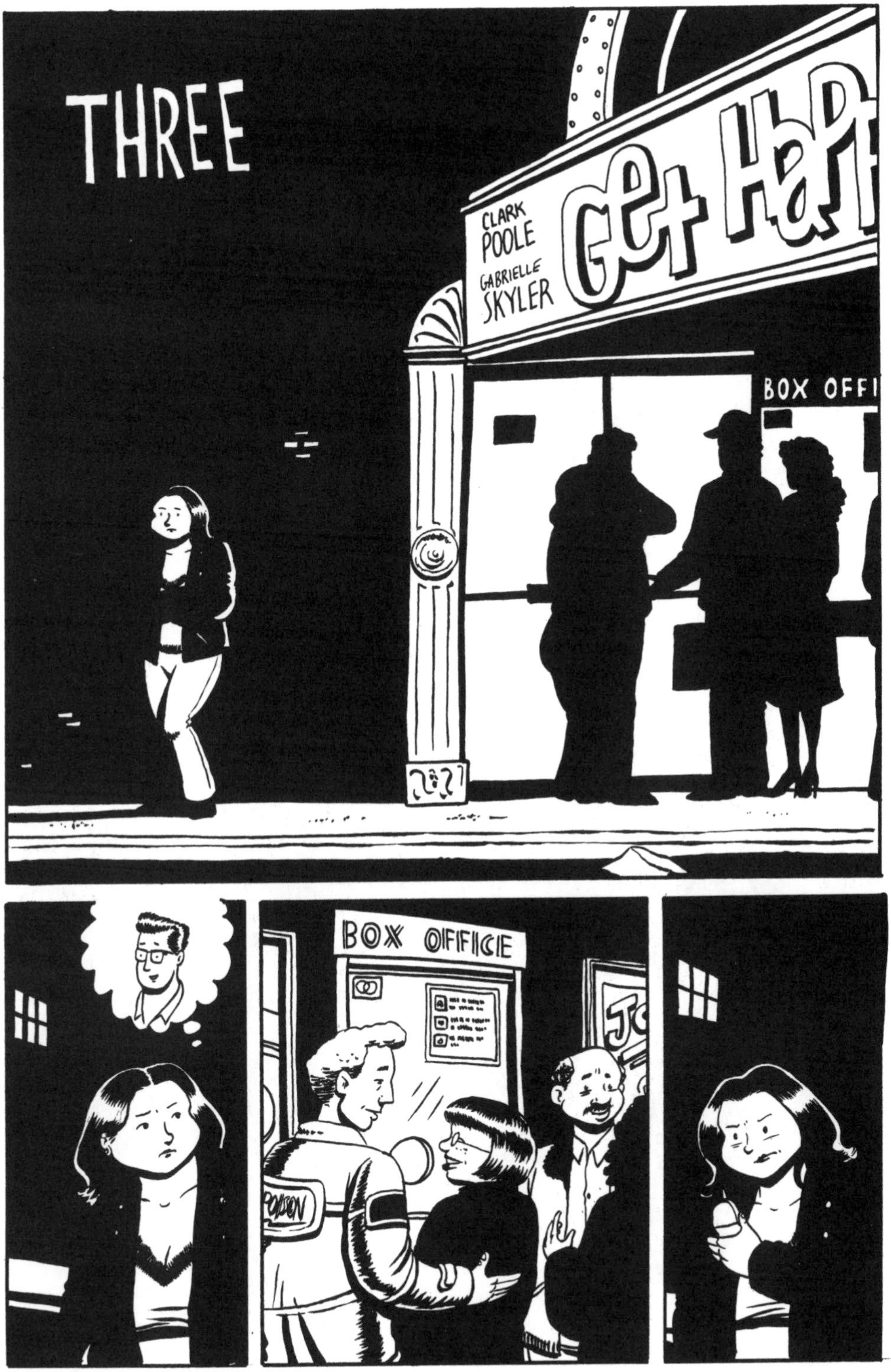
THREE
CLARK POOLE
GABRIELLE SKYLER
Get Hap
BOX OFFI
BOX OFFICE

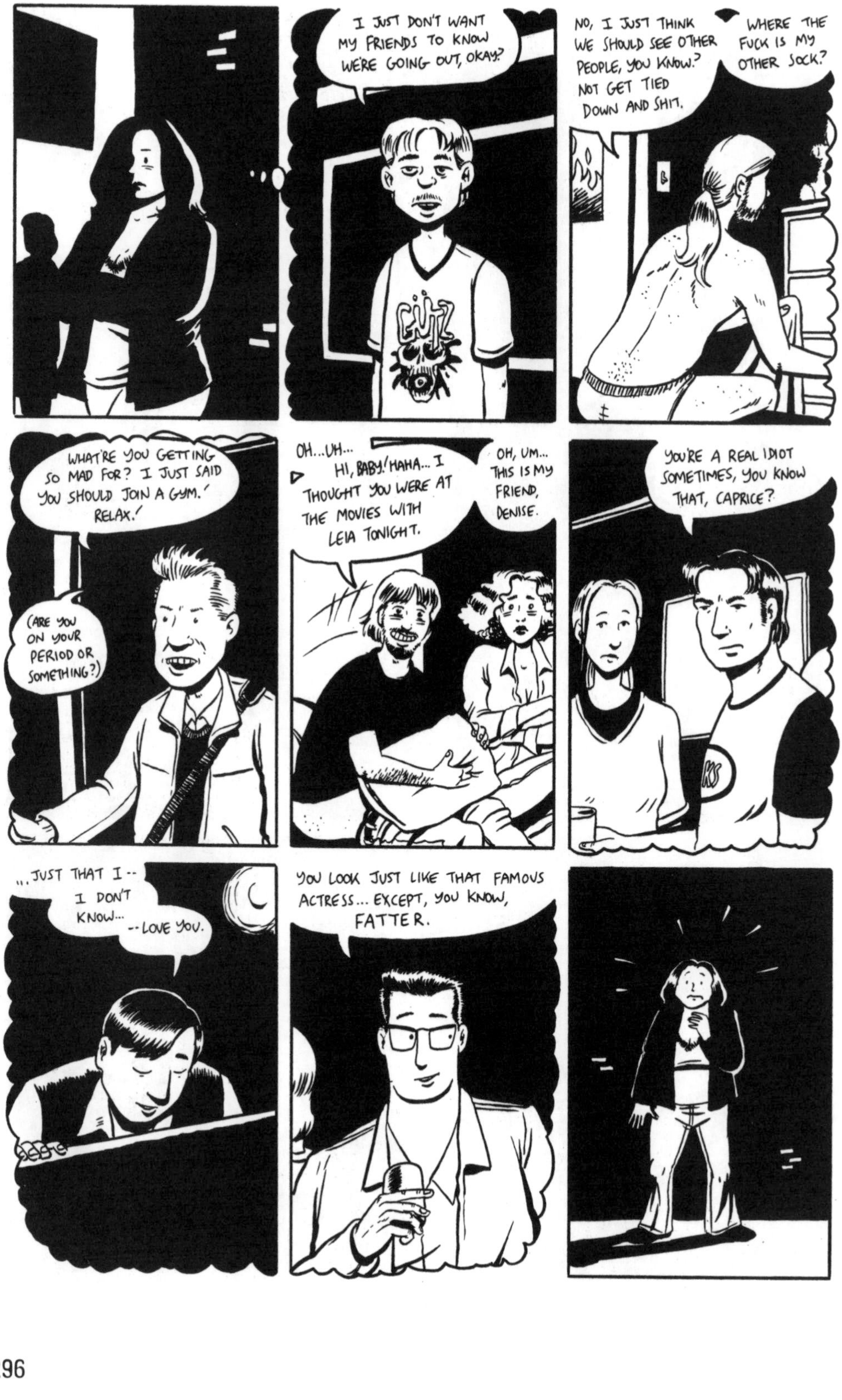
I JUST DON'T WANT MY FRIENDS TO KNOW WE'RE GOING OUT, OKAY?
NO, I JUST THINK WE SHOULD SEE OTHER PEOPLE, YOU KNOW? NOT GET TIED DOWN AND SHIT.
WHERE THE FUCK IS MY OTHER SOCK?
WHAT'RE YOU GETTING SO MAD FOR? I JUST SAID YOU SHOULD JOIN A GYM! RELAX!
(ARE YOU ON YOUR PERIOD OR SOMETHING?)
OH...UH... HI, BABY! HAHA... I THOUGHT YOU WERE AT THE MOVIES WITH LEIA TONIGHT.
OH, UM... THIS IS MY FRIEND, DENISE.
YOU'RE A REAL IDIOT SOMETIMES, YOU KNOW THAT, CAPRICE?
...JUST THAT I -- I DON'T KNOW... --LOVE YOU.
YOU LOOK JUST LIKE THAT FAMOUS ACTRESS... EXCEPT, YOU KNOW, FATTER.

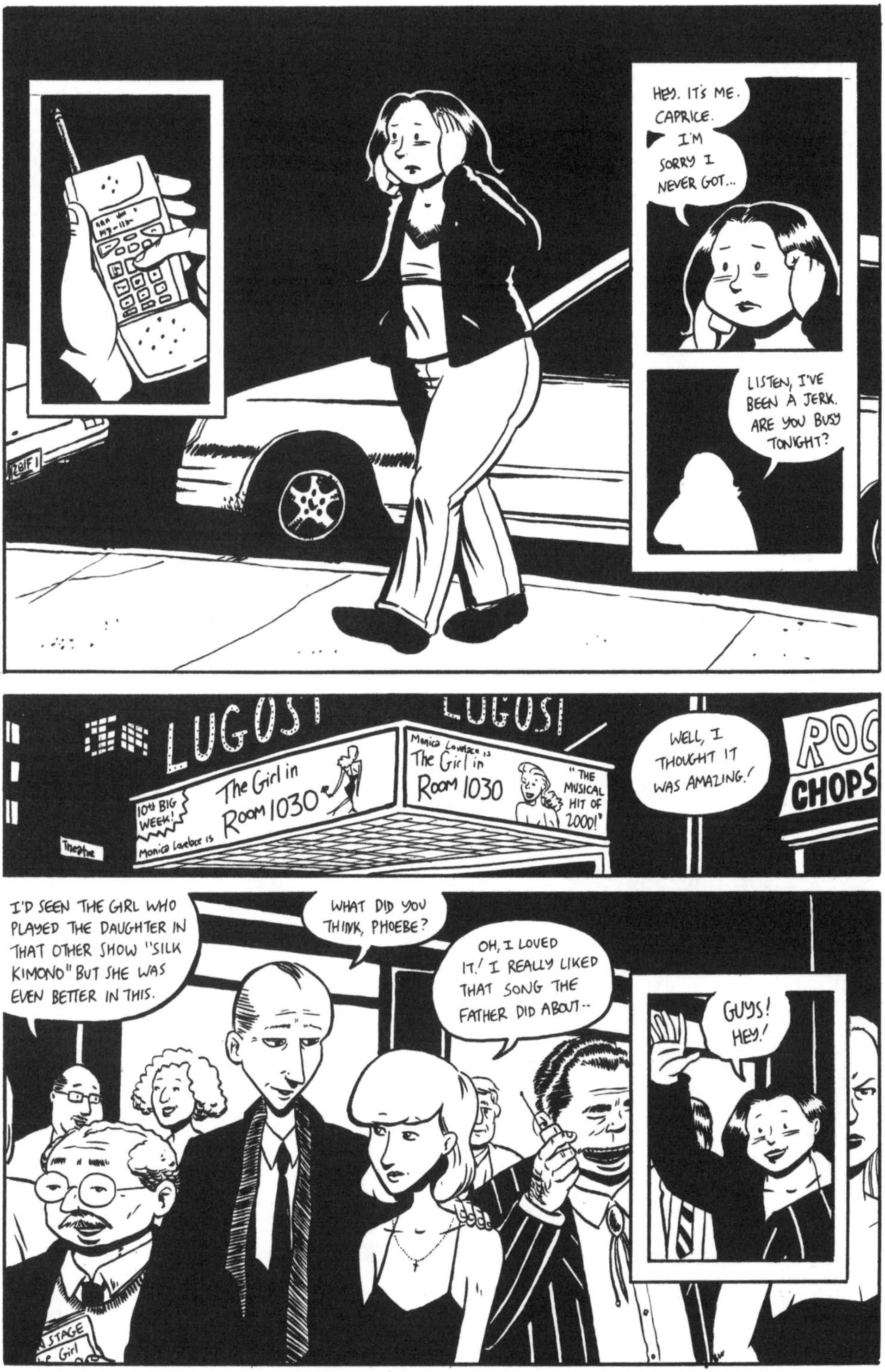
HEY. IT'S ME. CAPRICE. I'M SORRY I NEVER GOT...
LISTEN, I'VE BEEN A JERK. ARE YOU BUSY TONIGHT?
LUGOSI
LUGOSI
Monica Lovelace is The Girl in Room 1030
"THE MUSICAL HIT OF 2000!"
10th BIG WEEK!
The Girl in Room 1030
Monica Lovelace is
Theatre
WELL, I THOUGHT IT WAS AMAZING!
CHOPS
I'D SEEN THE GIRL WHO PLAYED THE DAUGHTER IN THAT OTHER SHOW "SILK KIMONO" BUT SHE WAS EVEN BETTER IN THIS.
WHAT DID YOU THINK, PHOEBE?
OH, I LOVED IT! I REALLY LIKED THAT SONG THE FATHER DID ABOUT--
GUYS! HEY!

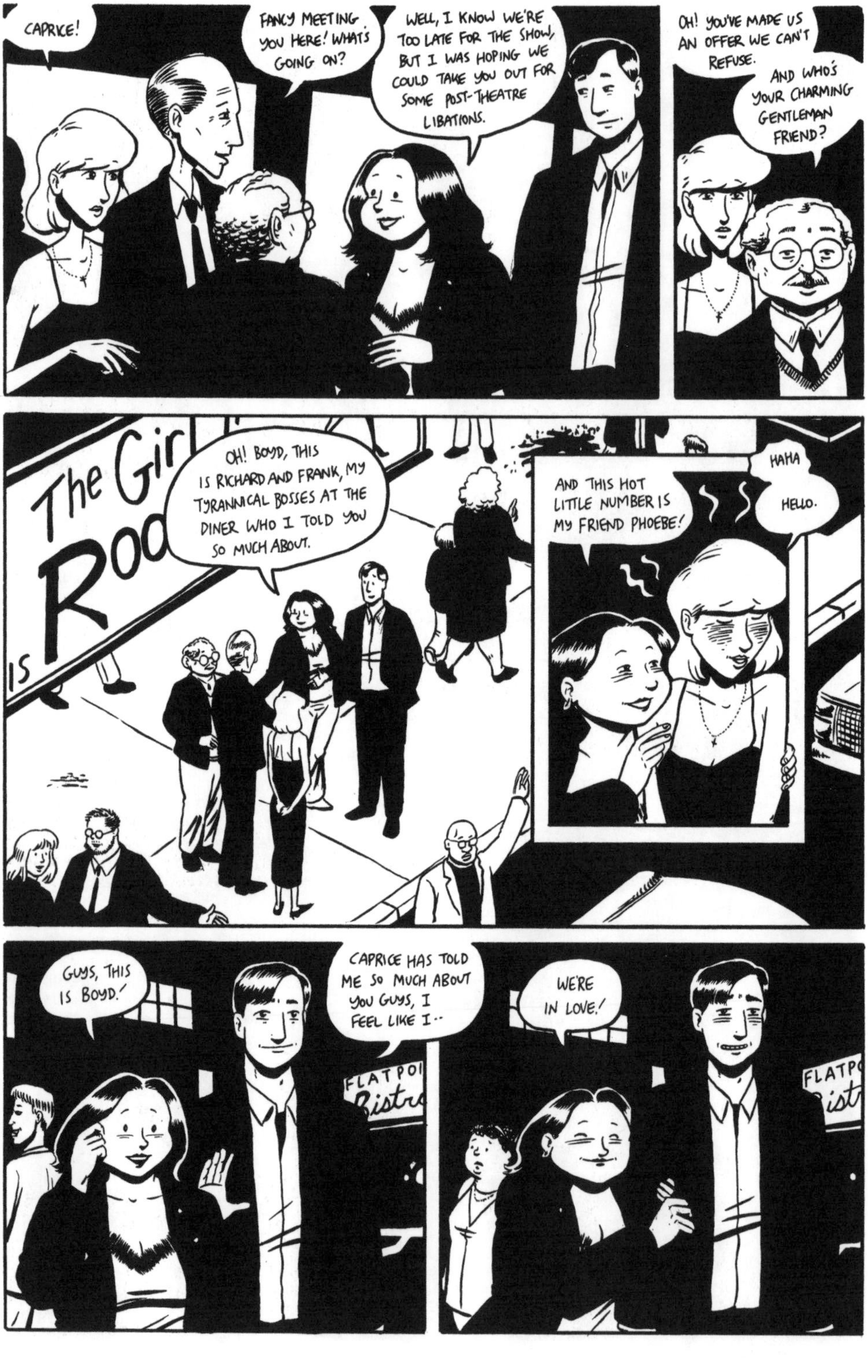
CAPRICE!
FANCY MEETING YOU HERE! WHAT'S GOING ON?
WELL, I KNOW WE'RE TOO LATE FOR THE SHOW, BUT I WAS HOPING WE COULD TAKE YOU OUT FOR SOME POST-THEATRE LIBATIONS.
OH! YOU'VE MADE US AN OFFER WE CAN'T REFUSE.
AND WHO'S YOUR CHARMING GENTLEMAN FRIEND?
The Gir
is Roo
OH! BOYD, THIS IS RICHARD AND FRANK, MY TYRANNICAL BOSSES AT THE DINER WHO I TOLD YOU SO MUCH ABOUT.
AND THIS HOT LITTLE NUMBER IS MY FRIEND PHOEBE!
HAHA
HELLO.
GUYS, THIS IS BOYD!
CAPRICE HAS TOLD ME SO MUCH ABOUT YOU GUYS, I FEEL LIKE I..
FLATPOI
Bistr
WE'RE IN LOVE!
FLATPO
Bistr

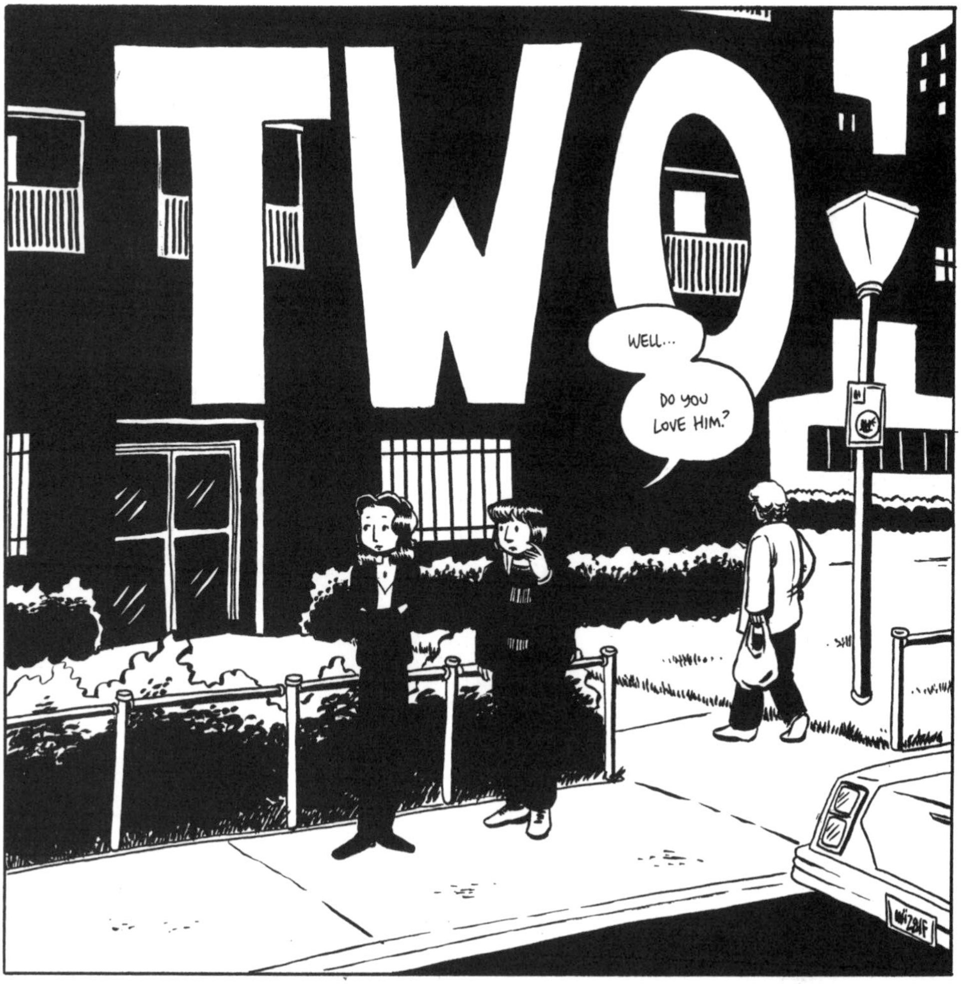
TWO
WELL...
DO YOU LOVE HIM?

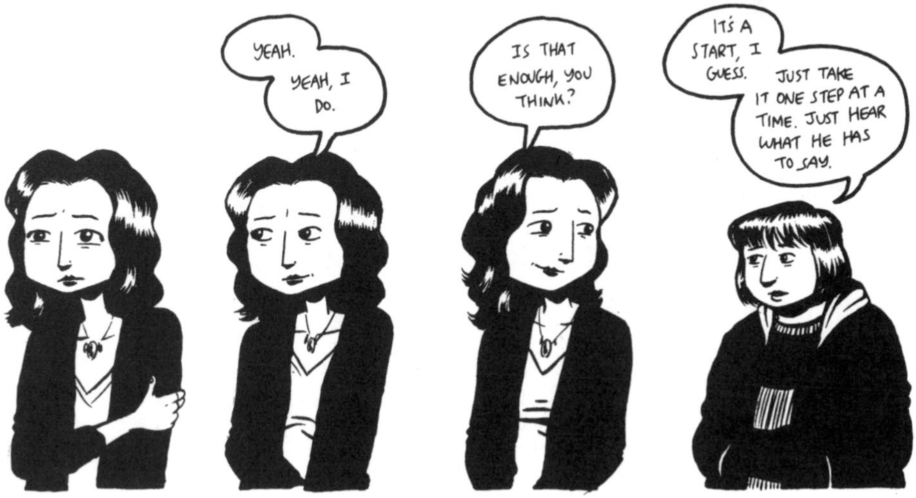
YEAH.
YEAH, I DO.
IS THAT ENOUGH, YOU THINK?
IT'S A START, I GUESS.
JUST TAKE IT ONE STEP AT A TIME. JUST HEAR WHAT HE HAS TO SAY.

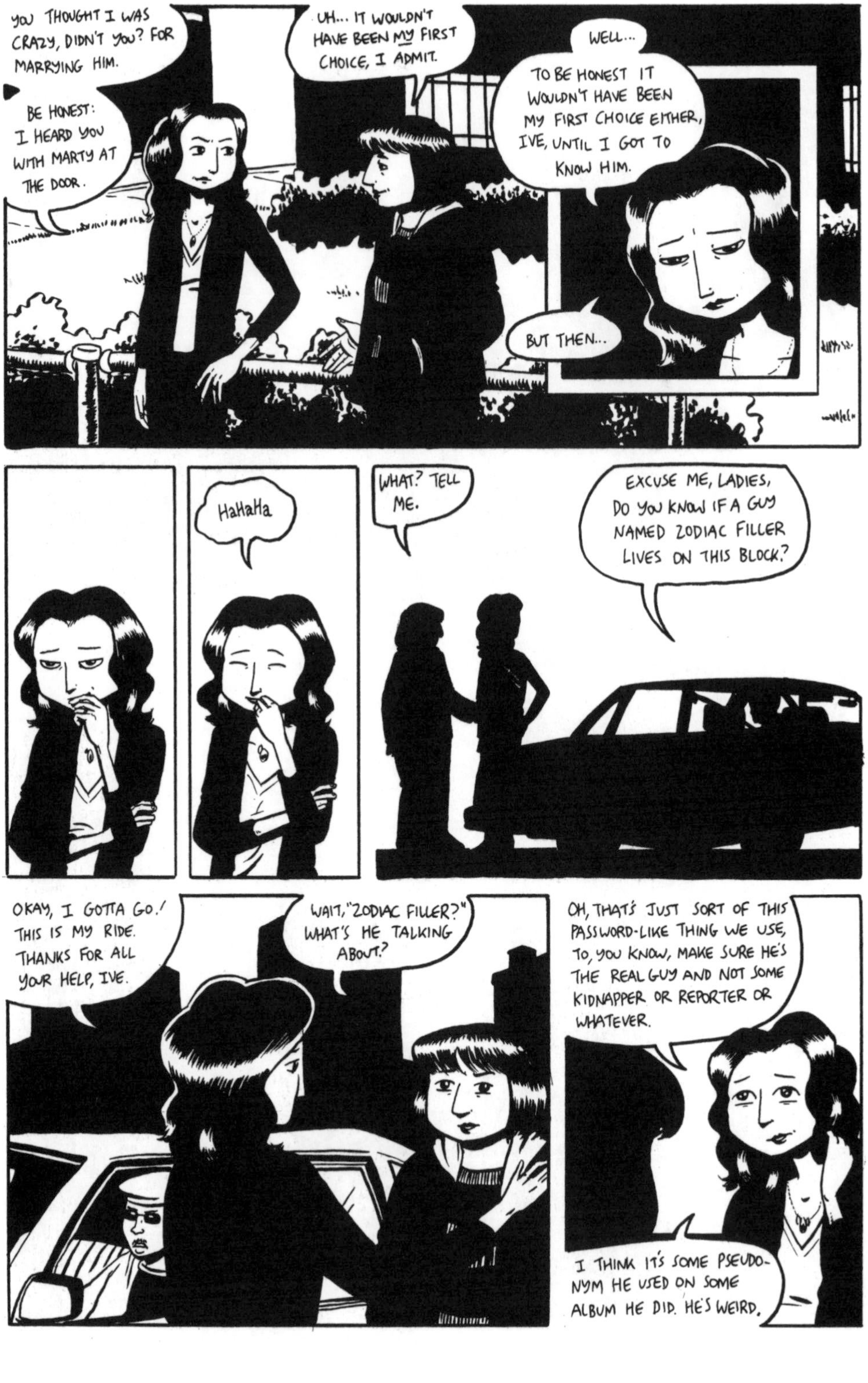
YOU THOUGHT I WAS CRAZY, DIDN'T YOU? FOR MARRYING HIM.
BE HONEST: I HEARD YOU WITH MARTY AT THE DOOR.
UH... IT WOULDN'T HAVE BEEN MY FIRST CHOICE, I ADMIT.
WELL...
TO BE HONEST IT WOULDN'T HAVE BEEN MY FIRST CHOICE EITHER, IVE, UNTIL I GOT TO KNOW HIM.
BUT THEN...
HaHaHa
WHAT? TELL ME.
EXCUSE ME, LADIES, DO YOU KNOW IF A GUY NAMED ZODIAC FILLER LIVES ON THIS BLOCK?
OKAY, I GOTTA GO.! THIS IS MY RIDE. THANKS FOR ALL YOUR HELP, IVE.
WAIT, "ZODIAC FILLER?" WHAT'S HE TALKING ABOUT?
OH, THAT'S JUST SORT OF THIS PASSWORD-LIKE THING WE USE, TO, YOU KNOW, MAKE SURE HE'S THE REAL GUY AND NOT SOME KIDNAPPER OR REPORTER OR WHATEVER.
I THINK IT'S SOME PSEUDONYM HE USED ON SOME ALBUM HE DID. HE'S WEIRD.

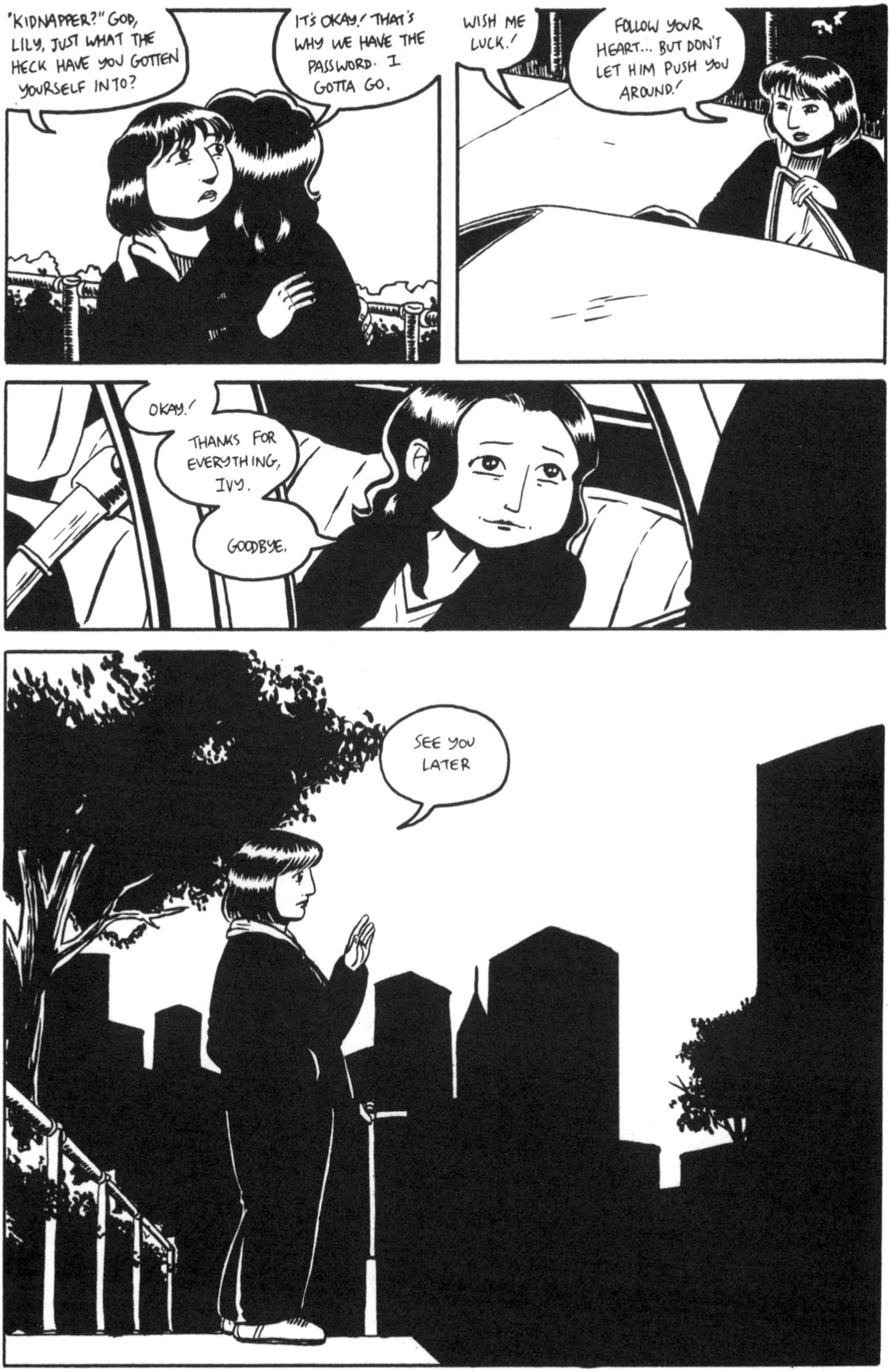
"KIDNAPPER?" GOD, LILY, JUST WHAT THE HECK HAVE YOU GOTTEN YOURSELF INTO?
IT'S OKAY! THAT'S WHY WE HAVE THE PASSWORD. I GOTTA GO.
WISH ME LUCK!
FOLLOW YOUR HEART... BUT DON'T LET HIM PUSH YOU AROUND!
OKAY!
THANKS FOR EVERYTHING, IVY.
GOODBYE.
SEE YOU LATER

ONE

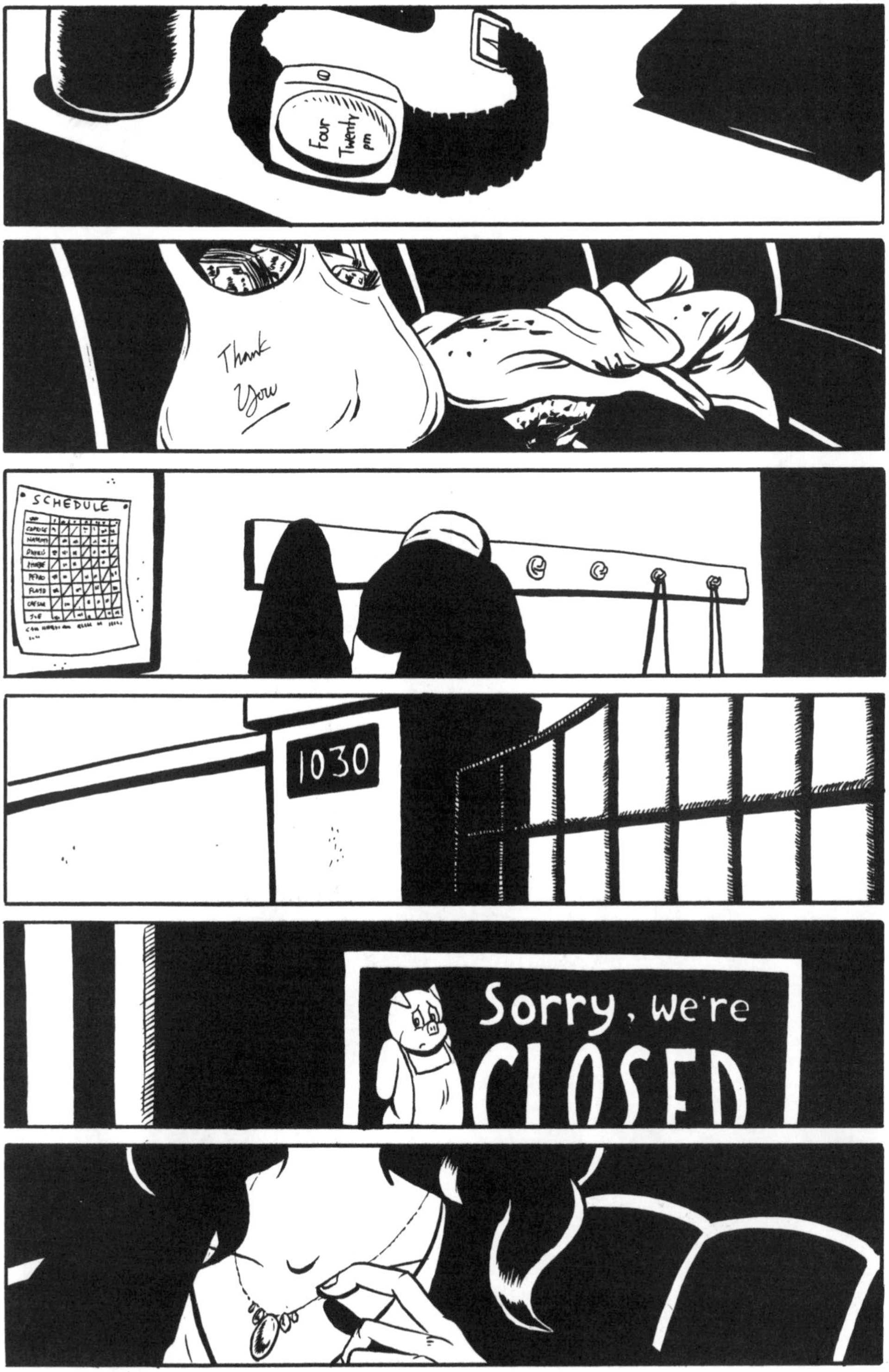
Four Twenty pm
Thank You
SCHEDULE
1030
Sorry, we're
CLOSED

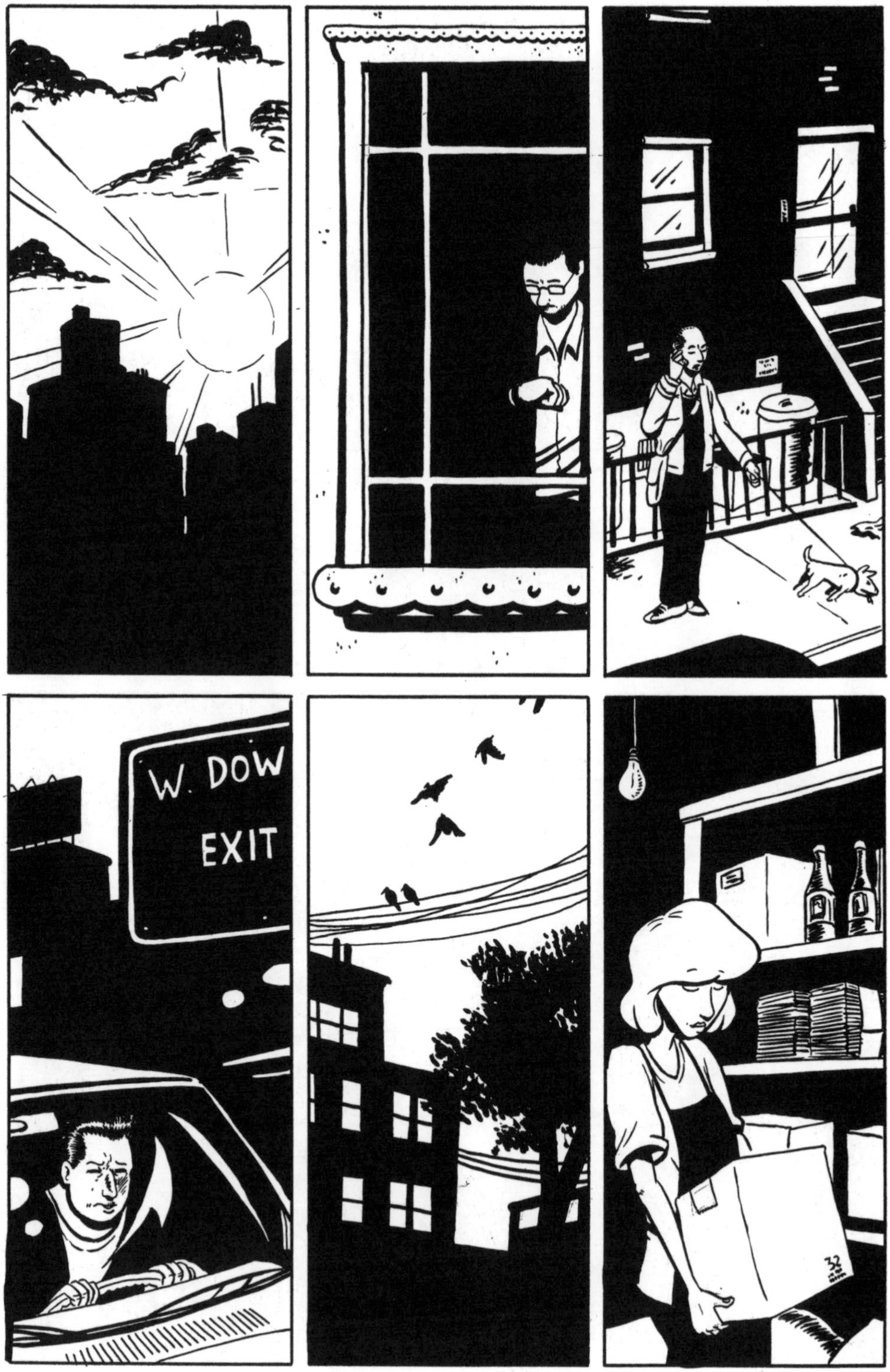
W. DOW
EXIT

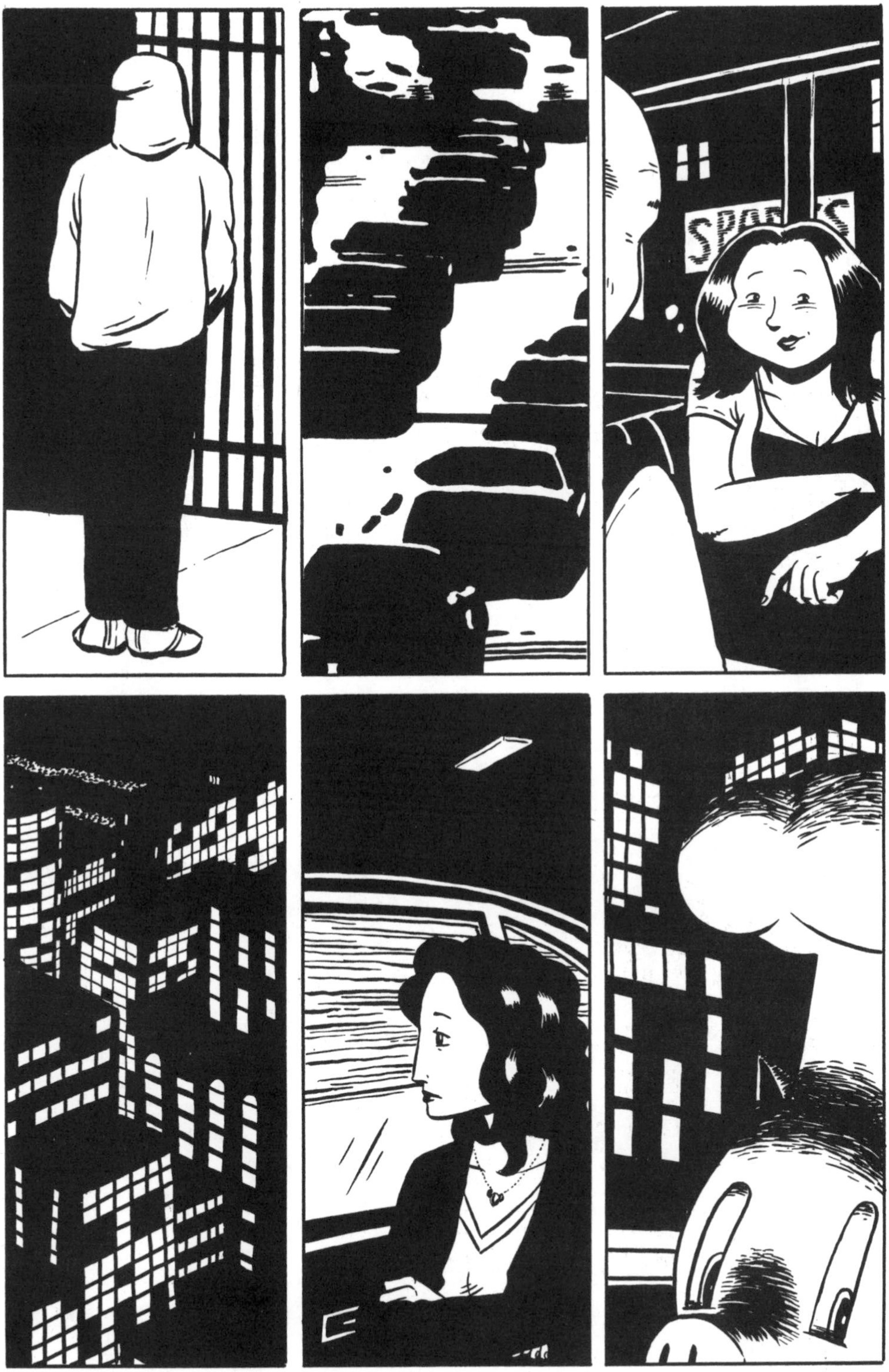

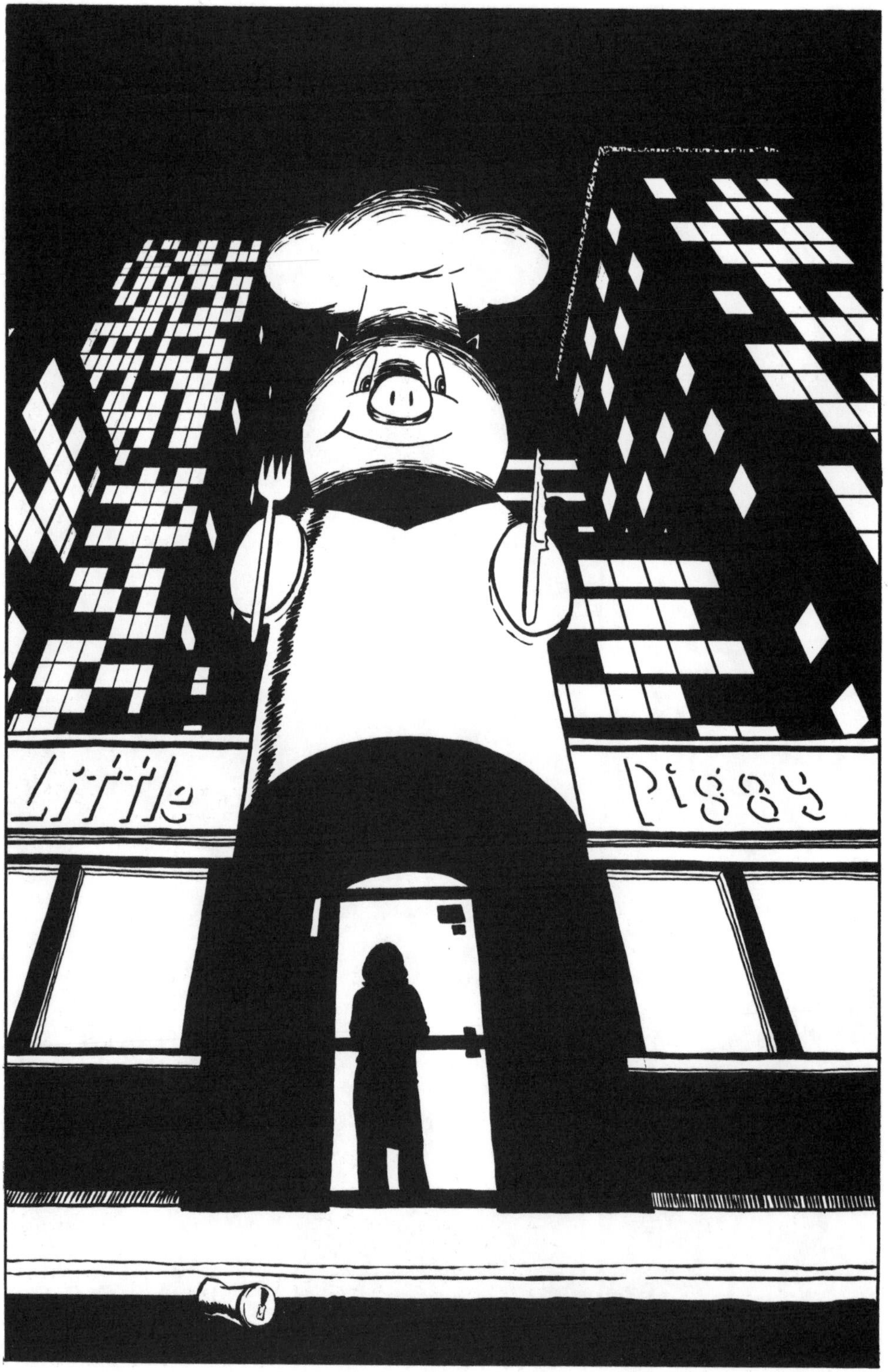
Little
Piggy

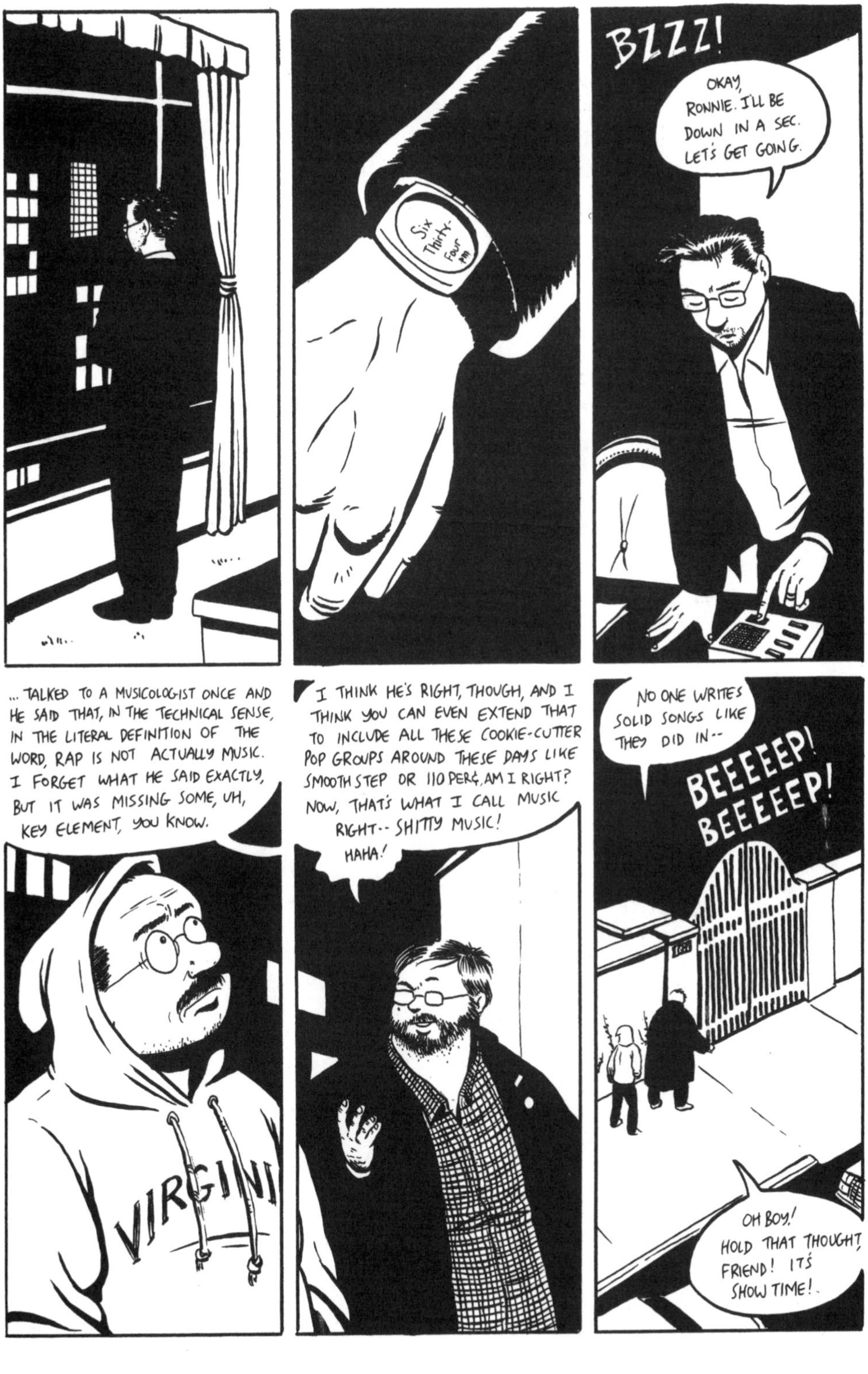
Six Thirty-Four AM
BZZZ!
OKAY, RONNIE. I'LL BE DOWN IN A SEC. LET'S GET GOING.
... TALKED TO A MUSICOLOGIST ONCE AND HE SAID THAT, IN THE TECHNICAL SENSE, IN THE LITERAL DEFINITION OF THE WORD, RAP IS NOT ACTUALLY MUSIC. I FORGET WHAT HE SAID EXACTLY, BUT IT WAS MISSING SOME, UH, KEY ELEMENT, YOU KNOW.
VIRGINI
I THINK HE'S RIGHT, THOUGH, AND I THINK YOU CAN EVEN EXTEND THAT TO INCLUDE ALL THESE COOKIE-CUTTER POP GROUPS AROUND THESE DAYS LIKE SMOOTH STEP OR 110 PER¢. AM I RIGHT? NOW, THAT'S WHAT I CALL MUSIC RIGHT-- SHITTY MUSIC! HAHA!
NO ONE WRITES SOLID SONGS LIKE THEY DID IN--
BEEEEEP! BEEEEEP!
OH BOY! HOLD THAT THOUGHT, FRIEND! IT'S SHOW TIME!

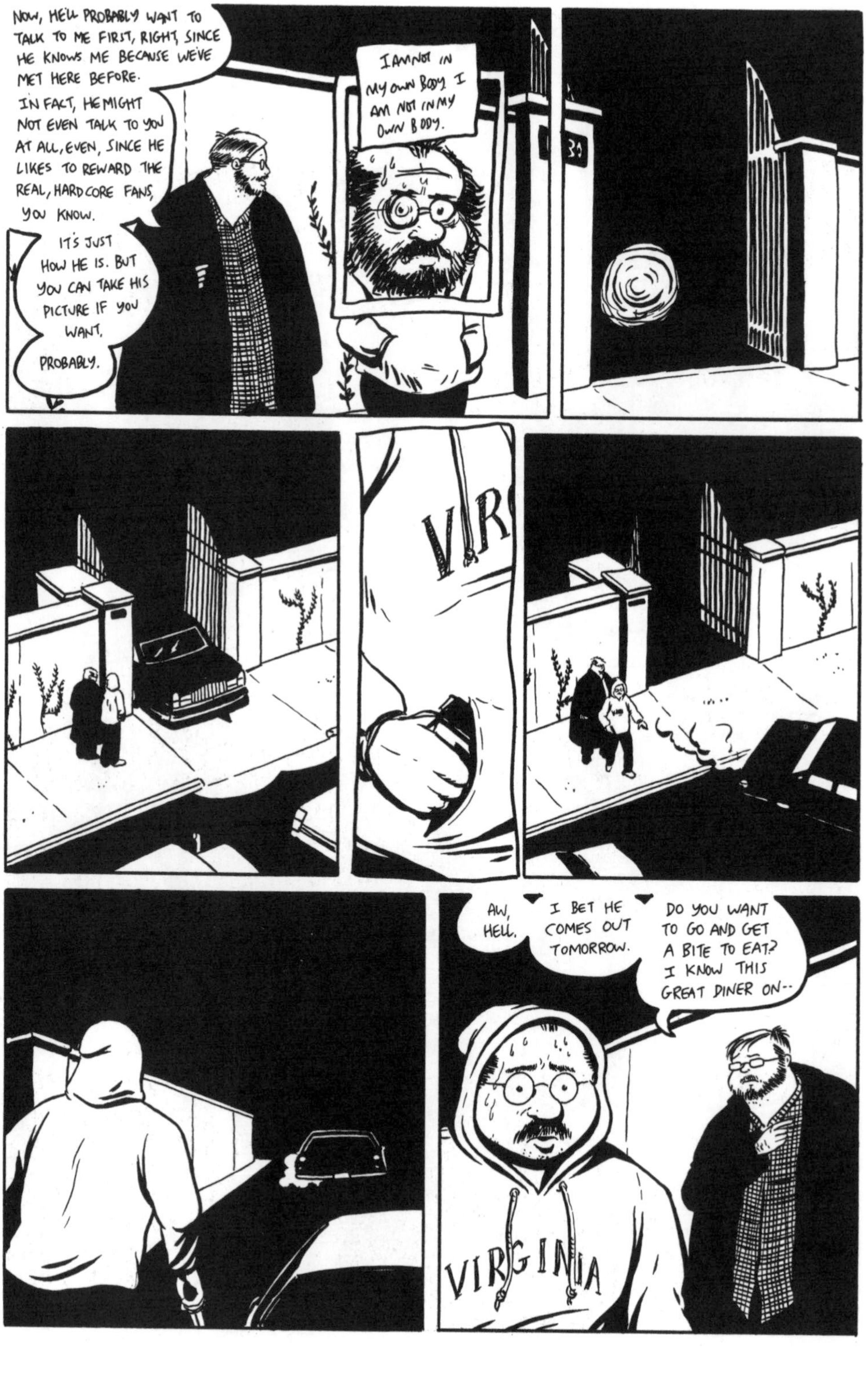
NOW, HE'LL PROBABLY WANT TO TALK TO ME FIRST, RIGHT, SINCE HE KNOWS ME BECAUSE WE'VE MET HERE BEFORE.
IN FACT, HE MIGHT NOT EVEN TALK TO YOU AT ALL, EVEN, SINCE HE LIKES TO REWARD THE REAL, HARDCORE FANS, YOU KNOW.
IT'S JUST HOW HE IS. BUT YOU CAN TAKE HIS PICTURE IF YOU WANT, PROBABLY.
I AM NOT IN MY OWN BODY. I AM NOT IN MY OWN BODY.
VIR
AW, HELL.
I BET HE COMES OUT TOMORROW.
DO YOU WANT TO GO AND GET A BITE TO EAT? I KNOW THIS GREAT DINER ON--
VIRGINIA

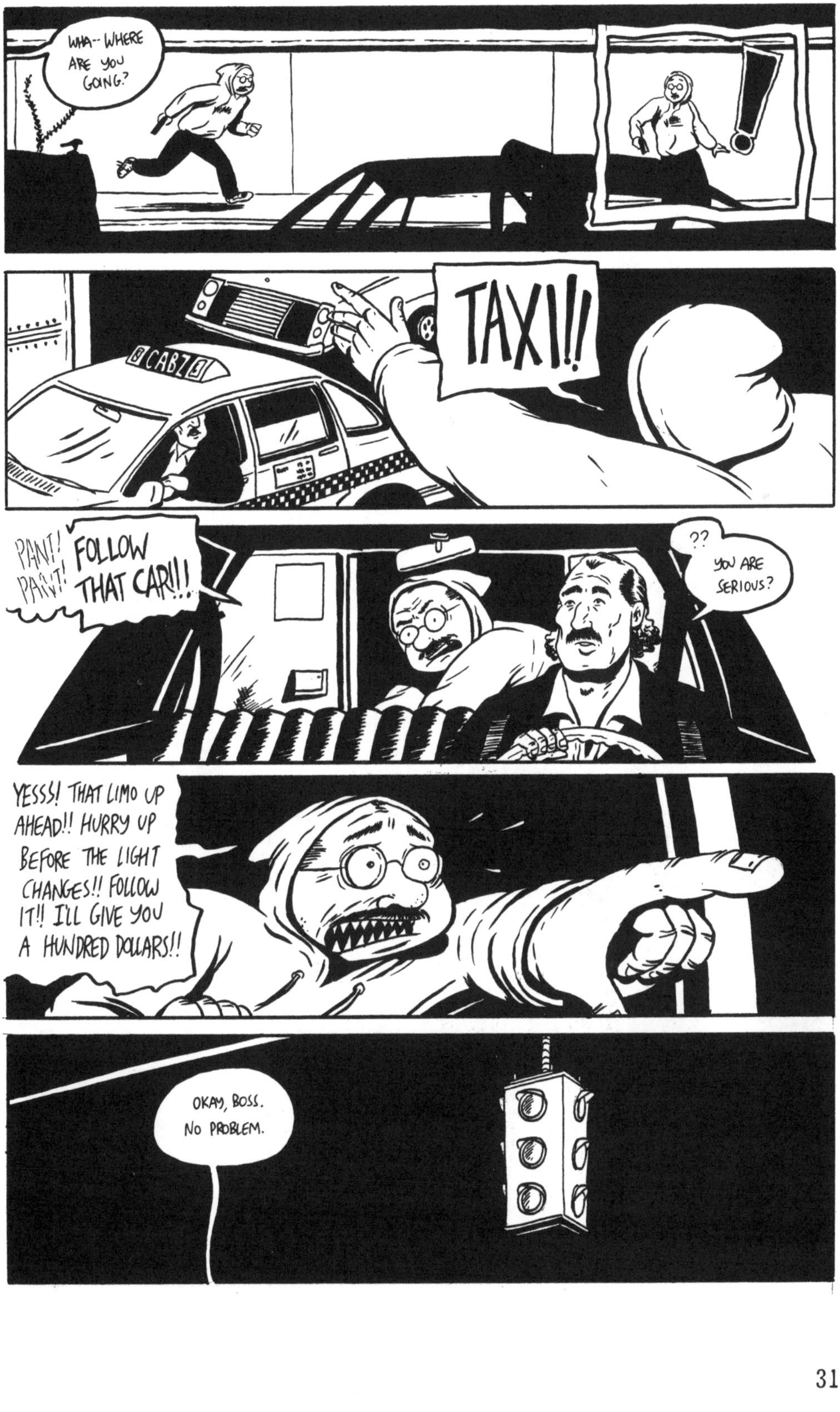
WHA-- WHERE ARE YOU GOING?
!
TAXI!!!
PANT! PANT!
FOLLOW THAT CAR!!!
??
YOU ARE SERIOUS?
YESSS! THAT LIMO UP AHEAD!! HURRY UP BEFORE THE LIGHT CHANGES!! FOLLOW IT!! I'LL GIVE YOU A HUNDRED DOLLARS!!
OKAY, BOSS. NO PROBLEM.

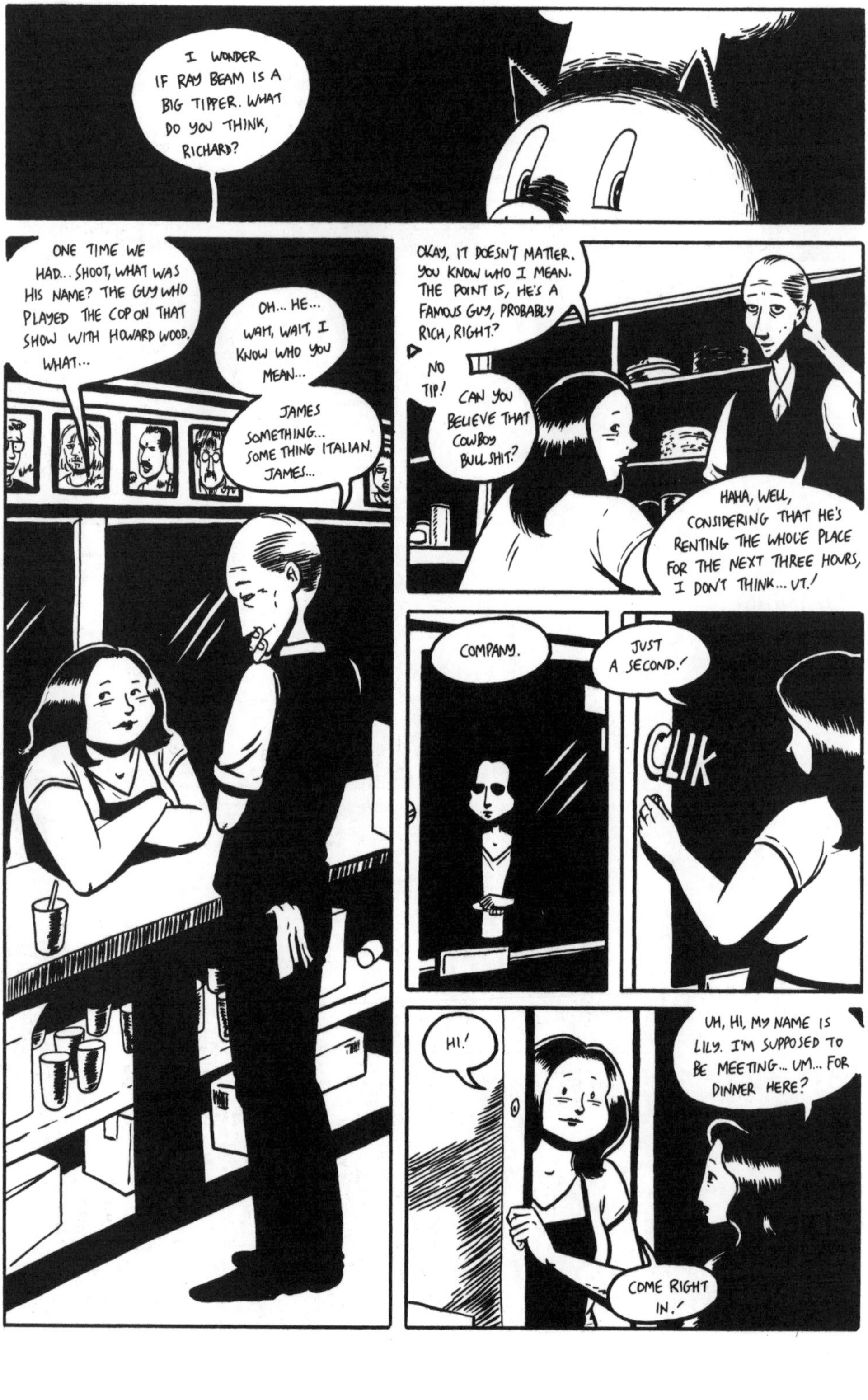
I WONDER IF RAY BEAM IS A BIG TIPPER. WHAT DO YOU THINK, RICHARD?
ONE TIME WE HAD... SHOOT, WHAT WAS HIS NAME? THE GUY WHO PLAYED THE COP ON THAT SHOW WITH HOWARD WOOD. WHAT...
OH... HE... WAIT, WAIT, I KNOW WHO YOU MEAN...
JAMES SOMETHING... SOME THING ITALIAN. JAMES...
OKAY, IT DOESN'T MATTER. YOU KNOW WHO I MEAN. THE POINT IS, HE'S A FAMOUS GUY, PROBABLY RICH, RIGHT?
NO TIP!
CAN YOU BELIEVE THAT COWBOY BULLSHIT?
HAHA, WELL, CONSIDERING THAT HE'S RENTING THE WHOLE PLACE FOR THE NEXT THREE HOURS, I DON'T THINK... UT.!
COMPANY.
JUST A SECOND.!
CLIK
HI.!
UH, HI, MY NAME IS LILY. I'M SUPPOSED TO BE MEETING... UM... FOR DINNER HERE?
COME RIGHT IN.!

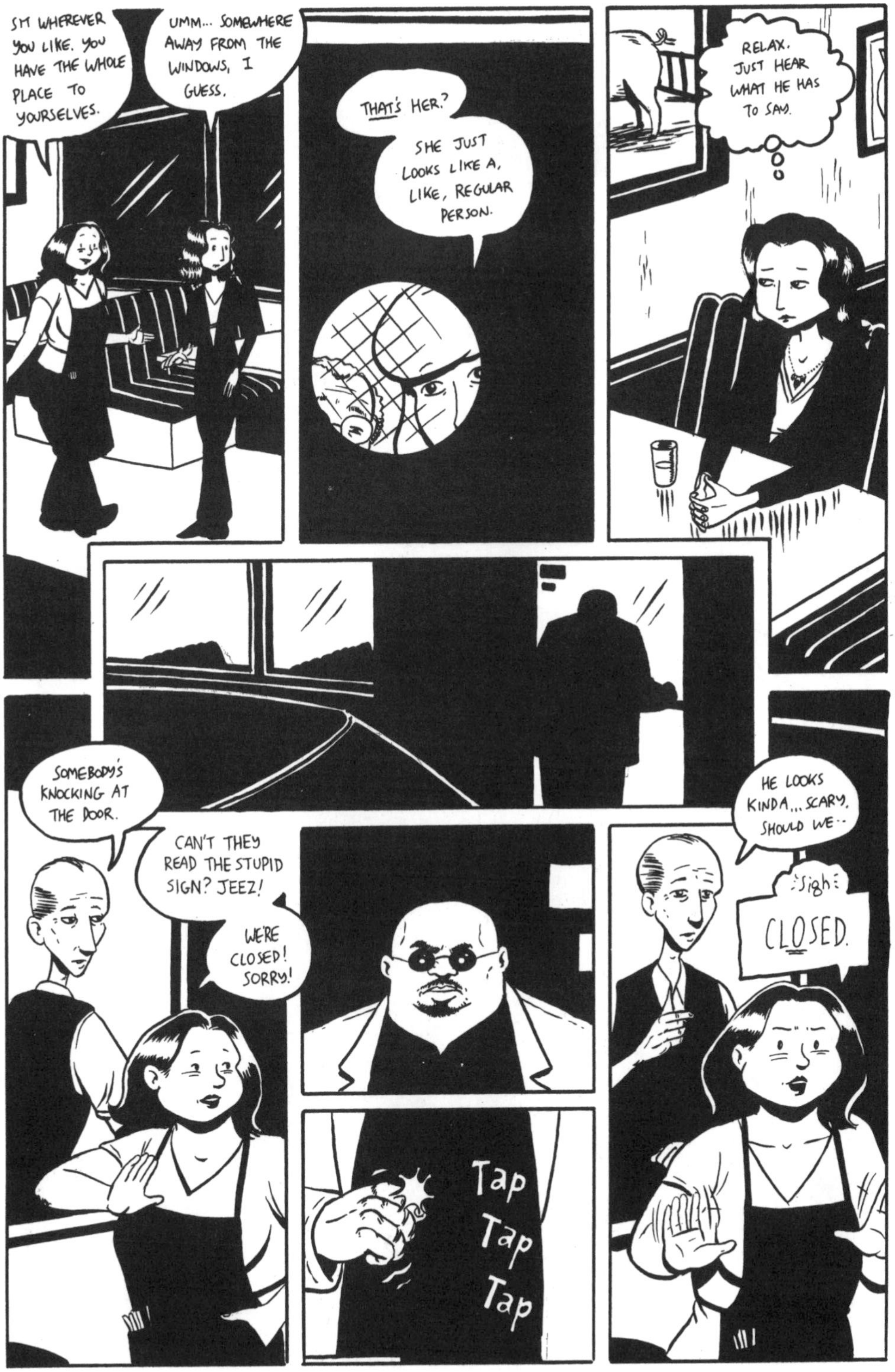
SIT WHEREVER YOU LIKE. YOU HAVE THE WHOLE PLACE TO YOURSELVES.
UMM... SOMEWHERE AWAY FROM THE WINDOWS, I GUESS.
THAT'S HER?
SHE JUST LOOKS LIKE A, LIKE, REGULAR PERSON.
RELAX. JUST HEAR WHAT HE HAS TO SAY.
SOMEBODY'S KNOCKING AT THE DOOR.
CAN'T THEY READ THE STUPID SIGN? JEEZ!
WE'RE CLOSED! SORRY!
Tap
Tap
Tap
HE LOOKS KINDA... SCARY. SHOULD WE--
Sigh
CLOSED.

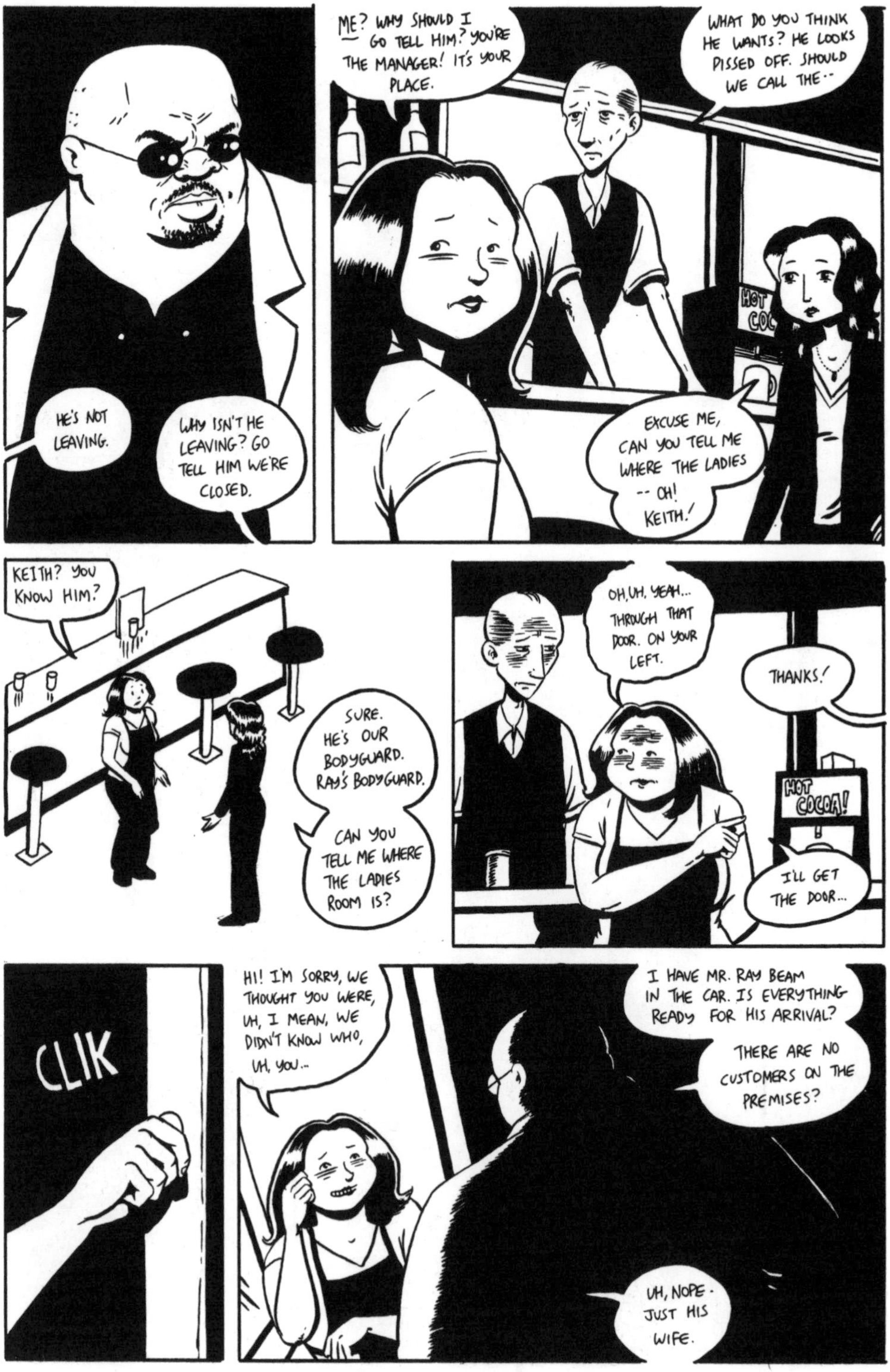
HE'S NOT LEAVING.
WHY ISN'T HE LEAVING? GO TELL HIM WE'RE CLOSED.
ME? WHY SHOULD I GO TELL HIM? YOU'RE THE MANAGER! IT'S YOUR PLACE.
WHAT DO YOU THINK HE WANTS? HE LOOKS PISSED OFF. SHOULD WE CALL THE--
HOT COCO
EXCUSE ME, CAN YOU TELL ME WHERE THE LADIES -- OH! KEITH!
KEITH? YOU KNOW HIM?
SURE. HE'S OUR BODYGUARD. RAY'S BODYGUARD.
CAN YOU TELL ME WHERE THE LADIES ROOM IS?
OH, UH, YEAH... THROUGH THAT DOOR. ON YOUR LEFT.
THANKS!
HOT COCOA!
I'LL GET THE DOOR...
CLIK
HI! I'M SORRY, WE THOUGHT YOU WERE, UH, I MEAN, WE DIDN'T KNOW WHO, UH, YOU...
I HAVE MR. RAY BEAM IN THE CAR. IS EVERYTHING READY FOR HIS ARRIVAL?
THERE ARE NO CUSTOMERS ON THE PREMISES?
UH, NOPE. JUST HIS WIFE.

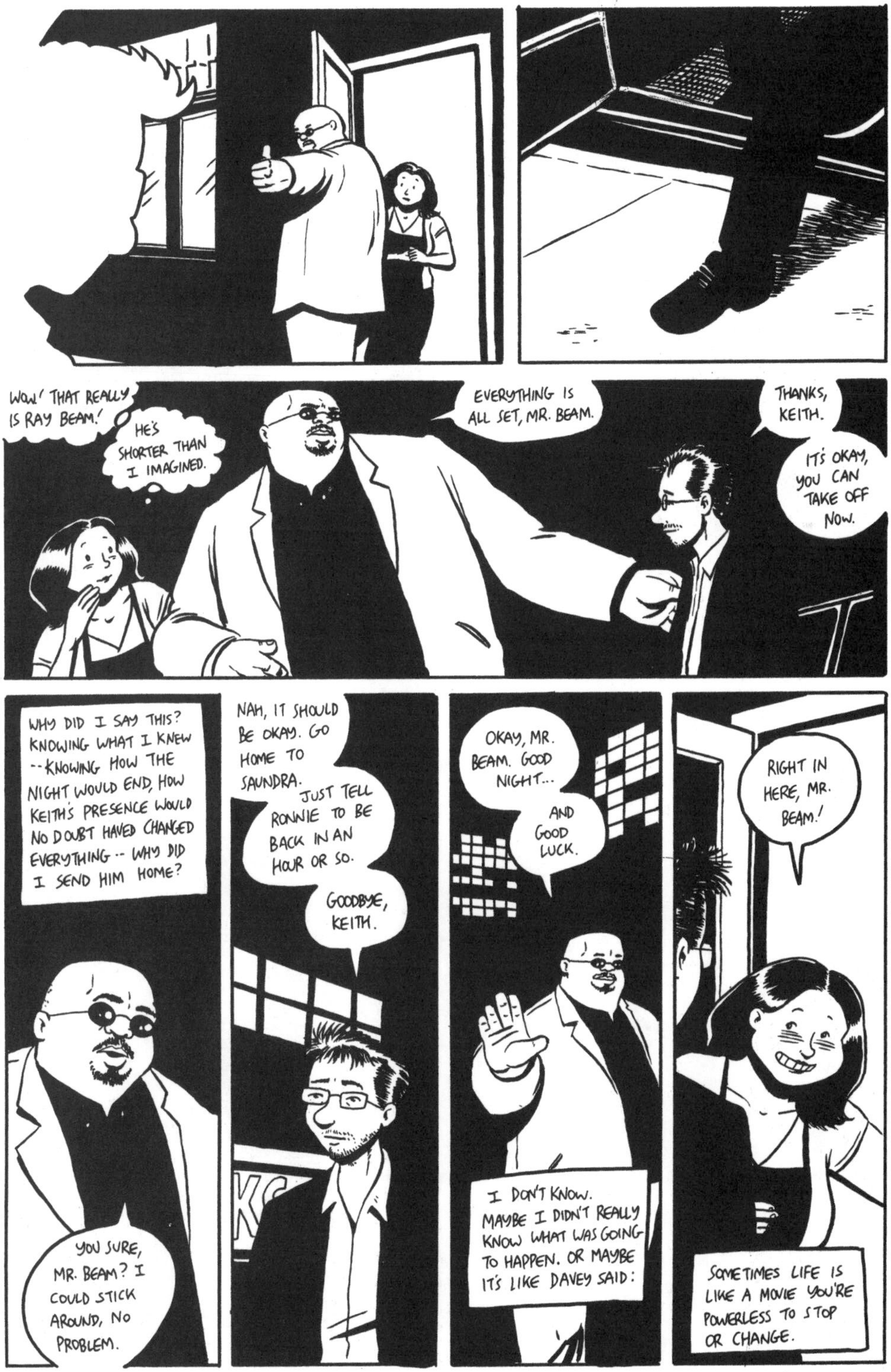
WOW! THAT REALLY IS RAY BEAM!
HE'S SHORTER THAN I IMAGINED.
EVERYTHING IS ALL SET, MR. BEAM.
THANKS, KEITH.
IT'S OKAY, YOU CAN TAKE OFF NOW.
WHY DID I SAY THIS? KNOWING WHAT I KNEW --KNOWING HOW THE NIGHT WOULD END, HOW KEITH'S PRESENCE WOULD NO DOUBT HAVED CHANGED EVERYTHING -- WHY DID I SEND HIM HOME?
YOU SURE, MR. BEAM? I COULD STICK AROUND, NO PROBLEM.
NAH, IT SHOULD BE OKAY. GO HOME TO SAUNDRA.
JUST TELL RONNIE TO BE BACK IN AN HOUR OR SO.
GOODBYE, KEITH.
OKAY, MR. BEAM. GOOD NIGHT...
AND GOOD LUCK.
I DON'T KNOW. MAYBE I DIDN'T REALLY KNOW WHAT WAS GOING TO HAPPEN. OR MAYBE IT'S LIKE DAVEY SAID:
RIGHT IN HERE, MR. BEAM!
SOMETIMES LIFE IS LIKE A MOVIE YOU'RE POWERLESS TO STOP OR CHANGE.

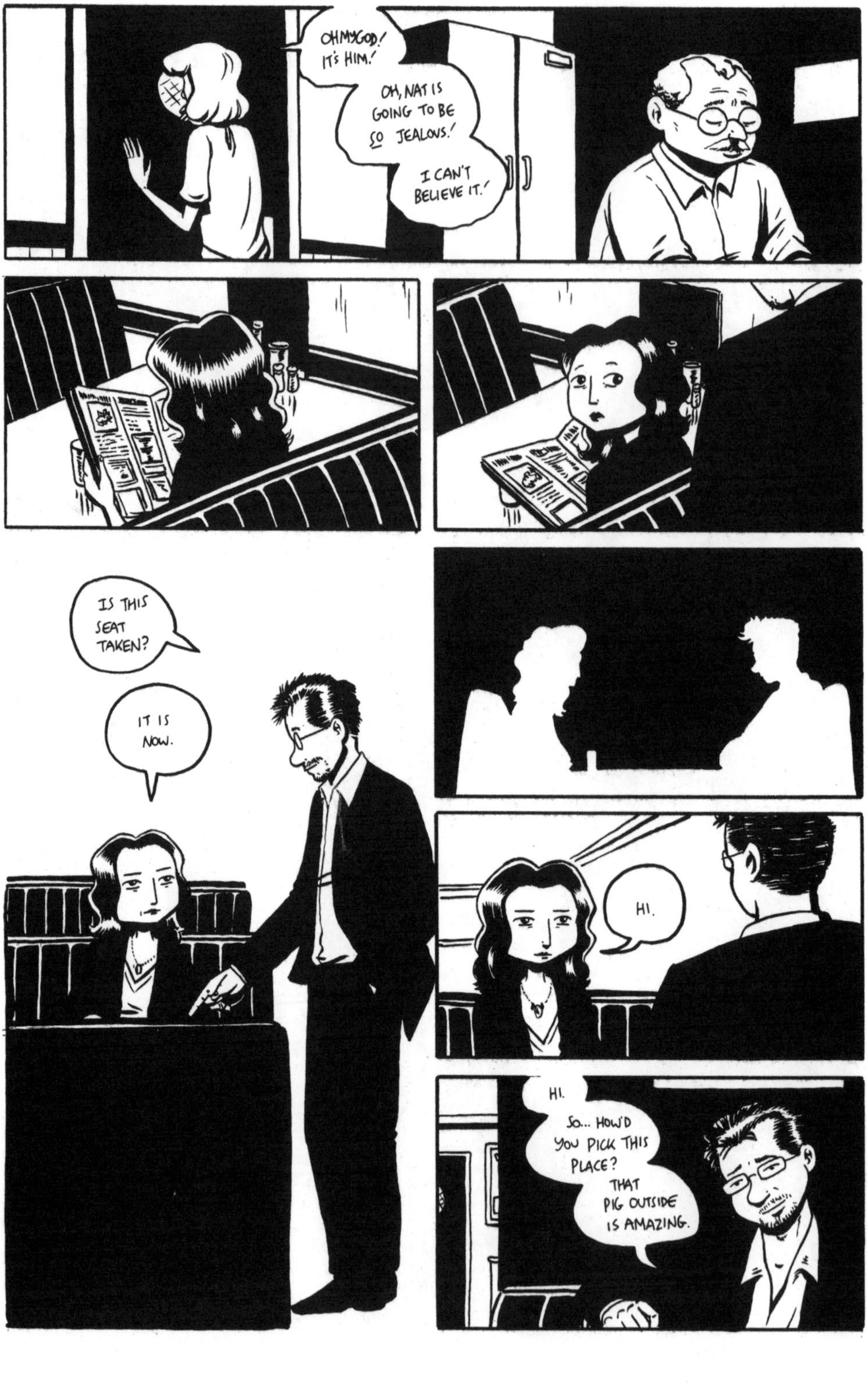
OHMYGOD! IT'S HIM!
OH, NAT IS GOING TO BE SO JEALOUS!
I CAN'T BELIEVE IT!
IS THIS SEAT TAKEN?
IT IS NOW.
HI.
HI.
SO... HOW'D YOU PICK THIS PLACE?
THAT PIG OUTSIDE IS AMAZING.

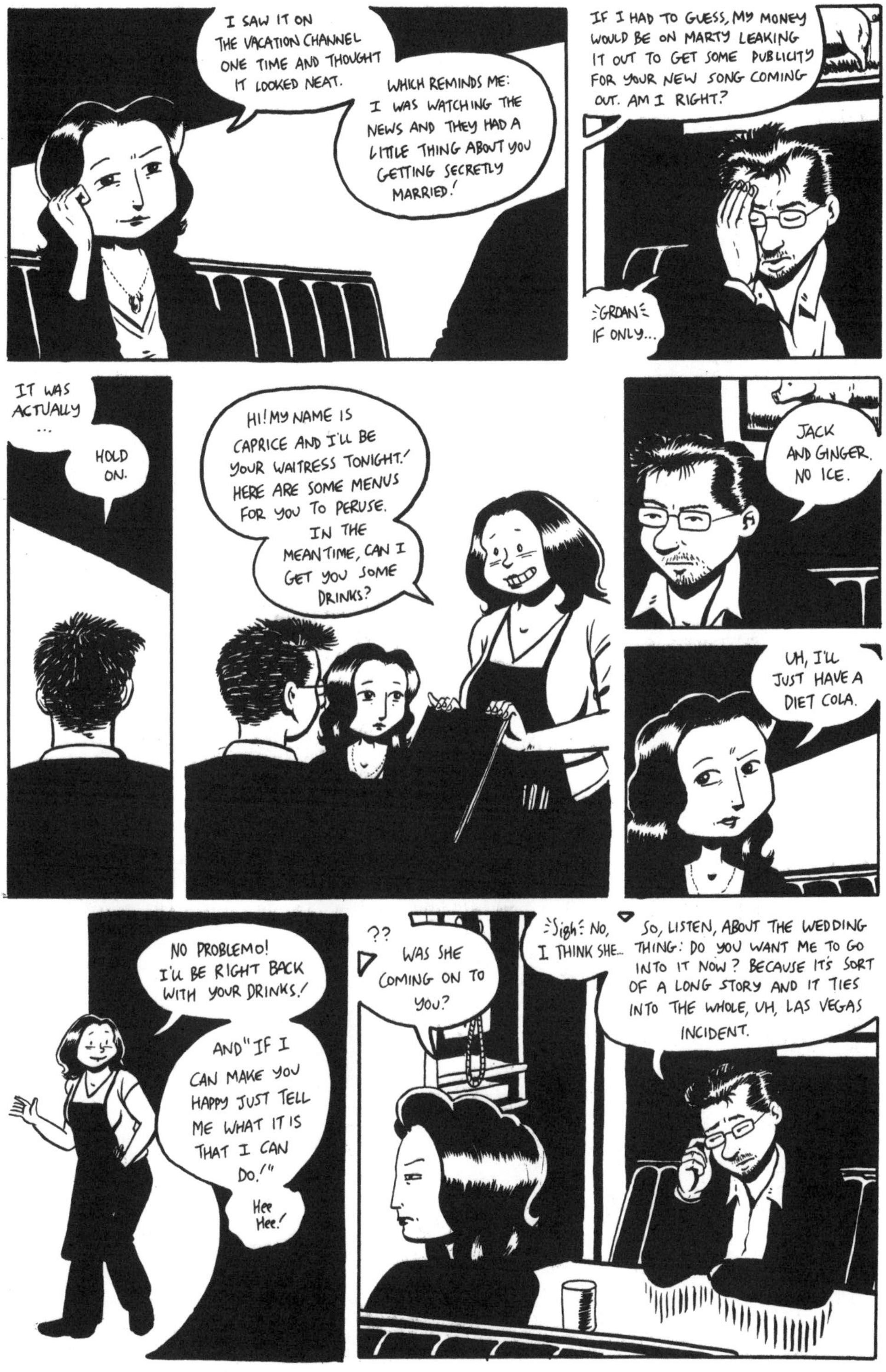
I SAW IT ON THE VACATION CHANNEL ONE TIME AND THOUGHT IT LOOKED NEAT.
WHICH REMINDS ME: I WAS WATCHING THE NEWS AND THEY HAD A LITTLE THING ABOUT YOU GETTING SECRETLY MARRIED!
IF I HAD TO GUESS, MY MONEY WOULD BE ON MARTY LEAKING IT OUT TO GET SOME PUBLICITY FOR YOUR NEW SONG COMING OUT. AM I RIGHT?
GROAN IF ONLY...
IT WAS ACTUALLY ...
HOLD ON.
HI! MY NAME IS CAPRICE AND I'LL BE YOUR WAITRESS TONIGHT! HERE ARE SOME MENUS FOR YOU TO PERUSE.
IN THE MEANTIME, CAN I GET YOU SOME DRINKS?
JACK AND GINGER. NO ICE.
UH, I'LL JUST HAVE A DIET COLA.
NO PROBLEMO! I'LL BE RIGHT BACK WITH YOUR DRINKS!
AND "IF I CAN MAKE YOU HAPPY JUST TELL ME WHAT IT IS THAT I CAN DO!"
Hee Hee!
??
WAS SHE COMING ON TO YOU?
Sigh No, I THINK SHE...
SO, LISTEN, ABOUT THE WEDDING THING: DO YOU WANT ME TO GO INTO IT NOW? BECAUSE IT'S SORT OF A LONG STORY AND IT TIES INTO THE WHOLE, UH, LAS VEGAS INCIDENT.

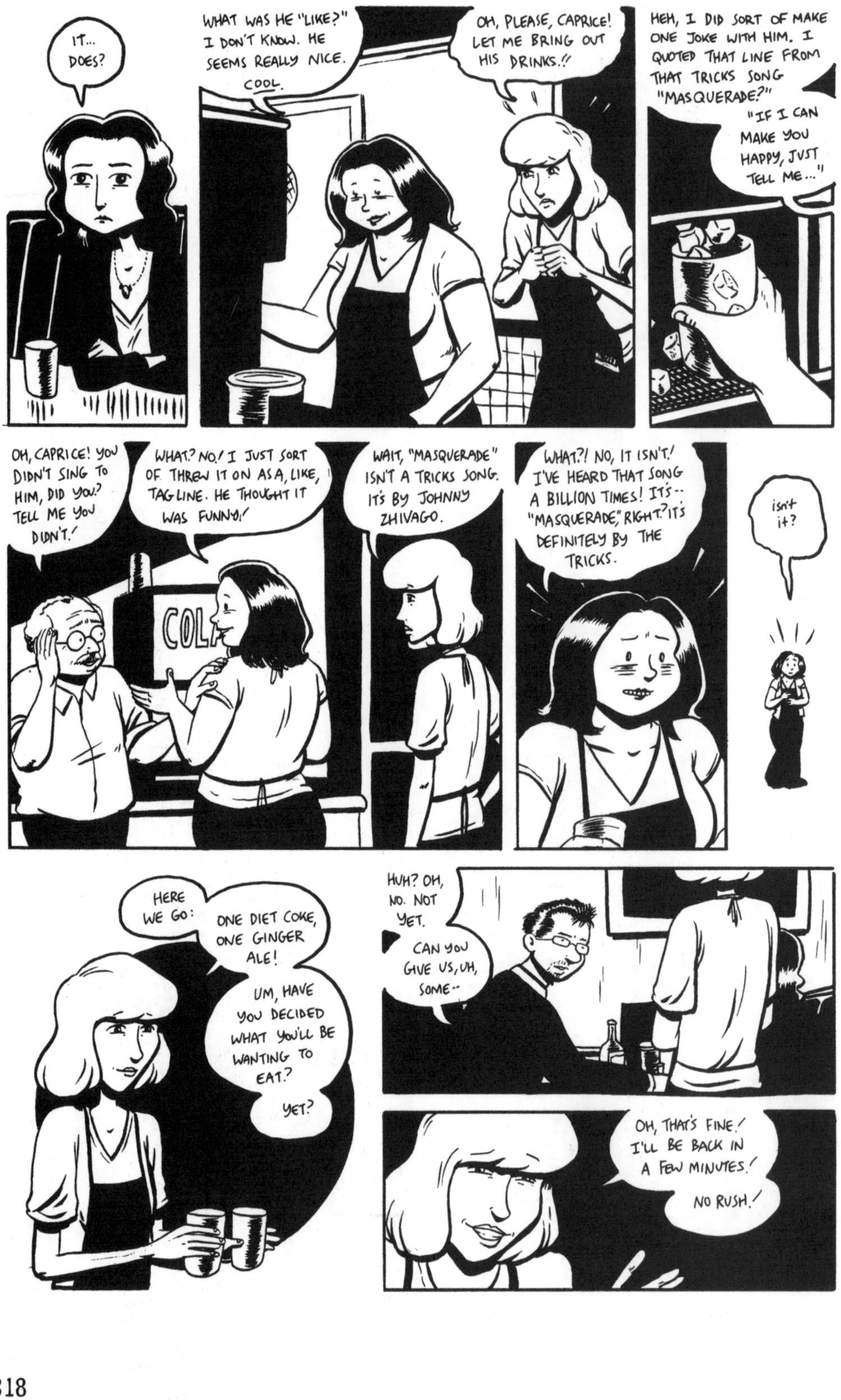

IT... DOES?
WHAT WAS HE "LIKE?" I DON'T KNOW. HE SEEMS REALLY NICE.
COOL.
OH, PLEASE, CAPRICE! LET ME BRING OUT HIS DRINKS!!
HEH, I DID SORT OF MAKE ONE JOKE WITH HIM. I QUOTED THAT LINE FROM THAT TRICKS SONG "MASQUERADE?"
"IF I CAN MAKE YOU HAPPY, JUST TELL ME..."
OH, CAPRICE! YOU DIDN'T SING TO HIM, DID YOU? TELL ME YOU DIDN'T!
WHAT? NO! I JUST SORT OF THREW IT ON AS A, LIKE, TAG LINE. HE THOUGHT IT WAS FUNNY!
COLA
WAIT, "MASQUERADE" ISN'T A TRICKS SONG. IT'S BY JOHNNY ZHIVAGO.
WHAT?! NO, IT ISN'T! I'VE HEARD THAT SONG A BILLION TIMES! IT'S-- "MASQUERADE," RIGHT? IT'S DEFINITELY BY THE TRICKS.
isn't it?
HERE WE GO:
ONE DIET COKE, ONE GINGER ALE!
UM, HAVE YOU DECIDED WHAT YOU'LL BE WANTING TO EAT?
YET?
HUH? OH, NO. NOT YET.
CAN YOU GIVE US, UH, SOME--
OH, THAT'S FINE! I'LL BE BACK IN A FEW MINUTES!
NO RUSH!

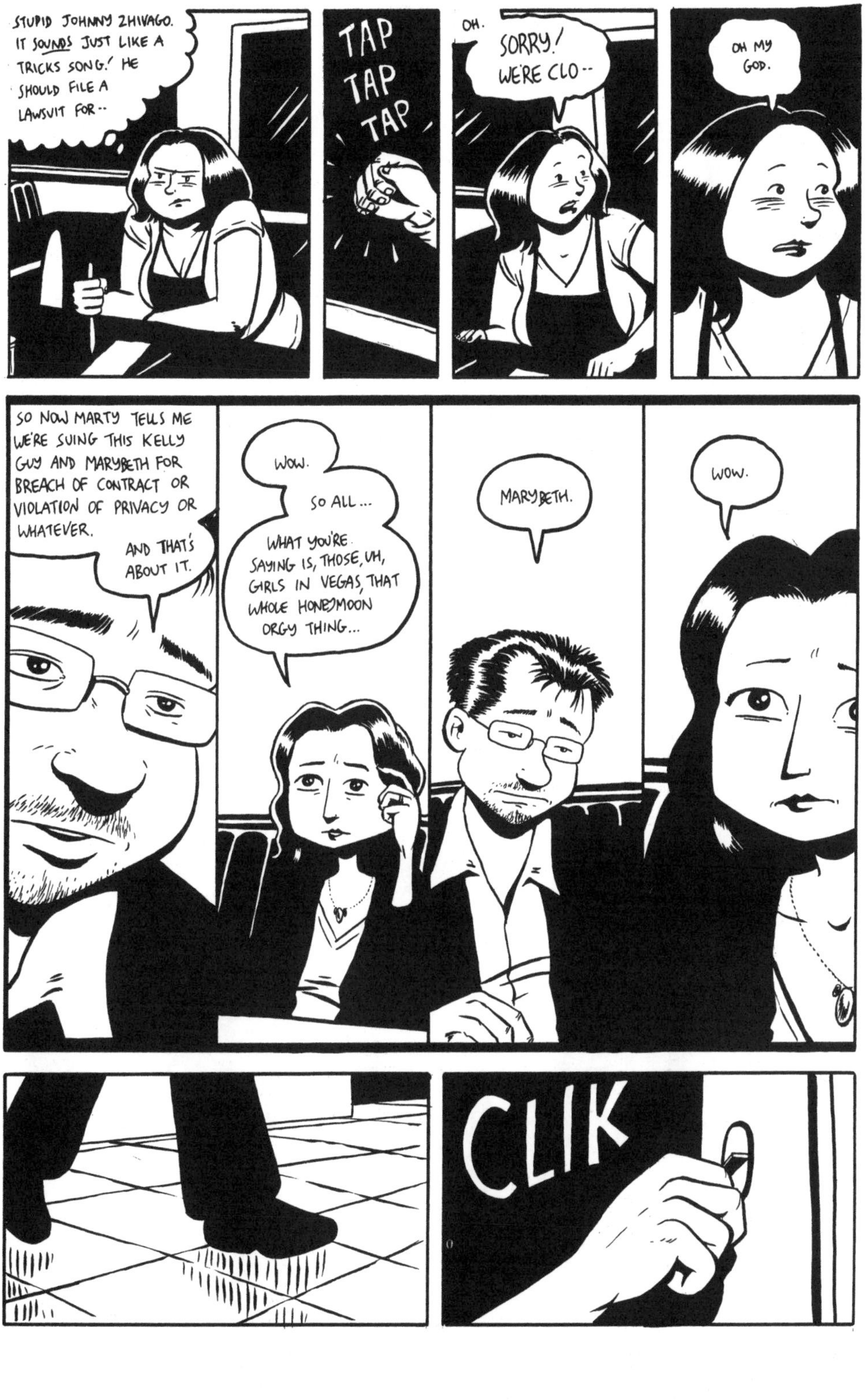
STUPID JOHNNY ZHIVAGO. IT SOUNDS JUST LIKE A TRICKS SONG! HE SHOULD FILE A LAWSUIT FOR--
TAP TAP TAP
OH.
SORRY! WE'RE CLO--
OH MY GOD.
SO NOW MARTY TELLS ME WE'RE SUING THIS KELLY GUY AND MARYBETH FOR BREACH OF CONTRACT OR VIOLATION OF PRIVACY OR WHATEVER.
AND THAT'S ABOUT IT.
WOW.
SO ALL...
WHAT YOU'RE SAYING IS, THOSE, UH, GIRLS IN VEGAS, THAT WHOLE HONEYMOON ORGY THING...
MARYBETH.
WOW.
CLIK

RAY! OH MY GOD, WHAT HAPPENED TO YOU?!

WHAT'RE YOU DOING HERE?

HEY, I'M SORRY TO BOTHER YOU AT WORK BUT I HAD TO TALK TO YOU.

CAN I COME INSIDE? CAN I TALK TO YOU REAL QUICK?

Let's Get AWESOME

UHHH... SURE. BUT JUST FOR A SECOND. WE HAVE THIS THING...

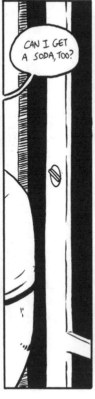

CAN I GET A SODA, TOO?

...UH, AND THE SUPER CRISPY ONION RINGS.

CAN I HAVE IT WITH THE DRESSING ON THE SIDE, PLEASE?

I'LL BE RIGHT BACK WITH YOUR APPETIZER!

320

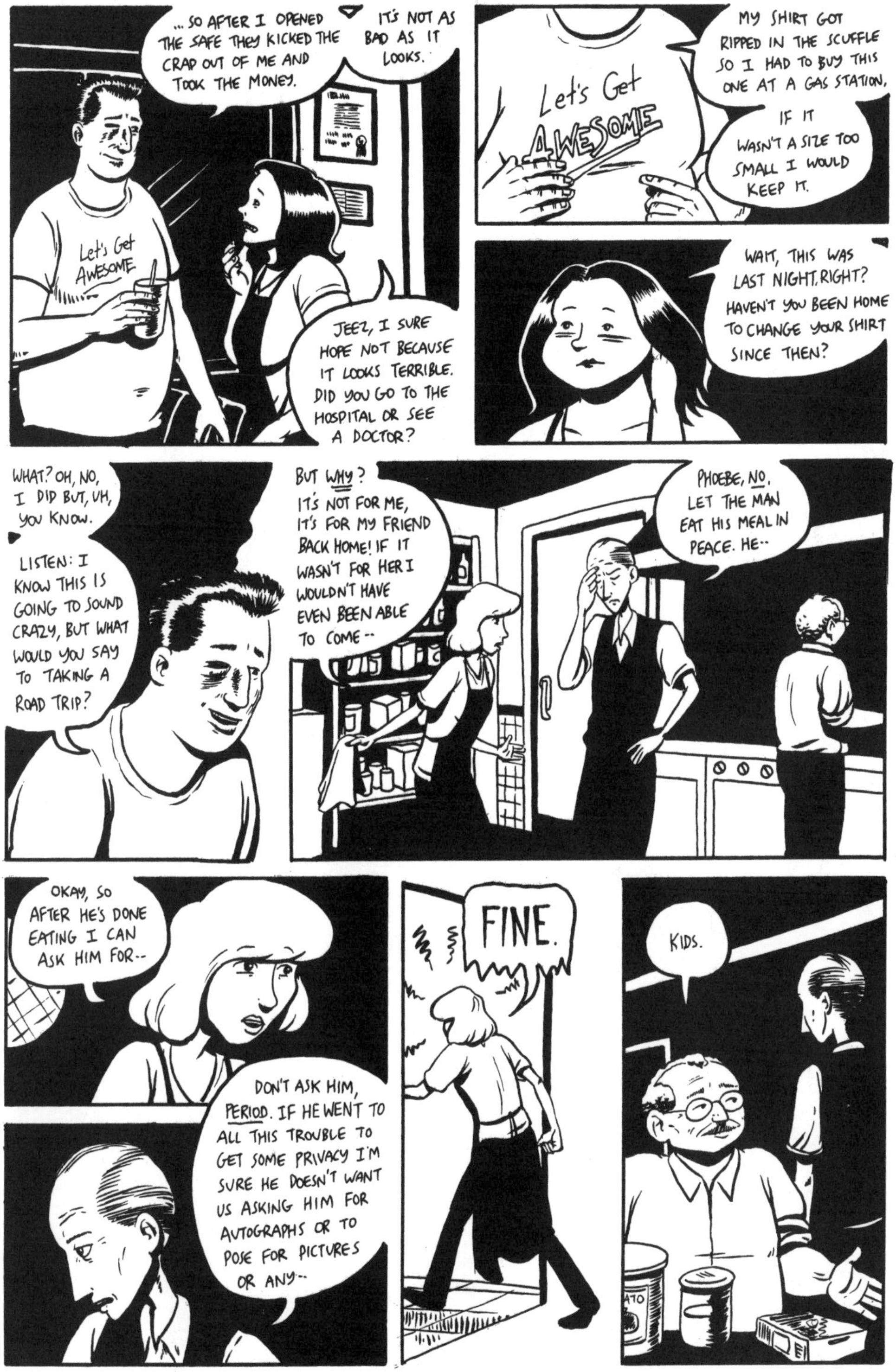
...SO AFTER I OPENED THE SAFE THEY KICKED THE CRAP OUT OF ME AND TOOK THE MONEY.
IT'S NOT AS BAD AS IT LOOKS.
Let's Get AWESOME
JEEZ, I SURE HOPE NOT BECAUSE IT LOOKS TERRIBLE. DID YOU GO TO THE HOSPITAL OR SEE A DOCTOR?
Let's Get AWESOME
MY SHIRT GOT RIPPED IN THE SCUFFLE SO I HAD TO BUY THIS ONE AT A GAS STATION.
IF IT WASN'T A SIZE TOO SMALL I WOULD KEEP IT.
WAIT, THIS WAS LAST NIGHT, RIGHT? HAVEN'T YOU BEEN HOME TO CHANGE YOUR SHIRT SINCE THEN?
WHAT? OH, NO, I DID BUT, UH, YOU KNOW.
LISTEN: I KNOW THIS IS GOING TO SOUND CRAZY, BUT WHAT WOULD YOU SAY TO TAKING A ROAD TRIP?
BUT WHY? IT'S NOT FOR ME, IT'S FOR MY FRIEND BACK HOME! IF IT WASN'T FOR HER I WOULDN'T HAVE EVEN BEEN ABLE TO COME--
PHOEBE, NO. LET THE MAN EAT HIS MEAL IN PEACE. HE--
OKAY, SO AFTER HE'S DONE EATING I CAN ASK HIM FOR--
DON'T ASK HIM, PERIOD. IF HE WENT TO ALL THIS TROUBLE TO GET SOME PRIVACY I'M SURE HE DOESN'T WANT US ASKING HIM FOR AUTOGRAPHS OR TO POSE FOR PICTURES OR ANY--
FINE.
KIDS.

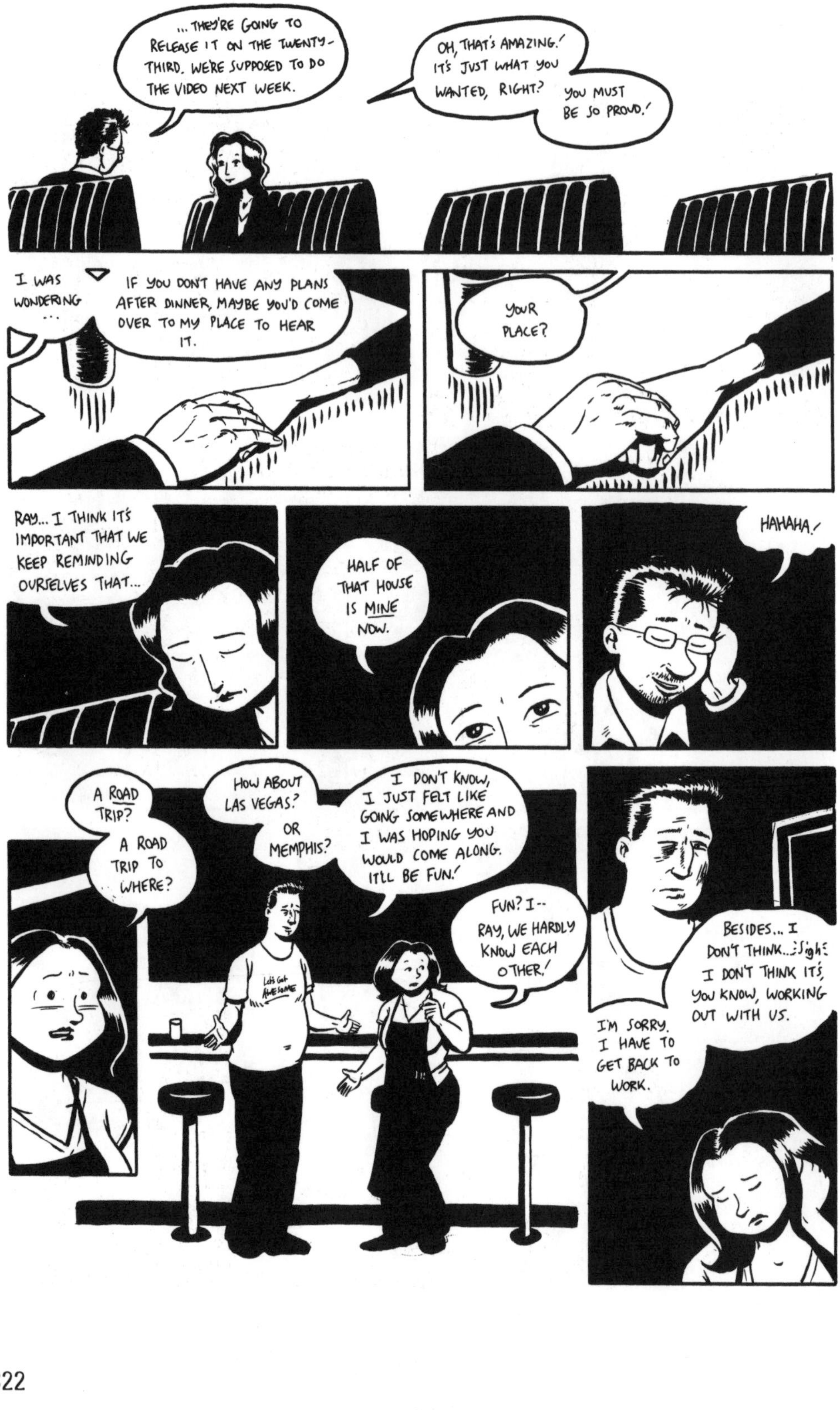
... THEY'RE GOING TO RELEASE IT ON THE TWENTY-THIRD. WE'RE SUPPOSED TO DO THE VIDEO NEXT WEEK.
OH, THAT'S AMAZING! IT'S JUST WHAT YOU WANTED, RIGHT?
YOU MUST BE SO PROUD!
I WAS WONDERING ...
IF YOU DON'T HAVE ANY PLANS AFTER DINNER, MAYBE YOU'D COME OVER TO MY PLACE TO HEAR IT.
YOUR PLACE?
RAY... I THINK IT'S IMPORTANT THAT WE KEEP REMINDING OURSELVES THAT...
HALF OF THAT HOUSE IS MINE NOW.
HAHAHA!
A ROAD TRIP?
A ROAD TRIP TO WHERE?
HOW ABOUT LAS VEGAS?
OR MEMPHIS?
I DON'T KNOW, I JUST FELT LIKE GOING SOMEWHERE AND I WAS HOPING YOU WOULD COME ALONG. IT'LL BE FUN!
FUN? I-- RAY, WE HARDLY KNOW EACH OTHER!
BESIDES... I DON'T THINK... :Sigh: I DON'T THINK IT'S, YOU KNOW, WORKING OUT WITH US.
I'M SORRY. I HAVE TO GET BACK TO WORK.

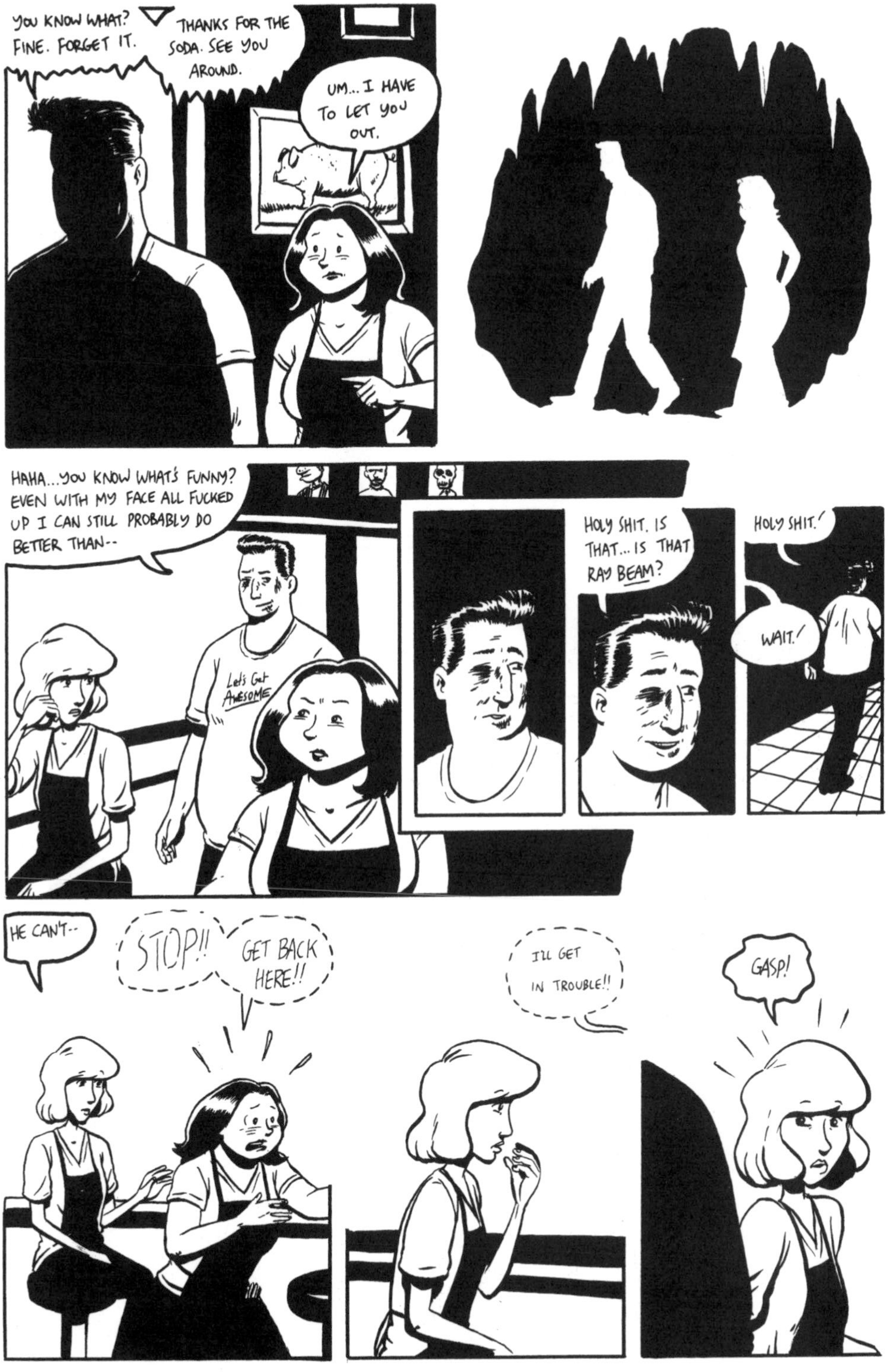
YOU KNOW WHAT? FINE. FORGET IT.
THANKS FOR THE SODA. SEE YOU AROUND.
UM... I HAVE TO LET YOU OUT.
HAHA...YOU KNOW WHAT'S FUNNY? EVEN WITH MY FACE ALL FUCKED UP I CAN STILL PROBABLY DO BETTER THAN--
Let's Get AWESOME
HOLY SHIT. IS THAT... IS THAT RAY BEAM?
HOLY SHIT!
WAIT!
HE CAN'T--
STOP!!
GET BACK HERE!!
I'LL GET IN TROUBLE!!
GASP!

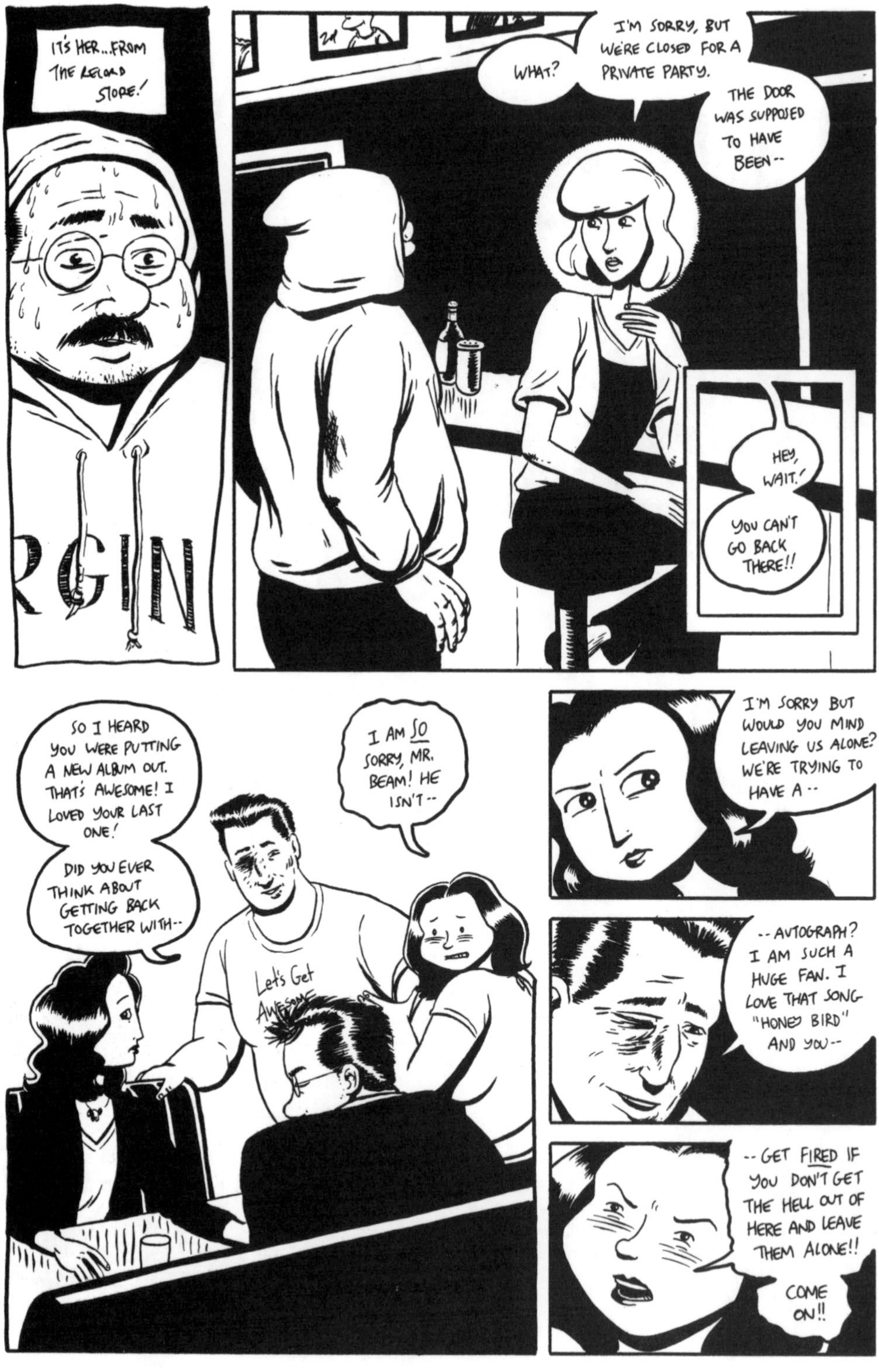
IT'S HER...FROM THE RECORD STORE!
RGIN
WHAT?
I'M SORRY, BUT WE'RE CLOSED FOR A PRIVATE PARTY.
THE DOOR WAS SUPPOSED TO HAVE BEEN--
HEY, WAIT!
YOU CAN'T GO BACK THERE!!
SO I HEARD YOU WERE PUTTING A NEW ALBUM OUT. THAT'S AWESOME! I LOVED YOUR LAST ONE!
DID YOU EVER THINK ABOUT GETTING BACK TOGETHER WITH--
I AM SO SORRY, MR. BEAM! HE ISN'T--
Let's Get Awesome
I'M SORRY BUT WOULD YOU MIND LEAVING US ALONE? WE'RE TRYING TO HAVE A--
--AUTOGRAPH? I AM SUCH A HUGE FAN. I LOVE THAT SONG "HONEY BIRD" AND YOU--
--GET FIRED IF YOU DON'T GET THE HELL OUT OF HERE AND LEAVE THEM ALONE!!
COME ON!!

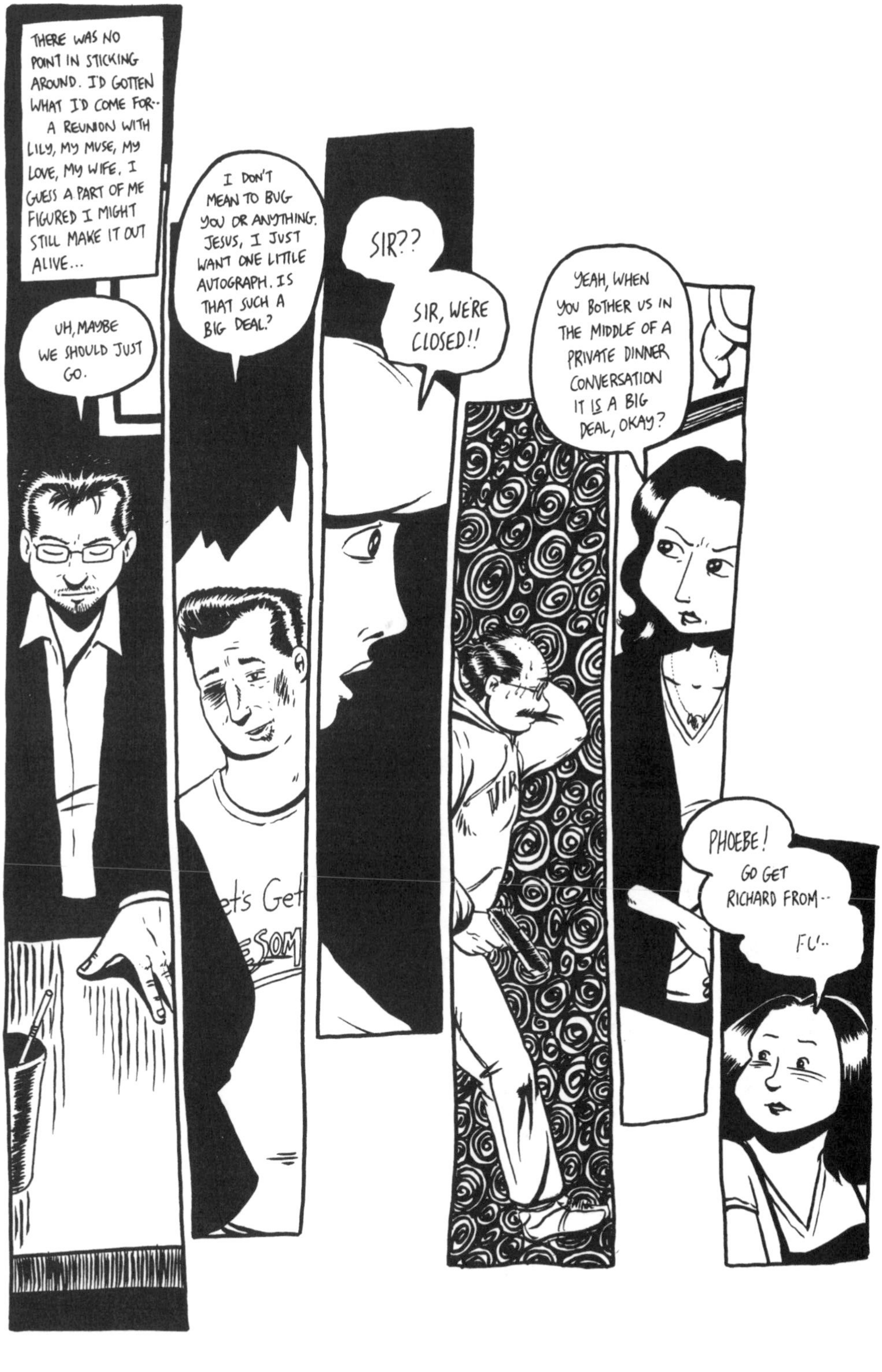
THERE WAS NO POINT IN STICKING AROUND. I'D GOTTEN WHAT I'D COME FOR.. A REUNION WITH LILY, MY MUSE, MY LOVE, MY WIFE. I GUESS A PART OF ME FIGURED I MIGHT STILL MAKE IT OUT ALIVE...
UH, MAYBE WE SHOULD JUST GO.
I DON'T MEAN TO BUG YOU OR ANYTHING. JESUS, I JUST WANT ONE LITTLE AUTOGRAPH. IS THAT SUCH A BIG DEAL?
SIR??
SIR, WE'RE CLOSED!!
YEAH, WHEN YOU BOTHER US IN THE MIDDLE OF A PRIVATE DINNER CONVERSATION IT IS A BIG DEAL, OKAY?
PHOEBE! GO GET RICHARD FROM..
FU..

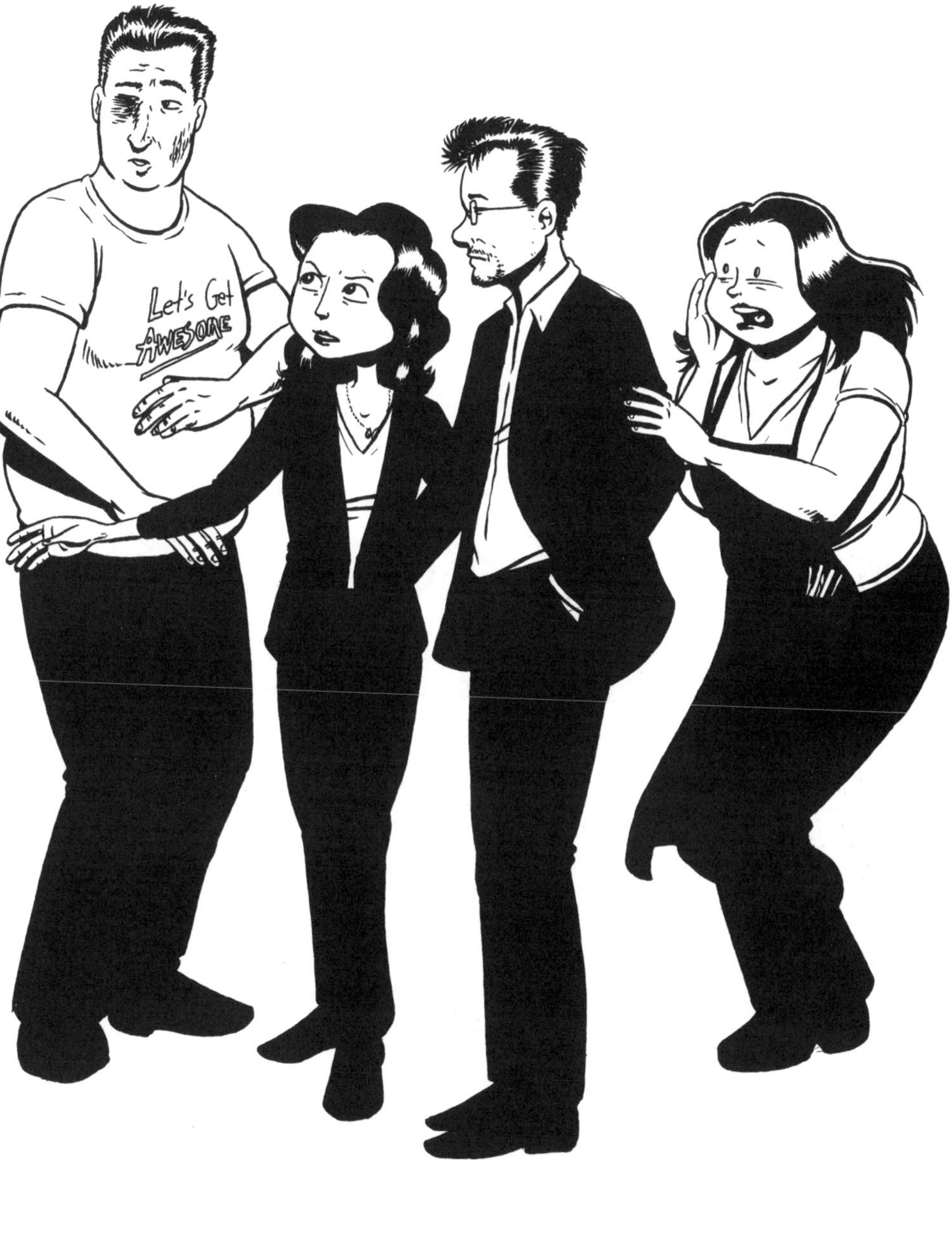
Let's Get
AWESOME

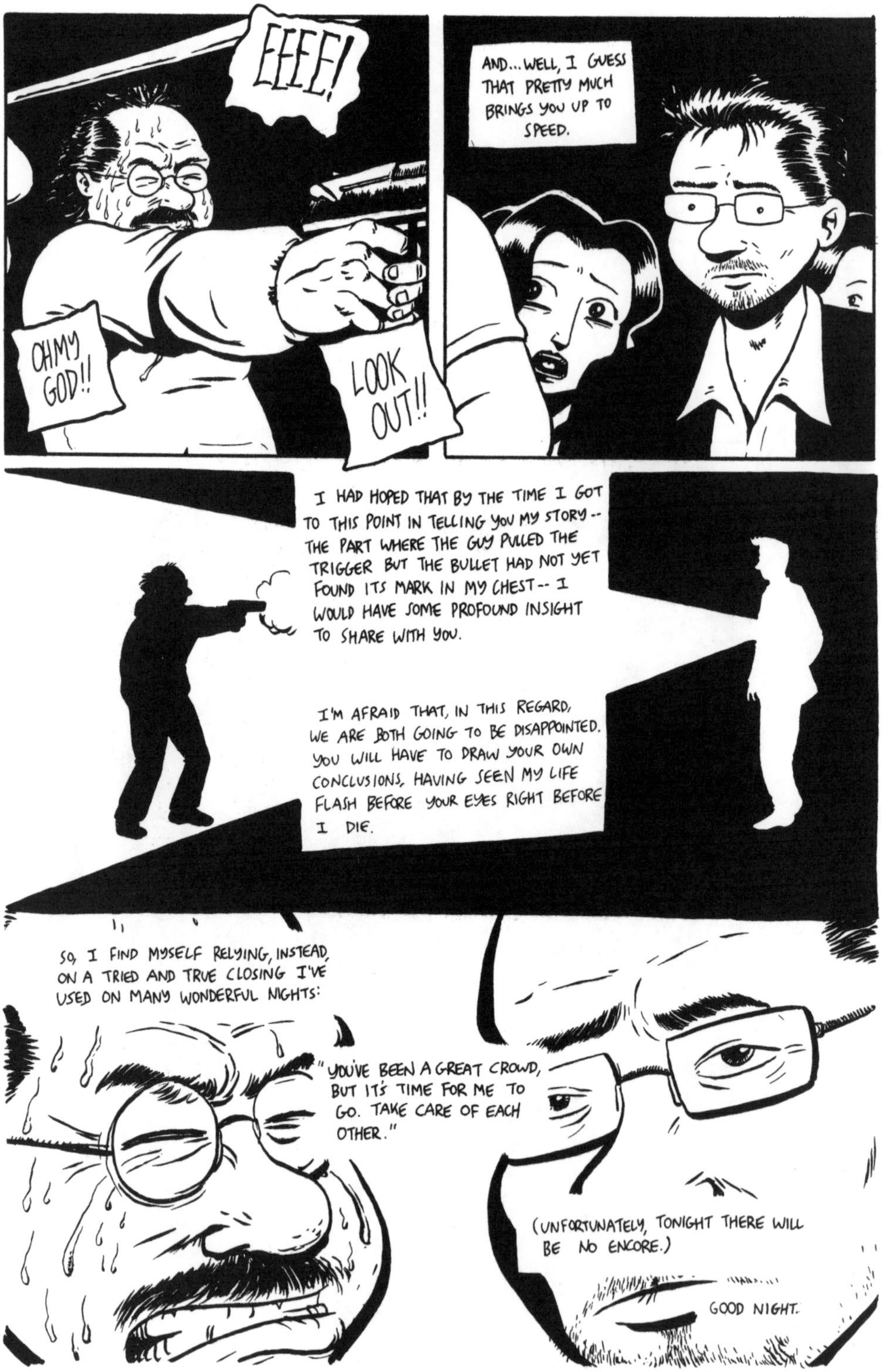
EEEE!
OHMY GOD!!
LOOK OUT!!
AND... WELL, I GUESS THAT PRETTY MUCH BRINGS YOU UP TO SPEED.
I HAD HOPED THAT BY THE TIME I GOT TO THIS POINT IN TELLING YOU MY STORY -- THE PART WHERE THE GUY PULLED THE TRIGGER BUT THE BULLET HAD NOT YET FOUND ITS MARK IN MY CHEST -- I WOULD HAVE SOME PROFOUND INSIGHT TO SHARE WITH YOU.
I'M AFRAID THAT, IN THIS REGARD, WE ARE BOTH GOING TO BE DISAPPOINTED. YOU WILL HAVE TO DRAW YOUR OWN CONCLUSIONS, HAVING SEEN MY LIFE FLASH BEFORE YOUR EYES RIGHT BEFORE I DIE.
SO, I FIND MYSELF RELYING, INSTEAD, ON A TRIED AND TRUE CLOSING I'VE USED ON MANY WONDERFUL NIGHTS:
"YOU'VE BEEN A GREAT CROWD, BUT IT'S TIME FOR ME TO GO. TAKE CARE OF EACH OTHER."
(UNFORTUNATELY, TONIGHT THERE WILL BE NO ENCORE.)
GOOD NIGHT.

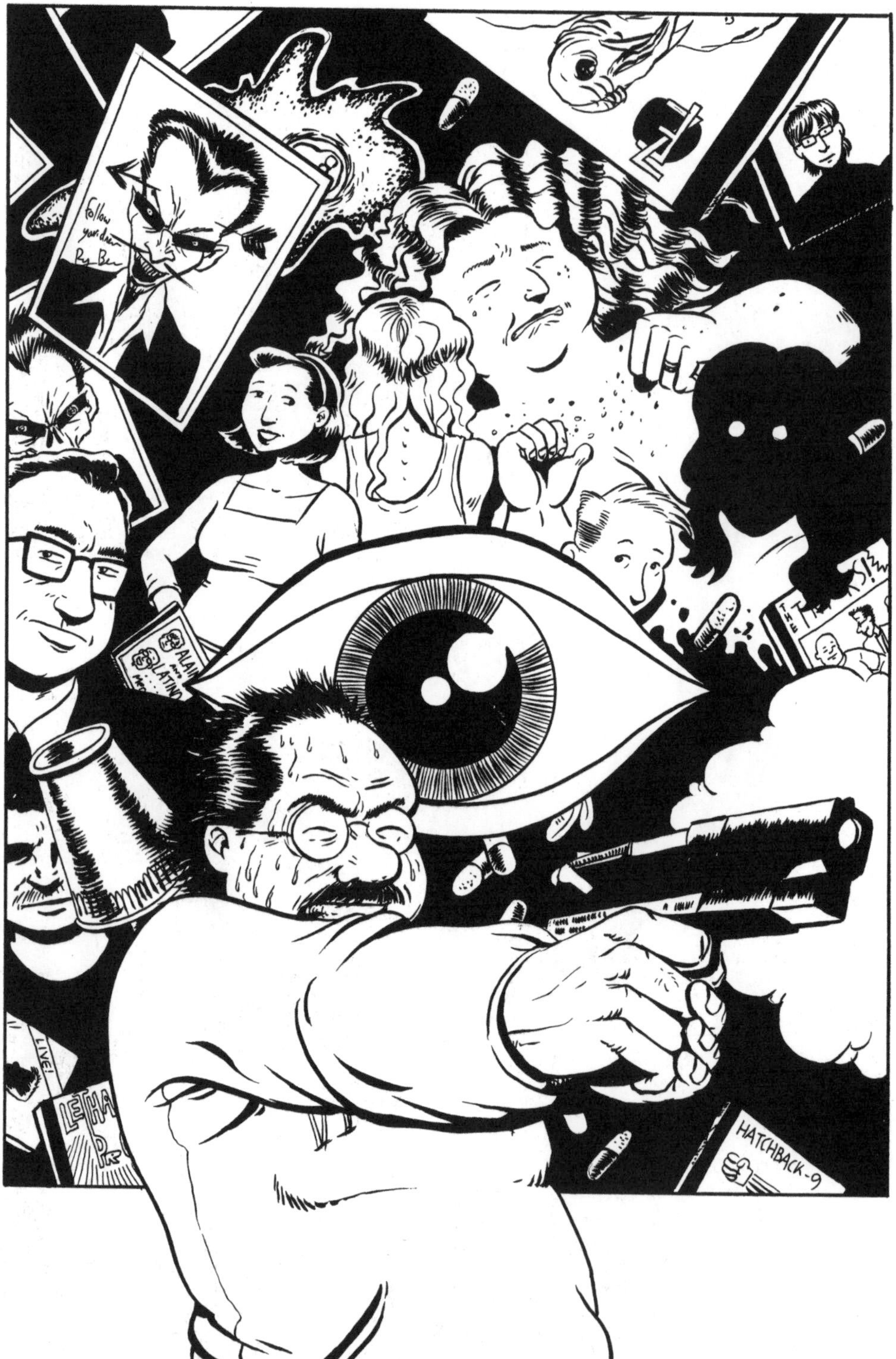
Follow
HATCHBACK-9
LIVE!

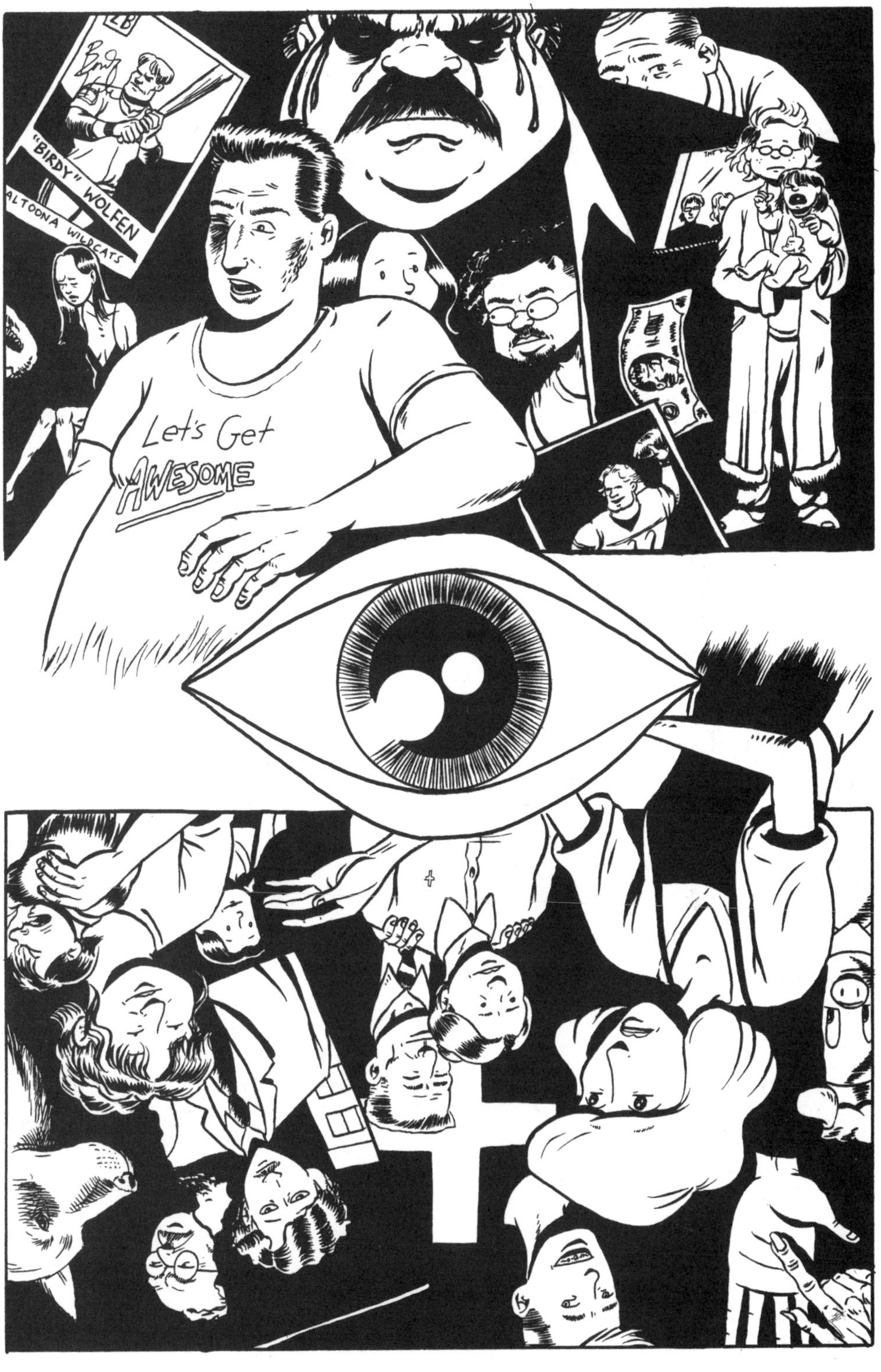

"BIRDY" WOLFEN
ALTOONA WILDCATS
Let's Get
AWESOME

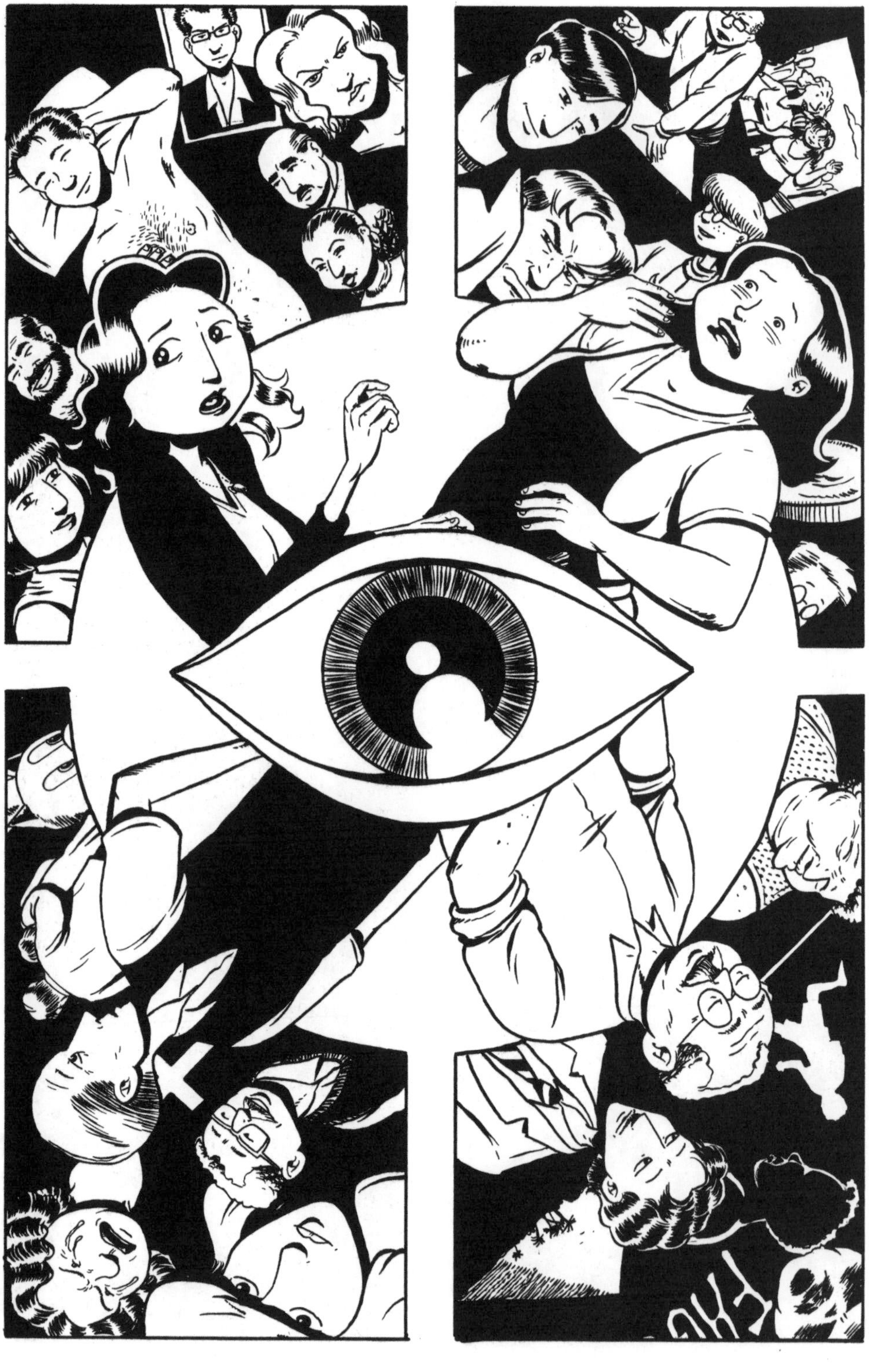

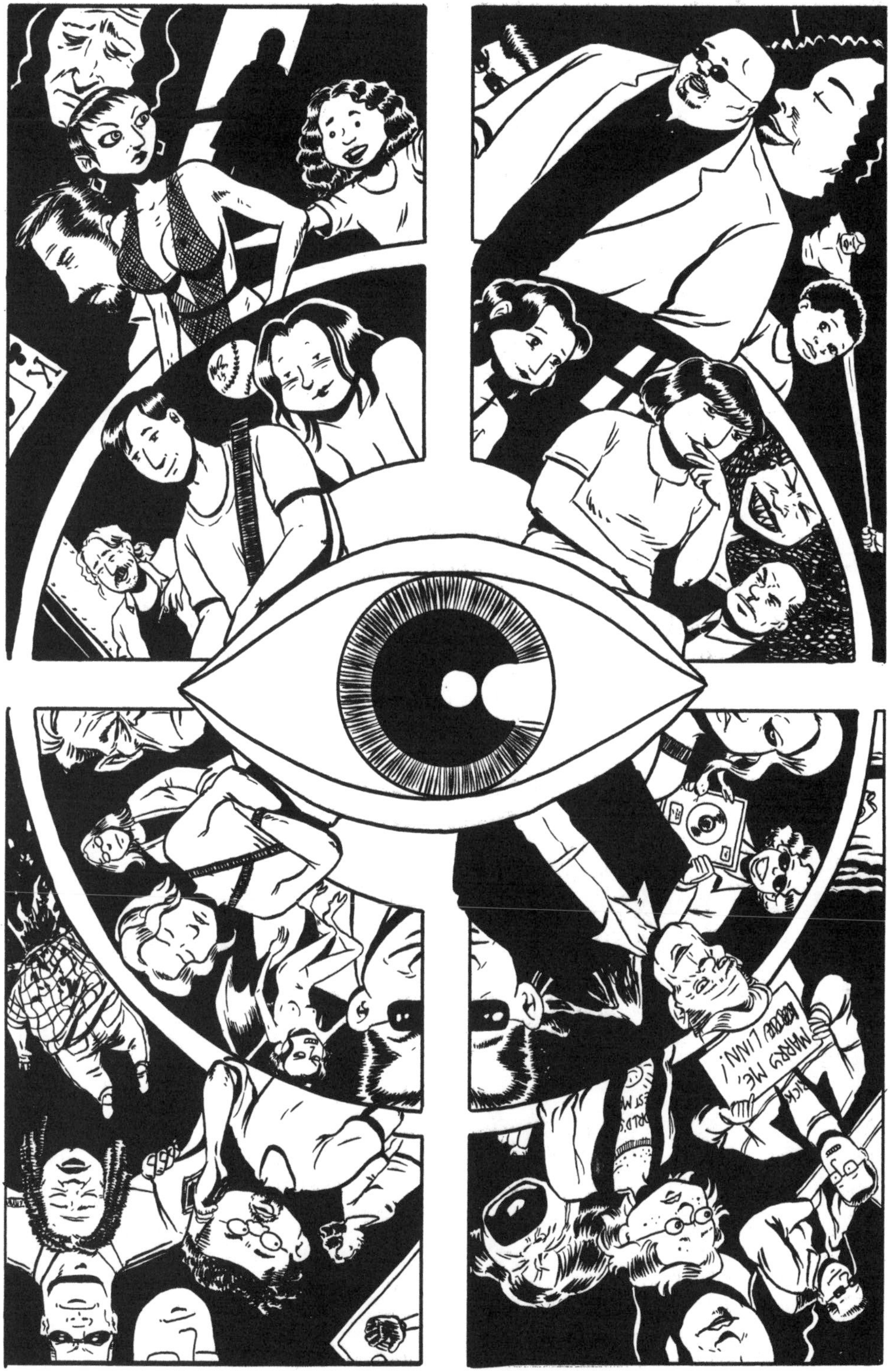
MARRY ME, LINN!

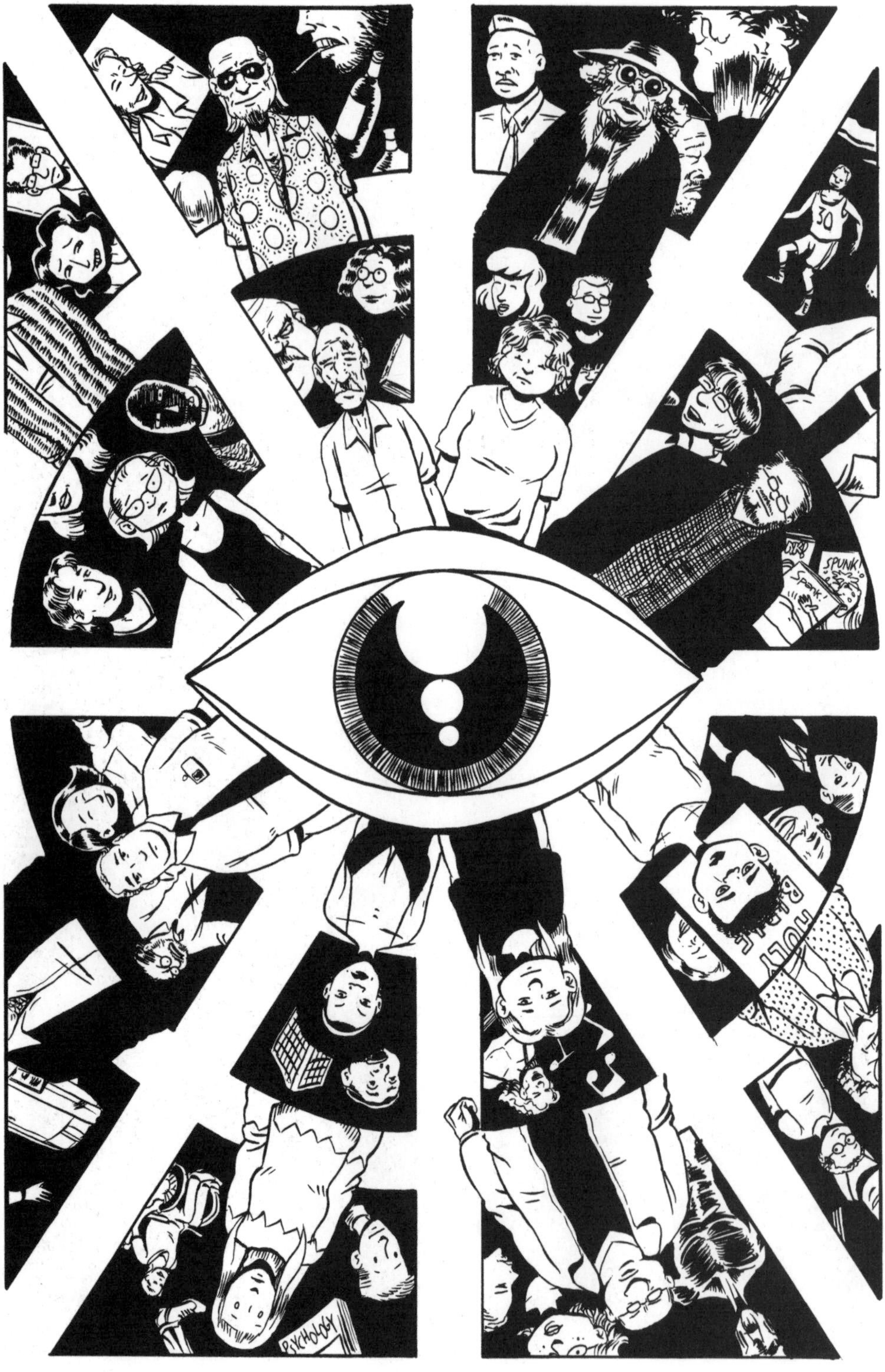
SPUNK!
Spunk!
PSYCHOLOGY

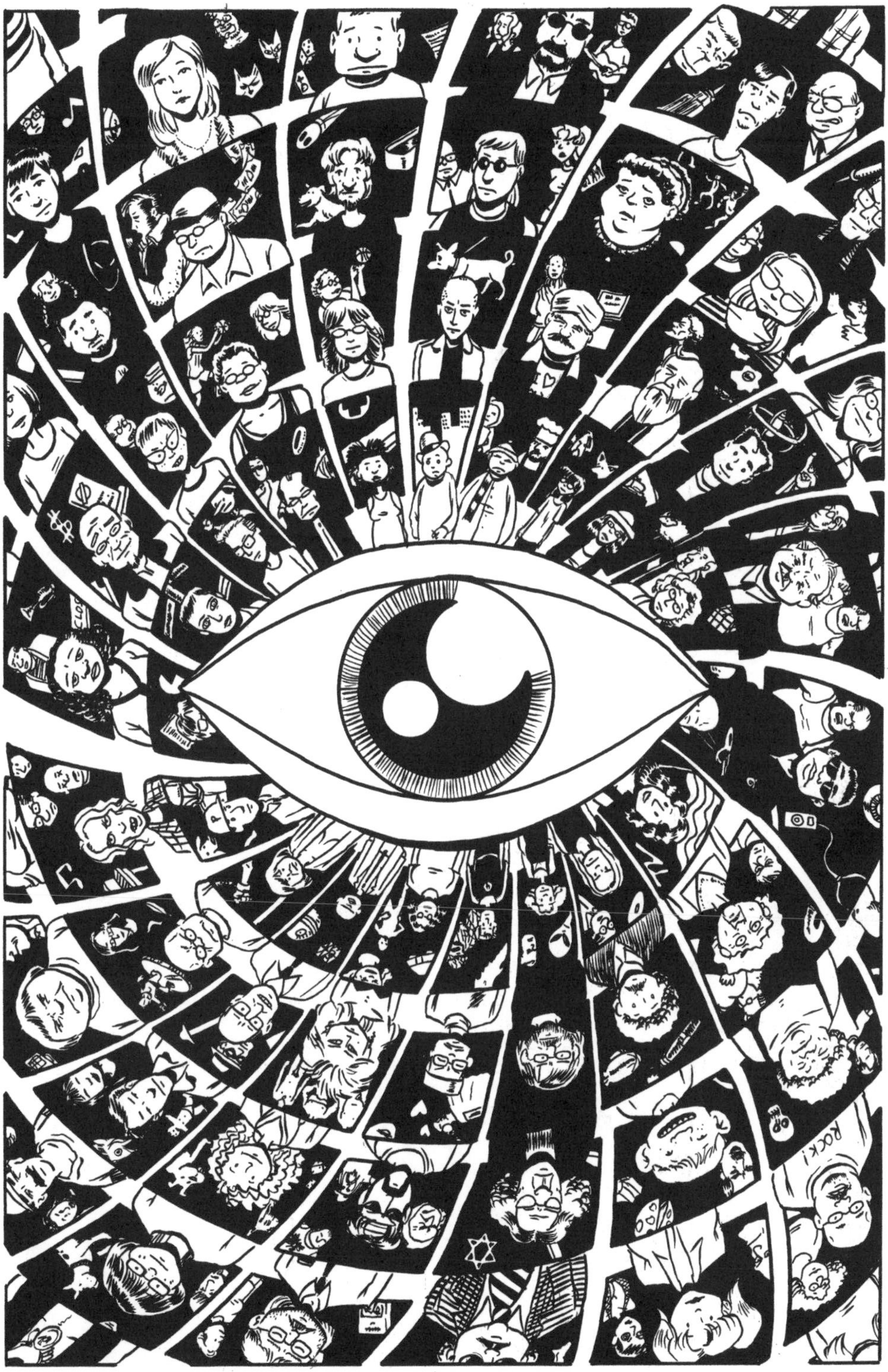
ROCK!

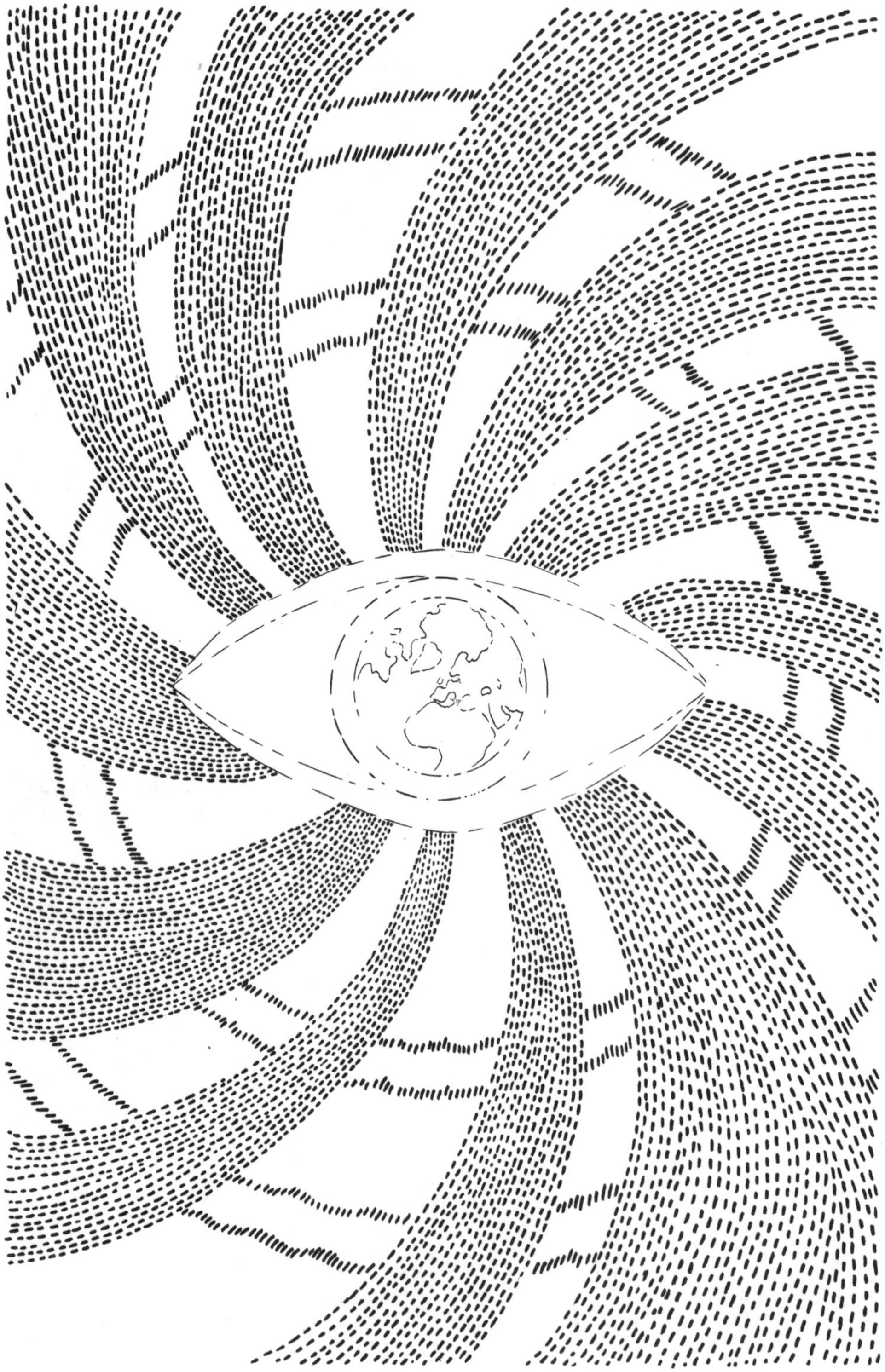

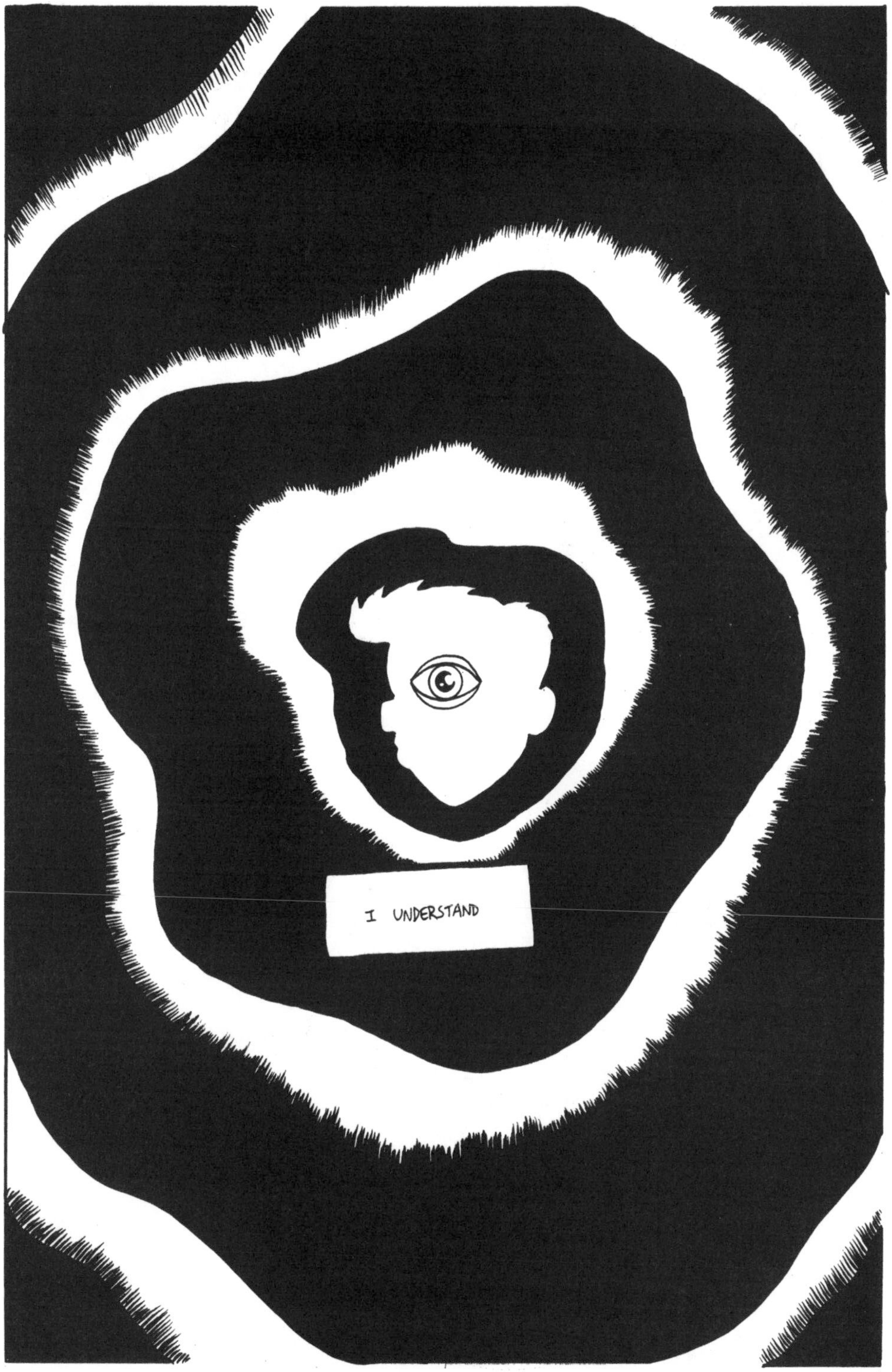
I UNDERSTAND

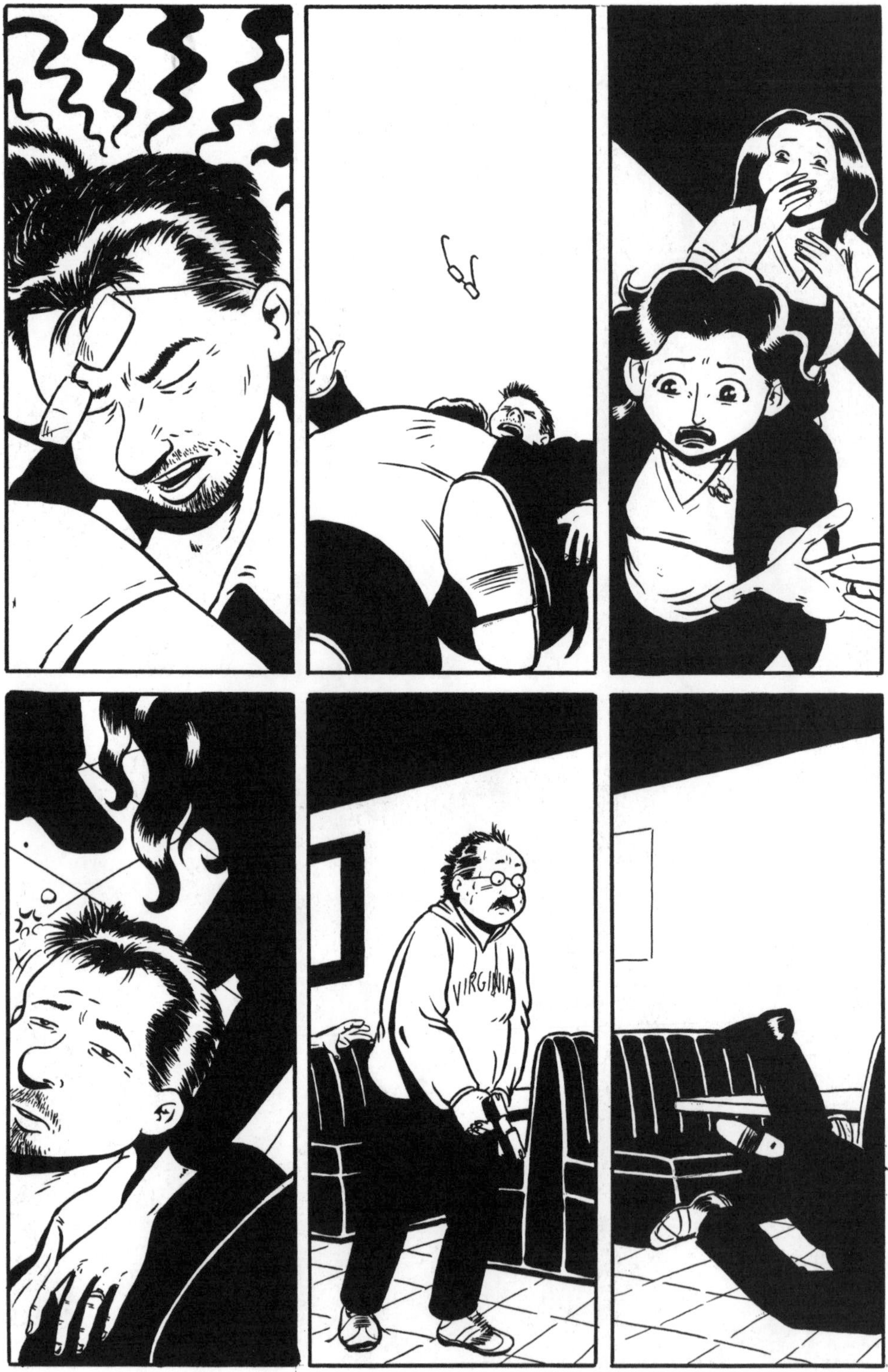
VIRGINIA

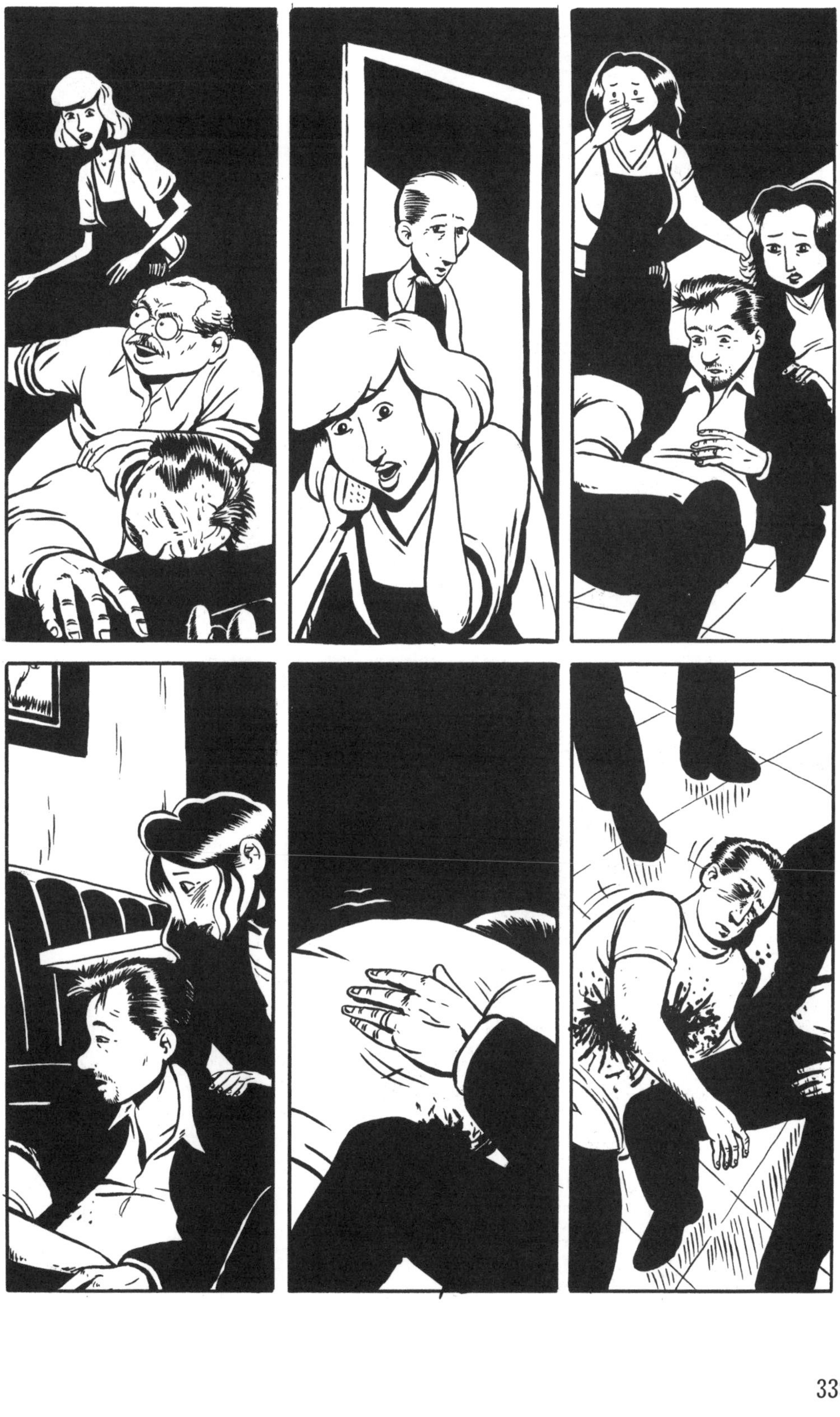

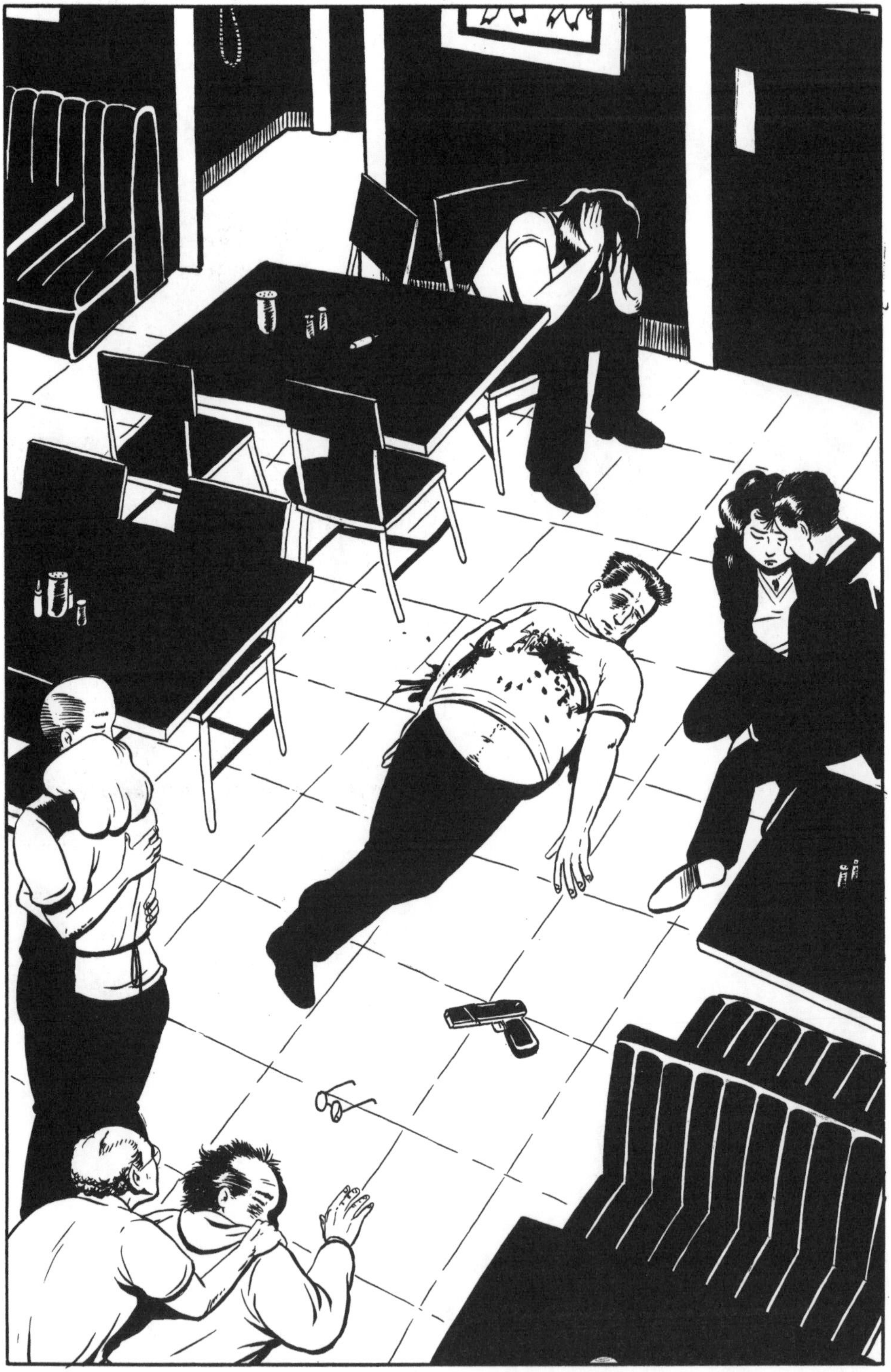

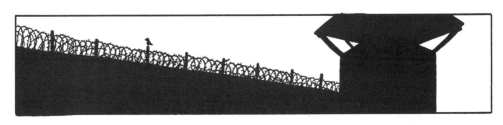

CODA

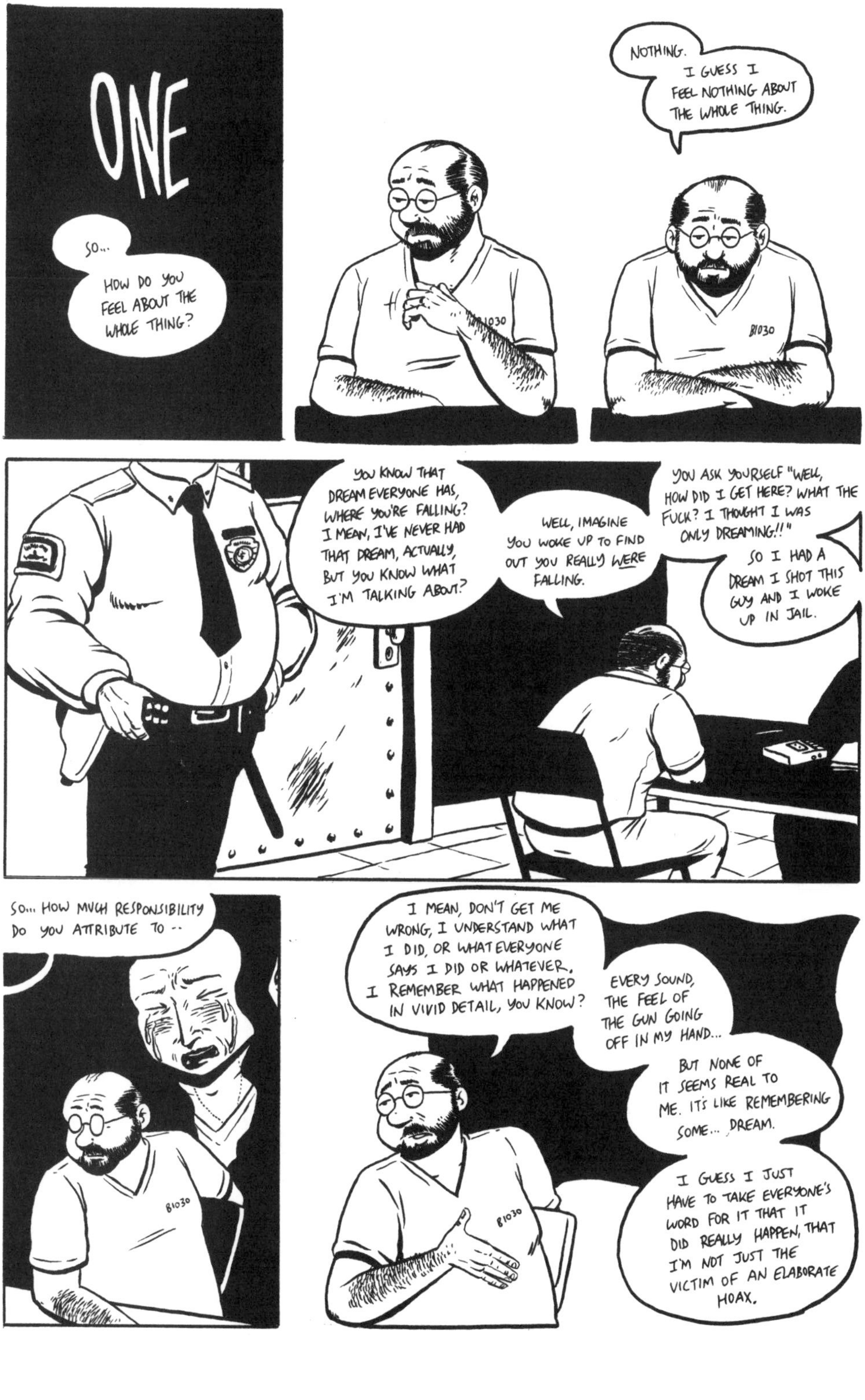
ONE
SO... HOW DO YOU FEEL ABOUT THE WHOLE THING?
NOTHING. I GUESS I FEEL NOTHING ABOUT THE WHOLE THING.
B1030
B1030
YOU KNOW THAT DREAM EVERYONE HAS, WHERE YOU'RE FALLING? I MEAN, I'VE NEVER HAD THAT DREAM, ACTUALLY, BUT YOU KNOW WHAT I'M TALKING ABOUT?
WELL, IMAGINE YOU WOKE UP TO FIND OUT YOU REALLY WERE FALLING.
YOU ASK YOURSELF "WELL, HOW DID I GET HERE? WHAT THE FUCK? I THOUGHT I WAS ONLY DREAMING!!"
SO I HAD A DREAM I SHOT THIS GUY AND I WOKE UP IN JAIL.
SO... HOW MUCH RESPONSIBILITY DO YOU ATTRIBUTE TO --
B1030
I MEAN, DON'T GET ME WRONG, I UNDERSTAND WHAT I DID, OR WHAT EVERYONE SAYS I DID OR WHATEVER. I REMEMBER WHAT HAPPENED IN VIVID DETAIL, YOU KNOW?
EVERY SOUND, THE FEEL OF THE GUN GOING OFF IN MY HAND...
BUT NONE OF IT SEEMS REAL TO ME. IT'S LIKE REMEMBERING SOME... DREAM.
I GUESS I JUST HAVE TO TAKE EVERYONE'S WORD FOR IT THAT IT DID REALLY HAPPEN, THAT I'M NOT JUST THE VICTIM OF AN ELABORATE HOAX.
B1030

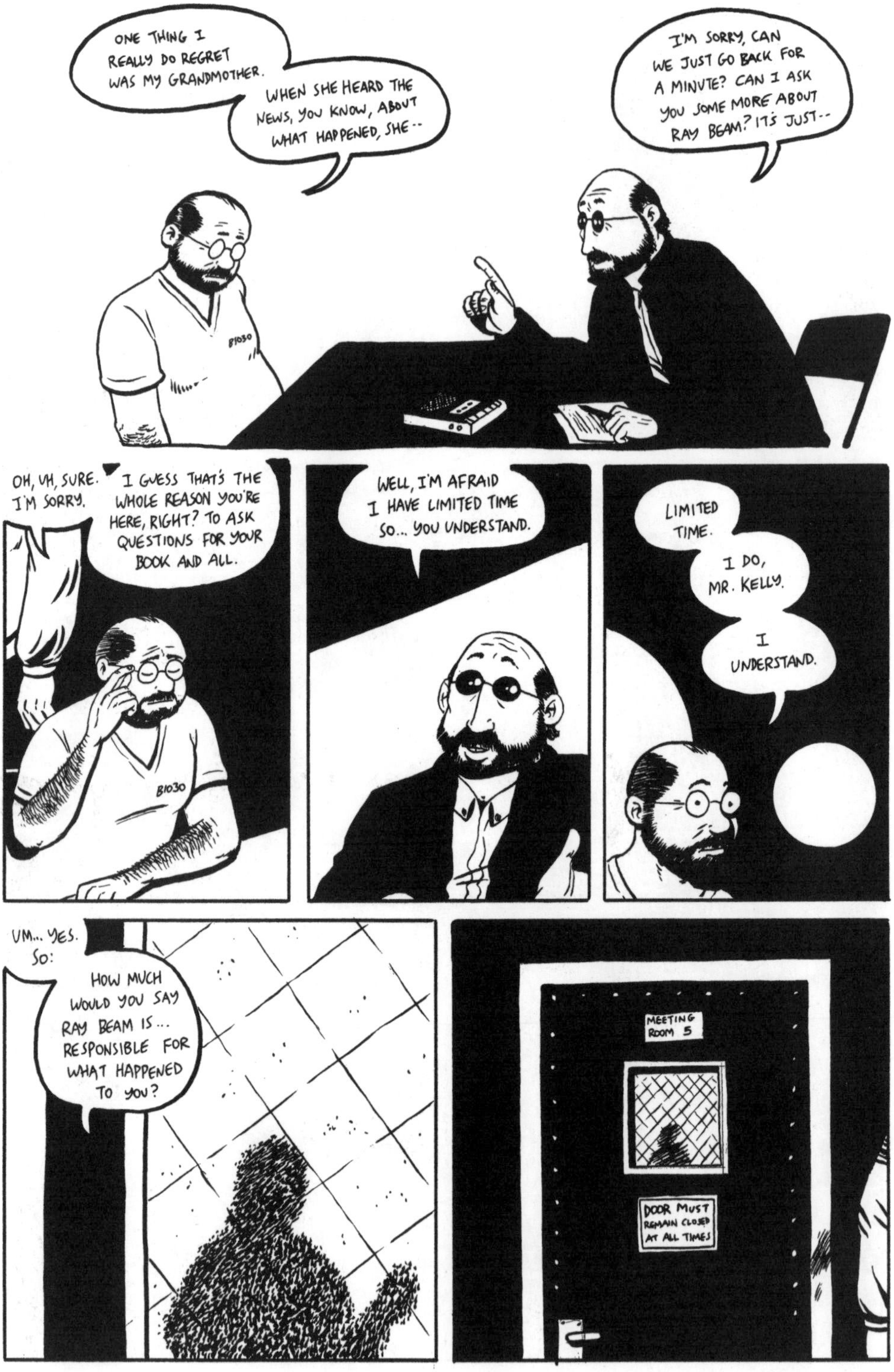

ONE THING I REALLY DO REGRET WAS MY GRANDMOTHER.
WHEN SHE HEARD THE NEWS, YOU KNOW, ABOUT WHAT HAPPENED, SHE--
I'M SORRY, CAN WE JUST GO BACK FOR A MINUTE? CAN I ASK YOU SOME MORE ABOUT RAY BEAM? IT'S JUST--
B1030
OH, UH, SURE. I'M SORRY.
I GUESS THAT'S THE WHOLE REASON YOU'RE HERE, RIGHT? TO ASK QUESTIONS FOR YOUR BOOK AND ALL.
B1030
WELL, I'M AFRAID I HAVE LIMITED TIME SO... YOU UNDERSTAND.
LIMITED TIME.
I DO, MR. KELLY.
I UNDERSTAND.
UM... YES. SO:
HOW MUCH WOULD YOU SAY RAY BEAM IS... RESPONSIBLE FOR WHAT HAPPENED TO YOU?
MEETING ROOM 5
DOOR MUST REMAIN CLOSED AT ALL TIMES

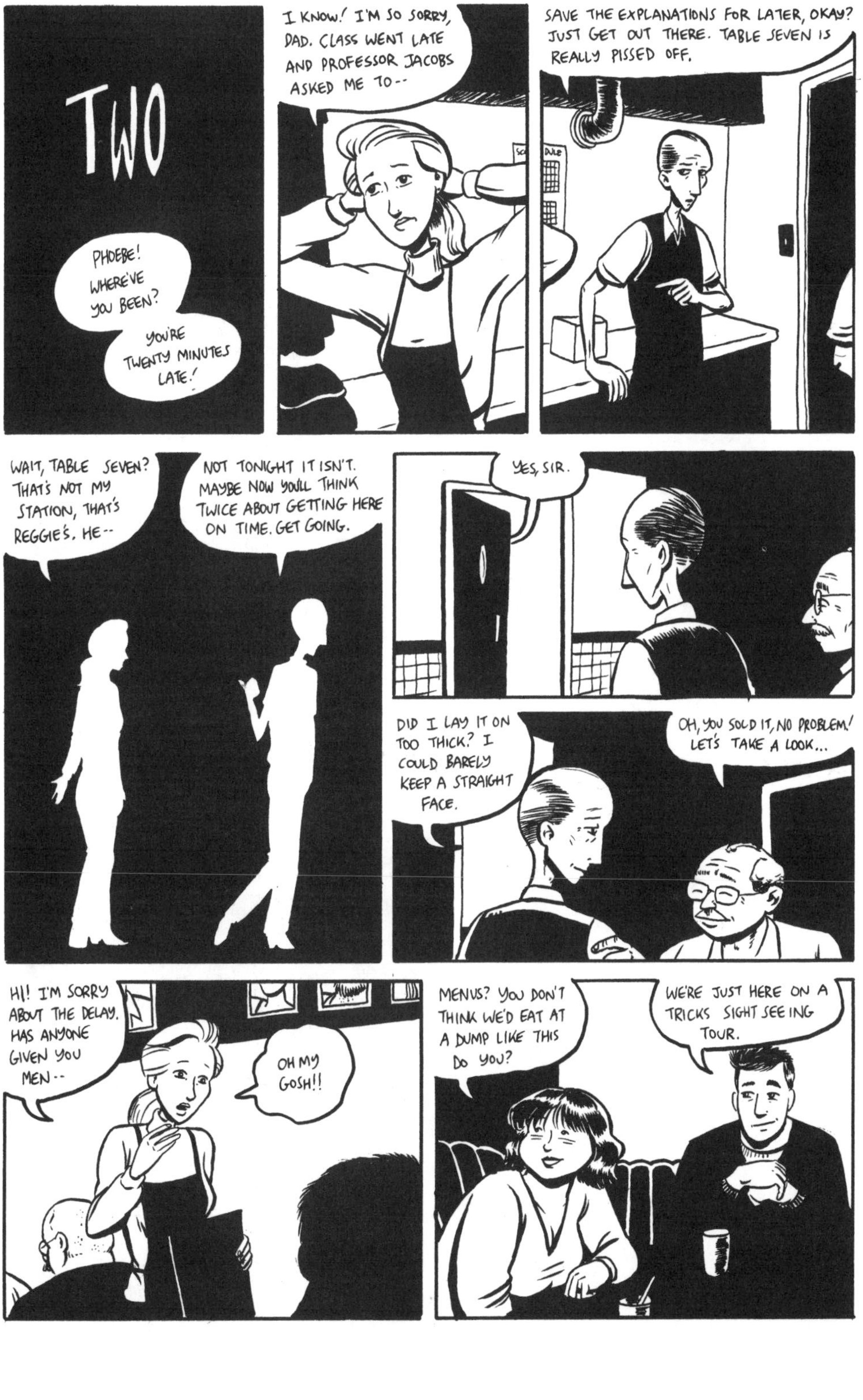
TWO
PHOEBE! WHERE'VE YOU BEEN?
YOU'RE TWENTY MINUTES LATE!
I KNOW! I'M SO SORRY, DAD. CLASS WENT LATE AND PROFESSOR JACOBS ASKED ME TO--
SAVE THE EXPLANATIONS FOR LATER, OKAY? JUST GET OUT THERE. TABLE SEVEN IS REALLY PISSED OFF.
WAIT, TABLE SEVEN? THAT'S NOT MY STATION, THAT'S REGGIE'S. HE--
NOT TONIGHT IT ISN'T. MAYBE NOW YOU'LL THINK TWICE ABOUT GETTING HERE ON TIME. GET GOING.
YES, SIR.
DID I LAY IT ON TOO THICK? I COULD BARELY KEEP A STRAIGHT FACE.
OH, YOU SOLD IT, NO PROBLEM! LET'S TAKE A LOOK...
HI! I'M SORRY ABOUT THE DELAY. HAS ANYONE GIVEN YOU MEN--
OH MY GOSH!!
MENUS? YOU DON'T THINK WE'D EAT AT A DUMP LIKE THIS DO YOU?
WE'RE JUST HERE ON A TRICKS SIGHT SEEING TOUR.

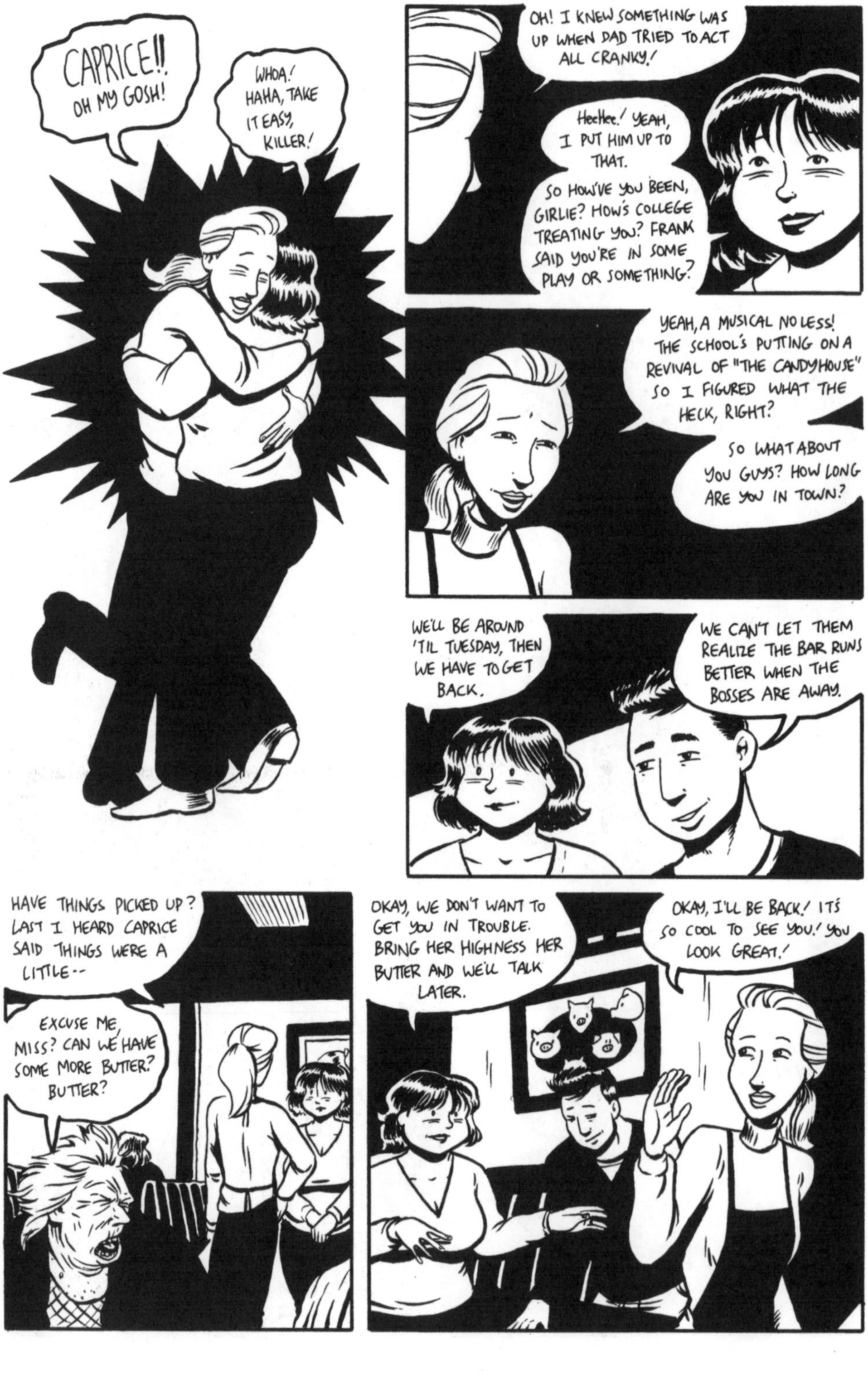
CAPRICE!! OH MY GOSH!
WHOA! HAHA, TAKE IT EASY, KILLER!
OH! I KNEW SOMETHING WAS UP WHEN DAD TRIED TO ACT ALL CRANKY!
HeeHee! YEAH, I PUT HIM UP TO THAT.
SO HOW'VE YOU BEEN, GIRLIE? HOW'S COLLEGE TREATING YOU? FRANK SAID YOU'RE IN SOME PLAY OR SOMETHING?
YEAH, A MUSICAL NO LESS! THE SCHOOL'S PUTTING ON A REVIVAL OF "THE CANDYHOUSE" SO I FIGURED WHAT THE HECK, RIGHT?
SO WHAT ABOUT YOU GUYS? HOW LONG ARE YOU IN TOWN?
WE'LL BE AROUND 'TIL TUESDAY, THEN WE HAVE TO GET BACK.
WE CAN'T LET THEM REALIZE THE BAR RUNS BETTER WHEN THE BOSSES ARE AWAY.
HAVE THINGS PICKED UP? LAST I HEARD CAPRICE SAID THINGS WERE A LITTLE--
EXCUSE ME, MISS? CAN WE HAVE SOME MORE BUTTER? BUTTER?
OKAY, WE DON'T WANT TO GET YOU IN TROUBLE. BRING HER HIGHNESS HER BUTTER AND WE'LL TALK LATER.
OKAY, I'LL BE BACK! IT'S SO COOL TO SEE YOU! YOU LOOK GREAT!

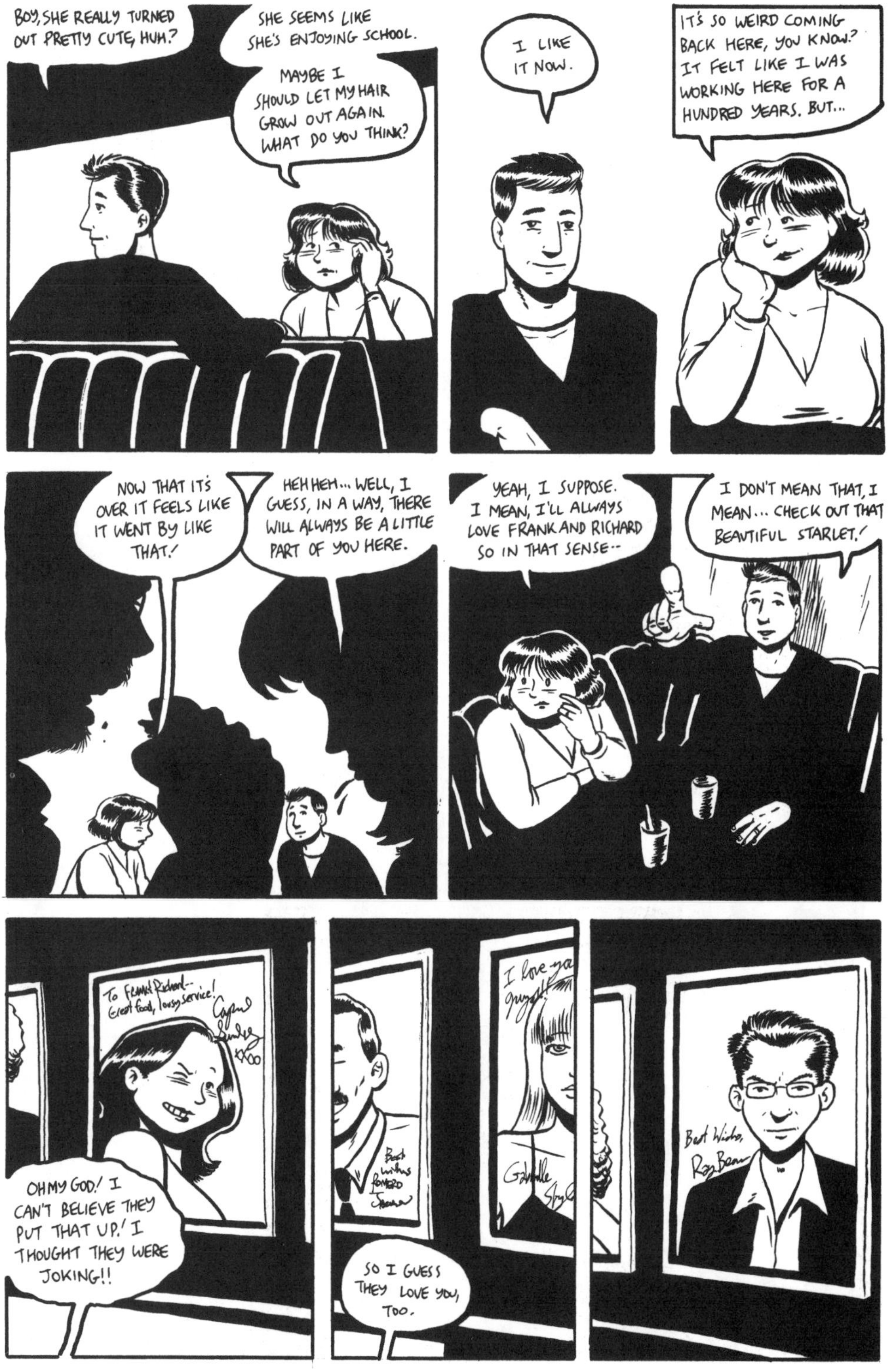
BOY, SHE REALLY TURNED OUT PRETTY CUTE, HUH?
SHE SEEMS LIKE SHE'S ENJOYING SCHOOL.
MAYBE I SHOULD LET MY HAIR GROW OUT AGAIN. WHAT DO YOU THINK?
I LIKE IT NOW.
IT'S SO WEIRD COMING BACK HERE, YOU KNOW? IT FELT LIKE I WAS WORKING HERE FOR A HUNDRED YEARS. BUT...
NOW THAT IT'S OVER IT FEELS LIKE IT WENT BY LIKE THAT!
HEH HEH... WELL, I GUESS, IN A WAY, THERE WILL ALWAYS BE A LITTLE PART OF YOU HERE.
YEAH, I SUPPOSE. I MEAN, I'LL ALWAYS LOVE FRANK AND RICHARD SO IN THAT SENSE--
I DON'T MEAN THAT, I MEAN... CHECK OUT THAT BEAUTIFUL STARLET!
To Frank and Richard-- Great food, lousy service!
OH MY GOD! I CAN'T BELIEVE THEY PUT THAT UP! I THOUGHT THEY WERE JOKING!!
Best wishes
SO I GUESS THEY LOVE YOU, TOO.
Best Wishes,

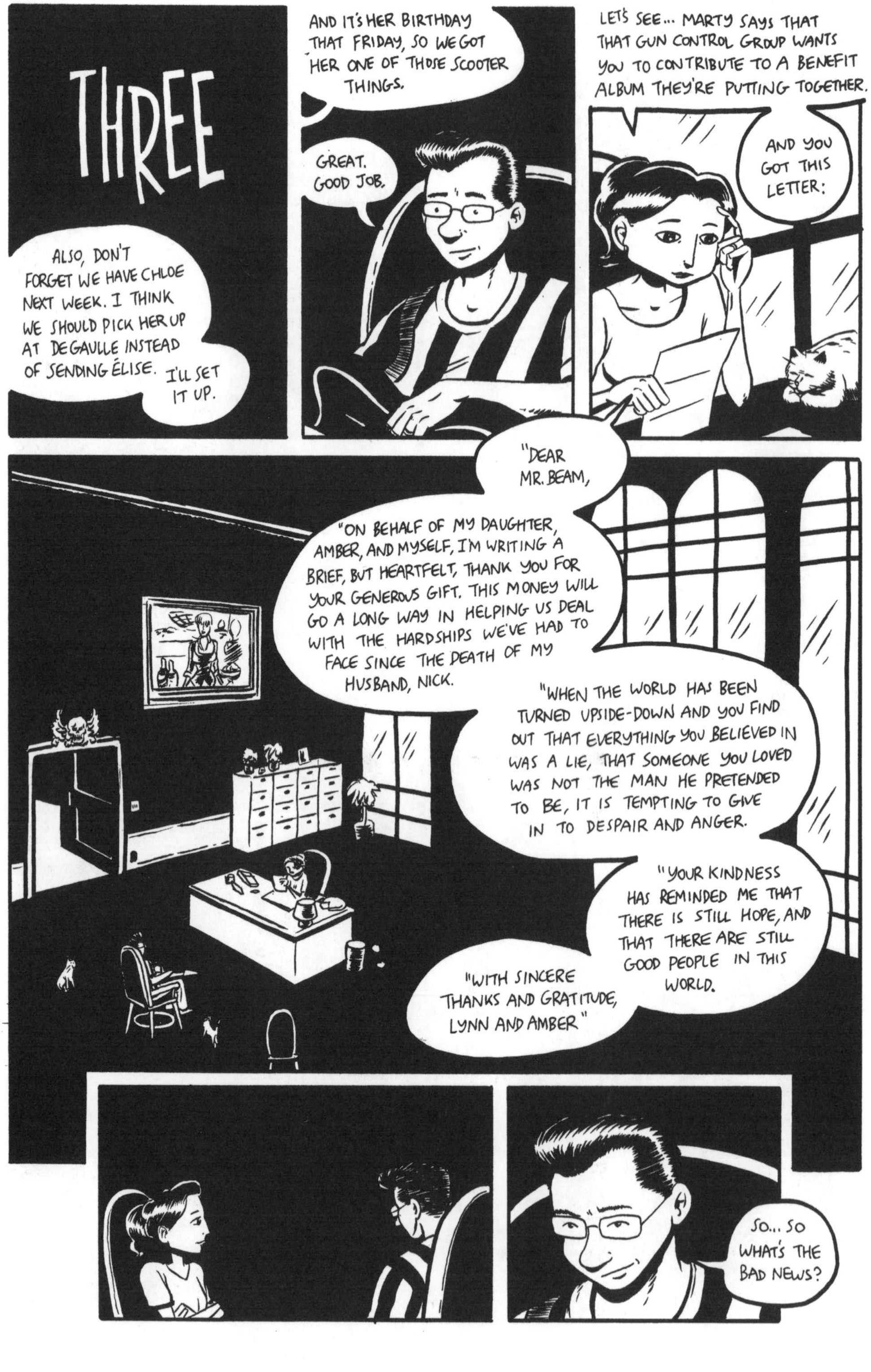
THREE
ALSO, DON'T FORGET WE HAVE CHLOE NEXT WEEK. I THINK WE SHOULD PICK HER UP AT DEGAULLE INSTEAD OF SENDING ÉLISE. I'LL SET IT UP.
AND IT'S HER BIRTHDAY THAT FRIDAY, SO WE GOT HER ONE OF THOSE SCOOTER THINGS.
GREAT. GOOD JOB.
LET'S SEE... MARTY SAYS THAT THAT GUN CONTROL GROUP WANTS YOU TO CONTRIBUTE TO A BENEFIT ALBUM THEY'RE PUTTING TOGETHER.
AND YOU GOT THIS LETTER:
"DEAR MR. BEAM,
"ON BEHALF OF MY DAUGHTER, AMBER, AND MYSELF, I'M WRITING A BRIEF, BUT HEARTFELT, THANK YOU FOR YOUR GENEROUS GIFT. THIS MONEY WILL GO A LONG WAY IN HELPING US DEAL WITH THE HARDSHIPS WE'VE HAD TO FACE SINCE THE DEATH OF MY HUSBAND, NICK.
"WHEN THE WORLD HAS BEEN TURNED UPSIDE-DOWN AND YOU FIND OUT THAT EVERYTHING YOU BELIEVED IN WAS A LIE, THAT SOMEONE YOU LOVED WAS NOT THE MAN HE PRETENDED TO BE, IT IS TEMPTING TO GIVE IN TO DESPAIR AND ANGER.
"YOUR KINDNESS HAS REMINDED ME THAT THERE IS STILL HOPE, AND THAT THERE ARE STILL GOOD PEOPLE IN THIS WORLD.
"WITH SINCERE THANKS AND GRATITUDE, LYNN AND AMBER"
SO... SO WHAT'S THE BAD NEWS?

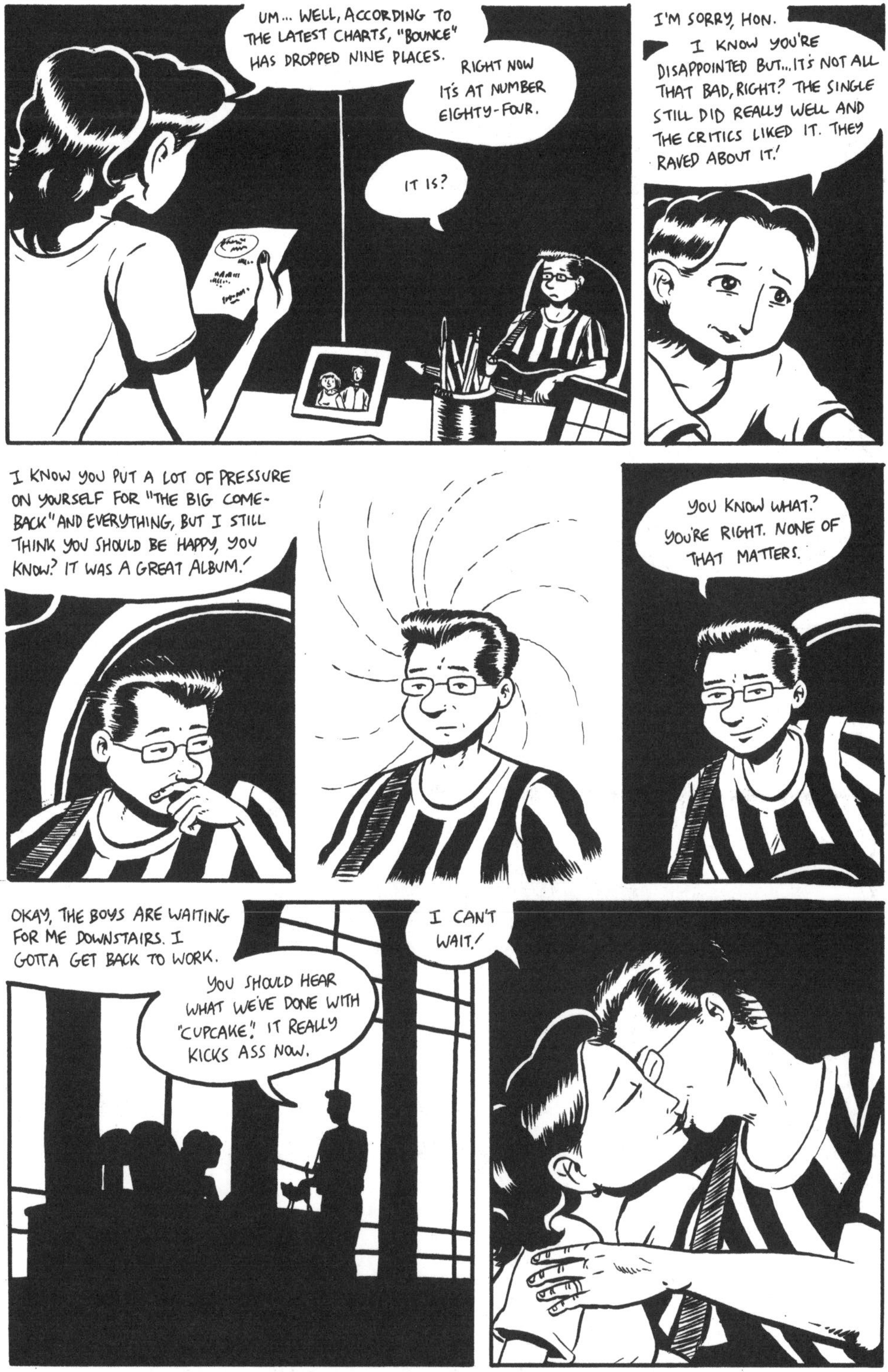
UM... WELL, ACCORDING TO THE LATEST CHARTS, "BOUNCE" HAS DROPPED NINE PLACES.
RIGHT NOW IT'S AT NUMBER EIGHTY-FOUR.
IT IS?
I'M SORRY, HON.
I KNOW YOU'RE DISAPPOINTED BUT... IT'S NOT ALL THAT BAD, RIGHT? THE SINGLE STILL DID REALLY WELL AND THE CRITICS LIKED IT. THEY RAVED ABOUT IT!
I KNOW YOU PUT A LOT OF PRESSURE ON YOURSELF FOR "THE BIG COME-BACK" AND EVERYTHING, BUT I STILL THINK YOU SHOULD BE HAPPY, YOU KNOW? IT WAS A GREAT ALBUM!
YOU KNOW WHAT? YOU'RE RIGHT. NONE OF THAT MATTERS.
OKAY, THE BOYS ARE WAITING FOR ME DOWNSTAIRS. I GOTTA GET BACK TO WORK.
YOU SHOULD HEAR WHAT WE'VE DONE WITH "CUPCAKE." IT REALLY KICKS ASS NOW.
I CAN'T WAIT!

Alex Robinson lives in New York with his wife and their two cats. His previous books, BOX OFFICE POISON, and BOP!: MORE BOX OFFICE POISON are also available from Top Shelf. To learn more about Alex, check out his website http://members.aol.com/ComicBookAlex. He welcomes your comments.

This book would not have been possible without the patience of Chris Staros and Brett Warnock, and the proofreading powers of Robert Venditti. Thanks to Andrew Robinson and Luba Reife for their generous help translating the Spanish and Russian portions of the text. However, the blame for any errors in these sections rests entirely with me.

The friendship, support and unheeded advice from Tony Consiglio, Michael Dawson and Chris Radtke has been invaluable over the past four years.

Finally, extra thanks and much love to my wife, Kristen Siebecker, without whom you would not be reading this book.